The Protection of Cultural Property in Armed Conflict

Charting in detail the evolution of the international rules on the protection of historic and artistic sites and objects from destruction and plunder in war, this book analyses in depth their many often-overlapping provisions. It serves as a comprehensive and balanced guide to a subject of increasing public profile, which will be of interest to academics, students and practitioners of international law and to all those concerned with preserving the cultural heritage.

ROGER O'KEEFE is University Lecturer in Law and Deputy Director of the Lauterpacht Research Centre for International Law, University of Cambridge. He is also a Fellow and College Lecturer in Law at Magdalene College, Cambridge.

CAMBRIDGE STUDIES IN INTERNATIONAL AND COMPARATIVE LAW

Established in 1946, this series produces high-quality scholarship in the fields of public and private international law and comparative law. Although these are distinct legal sub-disciplines, developments since 1946 confirm their interrelation.

Comparative law is increasingly used as a tool in the making of law at national, regional and international levels. Private international law is now often affected by international conventions, and the issues faced by classical conflicts rules are frequently dealt with by substantive harmonisation of law under international auspices. Mixed international arbitrations, especially those involving state economic activity, raise mixed questions of public and private international law, while in many fields (such as the protection of human rights and democratic standards, investment guarantees and international criminal law) international and national systems interact. National constitutional arrangements relating to 'foreign affairs', and to the implementation of international norms, are a focus of attention.

The Board welcomes works of a theoretical or interdisciplinary character, and those focusing on the new approaches to international or comparative law or conflicts of law. Studies of particular institutions or problems are equally welcome, as are translations of the best work published in other languages.

General Editors   James Crawford SC FBA
Whewell Professor of International Law, Faculty of Law, and Director, Lauterpacht Research Centre for International Law, University of Cambridge
John S. Bell FBA
Professor of Law, Faculty of Law, University of Cambridge

Editorial Board   Professor Hilary Charlesworth *Australian National University*
Professor Lori Damrosch *Columbia University Law School*
Professor John Dugard *Universiteit Leiden*
Professor Mary-Ann Glendon *Harvard Law School*
Professor Christopher Greenwood *London School of Economics*
Professor David Johnston *University of Edinburgh*
Professor Hein Kötz *Max-Planck-Institut, Hamburg*
Professor Donald McRae *University of Ottawa*
Professor Onuma Yasuaki *University of Tokyo*
Professor Reinhard Zimmermann *Universität Regensburg*

Advisory Committee   Professor D. W. Bowett QC
Judge Rosalyn Higgins QC
Professor J. A. Jolowicz QC
Professor Sir Elihu Lauterpacht CBE QC
Professor Kurt Lipstein
Judge Stephen Schwebel

A list of books in the series can be found at the end of this volume.

The Protection of Cultural Property in Armed Conflict

Roger O'Keefe

CAMBRIDGE UNIVERSITY PRESS
Cambridge, New York, Melbourne, Madrid, Cape Town, Singapore,
São Paulo, Delhi, Dubai, Tokyo, Mexico City

Cambridge University Press
The Edinburgh Building, Cambridge CB2 8RU, UK

Published in the United States of America by Cambridge University Press, New York

www.cambridge.org
Information on this title: www.cambridge.org/9780521172875

© Roger O'Keefe 2006

This publication is in copyright. Subject to statutory exception
and to the provisions of relevant collective licensing agreements,
no reproduction of any part may take place without the written
permission of Cambridge University Press.

First published 2006
First paperback edition 2010

A catalogue record for this publication is available from the British Library

Library of Congress Cataloguing in Publication Data

O'Keefe, Roger, 1968-
The protection of cultural property in armed conflict / Roger O'Keefe.
    p. cm.
Includes bibliographical references and index.
ISBN-13: 978-0-521-86797-9 (hardback)
ISBN-10: 0-521-86797-5 (hardback)
1. Cultural property–Protection (International law) 2. War (International law) 3.
Art treasures in war. 4. Art thefts. I. Title.
K3791.O44 2006
344'.09–dc22   2006023549

ISBN 978-0-521-86797-9 Hardback
ISBN 978-0-521-17287-5 Paperback

Cambridge University Press has no responsibility for the persistence or
accuracy of URLs for external or third-party internet websites referred to in
this publication, and does not guarantee that any content on such websites is,
or will remain, accurate or appropriate.

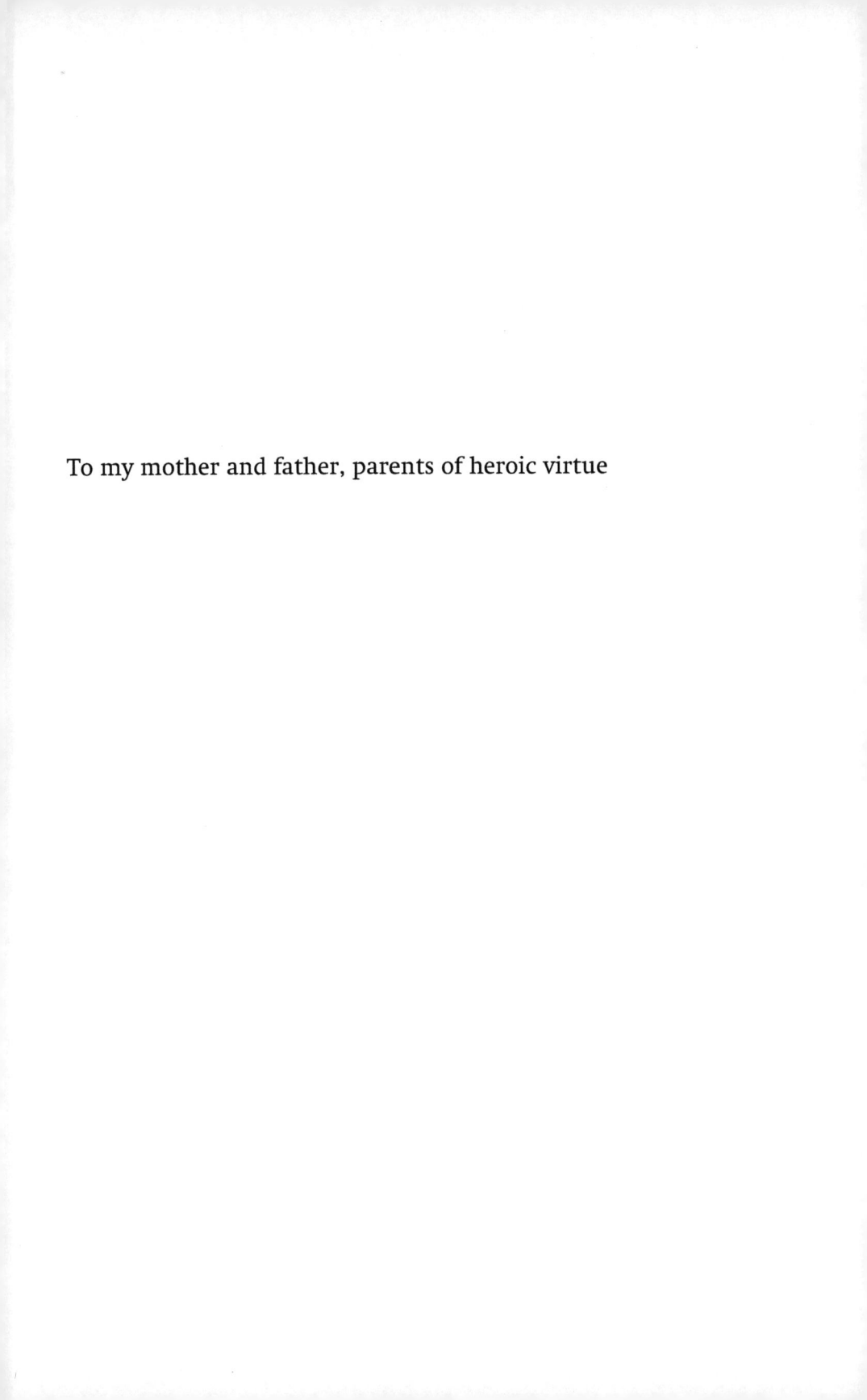

To my mother and father, parents of heroic virtue

Contents

Acknowledgements		page ix
Table of cases		x
Table of treaties and other international instruments		xiv
List of abbreviations		xviii
	Prologue	1
1	**From the high Renaissance to the Hague Rules**	5
	The classical law	5
	The French Revolution, the Napoleonic Wars and the nineteenth century	13
	The Hague Rules	22
2	**1914 to 1954**	35
	The First World War	36
	The inter-war years	44
	The Second World War	61
3	**The 1954 Hague Convention and First Hague Protocol**	92
	Preamble	94
	Scope of application	96
	General provisions regarding protection	100
	Special protection	140
	Transport of cultural property	162
	Execution of the Convention	165
	Special agreements	195
	The First Protocol	195

vii

4	**The 1977 Additional Protocols**	202
	Additional Protocol I	203
	Additional Protocol II	229
	The role of the ICRC	234
5	**The 1999 Second Hague Protocol**	236
	Relationship to the Convention	242
	Scope of application	245
	General provisions regarding protection	248
	Enhanced protection	263
	Penal sanctions	274
	Institutional issues	288
	Dissemination, co-operation and assistance	294
	Execution of the Protocol	297
6	**Other relevant bodies of law**	302
	Treaties	302
	Customary international law	316
	UNESCO Declaration concerning the Intentional Destruction of Cultural Heritage	356
	Epilogue	360
	Bibliography	362
	Index	393

Acknowledgements

I would like to thank the following people: my colleague, friend and PhD supervisor Dr Susan Marks, for guiding me through the doctoral version of this work, submitted in 1999 at the University of Cambridge; Tami Rex, for putting up with the same; the Cambridge Commonwealth Trust, the Overseas Research Student Awards and the Leslie Wilson Research Scholarships at Magdalene College, Cambridge, for funding my PhD; Jan Hladík, Programme Specialist, International Standards Section, Division of Cultural Heritage, UNESCO, for his generosity and invaluable assistance in making available to me numerous hard-to-come-by documents; Jake Soll, for introducing me to the seventeenth-century republic of letters; Eyal Rak and Morris Schonberg for translating the Israeli cases; my colleagues at the Faculty of Law and the Lauterpacht Research Centre for International Law at the University of Cambridge, and those at Magdalene College, for accommodating my sabbatical in 2004–5; Cambridge University Press, for taking on the manuscript and turning it into a book; Dr Roger Bacon, for the third most precious gift of all, health; and my parents, Barry and Jan, for the first and second, life and love.

Table of cases

Admission of a State to the United Nations (Charter, Art. 4), Advisory Opinion, ICJ Reports 1948, p. 57   110
Armed Activities on the Territory of the Congo (New Application: 2002) (Democratic Republic of the Congo v. Rwanda), ICJ General List No. 126, Jurisdiction and Admissibility, 3 February 2006   354
Armed Activities on the Territory of the Congo (Democratic Republic of the Congo v. Uganda), ICJ General List No. 116, Judgment, 19 December 2005   97, 307, 309, 318, 321, 333, 336–9
Arrest Warrant of 11 April 2000 (Democratic Republic of the Congo v. Belgium), ICJ Reports 2002, p. 3   225, 284
Autocephalous Greek-Orthodox Church of Cyprus and the Republic of Cyprus v. Goldberg and Feldman Fine Arts, Inc., 108 ILR 488 (7th Cir. 1990)   316
Candu v. Minister of Defence, 43(1) PD 738 (1989)   341
Coard v. United States of America, 123 ILR 156 (1999)   308
Coenca Brothers v. Germany, 4 AD 570 (1927)   27
Decision on Request for Precautionary Measures (Detainees at Guantánamo Bay, Cuba), 41 ILM 532 (2002)   308
Decision Regarding the Delimitation of the Border between The State of Eritrea and The Federal Democratic Republic of Ethiopia, 41 ILM 1057 (2002)   150
Delimitation of the Maritime Boundary in the Gulf of Maine Area (Canada/United States of America), ICJ Reports 1984, p. 246   127, 316
Dole v. Carter, 444 F Supp 1065 (1977), affirmed 569 F 2d 1109 (10th Cir. 1977)   164
Frontier Dispute (Burkina Faso/Mali), ICJ Reports 1986, p. 554   150, 268
Gabčíkovo-Nagymaros Project (Hungary/Slovakia), Judgment, ICJ Reports 1997, p. 7   109

Hess v. Commander of the IDF in the West Bank, HCJ 10356/02, Interim decision, 12 February 2003   131
Hess v. Commander of the IDF in the West Bank, 58(3) PD 443 (2004)   103, 131, 332, 342
In re von Lewinski (called von Manstein), 16 AD 509 (1949)   90–1
Judgment of the International Military Tribunal for the Trial of German Major War Criminals, Nuremberg, Misc. No. 12 (1946), Cmd 6964   81, 88–9, 333, 336, 349–50
Kiriadolou v. Germany, 5 AD 516 (1930)   27
Legal Consequences of the Construction of a Wall in the Occupied Palestinian Territory, ICJ General List No. 131, Advisory Opinion, 9 July 2004   97, 306–8, 321, 333, 339
Legality of the Threat or Use of Nuclear Weapons, Advisory Opinion, ICJ Reports 1996, p. 226   148, 306–8, 318
Maritime Delimitation in the Area between Greenland and Jan Mayen (Denmark v. Norway), ICJ Reports 1993, p. 4   128
Military and Paramilitary Activities In and Against Nicaragua (Nicaragua v. United States of America), Merits, ICJ Reports 1986, p. 14   247
North Sea Continental Shelf Cases (Federal Republic of Germany/Denmark; Federal Republic of Germany/Netherlands), ICJ Reports 1969, p. 3   318
Nuclear Tests (Australia v. France), ICJ Reports 1974, p. 253   150, 268
Nuclear Tests (New Zealand v. France), ICJ Reports 1974, p. 457,   150, 268
Padfield v. Minister for Agriculture, Fisheries and Foods [1968] AC 997   109
Partial Award: Central Front. Eritrea's Claims 2, 4, 6, 7, 8 & 22, 43 ILM 1249 (2004)   131, 214, 333
Partial Award: Western Front, Aerial Bombardment and Related Claims. Eritrea's Claims 1, 3, 5, 9–13, 14, 21, 25 & 26, Eritrea Ethiopia Claims Commission, 12 December 2005   129, 205, 318
Prosecutor v. Blaškić, IT-95-14-A, Appeals Chamber Judgment, 29 July 2004   318, 328–9, 346
Prosecutor v. Blaškić, IT-95-14-T, Trial Chamber Judgment, 3 March 2000   321, 332–3, 344–5, 347, 350
Prosecutor v. Brdjanin, IT-99-36-T, Trial Chamber Judgment, 1 September 2004   320–1, 344, 347, 350–1
Prosecutor v. Delalić, Mucić, Delić and Landžo (Čelebići case), IT-96-21-A, Appeals Chamber Judgment, 20 February 2001   283
Prosecutor v. Galić, IT-98-29-T, Trial Chamber Judgment, 5 December 2003   328–30, 346

Prosecutor v. Hadžihasanović and Kubura, IT-01-47-AR73.3, Appeals Chamber Decision on Joint Defence Interlocutory Appeal of Trial Chamber Decision on Rule 98 *bis* Motions for Acquittal, 11 March 2005   324–5, 337, 343, 349

Prosecutor v. Jokić, IT-01-42/1-S, Trial Chamber Sentencing Judgment, 18 March 2004   183, 281, 344, 347–8

Prosecutor v. Kordić and Čerkez, IT-95-14/2-A, Appeals Chamber Judgment, 14 December 2004   101, 210–11

Prosecutor v. Kordić and Čerkez, IT-95-14/2-T, Trial Chamber Judgment, 26 February 2001   127, 158–9, 321, 332–3, 344–5, 347, 350–1

Prosecutor v. Krstić, IT-98-33-A, Appeals Chamber Judgment, 19 April 2004   356

Prosecutor v. Krstić, IT-98-33-T, Trial Chamber Judgment, 2 August 2001   355–6

Prosecutor v. Kunarac, Kovač and Vuković, IT-96-23 & IT-96-23/1-A, Appeals Chamber Judgment, 12 June 2002   99, 350, 352–3

Prosecutor v. Kupreškić and others, IT-95-16-T, Trial Chamber Judgment, 14 January 2000   330–1

Prosecutor v. Naletilić and Martinović, IT-98-34-T, Trial Chamber Judgment, 31 March 2003   321, 332–3, 339–40, 344–5, 347, 351

Prosecutor v. Plavšić, IT-00-39 & 40/1-S, Trial Chamber Sentencing Judgment, 27 February 2003   348, 351

Prosecutor v. Rutaganda, ICTR-96-3-A, Appeals Chamber Judgment, 26 May 2003   99

Prosecutor v. Strugar, Jokić and others, IT-01-42-AR72, Appeals Chamber Decision on Interlocutory Appeal, 22 November 2002   318, 343

Prosecutor v. Strugar, IT-01-42-T, Trial Chamber Judgment, 31 January 2005   127, 183, 190, 210, 217, 227–8, 232, 281, 312, 321, 325, 333, 343–8

Prosecutor v. Tadić, IT-94-1, Appeals Chamber Decision on Defence Motion for Interlocutory Appeal on Jurisdiction, 2 October 1995, 99, 324–5, 328–9, 333–4, 338–9

Prosecutor v. Tadić, IT-94-1-A, Appeals Chamber Judgment, 15 July 1999   282–3, 353

Prosecutor v. Tadić, IT-94-1-T, Trial Chamber Judgment, 7 May 1997   346, 350–2

Queensland v. Commonwealth of Australia, 90 ILR 115 (1988)   312

Reservations to the Convention on Genocide, Advisory Opinion, ICJ Reports 1951, p. 15   354

Richardson v. Forestry Commission, 90 ILR 58 (1988)   312

Rights of Nationals of the United States of America in Morocco (France v. United States of America), ICJ Reports 1952, p. 176   109
Rosenberg v. Fischer, 15 ILR 467 (1948)   83
Ruidi and Maches v. Military Court of Hebron, 24(2) PD 419 (1970)   342
Sansolini v. Bentivegna, 24 ILR 986 (1957)   80
Serbian Loans, PCIJ Reports Series A Nos. 20/21 (1929)   150
Shikhrur v. Military Commander of the Judea and Samaria Region, 44(2) PD 233 (1990)   341
Temple of Preah Vihear (Cambodia v. Thailand), Merits, ICJ Reports 1962, p. 6   150
The Marquis de Somerueles, Stewart's Vice-Admiralty Reports (Nova Scotia) 482 (1813)   16, 40
The S.S. 'Lotus' (France v. Turkey), PCIJ Reports Series A No. 10 (1927)   276, 284
Trial of Karl Lingenfelder, 9 LRTWC 67 (1947)   89
US v. List (Hostages case), 11 TWC 757 (1948)   90
US v. Ohlendorf (Einsatzgruppen case), 4 TWC 1 (1948)   89–90

Table of treaties and other international instruments

1874 Draft International Regulations on the Laws and Customs of War (Brussels Declaration) 18–23, 27

1899 Regulations concerning the Laws and Customs of War on Land annexed to Convention concerning the Laws and Customs of War on Land 22, 27

1907 Convention concerning the Laws and Customs of War on Land
Regulations concerning the Laws and Customs of War on Land annexed to Convention concerning the Laws and Customs of War on Land (Hague Rules) 5, 22–39, 43–7, 55–6, 63, 74, 83–4, 88–9, 91, 95, 97, 101–2, 126–7, 130–1, 133–6, 317, 321, 323, 326, 331–2, 336–40, 342, 359
Convention concerning Bombardment by Naval Forces in Time of War 22, 24, 45–7, 56, 117

1923 Hague Draft Rules of Air Warfare 44–51, 56–8, 64–5, 131, 204

1935 Treaty on the Protection of Artistic and Scientific Institutions and Historic Monuments (Roerich Pact) 51–2, 95, 102, 114, 117, 218, 223, 226, 232, 255, 320

1938 Preliminary Draft International Convention for the Protection of Historic Buildings and Works of Art in Times of War 53–61, 80, 93–5, 101, 140–1, 151, 195
Regulations for the Execution of the Preliminary Draft International Convention for the Protection of Historic Buildings and Works of Art in Times of War 54, 58–9

1943 Inter-Allied Declaration Against Acts of Dispossession Committed in Territories Under Enemy Occupation or Control 77, 82

1945 Charter of the International Military Tribunal, Nuremberg annexed to Agreement by the Government of the United

Kingdom of Great Britain and Northern Ireland, the Government of the United States of America, the Provisional Government of the French Republic and the Government of the Union of Soviet Socialist Republics for the Prosecution and Punishment of the Major War Criminals of the European Axis   88, 336, 348–51

Constitution of the United Nations Educational, Scientific and Cultural Organisation   92, 139, 176, 178, 184–7, 236–7, 291

1947   Convention on the Privileges and Immunities of Specialized Agencies   171

1948   Convention on the Prevention and Punishment of the Crime of Genocide   95, 353–6

Universal Declaration of Human Rights   305

1949   Convention for the Amelioration of the Condition of the Wounded and Sick in Armed Forces in the Field (Geneva Convention I)   4, 96–8, 119, 148, 166–7, 182, 190, 195, 197, 202–4, 221, 224–5, 228–9, 233, 245, 276, 284, 294–5, 302, 304, 324

Convention for the Amelioration of the Condition of Wounded, Sick and Shipwrecked Members of Armed Forces at Sea (Geneva Convention II)   4, 96–8, 119, 148, 166–7, 182, 190, 195, 197, 202–4, 221, 224–5, 228–9, 233, 245, 276, 284, 294–5, 302, 304, 324

Convention relative to the Treatment of Prisoners of War (Geneva Convention III)   4, 96–8, 119, 148, 166–7, 182, 190, 195, 197, 202–4, 221, 224–5, 229, 233, 245, 276, 284, 294–5, 302, 304, 324

Convention relative to the Protection of Civilian Persons in Time of War (Geneva Convention IV)   4, 96–8, 119, 130–1, 133, 148, 166–7, 182, 190, 195, 197, 202–4, 221, 224–5, 228–9, 233–4, 245, 276, 284, 294–5, 302, 304, 324, 331, 339, 341

1954   Convention for the Protection of Cultural Property in the Event of Armed Conflict   92–198, 200–2, 204–5, 208–14, 217, 219, 221, 223–4, 226–7, 229–32, 234–5, 302–4, 310, 316–27, 331–6, 338–41, 348, 357–9

Regulations for the Execution of the Convention for the Protection of Cultural Property in the Event of Armed Conflict   93, 115, 117, 119–20, 163–72, 237, 289–90

(First) Protocol to the Convention for the Protection of Cultural Property in the Event of Armed Conflict   3, 94, 132, 172, 174, 179, 182, 187, 195–201, 234, 250, 260–1, 267, 342

Final Act of the Intergovernmental Conference on the Protection of Cultural Property in the Event of Armed Conflict   99, 115–16, 176, 179

Draft Code of Offences against the Peace and Security of Mankind   95

1956 Draft Rules for the Limitation of the Dangers incurred by the Civilian Population in Time of War   131, 200

Recommendation on International Principles Applicable to Archaeological Excavations   138, 261–2

1958 Geneva Convention on the Continental Shelf   127

1966 Convention on the Elimination of All Forms of Racial Discrimination   310

International Covenant on Civil and Political Rights   277, 306–7, 310

International Covenant on Economic, Social and Cultural Rights   305–10

1969 Vienna Convention on the Law of Treaties   106, 108–9, 126, 147, 189, 227, 232, 242–3, 245, 285

1970 Convention on the Means of Prohibiting the Illicit Import, Export and Transfer of Ownership of Cultural Property 3, 260–1, 314–16, 342–3, 357

1972 Convention concerning the Protection of the World Cultural and Natural Heritage   108, 223, 226, 248–9, 265–6, 268, 288–94, 310–14, 348, 357

1977 Protocol Additional to the Geneva Conventions of 12 August 1949, and Relating to the Protection of Victims of International Armed Conflicts   4, 100, 128, 132, 148, 202–35, 251–9, 272–7, 282, 284, 286, 294, 299, 302–3, 316, 318–20, 323, 327–31, 334–5, 345

Protocol Additional to the Geneva Conventions of 12 August 1949, and Relating to the Protection of Victims of Non-International Armed Conflicts   4, 202–3, 229–35, 245–6, 251, 253, 255–6, 272–3, 294, 299, 303, 324–6, 328, 330, 333–4, 337

1980	Protocol on Prohibitions or Restrictions on the Use of Mines, Booby-Traps and Other Devices to the Convention on Prohibitions or Restrictions on the Use of Certain Conventional Weapons Which May be Deemed to be Excessively Injurious or to have Indiscriminate Effects 302–4, 318–19, 328
1993	Statute of the International Criminal Tribunal for the former Yugoslavia 274, 281–3, 332, 336–7, 345–7, 349–52, 354
1994	Statute of the International Criminal Tribunal for Rwanda 281–3, 350–2, 354
1996	Amended Protocol on Prohibitions or Restrictions on the Use of Mines, Booby-Traps and Other Devices to the Convention on Prohibitions or Restrictions on the Use of Certain Conventional Weapons Which May be Deemed to be Excessively Injurious or to have Indiscriminate Effects 304–5, 318–19, 328
	Draft Code of Crimes Against the Peace and Security of Mankind 354–5
1998	Rome Statute of the International Criminal Court 128, 190, 281–2, 322, 324–6, 328–9, 332–3, 337–8, 344–7, 349–52, 355, 360
1999	Second Protocol to the Convention for the Protection of Cultural Property in the Event of Armed Conflict 108, 139, 234, 236–301, 317, 322, 325–6, 328–31, 333–5, 343, 360
	Final Act of the Diplomatic Conference on the Second Protocol to the Hague Convention for the Protection of Cultural Property in the Event of Armed Conflict 243, 285
2001	Articles on Responsibility of States for Internationally Wrongful Acts 148, 295
2002	Statute of the Special Court for Sierra Leone 281
2003	UNESCO Declaration concerning the Intentional Destruction of Cultural Heritage 356–9
	Agreement between the United Nations and the Royal Government of Cambodia concerning the Prosecution under Cambodian Law of Crimes Committed During the Period of Democratic Kampuchea 193, 350, 356
2004	UNESCO-Italy Joint Declaration for the Safeguarding, Rehabilitation and Protection of Cultural and Natural Heritage
	Statute of the Iraqi Special Tribunal 292

List of abbreviations

AD	*Annual Digest of Public International Law Cases*
AIDI	*Annuaire de l'Institut de Droit International*
AJIL	*American Journal of International Law*
AJIL Supp.	*Supplement to the American Journal of International Law*
BFSP	*British and Foreign State Papers*
BYIL	*British Yearbook of International Law*
CICI	Commission Internationale de Coopération Intellectuelle (International Commission on Intellectual Co-operation)
Dept St. Bull.	*Department of State Bulletin*
EJIL	*European Journal of International Law*
FRUS	*Foreign Relations of the United States*
ICA	International Council on Archives
ICBS	International Committee of the Blue Shield
ICC	International Criminal Court
ICCROM	International Centre for the Study of the Preservation and Restoration of Cultural Property
ICJ	International Court of Justice
ICOM	International Council of Museums
ICOMOS	International Council on Museums and Sites
ICRC	International Committee of the Red Cross
ICTR	International Criminal Tribunal for Rwanda
ICTY	International Criminal Tribunal for the former Yugoslavia
IFLA	International Federation of Library Associations and Institutions
IICI	Institut International de Coopération Intellectuelle (International Institute for Intellectual Co-operation)
IMT	International Military Tribunal

IRRC	*International Review of the Red Cross*
Isr. LR	*Israel Law Review*
Isr. YHR	*Israel Yearbook on Human Rights*
J. Air L.	*Journal of Air Law*
JNA	Jugoslovenska Narodna Armija (Yugoslav National Army)
JORF	*Journal Officiel de la République Française*
LNOJ	*League of Nations Official Journal*
LNTS	*League of Nations Treaty Series*
LRTWC	*Law Reports of Trials of War Criminals*
MFA&A	Monuments, Fine Arts and Antiquities
NOB	Nederlandsche Oudheidkundige Bond (Netherlands Archaeological Society)
Mich. LR	*Michigan Law Review*
OIM	Office International des Musées (International Museums Office)
RAF	Royal Air Force
RCADI	*Recueil des Cours de l'Académie de Droit International*
RDI	*Revue de Droit International*
RDI (Paris)	*Revue de Droit International* (Paris)
RDI (2 sér.)	*Revue de Droit International (2ème série)*
RDI (3 sér.)	*Revue de Droit International (3ème série)*
RDPMDG	*Revue de Droit Pénal Militaire et Droit de la Guerre*
RGDIP	*Revue Générale de Droit International Public*
RHDI	*Revue Hellénique de Droit International*
RICR	*Revue Internationale de la Croix-Rouge*
Riv. Dir. Int.	*Rivista di Diritto Internazionale*
TWC	*Trials of War Criminals before the Nuernberg Military Tribunals*
UN	United Nations
UNESCO	United Nations Educational, Scientific and Cultural Organisation
UNTS	*United Nations Treaty Series*
UNWCC	United Nations War Crimes Commission
USAAF	United States Army Air Forces

Prologue

This book does not set out to prove a point or to make grand claims. It offers a more basic service, namely to give a thorough and accurate account of a body of international law, outlining the relevant rules, setting them in a form of historical context and providing a guide to their interpretation and application by states, in accordance with orthodox positivist methodology.

What emerges, however, in some small way, is also the story of an idea — the idea that cultural property constitutes a universal heritage. What the record shows is that this imaginative construct-cum-metaphysical conviction has inspired the development of international rules and institutions reflective of its logic, has served in its own right as an internal and external restraint on the wartime conduct of states, and continues to inform how they interpret and apply the positive law.

On a less abstract level, the material presented in the following chapters points towards three broad conclusions.

First, states and other past parties to armed conflict have placed more and more sincere value over the last two hundred years on sparing and safeguarding immovable and movable cultural property than might be assumed. Perhaps this is not saying much, given the popular assumption that cultural property has always been deliberately attacked and looted in war, or its protection at best ignored. It is, nonetheless, a useful corrective to such unhistorical thinking. As this book details, states have expended considerable energies over the past two centuries on elaborating an increasingly demanding and sophisticated body of international rules specifically directed towards the protection of cultural property in armed conflict. Nor is this protection just on paper. The fact is that, since the end of the Napoleomic Wars, malicious destruction and plunder by armed forces and flagrant disregard for the wartime fate of cultural property have been exceptions – devastating and not uncommon exceptions, but exceptions all the same, and condemned by other states on each occasion. Good will, conscientiousness and a consensus that the cultural heritage should, where at all possible, be spared in armed conflict have tended to be the order of the day. Where these qualities have been lacking, a fear of the consequences, especially in terms of public opinion, has generally compelled compliance.

Secondly, the protection of cultural property in armed conflict by means of international law is not a pipe-dream. The signal failure of international law in the Second World War to prevent the levelling from the air of the cultural heritage of Germany and Japan was in many ways anomalous, a function of a specific moment in both the laws of armed conflict and military technology: legally, the classical law on bombardment had been rendered obsolete but the regime that would come to replace it was still underdeveloped; technologically, the massive increase in the explosive yield of ordnance and the capacity to deliver it from the air had not been adequately matched by advances in the precision with which it could be targeted. But thanks to crucial legal and technological developments since 1945, today there is a greater possibility than ever before of sparing cultural property from damage and destruction in wartime. That said, the limits of what international law can do to civilise war leave no room for triumphalism. No rules will ever stop parties to an armed conflict or individual combatants who, motivated by ideology or malice and convinced of their impunity, show contemptuous disregard for law itself. The Nazis' devastation and seizure of the cultural heritage of the occupied East was a phenomenon beyond the power of law to prevent, although not to punish. The same is true of Iraq's plunder of the museums of Kuwait in 1990, and the destruction of historic and religious sites in the former Yugoslavia. Moreover, the gravest threat to cultural property in armed conflict today is its theft by private, civilian actors not bound in this regard by the laws of war. The breakdown of order that accompanies armed conflict and the corrupting lure of the worldwide illicit market in art and antiquities continue to drive the looting of archaeological sites and museums in war-zones and occupied territory. The point to be made, however, is that insofar as the laws of war are capable of changing behaviour, the rules to protect cultural property are as capable as any.

The last conclusion to be drawn is that the common charge that a concern for the wartime fate of cultural property shows a callousness towards the wartime fate of people is misplaced. The argument could be rebutted as a matter of formal logic: there is no necessary reason why an interest in the one should mean a disregard for the other. One could also have recourse to a sort of metaphysical ethics, in that the ultimate end of protecting the cultural heritage is human flourishing. But the more pragmatic answer suggested by Chapter 2 of this book is that the protection of cultural property in armed conflict is flatly impossible without an equal or greater concern for the protection of civilians. If the civilian population is targeted, the cultural property in its midst will suffer with it. Conversely, as the inhabitants of Rome and Kyoto could attest, a concern to spare the cultural heritage from the destructive effects of war can end up saving the lives of the local people.

It should be made clear at the outset that the following chapters deal with the protection of cultural property in armed conflict from damage and destruction and from all forms of misappropriation. They do not address the distinct, albeit related question of the restitution of cultural property illicitly removed during hostilities and belligerent occupation – a vast topic in its own right implicating, in many instances, both private law and private international law, fields outside the author's expertise. As a consequence, articles 3 and 4 of the First Protocol to the 1954 Hague Convention are merely outlined. The restitution arrangements after Waterloo, the First World War, the Second World War, the first Gulf War and the invasion of Iraq, the restitution provisions of the Convention on the Means of Prohibiting and Preventing the Illicit Import, Export and Transfer of Ownership of Cultural Property, UNESCO's Intergovernmental Committee for Promoting the Return of Cultural Property to its Countries of Origin or its Restitution in case of Illicit Appropriation, the UNIDROIT Convention on Stolen or Illegally Exported Cultural Objects and the resolutions adopted on the question by the United Nations General Assembly are not considered.

It should also be said that the book does not attempt to catalogue every instance of state practice on point from the sixteenth and seventeenth centuries to the present. This is clearly impossible, and would not always add to the argument: a tally of compliance and breach is a waste of time if it tells us nothing significant about the law. Rather, the book deals with state practice only insofar as it is relevant to the evolution of customary or conventional rules, or to their interpretation, or to their proper or permissible application.

Turning to terminology, the meaning of 'cultural property', as used in this book, depends on the context. In relation to the 1954 Hague Convention and its two Protocols, the term is used in the formal legal sense embodied in article 1 of the Convention, which defines cultural property to mean 'movable or immovable property of great importance to the cultural heritage of every people'. For all other purposes, it is used in a lay sense. For example, as regards the 1907 Hague Rules, 'cultural property' is shorthand variously for the buildings and historic monuments referred to in article 27 – with the exception of hospitals and places where the sick and wounded are collected – and for the institutions, historic monuments and works of art and science referred to in article 56. As regards article 53 of Additional Protocol I and article 16 of Additional Protocol II, 'cultural property' means the 'historic monuments, works of art and places of worship which constitute the cultural and spiritual heritage of peoples' protected by these provisions. The word 'war' is also used in a lay sense, at least in reference to international law and practice since the 1949 Geneva Conventions. It is used as a synonym for armed conflict, within the meaning of modern international humanitarian law, and is not intended to denote a formal legal state which can only commence with a declaration and end with a treaty of peace. On the other hand, the word 'attack' is used in the special sense given it by article 49 of Additional Protocol I, referring to 'acts of violence against the adversary, whether in offence or in defence'.

Unless otherwise stated, translations from foreign languages are the author's own. Information is given as of 1 February 2006.

1   From the high Renaissance to the Hague Rules

As early as the 1500s, moral theologians and writers on the law of nations were enunciating rules which sought to regulate both the destruction and the plunder of cultural property in war. The same period also saw the birth of the metaphysical vision of such property as a universal estate, later to be termed a 'heritage', common to all peoples, a vision sometimes *ad idem* and sometimes at odds with the international legal position. Modified in the wake of the Napoleonic Wars and challenged by the technological and strategic revolutions of the nineteenth century, the customary international rules regulating the wartime treatment of cultural property came to be codified in the 1907 Hague Rules, which aimed to temper the conduct of war on land.

The classical law

As conceived in the sixteenth and seventeenth centuries, the rationale of the laws governing the conduct of hostilities was to minimise the harm inflicted in a sovereign's exercise of his right to wage just war. The balance of evil and good was sought to be struck by reference to the doctrine of necessity. It was held to be a 'general rule from the law of nature'[1] that as long as the end pursued by the war was just,[2] armed violence necessary

---

[1] See the heading 'General Rules from the Law of Nature regarding What is Permissible in War ...', in H. Grotius, *De Jure Belli ac Pacis Libri Tres*, first published 1625, text of 1646, translated by F. W. Kelsey (Oxford: Clarendon Press, 1925), book 3, chap. 1.

[2] The classical rules on the conduct of war were logically premised on the justice of the cause. In this respect, and especially in the specific area of the lawful destruction of enemy property, the wholly artefactual labels '*jus in bello*' and '*jus ad bellum*' are apt to mislead, the latter regulating as it did not simply the legality of the commencement of war but also the legality of each discrete act of armed violence committed therein. In the form of the rule of necessity, what later came to be called the *jus ad bellum* constantly penetrated what was later termed the *jus in bello*.

to achieve that end, including destruction of enemy property, was permissible.[3] No distinction was drawn *per se* between soldiers and civilians, nor between military and civilian property, although reason dictated that the killing of civilians and the destruction of civilian property was usually unnecessary and therefore unlawful. Works of art, grand edifices, monuments and ruins were treated no differently from other civilian property of which they were a species, at least according to the bare law of nations. The destruction of all types of enemy property was permissible, strictly speaking.[4] At the same time, Grotius believed that reason compelled the sparing of 'those things which, if destroyed, do not weaken the enemy, nor bring gain to the one who destroys them', such as 'colonnades, statues, and the like'[5] – that is, 'things of artistic value'.[6] Gentili had earlier come to the same conclusion,[7] as did Textor later.[8]

As well as regulating the infliction of direct injury or damage, the rule of necessity governed the common situation where persons or property to be spared, such as civilians or things of artistic or historic value, were incidentally harmed in the course of destroying permissible targets. Applying scholastic moral philosophy's doctrine of 'double effect', Grotius[9] – along with Suárez,[10] Vitoria[11] and Ayala[12] before him, and

---

[3] Grotius, *De Jure Belli ac Pacis*, book 3, chap. 1, s. 2. See also, previously, F. de Vitoria, 'De Indis Relectio Posterior, sive De Jure Belli Hispanorum in Barbaros', first published 1557, text of 1696, in *De Indis et De Jure Belli Relectiones*, translated by J. P. Bate (Washington, DC: Carnegie Institution, 1917), p. 163 at para. 18; F. Suárez, 'On Charity', text of 1621, in *Selections from Three Works of Francisco Suárez, S.J.*, translated by G. L. Williams *et al.* (Oxford: Clarendon Press, 1944), p. 797, disputation 13, s. 7, para. 6; and, subsequently, S. Pufendorf, *De Jure Naturae et Gentium Libri Octo*, first published 1672, text of 1688, translated by C. H. and W. A. Oldfather (Oxford: Clarendon Press, 1934), book 8, chap. 6, para. 7.

[4] Grotius, *De Jure Belli ac Pacis*, book 3, chap. 5; S. Rachel, *De Jure Naturae et Gentium Dissertationes*, text of 1676, translated by J. P. Bate (Washington, DC: Carnegie Institution, 1916), second dissertation, para. 48.

[5] Grotius, *De Jure Belli ac Pacis*, book 3, chap. 12, s. 5.

[6] *Ibid.*, s. 6.

[7] A. Gentili, *De Jure Belli Libri Tres*, first published 1598, text of 1612, translated by J. C. Rolfe (Oxford: Clarendon Press, 1933), book 2, chap. 23, p. 270.

[8] J. W. Textor, *Synopsis Juris Gentium*, text of 1680, translated by J. P. Bate (Washington, DC: Carnegie Institution, 1916), chap. 18, para. 33, as regards 'palaces and other fine buildings'.

[9] Grotius, *De Jure Belli ac Pacis*, book 3, chap. 1, s. 4.

[10] Suárez, 'On Charity', disputation 13, s. 7, para. 17.

[11] Vitoria, 'De Indis Relectio Posterior', para. 37.

[12] B. Ayala, *De Jure et Officiis Bellicis et Disciplina Militari Libri III*, text of 1582, translated by J. P. Bate (Washington, DC: Carnegie Institution, 1912), book 1, chap. 4, para. 9.

Textor[13] afterwards — declared, as one of his 'general rules from the law of nature', that things which were unlawful to do directly were lawful if unavoidable in pursuit of a lawful end. In other words, no rule of law was broken if civilians were unavoidably killed or things of artistic or historic value unavoidably destroyed in an attack on a defended position.

Vitoria, however, looked to temper the strict rule by weighing the evil to be caused against the good to be had:

Great attention, however, must be paid to [this] point ..., namely, the obligation to see that greater evils do not arise out of the war than the war would avert. For if little effect upon the ultimate issue of the war is to be expected from the storming of a fortress or fortified town wherein are many innocent folk, it would not be right, for the purpose of assailing a few guilty, to slay the many innocent by use of fire or engines of war or other means likely to overwhelm indifferently both innocent and guilty. In sum, it is never right to slay the guiltless, even as an indirect and unintended result, except when there is no other means of carrying on the operations of a just war, according to the passage (*St Matthew*, ch. 13) 'Let the tares grow, lest while ye gather up the tares ye root up also the wheat with them'.[14]

Grotius too sought to limit the wrong inflicted in pursuit of a right by reference to identical scriptural authority:

[W]e must also beware of what happens, and what we foresee may happen, beyond our purpose, [to ensure that] the good which our action has in view is much greater than the evil which is feared, or, [if] the good and the evil balance, [that] the hope of the good is much greater than the fear of the evil. The decision in such matters must be left to a prudent judgement, but in such a way that when in doubt we should favour that course, as the more safe, which has regard for the interest of another rather than our own. 'Let the tares grow', said the best Teacher, 'lest haply while ye gather up the tares ye root up the wheat with them.' Said Seneca: 'To kill many persons indiscriminately is the work of fire and desolation.'[15]

Suárez, however, rejected this restriction.[16]

---

[13] Textor, *Synopsis Juris Gentium*, chap. 18, para. 10.
[14] Vitoria, 'De Indis Relectio Posterior', para. 37.
[15] Grotius, *De Jure Belli ac Pacis*, book 3, chap. 1, s. 4. See also Textor, *Synopsis Juris Gentium*, chap. 18, paras. 10–11, seemingly endorsing Grotius.
[16] Suárez, 'On Charity', disputation 13, s. 7, para. 19.

As for the appropriation of enemy property in war, the general view was that the law of nations permitted a belligerent to capture and carry off movable property in pursuit of a just cause 'without limit or restriction'.[17] All chattels captured from the enemy population became the property either of the capturing power or of the individual captor. At the same time, considerations of justice, or at the very least humanity, dictated moderation.[18] As with destruction, when it came to appropriation most early modern writers made no distinction between different types of movables. Gentili expressly included 'statues and other ornaments' within the freedom to capture and remove.[19] If a town was captured by assault after refusing to surrender, a commander was entitled to turn it over to pillage[20] – that is, to every-man-for-himself looting by the soldiery, with each permitted to keep what he laid his hands on. Vitoria, however, thought pillage lawful only 'if necessary for the conduct of the war or as a deterrent to the enemy or as a spur to the courage of the troops'.[21] Either way, it was forbidden for soldiers to pillage other than with express permission.[22]

Nonetheless, while not yet reflected in the law of nations, the notion was already prevalent in the sixteenth century that monuments and works of art constituted a distinct category of property – an emergent consciousness which inspired the earliest domestic examples of historical preservation. In parallel with this, a conviction took shape in the Renaissance among the educated elites of Europe that the learned arts and sciences comprised a transnational common weal. By the end of the seventeenth century, this *respublica literaria* – known in its later francophone incarnation as the 'République des Lettres' or 'republic of letters' – was axiomatic as a metaphysical estate spanning literate

---

[17] Grotius, *De Jure Belli ac Pacis*, book 3, chap. 6, s. 2. See also, previously, Gentili, *De Jure Belli*, book 3, chap. 6, p. 310 and chap. 7, p. 315; and, subsequently, R. Zouche, *Iuris et Iudicii Fecialis, sive, Iuris Inter Gentes, et Quaestionum de Eodem Explicatio*, text of 1650, translated by J. L. Brierly (Washington, DC: Carnegie Institution, 1911), part 1, s. 8, para. 1; Rachel, *De Jure Naturae*, dissertation 2, para. 48.

[18] Gentili, *De Jure Belli*, book 3, chap. 6, pp. 313–14 and chap. 7, p. 315; Suárez, 'On Charity', disputation 13, s. 7, para. 7; Grotius, *De Jure Belli ac Pacis*, book 3, chap. 13.

[19] Gentili, *De Jure Belli*, book 3, chap. 6, p. 310, quoting Cicero.

[20] Grotius, *De Jure Belli ac Pacis*, book 3, chap. 6, s. 18; Zouche, *Iuris et Iudicii Fecialis*, s. 8, para. 1.

[21] Vitoria, 'De Indis Relectio Posterior', para. 52.

[22] *Ibid.*, para. 53; Suárez, 'On Charity', disputation 13, s. 7, para. 7.

European circles. A central feature of this cosmopolitan intellectual domain was the scholarly interest in the fine arts, architecture and antiquities that was the mark of high Renaissance and early modern cultivation. For instance, Pope Pius II, dubbed by Burckhardt 'the personal head of the republic of letters', 'was wholly possessed by antiquarian enthusiasm'.[23] The later French polymath and patron Nicolas-Claude Fabri de Peiresc — the man considered by the seventeenth century historian Pierre Bayle, editor of the journal *Nouvelles de la République des Lettres*, to have rendered more services than any other to the republic of letters (and, coincidentally, Hugo Grotius's chief encouragement and material support during the writing of *De Jure Belli ac Pacis*[24]) — 'used his income to buy or have copied the rarest and most useful monuments', and 'works of art [and] antiquities ... were equally the object of his concern and curiosity'.[25] In turn, it soon came to pass that the vision of a transnational commonwealth of the learned became the vision of a transnational commonwealth of what they were learned in: artworks, architecture and antiquities — that is, the actual paintings and sculptures, grand buildings and monuments, ruins and relics — themselves came to be viewed as a universal metaphysical estate whose well-being was a common human concern.

The Enlightenment was the heyday of the republic of letters, as well as of the specific vision of a pan-continental republic of the fine arts, architecture and antiquities. Indicative of the age, Diderot and Alembert's *Encyclopédie* sought to 'bring together the enlightened of all nations in a single work that [would] be like a ... universal library of what is beautiful, grand [and] luminous ... in all the noble arts'.[26] To this end, '[a]ll the great masters in Germany, in England, in Italy and throughout the whole of Europe call[ed] on all the scholars and artists of the confraternity' of 'belles-lettres and fine arts'[27] to contribute to a single work embracing, *inter alia*, 'Architecture', 'Buildings', 'Sculpture',

---

[23] J. Burckhardt, *The Civilization of the Renaissance in Italy*, text of 1860, translated by S. G. C. Middlemore (London: Penguin, 1990), p. 147.

[24] See J. Brown Scott, 'La genèse du traité du Droit de la Guerre et de la Paix' (1925) 6 RDI (3 sér.) 481 at 503.

[25] P. Bayle, *Dictionnaire Historique et Critique Par Monsieur Bayle*, 4 vols. (Rotterdam: Reinier Leers, 1697), vol. II, part 2, pp. 767–8.

[26] Andrew Michael Ramsay, quoted in J. Lough, *The Encyclopédie* (London: Longman, 1971), p. 6.

[27] Ibid.

'Painting', 'Monuments', 'Antiquities', 'Relics' and 'Ruins'.[28] The eighteenth century also witnessed the discovery of the archaeological sites at Pompeii, Herculaneum and Paestum, as well as the first excavations in Italy and Sicily. Le Roy's *The Ruins of the Most Beautiful Monuments of Greece* (1758), the first volume of Stuart and Revett's *The Antiquities of Athens* (1762) and Winckelmann's *History of Ancient Art* (1767) triggered trips by *érudits* of many nationalities to the cradle of classical European civilisation. A growing number of antiquarians ventured even further, to Egypt, the Sudan and the Middle East.

Writing in the Enlightenment as well, the jurists Vattel, Wolff and Burlamaqui, speaking of the lawful conduct of war, affirmed the general rule maintained by the early moderns that a belligerent had the right to use the armed force necessary to pursue a just end.[29] This included the destruction of enemy property,[30] even if Vattel was at pains to emphasise that '[a]ll harm done to the enemy unnecessarily, every act of hostility not directed towards securing victory and the end of the war, is mere licence, which the natural law condemns'.[31] As for specific types of property, Burlamaqui thought it scarcely necessary to wreck statues after a town had been taken.[32] Nor did Wolff believe there was any gain to be had in destroying ornamental goods.[33] For Vattel, the 'wilful destruction of public monuments, places of worship, tombs, statues, paintings, etc.' was 'absolutely condemned, even by the voluntary law of nations, as never being conducive to the rightful object of war'.[34]

---

[28] See D. Diderot and J. L. d'Alembert (eds.), *Encyclopédie, ou Dictionnaire Raisonné des Sciences, des Arts et des Métiers, par une Société des Gens de Lettres*, 17 vols. (Paris: Briasson, David, Le Breton, Durand, 1751–7).

[29] E. de Vattel, *Le Droit des Gens, ou Principes de la Loi Naturelle, appliqués à la Conduite et aux Affaires des Nations et des Souverains*, text of 1758 (Washington, DC: Carnegie Institution, 1916), book 3, chap. 8, paras 136–8; C. Wolff, *Jus Gentium Methodo Scientifica Pertractatum*, first published 1740–9, text of 1764, translated by J. H. Drake (Oxford: Clarendon Press, 1934), chap. 7, paras. 781–2; J.J. Burlamaqui, *Principes du Droit Politique*, 2 vols. (Amsterdam: Zacharie Chatelain, 1751), vol. II, part 4, chap. 5, para. 3 and chap. 6, para. 3.

[30] Vattel, *Droit des Gens*, book 3, chap. 9, paras. 166–7; Wolff, *Jus Gentium*, chap. 7, para. 823; Burlamaqui, *Principes*, vol. II, part 4, chap. 7, para. 8.

[31] Vattel, *Droit des Gens*, book 3, chap. 9, para. 172.

[32] Burlamaqui, *Principes*, vol. II, part 4, chap. 7, para. 8.

[33] Wolff, *Jus Gentium*, chap. 7, para. 823.

[34] Vattel, *Droit des Gens*, book 3, chap. 9, para. 173.

That is, harm to these things was prohibited not just by the law of nature but also by positive law. He declared:

> For whatever reason a country be ravaged, those buildings must be spared which do honour to humanity and which do not contribute to the enemy's strength, such as temples, tombs, public buildings and all works of remarkable beauty. What is to be gained by destroying them? It is the act of a sworn enemy of the human race to deprive it lightly of such monuments of the arts . . .[35]

Yet the doctrine of necessity still cut both ways. If it were 'necessary to destroy buildings of this sort to pursue military operations or to erect siegeworks', a belligerent 'no doubt had the right to do so'.[36] The same rule applied in defence: the besieged were permitted to destroy such buildings when, for example, they found it necessary to set fire to outlying districts in order to deny a siege party ground.[37]

Nowhere did necessity tend more towards permissiveness than in bombardment, the most destructive of prevailing methods of warfare. As classically viewed, bombardment was a means to the occupation, not devastation, of a fortified town or city, to be preceded by siege and, if the terms of surrender were refused, followed by assault. Its usual aim was to damage or destroy the town's perimeter defences (the cannon emplacements, redoubts and battlements), so as to enable troops to enter unopposed. It was considered a last resort to be employed sparingly, on account of its guaranteed killing of civilians and destruction of their property with the grossly inaccurate artillery typical of the times; and given that the rigours of siege often forestalled the need to fire on a town, it was a relatively rare occurrence. As for the rules of warfare regulating the bombardment of towns, it went without saying that it was absolutely impermissible to bombard an unfortified town, since it was unnecessary: the town could be entered and occupied without resistance. As regards defended towns, a debate arose in the eighteenth century over whether it could ever be necessary, and hence permissible, to fire on the civilian quarters. Vattel thought it could be:

> These days the besieger usually bombards the ramparts and everything to do with the place's defence: to destroy a town with bombs and hot shot is a last resort

[35] *Ibid.*, para. 168.
[36] *Ibid.*
[37] *Ibid.*

to which one does not go without grave reasons. But it is a resort nonetheless permitted by the laws of war, if there is no other way to break the resistance of an important locale on which the success of the war may hang, or which serves as a base for hazardous strikes against us.[38]

At the same time, his emphasis was on restraint.

All care was to be taken during bombardment not to kill civilians or to damage civilian property, including cultural property; but unavoidable incidental damage, while regrettable, was permissible. There was no call to question whether, in a given situation, the degree of necessity to shell a military position justified the scale of foreseeable death and destruction. Vattel was seemingly unqualified in his acceptance of the inevitability of incidental damage, and placed no upper threshold on its lawful extent, noting sanguinely that it 'is difficult to spare the most beautiful buildings when one is bombarding a town':[39] if, in furthering military operations, a commander 'thereby destroy[ed] some work of art', it was simply 'an accident, an unfortunate consequence of the war'.[40] Burlamaqui had earlier come to a similar conclusion when, restating the classical doctrine of double effect, he posited that, as a strict matter of natural law, what was otherwise impermissible in war was rendered permissible if it was the unintended and inevitable consequence of a permissible act,[41] even if the principles of humanity called for moderation.[42]

But whatever the inexorable dictates of the law, the stress remained on distinguishing things military, on the one hand, from the populace and its property, on the other. It was an emphasis endorsed by Jean-Jacques Rousseau. Writing in *The Social Contract*, Rousseau crystallised in politico-philosophical terms the principle of distinction inchoate in the doctrine of limited war espoused since the scholastics, that is, that a belligerent must distinguish at all times between the military forces of the state and the civilian population and its property, making every effort to spare the latter:

War ... is not a relation between men, but between states; in war individuals are enemies wholly by chance, not as men, not even as citizens, but only as soldiers;

---

[38] *Ibid.*, para. 169.
[39] *Ibid.*
[40] *Ibid.*, para. 168. The precise context for the quote was the right of the governor of a besieged town to destroy his own districts in pursuit of the war.
[41] Burlamaqui, *Principes*, part 4, chap. 5, paras. 5–6.
[42] *Ibid.*, para. 8.

not as members of their country, but only as its defenders ... Since the aim of war is to subdue a hostile state, a combatant has the right to kill the defenders of that state while they are armed; but ... [i]t is sometimes possible to destroy a state without killing a single one of its members, and war gives no right to inflict any more destruction than is necessary for victory. These principles were not invented by Grotius ...; they are derived from the nature of things; they are based on reason.[43]

The principle enjoyed a rapid reception after the coming to power in France of revolutionary leaders 'nourished on the writings of Rousseau'.[44]

As for appropriation, Vattel, Wolff and Burlamaqui all recognised a right of capture and removal to the value of any debt, plus varying sums.[45] No property was exempt. But here also the stress came to be laid on distinction, with the French jurist Portalis quoting Rousseau's maxim at the inauguration of a prize court in 1801. As for pillage, Vattel thought it permitted if the commander gave permission.[46] Wolff allowed it too, but cautioned that 'it should hardly be resorted to unless the greatest necessity should demand it'.[47]

The French Revolution, the Napoleonic Wars and the nineteenth century

As well as hastening the reception of the doctrine of distinction, the French Revolution and the Napoleonic Wars marked a turning point in attitudes to the legal protection of monuments and works of art, domestically as much as internationally and in peace as much as in war.

The passions inflamed by the Revolution posed a grave threat to the artworks and monuments of France. Partly with this in mind, a Commission on Monuments was established in 1790, after the nationalisation of royal, émigré and church assets, to amass, inventory and assume stewardship over confiscated cultural property, which, in the words of the Comte de Kersaint, was now 'the heritage ['patrimoine']

---

[43] J.-J. Rousseau, *The Social Contract*, text of 1762, translated by M. Cranston (London: Penguin, 1968), pp. 56–7.
[44] M. Vauthier, 'La doctrine du contrat social' (1914) 16 RDI (2 sér) 325 at 340.
[45] Vattel, *Droit des Gens*, book 3, chap. 9, paras. 160 and 164; Wolff, *Jus Gentium*, chap. 7, para. 849; Burlamaqui, *Principes*, part 4, chap. 7, para. 11.
[46] Vattel, *Droit des Gens*, book 3, chap. 9, para. 164.
[47] Wolff, *Jus Gentium*, chap. 7, para. 846.

of all'[48] – a 'national heritage' ('patrimoine national'), according to François Puthod de Maisonrouge.[49] On 3 March 1791, the National Constituent Assembly promulgated nine conditions for the conservation of condemned treasures and monuments,[50] and when, after the Paris uprising in 1792, the Legislative Assembly and later the National Convention issued respective decrees ordering the destruction of the vestiges of despotism, an exception was made in the event that the Commission on Monuments requested the preservation of 'objects which may be of interest to the arts'.[51] The confusion surrounding this exception was sought to be dispelled by a decree of 16 September 1792 calling for the preservation of 'masterpieces of the arts'.[52] But further and more inflammatory incitements to destruction followed the launch of the Terror in 1793. Some of the revolutionaries looked to stanch the loss, among them Joseph Lakanal, a deputy to the Convention, who appealed for protective legislation, declaring – as was literally true after their expropriation – that works of art 'belong[ed] to all citizens in general; not to any one of them in particular'.[53] On 13 April 1793, a penal decree was issued to safeguard certain 'masterpieces of sculpture',[54] followed by a 70-page 'Directive on the means of inventorying and conserving throughout the Republic all objects capable of serving the arts, sciences and teaching', written by Félix Vicq d'Azyr and referring to such objects as an inheritance ('héritage').[55] A further decree of 24 October 1793 forbade persons 'to remove, destroy, mutilate or alter in any way – on the pretext of effacing signs of feudalism and royalty – books, drawings, ... paintings, statues, bas-reliefs, ... antiquities ... and other objects of interest to the arts, history or teaching located in libraries, collections or ... artists' residences'.[56] In spite of these efforts, citizens set upon the cultural property of the *ancien régime* with gusto.

---

[48] F. Choay, *The Invention of the Historic Monument*, translated by L. M. O'Connell (Cambridge: Cambridge University Press, 2001), p. 195 n. 9.
[49] A. Desvallées, 'Emergence et cheminements du mot patrimoine', *Musées & Collections publiques de France*, No. 208, September 1995, p. 6 at p. 8.
[50] Reproduced in Choay, *Invention of the Historic Monument*, pp. 197–8 n. 27.
[51] J.-P. Babelon and A. Chastel, 'La notion de patrimoine' (1980) 49 *Revue de l'art* 5 at 18.
[52] *Ibid.*, at 19.
[53] J. L. Sax, 'Heritage Preservation as a Public Duty: The Abbé Grégoire and the Origins of an Idea' (1990) 88 Mich. LR 1142 at 1157 n. 76.
[54] Choay, *Invention of the Historic Monument*, pp. 72 and 198 n. 34.
[55] Desvallées, 'Emergence et cheminements', at p. 9.
[56] Choay, *Invention of the Historic Monument*, p. 72.

Finally, after the fall of Robespierre in 1794, the abbé Grégoire, a deputy to the Convention, produced three commissioned reports on revolutionary vandalism⁵⁷ (a word coined by Grégoire himself⁵⁸). Grégoire sought to preserve France's architectural, archaeological and artistic property by emphasising that they were 'the nation's objects, which, belonging to no one, are the property of all'.⁵⁹ He chided that '[t]he man with a measure of common decency will have the sense that, while he is free to be lavish with what is his, he is entitled only to be sparing with what is the nation's'.⁶⁰ The abbé undertook to 'pass on this ... inheritance ['héritage'] to posterity'.⁶¹ Indeed, the Convention 'owe[d] it to its own glory and to the people to hand down to posterity both [France's] monuments and its horror at those who wish to destroy them'.⁶²

At the international level, in a policy initiated by the Directory in spring 1796, Napoleon's military conquests were accompanied by the systematic appropriation, by plunder and coerced treaty, of a vast collection of artworks from France's defeated enemies. Ironically, the publicly-espoused inspiration for this was the vision of a pan-European artistic culture, of which France, as a republic among tyrannies, was best placed to act as custodian. But the same vision inspired the policy's critics. In 1796, affirming that 'for a long time in Europe the arts and sciences [had] constituted a republic',⁶³ the fine arts scholar Antoine Quatremère de Quincy published a set of open letters condemning the removal of treasures of art from Italy. The arts and sciences 'belong[ed] to all of Europe, and were no longer the exclusive property of one nation';⁶⁴ indeed, 'the riches of the sciences and arts ... belong[ed] to all the world'.⁶⁵ France's plunder was a 'violation of common

---

[57] See l'abbé Grégoire, 'Rapport sur les destructions opérées par le Vandalisme, et sur les moyens de le réprimer', in Œuvres de l'abbé Grégoire. Tome II. Grégoire député à la Convention nationale (Nendeln/Paris: KTO Press/EDHIS, 1977), p. 257; l'abbé Grégoire, 'Second Rapport sur le Vandalisme', in ibid., p. 321; l'abbé Grégoire, 'Troisième Rapport sur le Vandalisme', in ibid., p. 335.
[58] See l'abbé Grégoire, 'Rapport sur les inscriptions des monumens publics', in ibid., p. 141 at p. 149.
[59] Grégoire, 'Rapport sur les destructions', at p. 277.
[60] Grégoire, 'Second Rapport', at p. 328.
[61] Grégoire, 'Rapport sur les destructions', at p. 268.
[62] Grégoire, 'Troisième Rapport', at p. 352.
[63] A. C. Quatremère de Quincy, Lettres à Miranda sur le déplacement des monuments de l'art de l'Italie (1796), 2nd edn, introduction and notes by E. Pommier (Paris: Macula, 1996), p. 88.
[64] Ibid.
[65] Ibid., p. 123.

property'.[66] Quatremère declared that 'in civilised Europe, everything belonging to the culture of the arts and sciences is above the rights of war and victory'.[67] After Napoleon's eventual defeat, the sculptor Antonio Canova, a leading figure in negotiations for the return of collections to the Papal States, called in aid 'the good of the republic of the arts'[68] to claim once more, in the words of Quatremère, that '[e]verything belonging to the culture of the arts and sciences is above the rights of war and victory'.[69] In a letter to the Plenipotentiaries of Austria, Prussia and Russia, Lord Castlereagh, the British Foreign Secretary, characterised Napoleon's plunder as 'in contravention of the Laws of modern War'.[70] Meanwhile, on the other side of the Atlantic, a British Court of Vice-Admiralty in Halifax, Nova Scotia, decreeing in *The Marquis de Somerueles* the return of Italian artworks seized *en route* to Philadelphia by a British ship in the Anglo-American War of 1812, reasoned that '[t]he arts ... are considered not as the peculium of this or of that nation, but as the property of mankind at large, and as belonging to the common interest of the whole species'; as such, they were 'admitted amongst all civilized nations, as forming an exception to the severe rights of warfare, and as entitled to favour and protection'.[71]

Back in France, efforts set in train by the likes of Lakanal, Vicq d'Azyr and Grégoire bore fruit with the setting up in 1830 of the Comité des travaux historiques; with the first allocation of funds for the preservation of historic monuments in 1831; with the establishment in 1833 of the Historic Monuments Inspectorate, whose task it was to determine which buildings deserved that status; with the creation of a Commission on Historic Monuments in 1837; and with the first law on historic monuments in 1887. Between 1840 and 1849 alone, the number of listed monuments went from 934 to 3,000.[72] The French lead was followed elsewhere. By 1850, 'most European countries would grant to the historic monument the official blessing of institutionalization',[73]

---

[66] *Ibid.*, p. 89.
[67] *Ibid.*, p. 109.
[68] E. Jayme, 'Antonio Canova, la repubblica delle arti ed il diritto internazionale' (1992) 75 Riv. Dir. Int. 889 at 890.
[69] *Ibid.*, at 891.
[70] 3 BFSP (1815–1816) 203 at 206. See also *ibid.*, at 204 ('contrary ... to the usages of modern warfare'), and the Duke of Wellington to Castlereagh, *ibid.*, 207 at 210 ('contrary to the practice of civilized warfare').
[71] *The Marquis de Somerueles*, Stewart's Vice-Admiralty Reports (Nova Scotia), p. 482 (1813).
[72] Choay, *Invention of the Historic Monument*, p. 97.
[73] *Ibid.*, p. 84.

and by 1860 Burckhardt was able to state that '[t]he age in which we live is loud ... in proclaiming the worth of culture, and especially of the culture of antiquity'.[74] The newly-independent republics of Central and South America joined in, as did Meiji Japan. As for the UK, in 1845 an Act for the better Protection of Works of Art introduced criminal penalties for malicious destruction or damage to, *inter alia*, 'any Statue or Monument exposed to public View';[75] in 1877 William Morris founded the Society for the Protection of Ancient Buildings, borrowing from John Ruskin in seeing such sites as belonging 'partly to all generations of mankind who are to follow us';[76] in 1882 the Ancient Monuments Protection Act was passed, being updated in 1900;[77] in 1895 the National Trust was established as a private body voluntarily charged with the acquisition of historic sites to be held on trust for the nation, a task lent a degree of state support by the National Trust Act 1907;[78] and in 1908 the Royal Commission on Historical Monuments was set up.

Rather than undermining cultural ecumenism, this material cultural nationalism 'retained ... a cosmopolitan colouring'.[79] Preservationism at home flowed easily into a concern for the architecture, art and antiquities of other countries. Ruskin and Morris militated for the preservation of the monuments and old towns and cities of France, Switzerland and Italy. In 1854, the former coined the idea of the common 'European asset', and proposed setting up a Europe-wide private conservation organisation along the lines of the Society for the Protection of Ancient Buildings and the National Trust. Morris was vocal in defence of a working-class district in Naples, and later called for the protection of monuments in Turkey and of the Arabic and Coptic architecture of Egypt. At the popular level, Champollion's archaeological exploits in Egypt and Layard and Botta's in Mesopotamia, along with Elgin's Marbles and Schliemann's excavations at Troy and Mycaenae,

---

[74] Burckhardt, *Civilization of the Renaissance*, p. 146.
[75] 8 & 9 Vict. 44, s. 1.
[76] Quoted in N. Boulting, 'The law's delays: conservationist legislation in the British Isles', in Fawcett, J. (ed.), *The Future of the Past. Attitudes to Conservation 1174–1974* (London: Thames and Hudson, 1976), p. 9 at p. 16.
[77] 45 & 46 Vict. 73 and 63 & 64 Vict. 34 respectively.
[78] 7 Edw. VII 136.
[79] G. Best, *Humanity in Warfare. The Modern History of the International Law of Armed Conflicts* (London: Weidenfeld and Nicolson, 1980), p. 46, referring more generally to nineteenth century nationalism.

did much to raise public awareness of the historico-artistic wonders of the world. The birth of mass tourism played its part too, as the well-heeled Grand Tourists of the eighteenth century, armed with their Vasaris, gave way to the sensible-shoed '"Cook's Tourists"... carrying their Murrays and Baedekers'.[80] By 1903, in his landmark book *The Modern Cult of Monuments*, the Viennese art historian and theorist Alois Riegl was able to identify an interest in historic monuments in its 'modern form', that is, 'a concern for every accomplishment, however slight, of every people, whatever the differences that separate us from them; a concern for the history of humanity in general, each of its members appearing to us as an integral part of ourselves'.[81]

As for international legal protection in time of war, despite the demise of just war doctrine which had ethically underpinned the rule of necessity, the jurists of the early to mid-nineteenth century restated, for the most part, Vattel's positions on the destruction of civilian property and of cultural property in particular.[82] In 1863, Francis Lieber's Instructions for the Government of Armies of the United States in the Field (the Lieber Code),[83] the first codification of the laws of war, spoke of 'the distinction between the private individual belonging to a hostile country and the hostile country itself, with its men in arms', noting that '[t]he principle has been more and more acknowledged that the unarmed citizen is to be spared in person, property, and honor as much as the exigencies of war will admit'.[84] All direct destruction of property indispensable for securing the ends of the war, or incidentally unavoidable in the securing of such ends, remained permissible;[85] or, in the prohibitive wording of the 1874 Draft International Regulations on the Laws and Customs of War (the Brussels Declaration[86]), the first intergovernmental, albeit non-binding

---

[80] G. Lindop, 'With a cold tongue or a piece of beef', *Times Literary Supplement*, 31 July 1998, p. 9.
[81] A. Riegl, *Le Culte Moderne des Monuments: Son Essence et Sa Genèse*, text of 1903, translated by D. Wieczorek (Paris: Seuil, 1984), p. 51.
[82] See e.g. J.-L. Klüber, *Droit des gens moderne de l'Europe*, 2 vols. (Paris: J.-P. Aillaud, 1831), vol. I, paras. 262 and 253 respectively.
[83] D. Schindler and J. Toman (eds.), *The Laws of Armed Conflicts. A Collection of Conventions, Resolutions and Other Documents*, 4th revised and completed edn (Leiden/Boston: Martinus Nijhoff, 2004), p. 3.
[84] Lieber Code, art. 22.
[85] *Ibid*, arts. 14 and 15.
[86] Brussels, 27 August 1874, in Schindler and Toman, *Laws of Armed Conflicts*, p. 21.

codification of the laws of war, and of the so-called Oxford Manual,[87] a private initiative of the newly-formed Institut de droit international, all destruction of the enemy's property which was not 'imperatively demanded by the necessity of war' was forbidden.[88] 'Open towns, agglomerations of dwellings, or villages' which were undefended could not be attacked or bombarded.[89] But when it came to defended places, even if the Oxford Manual and late nineteenth century jurists underlined that 'considerations of humanity' required that 'this means of coercion be hedged with certain restraints',[90] the strict legal position — strongly contested though it was by a few — remained that the bombardment of civilian quarters of fortified towns was permissible if demanded by the exigencies of war.[91]

And by the late nineteenth century, the strategic and technological revolution signalled by the American Civil War and the Franco-Prussian War meant that such 'exigencies' threatened to become the rule rather than the exception. Strategically, the rise and extension of participatory democracy in several European countries and North America, along with the centralisation of the modern state, led to a reassessment of the rationale behind bombardment. With defending garrisons ultimately controlled by politicians responsive to the electorate, it now made sense to make the inhabitants suffer when seeking to occupy fortified towns and cities.[92] More to the point, the overrunning of particular towns and cities was less and less bombardment's *raison d'être*: rather than the collapse of individual garrisons, the incipient aim of bombardment was the surrender of the national government through the demoralisation

---

[87] Institut de droit international, 'Les lois de la guerre sur terre. Manuel publié par l'Institut de droit international' (1881–2) 5 AIDI 157.
[88] Brussels Declaration, art. 13(g). See also Oxford Manual, art. 32(b).
[89] Brussels Declaration, art. 15. See also Oxford Manual, art. 32(c).
[90] Oxford Manual, art. 32(c), explanatory note. Such restraints were 'to restrict the effects as far as possible to the hostile military force and its means of defence': *ibid*. See also G. Rolin-Jaequemyns, 'La guerre actuelle' (1870) 2 RDI 643 at 674; J.-C. Bluntschli, *Le droit international codifié*, 3rd edn, translated by M. C. Lardy (Paris: Guillaumin, 1881), para. 554 bis; J. Guelle, *Précis des lois de la guerre sur terre. Commentaire pratique à l'usage des officiers de l'armée active, de la réserve et de la territoriale*, 2 vols. (Paris: Pedone-Lauriel, 1884), vol. I, pp. 117–18.
[91] Bluntschli, *Droit international*, para. 554 bis; Guelle, *Précis*, vol. I, pp. 117–18; C. Calvo, *Le droit international théorique et pratique*, 5th edn, 5 vols. (Paris: Rousseau, 1896), vol. IV, para. 2073.
[92] An early instance of this thinking and practice was the bombardment of revolutionary Venice in 1849 by Austrian forces under Field Marshal Radetzky.

of the populace.⁹³ Technological advances made this feasible. Modern metallurgical techniques applied to artillery and the spread of railways capable of hauling heavy freight to the front with maximum expedition meant that resort to bombardment became much easier. Indeed, it became more convenient to do away with the time-consuming entr'acte of siege and to proceed post-haste to shelling as the technique of choice. Added to this, the vastly increased range of cannon meant that shells penetrated far deeper into the civilian heart of a city than in the past, when they rarely flew much further than the walls.⁹⁴

But despite the creeping tendency towards 'morale' bombardment, it was never suggested that it was permissible to target monuments and works of art in the hope of breaking a population's will to resist. Indeed, there was by now a consensus in the Western world that such property was deserving of legal privilege, a consensus crystallised during the Franco-Prussian War by the international outcry, both scholarly and public, at the Prussians' unintended bombardment of the abbey of St Denis and of historico-artistic sites in Strasbourg and Paris. While apportioning blame differently, the Royal Academy of Ireland and the University of Göttingen both characterised the threatened treasures of Paris as the 'property of humanity as a whole'.⁹⁵ The protest lodged by the Institut de France at the shelling of Strasbourg cathedral similarly described such buildings as 'belonging to humanity as a whole, forming, so to speak, the common heritage of cultured nations'.⁹⁶ The upshot was that the Brussels Declaration, the Oxford Manual and leading jurists were all in agreement that, in the event of bombardment of a defended place, 'all necessary steps must be taken to spare, as far as possible, buildings dedicated to art, science, and charitable purposes, ... on condition they are not being used at the time for military purposes'.⁹⁷

---

⁹³ 'Bismarck was much impressed in September 1870 by General Sheridan's advice, based on his experience in the American Civil War, to cause "the inhabitants so much suffering that they must long for peace, and force their government to demand it".': R. Tombs, 'The Wars against Paris', in S. Förster and J. Nagler (eds.), *On the Road to Total War. The American Civil War and the German Wars of Unification, 1861–1871* (Washington, DC/Cambridge: German Historical Institute/Cambridge University Press, 1997), p. 541 at p. 561.
⁹⁴ The Prussian artillery around Paris in 1871 had a range of 8 km.
⁹⁵ Quoted in G. Rolin-Jaequemyns, 'Essai complémentaire sur la guerre franco-allemande dans ses rapports avec le droit international' (1871) 3 RDI 288 at 302.
⁹⁶ Quoted in Guelle, *Précis*, vol. II, p. 133 n. 1 and Calvo, *Droit international*, para. 2086 n. 1.
⁹⁷ Brussels Declaration, art. 17. See also Oxford Manual, art. 34; T. Twiss, *The Law of Nations Considered as Independent Political Communities. On the Rights and Duties of Nations in Time*

The late nineteenth century also saw the rise of rules governing the treatment of cultural property during belligerent occupation, rules catalysed earlier by the Napoleonic Wars and consolidated by the furore over the plunder and torching of the Chinese imperial summer palace by Anglo-French forces in the Second Opium War of 1860. Guelle, in his handbook on the laws of war for use by French officers, declared:

> One act particularly contrary to international law is the destruction or carrying off of artistic collections, libraries and archives. These riches are the heritage of the whole of humankind, so it is in the interests of all that they escape the effects of war as much as possible ...[98]

A prohibition on injury to or destruction of monuments and works of art during belligerent occupation was endorsed by the Lieber Code, the Brussels Declaration, the Oxford Manual and contemporary jurists,[99] and once more gave voice to the belief that such behaviour was in no way necessary. As for appropriation, while an Occupying Power had certain rights in respect of the movable and immovable property of the occupied territory, the property of establishments devoted to the arts and sciences was to be treated as private property,[100] and was thus not to be seized.[101] For his part, Lieber permitted the removal of 'works of art, libraries, collections, or instruments belonging to a hostile nation' for the benefit of that nation, if it could be done without injury to them, with the ultimate ownership to be settled by the ensuing treaty of peace.[102] But under no circumstances were they to be sold or given away; nor were they to be privately appropriated.[103] Lieber's limited permission

---

 of War, 2nd edn revised (Oxford/London: Clarendon Press/Longmans, Green, 1875), para. 69; Bluntschli, *Droit international*, para. 554*ter*; Guelle, *Précis*, vol. II, p. 131.

[98] Guelle, *Précis*, vol. II, p. 136.
[99] Lieber Code, art. 36 (not to be 'wantonly destroyed or injured'); Brussels Declaration, art. 8; Oxford Manual, art. 53 ('save when urgently demanded by military necessity'); Twiss, *Law of Nations*, paras. 68–9; Bluntschli, *Droit international*, paras. 649–50; F. de Martens, *Traité de Droit International*, 2 vols. (Paris: Librairie Maresq Ainé, 1887), vol. II, p. 261; H. S. Maine, *International Law*, 2nd edn (London: John Murray, 1894), p. 195.
[100] Lieber Code, art. 34; Brussels Declaration, art. 8.
[101] Brussels Declaration, arts. 8 and 38; Oxford Manual, art. 53; P. Fiore, *Trattato di diritto internazionale pubblico*, 2nd edn, 3 vols. (Turin: Unione Tipografico-Editrice, 1884), vol. III, paras. 1664 and 1747; Martens, *Traité*, vol. II, p. 261; Maine, *International Law*, pp. 194–5; A. Pillet, *Les lois actuelles de la guerre* (Paris: Rousseau, 1898), para. 222.
[102] Lieber Code, art. 36.
[103] *Ibid.*

was not, however, included in either the Brussels Declaration or Oxford Manual, and found no favour with other jurists. The Brussels Declaration provided explicitly that all seizure or destruction of, or wilful damage to, institutions dedicated to religion, charity and education, the arts and sciences, historic monuments, or works of art or science should be made the subject of legal proceedings by the competent authorities.[104]

Article 18 of the Brussels Declaration and article 32(a) of the Oxford Manual flatly forbade the pillage of a town or place, even when taken by assault. The prohibition reflected a now-settled conviction that looting of this sort, even when permitted by a commanding officer, was not militarily necessary: with resistance to entry and occupation overcome, such conduct was in no way conducive to the ends of the war. In addition, article 39 of the Brussels Declaration forbade pillage during belligerent occupation, as did the Lieber Code and contemporary jurists.[105]

The Hague Rules

In 1899, the Brussels Declaration served as the basis for the Regulations concerning the Laws and Customs of War on Land annexed to the Convention concerning the Laws and Customs of War on Land[106] adopted at the First Hague Peace Conference. In 1907, a Second Peace Conference was convened in The Hague 'to complete and explain in certain particulars the work of the First Peace Conference, ... following on the Brussels Conference of 1874'.[107] This second conference produced revised rules for the conduct of war on land, as well as a specific convention on bombardment by sea.[108] The former were embodied in the Regulations

---

[104] Brussels Declaration, art. 8.
[105] Lieber Code, art. 44; Bluntschli, *Droit international*, para. 661; Fiore, *Trattato*, vol. III, para. 1670. Despite this, German troops looted the imperial astronomical observatory in Peking during the Boxer Rebellion, an act protested at by the US, which had strictly forbidden, and whose troops had refrained from, such conduct in the Spanish-American War.
[106] The Hague, 29 July 1899, UKTS No. 1 (1901), Cd 800.
[107] Convention concerning the Laws and Customs of War on Land, The Hague, 18 October 1907, UKTS No. 9 (1910), Cd 5030, preamble.
[108] The rules on naval bombardment are found in the Convention concerning Bombardment by Naval Forces in Time of War, The Hague, 18 October 1907, UKTS No. 13 (1910), Cd 5117.

concerning the Laws and Customs of War on Land, better known as the Hague Rules, annexed to the Convention concerning the Laws and Customs of War on Land (1907 Hague Convention IV). In terms of the destruction and appropriation of enemy property, including cultural property, the Hague Rules endorsed in binding form the positions staked out in the Brussels Declaration.

Hostilities

The overarching rule as to the treatment of enemy property in the course of hostilities is embodied in article 23(g) of the Hague Rules. Article 23(g) states that it is forbidden to destroy or seize the enemy's property, 'unless such destruction or seizure be imperatively demanded by the necessities of war'. In other words, destruction and seizure of enemy property is permissible only if and to the extent that it is militarily necessary.[109]

A special rule governs recourse to bombardment. Article 25 provides that the 'attack or bombardment, by whatever means, of towns, villages, dwellings or buildings which are undefended is prohibited'. The phrase 'by whatever means' is an implied reference to attack from the air,[110] the possibility of which had dawned with the advent of dirigibles. The basis for the distinction between 'undefended' and 'defended' lay in bombardment's original rationale as a last resort by which to enter and occupy a town: if a town was undefended,

---

[109] The concept of military necessity is not defined in the Hague Rules, but the orthodox view at the time was stated in L. Oppenheim, *International Law. A Treatise*, 2 vols., 2nd edn (London: Longmans, Green, 1912), vol. II, para. 150, original emphasis: 'All destruction of and damage to enemy property for the purpose of offence and defence is *necessary* destruction and damage, and therefore lawful. It is not only permissible to destroy and damage all kinds of property on the battlefield during battle, but also in preparation for battle or siege. To strengthen a defensive position a house may be destroyed or damaged. To cover the retreat of an army a village on the battlefield may be fired. The district around an enemy fortress held by a belligerent may be razed, and, therefore, all private and public buildings ... may be destroyed, and all bridges blown up within a certain area. If a farm, a village, or even a town is not to be abandoned but prepared for defence, it may be necessary to damage in many ways or entirely destroy private and public property.'

[110] See *The Proceedings of the Hague Peace Conferences. Translation of the Official Texts*, 4 vols. (New York: Oxford University Press, 1920–1), vol. III, pp. 14–15. See also J. E. Edmonds and L. Oppenheim, *Land Warfare. An Exposition of the Laws and Usages of War on Land, for the Guidance of Officers of His Majesty's Army* (London: HMSO, 1911), para. 117 note (i).

bombardment was unnecessary and, applying the general rule embodied in article 23(g), unlawful.

Neither article 25 nor any other rule forbade the bombardment of civilian districts. Indeed, the view of the Great Powers was that, apart from cultural property protected by article 27, it was lawful to bombard all property in a defended town.[111] The rule eventually embodied in article 25 may have been envisaged in the nineteenth century as a gloss on the fundamental rule of military necessity; but by the early twentieth, military necessity was taken to impose no restraints. On the contrary, it justified general bombardment, since the 'destruction of private and public buildings by bombardment ... [was] one of the means to impress upon the local authorities the advisability of surrender'.[112]

But express exception was made for cultural property. Article 27 of the Hague Rules provides that in sieges and bombardments 'all necessary steps must be taken to spare, as far as possible, buildings dedicated to religion, art, science, or charitable purposes, [and] historic monuments, ... provided they are not being used at the time for military purposes'. The verb 'to spare' encompasses both direct injury and avoidable incidental damage inflicted by percussion, shrapnel, debris or wayward ordnance in the course of bombarding nearby targets. The proviso 'as far as possible' makes it clear, however, that damage caused to privileged buildings and historic monuments as an unavoidable incident of the bombardment of other targets was not unlawful.[113] No positive rule compelled a belligerent to ask whether the military need to destroy a lawful target outweighed the damage likely to be caused to cultural property. For its part, the Convention concerning Bombardment by Naval Forces in Time of War (1907 Hague Convention IX) — article 5 of which was analogous to article 27 of the Hague Rules — stated in article 2 that as long as a naval commander was bombarding a military objective, he incurred no responsibility for any unavoidable damage which might be occasioned; and, according to its preamble, the Convention sought to apply

---

[111] Edmonds and Oppenheim, *Land Warfare*, para. 122, express exception being made in para. 133 for Hague Rules, art. 27; *Kriegsbrauch im Landkriege*, 1902, translated as *The German War Book being "The Usages of War on Land" Issued by the Great General Staff of the German Army*, translated by J. H. Morgan (London: John Murray, 1915), pp. 79 and 81.
[112] Edmonds and Oppenheim, *Land Warfare*, para. 122.
[113] See also *ibid.*, para. 123 note (c).

to bombardment by sea, as far as was possible, the principles applicable to bombardment by land.

Article 27 lays down a crucial precondition for the protection of the property in question – namely, that it is not being used at the time for 'military purposes'. What 'military purposes' encompasses is not specified, but it was generally agreed at the time that it included the use of buildings as offices and quarters for soldiers, or as signalling stations or observation posts to help target artillery.[114] What is also not specified is that, even if such property is used for military purposes, its destruction is not necessarily justified in all circumstances: reference back to the general restriction articulated in article 23(g) that the destruction of enemy property is only justified when imperatively demanded by the necessities of war makes it clear that a privileged building or historic monument put to military use by the enemy is only to be attacked if this is necessary, and only to the extent that it is necessary. There is also a temporal element to the condition precedent. Prior but discontinued military use is insufficient to deny a place protection. Finally, it is important to note that, while the relevant property is protected by article 27 as long as it is not used for military purposes, the provision imposes no positive obligation on the defending party to desist from such use. Use of cultural property for military purposes does not constitute a violation of the Hague Rules.

When it comes to targeting cultural property by way of bombardment, as distinct from damaging it unavoidably while targeting objects nearby, article 27 makes no general allowance on its face for military necessity, in the permissive sense of the term. The sole situation of military necessity which expressly justifies the direct bombardment of historic monuments and buildings dedicated to religion, art, science or charitable purposes is if they are being used at the time for military purposes. This created something of an anomaly, since the destruction of cultural property by any other military means in the course of hostilities was permitted, in accordance with article 23(g), if imperatively demanded by the necessities of war. In other words, while its use for military purposes appeared to be the only lawful reason for bombarding cultural property, it could be torched, dynamited, bulldozed, demolished by hand or raked with machine-gun fire if it 'served to obstruct a line of attack, or ... to provide a shelter to which the enemy might

---

[114] See e.g. *ibid.*, para. 136.

retire',[115] or in order to impede the enemy's advance, or the like. In this light, one school of thought construed the provision, possibly relying on the expressions 'all necessary steps' and 'as far as possible', to reflect the general rule on the destruction of enemy property embodied in article 23(g). On this view, what article 27 prohibited was any bombardment directed at or likely to cause avoidable incidental injury to churches, art galleries, museums, historic monuments and so on, unless such attack or injury was imperatively demanded by the necessities of war. Oppenheim, for example, referred to the '[u]nnecessary bombardment of historical monuments'.[116] This interpretation of article 27 accorded more with the classical customary position. At the same time, it is unclear whether article 27 was intended to reflect or circumscribe the classical law's allowance for military necessity. Moreover, Oppenheim's was a less satisfactory reading of the text. First, it rendered the proviso as to use for military purposes redundant: if the phrase 'as far as possible' encompasses military necessity in general, there would be no need to cite a specific instance thereof. Secondly, applying the maxim *expressio unius exclusio alterius*, the mention of use for military purposes would seem to exclude *a contrario* all other situations of military necessity. Nonetheless, Oppenheim's interpretation of article 27 appeared to be endorsed in the list of war crimes drawn up by Sub-Commission III, on the Responsibility for the Violation of the Laws and Customs of War, of the Commission on Responsibilities established in 1919 by the Preliminary Peace Conference of Paris.[117] The Sub-Commission cited the war crime of 'wanton destruction of religious, charitable, educational and historic buildings and monuments', just as it referred more generally to the 'wanton devastation and destruction of property', the adjective 'wanton' seemingly shorthand for 'not imperatively demanded by the necessities of war'.[118]

Although not made explicit in the *travaux*, it is logical to assume that article 27 applies to bombardment from the air, as well as by land. If article 25, which undoubtedly applies to aircraft, lays down the general

---

[115] B. C. Rodick, *The Doctrine of Necessity in International Law* (New York: Columbia University Press, 1928), p. 63.
[116] Oppenheim, *International Law*, 2nd edn, vol. II, para. 253.
[117] Reproduced in United Nations War Crimes Commission (UNWCC), *History of the United Nations War Crimes Commission and the Development of the Laws of War* (London: HMSO, 1948), pp. 34–5.
[118] *Ibid.*, p. 34.

rule as to the legality of bombardment, and article 27 refines it, it stands to reason that they cover the same types of bombardment. A similar logic was adopted in 1927 by the Greco–German Mixed Arbitral Tribunal in *Coenca Brothers* v. *Germany*,[119] which held that article 26 of the Hague Rules, dealing with pre-bombardment warnings to the civilian population, applied to aerial bombardment. The Tribunal considered it 'generally recognised that there was no reason why the rules as to land bombardment should not apply to bombardment from the air'.[120] Contemporary jurists also recognised the applicability of article 27 to aerial bombardment.[121]

Compared to its forerunner in 1899, article 27's only innovation was the inclusion of 'historic monuments' among the several types of property to be spared in bombardment. Reflecting, perhaps, the absence of peacetime monuments legislation and, indeed, of a monuments consciousness in the US of the mid-nineteenth century, article 35 of the Lieber Code, while prohibiting the unnecessary destruction of cultural movables, had not expressly encompassed within its rule immovable property worthy in its own right of preservation on historic or artistic grounds. For their part, in what may merely have been a drafting oversight, given the inclusion of historic monuments in the relevant provision of each relating to belligerent occupation, the Brussels Declaration, the Oxford Manual and the 1899 Hague Rules cast their protection over, *inter alia*, buildings devoted to art but not over buildings of artistic or historic value themselves.[122] The insertion of historic monuments into the text of article 27 at the Second Hague Peace Conference – at the suggestion of the Greek delegate, who had earlier successfully inserted reference to historic monuments into Hague Convention IX – was 'greeted with applause and unanimously approved'.[123]

By 1907, the term 'historic monuments' had a well-established meaning in national legislation throughout Europe and the New World, referring to immovable property, whether public or private, deserving of legal protection on its own historical, artistic or architectural terms,

---

[119] 4 AD 570 (1927), followed in *Kiriadolou* v. *Germany*, 5 AD 516 (1930).
[120] *Coenca Brothers*, at 571. See also *Kiriadolou*, at 517.
[121] See e.g. 'The Use of Balloons in the War between Italy and Turkey' (1912) 6 AJIL 485 at 487.
[122] Brussels Declaration, art. 17; Oxford Manual, art. 34; 1899 Hague Rules, art. 27.
[123] *Proceedings of the Hague Peace Conferences*, vol. III, p. 136. See also *ibid.*, pp. 12, 23 and 353–4.

rather than on account of its contents or purpose. Buildings, archaeological sites and ruins, city walls and so on were all capable of being characterised as 'historic monuments'. Nor did the adjective 'historic' imply that the structure had to be linked to an important event or person: artistic or architectural note sufficed to make a monument historic; indeed, as elaborated by Alois Riegl in 1903, the word 'historic' did not even necessarily denote a certain age, as long as the structure was of enduring artistic or architectural significance, although it is unclear whether general usage had caught up with Riegl's theory by 1907. The term 'historic monument' was particularly resonant in the authentic French text. The word 'monument' had been used in France to denote immovable cultural property since as early as the seventeenth century, and Quatremère de Quincy was able to explain in 1798 that '*monument*, referring more to the effect of the edifice than to its intention or purpose, can suit and be applied to all types of building'.[124] The full term 'historic monument' ('monument historique') dates in French from at least 1790, when it was used in the first volume of Aubin-Louis Millin de Grandmaison's *Antiquités nationales*,[125] and it would be defined in the law on historic monuments of 1913 as a building 'whose conservation is, from the point of view of history or art, in the public interest'.[126] The term was also current in English. As far back as 1560, Elizabeth I had sought to quell Reformation iconoclasm with a 'Proclamation against breaking or defacing of Monuments of antiquity set up in churches...',[127] and the extant conservation legislation in the UK was the Ancient Monuments Protection Act 1900,[128] soon to become the Ancient Monuments Consolidation and Amendment Act 1913.[129] 'Monument' was also the accepted term in Spanish ('monumento') and German ('Denkmal').

Historic monuments are not the only property protected by article 27. The provision applies equally to 'buildings dedicated to religion, art,

---

[124] Choay, *Invention of the Historic Monument*, p. 7, original emphasis.
[125] A.-L. Millin de Grandmaison, *Antiquités nationales, ou Recueil de monumens pour servir à l'histoire générale et particulière de l'empire françois, tels que tombeaux, inscriptions, statues, vitraux, fresques, etc.; tirés des abbayes, monastères, châteaux, et autres lieux devenus domaines nationaux*, 5 vols. (Paris: Drouhin, 1790–9), vol. I.
[126] Loi du 31 décembre 1913 sur les monuments historiques, JORF, 4 January 1914, chap. I, art. 1.
[127] Boulting, 'The law's delays', pp. 11 and 153 n. 7.
[128] 63 & 64 Vict. 34.
[129] 3 & 4 Geo. V 32.

science, or charitable purposes' — in the authoritative French text, to 'les édifices consacrés aux cultes, aux arts, aux sciences et à la bienfaisance' — and it applies to these regardless of whether they are historically or artistically significant in any way.[130] In other words, article 27 seeks to spare every single example, no matter how banal, of the several sorts of buildings to which it refers. What constitutes a building dedicated to religion is relatively straightforward; so too a building dedicated to art or, adhering more closely to the French, to 'the arts'. Next, the authoritative French text speaks of 'les sciences', which has a wider import than the English 'science' as it is used today, encompassing at a minimum all material manifestations of research and learning. The result is that article 27 covers museums, libraries and at least certain sorts of archives. The phrase 'charitable purposes' is also compendious, and includes not only orphanages, retirement homes, homes for those with disabilities *et ejusdem generis*, but also kindergartens, schools and, insofar as they are not already accounted for, universities. In this regard, it is true that article 27, in contradistinction to article 56, does not mention education as such; but a close comparison of the two provisions, especially in the authentic French text, makes it sufficiently clear that 'charitable purposes' ('la bienfaisance'), as used in the former, is synonymous with the latter's 'charity and education' ('la charité et ... l'instruction').[131]

To facilitate the sparing of the property in question, the second limb of article 27 states that it is 'the duty of the besieged to indicate the presence of such buildings or places by distinctive and visible signs, which shall be notified to the enemy beforehand'. While it is not clear from the English text whether 'beforehand' means before the outbreak of hostilities or before the commencement of bombardment during each siege, the authentic French text ('par des signes visibles spéciaux qui seraient notifiés d'avance à l'assiégeant') indicates the latter. The stipulation is purely facultative. That is, failure by the besieged to acquit the duty to indicate the relevant buildings does not relieve the

---

[130] Article 27 also covers 'hospitals, and places where the sick and wounded are collected'. This category of privileged property is not considered here, since the concept of 'cultural property', the focus of this book, does not extend to hospitals and other medical places as such. Some specific hospitals, however, such as (formerly) Santa Maria della Scala in Siena or the Hadassah Hospital in Jerusalem, with its windows by Chagall, may qualify as historic monuments and hence, in generic terms, as cultural property.

[131] As with hospitals and the like, not necessarily every type of building dedicated to these various ends can, as such, be considered 'cultural property'.

besieging Party of its obligation to spare them when their location is known. Although it is unclear whether the non-reciprocal character of all international humanitarian rules – accepted today as a fundamental principle of the laws of armed conflict, and hence applicable now to the Hague Rules as a whole – was agreed on when the Rules were adopted, this second limb of article 27 is phrased in such a way as to made it clear on its face that the besieging Party may not invoke the principle *inadimplenti non est adimplendum* in the event that the besieged fail in their duty to indicate protected buildings by distinctive signs. The *inadimplenti* maxim, if a general principle of international law at all, could only be invoked if the default were that of the other Contracting State, the juridical entity which has agreed to the international undertakings embodied in and annexed to 1907 Hague Convention IV – an entity generally denoted in the Hague Rules by the terms 'State', 'Government' or 'hostile party'.[132] The term 'the besieged', however, is unspecific as to the bearer of the duty in question, and tends *a contrario* to suggest the general populace and/or those linked with the protected institutions. Moreover, the word 'duty' ('devoir') is used, as distinct from 'obligation' ('obligation'), the term usually employed to denote a formal international legal rule.[133] The feasibility and utility of this second limb of article 27 was already open to doubt when drafted, given the reality even in 1907 of architecturally dense cities of wide radius bombarded by field artillery tens of miles distant or by aircraft.

Article 28 of the Hague Rules provides that the pillage of a town or place, even when taken by assault, is prohibited. In other words, the soldiery is not to be given free rein to ransack and pilfer enemy property. An identical rule applicable to marine forces is found in article 7 of Hague Convention IX.

Belligerent occupation

Article 42 of the Hague Rules provides that territory is considered occupied 'when it is actually placed under the authority of the hostile army', adding that the occupation 'extends only to the territory where such authority has been established and can be exercised'. The satisfaction of article 42 – that is, the legal existence of a state of belligerent occupation – renders applicable the provisions of section III of the Hague

---

[132] See Hague Rules, arts. 6 and 55 ('State'), arts. 7, 10, 11, 14 and 17 ('Government'), and arts. 23(h) and 29 ('hostile party').

[133] *Cf.* e.g. Hague Rules, art. 21.

Rules, entitled 'Military Authority over the Territory of the Hostile State'. It does not, however, exclude the continuing application of other provisions of the Rules insofar as they may be relevant. Crucially, if the military forces of an Occupying Power are involved in military operations during belligerent occupation, whether to quell armed resistance to the occupation, to defend against the enemy's attempt to recapture the territory or to cover a retreat from it, the provisions on hostilities apply.

Article 56 of the Hague Rules lays down the *lex specialis* on the treatment of cultural property during belligerent occupation. Its first limb states that '[t]he property of municipalities, that of institutions dedicated to religion, charity and education, the arts and sciences, even when State property, shall be treated as private property'. In accordance with article 46, private property must be respected — that is, not interfered with, and especially neither damaged nor appropriated — and cannot be confiscated. The term 'property' covers immovables and movables alike, with the result that, in terms of cultural property, the rule applies as much to works of art, antiquities and so on housed in the relevant institutions, or owned by municipalities, as to the buildings that house them. The second limb of article 56 provides that '[a]ll seizure of, destruction or wilful damage done to institutions of this character, historic monuments, works of art and science, is forbidden, and should be made the subject of legal proceedings'. This is the only provision in the Hague Rules to refer explicitly to the legal responsibility of individuals who violate it, although it does not specify whether the proceedings in question should be penal or merely disciplinary. The prohibition embodied in the second limb of article 56 is absolute.

It is important to appreciate, however, that — leaving aside the seizure of cultural property, for which it is impossible to imagine a legitimate military purpose — what the provision forbids is all destruction of and damage to protected institutions and historic monuments unconnected with military operations. Insofar as any destruction or damage is for the purpose of furthering military operations, it is governed not by article 56 but by article 23(g), regulating the destruction of enemy property in the context of hostilities. In this light, the demolition of institutions of a cultural character or historic monuments is not prohibited by article 56 if, in the words of article 23(g), it is imperatively demanded by the necessities of war.[134] This reading of the interaction of the two provisions

---

[134] Indeed, art. 53 of the Oxford Manual, the forerunner to art. 56 of the Hague Rules, had included the proviso 'save when urgently demanded by military necessity'.

was subsequently lent support by the list of war crimes drawn up by Sub-Commission III, on the Responsibility for the Violation of the Laws and Customs of War, of the Commission on Responsibilities established in 1919 by the Preliminary Peace Conference of Paris. In a provision which equally covered the bombardment and other destruction of such property in the course of hostilities, the Sub-Commission listed the war crime of 'wanton destruction of religious, charitable, educational and historic buildings and monuments',[135] just as it spoke more generally of the 'wanton devastation and destruction of property', the adjective 'wanton' seemingly standing for 'not imperatively demanded by the necessities of war'.

As for the relevant *lex generalis*, article 43 provides that, '[t]he authority of the legitimate power having in fact passed into the hands of the occupant, the latter shall take all the measures in his power to restore, and ensure, as far as possible, public order and safety, while respecting, unless absolutely prevented, the laws in force in the country'. The second limb of the provision ('while respecting. . .') obviously obliges a belligerent occupant, unless absolutely prevented from doing so, to leave in place and abide by existing laws providing for the protection and preservation of immovable and movable cultural property in the territory, and this logically entails an obligation to allow the competent local authorities to fulfil any duties or exercise any rights they have under such laws. An important corollary of the second limb of article 43 is that the Occupying Power must comply, unless absolutely prevented from doing so, with any existing local laws relating to the authorisation of archaeological excavations: where a local legal regime regulating archaeological excavations is in place, a belligerent occupant may not engage in or sponsor digs except in accordance with local law, and may not usurp the authority of competent local authorities in this regard, for example by purporting to authorise digs itself. The same goes for any laws regarding the alteration of cultural property and laws regulating the trade in art and antiquities. As for the first limb of article 43, where the English version speaks of 'public order and safety', the authoritative French text uses the expression 'l'ordre et la vie publics'. While 'l'ordre public' can encompass more than the mere absence of civil unrest connoted by the English 'public order', and is often more accurately translated as 'the public good' or 'the public interest', the word 're-establish' here suggests that 'public order' or 'law and order' is

[135] UNWCC, *History of the United Nations War Crimes Commission*, p. 34.

indeed the meaning intended. As for the expression 'la vie [publique]', this is better rendered as 'civil life'[136] or 'civil affairs'. The implications for cultural property of the first limb of article 43 are therefore severalfold. An Occupying Power has a clear obligation to put a stop to and prevent, as far as possible, the breakdown of law and order, in the context of which looting and vandalism of cultural property commonly takes place. More generally, a belligerent occupant must ensure, as far as possible, that existing laws which aim to prevent any form of misappropriation of and wilful damage to cultural property in the territory are adequately enforced. The same goes for local laws aimed at the preservation more broadly of cultural property, such as town planning laws requiring permits for construction on sensitive sites, laws regulating the upkeep and alteration of historic buildings, laws relating to the authorisation of archaeological excavations and those governing the trade in art and antiquities, including export controls. In other words, where the second limb of article 43 requires the Occupying Power to leave in place and abide by local cultural property laws itself, unless absolutely prevented from doing so, the first limb requires it to ensure, as far as possible, that others abide by them too. This may simply involve not hindering the competent local authorities, the local police and the local courts in their enforcement of the relevant laws. It may involve assisting them. It may involve enforcing the laws itself. It will all depend on the circumstances. Finally, the first limb of article 43 permits, where necessary, the promulgation by the Occupying Power itself of laws for the maintenance of public order and civil affairs, and this includes laws for all forms of protection and preservation of cultural property, the aim of such laws being to maintain, in the material cultural context, the maintenance of the *status quo ante* to which article 43 is largely directed.[137]

Article 47 states that pillage 'is formally forbidden' during belligerent occupation. The provision picks up where article 28, the analogous prohibition applicable immediately upon the capture of a place, leaves off.

*

---

[136] E. Benvenisti, *The International Law of Occupation*, with new preface by the author (Princeton, NJ: Princeton University Press, 2004), p. 9; M. Sassòli, 'Legislation and Maintenance of Public Order and Civil Life by Occupying Powers' (2005) 16 EJIL 661 at 663–4.

[137] Moreover, suppressing misappropriation of and damage to cultural property in occupied territory is recognised as a legitimate legislative role for an Occupying Power in art. 56.

The Hague Rules provided cultural property with a degree of legal protection in war. But in the case of bombardment, the most destructive and indiscriminate method of warfare, the reality was that the preservation of cultural property was dependent at the time on the rules protecting the other civilian property around it. And this property, not to mention its inhabitants, was in greater danger than ever, since no rule forbade the bombardment of civilian districts in defended towns, and the new strategic logic militated for it. Nor did any rule prohibit bombardment where the foreseeable damage to cultural property outweighed the military advantage to be gained. The fate of cultural property in the course of bombardment hung in practice on the concept of a 'defended' town – and this concept, in its prime in the days of Wellington and Blücher, looked infirm in the age of Zeppelin.

2   1914 to 1954

The period 1914 to 1954, spanning the two most murderous and destructive conflicts in history, witnessed an upheaval in the laws of war relating to the protection of civilians and civilian property in bombardment. The advent of aerial bombing and the realisation of the logic of total war led to the eclipse in the First World War of the relevant Hague Rules, with baleful incidental consequences for cultural property. In their place emerged the outlines in the interwar years of a new law of aerial bombardment. But these rudiments were insufficient during the Second World War to prevent the devastation from the air of the civilian populations and cities – and, with them, the material cultural heritage – of Germany and Japan. When it came to the destruction of cultural property by other means, however, and to its plunder, the rules codified in the Hague provisions, although flouted by Germany on an almost unimaginable scale in the Second World War, survived and were lent criminal sanction at Nuremberg.

The close of the First World War and the interwar period also saw early moves towards a specialised legal regime for the protection of cultural property in time of war, a regime which, while not formally in place in the Second World War, informed many of the measures adopted by the belligerents with a view to safeguarding monuments and other cultural treasures. These textual and practical efforts would inform the post-war drafting of a specific treaty on the protection of cultural property in the event of armed conflict.

The First World War

Bombardment

The outbreak of the First World War exposed the inadequacy of the rule on bombardment embodied in article 25 of the Hague Rules.[1] With the lines on the Western Front stretching from Flanders to Verdun and beyond, every town behind them could only be captured by fighting and was therefore, in effect, defended. Moreover, the scale of mobilisation meant that towns were full of troops, making them defended in a second sense.[2] They were usually also within range of defensive artillery. As it was, the defence of towns from 1916 'tend[ed] to take the form of aerial counteraction ... perhaps based on some fairly distant aerodrome'.[3] So the assumption was that virtually every single town (and village and city) was liable to bombardment. And in the absence of any positive restraint on bombarding civilian districts in defended towns, all civilian property, except for cultural property covered by article 27, was open to attack.

Not only did the impact of technology make it lawful to attack towns deep behind enemy lines. It also made it feasible. German forces fired on Paris in March 1918 using field artillery, the legendary 'Big Bertha', with a range of 120 kilometres. Zeppelins and Gothas dropped bombs on London, British and French planes attacked towns in western Germany and Austrian aircraft bombarded northern Italy.

Furthermore, there was now an incentive to do so beyond the demoralisation of the populace — although morale bombing, disguised or unabashed, was no less a feature of the war. With the mechanisation and industrialisation of warfare, strategy no longer sought simply to disable the army in the field but also to cripple the productive base, infrastructure and communications without which it was powerless. The munitions factories, the foundries, the chemical-works, the production lines of aircraft, tanks and trucks, the railways, roads, airfields and docks, the telegraph lines and telephone lines — shut these down and the

---

[1] Article 2 of Hague Convention IV, to which the Rules were annexed, was a general participation (*si omnes*) clause, providing that the convention applied only if all the belligerents were Parties to it. Italy, Serbia, Montenegro, Bulgaria and Turkey had not ratified it. But the provisions on the destruction and appropriation of enemy property merely codified custom. As it was, the belligerents invoked the Hague Rules in official statements.

[2] The prevailing view was that the presence of troops rendered a town defended: see e.g. Edmonds and Oppenheim, *Land Warfare*, para. 119; *Kriegsbrauch*, p. 78.

[3] J. M. Spaight, *Air Power and War Rights* (London: Longmans, Green, 1924), p. 197.

war was won. In this way, the First World War spawned the doctrine of economic warfare, in which the path to victory lay in the cities and suburbs.

Belligerent reprisals also played a part in the aerial bombardment of undefended towns,[4] even if, despite the ambiguous official line, the policy was less one of reprisal aimed at the enemy's return to compliance than of retaliation based on a determination not to be worsted. With the law on aerial attacks in disarray, almost any raid could be characterised by the adversary as illegal, justifying a reciprocal illegality in the form of an attack against an undefended town. This reprisal would in turn be seen as a violation, demanding a counter-reprisal.

In this free-for-all environment, where nearly all civilian property was fair game, article 27 of the Hague Rules proved insufficient to save some cultural property from destruction. Advances in the science of explosives were unaccompanied by improvements in the precision with which they could be targeted. The immense destructive power of modern ordnance and the gross inaccuracy of its delivery meant that, even if monuments situated in a defended town were not themselves the object of attack, they were often damaged in attacks on surrounding property, as when, in March 1918, a German shell destroyed the nave of the thirteenth-century church of St Gervais in Paris, killing eighty-eight people. If such damage was unavoidable in the bombardment of lawful targets, it was not unlawful. The resultant destruction of history and art was not only by land and air[5] but by sea as well, with German naval forces hitting the ruins of Whitby Abbey and the Austrian navy raining shells on Ancona.

In addition, article 27's proviso as to military use was regularly invoked by artillery units and air crews – as with infantry units, usually on flimsy grounds – to justify direct attacks on monuments. The cathedral at Rheims was partially destroyed by German forces in September 1914 on

---

[4] It is unclear if cultural property was targeted by way of reprisal, although it was asserted that the Austrians 'appear to have defended' the bombardment of churches and historic monuments in Venice 'as a legitimate measure of reprisal against Italy for the bombardment of Trieste by Italian aviators': J.W. Garner, *International Law and the World War*, 2 vols. (London: Longmans, Green, 1920), vol. I, para. 294. See also L. Rolland, 'Les pratiques de la guerre aérienne dans le conflit de 1914 et le droit des gens' (1916) 23 RGDIP 497 at 544–5 and 563; A. Mérignhac and E. Lémonon, *Le Droit des Gens et la Guerre de 1914–1918*, 2 vols. (Paris: Recueil Sirey, 1921), vol. I, p. 638.

[5] Inaccuracy of bombing from the air was supposedly offered by the Austrians as a further excuse for hitting historic buildings in Venice: Mérignhac and Lémonon, *Droit des Gens et Guerre de 1914–1918*, vol. I, p. 638.

the supposition, based on the accuracy of the French artillery, that its belltower was being used to reconnoitre the German positions.[6] At the same time, an element of blame can be pinned on the failure of article 27 to prohibit the use of monuments for military purposes. Steeples and bell-towers were routinely used by both sides for artillery-spotting, leading to the laying waste of hundreds of village churches. Châteaux were regularly converted into officers' mess and quarters, with little regard for the risk of drawing fire.[7]

Some historic property gave rise to the problem that, whatever its contemporary function or significance, it originally constituted a form of defence for the purposes of article 25. Equating historic and militarily obsolete castles, fortifications and gun emplacements with defences proper, the Central Powers not only characterised towns endowed with such objects as defended, and thus liable to bombardment, but also saw these monuments as military targets in themselves. While one writer objected that '[a] modern town is not defended merely because it includes an ancient Roman camp or a ruinous mediaeval fortress',[8] Austria nonetheless sought to justify its attacks on Venice by reference to, *inter alia*, the historic arsenal of the Venetian republic.[9] The Germans bombarded Belgrade in October 1914, destroying the old royal palace, the national museum and the university, even though the city's defence consisted of 'an ancient Turkish fortress', which was 'nothing but a historical monument'.[10]

The saving grace was that aerial bombardment was still in its infancy in the First World War. Despite the range of modern field artillery, serious penetration of the civilian heartland did not occur until the Zeppelin raids on London in late 1915, and even then its scale and power were comparatively limited in hindsight. Although a trend was clearly developing by the end of the war, with the advent of long-range bomber aircraft, the destruction of civilian property in general and of cultural property in particular was, for the most part, still a tactical, rather than strategic affair. The legal lacunae, technological advances

---

[6] German government communiqué, in *La Guerre de 1914. Recueil de documents intéressant le droit international*, 2 vols. (Paris: Pedone, undated), vol. I, para. 175.

[7] Edmonds and Oppenheim, *Land Warfare*, para. 429, stated that troops could be housed in such places if militarily necessary.

[8] T. J. Lawrence, *The Principles of International Law*, 7th edn, edited by P. H. Winfield (London: Macmillan, 1930), p. 523.

[9] Mérignhac and Lémonon, *Droit des Gens et Guerre de 1914–1918*, vol. I, p. 639.

[10] Garner, *International Law and the World War*, vol. I, para. 269.

and fundamental shifts in strategic logic were not to plumb their potential by 11 November 1918.

Other military operations

The general rule governing the destruction of enemy property – that such destruction was prohibited unless imperatively demanded by the necessities of war, as laid down in article 23(g) of the Hague Rules – emerged from the war battered by infantry on both sides but essentially intact. It was flouted and invoked in bad faith, particularly by German forces in France and Belgium, who in the process devastated many cultural treasures, such as the Cloth Hall at Ypres and the Flemish university town of Louvain (Leuven), where the university library was burnt to the ground, along with its priceless and sometimes irreplaceable contents. In addition, historic villages, churches, châteaux, archives, museums, galleries and monuments were destroyed or severely damaged and works of art vandalised, especially during the German invasion of 1914 and retreat of 1917–18. Yet such conduct was generally characterised by the opposing party as a violation of the laws of war, and those responsible often sought simply to deny the facts. Even when the principle was invoked in good faith, however, the standard of military necessity was debased to the extent that there was very little, if any, difference between what was 'imperatively demanded by the necessities of war' and was merely advantageous.

Mobilisation for protection

Although a few cultural treasures and countless other monuments were damaged or destroyed in the First World War, the value placed on the wartime protection of cultural property was, if anything, reinforced. 'The damage caused to major Belgian and French works of architecture, especially the Library in Louvain and the cathedral in Rheims, became an instrument of national and international mobilization...'[11] Political and popular condemnation, while fuelled by jingoism[12] and hysteria, affirmed the legitimacy and purchase of the relevant international rules

---

[11] D. Gamboni, *The Destruction of Art. Iconoclasm and Vandalism since the French Revolution* (London: Reaktion, 1997), p. 42, reference omitted.

[12] That propagandists could count on outrage at the devastation of such places proves the point. See e.g. Gamboni, *Destruction of Art*, pp. 42–3 and 344 n. 56; J. Horne and A. Kramer, *German Atrocities, 1914. A History of Denial* (New Haven/London: Yale University Press, 2001), pp. 218–21 and 306–8.

and the vision that inspired them. Protesting the bombardment at Rheims, the French minister for foreign affairs declared that 'this revolting act of vandalism ..., by consigning to the flames a sanctuary of our history, robs humanity of an incomparable portion of its artistic heritage'.[13] In 1917, when the pope sent an envoy to Berlin to protest the destruction of Belgian churches, the Kaiser is reputed to have replied that he was attempting 'to spare from the horrors of war ... monuments of art considered by him the common property of all humanity'.[14] A publicised manifesto declared that, '[f]or their part, the French Universities continue to think that civilisation is the work not of a single people, but of all peoples, that the intellectual and moral richness of humanity is created by the inherent natural variety and independence of every national spirit'.[15] Nikolai Roerich, the first designer for Diaghilev's Ballets Russes, produced a popular poster in late 1914 emblazoned 'Enemy of mankind', denouncing the devastation in Louvain and Rheims. International lawyers took up the refrain. Phillipson deplored the burning of Louvain as 'an outrage to humanity'.[16] Garner decried the bombardment of Rheims cathedral, 'which not only was regarded as one of the architectural glories of France, but which in a sense belonged to all mankind'. Dubbing such monuments 'a part of the common heritage of civilization', he thought that what was said in the *Marquis de Somerueles* 'might be said equally of such architectural and historical landmarks', 'namely, that "the arts and sciences are considered not as the peculium of this or that nation, but as the property of mankind at large"'.[17]

The indignation led to the adoption by both sides of special measures to supplement the prohibitions of the Hague Rules. In 1915, Britain and the Allied Powers pledged 'that so long as pilgrims were not seriously interfered with no hostile action would be taken against the port of Jeddah or the holy places in Arabia or Mesopotamia'.[18]

---

[13] Protest of the French government sent to neutral states, 21 September 1914, in *Guerre de 1914*, vol. I, para. 172. See also the near-identical statement of 20 April 1918 after the cathedral's further devastation: Garner, *International Law and the World War*, vol. I, para. 285.

[14] Mérignhac and Lémonon, *Droit des Gens et Guerre de 1914–1918*, vol. I, p. 219.

[15] Manifesto of the French universities in reply to the protest of the German universities, 3 November 1914, in *Guerre de 1914*, vol. I, para. 189.

[16] C. Phillipson, *International Law and the Great War* (London: T. Fisher Unwin/Sweet & Maxwell, 1915), p. 168.

[17] Garner, *International Law and the World War*, vol. I, para. 286. See also J. W. Garner, 'Some Questions of International Law in the European War' (1915) 9 AJIL 72 at 108.

[18] *Hansard*, HC, vol. 73, col. 1493, 21 July 1915.

The Kaiser is reputed to have authorised the bombing of London by German airships on the express condition that they spare 'the monuments and especially St Paul's Cathedral'.[19] A Kunstschutz (art protection) corps, headed by Paul Clemen, professor of art history in Bonn, was set up in the German army in 1915 for the preservation and 'rescue' of threatened monuments.[20] The French and Italian armies did the like. In Russia, an early act in the wake of the first revolution was the establishment, in March 1917, of the Council for the Protection of Cultural Treasures of the Provisional Government, 'a special militia to protect art and museums [with] the right to give orders necessary for this end',[21] which organised the evacuation of two trainloads of artistic treasures from the Hermitage Museum in St Petersburg to Moscow, with a third prevented from leaving by the Bolshevik revolution.

In April 1918, as the devastation visited by the retreating German forces in France and Belgium reached a peak, a private body, the Netherlands Archaeological Society (Nederlandsche Oudheidkundige Bond or NOB), proposed that the Netherlands call an intergovernmental conference, at least of neutral powers, with the aim of improving the protection afforded historic and artistic monuments and objects in war. It offered to draft a report suggesting measures which might fruitfully be discussed at the conference. The Ministry of Foreign Affairs responded with interest and invited the NOB to prepare its report. The NOB established an interdisciplinary commission which, on 31 October 1918, submitted its findings, calling on the Ministry to bring them to the attention of every state. The Ministry, unable to do so under the circumstances, suggested that the NOB distribute the report to analogous organisations worldwide. On 15 May 1919, the report was disseminated internationally, taking the curious form of thirteen questions with an annexed explanatory memorandum,[22] proclaiming that damage to monuments and works of art was an injury not just to their owners and to the states in which they were but also 'to humanity as a whole'.[23]

---

[19] J. M. Spaight, *Air Power and War Rights*, 2nd edn (London: Longmans, Green, 1933), p. 269.
[20] See P. Clemen, *Kunstschutz im Kriege: Berichte über den Zustand der Kunstdenkmäler auf den verschiedenen Kriegsschauplätzen und über die deutschen und österreichischen Massnahmen zu ihrer Erhaltung, Rettung, Erforschung* (Leipzig: Seeman, 1919).
[21] G. Norman, *The Hermitage. The Biography of a Great Museum* (London: Pimlico, 1999), p. 138.
[22] Draft questionnaire on the protection of works of art in wartime, with explanatory memorandum, in 'Pays-Bas. La protection des monuments et objets historiques et artistiques contre les destructions de la guerre. Proposition de la Société néerlandaise d'archéologie' (1919) 26 RGDIP 329 at 331.
[23] *Ibid.*, at 334.

The NOB's report, dealing with both immovables and movables, proposed, if only tentatively and impressionistically, a reorientation of the conceptual basis for their protection away from a reliance on restraint in attack towards what was later called 'material' protection, namely the geographical isolation and physical insulation of cultural property. It suggested the creation, where possible, of demilitarised zones in the immediate vicinity of the most significant monuments, and proposed that they be given an 'international status', which 'would not be established by each State individually, but by all States together, for example through the establishment of an international Office'.[24] In return for the monuments' immunity from attack, the state on whose territory they were situated could be placed under an obligation not to use them for military purposes. The report left open whether these obligations might be abrogated on the grounds of military necessity or belligerent reprisals. It also asked whether the prohibition on attack should be phrased so as to apply 'as far as military technology permits',[25] in order to take into account the inaccuracy of very long-range artillery and bomber aircraft. The report recognised that in some defended towns there would be so many monuments, each surrounded by its own demilitarised zone, as to create the legally intolerable situation of a defended town that in practice could not be attacked. In a few such cases – 'for example Bruges, Florence, Nuremberg, Oxford, Paris's Cité, Rome, Rothenburg, Venice'[26] – where concern was of such a degree of interest to 'the whole world'[27] as to rule out preserving some monuments at the expense of others, it suggested that whole towns might be protected by specific agreements providing for complete demilitarisation in return for absolute immunity. These demilitarised towns would act as 'sanctuaries of art'.[28] The report further queried whether, in addition to the obligation not to damage monuments and works of art in occupied territory, a belligerent occupant might be placed under some limited duty to take positive steps, if and only insofar as was strictly necessary, to shore up monuments damaged in the course of operations. In addition, it asked whether an Occupying Power should have an obligation to support, as far as possible, any measures taken by local authorities with a view to protecting works of art and history.

[24] Ibid., at 336.
[25] Ibid., at 333 and 335–6.
[26] Ibid., at 333.
[27] Ibid., at 335.
[28] Ibid., at 336.

The NOB recommended an obligatory system of peacetime preparation or 'mobilisation', to which a national inventory of monuments was 'indispensable',[29] in order to ready relevant property in advance for the dangers of war – a preparation considered necessary in light of the sudden violence with which modern wars broke out. Measures taken might be communicated, as far as military considerations permitted, to the other High Contracting Parties to any eventual treaty, to the relevant cultural institutions and to the public at large. The report also called for international compliance mechanisms. It suggested that some sort of international office be made responsible in peacetime for the regime of demilitarised zones around monuments. It also proposed an international system of wartime control, prepared in peace by drafting a list of people of high repute ready to shoulder the task on the outbreak of hostilities. To avoid a repeat of the mutual recriminations of the First World War, contested facts, especially whether a particular monument was being used for military purposes, would be determined by arbitration or by a commission of inquiry. The report left open whether criminal responsibility was necessary for breaches of the duties of preparation and demilitarisation, and, if so, whether trials should be heard by national or international judges.

The post-war draft list of war crimes

In January 1919, Sub-Commission III, on the Responsibility for the Violation of the Laws and Customs of War, of the Commission on Responsibilities of the Preliminary Peace Conference of Paris was mandated with investigating and making recommendations as to violations of the laws and customs of war committed by Germany and the Central Powers. The Sub-Commission produced a draft list of war crimes[30] which reaffirmed the binding force of the customary laws of war, of which the Hague Rules were largely declaratory, and which explicitly asserted individual criminal responsibility for their violation. The Sub-Commission characterised as a war crime the 'wanton devastation and destruction of property', that is, the violation of the customary rule codified in article 23(g) of the Hague Rules, the adjective 'wanton' being shorthand for 'not imperatively demanded by the necessities of war'. The 'deliberate bombardment of undefended places', as prohibited by article 25, was also recognised as criminal.

[29] *Ibid.*, at 335.
[30] Reproduced in UNWCC, *History of the United Nations War Crimes Commission*, p. 34.

In addition, the Sub-Commission declared as a war crime the 'wanton destruction of religious, charitable, educational and historic buildings and monuments'. This covered the violation of article 27, as well as the destruction of protected buildings and monuments in violation of articles 23(g) and 56. The confiscation of any form of private property, as prohibited by article 46, was deemed a war crime too, as was pillage, prohibited by articles 28 and 47.

In the event, political disagreement thwarted trials before an inter-Allied criminal tribunal. Instead, the Allied Powers sought the extradition from Germany of over one thousand suspected war criminals for trial by national courts.[31] This included sixteen requests by France in respect of offences of a cultural nature.[32] But extradition proved elusive as well.[33]

The inter-war years

The First World War proved a potent catalyst to the refinement of the general law on aerial bombardment, with significant implications for monuments, and to the development of a specialised international legal regime to protect cultural property in war. Both were given another shot in the arm by the Spanish Civil War. But crucial aspects of the law on bombing from the air were in an unsatisfactory state, and a draft international convention on the wartime preservation of historic and artistic treasures remained unadopted, when Panzer divisions crossed into Poland on 1 September 1939.

The Hague Draft Air Rules

There was general agreement after the First World War that the Hague Rules embodied an 'obsolete and unworkable test of liability to bombardment'.[34] The specific problem in the minds of statesmen and writers was that of bombardment from the air. In 1922, the Washington Conference on the Limitation of Armament appointed a Commission of

---

[31] See Horne and Kramer, *German Atrocities, 1914*, appendix 4, p. 449.
[32] See *ibid.*, p. 448.
[33] As a result of an Allied–German compromise, trials of some suspected German war criminals took place in Leipzig, but to little avail, while some were tried *in absentia* in France and Belgium.
[34] L. Oppenheim, *International Law. A Treatise*, 5th edn, edited by H. Lauterpacht, 2 vols. (London: Longmans, Green, 1935–7), vol. II, para. 214*e*.

Jurists, headed by John Bassett Moore, to study and make proposals on the law governing aerial bombardment. The Commission's findings were reflected in the 1923 Hague Draft Rules of Aerial Warfare[35] (the Air Rules). But despite a proposal to the effect by the USA, the Air Rules were never adopted in binding form.

The Air Rules made no attempt to define in aerial terms what made a town 'defended' within the meaning of article 25 of the Hague Rules. They sought, rather, to recast the conceptual foundations of the law of aerial bombardment by replacing the dichotomy between undefended and defended towns with the more specific concept of individual military objectives, thereby aligning necessity more closely with distinction and eliding the legality of the recourse to bombardment with the legality of its conduct. Recognising the common strategic logic of neutralising the enemy's strength rather than capturing its territory, the Air Rules' drafters transposed the principles of naval bombardment[36] to aerial attack, declaring that any town or city could, in principle, be bombed from the air but that bombing was to be restricted to a finite list of military and related infrastructural targets. In addition, as specifically regards historic monuments, the Air Rules proposed an optional, supplementary regime of material protection along the lines suggested by the NOB, which sought to preserve monuments from damage by means of a *cordon sanitaire*.

Article 24 of the Air Rules substituted for the duty to distinguish between undefended and defended localities an obligation to distinguish between individual military objectives and the civilian populace, with paragraph 1 stating that aerial bombardment was 'legitimate only when directed at a military objective, that is to say, an object of which the destruction or injury would constitute a distinct military advantage to the belligerent'. Paragraph 2 elaborated, continuing that aerial bombardment was 'legitimate only when directed exclusively at the following objectives: military forces; military works; military establishments or depots; factories constituting important and well-known centres engaged in the manufacture of arms, ammunition or distinctively military supplies; lines of communication or transportation used for military purposes'. But the relationship between the two paragraphs was unclear. The exhaustive list enunciated in the latter seemed to render superfluous

---

[35] UK Misc. No. 14 (1924), Cmd 2201.
[36] See Hague Convention IX, art. 2.

the abstract definition of a military objective posited in the former. The Commission of Jurists was silent on the point.

Article 22, applying the general rule of distinction laid down in article 24(1), declared that aerial bombardment 'for the purpose of terrorizing the civilian population, of destroying or damaging private property not of military character, or of injuring non-combatants' was prohibited. 'No difficulty was found in reaching an agreement'[37] on this provision, a reflection of discomfort at morale bombing.

As specifically regards cultural property, article 25 provided that, in bombardment by aircraft, 'all necessary steps must be taken by the commander to spare as far as possible buildings dedicated to public worship, art, science, or charitable purposes [and] historic monuments, ... provided such buildings, objects or places are not at the time used for military purposes'. It further stipulated that such buildings, objects and places 'must by day be indicated by marks visible to aircraft', adding that the use of marks to indicate other buildings, objects or places than those specified was to be deemed an act of perfidy. This was no more than an affirmation of the customary prohibition on bombarding such property codified in article 27 of the Hague Rules and in article 5 of Hague Convention IX, and was actually redundant within the logic of the Air Rules, since a straightforward application of articles 24(1) and 24(2) made it plain that cultural property was not a military objective.

The second limb of article 24(3) represented a landmark in the evolution of the law of bombardment and of the legal protection afforded civilians and civilian property, including cultural property, in war. It stated that in cases 'where the objectives specified in paragraph 2 are so situated, that they cannot be bombarded without the indiscriminate bombardment of the civilian population, the aircraft must abstain from bombardment'. What the provision purported to outlaw was aerial bombardment which visited on the civilian population injury 'out of proportion to the interest that the belligerents have in destroying the objective'[38] – bombardments which, 'while of military value, are likely to cause devastation or suffering *disproportionate* to their military efficacy'.[39]

---

[37] 'Commission of Jurists to Consider and Report upon the Revision of the Rules of Warfare. General Report' (1938) 32 AJIL Supp. 1 at 23.

[38] M. Sibert, 'Les bombardements aériens et la protection des populations civiles' (1930) 37 RGDIP 621 at 648.

[39] J. L. Kunz, 'Plus de lois de la guerre?' (1934) 41 RGDIP 22 at 39, original emphasis, referring synonymously to 'suffering ... out of proportion to the military advantage gained'.

In short, in a rejection of the doctrine of double effect, article 24(3) asserted a cap on incidental damage.

The ideas for the material protection of cultural property put forward by the NOB were promoted by the Italian delegate to the Commission of Jurists and eventually embodied in article 26. Article 26 represented an optional, supplementary regime imposing more onerous duties on the state in whose territory the property was situated but guaranteeing, in return, greater protection than under the *lex generalis* of articles 24 and 25. Of the various types of cultural property protected by article 25, only 'important historic monuments'[40] and, by implication, groups of such monuments[41] were to be eligible for article 26. Moreover, despite the Italian delegate's recommendation that the Air Rules cover 'artistic' as well as historic monuments, reference was made only to the latter. But this was for no other reason than to reproduce verbatim the terminology of article 27 of the Hague Rules and article 5 of Hague Convention IX.[42] The Commission of Jurists adopted a broad interpretation of 'historic monument' which included 'all monuments which by reason of their great artistic value are historic today or will become historic in the future'.[43] In this regard, '[n]o standard of artistic excellence or of other qualifications entitling a building to benefit under the Article [was] laid down', with each state 'free to use its own judgment in this matter'.[44]

Article 26 entitled a state, if it wished, 'to establish a zone of protection [a]round such monuments situated in its territory'[45] up to 500 metres in width.[46] The benefit of such a zone was its immunity from bombardment,[47] by which was apparently meant a protection unqualified by considerations of military necessity. The price of this immunity was the willingness on the part of the state in whose territory the relevant monument was found to 'abstain from using the monument and the surrounding zone for military purposes, or for the benefit in any way whatever of its military organization, or from committing within such monument or zone any act with a military purpose in view'.[48] This condition was to be 'very strictly interpreted', according to the

---

[40] Air Rules, art. 26, chapeau.
[41] See Air Rules, art. 26(3).
[42] 'Commission of Jurists', at 25–6.
[43] *Ibid.*, at 26.
[44] Spaight, *Air Power and War Rights*, 2nd edn, p. 269.
[45] Air Rules, art. 26(1).
[46] *Ibid.*, art. 26(3).
[47] *Ibid.*, art. 26(1).
[48] *Ibid.*, art. 26(7).

Commission of Jurists: there was to be 'a complete cessation of the use of any place, including, for instance, factories and railway lines, with a military purpose in view',[49] and it was to be monitored by an inspection committee consisting of three neutral representatives.[50] In the case of certain cities, such as Venice and Florence, the Commission foresaw that the zones of protection might overlap to such an extent that the majority of the city would be immune from attack, at the cost of its demilitarisation.[51] Unlike the NOB, the Commission predicted no problem with this, presumably since the concept of the defended town, central to the former's concern, played no part in the Air Rules' scheme.

Borrowing a further element from the NOB's report, article 26 required a state to notify other states during peacetime of the existence and boundaries of any zones established around monuments in its territory, a notification not to be withdrawn in time of war.[52] As well as facilitating the immunity of such monuments, notification in peacetime permitted a state receiving it, 'if it [thought] it necessary to do so, to question within a reasonable time the propriety of regarding a particular place as an historic monument'.[53] A compulsory system of marking also applied to enable hostile air crews to identify protection zones.[54] But the Commission of Jurists agreed 'that if the belligerents did not for military reasons place the signs indicated in the article, enemy aviators had no right by reason merely of their absence to bombard the zone in question, if it had been duly determined and notified'.[55]

Article 26 was severely criticised by Spaight, for whom it amounted to 'an admission that the ordinary rule that non-military objectives may not be bombarded, supplemented by the further rule that where such non-military objectives are ... historic monuments, *et hoc genus*, special care must be taken to spare them, is so unlikely to be adhered to in practice that it is necessary, when one comes to a class of property which one wants really to protect, to super-add an elaborate system of demarcation of zones, notification, special markings, and neutral inspection, which are unnecessary in other cases'.[56] A main concern underpinning

---

[49] 'Commission of Jurists', at 26.
[50] Air Rules, art. 26(8).
[51] 'Commission of Jurists', at 26.
[52] Air Rules, art. 26(2).
[53] 'Commission of Jurists', at 26.
[54] Air Rules, art. 26(4) to (6).
[55] 'Commission of Jurists', at 26.
[56] Spaight, *Air Power and War Rights*, 2nd edn, p. 271.

article 26, however, was not that historic monuments would be bombarded in violation of articles 24 and 25 but that they could be damaged or destroyed even in accordance with the lawful operation of article 24(3), which contemplated proportionate and thus permissible incidental harm.[57] Added to this, as Spaight conceded, it was technologically unfeasible when the Air Rules were drafted to 'pick out a particular building and bomb it'.[58] It was, however, possible to confine bombing within a given radius and, when percussive force was factored into the equation, the 500-metre zone provided for by article 26 dramatically narrowed the chances of incidental damage.

The Air Rules, while not binding, 'enjoyed considerable status' and 'were respectfully quoted'.[59] But while their gist found favour, the devil was in the detail. Deeply influential was the approach taken by the UK's Royal Air Force (RAF), at that time the only strategic bombing force in the world. On 2 May 1928, Sir Hugh Trenchard, Marshal of the RAF and Chief of the Air Staff, forwarded to the Chiefs of Staff Sub-Committee a memorandum on the use of air power in a future war in Europe,[60] in which he discarded article 25 of the Hague Rules in favour of the Air Rules' general approach:

As regards the question of legality, no authority would contend that it is unlawful to bomb military objectives, wherever situated. There is no written international law as yet upon this subject, but the legality of such operations was admitted by the Commission of Jurists who drew up a draft code of rules for air warfare at The Hague in 1922–23. Although the code then drawn up has not been officially adopted it is likely to represent the practice which will be regarded as lawful in any future war.[61]

---

[57] 'Commission of Jurists', at 25.
[58] Spaight, *Air Power and War Rights*, 2nd edn, p. 21.
[59] Best, *Humanity in Warfare*, p. 273.
[60] Reproduced in C. Webster and N. Frankland, *The Strategic Air Offensive Against Germany 1939–1945*, 4 vols. (London: HMSO, 1961), vol. IV, appendix 2 (i), p. 71.
[61] Ibid., at p. 73. See also the note from the legal service of the French Ministry of Foreign Affairs, 6 April 1936, in A.-C. Kiss (ed.), *Répertoire de la Pratique Française en matière de Droit International Public*, 7 vols. (Paris: Editions du CNRS, 1962–72), vol. 6, para. 129, not mentioning the Air Rules by name. The Air Rules were included in the Luftwaffe's regulations and were supposed to apply to strategic bombing: see German Air Force regulation L. Dv. 64 II, 1 October 1939, introduction, cited in H. Boog, 'The Luftwaffe and Indiscriminate Bombing up to 1942', in H. Boog (ed.), *The Conduct of the Air War in the Second World War. An International Comparison* (New York/Oxford: Berg, 1992), p. 373 at pp. 377–8. The RAF at that time had no chapter in its service manual on the laws of aerial bombardment: see *Manual of Air Force Law*, 2nd edn (London: HMSO, 1933, reprinted without change 1939).

But while he accepted as military objectives the objects cited in article 24(2), he did not hold the list to be exhaustive, adding to it economic assets and civil infrastructure. In addition, he adopted a permissive misconstruction of article 24(3)'s rule on indiscriminate harm:

> [Legitimate military] objectives may be situated in centres of population in which their destruction from the Air will result ... in the incidental destruction of civilian life and property. The fact that air attack may have that result is no reason for regarding the bombing as illegitimate provided all reasonable care is taken to confine the scope of the bombing to the military objective. Otherwise a belligerent would be able to secure complete immunity for his war manufactures and depots merely by locating them in a large city, ... a position which the opposing belligerent would never accept.[62]

In short, Trenchard neutered article 24(3): instead of prohibiting disproportionate incidental harm, it imposed a mere duty of diligence. He also subtly rewrote article 22's prohibition on morale bombing: rather than outlawing aerial bombardment 'for the purpose of terrorizing the civilian population', article 22 became a rule against the indiscriminate bombing of a city 'for the sole purpose of terrorising the civilian population'.[63] Any effect on morale that accompanied a lawful operation of war, namely the bombing of a legitimate military objective, was itself lawful.[64]

Subsequently, in the late 1930s, international outrage occasioned by Japanese air attacks against civilian centres in the Sino-Japanese War and by the aerial devastation of Guernica in the Spanish Civil War lent renewed impetus to the clarification of the laws of aerial bombardment. In 1938, the Third Committee of the League of Nations Assembly adopted a report on the Protection of Civilian Populations against Bombing from the Air in Case of War. Echoing a statement by the British prime minister to the House of Commons,[65] the Third Committee '[r]ecognise[d] the following principles as a necessary basis for any subsequent regulations':

(1) The intentional bombing of civilian populations is illegal.

---

[62] Webster and Frankland, *Strategic Air Offensive*, vol. IV, appendix 2 (i), p. 73.
[63] Ibid.
[64] Ibid.
[65] *Hansard*, HC, vol. 337, cols. 937–8, 21 June 1938. The prime minister's statement was reiterated by the UK representative to the Third Committee: LNOJ Special Supplement No. 186 (1938), p. 20.

(2) Objectives aimed at from the air must be legitimate military objectives and must be identifiable.
(3) Any attack on legitimate military objectives must be carried out in such a way that civilian populations in the neighbourhood are not bombed through negligence.[66]

But while states agreed that only legitimate military objectives could be attacked, there was debate over what constituted such an objective,[67] with controversy over factories not engaged in munitions production and civil infrastructure with military applications, such as railways and roads. Furthermore, the last of the Third Committee's propositions effectively endorsed Trenchard's view on incidental damage, namely that as long as care was taken to avoid civilians, their incidental bombing was lawful, regardless of its extent, if it was incidentally unavoidable when neutralising military objectives.

The Roerich Pact

As early as the Russo-Japanese War of 1904–5, Nikolai Roerich – designer of the popular 'Enemy of mankind' poster decrying German destruction of cultural sites in the First World War – had given thought to the creation of a comprehensive system for the international protection of monuments in the course of hostilities. In the event, it was not until 1930 that Georges Chklaver of the Institut des Hautes-Études Internationales in Geneva set about drafting, on Roerich's initiative, a treaty exclusively dedicated to the legal protection, in both war and peace, of certain cultural property. Roerich and Chklaver approached the Bureau of the League of Nations' International Museums Office (Office International des Musées or OIM) with a draft text,[68] the preamble to which spoke of 'the sacred obligation to promote the well-being of [the] respective Nations and the advancement of the Arts and Sciences, in the common interest of humanity', declaring that '[i]nstitutions dedicated ... to the Arts and Sciences constitute a treasure common to all the Nations

---

[66] LNOJ Special Supplement No. 186 (1938), p. 48.
[67] See *ibid.*, p. 20; Spaight, *Air Power and War Rights*, 2nd edn, pp. 226–35; F. E. Quindry, 'Aerial Bombardment of Civilian and Military Objectives' (1931) 2 J. Air L. 474 at 478, 489–90 and 501–7.
[68] G. Chklaver, 'Projet d'une Convention pour la Protection des Institutions et Monuments consacrés aux Arts et aux Sciences' (1930) 6 RDI (Paris) 589, referring in a commentary to the protection of monuments and buildings which constitute 'the common heritage of humanity': *ibid.*, at 590. The text presented to the Bureau by Roerich and Chklaver is reproduced at (1930) 6 RDI (Paris) 593.

of the World'. In turn, at the instigation of its Bureau, the OIM held consultations on the possibility of adopting such a convention. In the end, the proposal for a convention stalled and the OIM remained content to circulate, at the request of some states, a 1934 set of recommendations to national authorities, based heavily on the report of the NOB, on peacetime preparations for the protection of historic monuments in war.[69] Roerich and Chklaver instead took their text to the Governing Board of the Pan-American Union, where a final draft was prepared, and in 1935 the Treaty on the Protection of Artistic and Scientific Institutions and Historic Monuments, also known as the Washington Pact or Roerich Pact, was adopted.[70]

In accordance with article 1, the Roerich Pact applies during peacetime and war to historic monuments, museums and scientific, artistic, educational and cultural institutions. No mention is made of movable cultural property, which is protected only insofar as it is housed in a museum or other protected institution. Article 1 also lays down the Pact's essential obligations. Protected property is to be considered 'neutral' and is to be 'respected and protected' by belligerents. Parties undertake in article 2 to adopt legislation necessary to ensure protection and respect. Pursuant to article 5, monuments, museums and institutions cease to enjoy the privileges of respect and protection if used for military purposes, but military use is the sole ground on which a belligerent may withdraw these privileges: military necessity as such is no justification. The Pact establishes a dual system for identifying the monuments, museums and institutions covered by its provisions. Article 3 provides for voluntary marking with a distinctive flag.[71] Article 4 obliges Parties to send to the Pan-American Union (now the General Secretariat of the Organization of American States) a list of the monuments and institutions 'for which they desire the protection agreed to', and obliges the Pan-American Union to send all the Parties copies of these lists and to inform them of changes to them.

---

[69] Reproduced in J. Vergier-Boimond, *Villes sanitaires et cités d'asile* (Paris: Éditions Internationales, 1939), pp. 122–3 and 318–19. The OIM invited the responsible national authorities 'to prepare by their own means the defence of their artistic and historical heritage' in accordance with its recommendations: LNOJ, 18th Year, No. 12 (December 1937), p. 1047.

[70] Washington, DC, 15 April 1935, 167 LNTS 290. The Pact remains in force among eleven American states, including the US.

[71] This is a 'red circle with a triple red sphere in the circle on a white background'.

The Preliminary Draft International Convention for the Protection of Historic Buildings and Works of Art in Times of War

In 1936, 'events in Spain ... again brought the question, in an acute form, to the attention of national administrations and of public opinion'.[72] The destruction of irreplaceable works of art and history in the Spanish Civil War spurred the League into action. In the Sixth Committee of the League Assembly, the Bolivian delegate's proposal to help safeguard Spain's cultural property, 'the preservation of which was a matter of importance to civilisation as a whole', was 'welcomed' by the Spanish delegate and 'favourably greeted by all the other delegations'.[73] Pursuant to an 'implicit mandate',[74] the League's International Commission on Intellectual Co-operation (Commission Internationale de Coopération Intellectuelle or CICI) referred the question to the OIM. In turn, the OIM commissioned Professor Charles de Visscher to prepare a report on the protection of historic monuments and works of art 'menaced in the course of wars or civil strife'.[75] It specifically requested him to give 'due consideration to earlier labours and action, and in particular to the proposals of the Committee of Jurists, set up in 1922 by the Washington Conference, and to the inquiry carried out in 1919 by the NOB'.[76] The resulting report and proposals were endorsed by the Directors' Committee of the OIM, which prepared and presented the Office's report to the CICI. In July 1937, the CICI approved the OIM's proposals and requested it to continue its efforts with a view to the preparation of a draft convention. Reporting to the Assembly in September on the CICI's progress, and with specific reference to the Sino-Japanese War which had just broken out, the Sixth Committee 'unanimously urge[d] that, in armed conflicts, artistic monuments and cultural institutions representing the high-water mark of civilisations should be spared'.[77] The Directors' Committee of the OIM proceeded to appoint a committee of experts, which held sessions in November 1937 and April 1938 with

---

[72] LNOJ, 18th Year, No. 12 (December 1937), p. 1047.
[73] LNOJ, Special Supplement No. 161 (1936), p. 57.
[74] Ibid., p. 39.
[75] LNOJ, 18th Year, No. 12 (December 1937), p. 1047.
[76] Ibid.
[77] LNOJ, Special Supplement No. 175 (1937), p. 83. As for the civil war in Spain, the Spanish authorities had by this point supposedly adopted technical measures to protect historic monuments and works of art threatened by the fighting, along the lines recommended by the OIM in 1934: Report of the Directors' Committee of the OIM 1936, in Vergier-Boimond, *Villes sanitaires*, pp. 316–17.

a view to preparing a text. The upshot was a Preliminary Draft International Convention for the Protection of Historic Buildings and Works of Art in Times of War, with annexed Regulations for the Execution of the Convention.[78] The CICI transmitted this to the Council of the League soon afterwards, for dissemination among national governments, and the Netherlands offered to convene a diplomatic conference in the event that 'their replies showed the possibility of arriving at an international agreement'.[79]

In commenting on the draft convention, the director of the CICI's International Institute for Intellectual Co-operation (Institut International de Coopération Intellectuelle or IICI), the official with overall responsibility for the OIM, emphasised that the problem was 'rightly a matter of concern . . . to all Governments and peoples who care for the preservation of their common artistic and historic heritage'.[80] This echoed an earlier resolution of the CICI, which had declared that 'the preservation of the artistic and archaeological heritage of mankind is a matter of interest to the community of States, as the guardians of civilisation',[81] a resolution which in turn borrowed from the General Conclusions of the OIM-convened First International Congress of Architects and Technicians of Historic Monuments, held in Athens in 1931.[82] The text of the OIM draft itself also sought from the outset to affirm the legitimacy of international concern in the fate of a state's cultural property and of co-operative measures to protect it, with the preamble declaring that 'the preservation of artistic treasures is a concern of the community of States and it is important that such measures should receive international attention', and that 'the destruction of a masterpiece, whatever nation may have produced it, is a spiritual impoverishment for the entire international community'. Similarly, in article 5(1), the High Contracting Parties 'acknowledg[ed] it to be their joint and several duty to respect and protect all monuments of artistic or historic interest in time of war', and article 7(6) spoke of 'buildings the preservation of which is the concern of the entire international community'. The theme was taken up by one delegate to

---

[78] LNOJ, 19th Year, No. 11 (November 1938), p. 937.
[79] LNOJ, Special Supplement No. 190 (1938), p. 43.
[80] LNOJ, 19th Year, No. 11 (November 1938), p. 937.
[81] LNOJ, 13th Year, No. 11 (November 1932), p. 1776.
[82] See Conclusions générales, para. VII(a), in *Actes de la Conférence d'Athènes sur la conservation des monuments d'art et d'histoire* (Paris: Institut de coopération intellectuelle, 1933).

the Seventh Committee of the League Assembly, who spoke of preserving 'artistic treasures which belonged to humanity as a whole'.[83]

In drafting the text, however, the committee of experts adopted 'a certain attitude of resignation: past experience of observance of the laws of war, and the constant increase in the power of destructive weapons [left] few illusions as to the efficacy of any rules adopted in disregard of this experience and of the technique of modern warfare'.[84] The Committee 'carefully refrained from proposing any rules or measures which would prove inoperative or inapplicable when the time came ... preferr[ing] to confine itself to what seemed feasible in practice, rather than aim at a higher mark and a more complete programme which would inevitably involve breaches of the projected international convention'.[85] 'If sacrifices have to be made', the director of the IICI explained, 'the convention asks that they be made preferably by the States possessing the artistic treasures to be preserved',[86] given that '[t]he countries possessing artistic treasures are merely their custodians and remain accountable for them to the international community'.[87] In this light, the thrust of the text was the concept of material protection put forward by the NOB and partially reflected in article 26 of the Air Rules, which looked to save monuments through geographical isolation and physical insulation undertaken in advance by the state in whose territory they were situated.[88] Whereas the Hague Rules had 'sought to protect artistic monuments and works of art by restricting the destructive effects of war – often to the detriment of important military interests – the International Museums Office advocate[d] action in the opposite direction and deliberately base[d] the protection of the monuments on the absence of any serious military advantage in their destruction'.[89]

The precise scope of the draft convention's application in terms of the property it sought to protect was never formally outlined. The substantive provisions refer generically and variously to 'historic buildings and works of art',[90] 'artistic and historic treasures',[91] 'works of art or

---

[83] LNOJ, Special Supplement No. 190 (1938), p. 44.
[84] LNOJ, 19th Year, No. 11 (November 1938), p. 961.
[85] *Ibid.*, p. 937.
[86] *Ibid.*, p. 961.
[87] *Ibid.*
[88] The concept of material protection was 'one of the fundamental principles of the convention': *ibid.*
[89] *Ibid.*
[90] OIM Draft Convention, arts. 1, 3(1), 3(2), 8 and 10.
[91] *Ibid.*, arts. 2(2) and 10(1).

of historic interest',[92] 'all monuments of artistic or historic interest'[93] and 'masterpiece[s]'.[94] This phraseology, and the gist of the provisions themselves, at least made it clear that the text encompassed movable property in its own right, in addition to immovable property. As regards the latter, what was also agreed was that – in contrast to articles 27 and 56 of the Hague Rules, article 5 of Hague Convention IX and article 25 of the Air Rules – the OIM draft was not to extend to 'buildings dedicated to religion, art, science, or charitable purposes' as such, but was to apply *de lege* only to historic monuments.[95] It 'deliberately abandoned the old criterion of the Hague Conventions' which covered 'any building devoted to education, art, science or religious worship, and was therefore likely to cause difficulties in applying a convention'.[96] Nor, it seems, did the text aim to protect every historic monument: the Seventh Committee of the League Assembly spoke of it as aiming to preserve 'monuments of great artistic and historic importance'.[97]

Despite the pessimism of its drafters, the OIM draft convention did embody legal restraints on the conduct of belligerents. The first limb of article 5(1) reaffirmed the longstanding customary obligation to take all possible precautions to spare monuments in the course of bombardment. More innovatively, and plugging a costly gap in the Hague regime, the second limb of article 5(1) imposed in relation to monuments an obligation to take all possible precautions 'to ensure that their use or situation shall not expose them to attack'.[98] In addition, as part of the draft's multilateralisation of the question of compliance, article 8 sought to outlaw belligerent reprisals directed against historic buildings and works of art.

Material protection was nonetheless the gist of the text, with the tone being set in the very first provision. Article 1, based on the NOB report, imposed on states in whose territory relevant property was situated a duty 'to organise the defence of historic buildings and works of art against the foreseeable effects of war, and ... to prepare that defence in time of peace'. 'Defence' meant civil defence, such as contingency plans

[92] *Ibid.*, art. 4(1).
[93] *Ibid.*, art. 5(1).
[94] *Ibid.*, preamble.
[95] And *de facto* to buildings dedicated to art, by virtue of their contents.
[96] UNESCO Doc. CL/484, Annex, p. 9.
[97] LNOJ, Special Supplement No. 190 (1938), pp. 39 and 95.
[98] Failure to acquit this second obligation did not of itself excuse the attacking party from its duty to spare the cultural property in question: military necessity remained the touchstone of attack at all times.

for structural insulation and support, the mobilisation of the emergency services and the transport of movables to refuges, rather than defence in the military sense.[99] The second element of material protection, in this case modelled on article 26 of the Air Rules, was the supplementary level of 'special protection', over and above the protection afforded by article 5(1), to which some monuments or groups of monuments were to be eligible in accordance with article 5(2).[100] What this special protection involved in terms of legal restraints was never specified.[101] In practice, this was largely unimportant, since the criteria for eligibility were themselves the key to preservation: as under article 26 of the Air Rules, monuments or groups of monuments seeking special protection were to be isolated from any military objective within a radius of 500 metres[102] and were not to be used, directly or indirectly, for purposes of national defence.[103] Thirdly, article 4, based on the OIM's recommendations to national authorities in 1934, provided a scheme for the material protection of movables. A state was entitled to set up a 'limited' number of refuges for works of artistic or historic value, consisting either of buildings erected for the purpose, or of historic buildings or groups of buildings,[104] which were to be immune from all acts of hostility[105] — that is, the prohibition on their attack was to be absolute — provided they were not used directly or indirectly for purposes of national defence[106] and were 'situated at a distance of not less than 20 kilometres from the most likely theatres of military operations, from any military objective, from any main line of communication, and from any large industrial centre'.[107] Given the second criterion, which conferred *de facto* immunity

---

[99] The director of the IICI referred to 'technical defence': LNOJ, 19th Year, No. 11 (November 1938), p. 962.

[100] Under art. 5(2)(c), the identity and location of such monuments was to be made known in time of peace, presumably through bilateral diplomatic channels, as under the analogous Air Rules, art. 26(2).

[101] It may or may not have been the same as the immunity from attack afforded refuges for movables: see LNOJ, 19th Year, No. 11 (November 1938), p. 962, where a distinction appears to be drawn.

[102] OIM Draft Convention, art. 5(2)(a).

[103] *Ibid.*, art. 5(2)(b).

[104] *Ibid.*, art. 4(2).

[105] *Ibid.*, arts. 4(1) and 4(3), chapeau.

[106] *Ibid.*, art. 4(3)(c).

[107] *Ibid.*, art. 4(3)(a). The distance of 20 km could be reduced 'in certain cases in countries with a very dense population and small area'. The location of such refuges was to be notified in peacetime: *ibid.*, art. 4(3)(b). Refuges were to be distinguished by a 'protecting mark': *ibid.*, art. 7.

from attack, it was acknowledged that the regime of refuges would apply only to movables: while it was theoretically possible for 'monuments or groups of monuments of high artistic value' to be used as refuges and hence to benefit from the immunity themselves, the required radius of demilitarisation meant that 'in the majority of cases – if not all cases – this would be almost impossible', since it would 'amount to the neutralising of whole towns'.[108] Indeed, the director of the IICI conceded phlegmatically that the OIM 'was, unfortunately, unable to envisage protection on such an extensive scale for monuments situated in large urban centres'.[109]

At the same time, 'in order not to preclude all possibility of legal protection for cities noted for their artistic treasures',[110] article 6 provided that a Party to the proposed convention could at any time declare that it was prepared to conclude with any other Party, on a reciprocal basis, special agreements extending the immunity granted to refuges to certain monuments or groups of monuments the preservation of which, 'although they [did] not satisfy the conditions laid down in Article 4, [was] of fundamental importance to the international community'.[111] The idea of facilitating humanitarian protection through agreements to demilitarise whole towns and cities, known popularly as 'open' towns and cities, had been promoted in the 1930s by the ICRC, the International Association for the Protection of Humanity (the 'Monaco project') and the 'Lieux de Genève' movement, and had already been used, with limited success, in the Spanish Civil War and Sino-Japanese War. In the context of cultural property, it had formed an important element of the NOB report, and the Monaco project foresaw the potential for coextensive zones, combining the protection of the civilian population with the preservation of monuments and works of art.[112]

The OIM draft convention embodied a compliance regime that went further than article 26 of the Air Rules by envisaging an international system of wartime inspection designed to ensure not only the continued satisfaction of the criteria for special protection and for the immunity of refuges respectively[113] but also the satisfaction by both sides

---

[108] LNOJ, 19th Year, No. 11 (November 1938), p. 962.
[109] Ibid.
[110] Ibid.
[111] See also OIM Draft Regulations, art. 6.
[112] Vergier-Boimond, *Villes sanitaires*, p. 131.
[113] OIM Draft Convention, arts. 5(2)(d) and 4(3)(d). The task was to fall to an International Verification Commission: OIM Draft Regulations, arts. 2–5.

of the obligations incumbent on them during hostilities and belligerent occupation.[114] The draft also foresaw the establishment of a General Conference, meeting periodically,[115] with power 'to decide conjointly upon measures for ensuring the application of [the] Convention, and to review, if necessary, the Regulations for its execution'.[116] In turn, the General Conference was to appoint an executive Standing Committee with the authority 'to settle all questions relating to the application of the Convention' in the intervals between sessions of the Conference.[117] In the event of a disturbance or armed conflict within a country, the Standing Committee was authorised to extend its good offices towards the contending parties 'with a view to taking all necessary steps for the protection of monuments or works of art threatened by the operations'.[118] But the director of the IICI sought to play down these internationalist elements in order to maximise the chances of the text's adoption, 'point[ing] out that the draft reduces to a minimum the really new features of the organisation which would be responsible for applying the provisions of the convention', so that 'the financial burden on the contracting States was strictly limited to the special services which each was entitled to ask of this new organisation'.[119]

Tying in with the compliance regime, and reflecting its immediate origins in international concern over the fate of monuments in Spain, the OIM draft convention made a tentative foray into the realm of civil war. It did not go so far as to stipulate that the parties to a civil conflict were formally bound by its substantive provisions. Rather, in what at the time was nonetheless a notable penetration of the domestic sphere, article 10(1) provided that, in the event that monuments or works of art were threatened by 'disturbances or armed conflicts within a country', Parties to the proposed convention were entitled to 'lend their friendly assistance to the contending parties for the purposes of safeguarding

---

[114] OIM Draft Convention, art. 11. The job was to be given to an International Commission of Inspection: OIM Draft Regulations, arts. 7, 8 and 10. The individual members of the respective commissions were to be chosen from a list of 'persons of acknowledged impartiality': *ibid.*, art. 1.

[115] The Conference was to meet whenever necessary but at least once every five years: OIM Draft Regulations, art. 12(2).

[116] OIM Draft Convention, art. 12(1). See also OIM Draft Regulations, art. 12(5).

[117] OIM Draft Regulations, art. 12(7). See also OIM Draft Convention, art. 12(2). The Committee was to meet whenever necessary but at least once a year: OIM Draft Regulations, art. 12(8).

[118] OIM Draft Regulations, art. 11.

[119] LNOJ, 19th Year, No. 11 (November 1938), p. 961.

the threatened historic and artistic treasures'.[120] This right of diplomatic initiative mirrored the course of action proposed by Bolivia to the Sixth Committee of the League of Nations Assembly in October 1936. In response to the historical and artistic losses occasioned by the outbreak of the war in Spain, the Bolivian delegate, diplomatically eschewing talk of political intervention, proposed that the League offer *proprio motu* its purely technical assistance as an indirect means of safeguarding 'marvels of art which were the pride of the human race'.[121] In a judiciously phrased offer which placed the moral onus on the Spanish authorities, 'with no other object than an expression of human and cultural solidarity', 'he would ask delegates, as well as all his Spanish brethren there and elsewhere, whether they thought that, in the existing circumstances, a commission composed of foreign technicians chosen for their experience, and exclusive of any elements that might arouse the faintest political susceptibility, could, while there was yet time, co-operate urgently, by taking suitable technical measures, in safeguarding Spain's artistic treasures where they were in particular danger'.[122] Scrupulously avoiding any assignation of blame, the Bolivian delegate took the view that the League would be operating within its mandate:

> The chances of the struggle might unfortunately prove too much for the power of the opposing parties to protect such works of art. Neither side, therefore, could or should take umbrage at this proof of solidarity and sympathy. The League could co-operate, with the full consent of everyone, in preserving monuments and museums from any serious damage. That was not only within its powers; it was its duty.[123]

Likening his proposal to the work being done on both sides of the fighting by the ICRC, he agreed that '[n]on-interference in political matters was the whole foundation of wisdom', but believed that 'non-interference in humanitarian and artistic matters would be the expression of an

---

[120] Article 10(2) provided that Parties were also entitled to 'receive and shelter in their respective territories works of art coming from a country in which civil strife [was] prevalent, and endangered by acts arising out of such strife'. See also OIM Draft Convention, arts. 10(3) and 10(4). A textbook example of this practice occurred during the Spanish Civil War, when the contents of the Prado in Madrid were removed to Geneva for safekeeping. The Swiss authorities returned the collections after the war at the request of Franco's government.

[121] LNOJ, Special Supplement No. 161 (1936), p. 20.

[122] *Ibid.*

[123] *Ibid.*

indifference incompatible with the demands of contemporary sensibility and culture'.[124] In the event, justifying article 10(1), the director of the IICI declared that, as the convention was 'conceived in a spirit of international solidarity', it was 'only natural that it should ... envisage the dangers which threaten monuments and works of art during civil disturbances'.[125] For its part, the CICI 'considered it its duty to do its utmost to safeguard monuments and works of art menaced in the course of ... internal disturbances'.[126]

Finally, the High Contracting Parties undertook in article 3(3) 'to take steps to punish in time of war any person looting or damaging monuments and works of art'.

The Second World War

In the early hours of 1 September 1939, German Stukas squealed over Warsaw. 'The two beautiful and historic streets of the city, the Krakowskie Przedmiescie and the Nowy Swiat, with a number of fine old buildings, were reduced to a mass of débris.'[127] The Second World War had begun, and the diplomatic conference scheduled to adopt the Preliminary Draft International Convention for the Protection of Historic Buildings and Works of Art in Times of War was prevented from taking place. Instead, the OIM cobbled together a Declaration on the Protection of Cultural Property in the Course of Armed Conflict,[128] a statement of principles, ten articles in length, based on the draft convention but without its compliance regime. It was designed to form the basis of bilateral agreements between the belligerents. But hopes of securing such *ad hoc* accords, always brittle, were shattered by the German invasion of the Netherlands, Belgium and France in 1940.

The war could hardly have come at a worse time in the evolution of the law on aerial bombardment. The cultural heritage of Germany and Japan paid the price for the expansive approach taken at the time to the concept of a military objective and for the lack of a prohibition on disproportionate incidental harm, although one can only speculate whether even the most tightly formulated, well-established rules would have stood

---

[124] *Ibid.*, p. 21.
[125] LNOJ, 19th Year, No. 11 (November 1938), p. 962.
[126] LNOJ, 18th Year, No. 12 (December 1937), p. 994.
[127] J. M. Spaight, *Air Power and War Rights*, 3rd edn (London: Longmans, Green, 1947), p. 265.
[128] Reproduced in UNESCO Doc. 5 C/PRG/6, Annex I, para. 7.

in the way of action deemed necessary at what was held to be a time of supreme necessity threatening the life of several states and peoples. Indeed, when it comes to the settled and absolute prohibition on the destruction and plunder of cultural property during belligerent occupation, the Germans' razing of monuments in the Soviet Union – compelled, as it was, by Nazism's ideological hatred of Communism and contempt for the Slavs – and their systematic seizure and removal to the Reich, fuelled by colossal vainglory and venality, of many of the USSR's and Europe's public and Jewish-owned private collections, one is faced with the limitations of legal restraint in the face of moral perversity. On the other hand, measures voluntarily taken by all the belligerents during the war, in the absence of legal obligation, to secure and safeguard cultural property against damage attest to the adjectival quality of law, to an extent, where ethical and political motivations – in this case, the conviction that the property in question should be saved for humanity, present and future – have sufficient purchase.

Strategic air operations

By the end of the war, the Allied strategic bombing campaign[129] had devastated Germany and Japan. High explosives and incendiaries rained down with a yield, concentration and indiscriminateness unthinkable before or since, laying waste civilian districts and the civilian population, and with them monuments and works of art. Some saw this as a function of the desuetude of the pre-war rules brought about by their repeated violation. Indeed, it might even be said that to talk of violation is to overstate the role played by law in the war, especially since Air Chief Marshal Sir Arthur Harris, leader of Britain's Bomber Command from 1942 onwards, was to assert later that 'in this matter of the use of aircraft in war there is, it so happens, no international law at all ... with the

---

[129] The Germans' tactical use of the Luftwaffe in support of ground operations involved massive air-raids on cities such as Warsaw, Rotterdam and Belgrade. But independent strategic bombing of the sort seen relatively briefly over industrial cities in the UK did not feature in the Axis war effort to anywhere near the same extent as in the Allied. Moreover, despite the inevitable wartime propaganda surrounding German air-raids on Britain, there was little real difference in legal terms between most of these and Allied air-raids, at least before the advent of the V-series rockets. The Luftwaffe engaged in instances of deliberately indiscriminate terror-bombing over Britain, especially after November 1940, but surprisingly infrequently in hindsight. This uncharacteristic restraint on the Nazis' part was for reasons more pragmatic than principled: they feared retaliation by the more powerful RAF.

single exception that about the time of the siege of Paris in the war of 1870 the French and Germans came to an agreement between themselves that neither side should drop explosives from free balloons'.[130] But such views underestimate the extent to which the Allied powers continued to pay at least formal and public regard throughout the conflict to the concept of military objectives and to the need to limit incidental harm. '[T]he preservation of the notion of international law in war was an important concern of the Allies in 1939–45, in spite of all the problems presented by waging total war against a totalitarian foe.'[131]

Others were to characterise Allied bombing policy as an extended exercise in belligerent reprisals. But this too is belied by the record, and Telford Taylor, in his subsequent role as Chief Counsel for War Crimes at Nuremberg, rightly concluded that 'the ruins of German and Japanese cities were the results not of reprisal but of deliberate policy'.[132] The rhetoric of reprisal was less legal than political, serving to cloak the strategic air campaign in a populist legitimacy. Similarly, although the Germans sought to defend their 1942 'Baedeker raids' on Exeter, Bath, Norwich, York and Canterbury – undertaken with the perhaps-rhetorical intention of destroying every building in England marked with three stars in the Baedeker guidebook – as belligerent reprisals for the British firebombing of Lübeck, the sincerity of this claim is open to doubt, despite the Germans' insistence on cities of equivalent age to the Hanseatic port.

Rather, where not consciously unlawful (and this was uncommon), the devastation from the air of whole cities and towns was a product of the application of the law as it then stood, or, to be more precise, of the more permissive view of the *lex ferenda*. The war broke out 'before a clear understanding had been reached about the law of war governing bombardment from the air',[133] and what understanding there was was distinctly hawkish.

It was accepted that a regime premised on individual military objectives, rather than the old undefended/defended dichotomy, applied, in some essential form, as a matter of customary international law.[134]

---

[130] A. Harris, *Bomber Offensive* (London: Collins, 1947), p. 177.
[131] Horne and Kramer, *German Atrocities, 1914*, p. 425.
[132] Quoted in W. H. Parks, 'Air War and the Laws of War', in Boog, *Conduct of the Air War*, p. 310 at p. 346.
[133] J. M. Spaight, 'Legitimate Objectives in Air Warfare' (1944) 21 BYIL 158 at 161.
[134] That said, the Germans made self-serving reference to the Hague Rules in seeking to justify their Stuka attacks on Warsaw and Rotterdam.

After an appeal by President Roosevelt that the belligerents refrain from air attacks on civilians,[135] an appeal immediately endorsed by Germany,[136] Poland,[137] Britain[138] and France,[139] the last two issued a joint declaration on 3 September 1939 publicising instructions to their respective armed forces which prohibited 'the bombardment whether from the air, or the sea, or by artillery on land of any except strictly military objectives in the narrowest sense of the word'.[140] At the same time, both reserved the right not to conduct themselves in this way in the event that the enemy did not, and, on 10 May 1940, Britain formally retracted its declaration after Germany's invasion of the Low Countries, notorious for its aerial attacks on Rotterdam. The retraction, however, made little difference in the early stages of the war to the conduct of the British (later, Anglo-American) strategic air offensive, in which deliberate indiscriminateness was at least formally eschewed, with the then Air Marshal Sir Charles Portal being warned by the Air Staff that under 'no circumstances should night bombing be allowed to degenerate into mere indiscriminate action, which is contrary to the policy of His Majesty's Government'.[141]

But while the UK and, on its entry into the war, the USA accepted that bombing from the air was to be restricted to specific military objectives, the RAF had always taken the view that what was to be considered a legitimate military objective – that is, 'an object of which the destruction or injury would constitute a distinct military advantage to the belligerent', in the words of article 24(1) of the Air Rules – was not limited to the strictly military assets stipulated in paragraph 2 of that provision. Nor was it alone in this: the dominant view seemed to be that the bombardment 'of industrial centres, of great thoroughfares, of great cities, of every locality of the sort whose paralysis or destruction involves a weakening of the warmaking capacity of the enemy' was lawful.[142] One such locality was the residential districts where the industrial workforce slept. And while the targeting of the populace as such was

---

[135] [1939] 1 FRUS 541–2.
[136] Ibid., 543–4. But see Boog, 'The Luftwaffe', at p. 375, for evidence of Hitler's insincerity.
[137] [1939] 1 FRUS 544–5.
[138] Ibid., 544.
[139] Ibid., 545.
[140] Ibid., 547–8, quote at 548.
[141] Webster and Frankland, *Strategic Air Offensive*, vol. I, p. 145.
[142] G. Balladore Pallieri, *Diritto bellico*, 2nd edn (Padua: Cedam, 1954), pp. 240–2, quote p. 241.

publicly beyond the pale, its terrorisation was, at the very least, an intended by-product of bombing Germany and Japan.

The greater the number of military objectives, the greater the risk of incidental harm to cultural property, a risk rendered a virtual certainty by the RAF's indulgent approach to incidental damage – an approach endorsed by the Third Committee of the League of Nations Assembly in 1938, and accepted by the USA – whereby if otherwise legitimate military objectives could not be neutralised without harming non-objectives, the non-objectives had to go. Implicit in Bomber Command's reasoning after 1942 was the conviction that as long as it was lawful to attack the intended objective, any unavoidable incidental damage was subsumed within that lawfulness. The proportionality calculus laid down in article 24(3) was not a factor in decision-making, particularly where area bombing was considered an operational imperative. While the British and French governments expressed on the outbreak of war 'a firm desire ... to preserve in every way possible those monuments of human achievement which are treasured in all civilized countries',[143] it was not thought possible from the air, with the UK's secretary of state for air explaining the policy:

> We cannot be prevented from bombing important military targets because, unfortunately, they happen to be close to ancient monuments ... The same principles are applied to all centres. We must bomb important military objects. We must not be prevented from bombing important military objects, because beautiful or ancient buildings are near them.[144]

As long as damage to monuments was neither wanton nor grossly careless, it was lawful.

With the *reductio ad absurdum* of the concept of a military objective and the dispensing with any limit on incidental damage, the scheme of the Air Rules collapsed into the customary rule of military necessity. In most cases, if a given attack furthered the desired strategic end, that was as far as the inquiry went. But when it came to attacks likely to damage significant cultural sites, an informal qualitative notion of proportionality *grosso modo* retained some purchase in decision-making and came to shape the wartime fate of the cultural heritage of Europe. The military significance of the intended target and the risk posed to the lives of Allied servicemen by any measures designed to spare cultural property

---

[143] [1939] 1 FRUS 548.
[144] *Hansard*, HC, vol. 391, col. 1557, 28 July 1943.

was weighed against the cultural significance of the property at risk and the extent of likely damage to it. As for the likely loss of civilian life, this weighed in favour of bombing Axis centres and against bombing occupied countries. Judgements as to the historic and artistic significance of given monuments and works of art tended to reflect cultural and personal biases. They were also informed by the likely political repercussions, both domestic and international, of damage to the cultural property in question, and hence by a strategic imperative in the grandest sense, namely the need to maintain support for the war on the home front and abroad.

Germany

The orthodox view throughout the war was that the intensive and indiscriminate aerial bombing of German cities was a necessary means to Allied victory. The countervailing arguments did not convince. First and most conclusively, a scrupulous attachment in the case of the German people to the distinction between civilians and the state was deemed unfeasible and unwarranted in principle. Second, while one UK Member of Parliament thought many German buildings 'of enormous interest to the whole world',[145] this was neither a popular nor influential view. That said, if their preservation had not involved perceived operational and strategic costs, it might have been considered more favourably. But the degree of precision needed to spare individual sites involved flying lower and slower, in the teeth of anti-aircraft fire and fighter cover. Better-than-woeful accuracy also called for experienced crews, which proved harder and harder to find with the appalling casualty rate. As well as the problem of raw requisite manpower, bomber losses went directly to domestic support for the war, the maintenance of which was a grand strategic imperative. In short, saving monuments meant losing air-crews, probably crack ones, and, in a variation on Bismarck's verdict on the Balkans, Air Chief Marshal Sir Arthur Harris did not regard 'the whole of the remaining cities of Germany as worth the bones of one British Grenadier'.[146]

It was chiefly on account of the desire to shatter the morale of the German people and the need to conserve Allied air-crews that, from 1942

---

[145] *Ibid.*, vol. 406, col. 1762, 20 December 1944.
[146] Quoted in C. Messenger, 'Dresden, raid on', in I. C. B. Dear and M. R. D. Foot (eds.), *The Oxford Companion to the Second World War* (Oxford: Oxford University Press, 1995), p. 311 at p. 312.

onwards, the Allies opted for the technique of area bombing, the most destructive means open to them and devastating to cultural property and civilian lives. Area bombing, known in its most extensive form as general area bombing, was the predominantly British aerial practice of destroying numerous distinct military objectives scattered over an urban concentration by levelling the whole concentration indiscriminately. General area bombing 'worked almost on the principle that in order to destroy anything it [was] necessary to destroy everything'.[147] Each whole town or each whole city was treated, in effect, as a single objective. The target aimed at, for technical reasons, was the very centre of the city, usually the historic Altstadt (old town) common then to most German cities. Operationally, the rationale for area bombing was the need to hit multiple, dispersed targets with highly inaccurate delivery systems from high altitude, at night, in the face of concerted anti-aircraft defences and with hurriedly trained crews: the 'Butt Report',[148] presented to Bomber Command in August 1941, had suggested that 'the smallest targets which were operationally feasible at night with the aircraft and equipment in service were whole towns'.[149] Strategically, the inherent indiscriminateness of area bombing promised the side-effect of sapping the morale of the civilian population.[150] This largely explains why area bombing was used over Germany but not, as a matter of official policy, over German-occupied France, the Netherlands, Belgium, Poland, Czechoslovakia,

---

[147] Webster and Frankland, *Strategic Air Offensive*, vol. III, p. 44.
[148] Reproduced *ibid.*, vol. IV, appendix 13, p. 205.
[149] A. N. Frankland, 'Strategic air offensives. 1. Against Germany', in Dear and Foot, *Oxford Companion to the Second World War*, p. 1066 at p. 1071.
[150] The Deputy Chief of the Air Staff informed Air Chief Marshal Sir Arthur Harris in May 1942 that 'the primary aim of [his] operations must remain the lowering of the morale of the enemy civil population': Webster and Frankland, *Strategic Air Offensive*, vol. IV, appendix 8(xxiii), p. 148, para. 2. In January 1943, the Allies' Casablanca conference, which launched the Combined Bomber Offensive (CBO), announced the CBO's objective to be 'the progressive destruction and dislocation of the German military, industrial and economic system, and the undermining of the morale of the German people to a point where their capacity for armed resistance is fatally weakened': *ibid.*, appendix 8(xxviii), p. 153, para. 1; appendix 8(xxxii), p. 158, para. 5; appendix 23, p. 273, para. 1. In August the same year, the Quebec conference omitted reference to morale bombing: *ibid.*, appendix 8(xxxiii), p. 160; appendix 8(xxxvi), p. 164, para. 2(1); appendix 8(xxxviii), p. 167, para. 1; appendix 8(xxxix), p. 170 at p. 171, para. 3; appendix 8(xl), p. 172, para. 1. 'Formal decisions and official directives were, however, by no means the only ways in which the policy of the combined bomber offensive was made': *ibid.*, vol. III, p. 46. Bomber Command continued to pursue the earlier strategy actively, with the apparent acquiescence of the Combined Chiefs of Staff.

Yugoslavia and, after its surrender and occupation by Germany in July 1943, Italy.[151]

With the possible exception of some, the Allies were not untroubled by their recourse to the area bombing of Germany's historically and artistically significant cities and towns, as made clear by the UK's secretary of state for air:

> Monuments of art and antiquity are the common heritage of all mankind. We do not deliberately destroy them, but it is our policy to restore that greater heritage of mankind – freedom – and to do that we must and will destroy the enemy's means of making war – his defences, his factories, his stores and his means of transportation, wherever they may be found.[152]

Destroying the enemy's defences, factories, stores and means of transportation meant destroying everything around them. When a raid combined traditional high explosives with incendiaries, area bombing created an uncontrollable firestorm, incinerating and even melting everything and everyone in its path. By the end of the war, historic Lübeck, Hamburg, Cologne, Würzburg, Nuremberg, Munich and Berlin, along with scores of other cities and towns across Germany, had been reduced to ashes and rubble, and between 750,000 and 1,000,000 German civilians killed.[153] Most iconically, Dresden was incinerated on the night of 13 February 1945 'for complicated reasons not wholly connected with the general area campaign', in the sanguine words of the official British history.[154] Its renowned cultural treasures were destroyed and over fifty thousand people, many of them refugees, were asphyxiated or burnt alive. But the university towns of Heidelberg, Freiburg, Göttingen and Tübingen were almost completely spared, thanks to the combination of their great cultural significance and uncompelling strategic value.[155]

---

[151] See *ibid.*, vol. IV, appendix 8(iii), p. 112 at p. 115, para. 14; appendix 8(xxiv), p. 149 at p. 150, para. 3; appendix 8 (xxv), p. 150 at p. 151, para. 7; W. Jackson, *The Mediterranean and Middle East. Volume VI. Part III* (London: HMSO, 1988), pp. 246–7.

[152] Quoted in Spaight, *Air Power and War Rights*, 3rd edn, p. 291, citing *The Times*, 9 May 1942.

[153] Frankland, 'Strategic air offensives', at p. 1073.

[154] Webster and Frankland, *Strategic Air Offensive*, vol. III, p. 6. There is nothing, however, surrounding the raid on Dresden to suggest the malicious choice of a city famed for its architecture and collections.

[155] 'There is a widespread belief among *cognoscenti* that Oxford and Heidelberg benefited from a gentlemen's understanding among Rhodes Scholars and such, but none of the suitably placed survivors from that time I have asked has been able to substantiate it.': G. Best, *War and Law Since 1945* (Oxford: Clarendon Press, 1994), p. 285 n. 23.

Japan

By late 1944, the US Army Air Forces (USAAF) had penetrated Japan and were engaged in the general area bombing of cities such as Nagoya, Osaka, Kawasaki, Yokohama, Kobe and Tokyo. The operational and strategic reasons for this, and the attendant legal questions, were of a piece with the Allied bombing campaign over Germany. Early 1945 saw the launch of massive and indiscriminate fire-bombing raids, using napalm, on the major cities of Japan, especially Tokyo, leading to the deaths of hundreds of thousands of Japanese civilians in their largely wood-and-paper houses and the devastation of the country's cultural heritage. '[I]n ten days nearly half of the destruction that the whole bombing war had caused in Germany was visited on Japan',[156] and much more was to come by June. 'In all of Germany, seventy-nine square miles had been destroyed in five years – in Japan, 178 square miles in a half-year',[157] with sixty-six cities burned to the ground and two pulverised by atomic bombs.[158] But Kyoto and Nara were spared out of deference to their architectural and artistic heritage,[159] a deference made feasible by a lack of military necessity.

Italy

In contrast to decentralised Germany, around two-thirds of Italy's industrial output was generated by three cities, Milan, Turin and Genoa, all of them in the north. Once these were area-bombed with relative success, the need to hit Italy harder and more widely was, to an extent, obviated, although not eliminated. After the opening of the North African front, the potential bombardment of Rome was the subject of vigorous diplomacy and debate. The topic had first been raised when, in an effort to secure protection for two other historic cities, the UK government, via an official statement of 19 April 1941, informed the Axis powers that if either the monuments of Athens or the Islamic shrines in Cairo were bombed, Britain would bomb the Italian capital.[160] Subsequently, much of the diplomacy centred inconclusively on the possibility of mutually declaring Rome an 'open' city. During this time,

---

[156] S. Lindqvist, *A History of Bombing* (London: Granta, 2001), para. 228.
[157] Ibid.
[158] Ibid., para. 231.
[159] W. F. Craven and J. L. Cate (eds.), *The Army Air Forces In World War II*, 7 vols. (Chicago: University of Chicago Press, 1948–58), vol. V, p. 710.
[160] [1943] 2 FRUS 913 and 937.

although the British government reiterated that it would 'not hesitate to bomb Rome to the best of [its] ability and as heavily as possible if the course of the war should render such action convenient and helpful',[161] the course of the war favoured the city, and, despite political and public pressure, it remained unscathed until mid-1943. Throughout this period, the conclusive factor in Rome's preservation was that it was actually of little strategic importance, despite its being the capital of enemy Italy. The only potential military objectives were the San Lorenzo and Littorio marshalling yards, which it was unnecessary to destroy while the war was focused on North Africa, even though all north–south rail traffic bar a single set of routes passed through them.

With the Allied invasion of Sicily in July 1943, followed by Italy's surrender and occupation by Germany, all this changed. The Roman marshalling yards were now a vital and vulnerable choke-point for German troops and *matériel* on their way to the southern front, which was gradually creeping up the peninsula towards the capital. As the prevention of German reinforcement (and, later, retreat) became crucial to the success of the Allied drive north, so in the minds of strategists did the destruction of San Lorenzo and Littorio. The airfields at Ciampino, on the outskirts of the city, also assumed military significance. Additionally, German troop concentrations crossing the city by road posed an increasingly compelling target. In Radio Bulletin No. 175, President Roosevelt announced that, in order to save American and British lives, the USA would take whatever steps were necessary to stop Axis traffic through Rome.[162]

The competing considerations were encapsulated by the Holy See's cardinal secretary of state, when he said that, '[i]f it should be desired to justify [the bombing of Rome] on grounds of so-called war exigencies, it would be easy to rejoin first of all that it would appear that the consideration of military objectives (which do not seem to be of great importance in Rome) should not prevail over the very serious superior reasons of religion, civilization and humanity'.[163] Any bombs dropped 'might very well do irreparable damage to great works of art'.[164]

---

[161] *Hansard*, HC, vol. 374, col. 518, 30 September 1941. See also *ibid.*, HL, vol. 125, col. 526, 9 December 1942; *ibid.*, HC, vol. 386, col. 183, 20 January 1943; *ibid.*, vol. 389, col. 1081, 19 May 1943; *ibid.*, vol. 390, col. 1598, 30 June 1943.
[162] [1943] 2 FRUS 933 n. 37.
[163] *Ibid.*, 942.
[164] *Hansard*, HC, vol. 385, col. 114, 12 November 1942.

On 19 May 1943, Pope Pius XII appealed to President Roosevelt on behalf of the city's 'many treasured shrines of Religion and Art', which were the 'precious heritage not of one people but of all human and Christian civilization',[165] and expressed the desire that 'monuments [which] enshrine the memory and masterpieces of human genius be protected from destruction'.[166] Pius complained that '[w]ithout hope of helping itself the nation is forced to witness the obliteration of so many of its treasures of religion, art and culture which it has fondly safeguarded throughout the centuries not only for itself but for the world'.[167] In the UK Parliament, Lord Lang of Lambeth – who entered a Notice on the Paper 'call[ing] attention to the importance of preserving objects of special historical or cultural value within the theatres of war',[168] a call which occasioned heated debate – declared that 'Rome does not belong to Italy; it belongs to the world. It does not belong to any particular time; it belongs to all time.'[169] The position in which the Allies found themselves was summarised by one US under-secretary of state when he observed that, '[a]side from the religious significance of the city, the historical importance of its monuments to the Western World makes it highly desirable that we avoid the responsibility for destroying large sections of Rome while liberating it from the Germans'.[170]

In the event, the Allies' decision to bomb Rome 'was based upon both military and political considerations and with full appreciation of the possibility of unfavorable reaction from the Roman Catholic Church, as well as from many artists, architects, historians, and others throughout the world'.[171] The city was bombed, and on several occasions, over a period of a year commencing 19 July 1943. All told, however, the number of raids was sparing. In addition, the city was bombed with the utmost possible care, the UK's secretary of state

---

[165] [1943] 2 FRUS 917.
[166] *Ibid.*, 932, the day after the first air-raid, on 19 July 1943, damaged the papal basilica of San Lorenzo.
[167] [1944] 4 FRUS 1278.
[168] *Hansard*, HL, vol. 130, col. 813, 16 February 1944. Lord Lang pointed out the dangers posed not just to Rome but also to northern Italian towns such as Assisi, Siena, Florence, Padua, Perugia, Pisa, Ravenna and Venice, a warning endorsed by others.
[169] *Ibid.*, col. 814, 16 February 1944.
[170] [1943] 2 FRUS 948.
[171] Craven and Cate, *Army Air Forces*, vol. II, p. 463.

for air announcing that '[a]ll practical precautions were taken to avoid damage to religious and cultural buildings in Rome'.[172] The objectives selected – namely, the San Lorenzo and Littorio marshalling yards and the airfields at Ciampino – were all in the suburbs. Of the historic centre, not even the enemy's military headquarters were targeted. In terms of their execution, the raids were entrusted to the more accurate US bomber aircraft, flown by select, experienced crews under strict instructions to return with their bombs if the targets were obscured. The technique employed was precision-targeting of discrete and identifiable military objectives. Even then, it took a crucial operational determinant to make precision-targeting feasible, obviating recourse to area bombing: the relative weakness of Rome's antiaircraft defences and fighter cover – indeed, its already threadbare anti-bomber defences were largely dismantled after its unilateral declaration as an open city – enabled Allied bomber crews to fly lower and spend longer over their targets, and even allowed them to fly by day, all of which considerably improved their accuracy. Even so, despite every effort to restrict the radius of damage, the papal basilica of San Lorenzo Fuori le Mure was struck in the initial attack on the railyards and, 'together with its cloisters, was badly damaged'.[173] Later raids hit other Vatican property in and around the outskirts of Rome, and, as the land campaign inched closer, Allied bombs landed in the grounds of the papal villa of Castel Gandolfo. Eventually, even the heart of the Vatican City was struck. But with the notable exception of San Lorenzo, the damage inflicted on these sites was negligible.

Early in 1944, after the Allied landings on the mainland, Italian cities were classified into three categories:

Category A included Rome, Florence, Venice, and Torcello, which 'in no circumstances were to be bombed without authority from [Supreme Headquarters, Allied Expeditionary Force]' ... Category B covered such cities as Ravenna, Assisi, San Gimignano, Urbino, and Spoleto, which could be bombed if it was considered essential. ('Full responsibility will be accepted by ... HQ.') But Siena, Pisa, Orvieto, Padua, and scores of others in the last group,

---

[172] *Hansard*, HC, vol. 391, col. 1555, 28 July 1943. See also *ibid.*, HL, vol. 128, col. 606, 20 July 1943.

[173] Craven and Cate, *Army Air Forces*, vol. II, p. 465.

near which there were 'important military objectives ... which are to be bombed, and any consequential damage is accepted', were on their own.[174]

Special maps with aerial photographs of the important monuments, taken by the Air Force itself, were issued and 'had the advantage of showing the bombardier exactly what he would see through the bombsight'.[175]

The subsequent story of the aerial bombing of Florence in 'Operation Strangle' followed the same pattern as that of Rome. While Allied troops were far to the south, the need to hit the Florentine railyards, whose neutralisation appeared 'impossible ... without causing irreparable damage to works exceptionally precious to all humanity', seemed 'less real, more remote'.[176] As the war inched closer in mid-1944, however, the railyards and their regular through-traffic of munitions became more strategically significant, to the point where their destruction was deemed imperative. The feebleness of the city's anti-aircraft defences made precision-bombing operationally feasible, a task entrusted to the most accurate bomber aircraft and to US crews hand-picked from various squadrons and under strict instructions not to risk hitting certain buildings clearly pointed out by aerial photographic maps. The targets were all suburban, namely the railway stations at Campo di Marte and Rifredi, the rail offices at Porta al Prato and the train depot at Romito. No historic monuments were struck but there were relatively minor civilian casualties.

As with Florence, the bombing of other targets such as the rail centre at Siena and Venice's modern port 'were usually masterpieces of precision'.[177] In the words of the UK's secretary of state for air, the 'utmost precautions [were] taken to protect from damage all buildings of historic and artistic value, in so far as this [was] consistent with military necessity'.[178]

---

[174] National Archives (Washington, DC), Record Group doc. 165/463, CAD Section 4, Office of Director of Operations, 23 February 1944, quoted in L. H. Nicholas, *The Rape of Europa. The Fate of Europe's Treasures in the Third Reich and the Second World War* (London: Papermac, 1995), p. 248.
[175] *Ibid.*
[176] Lt B. McCartney, USAAF, quoted in A. Marcolin, *Firenze 1943–'45* (Florence: Edizioni Medicea, 1994), pp. 56–7.
[177] Nicholas, *Rape of Europa*, p. 248.
[178] *Hansard*, HC, vol. 406, col. 1761, 20 December 1944. Even so, losses sustained in air-raids included the Mantegna frescoes in the Church of the Eremitani in Padua.

Land and associated air operations

Although the Anglo-French declaration of 3 September 1939 accepted that bombardment by artillery on land was also to be restricted to 'strictly military objectives in the narrowest sense of the word',[179] this was later retracted. Moreover, and more to the point, the military objective approach soon collapsed, for essentially the same reasons as in relation to bombardment from the air, into the long-established rule of military necessity codified in article 23(g) of the Hague Rules and applicable to all aspects of land warfare.

In the context of cultural property, the rule of military necessity was expressly reiterated by the Allies during the Italian campaign, which brought the fate of monuments in the land war to the forefront of military and public attention. Given the plan to land in Sicily, cross to the mainland and fight up the peninsula to the Alps, it was clear to Allied strategists that a very great number of cultural treasures would be at risk. In this light, on 29 December 1943, about five months after the invasion of Sicily and a few weeks before the landings at Anzio, General Eisenhower (at that point, Allied Commander in the Mediterranean; within days, Supreme Commander, Allied Expeditionary Force) issued General Order No. 68,[180] on the preservation of historic monuments during the Italian campaign, with a covering memorandum addressed to all commanders:[181]

> Today we are fighting in a country which has contributed a great deal to our cultural inheritance, a country rich in monuments which by their creation helped and now in their old age illustrate the growth of the civilisation which is ours. We are bound to respect those monuments so far as war allows.

Declaring it a responsibility of higher commanders to determine through Allied Military Government officers the location of historic monuments, whether immediately ahead of the Allied front lines or in areas occupied by them, Eisenhower emphasised the restraints imposed by military necessity. He stressed that, in many cases, monuments could be spared 'without any detriment to operational needs', noting that 'the phrase "military necessity" is sometimes used where it would be more truthful

---

[179] [1939] 1 FRUS 548.
[180] Reproduced in *Hansard*, HC, vol. 396, col. 1115, 1 February 1944. General Order No. 68 reiterated in more emphatic form an order to the same effect issued by Allied Force Headquarters in April the same year.
[181] Reproduced *ibid.*, col. 1116, 1 February 1944.

to speak of military convenience or even personal convenience'. He did 'not want it to cloak slackness or indifference'. At the same time, he affirmed that '[n]othing [could] stand against the argument of military necessity', a point he developed in an analogous military directive and memorandum of 26 May 1944,[182] in respect of western and central Europe:

> In some circumstances the success of the military operation may be prejudiced in our reluctance to destroy these revered objects ... So, where military necessity dictates, commanders may order the required action even though it involves destruction of some honored site.[183]

As in the air war, one factor weighing on the permissive side of military necessity was the need to safeguard the lives of Allied soldiers. Eisenhower struck a hawkish note on this point in General Order No. 68, declaring that '[i]f we have to choose between destroying a famous building and sacrificing our own men, then our men's lives count infinitely more and the buildings must go'.

General Order No. 68 made it clear that the 'prevention of looting, wanton damage and sacrilege of buildings' was a command responsibility, and that the seriousness of this offence was to be explained to all Allied personnel.[184]

In the event, the adherence by both sides to a strict standard of military necessity during the land campaigns in southern and western Europe spared the majority of its most precious cultural sites. This was particularly the case in Italy. 'A bitter struggle was waged along the length of the peninsula' – not to mention Sicily – 'and in the course of it damage was inevitably caused to some treasures of antiquity; but,

---

[182] See also the draft Military Directive on Monuments and Fine Arts (Germany), reproduced at [1944] 2 FRUS 1046, which became Policy Statement No. 1186, chapter XVI ('Monuments, Fine Arts and Archives'), part III, of the *Handbook for Military Government in Germany Prior to Defeat or Surrender*; and General Alexander's military directive of 12 January 1945 on the protection of historic buildings and the civilian population, cited in Jackson, *Mediterranean and Middle East*, pp. 185–6.

[183] Covering memorandum to military directive of 26 May 1944, reproduced in J.H. Merryman, 'Two Ways of Thinking About Cultural Property' (1986) 80 AJIL 831 at 839 n. 28. 'But', Eisenhower continued, 'there are many circumstances in which damage and destruction are not necessary and cannot be justified. In such cases, through the exercise of restraint and discipline, commanders will preserve centers and objects of historical and cultural significance.'

[184] General Order No. 68, para. 2.

all things considered, it was extraordinarily little'.[185] Rome was spared assault through the reluctance of the Allies to launch one and through the scruples of its German defender, Field Marshal Kesselring. On 2 June 1944, seeing no point in turning the city into a battleground, Kesselring sent a firm request to Hitler, granted the next day, to abandon Rome without a fight, and promptly withdrew his forces, retreating north. Despite the military advantage in doing so, he refused to engage in the common practice of demolitions, designed to hinder the enemy's pursuit. On the night of 4–5 June 1944, the Allies entered Rome to find it completely intact. A desire to avoid 'useless loss of life and the destruction of works of art and historic monuments'[186] also partly explains General Weygand's decision of 11 June 1940 to order General Héring to withdraw his army from Paris. The official communiqué[187] states:

[T]he French Command aimed at sparing [Paris] the devastation which defence would have involved. The Command considered that no valuable strategic result justified the sacrifice of Paris.

Four years later, with the Allies closing on the city, the commander of the German occupation forces, General von Choltitz, deliberately delayed carrying out an initial order to destroy all the bridges over the Seine, and eventually ignored Hitler's command to defend the city 'stone by stone', choosing instead to surrender without a fight.

But military necessity was also invoked to justify the destruction of irreplaceable treasures of history and art. Having concluded that his decision not to do so in Rome had cost him too many men, Kesselring ordered swingeing demolitions to cover his retreat from Florence, reducing a swathe of the historic quarter to rubble, along with every bridge over the Arno bar the unpassable Ponte Vecchio, including the Ponte Santa Trinità, reputedly designed by Michelangelo. For their part,

---

[185] Spaight, *Air Power and War Rights*, 3rd edn, p. 288. Destruction of cultural property generally decreased as the campaign wore on. In Sicily, Messina and Catania were heavily damaged and Palermo suffered considerably, all as much through tactical aerial bombardment in support of land forces as by the land engagements themselves. The Italian mainland south of Rome was next worse off, especially around Cassino. But – leaving aside Milan, Genoa and Turin, all targets of strategic aerial bombardment – the north fared astonishingly well, with the exception of Florence.

[186] A. Cobban, 'The Fall of France', in A. Toynbee and V. M. Toynbee (eds.), *The Initial Triumph of the Axis* (London: Oxford University Press/Royal Institute of International Affairs, 1958), p. 190 at p. 195.

[187] Reproduced in R. Y. Jennings, 'Open Towns' (1945) 22 BYIL 258 at 258 n. 1.

Allied land forces, after months of losses in attritional fighting which stalled the advance on Rome, called in tactical air support in February 1944 to level the great Benedictine abbey at Monte Cassino, which the Germans, while not occupying (although this was not absolutely clear at the time), had incorporated into their defensive line.[188] (In both cases, movable cultural property had been largely evacuated.) The genuine military necessity for these actions remains hotly contested – and, in the case of Monte Cassino, was the subject at the time of marked differences of opinion among Allied commanders.

In addition, pillage and vandalism of cultural property occurred on both sides of the land war in southern and western Europe, sometimes extending to wanton devastation, most notably during the German retreats up the Italian peninsula and across France.

Special protective measures

Over and above the protection afforded by the general laws of war, the Allies also adopted, with mixed success, special measures for the protection of cultural property during hostilities and belligerent occupation. In mid-1943, prior to the Allied invasion of Sicily, President Roosevelt authorised the establishment of the American Commission for the Protection and Salvage of Artistic and Historic Monuments in Europe, headed by US Supreme Court Justice Owen Roberts and known as the 'Roberts Commission'. The word 'Europe' in the formal name was replaced by 'War Areas' when the scheme was extended to Asia. One of the Commission's tasks was to 'work with the appropriate branch of the United States Army, for the purpose of furnishing to the General Staff of the Army, museum officials and art historians, so that, so far as is consistent with military necessity, works of cultural value may be protected in countries occupied by armies of the [Allies]'.[189] A special section was formed, under the auspices of the War Department, within the School of Military Government at Charlottesville, VA, 'for the purpose of training certain officers in the Specialist Branch of the service so that

---

[188] It was only after the abbey was gutted that it was occupied by the Germans, serving as an effective redoubt.

[189] [1943] 1 FRUS 477. The Roberts Commission's main task was the investigation, salvage and return to their rightful owners of confiscated artworks, pursuant to the Inter-Allied Declaration against Acts of Dispossession committed in Territories under Enemy Occupation or Control, 5 January 1943, below. See [1945] 2 FRUS 933–57; *Report of the American Commission for the Protection and Salvage of Artistic and Historic Monuments in War Areas* (Washington, DC: Government Printing Office, 1946).

they could be attached to the staffs of [US] armies to advise the commanding officers of such troops as to the location of and the care to be given to the various artistic and historic objects in occupied territory'.[190] Monuments, Fine Arts and Archives (so-called 'MFA&A') officers accompanied or followed American forces through the Sicilian and Italian mainland theatres and, later, through France, the Low Countries and Germany. Using an operational definition of 'work of art' which encompassed immovables as well as movables,[191] they 'render[ed] such ... services as might be needed with respect to works of art, cathedrals and other cultural monuments in Europe, so that their destruction might be avoided if consistent with military operations'.[192] By December 1943, MFA&A officers had drawn up plans for the rapid protection of historic buildings on the fall of Rome, and, on its eventual capture in June 1944, an MFA&A officer entered the city before US troops. In Florence and the shattered towns of Normandy, MFA&A officers were obliged to restrain overzealous sappers keen to bulldoze and clear damaged architecture. For its part, after conceding that the informal measures of protection for monuments taken during its invasion and occupation of Italy's Libyan colonies left something to be desired, the UK government set up a Monuments, Fine Arts and Archives branch to perform the same function as its American counterpart, under an Archaeological Advisor to the Director of Civil Affairs, Lt Col. Sir Leonard Woolley (who, as a civilian archaeologist, had led the excavations at Ur in the 1920s).[193]

In response to criticism by Woolley and others of the use by the US military of certain monuments in Sicily and southern Italy as headquarters and billets, General Order No. 68 and the analogous military directive of 26 May 1944 placed restrictions on the use of monuments for military purposes in the widest sense. No buildings listed in the sections 'Works of Art' in the respective zone handbooks issued by the Political Warfare Executive were to be used for military purposes 'without the explicit permission of the Allied Commander-in-Chief or of the General Officer Commanding-in-Chief ... in each

[190] [1943] 1 FRUS 481–2.
[191] [1944] 2 FRUS 1033.
[192] Ibid., 1031.
[193] See *Hansard*, HC, vol. 391, cols. 2485–6, 5 August 1943; *ibid.*, vol. 396, cols. 1113–15, 1 February 1944; and, generally, L. Woolley, *A Record of the Work Done by the Military Authorities for the Protection of the Treasures of Art and History in War Areas* (London: HMSO, 1947).

individual case'¹⁹⁴ – a stipulation, it seems, honoured as much in the breach as in the observance. Commanders were also authorised to close and place out of bounds to troops any buildings listed in the zone handbooks that they deemed necessary, a measure to be enforced by guards if required.¹⁹⁵ A supplementary list of historical buildings of secondary importance was also prepared. These were permitted to be used for military purposes when it was deemed necessary, although commanders were reminded that 'buildings containing art collections, scientific objects, or those which when used would offend the religious susceptibilities of the people' ought not to be occupied when alternative accommodation was available.¹⁹⁶

The Germans were also solicitous of the cultural treasures of (but only of) southern and western Europe. The Kunstschutz corps, created in the First World War, was re-established after the defeat of France, although its activities were often undermined and even opposed by those charged with seizing and sending back to Germany notable artworks and antiquities.¹⁹⁷ Even in the absence of Kunstschutz officers, who were not to arrive in German-occupied Italy until October 1943, and in addition to measures adopted by the Italian authorities, Kesselring ordered the posting of 'off limits' notices around monuments, galleries, museums and libraries, along with the removal of historico-artistic movables out of combat and potential combat zones and into secure storage, in some cases in the Vatican. As the shifting frontline threatened refuge after refuge, the Germans packed up artworks and transported them further northwards out of harm's way, the most famous instance being twenty-two truckloads of Florentine treasures (532 paintings and 153 sculptures) spirited away to refuges in the mountains of Alto Adige.¹⁹⁸ On one occasion, the following telegram was sent via the German legation in Bern and, in turn, the Swiss Foreign Office

---

[194] General Order No. 68, para. I(a).
[195] Ibid., para. I(b).
[196] Ibid., para. I(c).
[197] For example, Himmler sent an armed detachment of the SS's special research division, the Ahnenerbe, to raid one of the houses of Count Aurelio Balleani outside Iesi, near Ancona, in an unsuccessful search for the Codex Aesinas of Tacitus' *Germania*: S. Schama, *Landscape and Memory* (London: HarperCollins, 1995), pp. 75–81.
[198] Nicholas, *Rape of Europa*, p. 251–2, tells how the Kunstschutz officer in charge of Florence, SS Standartenführer Dr Alexander Langsdorff, had worked with Sir Leonard Woolley before the war and left him a personal letter on his withdrawal from the city.

to the Department of State in Washington, DC, with similar announcements being made over the radio:

> German authorities Italy have stored in Villa Reale Poggio at Caiano ... valuable artistic collections and archives concerning Tuscan Renaissance works ... German Government states there are no (repeat no) German troops in neighborhood Villa Reale and villa itself not used (repeat not used) for military purpose ... German Government desires inform American and British Governments it desires avoid bombardment or destruction Villa Reale.[199]

A lull in the Allied artillery barrage followed,[200] although it is hard to attribute cause and effect.

In addition, in an effort to immunise certain exceptionally treasured monuments from the effects of hostilities, *ad hoc* agreements of the sort urged in the 1930s by the proponents of material protection were from time to time the subject of diplomacy. There was much discussion before 1943 of mutually declaring Rome an open city, along the lines proposed in article 6 of the OIM draft convention and by the NOB before it, as well as by the ICRC, the Monaco project and the Lieux de Genève movement, although no agreement was ever reached. In the event, the Italians declared Rome open unilaterally, but the act was devoid of international legal significance.[201] The same was the case when the Germans withdrew in 1944. The possibility of designating Assisi a 'hospital city' was also briefly floated as 'part of [the] overall problem of safeguarding religious and cultural objects as well as [the] civilian population of Italy'.[202] For what it was worth, when King Abdul Aziz ibn Saud announced Saudi Arabia's belated declaration of war against the Axis on 28 February 1945 (effective 1 March), he expressly excluded the zones of the Holy Shrines.[203]

Belligerent occupation

German occupation notoriously involved the systematic removal and transportation to the Reich, orchestrated at the highest levels of command, of staggering numbers of artworks and antiquities from, in the east, public galleries, museums and libraries, as well as, in both east and west, private

---

[199] National Archives (Washington, DC), Record Group doc. 239/19, Harrison to Secretary of State, no. 5428, 19 August 1944, quoted *ibid.*, p. 255.
[200] *Ibid.*, pp. 254–5.
[201] See *Sansolini v. Bentivegna*, 24 ILR 986 (1957).
[202] [1944] 4 FRUS 1308.
[203] Dept St. Bull., vol. XII, No. 297, 4 March 1945, p. 375.

Jewish-owned collections. At the centre of this meticulously organised project was Albert Rosenberg's Einsatzstab Rosenberg, a body decreed into being by Hitler himself with which the Wehrmacht was later directed by further decree to co-operate: during the period from March 1941 to July 1944, its unit for Pictorial Art alone 'brought into the Reich 29 large shipments, including 137 freight cars with 4,174 cases of art works'.[204] Operatives and detachments acting under the instructions of Goering were also involved, as was the Special Purposes Battalion of the Waffen SS of the Ministry of Foreign Affairs, directed by von Ribbentrop, and the archaeological corps of the SS's special research division, the Ahnenerbe, all usually working in competition with Rosenberg's men. Bormann, too, 'was interested in the confiscation of art . . . in the East'.[205] The Soviet Union – Slavic and Bolshevik, hence not conceded the services of the Kunstschutz – was especially hard hit:

Museums, palaces and libraries in the occupied territories of the USSR were systematically looted. Rosenberg's Einsatzstab, von Ribbentrop's special 'Battalion', the Reichscommissars, and representatives of the Military Command seized objects of cultural and historical value belonging to the people of the Soviet Union, which were sent to Germany. Thus, the Reichscommissar of the Ukraine removed paintings and objects of art from Kiev and Kharkov and sent them to East Prussia. Rare volumes and objects of art from the palaces of Peterhof, Tsarskoye Selo, and Pavlovsk were shipped to Germany. In his letter to Rosenberg of the 3rd October, 1941, Reichscommissar Kube stated that the value of the objects of art taken from Byelorussia ran into millions of roubles. The scale of this plundering can also be seen in the letter sent from Rosenberg's department to von Milde-Schreden in which it is stated that during the month of October, 1943 alone, about 40 box-cars loaded with objects of cultural value were transported to the Reich.[206]

'The intention [was] to enrich Germany, rather than to protect the seized objects',[207] as had been alleged. In response, in 'their determination

---

[204] Judgment of the International Military Tribunal for the Trial of German Major War Criminals, Nuremberg, 30 September and 1 October 1946, Misc. No. 12 (1946), Cmd 6964, p. 56.
[205] Ibid., p. 129.
[206] Ibid., p. 56.
[207] Ibid. Some of these objects were subsequently destroyed by Allied bombers or land forces. For example, it now appears that the famed Amber Room, removed by German forces from the Catherine Palace in Tsarskoye Selo (Pushkin) on the outskirts of St Petersburg and sent in crates to Königsberg, was destroyed in the fire, started by the Red Army, which destroyed the Knights' Hall in Königsberg Castle in 1945: see C. Scott-Clark and A. Levy, *The Amber Room* (London: Atlantic Books, 2004).

to combat and defeat the plundering by the enemy Powers of the territories which have been overrun or brought under enemy control', the Allies issued the Inter-Allied Declaration against Acts of Dispossession Committed in Territories under Enemy Occupation or Control of 5 January 1943.[208] It announced that the Allied governments 'reserve[d] all their rights to declare invalid any transfers of, or dealings with, property, rights and interests of any description whatsoever' which were, or had been, situated in the territories which had come under the occupation or control, direct or indirect, of the enemy states or which belonged, or had belonged to persons (including juridical persons) resident in these territories. The explanatory memorandum issued by the Parties noted that the Declaration covered 'all forms of looting to which the enemy ha[d] resorted', applying 'to the stealing or forced purchase of works of art just as much as to the theft or forced transfer of bearer bonds'.[209]

In addition to plunder, the German occupation of the Soviet Union brought with it the vicious premeditated devastation of historic, artistic and religious buildings and sites. In an order of 10 October 1941,[210] which seemed at odds with the Einsatzstab Rosenberg's perverse appreciation of the same, Field Marshal von Reichenau declared that '[n]o treasures of history and art in the East are of the slightest consequence'. German forces systematically destroyed, usually after stripping them, churches, cathedrals, monasteries, synagogues, palaces, museums, libraries, archives, cityscapes, townscapes and villages across the Ukraine, Byelorussia and western Russia. Other Slavic countries suffered too. In Poland, the Germans razed the historic centre of Warsaw after putting down the uprising there.

In turn, as the Red Army swept across eastern Europe and into the Reich in the closing stages of the war, its 'trophy units' — directed by the Arts Committee of the Council of the People's Commissars, as ordered by the Central Committee of the Communist Party of the Soviet Union, with the conscious aim of securing reparation for German depredations — seized and sent to the USSR huge numbers of equally significant artworks

---

[208] Inter-Allied Declaration against Acts of Dispossession committed in Territories under Enemy Occupation or Control, 5 January 1943 (with covering statement by His Majesty's Government in the UK and Explanatory Memorandum issued by the Parties to the Declaration), Misc. No. 1 (1943), Cmd 6418.

[209] Explanatory memorandum, *ibid.*, para. 4.

[210] Reproduced in G. Schwarzenberger, *International Law and Totalitarian Lawlessness* (London: Jonathan Cape, 1943), appendix 5, p. 150 at p. 151.

and antiquities from Germany and, less explicably, Poland, many of them previously plundered by the Germans not only from the USSR but from the rest of occupied Europe as well. The last removal did not occur until long after the war, when 98 paintings from the private collection of the German industrialist Otto Krebs were found in a specially equipped room in the cellar of his country-house near Weimar.

While the German occupation of the Netherlands, Belgium and France saw the confiscation and removal of private Jewish collections, its treatment of public collections and of immovable cultural property was a different story. The Kunstschutz played as active a role here during belligerent occupation as it did in the war-zone in Italy, albeit far more seriously compromised by the activities of the Einsatzstab Rosenberg and its ilk. In the Netherlands, the German military government co-operated with the Dutch authorities in constructing sophisticated humidity-controlled refuges to which the most precious artworks were transported. In the occupied zone of France, the Germans compiled lists of protected structures, limited the use of historic buildings as billets for troops, and posted armed guards at two of the refuges for artworks established by the French authorities. Added to this, the protection of monuments and works of art featured in directives issued to the Wehrmacht, and the latter was instructed that the Hague Rules regarding private property were to be observed.[211] The head of the Kunstschutz subsequently protested that the confiscation of private Jewish collections in France by the Einsatzstab Rosenberg violated article 46,[212] and the overborne military administration eventually declared, in the light of Goering's intervention ordering the removal of the collections, that it was 'exempt from any responsibility for [its] contravention'.[213] Towards the end of the German occupation in all three countries, however, as the Allies steadily drove the occupiers back towards their own border, certain Kunstschutz officers were involved in the removal of treasures from churches and public collections.

As for US and UK forces, the special measures adopted for the preservation of monuments and works of art were as applicable

---

[211] Nicholas, *Rape of Europa*, p. 119.
[212] *Ibid.*, p. 125. See also *Rosenberg* v. *Fischer*, 15 ILR 467 (1948) at 469. Relying on a specious argument not worth elaborating here, the Nazi leadership argued in response that the Hague Rules did not apply to Jews.
[213] National Archives (Washington, DC), Record Group doc. 239/82, 'Report on Measures for the Seizure of Jewish Property', 29 January 1941, quoted in Nicholas, *The Rape of Europa*, p. 132.

to belligerent occupation as to the conduct of hostilities. In addition, exercising the belligerent occupant's right and, indeed, acquitting its obligation to ensure public order and civil affairs, as provided for in article 43 of the Hague Rules, the British and US military governments enacted laws for the protection of immovable and movable cultural property from the local population and other civilians, as well as from their own troops. For example, on 24 November 1943, the British Military Administration in Italy's occupied Libyan colonies of Tripolitana and Cyrenaica issued a Proclamation on Preservation of Antiquities, which vested temporary rights over antiquities in the military government and forbade their excavation, removal, sale, concealment or destruction without licence.[214] Later, after the eventual surrender and occupation of Germany,[215] the Office of Military Government (OMG) for Germany in the US Zone of Occupation promulgated Title 18 ('Monuments, Fine Arts and Archives') of the Military Government Regulations,[216] which, in addition to putting in place measures aimed at the restitution of artworks looted under the Nazis, embodied in Part 2 a legal regime for the 'Protection and Preservation of Cultural Structures'.[217] Under this regime, MFA&A officers were to 'ensure that appropriate action [was] taken for the protection of all structures listed in the Supreme Headquarters Allied Expeditionary Forces "Official List of Protected Monuments in Germany", the "Official List (SHAEF List Revised) of Protected Structures or Installations of Architectural, Artistic, Historical or Cultural Importance in the United States Zone of Germany" . . . or any subsequent

---

[214] Ibid., p. 217.
[215] Whether the Allied occupation of Germany after the unconditional surrender of the Nazi government constituted belligerent occupation within the meaning of the Hague Rules as then understood is a difficult question. Some post-war tribunals said it did not, although their conclusions were not uncontested. It is reasonably clear, however, that the same situation would today be characterised as belligerent occupation, hence the consideration here and below of the relevant Allied acts. See A. Roberts, 'What is Military Occupation?' (1984) 55 BYIL 249 at 267–71; Benvenisti, *International Law of Occupation*, pp. 91–6.
[216] Reproduced in W. W. Kowalski, *Art Treasures and War*, edited by T. Schadla-Hall (Leicester: Institute of Art and Law, 1998), annex 10.
[217] The term 'cultural structures' was defined to include 'monuments and other buildings or sites of religious, artistic, archaeological, historic, or similar cultural importance, such as: statues and other immovable works of art; churches, palaces and similar public or private buildings of architectural or historic importance; museum, library and archival buildings; parks and gardens attached to such buildings; and ruins of historical or archaeological importance': Military Government Regulations 18–100.

official list as well as any additional structures which in their judgment are cultural structures'.[218] While it was the responsibility of the German authorities (namely, the Ministerpräsidenten of the various Länder within the US Zone) actually to protect and preserve the cultural structures in question and to mobilise or establish appropriate German agencies for this purpose, the OMG of the relevant Land, in co-ordination with unit commanders, was empowered to make available, if requested by the German authorities, 'such assistance in the protection of cultural structures as appear[ed] appropriate', including the posting of notices placing cultural structures or areas off limits to all personnel, the posting of guards, and aid 'in the procurement of critical supplies for emergency restoration and protection of cultural structures and materials'.[219] There was a general prohibition on the use of cultural structures in the US Zone 'for any purpose other than those for which they [were] normally intended', with exceptions for non-Germans being made only with the explicit permission of the director of the OMG for that Land, who was normally to act on the advice of his MFA&A officers, and for Germans by 'the competent German official responsible for cultural monuments', with the OMG retaining a right of review.[220] Where exceptions were made and cultural structures were used for military purposes, the MFA&A officer of the Land OMG concerned was to 'ensure, by regular inspections, that the commanding officer of the unit using the building [was] informed of the necessity of protecting it and its contents from pilfering and defacement; that portions of the building particularly liable to pilferage or defacement [were] placed off limits; and that valuable movable contents of the building [were] placed off limits or collected in locked rooms'.[221] When it came to cultural structures damaged in the course of hostilities, their further demolition by military personnel was prohibited 'except as a measure of public safety, and then only under supervision of an MFA&A officer'.[222] Special instructions were to be issued by the OMG on the preservation of historic castles

---

[218] *Ibid.*, 18–200. For the purpose of identifying additional structures not on any official list, MFA&A officers were to 'consult the more comprehensive list of cultural monuments in Germany contained in Army Service Forces Manual M 336–17, "Atlas on Churches, Museums, Libraries and other Cultural Institutions in Germany"': *ibid.*
[219] *Ibid.*, 18–201.
[220] *Ibid.*, 18–204.1.
[221] *Ibid.*, 18–204.2.
[222] *Ibid.*, 18–205.

and palaces.²²³ Finally, each Land MFA&A officer was 'to render such advice as the Demilitarization Branch of Armed Forces Division may request in the event of an appeal for the retention of structures, memorials and monuments on the basis of great aesthetic value which might otherwise be destroyed through the implementation of Control Council Directive No. 30',²²⁴ which pursued the eradication of German militarism and Nazi doctrines.

The home front

Labour-intensive and often costly measures of material protection were adopted by civil authorities in the various belligerent states with a view to safeguarding the collections of national galleries, museums and archives against the threat of damage.

In the UK, the contents of fourteen leading institutions were removed in September 1939, in accordance with plans made years earlier, and transported out of the capital for dispersal among over thirty country-houses situated away from likely military objectives, although a few items were secreted in unused tunnels in the London Underground. The collections of two of these, the British Museum and the Victoria & Albert Museum, were soon gathered together and stored for the remainder of the war in Westwood Quarry, a vast, specially converted underground repository in rural Wiltshire, while paintings from the National Gallery were moved to Manod Quarry in Wales.²²⁵ The endeavour proved worthwhile, in the light of the bomb-damage inflicted on the British Museum, the National Gallery and the Tate Gallery. Historic buildings, too, were prepared against air-raid damage, with sandbagging and the deposit of piles of earth to absorb percussion, and the boarding-up of windows. In the Soviet Union, the majority of the most important items in the Hermitage, around 1.5 million pieces, were transported by train from Leningrad to Sverdlovsk in the Urals, where they sat out the war. The evacuation of the remainder, packed up in 351 crates and ready to go, was prevented when the Germans cut the railway lines out of Leningrad,

---

²²³ *Ibid.*, 18–206.
²²⁴ *Ibid.*, 18–207.
²²⁵ This herculean task included the lowering of a road and the insertion of concrete footings under a railway bridge solely to accommodate the passage, in a specially constructed transit case on the tray of a lorry, of van Dyck's 'King Charles I on Horseback' – with three-quarters of an inch to spare: N. J. McCamley, *Saving Britain's Art Treasures* (Barnsley: Leo Cooper, 2003), p. 108.

and these pieces endured the 900-day siege of the city in the Rastrelli Gallery on the ground floor of the Winter Palace. Again, that 'very little of the collection was lost', despite the fact that '[t]he museum's magnificent architectural complex was hit by thirty-two shells and two bombs',[226] indicates the value of the undertaking. Treasures from other Russian collections were moved to Siberia. In Poland, art treasures began to be sent away for safekeeping even before the German invasion, with the Jagellonian tapestries from Wawel Castle in Cracow ending up, by a circuitous route, in Canada. Similar efforts were made in Belgium, France and even mainland USA.

On the Axis side, the Italian authorities were quick to store the nation's most precious movable treasures of art and antiquity in refuges, and to board up, reinforce and insulate immovables, the latter contributing to the miraculous survival of Leonardo da Vinci's fresco *The Last Supper* when the refectory of the convent of Santa Maria delle Grazie in Milan was struck during an Allied air-raid. The Germans too adopted measures to safeguard both the collections of their own great museums, galleries and libraries and those collections transported to Germany from countries plundered under their occupation. Enormous numbers of items were dispersed to thousands of depositories, including, in the latter stages of the war, to the vast underground refuge at Alt Aussee in Austria. Most were stored deep down mines of all varieties, in the cellars of castles and monasteries, in the crypts of churches or in caches located in remote villages, while the plundered contents of the Poznan, Tallinn and Riga museums were hidden in tunnels off an underground aircraft factory in Hohenwalde. The most important treasures from the state museums in Berlin, among them Schliemann's Pergamon frieze and Trojan gold, were deposited in the vaults of the Reichsbank and the New Mint or in 'two, virtually impregnable, anti-aircraft towers – their walls made of reinforced concrete two yards thick – which had been built, one in the Zoological Garden and one at Friedrichshain',[227] some being moved in February 1945 to a saltmine in the village of Merkers.[228]

---

[226] Norman, *Hermitage*, p. 241.
[227] *Ibid.*, p. 267.
[228] Some of the treasures left in Berlin would perish in a mysterious fire as the Russians overran the city, while the remainder would be captured and transported to the Soviet Union by trophy units. It now seems, too, that not all of the items sent to Merkers escaped misappropriation.

The post-war trials

Article 6 of the Charter of the International Military Tribunal, Nuremberg,[229] which provided for the trial of the major German war criminals before a criminal tribunal constituted by France, the UK, the USA and the USSR, and which was adhered to by nineteen other states, vested the tribunal with jurisdiction over, *inter alia*:

> (b) War crimes: Namely violations of the laws and customs of war. Such violations shall include ... plunder of public or private property, wanton destruction of cities, towns or villages, or devastation not justified by military necessity;
> (c) Crimes against humanity: [Including] ... inhumane acts committed against any civilian population, before or during the war, or persecutions on political, racial or religious grounds in execution of or in connection with any crime within the jurisdiction of the Tribunal ...

It was in this context that the Nuremberg judgment considered the seizure of public collections in the German-occupied states and of private Jewish collections, including those of German and Austrian Jews. Although not required to do so, the Tribunal held that the relevant war crimes over which article 6(b) vested it with jurisdiction were 'already recognized as war crimes under international law': they were covered by article 46 (private property) and article 56 (the property of municipalities and of religious, charitable, educational, artistic and scientific institutions) of the Hague Rules; these rules 'were recognised by all civilised nations, and were regarded as being declaratory of the laws and customs of war' referred to in article 6(b) of the Charter; and '[t]hat violations of these provisions constituted crimes for which the guilty individuals were punishable [was] too well settled to admit of argument'.[230] Added to this, 'from the beginning of the war in 1939 war crimes were committed on a vast scale, which were also crimes against humanity'.[231] In the event, those involved in organising the seizure and destruction of artworks and monuments in the occupied territories were convicted, on these and many other counts, of war crimes and crimes against humanity. Chief among them, Alfred Rosenberg was held

---

[229] Annexed to the Agreement by the Government of the United Kingdom of Great Britain and Northern Ireland, the Government of the United States of America, the Provisional Government of the French Republic and the Government of the Union of Soviet Socialist Republics for the Prosecution and Punishment of the Major War Criminals of the European Axis, London, 8 August 1945, 82 UNTS 279.
[230] Nuremberg Judgment, pp. 64–5.
[231] *Ibid.*, p. 65.

responsible for a system of organised plunder of both public and private property throughout the invaded countries of Europe. Acting under Hitler's orders of January, 1940, he set up the 'Hohe Schule', he organised and directed the 'Einsatzstab Rosenberg', which plundered museums and libraries, confiscated art treasures and collections and pillaged private houses. His own reports show the extent of the confiscations ... As of July 14th, 1944, more than 21,903 art objects, including famous paintings and museum pieces, had been seized by the Einsatzstab in the West [alone].[232]

Rosenberg had also 'directed that the Hague Rules of Land Warfare were not applicable in the Occupied Eastern Territories'.[233] He was sentenced to death by hanging.

Nor were lesser examples of crimes against cultural property ignored by the other war crimes tribunals established by the Allied powers. In the *Trial of Karl Lingenfelder*, the Permanent Military Tribunal set up under French jurisdiction at Metz found a German civilian guilty under a provision of the French penal code of destroying public monuments, on the order of a German official, contrary to article 56 of the Hague Rules. The accused had used horses to pull down a monument erected in a French town to honour the dead of the First World War and had destroyed the marble slabs bearing their names. He had also broken a statue of Joan of Arc.[234]

For what it might imply about the Allied campaign (and Lauterpacht thought not much[235]), none of the accused at Nuremberg was indicted for indiscriminate bombing from the air. According to the UN War Crimes Commission, 'the majority of the members of Committee I considered the problem too complex to be resolved in the short time remaining', and the question was 'left undecided, as indeed it has been in the minds of authorities on international law'.[236] But in the subsequent case of *Ohlendorf* before a US military tribunal, also sitting in Nuremberg, 'the bombing of a city, with a concomitant loss of civilian life' was characterised – wholly *obiter*, it should be emphasised – as 'an act of legitimate warfare'.[237]

A city is bombed for tactical purposes; communications are to be destroyed, railroads wrecked, ammunition plants demolished, factories razed, all for the

[232] *Ibid.*, p. 95.
[233] *Ibid.*, p. 96.
[234] *Trial of Karl Lingenfelder*, 9 LRTWC 67 (1947).
[235] See L. Oppenheim, *International Law. A Treatise*, 7th edn, edited by H. Lauterpacht, 2 vols. (London: Longmans, Green, 1948–52), vol. II, para. 214 *eb*; H. Lauterpacht, 'The Problem of the Revision of the Law of War' (1952) 29 BYIL 360 at 365–8.
[236] UNWCC, *History of the United Nations War Crimes Commission*, pp. 492–3.
[237] *US v. Ohlendorf* (*Einsatzgruppen* case), 4 TWC 1 (1948) at 467.

purpose of impeding the military. In these operations it inevitably happens that nonmilitary persons are killed. This is an incident, a grave incident to be sure, but an unavoidable corollary of battle action. The civilians are not individualized. The bomb falls, it is aimed at the railroad yards, houses along the tracks are hit and many of their occupants killed.[238]

The tribunal's dictum was premised on the assumption that aerial bombardment – in which it included, with what can only be called wilful judicial blindness, the atomic bomb – 'was not aimed at non-combatants' but 'was dropped to overcome military resistance'.[239] The tribunal, however, seemed to elide overcoming military resistance (tactical bombing) with destroying the enemy's economic and infrastructural capacity to make war and undermining the morale of the civilian population (strategic bombing, as conducted by the Allies over Germany); indeed, in an unselfconscious but eminently contestable acceptance of the legality of morale bombing, the tribunal continued:

Thus, as grave a military action as is an air bombardment, whether with the usual bombs or by the atomic bomb, the one and only purpose of the bombing is to effect the surrender of the bombed nation. The people of that nation, through their representatives, may surrender and, with the surrender, the bombing ceases, the killing is ended.[240]

In a related vein, although in a different context, the US military tribunal in the case of *List* declared, in a near-verbatim restatement of article 15 of the Lieber Code, that military necessity 'permits the destruction of life ... incidentally unavoidable by the armed conflicts of the war'.[241] On the other hand, in the case of *Lewinski*, a British military court sitting in Hamburg observed:

[The] first and obvious comment on the wording of [article 23(g) of the Hague Rules] is that the requirement is 'necessity' and not 'advantage'. The second is that that necessity must be an imperative one. [A particular action] may afford ... advantages ... That fact alone, if the words in this article mean anything at all, cannot afford a justification.[242]

---

[238] Ibid.
[239] Ibid.
[240] Ibid.
[241] US v. List (*Hostages* case), 11 TWC 757 (1948) at 1253.
[242] In re von Lewinski (called von Manstein), 16 AD 509 (1949) at 522.

'Were it to do so', the court concluded, 'the article would become meaningless.'²⁴³

Despite the insufficiency of the law on bombardment to protect the cultural heritage of Germany and Japan from the ravages of bombing from the air, and in the face of Germany's ruthless contempt for the Hague prohibitions on plunder and destruction of cultural property in occupied territory, there were many genuine efforts on both sides of the Second World War, often under pressure and facilitated by neutrals, to preserve what even the Nazis, with breathtaking temerity, called 'cultural monuments which are the eternal heritage of all humanity'.²⁴⁴ In much the same way that the First World War spurred eventually thwarted inter-war action to this end, the Second World War played a seminal role in the consciousness-building and political mobilisation necessary for concerted diplomatic movement on this front, movement which would bear fruit nine years later.

---

²⁴³ *Ibid.*
²⁴⁴ Broadcast of 13 February 1944, quoted in D. Hapgood and D. Richardson, *Monte Cassino* (London: Angus & Robertson, 1984), p. 181.

3   The 1954 Hague Convention and
    First Hague Protocol

In 1946, as heir to the ICIC, the United Nations Educational, Scientific and Cultural Organisation (UNESCO) was established as a specialised agency of the new United Nations Organisation. Given its constitutional mandate to maintain, increase and diffuse knowledge by 'assuring the conservation and protection of the world's inheritance of books, works of art and monuments of history and science, and recommending to the nations concerned the necessary international conventions',[1] it seemed natural that it should move quickly to revive the idea of a multilateral agreement on the protection of monuments and artworks in war. In 1949, UNESCO's General Conference instructed the Director-General of the Organisation to report to it the following year on 'measures suitable for ensuring the co-operation of interested States in the protection, preservation and restoration of antiquities, monuments and historic sites', giving particular attention 'to arrangements for the protection of such monuments, as well as to the protection of all objects of cultural value, particularly those kept in museums, libraries and archives, against the probable consequences of armed conflict'.[2] In pursuance of this mandate, the Director-General convened a meeting of experts in 1950, followed by two more in succeeding years, to prepare a draft convention on the protection of cultural property in the event

---

[1] Constitution of the United Nations Educational, Scientific and Cultural Organisation, London, 16 November 1945, 4 UNTS 275, art. I(2)(c). Paragraph D.23 of UNESCO's Basic Programme adopted in 1950 provided specifically that the Organisation would '[e]ncourage Member States to arrange for the protection of their monuments and other cultural treasures from the dangers of armed conflict': *Records of the General Conference of the United Nations Educational, Scientific and Cultural Organisation, Fifth Session, Florence, 1950: Resolutions*, p. 28.

[2] 4 C/Resolution 6.42.

of armed conflict.[3] Working from the OIM draft, progress towards a UNESCO draft convention was relatively swift, and, fifteen years after its earlier invitation had been thwarted, the Netherlands government eventually invited diplomatic representatives to an Intergovernmental Conference on the Protection of Cultural Property in the Event of Armed Conflict, which met at The Hague from 21 April to 14 May 1954.

Echoing those responsible for the OIM draft, the committee of governmental experts which in 1952 finalised the UNESCO draft spoke of aiming at 'a realistic draft, rather than at an "ideal" one',[4] introducing a theme that would dominate debate at the intergovernmental conference in The Hague. The balance to be struck was the perennial one between maximising participation in the convention and maximising the protection it afforded. The view of UNESCO's Director-General, virtually a restatement of the director of the IICI's in 1938, was that the experts had eschewed 'an ideal of unlimited protection' and had adopted instead 'a realistic and cautious attitude', in the belief that 'modest, but enforceable, provisions' would better serve the cause of saving monuments.[5] Fears that this approach might have come at the cost of the instrument's bite were hardly assuaged when, referring in his closing address to the tension between military necessity and cultural protection, the president of the conference admitted that '[t]he point of balance between these two requirements, charted in the present Convention, may be held by critics to have been placed in the wrong position', adding that 'whether or not [the] map be entirely accurate, it at least [gave] a number of co-ordinates that should enable those who have to apply the Convention to set their course'.[6]

In the event, less than a decade after the close of the Second World War, the Convention for the Protection of Cultural Property in the Event of Armed Conflict and the Regulations for the Execution of the Convention,[7] which constitute an integral part of it,[8] were adopted at The Hague

---

[3] UNESCO Docs. 5 C/PRG/6 and Annex I; 6 C/PRG/22 and CL/484, Annex; 7 C/PRG/7 and Annexes I to III. See also the comments by states on the UNESCO draft convention, UNESCO Doc. CBC/4.

[4] 7 C/PRG/7, Annex I, p. 6.

[5] *Records of the Conference convened by the United Nations Educational, Scientific and Cultural Organisation held at The Hague from 21 April to 14 May 1954* (The Hague: Staatsdrukkerij- en uitgeverijbedrijf, 1961), para. 3.

[6] *Records 1954*, para. 2206.

[7] The Hague, 14 May 1954, 249 UNTS 240.

[8] 1954 Hague Convention, art. 20.

on 14 May 1954, along with a separate optional Protocol,[9] now referred to as the First Protocol.[10] Both entered into force on 7 August 1956. The Convention currently has 114 High Contracting Parties[11] and the First Protocol 92.[12]

For the purposes of the Convention, the protection of cultural property is deemed to comprise both the safeguarding of and respect for such property,[13] a reference respectively to material protection and legal restraint. Such protection is divided into two categories: so-called 'general protection' extends to all immovables and movables satisfying the Convention's definition of cultural property, whereas 'special protection' imposes a supplementary and nominally stricter standard of respect in relation to a narrower range of property. There are also rules for the transport of cultural property during armed conflict and for the treatment of personnel engaged in its protection. To assist and promote its execution, the Convention and its Regulations establish an international regime of control. For its part, the First Protocol deals with questions regarding the exportation and importation of cultural property from occupied territory, and with the return of cultural property deposited abroad for the duration of hostilities.

Preamble

Situating the instrument in an intellectual tradition handed down from the high Renaissance, and echoing the words of the OIM draft, the Convention's preamble gives voice to the conviction of the Parties that 'damage to cultural property belonging to any people whatsoever means damage to the cultural heritage of all mankind, since each people makes its contribution to the culture of the world'. Since 'the preservation of the cultural heritage is of great importance for all peoples of the world', the Parties deem it 'important that this heritage should receive international protection'. As familiar as this internationalist cultural ethos was by the mid-twentieth century, the preamble to the Convention represents

---

[9] The Hague, 14 May 1954, 249 UNTS 358.
[10] See art. 1(k) of the Second Protocol to the Convention for the Protection of Cultural Property in the Event of Armed Conflict, The Hague, 26 March 1999, UN Reg. No. 3511.
[11] For an updated list, see <http://erc.unesco.org/cp/convention.asp?KO=13637&language=E>.
[12] For an updated list, see <http://erc.unesco.org/cp/convention.asp?KO=15391&language=E>.
[13] 1954 Hague Convention, art. 2.

its first explicit embodiment in a binding international legal agreement, establishing what would become the hallmark of a succession of UNESCO-sponsored cultural heritage treaties. It also constitutes the first formal legal usage anywhere in the English language, in the specific context of historico-artistic preservationism, of the now-standard term 'heritage', with its intergenerational fiduciary tenor[14] — a rhetorical resonance all the greater in the French text, in the light of Aubry and Rau's canonical elaboration of the legal concept of *patrimoine*.[15] The term 'peoples' was preferred by the drafters to 'states' probably to reflect the fact that the property protected by the Convention is ultimately, as an anthropological matter, 'cultural' property by virtue of social context — that is, by virtue of the meaning ascribed to it by a society, as distinct from the juridical personification of that society for the formal purposes of the prevailing international legal order. This terminological idiom was well established by 1954, being traceable to the 1932 resolution of the CICI which endorsed the landmark Athens Conference, with its vision of 'the artistic and architectural heritage of mankind' reflecting 'the national genius of the different peoples'.[16] Similarly, the preamble's use of 'mankind', in place of reference to 'the international community of states' or the like, reflects the Convention's humanitarian character, identifying more accurately, as it does, the ultimate beneficiary of its provisions.[17]

As for how the preservation of this 'cultural heritage of all mankind' is to be secured in the event of armed conflict, the preamble emphasises material protection undertaken in advance. The Parties declare themselves in the final recital to be of the opinion that the wartime protection of cultural property 'cannot be effective unless both national and international measures have been taken to organize it in time of peace'. In this light, the Convention, while paying preambular homage to the Hague Rules and the Roerich Pact, points to its ancestry in the report of the NOB and the OIM draft convention.

---

[14] A resolution of the first meeting of the High Contracting Parties to the Convention recalled subsequently 'that the purpose of the Convention ... is to protect the cultural heritage of all peoples for future generations': UNESCO Doc. CUA/120, para. 22.

[15] See e.g. C. Aubry and C. Rau, *Cours de droit civil français d'après la méthode de Zachariae*, 6th edn, 12 vols. (Paris: Marchal et Billard, 1935–1958), vol. IX, paras. 573–87.

[16] LNOJ, 13th Year, No. 11 (November 1932), p. 1776.

[17] See also Convention on the Prevention and Punishment of the Crime of Genocide, Paris, 9 December 1948, 78 UNTS 277, preamble; Draft Code of Offences against the Peace and Security of Mankind, *Report of the International Law Commission covering the work of its sixth session, 3 June–28 July 1954*, UN Doc. A/2693, para. 54.

Scope of application

The Convention's scope of application *ratione materiae* is a question both of the property and the armed conflicts encompassed by the instrument. The former is dealt with in article 1 (in relation to general protection) and article 8 (as regards special protection), and is considered below. In accordance with the Convention's slightly perverse schema, the relevant armed conficts are specified in chapter 6 (articles 18 and 19). Article 18, modelled on article 2 common to the four 1949 Geneva Conventions, deals with armed conflicts of an international character, while article 19 concerns conflicts not of an international character. Neither provision makes any distinction as among armed actions by land, sea or air, with the result that the Convention applies to all three.

Article 18(1) provides that, '[a]part from the provisions which shall take effect in time of peace, the present Convention shall apply in the event of declared war or of any other armed conflict which may arise between two or more of the High Contracting Parties, even if the state of war is not recognized by one or more of them'. The import of the provision is twofold. First, like common article 2 of the Geneva Conventions, it ensures that the Convention applies in international armed conflict whether or not a legal state of war exists between or among the belligerents, a crucial point in the light of the desuetude into which formal declarations of war have fallen.[18] Second, it lays down the condition precedent that there must be at least one Party on each side of the conflict before the Convention binds any of the Parties involved.[19] Article 18(3) makes it clear, however, that article 18(1) is not a *si omnes* clause, stating that '[i]f one of the Powers in conflict is not a Party to the present Convention, the Powers which are Parties thereto shall nevertheless remain bound by it in their mutual relations'. Paragraph 3 of article 18 continues that those Parties involved in the conflict shall be

---

[18] As for the term 'armed conflict' in the international context, the ICRC commentary to common art. 2 explains that '[a]ny difference arising between two [or more] States and leading to the intervention of members of the armed forces is an armed conflict': J. Pictet (ed.), *Geneva Convention relative to the Protection of Civilian Persons in Time of War. Commentary* (ICRC: Geneva, 1958), p. 20.

[19] Israel, a High Contracting Party, appeared to accept that the Convention applied to its 1982 invasion of Lebanon, also a Party, even though it sought to characterise the conflict as one between it and the Lebanon-based forces of the Palestine Liberation Organisation (PLO), a non-state actor and *a fortiori* not a Party to the Convention: see *Information on the Implementation of the Convention for the Protection of Cultural Property in the Event of Armed Conflict, The Hague 1954. 1984 Reports*, UNESCO Doc. CLT/MD/3, para. 18.

bound by the Convention in relation to any non-Party[20] involved in the conflict 'if the latter has declared that it accepts the provisions thereof and so long as it applies them'.[21]

Article 18(2) stipulates that the Convention 'shall also apply to all cases of partial or total occupation of the territory of a High Contracting Party, even if the said occupation meets with no armed resistance'. The article is not restricted in its application to those operative provisions of the Convention and its Regulations which refer specifically to occupation but relates, subject to express wording to the contrary (which is not, as it turns out, anywhere to be found) to every provision of the Convention. In other words, in international armed conflicts, the obligations imposed and the machinery of control established by the Convention are applicable as much to belligerent occupation as they are to active hostilities. Paragraph 2 of article 18 does not itself define the term 'occupation'. It presumably relies instead on the accepted customary[22] definition reflected in article 42 of the Hague Rules, which provides that territory is considered occupied 'when it is actually placed under the authority of the hostile army' and that the occupation 'extends only to the territory where such authority is established and can be exercised'.

Turning to non-international armed conflicts, article 19(1), modelled on article 3 common to the Geneva Conventions, states that in the event of an armed conflict not of an international character occurring within the territory of one of the Parties, 'each party to the conflict shall be bound to apply, as a minimum, the provisions of the present Convention

---

[20] While accepting that the *pacta tertiis* rule was a fundamental rule of treaty law, the 1952 committee of governmental experts commented during the drafting of the Convention that '[t]he cultural property of an adversary is no less a part of the cultural heritage of mankind by reason of the fact that such adversary is not a Party to the Convention': 7 C/PRG/7, Annex I, p. 12.

[21] In 1962, the Federal Republic of Germany (FRG), then a signatory, informed UNESCO, as depositary, that it would be some time before it would be in a position to ratify the Convention, owing to its federal system of government. At the same time, it declared that it accepted and applied the Convention's provisions and that, accordingly, all Parties to the Convention were bound in relation to it by virtue of art. 18(3): UNESCO Doc. ODG/SJ/2/467; *Information on the Implementation of the Convention for the Protection of Cultural Property in Case of Armed Conflict, The Hague 1954. 1967 Reports*, UNESCO Doc. SHC/MD/1, para. 6. The FRG ratified the Convention on 11 August 1967.

[22] *Legal Consequences of the Construction of a Wall in the Occupied Palestinian Territory*, ICJ General List No. 131, Advisory Opinion, 9 July 2004, para. 78; *Armed Activities on the Territory of the Congo (Democratic Republic of the Congo v. Uganda)*, ICJ General List No. 116, Judgment, 19 December 2005, para. 172.

which relate to respect for cultural property'. Article 19(2) adds that the parties to the conflict 'shall endeavour to bring into force, by means of special agreements, all or part of the other provisions'. The drafters sought to justify this imposition of treaty obligations on rebel forces not Parties to the Convention by invoking the argument that each adversary 'is bound by contractual arrangements undertaken by a community of which he is a part'.[23] In this regard, article 19(4) makes it clear that the application of article 19 shall not affect the legal status of the parties to the conflict. As with common article 3, the threshold of violence beyond which internal unrest becomes 'armed conflict not of an international character' is not specified in article 19, although it can at least be assumed that the latter was to have the same scope as the former. As for '[t]he provisions of the Convention which relate to respect for cultural property' mentioned in article 19(1), the reference is to paragraphs 1 to 5 of article 4 (headed 'Respect for cultural property'), which embody the Convention's most fundamental legal restraints, applicable to all movables and immovables falling within the definition of cultural property in article 1.[24]

It should be emphasised that there is no such thing as belligerent occupation in non-international armed conflict. The apparent assertion to the contrary by the director of UNESCO's Division of Cultural Heritage, Sector for Culture,[25] in relation to the destruction of the Buddhas of Bamiyan in 2001 by the Taliban government of Afghanistan is baseless. So too is the statement by the Director-General of UNESCO that the demolition of the statues 'was the act of an occupying power'.[26] It should also be noted that although a localised armed conflict, whether international or non-international, in one region of a state triggers the application of the Convention in the whole of that state, this does not mean that all acts performed on the territory of that state for the

---

[23] 7 C/PRG/7, Annex I, p. 13.
[24] See also A. P. V. Rogers, *Law on the Battlefield*, 2nd edn (Manchester: Manchester University Press, 2004), p. 140 n. 48. But cf. J. Toman, *The Protection of Cultural Property in the Event of Armed Conflict. Commentary on the Convention for the Protection of Cultural Property in the Event of Armed Conflict and its Protocol, signed on 14 May 1954 in The Hague, and on other instruments of international law concerning such protection* (Aldershot: Dartmouth/UNESCO Publishing, 1996), pp. 213–15; K. Chamberlain, *War and Cultural Heritage. An Analysis of the 1954 Convention for the Protection of Cultural Property in the Event of Armed Conflict and its Two Protocols* (Leicester: Institute of Art and Law, 2004), pp. 72–3.
[25] *Bureau of the World Heritage Committee, Twenty-Fifth Session, 25–30 June 2001. Report of the Rapporteur*, UNESCO Doc. WHC-2001/CONF.205/10, para. I.9.
[26] UNESCO Doc. DG/2001/115, p. 1.

duration of the conflict are governed by the Convention. The acts must be closely related to the armed conflict for them to be regulated by the laws of armed conflict,[27] and the demolition of the Buddhas was in no way related to the armed conflict. Contrary, then, to the view of Francioni and Lenzerini,[28] as adopted by the Director-General of UNESCO,[29] the destruction of the Buddhas of Bamyan in 2001 by the Taliban government of Afghanistan would not have been governed by the Convention had Afghanistan been a Party to it (or, indeed, by any other provision of the laws of armed conflict, conventional or customary).[30]

Finally, held as it was the year after the end of the Korean War, the intergovernmental conference was eager to make reference to United Nations military forces. The result was resolution I of the Final Act of the Intergovernmental Conference on the Protection of Cultural Property in the Event of Armed Conflict,[31] in which the hope was expressed 'that the competent organs of the United Nations should decide, in the event of military action being taken in implementation of the Charter, to ensure application of the provisions of the Convention by the armed forces taking part in such action'. The resolution was endorsed later that same year by the UNESCO General Conference.[32] The Director-General of the Organisation subsequently asked the UN Secretary-General to bring resolution I to the attention of the competent UN organs, which he did.[33] In this light, it is worth noting that the Secretary-General's Bulletin on the Observance by United Nations Forces of International Humanitarian Law, issued on 6 August 1999, states:

The United Nations force is prohibited from attacking monuments of art, architecture or history, archaeological sites, works of art, places of worship

---

[27] *Prosecutor* v. *Tadić*, IT-94-1, Appeals Chamber Decision on Defence Motion for Interlocutory Appeal on Jurisdiction, 2 October 1995, para. 70; *Prosecutor* v. *Kunarac, Kovač and Vuković*, IT-96-23 & IT-96-23/1-A, Appeals Chamber Judgment, 12 June 2002, paras. 55–60; *Prosecutor* v. *Rutaganda*, ICTR-96-3-A, Appeals Chamber Judgment, 26 May 2003, paras. 569–70.
[28] F. Francioni and F. Lenzerini, 'The Destruction of the Buddhas of Bamyan and International Law' (2003) 14 EJIL 619 at 632–3 and 635–7.
[29] UNESCO Doc. 32 C/3, p. 100.
[30] See also T. Georgopoulos, 'Avez-vous bien dit "crime contre la culture"? La protection internationale des monuments historiques' (2001) 54 RHDI 459 at 471–2; R. Goy, 'La destruction intentionnelle du patrimoine culturel en droit international' (2005) 109 RGDIP 273 at 282.
[31] *Records 1954*, p. 78.
[32] 8 C/Resolution 4.1.4.133, para. 5.
[33] *1967 Reports*, para. 8.

and museums and libraries which constitute the cultural or spiritual heritage of peoples. In its area of operation, the United Nations force shall not use such cultural property or their immediate surroundings for purposes which might expose them to destruction or damage. Theft, pillage, misappropriation and any act of vandalism directed against cultural property is strictly prohibited.[34]

The provision blends articles 1, 4(1) and 4(3) of the 1954 Hague Convention with articles 53(a) and (b) of 1977 Protocol I Additional to the Geneva Conventions.[35] The earlier draft model agreement between the United Nations and Member States contributing personnel and equipment to United Nations peacekeeping operations[36] states that the UN peacekeeping operation the subject of the agreement is to 'observe and respect the principles and spirit of the general international conventions applicable to the conduct of military personnel', among which it includes the 1954 Hague Convention.

General provisions regarding protection

Chapter I (articles 1 to 7) of the Convention lays down 'general provisions regarding protection' applicable to all movables and immovables satisfying the definition of cultural property. The label 'general protection' – nowhere, in fact, used in the Convention – tends to be applied to this regime, in contradistinction to the 'special protection' provided for in chapter II, but this can be misleading, since cultural property granted special protection still benefits from chapter I's general provisions to the extent that chapter II does not constitute *lex specialis* to them. In other words, chapter I comprises the baseline level of protection applicable to all cultural property covered by the Convention, which, with the exception of the provisions on the use of cultural property for purposes likely to expose it to destruction or damage and on acts of hostility directed against it, is supplemented, not supplanted, by chapter II.

---

[34] UN Doc. ST/SGB/1999/13, para. 6.6.
[35] Protocol Additional to the Geneva Conventions of 12 August 1949, and Relating to the Protection of Victims of International Armed Conflicts, Geneva, 8 June 1977, 1125 UNTS 3.
[36] UN Doc. A/46/185, Annex, para. 28.

Definition of 'cultural property'

The drafters of the Convention were fixated from the outset with the idea that the supposed failure of the provisions of the Hague Rules relevant to cultural property (in the lay sense) stemmed in part from their 'over-ambitious definitions' which, by 'aiming too high', risked 'getting too little'.[37] The unchallenged assumption was that it was unrealistic to hope to protect every building dedicated to religion, art, science or charitable purposes, every historic monument and every work of art in the event of armed conflict. What was wanted was a convention of narrower application, so as to render feasible a higher standard of protection. As a consequence, the committee of experts invited by UNESCO to prepare a draft text discarded the Hague formula[38] and cast about for a definition which embodied a more selective approach – not an easy task, given the intrinsic subjectivity of notions of historic and especially artistic significance, the basic criterion settled on for inclusion.

In the event, the Convention, unlike the OIM draft, employs a single, generic term to refer to property falling within its scope of application, namely 'cultural property'. The label is not used in a lay sense – as one might refer, for example, to the 'cultural property' protected by articles 27 and 56 of the Hague Rules – but is given a specific legal definition in article 1:

For the purposes of the present Convention, the term 'cultural property' shall cover, irrespective of origin or ownership:

(a) movable or immovable property of great importance to the cultural heritage of every people, such as monuments of architecture, art or history, whether religious or secular; archaeological sites; groups of buildings which, as a whole, are of historical or artistic interest; works of art; manuscripts, books and other objects of artistic, historical or archaeological interest; as well as scientific collections and important collections of books or archives or of reproductions of the property defined above;

---

[37] 7 C/PRG/7, Annex I, p. 7.
[38] For example, educational establishments are not protected as such by the Convention but only by the relevant Hague Rules: see e.g. *Prosecutor* v. *Kordić and Čerkez*, IT-95-14/2-A, Appeals Chamber Judgment, 17 December 2004, paras. 89–92. But the Convention does extend to educational establishments which qualify as 'cultural property' under art. 1.

(b) buildings whose main and effective purpose is to preserve or exhibit the movable cultural property defined in sub-paragraph (a) such as museums, large libraries and depositories of archives, and refuges intended to shelter, in the event of armed conflict, the movable cultural property defined in sub-paragraph (a);
(c) centres containing a large amount of cultural property as defined in sub-paragraphs (a) and (b), to be known as 'centres containing monuments'.

As the chapeau to the provision states, the definition is strictly for the purposes of the Convention. It is not cross-referable to the definitions of cultural property found in subsequent UNESCO standard-setting instruments in the field of cultural heritage, each of which is tailored to the object and purpose of its respective instrument. The sole exceptions are the Convention's two Protocols, which also apply the definition laid down in article 1.[39]

In contrast to the Roerich Pact, the Convention protects both immovables and movables. Article 1 underlines too that this protection accrues 'irrespective of origin or ownership'. The examples of specific types of property given in paragraphs (a) and (b) of article 1 are not intended to be exhaustive, as the phrase 'such as' makes clear. As under articles 27 and 56 of the Hague Rules, the term 'monuments' in subparagraph (a) was taken by the drafters to encompass 'constructions of a certain age and design, whatever their purpose, as well as monuments, in the more limited sense, erected to commemorate some event or person':[40] in other words, the label refers to immovables which are of historic or artistic importance in their own right, whatever the historic or artistic importance of any movables they may house.[41] The category 'groups of buildings which, as a whole, are of historical or artistic interest' was proposed by the Scandinavian countries to cover places, such as certain mediaeval villages, where the overall town fabric may be culturally important even if no individual building would necessarily be worthy of protection in and of itself. The inclusion of this category, opposed at the time by the UK and adopted by the Main Commission only by fourteen votes to ten, with fourteen abstentions, was an early reflection of the move in preservationist thinking away from the conservation of decontextualised 'monuments' and towards the

---

[39] First Hague Protocol, art. 1; Second Hague Protocol, art. 1(b).
[40] 7 C/PRG/7, Annex I, p. 7.
[41] 5 C/PRG/6, Annex I, para. 15.

protection of streetscapes and historic areas. It was precisely this category of cultural property which was at issue in *Hess v. Commander of the IDF in the West Bank*,[42] in which the Supreme Court of Israel, sitting as the High Court of Justice, upheld the revised order of the Commander of the Israel Defence Forces in the occupied West Bank to demolish, for security reasons, two and a half uninhabited buildings, including a structure which formed part of the historic streetscape of the Old City of Hebron. The protection of 'buildings whose main and effective purpose is to preserve or exhibit the movable cultural property defined in sub-paragraph (a) such as museums, large libraries and depositories of archives', as referred to sub-paragraph (b), is dependent on the cultural importance not of the buildings themselves but of the movable cultural property they are intended to house. The same goes for sub-paragraph (b)'s 'refuges intended to shelter, in the event of armed conflict, the movable cultural property defined in sub-paragraph (a)'. As for 'centres containing monuments', the term is somewhat misleading, since, in accordance with sub-paragraph (c), these are 'centres containing a large amount of cultural property as defined in sub-paragraphs (a) and (b)', and the definition of cultural property in sub-paragraph (a) is not limited to monuments. Indeed, a centre containing monuments might in principle contain no monuments, nor any immovable property of great cultural importance in its own right, but only movable cultural property, whether or not housed in buildings whose main and effective purpose is to preserve or exhibit such property. Nor, according to the experts who prepared the UNESCO draft, is there any reason why 'whole towns that are universally admired as great art centres – e.g. Venice, Bruges, and Toledo' cannot be considered centres containing monuments.[43]

The property encompassed by paragraphs (b) and (c) of article 1 depends on the general definition of cultural property given in paragraph (a), namely 'movable or immovable property of great importance to the cultural heritage of every people'. On its face, the phrase 'of every people' is capable of two meanings, that is, 'of all peoples jointly' or 'of each respective people',[44] and recourse to the French and Spanish texts, which are also authoritative, fails to establish which of these

---

[42] 58(3) PD 443 (2004).
[43] 7 C/PRG/7, Annex I, p. 17. But *cf. Records 1954*, para. 525 (US).
[44] The ambiguity is compounded by the secondary sources, which occasionally misrender the crucial phrase: see e.g. *The protection of movable cultural property. Compendium of legislative texts*, 2 vols. (Paris: UNESCO, 1984), vol. I, p. 17 ('of all peoples').

meanings is to be preferred.[45] It is clear, however, that the second alternative is the correct one: the term 'cultural property' in article 1 refers to movable or immovable property of great importance to the cultural heritage of each respective people – in other words, of great importance to the national cultural heritage of each respective Party. This follows from the preambular recital which declares 'that damage to cultural property belonging to any people whatsoever means damage to the cultural heritage of all mankind, since each people makes its contribution to the culture of the world', especially the words 'any people' and 'each people' and their use in contradistinction to 'all mankind' (as opposed to 'every people'). Some states have sought to echo this statement in their periodic implementation reports submitted in accordance with article 26(2). The former Ukrainian SSR referred to 'movable and immovable property of great importance for national consciousness which shows the contribution of the Ukrainian people to the world's cultural heritage'.[46] Jordan stated on one occasion that the sites on which it was reporting 'form part of the common heritage of mankind as a whole, as well as being the cultural heritage of the Jordanian nation and people'.[47] An Iranian report speaks of 'the unique, time-honoured cultural patrimony of Iran, which is indeed none but the cultural heritage of humanity',[48] and of the need 'to understand and interpret the cultural heritage of countries as a part of the cultural heritage of humanity'.[49] In this light, article 1's definition of cultural property reflects the conviction – in the words of a former president of the International Court of Justice, referring to the Convention – that 'cultural objects and properties which make up [one state's] national heritage [are], consequently, the world's heritage'.[50]

---

[45] Although the French and Spanish versions omit the word 'every', speaking only of 'the cultural heritage of peoples' ('le patrimoine culturel des peuples'/'el patrimonio cultural de los pueblos'), the genitive can still be read either way.

[46] *Information on the Implementation of the Convention for the Protection of Cultural Property in the Event of Armed Conflict, The Hague 1954. 1995 Reports*, UNESCO Doc. CLT-95/WS/13, p. 48. See also Hungary (*1967 Reports*, p. 23), the former Byelorussian SSR (*Information on the Implementation of the Convention for the Protection of Cultural Property in the Event of Armed Conflict, The Hague 1954. 1979 Reports*, UNESCO Doc. CC/MD/41, p. 15) and the former USSR (*ibid.*, p. 27).

[47] *1979 Reports*, p. 20.

[48] *1995 Reports*, p. 31.

[49] *Ibid.*, p. 34.

[50] Address by Nagendra Singh at the celebration of the thirtieth anniversary of the Hague Convention, *1984 Reports*, p. 14 at p. 15. See also the address by Manfred Lachs at the celebration of the thirtieth anniversary of the Hague Convention, *ibid.*, p. 12 at p. 13.

What all this means in practice is that article 1 devolves to each Party the discretionary competence to determine the precise property in its territory to which the Convention applies. There are several pointers to this. First, articles 6, 16 and 17 provide for a scheme under which cultural property protected by the Convention is rendered clearly identifiable through the affixing of a distinctive emblem by the authorities of the Party in whose territory it is situated, a competence premised on the competence of that Party to determine, as it sees fit, the cultural property to which the Convention applies in the first place. Secondly, an analysis of the implementation reports submitted over time by the Parties shows that those Parties which have proffered information apply the Convention to movable and immovable property which each considers of great importance to its own cultural heritage, according to its own criteria.[51] Finally, the *travaux préparatoires* confirm this approach to article 1. The drafters clearly envisaged that the Convention's application to specific property was to be left to the judgement of each Party acting on the basis of an open-textured international definition which merely implied, without seeking rigidly to structure, a degree of selectivity based on cultural significance. The committee of experts charged with preparing UNESCO's draft text 'pointed out that a multilateral instrument designed to secure the support of many States with different customs and legislations could not include all the definitions given in ... national regulations, some of which [were] far ahead of general usage' and that, as such, the Convention's aim was 'to establish an average standard which most States would be able to apply'.[52] In a similar vein, the Israeli delegate to the intergovernmental conference

---

[51] This approach is evidenced, with varying degrees of explicitness, in reports submitted by Bulgaria, *1995 Reports*, p. 19; Croatia, *ibid.*, p. 22; Germany, *ibid.*, p. 24; Iran, *ibid.*, p. 31; Liechtenstein, *ibid.*, p. 35; Madagascar, *ibid.*, p. 36; Slovenia, *ibid.*, p. 42; Switzerland, *ibid.*, pp. 43–4; Ukraine, *ibid.*, p. 48; India, *Information on the Implementation of the Convention for the Protection of Cultural Property in the Event of Armed Conflict, The Hague 1954. 1989 Reports*, UNESCO Doc. CC/MD-11, p. 16; Netherlands, *ibid.*, p. 27; USSR, *ibid.*, p. 38; Austria, *1984 Reports*, p. 21; Byelorussian SSR, *ibid.*, pp. 24–5; Hungary, *1979 Reports*, p. 19; Iraq, *ibid.*, p. 20; Jordan, *ibid.*, p. 20; Niger, *ibid.*, p. 25; Luxembourg, *Information on the Implementation of the Convention for the Protection of Cultural Property in the Event of Armed Conflict, The Hague 1954. 1970 Reports*, UNESCO Doc. SHC/MD/6, p. 16; San Marino, *1967 Reports*, pp. 32–3. The reports of several other Parties hint at the same approach, and during the drafting process, Israel referred in the context of art. 1 to cultural property 'as scheduled by the respective High Contracting Parties' and 'as ... scheduled by the respective Departments of Antiquities of the High Contracting Parties': CBC/4, p. 7.

[52] 7 C/PRG/7, Annex I, p. 7.

which finalised and adopted the Convention seemed to speak for many when he urged that article 1 embody a very general definition, with every state being 'left to decide what its respective cultural property was'.[53] The French representative was emphatic on this point, stressing that 'it was indispensable in international law to have a general definition' and that '[n]ational authorities should be able to decide, within the meaning of the general definition, the exact items of cultural property' covered.[54] As for the Italian delegation, it stated unequivocally after the adoption of article 1 that '[t]he choice of property to be placed under general protection had been left to each country'.[55] In support of this approach, the Soviet representative noted that, while the destruction of cultural property 'affected mankind as a whole', '[e]very people had its particular characteristics and the cultural heritages of the various countries differed accordingly'.[56] Anyway, as the West German delegate reminded the conference, 'whenever a country wanted to protect its own cultural property, it was also protecting that of other peoples'.[57] The only real controversy was over the degree of selectivity the definition was to imply, with some states tending more towards the exclusory than others. In the event, the phrase 'of great importance to the cultural heritage of every people' which found its way into article 1 was something of a compromise and, in the final analysis, is relatively non-committal, suggesting as great a degree of cultural importance as each Party sees fit, within the limits imposed by the ordinary meaning of the words[58] and the requirement of good faith.[59]

As to how the Parties have given effect to article 1, the overwhelming majority of states which have submitted implementation reports appear, in the case of immovable cultural property, to consider 'of great importance to [their] cultural heritage' either the full complement of monuments and sites on the official list of their national cultural heritage, as defined and formally identified by domestic law and procedure, or a not insubstantial, though considerably varying proportion thereof.[60]

---

[53] *Records 1954*, para. 163. See also *ibid.*, para. 869 (Denmark).
[54] *Ibid.*, para. 164.
[55] It was in this light that Italy proposed a permanent intergovernmental co-ordinating committee with a mandate to review the suitability of property nominated by each state (UNESCO Docs. CBC/DR/129 and 130, *ibid.*, pp. 388–9). The proposal was rejected.
[56] *Ibid.*, para. 136.
[57] *Ibid.*, para. 146.
[58] Vienna Convention on the Law of Treaties, Vienna, 23 May 1969, 1155 UNTS 331, art. 31.
[59] Good faith is demanded in both the interpretation and application of treaties: Vienna Convention on the Law of Treaties, arts. 31(1) and 26 respectively.
[60] This approach is made sufficiently clear in most of the reports cited above.

The numbers will differ depending on a raft of factors, although, on the whole, the figures for immovable cultural property protected in each state by the Convention might be considered to be of a very roughly comparable order of magnitude, namely tens of thousands. Of the Parties which have cited figures, the Netherlands has spoken in the past of 43,000 items of immovable cultural property under protection,[61] Bulgaria 39,412,[62] Germany 10,000 in the former West Germany alone bearing the Convention's distinctive sign (but whether more are considered protected is unclear),[63] Switzerland 8,000,[64] the former Byelorussian SSR over 6,000[65] and Slovenia 5,550.[66] The UK – which announced on the Convention's fiftieth anniversary, 14 May 2004, its intention to ratify the instrument and both of its Protocols – currently proposes to extend general protection to around 10,800 immovables.[67] In Iraq, formally registered and gazetted archaeological sites alone which that state in the past deemed covered by the Convention numbered 10,000.[68] Austria has cited a figure of 76,890,[69] which includes fixtures such as '[b]ells, organs, stained glass windows [and] murals classified in accordance with the Austrian law on the protection of historic monuments'.[70] In terms of movable cultural property, only Bulgaria has cited a figure, viz. 4,000,000 protected objects, housed in the country's 222 museums and art galleries.[71] The UK currently proposes to extend general protection to the contents of 102 museums, galleries and collections, as well as to the

---

[61] *1989 Reports*, p. 27. This number was expected to grow.
[62] *1995 Reports*, p. 19.
[63] *Ibid.*, p. 24. The FRG's national inventory of protected cultural property was decided 'in accordance with [a] distributive formula agreed on by the Federal and Land authorities' by which each Land was entitled to a certain fixed percentage of the national total of protected buildings based on population size and apparently regardless of how many buildings might actually have been capable of satisfying art. 1: *1984 Reports*, pp. 29–30, quote p. 29.
[64] *1989 Reports*, p. 35; *1995 Reports*, p. 43. A new edition of the inventory was to contain approximately 300 further items: *1995 Reports*, p. 44.
[65] *1979 Reports*, p. 15.
[66] *1995 Reports*, p. 42.
[67] Department for Culture, Media and Sport Cultural Property Unit, *Consultation Paper on The 1954 Hague Convention on the Protection of Cultural Property in the Event of Armed Conflict and its two Protocols of 1954 and 1999* (September 2005), p. 13.
[68] *1989 Reports*, p. 20.
[69] *1984 Reports*, p. 21.
[70] *1979 Reports*, p. 10. As regards the contents of museums, galleries, libraries and archives, 'the complete collection or all the [movable] cultural property preserved is regarded as a single item of cultural property for protection': *ibid.*
[71] *1995 Reports*, p. 20.

contents of the National Record Offices and the country's five legal deposit libraries.[72]

Until now, only one Party has explicitly favoured a highly restrictive approach, although others may have tended in this direction without stating so. In terms of immovables, Spain, referring in 1984 to its 'list of items of cultural property as defined under Article 1 of the Convention', described this as 'practically identical to the list ... transmitted to the World Heritage Committee' for consideration for inclusion on the World Heritage List.[73] Today, the number of cultural sites on Spain's tentative list[74] added to the number already inscribed on the World Heritage List makes for just over fifty items of cultural property. In this light, it is highly relevant that the twenty-seventh General Conference of UNESCO – comprising representatives of every Member State of the Organisation, many of them Parties to the Convention – requested the Director-General 'to draw the attention of States that are party to the [World Heritage Convention], but are not party to the 1954 Hague Convention, to the fact that the latter Convention offers protection to cultural property that is of national and local importance as well as to sites of outstanding universal importance'.[75] Indeed, the criterion for protection under the World Heritage Convention and for inclusion on the World Heritage List, namely 'outstanding universal value',[76] does seem at such variance with the ordinary meaning of the criterion for general protection under the 1954 Hague Convention, namely 'great importance to the cultural heritage of [a] people', as to suggest that Spain's application of article 1 is wrong in law. In addition, Spain's approach raises the question of what, by comparison with such a selective group of sites, could possibly be considered cultural property 'of very great importance'[77] to the cultural heritage of a people for the purposes of special protection under the Convention.

---

[72] Department for Culture, Media and Sport Cultural Property Unit, *Consultation Paper*, p. 13. Over and above this, the UK proposes to request enhanced protection under chap. 3 of the Second Hague Protocol for twenty-six of the museums, as well as for the National Records Offices and the UK's five legal deposit libraries: *ibid.*, pp. 30–3.
[73] *1984 Reports*, p. 39.
[74] For the latter, see UNESCO Doc. WHC-05/29.COM/8A, Annex 3, pp. 18–19.
[75] 27 C/Resolution 3.5, para. 3. See also 142 EX/Decision 5.5.2, para. 7(c); UNESCO Doc. 142 EX/15, para. 8.
[76] Convention concerning the Protection of the World Cultural and Natural Heritage, Paris, 16 December 1972, 1037 UNTS 151, art. 1.
[77] 1954 Hague Convention, art. 8(1), chapeau. The text of a treaty (that is, the provisions *in toto*) is part of the context by reference to which a given provision is to be interpreted, in accordance with Vienna Convention on the Law of Treaties, arts. 31(1) and 31(2).

Some Parties appear to condition their application of the Convention to specific property not just on a requisite degree of cultural importance but also on military considerations. Spain, for example, further reported in 1984 that an initial draft list of protected property was to be 'revised by the appropriate organizations, chiefly the Ministry of Defence'.[78] Conversely, there is always the possibility that some Parties seek to confer the Convention's protection on immovable property of strategic value but palpably undeserving of characterisation as greatly important to their cultural heritage. While the Convention's mere application does not necessarily mean that the building must be spared in the event of hostilities, given that an attacking Party ultimately has recourse to article 4(2)'s waiver in respect of military necessity, such practices still raise questions about the abuse of article 1. That said, there is no reason in principle why the Convention should not apply to strategically significant immovable cultural property if the latter genuinely satisfies the definition laid down in article 1. The issue in such a case, in terms of the conduct of the territorial Party, will be whether the use to which the immovable is put constitutes a breach of article 4(1)'s obligation not to use cultural property and its surroundings for purposes which are likely to expose it to destruction or damage in the event of armed conflict.

Although the power to evaluate the cultural importance of specific property rests with the authorities of the Party where it is situated, 'it is a power which must be exercised reasonably and in good faith',[79] in accordance with article 26 of the Vienna Convention on the Law of Treaties. The principle of good faith obliges the Parties to a treaty 'to apply it in a reasonable way and in such a manner that its purpose can be realized'.[80] In the present case, bad faith may be imputed where a Party to the Convention exercises its competence under article 1 in a manner manifestly unjustified by the facts, either by not applying the Convention

---

[78] *1984 Reports*, p. 39.
[79] *Rights of Nationals of the United States of America in Morocco (France v. United States of America)*, ICJ Reports 1952, p. 176 at p. 212.
[80] *Gabčíkovo-Nagymaros Project (Hungary/Slovakia)*, Judgment, ICJ Reports 1997, p. 7 at para. 142. Employing the analogous concept of abuse of rights, Lauterpacht states that 'in any case where international law gives discretionary powers to States to act, as it were, as trustees for the international community, ... States who exercise this power in an arbitrary manner, as an instrument exclusively of selfish national policy, are plainly guilty of an abuse of right': H. Lauterpacht, 'Règles générales du droit de la paix', 62 RCADI (1937-IV) 95 at 390. A domestic analogy can be drawn with the French administrative law doctrine of *détournement de pouvoir* – or, more precisely in this context, *détournement du but social*, where a power conferred for a communal purpose is used for private ends – and with the English administrative law doctrine enunciated in *Padfield v. Minister for Agriculture, Fisheries and Foods* [1968] AC 997.

to property of incontestably great importance to its cultural heritage as a blatant means of obviating article 4's obligation of respect where this might prove strategically inconvenient or by applying the Convention to property incontestably lacking the requisite cultural importance blatantly to secure protection for stategically valuable activities.[81] *Bona fide* value judgements on which reasonable people and peoples can differ are one thing, and are almost inevitable when dealing with notions as personally and culturally contingent as historic and, *a fortiori*, artistic significance. But some characterisations may fall so outside the penumbra of reasonable intersubjectivity as to raise legitimate doubts as to motive, especially when viewed in the light of other probative evidence.

Despite the fact that most Parties would appear to consider the Convention applicable to the full complement, or to a substantial and representative sample, of their respective national cultural heritages as identified by them, a considerable degree of uncertainty as to the instrument's proper scope of application seems to persist, no doubt owing to the ambiguity *prima facie* of article 1. A few scholars continue to place a restrictive construction on the provision.[82] The UK's *Manual of the Law of Armed Conflict* is also misleading in this regard.[83] It need hardly be said that any confusion, doubt or hesitancy over this most basic question of all — that is, the 'cultural property' to which the eponymous Convention properly applies — is unsatisfactory, and that the protection in the event of armed conflict which constitutes the object and purpose of the instrument would be 'strengthened by freeing the designation of cultural property, to a very large extent, from all possibility of dispute'.[84]

Finally, and crucially, while in principle the Convention leaves it to the Party in whose territory the relevant property is situated to determine whether or not that property is of great importance to its cultural heritage and is therefore protected by the Convention, in practice things are not so straightforward. It may well be that a Party has indeed identified the 'cultural property' within the meaning of article 1 located

---

[81] '[T]he right in question must be exercised in accordance with standards of what is normal, having in view the social purpose of the law': *Admission of a State to the United Nations (Charter, Art. 4)*, Advisory Opinion, ICJ Reports 1948, p. 57, ind. op. Azevedo at p. 80.

[82] See L. C. Green, *The Contemporary Law of Armed Conflict*, 2nd edn (Manchester: Manchester University Press, 2000), p. 46 n. 176, p. 153 n. 211 and p. 154 n. 214; Rogers, *Law on the Battlefield*, p. 140.

[83] See UK Ministry of Defence, *The Manual of the Law of Armed Conflict* (Oxford: Oxford University Press, 2004), para. 5.26.2 n. 116.

[84] 5 C/PRG/6, Annex I, para. 19.

in its territory. But unless it has also taken measures under article 3 to notify other Parties in advance of the identity and location of all such property by means of inventories and/or maps, or has marked all such property with the Convention's distinctive emblem as permitted by article 6, there will be no definitive way for an opposing Party to know what movables and immovables are considered by the territorial Party to be of great importance to its national cultural heritage: in short, there will be no conclusive indication of the applicability of the Convention to property situated in the territory of that state. In such a situation, which – given the Parties' discretion under both article 3 and article 6, and, it has to be acknowledged, their general, perhaps overwhelming lack of conscientiousness – is likely to be the rule rather than the exception, it will ultimately fall by default to the opposing Party to determine, for the purposes of compliance with its own obligations of respect under article 4 of the Convention, which movables and immovables situated in the territory of the first Party satisfy the definition of 'cultural property' laid down in article 1. In such an event, the opposing Party must always bear in mind that the criterion to be applied under article 1 is of great importance to the national cultural heritage of the territorial Party. In other words, the opposing Party must hazard an assessment as to the cultural importance of the property in question to the territorial Party. This is by no means unworkable: the safest course is to err on the side of caution and simply to presume that every example of the sorts of cultural property outlined in paragraph (a) of article 1, and hence every building of the sort mentioned in paragraph (b) and every centre containing monuments as in paragraph (c), is of great importance to the cultural heritage of the territorial Party and is therefore protected by the Convention.[85]

Safeguarding

The Convention's first substantive provision, article 3, obliges the High Contracting Parties 'to prepare in time of peace for the safeguarding of cultural property situated within their own territory against the foreseeable effects of an armed conflict, by taking such measures as they consider appropriate'. What the drafters had in mind were '[s]pecial

---

[85] When it comes to the twin obligations imposed by art. 4(1) of the Convention, a presumption of protection will not render such property absolutely off-limits to military use or attack, given the waiver in respect of military necessity provided for in art. 4(2).

measures of an architectonic nature' designed to protect immovable cultural property, 'particularly against the dangers of fire and collapse'; special measures designed to protect movable cultural property 'in the building where it is generally to be found or in the immediate neighbourhood of the latter (organization, stocking of packing material, etc.)'; the establishment of refuges for movables and the organisation of transport to them in the event of armed conflict; and the institution of a civilian service to execute such measures.[86] The measures taken in Croatia on the eve of the armed conflict there in the early 1990s are textbook examples of the application of article 3:

> As ordered by the Ministry of Culture and Education, permanent exhibits of museums and galleries were relocated to safer places. Due to the imminent war danger, the most important treasures were selected, packed and evacuated to areas and buildings ensuring safer storage. The participants in these actions were conservators, restorers, museum experts, special units of the Croatian Army and police, local authorities and enterprises ... Buildings and premises for safe storage of evacuated objects were agreed with local authorities after an opinion given by conservation experts ... For protection of immovable treasures technical measures were taken, such as installing wooden structures, panelling and sand [bags] ... Priority was given to important architectural decoration and weak structural spots. Protected in this way were also sculptures, open space groups of sculptures and public statues in towns. These measures proved to be highly useful. In churches, from which transportable or highly valuable objects were evacuated such as dishes, paintings and statues, the fixed inventory like altars and organs had to be left behind. Efforts were made to protect them *in situ* by proper materials and structures.[87]

That said, the text of article 3 leaves the choice of measures to be adopted to the complete discretion of the Party in whose territory the cultural property is situated, and the ordinary meaning of the key phrase 'such measures as [the Parties] consider appropriate' is capable of encompassing all conceivable sorts of measures. For example, Bulgaria once studied the possibility of totally or partially dismantling some of its monuments in the event of armed conflict.[88] It is worth noting in this connection that, under article 23(1) of the Convention, the Parties may call upon UNESCO for technical assistance in organising the protection of their cultural property.

---

[86] 7 C/PRG/7, Annex I, p. 8.
[87] *1995 Reports*, p. 22. Such measures continued to be taken after the outbreak of hostilities.
[88] *1967 Reports*, p. 14.

Despite the emphasis since the report of the NOB on peacetime preparation for the safeguarding of cultural property in war, it was proposed at an early stage to exclude from the Convention any obligation along the lines of article 3, on the ground that this was a matter for municipal law.[89] The provision was eventually included on express account of the importance of such property to all humanity: article 3's 'international undertaking to take internal measures for the material preservation of national cultural property [was] founded on the idea that the cultural heritage, and therefore its preservation, is the concern of the entire community of States, and that countries possessing such cultural riches are accountable for them to mankind'.[90] By not taking such measures, a state was considered to have 'done harm to itself and to the common heritage of mankind'.[91]

Since the obligation imposed by article 3 is to take such measures as they consider appropriate, the Parties are not compelled to undertake equally rigorous preparations in relation to each item of cultural property in their territory. The wording of the provision takes into account financial and technical constraints on the Parties, leaving it to each to prioritise its resources as it sees fit.[92] In the case of immovables, the drafters themselves foresaw that measures of safeguard would be taken only in relation to 'a certain number of buildings of great value and of buildings containing collections of cultural property (museums, archives, libraries, etc.)',[93] and this likelihood is acknowledged in article 4(5) of the Convention, which provides that no High Contracting Party 'may evade the obligations incumbent upon it under the present Article, in respect of another High Contracting Party, by reason of the fact that the latter has not applied the measures of safeguard referred to in Article 3'. This selectivity has been borne out in the Parties' practice. Those Parties which in principle apply the Convention to the whole of their national cultural heritage seem generally to take fully fledged measures of safeguard in relation to only a very small fraction of immovables. For example, the Netherlands has instituted such measures for between 70 and 100 of the 43,000 listed monuments in the country.[94] As regards movables, many Parties make provision for the evacuation

---

[89] 7 C/PRG/7, Annex I, p. 8.
[90] Ibid.
[91] CBC/4, p. 17 (Switzerland).
[92] 7 C/PRG/7, Annex I, p. 8.
[93] Ibid., emphasis omitted.
[94] 1989 Reports, p. 28.

in the event of armed conflict of only the most important artworks and antiquities, as effected in Croatia in 1991.[95]

In light of the fact that article 1 leaves it to each Party to determine the applicability of the Convention to given cultural property in its territory, the measure *sine qua non* that a Party can and should take in pursuance of the obligation laid down in article 3 is the identification of the property in question. Linked to this, a useful practical measure of peacetime preparation undertaken in the past by some Parties is the compilation and submission to UNESCO, as the Convention's depositary, of updated inventories of immovable cultural property and collections of movable cultural property in their territories, for dissemination among the Parties.[96] Indeed, the drafters of the Convention themselves recognised that the encouragement of a standard practice of notification had, 'to a very large extent, become the essential factor in identifying property and facilitating its protection'.[97] The former West Germany once sensibly proposed that 'lists of immovable cultural property be deposited with Unesco so that they will be accessible to the High Contracting Parties to the Convention'.[98] Even better still, in the spirit of the drafters' view that '[c]ultural treasures will not be safe from bombardment ... unless their location is known',[99] Switzerland has previously sent to the Director-General of UNESCO a map showing the location of cultural property in its territory and in Liechtenstein;[100] in turn, the Director-General transmitted copies of the map to all the Parties.[101] An updated topographic map showing 1,500 high-priority objects in Swiss territory and an inventory of the complete 8,000 'cultural items that Switzerland wished to protect and have protected' were subsequently circulated.[102] For their part, after an artillery attack in July 1991 on the town of Erdut

---

[95] *1995 Reports*, p. 22.
[96] Recall, in this light, the obligations laid down in art. 4 of the Roerich Pact.
[97] CL/484, Annex, p. 14.
[98] *1989 Reports*, p. 15.
[99] CL/484, Annex, p. 11.
[100] *1967 Reports*, p. 34. See also the recommendation to this end in para. 3.5 of the Final Communiqué of the NATO-Partnership for Peace (PfP) Conference on Cultural Heritage Protection in Wartime and in State of Emergency, 21 June 1996, <http://www.icomos.org/blue_shield/krakowna.html>, and the analogous suggestion in 'Practical advice for the protection of cultural property in the event of armed conflict', in M. T. Dutli (ed.), *Protection of Cultural Property in the Event of Armed Conflict. Report on the Meeting of Experts (Geneva, 5–6 October 2000)* (Geneva: ICRC, 2002), p. 143 at p. 178.
[101] *1967 Reports*, para. 13.
[102] *1995 Reports*, p. 43.

damaged its medieval fortress, the Croatian authorities sent lists of cultural monuments marked with the Convention's distinctive sign to the Yugoslav Federal Defence Secretariat and to all headquarters of the Yugoslav National Army.[103]

Article 15 becomes relevant if, pursuant to article 3, a Party establishes a civilian service to put other measures of safeguard into effect. Article 15 provides that, as far as is consistent with the interests of security, personnel engaged in the protection of cultural property 'shall, in the interests of such property, be respected and, if they fall into the hands of the opposing Party, shall be allowed to continue to carry out their duties whenever the cultural property for which they are responsible has also fallen into the hands of the opposing Party'. That is, as far as is consistent with the interests of security, acts of hostility must not be directed against such personnel and they must be permitted to carry out their duties should the opposing Party capture them and take control of cultural property within their remit – a situation which encompasses, but is not limited to, belligerent occupation. In accordance with article 17(2)(c) of the Convention and article 21 of the Regulations, such personnel may wear an armlet bearing the distinctive emblem of the Convention, issued and stamped by the competent authorities,[104] and must carry a special identity card bearing the emblem, as well as the embossed stamp of the competent authorities.[105] They may not, without legitimate reason, be deprived of this card or of the right to wear the armlet.[106]

Linked to the idea of a civilian service specially dedicated to safeguarding cultural property is resolution II of the Final Act of the Intergovernmental Conference on the Protection of Cultural Property in the Event of Armed Conflict.[107] Resolution II reads in full:

The Conference expresses the hope that each of the High Contracting Parties, on acceding to the Convention, should set up, within the framework of its constitutional and administrative system, a national advisory committee consisting of a small number of distinguished persons: for example, senior

---

[103] Ibid., p. 22.
[104] 1954 Hague Regulations, art. 21(1).
[105] Ibid., art. 21(2).
[106] Ibid., art. 21(4).
[107] Records 1954, p. 78. The part to be played, in accordance with resolution II, by National Committees was stressed by the first meeting of the High Contracting Parties, held in 1962: CUA/120, para. 21.

officials of archaeological services, museums, etc., a representative of the military general staff, a representative of the Ministry of Foreign Affairs, a specialist in international law and two or three other members whose official duties or specialized knowledge are related to the fields covered by the Convention.

The Committee should be under the authority of the minister of State or senior official responsible for the national service chiefly concerned with the care of cultural property. Its chief functions would be:

(a) to advise the government concerning the measures required for the implementation of the Convention in its legislative, technical or military aspects, both in time of peace and during armed conflict;
(b) to approach its government in the event of an armed conflict or when such a conflict appears imminent, with a view to ensuring that cultural property situated within its own territory or within that of other countries is known to, and respected and protected by the armed forces of the country, in accordance with the provisions of the Convention;
(c) to arrange, in agreement with its government, for liaison and co-operation with other similar national committees and with any competent international authority.

The model the conference had in mind was the Roberts Commission established by President Roosevelt in 1943.

Distinctive marking

One measure which a High Contracting Party can take in peacetime to promote respect for cultural property under general protection in the event of hostilities is to mark it with the Convention's distinctive emblem. Article 6 provides that, in accordance with the provisions of article 16, 'cultural property may bear a distinctive emblem so as to facilitate its recognition'. The emblem in question comprises a shield, pointed below, per saltire blue and white, in the technical heraldic language of article 16(1);[108] and when used alone, the distinctive emblem indicates general protection.[109] In principle, the single emblem may be

---

[108] 1954 Hague Convention, art. 16(1). What this means is explained parenthetically, namely 'a shield consisting of a royal-blue square, one of the angles of which forms the point of a shield, and of a royal-blue triangle above the square, the space on either side being taken up by a white triangle'.

[109] *Ibid.*, arts. 16(2) and 17(2)(a). In accordance with arts. 17(2)(b), (c) and (d) respectively of the Convention, a single distinctive emblem may also be used to identify the persons responsible for the duties of control laid down in the Regulations, the personnel engaged in the protection of cultural property, and the identity cards provided for in the Regulations.

used on both immovable and movable cultural property, although practicality and aesthetics militate against the latter.

As the wording of article 6 makes clear, the distinctive marking of protected cultural property is not obligatory. Conversely, during armed conflict,[110] the marking with the distinctive emblem of property not satisfying article 1's definition of cultural property is forbidden by article 17(3). The same goes for the use 'for any purpose whatever' of a sign resembling the distinctive emblem. Article 17(4) stipulates that the distinctive emblem may not be placed on immovable cultural property unless at the same time there is displayed 'an authorization duly dated and signed by the competent authority of the High Contracting Party'.

In practice, the distinctive marking in peacetime of cultural property under general protection is rare among Parties to the Convention.[111] There are several possible reasons for this. Given the numbers of buildings typically protected by the Convention in each state, marking is an expensive business. It is also time-consuming, especially when one takes into account article 17(4)'s requirement of a duly dated and signed authorisation each time the emblem is used. Ironically, a concern for the preservation, not to mention aesthetics, of the cultural property in question can contraindicate marking.[112] Nor do the advantages appear to outweigh the disadvantages: the effectiveness of a small plaque in the event of an attack must seriously be questioned in the age of high-altitude bombing, ship-launched cruise missiles[113] and very long-range artillery, and no less so when military objectives are identified by satellites and

---

[110] The abuse of the distinctive emblem in peacetime is apparently unregulated.

[111] That said, some states supply emblems to owners or curators of protected buildings with instructions to affix them in the event of armed conflict. The Croatian authorities embarked on distinctive marking in 1991 only when war was imminent: *ibid.*, p. 22.

[112] See e.g. 7 C/PRG/7, Annex I, p. 12; *Records 1954*, para. 399 (Greece). The use of the distinctive emblem has been criticised by curators of museums, galleries and monuments. Note that, in accordance with art. 20 of the Regulations, the placing of the distinctive emblem and its degree of visibility is left to the discretion of the competent authorities of each Party, and it may be displayed on flags, painted on an object 'or represented in any other appropriate form'.

[113] While in practice it cannot be said to matter, it is not ideal that the Convention's distinctive emblem differs from the 'visible signs' stipulated by Hague Convention IX, art. 5 ('large, stiff rectangular panels divided diagonally into two colored triangular portions, the upper portion black, the lower portion white') and from the 'distinctive flag' prescribed by art. 3 of the Roerich Pact (a 'red circle with a triple red sphere in the circle on a white background'). But as between Parties to both the Convention and Hague Convention IX, the distinctive emblem of the former replaces the signs prescribed by the latter, and the same goes *mutatis mutandis* for the Convention and the Roerich Pact: 1954 Hague Convention, art. 36.

very high-altitude spy planes. In 1996, the NATO-Partnership for Peace Conference on Cultural Heritage Protection in Wartime and in State of Emergency suggested incorporating new technology into the emblem,[114] by which it presumably meant a microchip or transmitter 'visible' electronically, but the bill for installation and upkeep would surely be prohibitive.

Nonetheless, the marking of cultural property can scarcely undermine its protection from attack.[115] Moreover, it might help to prevent the use of such property for purposes likely to expose it to damage or destruction. There are also foreseeable advantages when it comes to belligerent occupation.

If a Party does opt to mark immovable cultural property in its territory, prudence suggests that it should be all or nothing. While the absence of the distinctive emblem does not, as a matter of law, denote the absence of protection under the Convention, the assumption made in practice by an opposing Party might well be *expressio unius exclusio alterius*. In this way, the selective use of the emblem, which seems not uncommon among the Parties,[116] poses a threat to the protection of the property it is meant to facilitate.

Military measures

In accordance with article 7(1), the High Contracting Parties undertake 'to introduce in time of peace into their military regulations or instructions such provisions as may ensure observance of the ... Convention, and to foster in the members of their armed forces a spirit of respect for the culture and cultural property of all peoples'.[117] This is a critical provision

---

[114] NATO-PfP Conference on Cultural Heritage Protection, Final Communiqué, para. 3.4.

[115] That said, the fear was expressed during the drafting of the Convention that marking cultural property might help an attacking force to get its bearings: 6 C/PRG/22, Annex, p. 13; 7 C/PRG/7, Annex I, p. 12; and Iraq defended its failure to mark protected cultural property during the Iran–Iraq War by claiming that the distinctive emblem might be seen by the Iranian aircraft, missile batteries and artillery positions which were attacking Iraqi towns: *1989 Reports*, p. 20.

[116] For example, in 1991, the Croatian authorities affixed the emblem to 794 historic buildings, a fraction of the total immovable cultural heritage in the republic: *1995 Reports*, p. 22.

[117] Some states not Parties to the Convention also follow this practice. The UK included the text of the Convention in appendix XVI to its now-superseded *The Law of War on Land being Part III of the Manual of Military Law* (London: HMSO, 1958), and considers the Convention's provisions in its current military handbook: *UK Manual*, paras. 5.26–5.26.8, *inter alia*. US forces include the Convention in their doctrine, instruction and training.

given that, in most cases, it is the armed forces which will ultimately execute the provisions of the Convention, and it goes hand in hand with the obligation to disseminate the Convention laid down in article 25.[118] Article 7(2), inspired by the examples of the Monuments, Fine Arts and Archives officers, the Kunstschutz and their various equivalents in the Second and First World Wars, imposes on Parties the obligation to 'plan or establish in peace-time, within their armed forces, services or specialist personnel whose purpose will be to secure respect for cultural property and to co-operate with the civilian authorities responsible for safeguarding it'. The reference to safeguarding is to measures taken under article 3 and the civilian authorities mentioned include the competent national authorities in occupied territory. The services or specialist personnel established within the armed forces pursuant to article 7(2) enjoy protection under article 15, so that, as far as is consistent with the interests of security, acts of hostility must not be directed against them and they must be permitted to carry out their duties in the event that the opposing Party captures them and takes control of cultural property within their remit, a situation which includes but is not limited to belligerent occupation. In accordance with article 17(2)(c) of the Convention and article 21 of the Regulations, they may wear an armlet bearing the distinctive emblem, issued and stamped by their competent authorities,[119] and must carry an identity card bearing the emblem and the embossed stamp of the competent authorities.[120] They may be deprived of neither the card nor the right to wear the armlet without legitimate reason.[121] Should they in fact fall into the hands of the

---

[118] Article 25 provides: 'The High Contracting Parties undertake, in time of peace as in time of armed conflict, to disseminate the text of the present Convention and the Regulations for its execution as widely as possible in their respective countries. They undertake, in particular, to include the study thereof in their programmes of military and, if possible, civilian training, so that its principles are made known to the whole population, especially the armed forces and personnel engaged in the protection of cultural property.' Article 25 is modelled on an analogous provision common to the four Geneva Conventions: see Convention for the Amelioration of the Condition of the Wounded and Sick in Armed Forces in the Field, Geneva, 12 August 1949, 75 UNTS 31, art. 47; Convention for the Amelioration of the Condition of Wounded, Sick and Shipwrecked Members of Armed Forces at Sea, Geneva, 12 August 1949, 75 UNTS 85, art. 48; Convention Relative to the Treatment of Prisoners of War, Geneva, 12 August 1949, 75 UNTS 135, art. 127; Convention Relative to the Protection of Civilian Persons in Time of War, Geneva, 12 August 1949, 75 UNTS 287, art. 144.
[119] 1954 Hague Regulations, art. 21(1).
[120] Ibid., art. 21(2).
[121] Ibid., art. 21(4).

opposing Party, they are entitled to the protection of the third Geneva Convention. In short, their status is not unlike that of medical personnel in the armed forces.[122]

Respect

The most fundamental obligation undertaken by High Contracting Parties to the Convention is the obligation of respect for cultural property embodied in article 4, although it is more accurate to speak in the plural of the provision's obligations of respect. The concept of respect, within the meaning of article 4, has four distinct aspects – refraining from any use of cultural property and its immediate surroundings for purposes which are likely to expose it to destruction or damage in the event of armed conflict; refraining from any act of hostility directed against such property; prohibiting, preventing and, if necessary, putting a stop to theft, pillage, misappropriation and vandalism of such property, as well as refraining from requisitioning such property; and refraining from reprisals against such property.

The obligations of respect imposed by article 4 of the Convention apply as much to cultural property situated within a Party's own territory as to cultural property in the territory of an opposing Party. They also apply as much to belligerent occupation as to active hostilities: nothing in the wording of the various provisions displaces the Convention's usual scope of application, as laid down, in the case of belligerent occupation, in article 18(2); and while article 5 is headed 'Occupation', any implication from this *a contrario* is insufficiently unambiguous, since there is no reason why the obligations the latter provision imposes, which clearly apply only to belligerent occupation and which relate specifically to the relations between the Occupying Power and the competent national authorities, cannot be treated as additional to those posited in article 4. As it is, the application of article 4 during belligerent occupation is made clear in both article 5(3) of the Convention[123] and article 19 of the Regulations for the Execution of the Convention,[124] and is conclusively

---

[122] Rogers, *Law on the Battlefield*, p. 148.
[123] Paragraph 3 of art. 5 ('Occupation') reads: 'Any High Contracting Party whose government is considered their legitimate government by members of a resistance movement, shall, if possible, draw their attention to the obligation to comply with those provisions of the Convention dealing with respect for cultural property.'
[124] Article 19 of the Regulations states: 'Whenever a High Contracting Party occupying territory of another High Contracting Party transfers cultural property to a refuge

confirmed by the chapeau to article 9(1) of the Second Protocol.[125] The provisions of article 4 are further applicable to conflicts not of an international character occurring within the territory of one of the Parties: article 19(2) stipulates that, in the event of such a conflict, 'each party to the conflict shall be bound to apply, as a minimum, the provisions of the ... Convention which relate to respect for cultural property'. Finally, article 4(5) provides that the obligation to respect cultural property applies whether or not the Party in whose territory the relevant cultural property is found has applied the measures of safeguard referred to in article 3.

Use and acts of hostility

The first two obligations laid down in article 4 — that is, the obligations in article 4(1) to refrain respectively from any use of cultural property and its immediate surroundings for purposes which are likely to expose it to destruction or damage in the event of armed conflict and from any act of hostility directed against such property — are not absolute. They must be read subject to article 4(2), which provides that the obligations in paragraph 1 of article 4 'may be waived only in cases where military necessity imperatively requires such a waiver'. Although military necessity is not accommodated in the text of the prohibitions themselves, which on the face of article 4(1) are unqualified, and while the word 'only' in article 4(2) is intended to emphasise the sparingness with which it is hoped the waiver will be invoked, these devices are merely rhetorical. The legal effect of the combination of paragraphs 1 and 2 of article 4 is that both of the obligations embodied in article 4(1) may be waived in cases where military necessity imperatively requires such a waiver.

The inclusion of a waiver in respect of military necessity was the subject of intense and acrimonious controversy at the intergovernmental conference of 1954. The Soviet delegate objected that it allowed 'a right

situated elsewhere in that territory, without being able to follow the procedure provided for in Article 17 of the Regulations, the transfer in question shall not be regarded as misappropriation within the meaning of Article 4 of the Convention, provided that the Commissioner-General for Cultural Property certifies in writing, after having consulted the usual custodians, that such transfer was rendered necessary by circumstances.'

[125] The chapeau to para. 1 of art. 9 ('Protection of cultural property in occupied territory') reads: 'Without prejudice to the provisions of Articles 4 and 5 of the Convention, a Party in occupation of the whole or part of the territory of another Party shall prohibit and prevent in relation to the occupied territory.'

of destruction' to two or several countries, in spite of the aim of the Convention to protect 'all the cultural values of the nations of the world'.[126] Other opponents looked more to practice than principle, focusing on the uncalibrated nature of the discretion and its potential, regularly fulfilled in the past, for abuse, with criticism being directed towards 'vague terms offering themselves to subterfuge'.[127] But the committee of experts convened by UNESCO to prepare a draft text had sanguinely noted at the outset that the law regulating the protection of cultural property in the course of hostilities had always been qualified by reference to military necessity, and declared the need to preserve this qualification.[128] The Turkish delegate to the conference stated plainly what many supporters of a waiver probably assumed, namely that '[t]he defence of the nation came first, and a cultural monument should be sacrificed if necessary'.[129] The Netherlands representative reminded the conference that the invocation of military necessity might save the lives of thousands of soldiers.[130] Of the proponents of a waiver, the USA and the UK, warning against 'clos[ing] the door to those things which were militarily unavoidable in the face of a mission assigned by competent governmental authorities',[131] were the most influential, and ultimately conditioned their signatures on the point. The waiver was eventually included, attracting a considerable degree of support.[132]

The drafters of the Convention made no attempt to elaborate textually on the circumstances which might imperatively require the use of cultural property and its surroundings for purposes likely to expose it to damage or destruction or which might justify an act of hostility against it. The concept of imperative military necessity was a long-established one, and the difficult questions of factual appreciation called for were a matter for the discretion of each party to the conflict. As it is, the language of article 4(2) is relatively transparent and straightforward. As emphasised by Eisenhower, military necessity is not the same as

---

[126] *Records 1954*, para. 299.
[127] Ibid., para. 133 (Spain). See also *ibid.*, paras 275 (Ecuador), 299 and 903 (USSR); CBC/4, p. 6 (Greece).
[128] 5C/PRG/6, Annex I, para. 17.
[129] *Records 1954*, para. 294. See also *ibid.*, para. 855.
[130] Ibid., para. 277.
[131] Ibid., para. 264 (US).
[132] The motion in the Main Commission to delete art. 4(2) was rejected 8:22:8, with 8 absentees. The motion in the Plenary Session on including the waiver in the final text was adopted 26:7:8. The US is still not a Party to the Convention. The UK announced on 14 May 2004 its intention to ratify the Convention and both of its Protocols.

military convenience,[133] a view reiterated in 1997 by the third meeting of the High Contracting Parties to the Convention[134] and the following year by a meeting of governmental experts drawn from fifty-seven High Contracting Parties.[135] 'It is not sufficient that the objective could be more easily attained by endangering the protected object'; rather, 'an imperative necessity presupposes that the military objective cannot be reached in any other manner'.[136] Military necessity also serves to calibrate the gravity of any damage or destruction compelled by military considerations: harm to cultural property occasioned by the invocation of article 4(2) must be only to a degree that is imperatively necessary.[137]

The first limb of article 4(1) imposes an obligation on the Parties 'to respect cultural property situated within their own territory as well as within the territory of other High Contracting Parties by refraining from any use of the property and its immediate surroundings or of the appliances in use for its protection for purposes which are likely to expose it to destruction or damage in the event of armed conflict'. In this way, article 4(1) fills a lacuna which had led in both World Wars to the deterioration, damage and in some cases destruction of important cultural property. It is significant too that the obligation not to use cultural property for purposes likely to expose it to destruction or damage applies not just to property situated in the territory of another Party but also to property situated in a Party's own territory. The motivation for this was explained by the delegation from the Netherlands:

The idea behind the Convention is that the cultural heritages of individual countries should be protected against the consequences of an armed conflict in

---

[133] Covering memorandum to General Order No. 68, 29 December 1943, reproduced in *Hansard*, HC, vol. 396, col. 1116, 1 February 1944.
[134] UNESCO Doc. CLT-97/CONF.208/3, para. 5(ii). Sixty-five Parties were represented.
[135] UNESCO Doc. 155 EX/51, Annex, para. 14.
[136] K.J. Partsch, 'Protection of Cultural Property', in D. Fleck (ed.), *The Handbook of Humanitarian Law in Armed Conflicts* (Oxford: Oxford University Press, 1995), p. 377 at para. 906(1). See also *UK Manual*, paras. 5.26.3 n. 120 and 5.26.8; Rogers, *Law on the Battlefield*, p. 144; R. Wolfrum, 'Protection of Cultural Property in Armed Conflict' (2003) 32 Isr. YHR 305 at 325. See also Grotius, *De Jure Belli ac Pacis*, book II, chap. 22, s. 6 ('Advantage does not confer the same right as necessity.').
[137] Article 6 of the Second Protocol now clarifies the conditions under which a Party to the Convention which also a Party to the Second Protocol may invoke military necessity so as to waive its obligations under art. 4(1).

the interests of the whole international community of nations. Hence there seems no reason for imposing, in respect of the protection ... of cultural property situated in a given country, fewer obligations on that country than on another country.[138]

The historical significance of the first limb of article 4(1) is further amplified by its applicability to international and non-international armed conflicts equally by virtue of article 19(2).

The wording of the first limb of article 4(1) makes the provision more than a prohibition on the use of cultural property for hostile purposes. The reference to 'its immediate surroundings' and to 'any use ... for purposes which are likely to expose it to destruction or damage' means that the prohibition extends to the *de facto* or passive use of a monument or other relevant immovable cultural property in any manner likely to draw fire on it.[139] Article 4(1) therefore prohibits the deliberate interposition of cultural property in the line of fire, for example by retreating to a position obscured by a monument from the opposing party's view. The provision also serves to forbid the effective incorporation of a monument into a defensive line, as with the German 'Gustav line' around the abbey at Monte Cassino in the Second World War. Nor is it only used in combat which article 4(1) prohibits. If it is foreseeable that the use of a protected building as a field headquarters or barracks, for example, will expose it to attack, such use is forbidden. The first limb of article 4(1) would also prohibit parking military aircraft in the immediate surroundings of cultural property,[140] as Iraq did in the Gulf War of 1991.[141] Nor, indeed, need such use expose the property in question to attack for it to fall foul of the first limb of article 4(1). The provision forbids any use likely to expose cultural property to damage during armed conflict [which, in accordance with article 18(2), includes belligerent occupation], with the result that the likelihood of more than *de minimis* deterioration in the fabric of a monument, and *a fortiori* the risk of vandalism, through its use as headquarters, barracks or the like – the source of considerable harm to historic buildings during

---

[138] CBC/4, p. 12. See also, less explicitly, *ibid.*, p. 5 (France).
[139] Partsch speaks in this respect of the 'indirect' use of cultural property: Partsch, 'Protection of Cultural Property', para. 903(2).
[140] Rogers, *Law on the Battlefield*, p. 146 n. 95.
[141] Department of Defense, *Report to Congress on the Conduct of the Persian Gulf War, Appendix O: The Role of the Law of War*, 31 ILM 612 (1992) at 626.

the Second World War and to the archaeological site at Babylon since 2003[142] – is enough to render such use impermissible. Finally, it is important to note that the first limb of article 4(1) prohibits the use of cultural property and its surroundings in any manner likely to expose it to damage or destruction 'in the event of armed conflict'. In other words, if such use in peacetime is likely to expose cultural property to attack on the outbreak of hostilities, it is not permitted.[143]

It must, of course, be borne in mind that article 4(1) is qualified by article 4(2)'s waiver as to military necessity. As such, if 'military necessity imperatively requires' the use of cultural property and its surroundings for purposes likely to expose it to attack, such use is not prohibited. An example of one of the '*rare* cases where it is essential to use cultural property for military purposes' given by the UK *Manual* is a historic bridge which constitutes the only available river crossing.[144] A further example given in the 1964 German manual on the protection of cultural property in armed conflict is the positioning of an artillery piece in the immediate vicinity of cultural property if that is the only point from which an enemy stronghold dominating the battlefield can be attacked.[145]

It should be emphasised that a Party's use of cultural property and its surroundings in any manner likely to expose it to destruction or damage does not as such make it lawful for an opposing Party to attack it: that is, a Party's breach of the first limb of article 4(1) does not *ipso facto* relieve an opposing Party from its obligation under the second limb of the provision.[146] The obligation to refrain from any act of hostility directed against cultural property imposed on Parties by the second limb of article 4(1) 'may be waived only in cases where military necessity

---

[142] A military camp was established by US forces on the archaeological site at Babylon in April 1993. Control of the camp was transferred to Polish forces in September that year. While the USA is not a Party to the Convention, Poland and Iraq are, and it would be hard to conclude, in the words of art. 4(2), that imperative military necessity required Poland to waive art. 4(1)'s obligation not to use the site.

[143] So, for example, the former Ukrainian SSR reported that, even in peacetime, Soviet armed forces were not allowed to be quartered, to stock arms or to install military targets in the immediate surroundings of historic monuments or groups of historic monuments, 'as stated in Article 4, paragraph 1 of the Convention': *1989 Reports*, p. 38. That certain provisions of the Convention apply in peacetime is made clear in 1954 Hague Convention, art. 18(1).

[144] *UK Manual*, para. 5.25.3, original emphasis.

[145] *Der Schutz von Kulturgut bei bewaffneten Konflikten*, Federal Ministry of Defence publication Zdv 15/9 (15 July 1964), p. 16, cited in Rogers, *Law on the Battlefield*, pp. 144–5.

[146] Toman, *Protection of Cultural Property*, pp. 70 and 75; *UK Manual*, paras. 5.26.3 n. 120 and 5.26.8. See also Partsch, 'Protection of Cultural Property', para. 906(4).

imperatively requires such a waiver', as stressed by the Legal Committee during the drafting of the Convention:

> The obligation to respect an item of cultural property remained even if that item was used by the opposing party for military purposes. The obligation of respect was therefore only withdrawn in the event of imperative military necessity.[147]

As it is, unless it is clearly specified in the text, conventional obligations of a humanitarian nature are not conditioned on reciprocity;[148] and Provost further suggests that the express provision for reciprocity made in article 11(1) of the Convention in respect of property under special protection points even more strongly *a contrario* to the inapplicability of the maxim *inadimplenti non est adimplendum* in the context of articles 4(1) and 4(2).[149]

The second limb of article 4(1), applicable to combat operations and belligerent occupation alike, obliges Parties 'to respect cultural property situated within their own territory as well as within the territory of other High Contracting Parties ... by refraining from any act of hostility directed against such property'. The term 'any act of hostility' is significant in forbidding not just attacks against cultural property but also its demolition,[150] whether by way of explosives or bulldozers or other wrecking equipment. Insofar as it applies to attacks, it applies to all attacks, whether by land, sea or air.

Like the first limb of the provision, this second limb of article 4(1) is to be read subject to article 4(2)'s waiver in respect of imperative military necessity. In this light, given that the term 'act of hostility' treats all destructive acts alike, articles 4(1) and (2) of the Convention could be seen in the specific context of bombardment as a regression from article 27 of the Hague Rules, which, rather than making general allowance for

---

[147] *Records 1954*, para. 1170.
[148] See e.g. Pictet, *Commentary (IV)*, p. 15; C. Greenwood, 'Historical Development and Legal Basis', in Fleck, *Handbook*, p. 1 at para. 102(2). The non-reciprocity of humanitarian undertakings is reflected in Vienna Convention on the Law of Treaties, art. 60(5).
[149] R. Provost, 'Reciprocity in Human Rights and Humanitarian Law' (1994) 65 BYIL 383 at 407–8. Provost also notes that reciprocity is expressly rejected in art. 4(4) (the prohibition on reprisals against cultural property) and art. 4(5) (art. 4 applicable notwithstanding the opposing Party's failure to take measures of safeguard under art. 3).
[150] M. Bothe, K. J. Partsch and W. A. Solf, *New Rules for Victims of Armed Conflicts* (The Hague: Martinus Nijhoff, 1982), para. 2.5.2; Y. Sandoz, C. Swinarski and B. Zimmermann, *Commentary on the Additional Protocols of 8 June 1977 to the Geneva Conventions of 12 August 1949* (Geneva: ICRC/Martinus Nijhoff, 1987), para. 2070; Toman, *Protection of Cultural Property*, p. 389.

military necessity, permits, on its face, the bombardment of cultural property only when it is used for military purposes. That said, since it is unthinkable that the drafters of the Convention would have wanted to derogate from the existing customary rule on bombardment, it must have been that case that they read article 27 in the light of the general rule on the destruction of enemy property laid down in article 23(g) of the Hague Rules, with the result that – just like the first limb of article 4(1) of the Convention, as modified by article 4(2) – it forbade only the unnecessary bombardment of cultural property.[151] Either way, the suggestion by the Trial Chambers of the ICTY in *Kordić* that the use of cultural property for military purposes is the sole reason for invoking military necessity under article 4(2) of the Convention is incorrect:[152] the ordinary meaning of the expression 'where military necessity imperatively requires such a waiver', which is in no way contraindicated by the *travaux* or by the subsequent practice of the Parties, is, as a formal matter, wider than 'if used for military purposes' or the equivalent.

On the face of it, the phrase 'where military necessity imperatively requires' is an open-textured one. But at least in the case of so-called 'law-making' conventions (that is, multilateral treaties of a general, standard-setting nature), treaty provisions must be interpreted and applied in the light of directly relevant rules of customary international law which emerge subsequent to their adoption. In the *Gulf of Maine* case, a Chamber of the International Court of Justice stated that what it called 'general conventions' – that is, conventions in which 'principles and rules of general application can be identified' – 'must ... be seen against the background of customary international law and interpreted in its light',[153] the customary rules at issue in that case having arisen after the conclusion of the convention. Similarly, in the *Jan Mayen* case, the ICJ, when called on to apply article 6 of the 1958 Geneva Convention on the Continental Shelf, observed: 'The fact that

---

[151] Recall, in this light, the war crime of 'wanton destruction of religious, charitable, educational and historic buildings and monuments' listed by Sub-Commission III of the Commission on Responsibilities of the 1919 Preliminary Peace Conference of Paris, with 'wanton' apparently meaning 'not imperatively demanded by the necessities of war': UNWCC, *History of the United Nations War Crimes Commission*, p. 34. Article 27 was not considered by any of the post-Second World War criminal tribunals.

[152] *Prosecutor v. Kordić and Čerkez*, IT-95-14/2-T, Trial Chamber Judgment, 26 February 2001, para. 362. See also *Prosecutor v. Strugar*, IT-01-42-T, Trial Chamber Judgment, 31 January 2005, paras. 310 and 312.

[153] *Delimitation of the Maritime Boundary in the Gulf of Maine Area (Canada/United States of America)*, ICJ Reports 1984, p. 246 at para. 83.

it is the 1958 Convention which applies to the continental shelf delimitation in this case does not mean that Article 6 thereof can be interpreted and applied ... without reference to customary law on the subject',[154] the customary rules in this case again having arisen after the Convention. The principles enunciated by the court in these cases apply with even greater force to conventions on the laws of war and subsequent, stricter custom. The object and purpose of such treaties dictate that their provisions may not have the effect of derogating from any higher humanitarian standards that the customary laws of armed conflict may later impose. In this light, in its application to the specific question of attacks under the second limb of article 4(1), the waiver in article 4(2) must today be read through the lens of the customary international rules on targeting, applicable to both international and non-international armed conflict, which have emerged since the adoption of the Convention, specifically the subsequent definition of a military objective, as consonant with article 52(2) of 1977 Protocol I Additional to the Geneva Conventions.[155] This is in line with the approach taken to the phrase 'not justified by military necessity' by the ICTY.[156] The upshot is that a Party may invoke the waiver embodied in article 4(2) to justify attacking cultural property only in cases where the cultural property in question, by its nature, location, purpose or use, makes an effective contribution to military action and where its total or partial destruction, capture or neutralisation, in the circumstances ruling at the time, offers a definite military advantage.

Applying this test, in certain circumstances cultural property can be considered a military objective, although these circumstances will be rare. It is not wholly absurd to suggest that very specific cultural property – historic fortresses, barracks, arsenals and the like – can, by its nature, make an effective contribution to military action. That said, if it is decommissioned, an eighteenth-century fortress, to take an example,

---

[154] *Maritime Delimitation in the Area between Greenland and Jan Mayen (Denmark v. Norway)*, ICJ Reports 1993, p. 38 at para. 46.

[155] See also Sandoz et al., *Commentary*, para. 2079 n. 30; Toman, *Protection of Cultural Property*, p. 389; *UK Manual*, para. 5.26.8. The development of these rules is dealt with in more detail in the following chapters.

[156] *Strugar*, Trial Chamber Judgment, para. 295. Consider also the Rome Statute of the International Criminal Court, Rome, 17 July 1998, 2187 UNTS 90, arts. 8(2)(b)(ix) (international armed conflict) and 8(2)(e)(iv) (non-international armed conflict), providing for the war crime of directing attacks against historic monuments 'provided they are not military objectives'; and, identically, Statute of the Iraqi Special Tribunal, 43 ILM 231 (2004), arts. 13(b)(10) and 13(d)(4).

is better characterised by its nature as a historic monument, rather than a fortress; and if it is still in service, any effective contribution it may make to military action will be through its use, rather than its nature. Similarly, while the vast majority of cultural property cannot make an effective contribution to military action through its purpose (defined as 'the future intended use of an object'[157]), a historic bridge, railway station or dock could conceivably, by its purpose, make such a contribution, although whether this contribution is genuinely effective will depend on the circumstances. Generally speaking, one would not expect infrastructure built in and for another age to play a significant military role today. As for location, it is not unimaginable that the position of cultural property during a battle could serve to block a party's line of sight or line of fire. At the same time, any contribution this may make to the military action of the opposing party is arguably better seen as a function of the property's passive or *de facto* use.[158] In the final analysis, then, it is principally through its use, if it all, that cultural property could be expected to make an effective contribution to military action.[159] In other words, use in support of military action is the principal reason for which a Party could be expected to invoke article 4(2) to justify attacking cultural property. Indeed, it is inconceivable today that a Party would cite the nature of cultural property to this end, scarcely imaginable that it would cite its purpose, and highly unlikely that it would cite its location.

It is crucial, furthermore, to note in all of the above cases that, whatever contribution cultural property may make to military action, an attack against it is lawful only when its total or partial destruction, capture or neutralisation, in the circumstances ruling at the time, offers a definite military advantage. '[A]nd even then', in the words of the UK *Manual*, 'attacks on it may not be necessary.'[160] For example, as Rogers points out, if enemy snipers have installed themselves in cultural

---

[157] *Partial Award: Western Front, Aerial Bombardment and Related Claims. Eritrea's Claims 1, 3, 5, 9–13, 14, 21, 25 and 26*, Eritrea Ethiopia Claims Commission, 19 December 2005, para. 120, endorsing *UK Manual*, para. 5.4.4, in turn endorsing Sandoz *et al.*, *Commentary*, para. 2022.

[158] See also Sandoz *et al.*, *Commentary*, para. 2078. For example, the defending German forces can be taken to have made passive or *de facto* use of the abbey of Monte Cassino in the Second World War.

[159] See also J.-M. Henckaerts, 'New rules for the protection of cultural property in armed conflict' (1999) 81 IRRC 593 at 602–6. Indeed, the *UK Manual* states that waiver under art. 4(2) 'only arises where the enemy unlawfully uses such property for military purposes': para. 5.26.3 n. 120. See also Wolfrum, 'Protection of Cultural Property', at 321.

[160] *UK Manual*, para. 5.26.3 n. 120.

property, it may be possible simply to bypass it.[161] Equally, it may be possible to surround it and to wait, while pursuing a peaceful resolution through negotiation and reliance on diplomatic good offices, as the Israel Defence Forces did for over a month in 2002 at the Church of the Nativity in Bethlehem, in which a large number of armed Palestinian militants had taken up position. In short, there must be 'no feasible alternative method for dealing with the situation' before an attack on cultural property on the basis of military necessity can be held permissible.[162] In this light, it would be extremely difficult to conclude that no realistic alternative to attacking cultural property exists unless and until the prospective attacking party has issued a warning to the opposing party and given it a reasonable opportunity to desist from using the cultural property in question.[163]

Demolitions – whether to impede the progress of enemy columns, to clear a field of fire, to deny cover to enemy fighters or, *a fortiori*, for motives other than military – are not, however, amenable to an analysis based on the definition of a military objective, since the latter applies only to 'attacks',[164] as distinct from the broader concept of 'acts of hostility' by which article 4(1) encompasses demolitions. One must revert to the unvarnished words of article 4(2) of the Convention, so that the demolition of cultural property in support of military operations, including during belligerent occupation, is permissible only in cases where military necessity imperatively requires it – that is, where there is no feasible alternative for dealing with the situation. This accords with the classical customary rule on the destruction of enemy property reflected in article 23(g) of the Hague Rules and, in the case of belligerent occupation, with article 53 of the fourth Geneva Convention.[165] Reasoning roughly of this sort was relied on by the Supreme Court of Israel, sitting as the High Court of Justice, in *Hess* v. *Commander of the IDF in*

---

[161] Rogers, *Law on the Battlefield*, p. 144. See also *ibid*., n. 79.
[162] *UK Manual*, para. 5.26.8.
[163] Israel argued that its shelling of the archaeological site at Tyre during its 1982 invasion of Lebanon was undertaken out of military necessity, alleging that active units of the PLO were using it as an ammunition depot and artillery emplacement: *1984 Reports*, para. 18. It is impossible to assess whether this invocation of art. 4(2) was justified, although Israel's apparent failure to issue an ultimatum would militate against this.
[164] Additional Protocol I, art. 52(2), as consonant with custom.
[165] Geneva Convention IV, art. 53 provides: 'Any destruction by the Occupying Power of real or personal property belonging individually or collectively to private persons, or to the State, or to other public authorities, or to social or co-operative organizations,

the West Bank, where the court upheld a revised order of the commander of Israeli occupation forces in the West Bank to demolish, *inter alia*, a structure forming part of the historic streetscape of the Old City of Hebron in order to prevent armed attacks by Palestinian militants on Israeli settlers en route to the Cave of the Patriarchs.[166] Of course, like the destruction of any other enemy property, demolition of cultural property must be only to a degree that is imperatively necessary. In *Hess*, the commander revised his original order, which would have involved the destruction of twenty-two Ottoman and Mameluke buildings, some dating from the fifteenth century, on the earlier urging of the court.[167] Moreover, although eventually upholding the order to demolish one building comprising cultural property, the court ruled that the demolition had to be supervised by an expert in the preservation of historic buildings and an archaeologist, so as to protect as much heritage value as possible.[168]

The second limb of article 4(1) deals only with acts of hostility 'directed against' cultural property. It says nothing about what had been – since the late nineteenth century and, most devastatingly, during the Second World War – the far more significant threat to cultural property in the course of hostilities, namely incidental damage. Indeed, the question of incidental damage was never broached by the Convention's drafters. The fact was that in 1954 any restraint on the permissible extent of damage to non-military objectives, such as cultural property, caused by the bombardment of nearby military objectives remained inchoate.[169] The inclusion of a rule of proportionality in relation to incidental damage, as proposed in article 24(3) of the Air Rules, was simply a

is prohibited, except where such destruction is rendered absolutely necessary by military operations.' The customary status of art. 53 was endorsed by the Eritrea Ethiopia Claims Commission in *Partial Award: Central Front. Eritrea's Claims 2, 4, 6, 7, 8 & 22*, 43 ILM 1249 (2004), paras. 21 and 87.

[166] The court, applying international law via Israeli public law, referred to the Hague Rules, Geneva Convention IV and the 1954 Hague Convention without citing provisions, although it seems to have relied on a combination of arts. 23(g) and 43 of the Hague Rules, the exception to art. 53 of Geneva Convention IV 'where such destruction is rendered absolutely necessary by military operations', and art. 4(2) of the 1954 Hague Convention.

[167] *Hess v. Commander of the IDF in the West Bank*, HCJ 10356/02, Interim decision, 12 February 2003.

[168] *Hess*, Judgment, para. 21.

[169] That said, the ICRC included a rule of proportionality in art. 8(b) of its 1956 Draft Rules for the Limitation of the Dangers incurred by the Civilian Population in Time of War, reproduced in Schindler and Toman, *Laws of Armed Conflicts*, p. 339.

non-starter. In this light, whatever benefits the second limb of article 4(1) may have offered, it was, to this extent, beside the point.

That said, with the subsequent rise and consolidation of the rule of proportionality under the customary laws of armed conflict, Parties to the Convention are today bound to refrain from attacks which may be expected to cause incidental damage to cultural property which would be excessive in relation to the concrete and direct military advantage anticipated.[170] They are bound to do so, however, not by the Convention itself but by a freestanding rule of customary international law.[171]

Theft, pillage, misappropriation, vandalism and requisition

Article 4(3) has, in the fifty years since its adoption, taken on a crucial role in the protection of cultural property in armed conflict, as the main threat has shifted from the destruction of immovables and their contents during attack to the plunder of archaeological sites and museums.[172] In accordance with the first limb of article 4(3), the High Contracting Parties to the Convention must 'prohibit, prevent and, if necessary, put a stop to any form of theft, pillage or misappropriation of, and any acts of vandalism directed against, cultural property'.[173] Curiously, the provision does not in terms prohibit the actual commission of such acts by a Party's armed forces, but a prohibition to this effect must be implied, reasoning *a fortiori*: any other outcome would fly in the face of the article's object and purpose. This implication is strengthened by the adoption of article 15(1)(e) of the Second Protocol to the Convention, which recognises

---

[170] Additional Protocol I, art. 51(5)(b), as consonant with custom.

[171] And, equally, by art. 51(5)(b) of Additional Protocol I, if they are a Party to the latter. States Parties to the Second Protocol to the 1954 Hague Convention are now also bound by the rule of proportionality embodied in arts. 7(c) and 7(d)(ii) of the Second Protocol.

[172] In a resolution entitled 'Return or restitution of cultural property to the countries of origin', the UN General Assembly – expressing concern at 'the loss, destruction, removal, theft, pillage, illicit movement or misappropriation of and any acts of vandalism or damage directed against cultural property, in particular in areas of armed conflict, including areas that are occupied, whether such conflicts are international or internal' – reaffirmed the importance of the principles and provisions of the Convention in this respect, and invited states not Parties to it to become so and to promote its implementation: GA res. 58/17, 3 December 2003, preamble, fourteenth recital and para. 4. See also GA res. 56/97, 14 December 2001; GA res. 54/190, 17 December 1999.

[173] Parties to the Convention which are also Parties to the First Protocol are further obliged by art. 1 of the latter to prevent the exportation of cultural property from territory occupied by them in armed conflict. Article 9(1)(a) of the Second Protocol also makes provision in this regard.

as a war crime, when committed intentionally and in violation of the Convention, 'theft, pillage or misappropriation of, or acts of vandalism directed against cultural property protected under the Convention'. The second limb of article 4(3), for its part, obliges Parties to refrain from requisitioning movable cultural property situated in the territory of another Party. Neither limb is subject to article 4(2)'s waiver in respect of military necessity. As with the rest of article 4, article 4(3) applies as much to belligerent occupation as to hostilities. Indeed, it is during belligerent occupation that the provision will really bite.

The undertaking in article 4(3) to prohibit, prevent and, if necessary, put a stop to the various impugned acts is not limited to the commission of such acts by a Party's own armed forces but extends to commission by the local populace and by remnants of the opposing armed forces. This explains why the first limb of the provision is formulated as an obligation 'to prohibit, prevent and, if necessary, put a stop to' the relevant conduct, instead of merely an obligation to refrain from it, as is the case with the second limb of the provision and with articles 4(1) and 4(4). The obligation accords with, and was in all probability inspired by, the practice during the Second World War of the USA, the UK and, in the western and southern European theatres, Germany in relation to cultural property which fell under their respective authorities. It serves to affirm, in the specific context of cultural property, the obligation imposed on an Occupying Power by article 43 of the Hague Rules, reflecting customary international law, to take all measures in its power to restore and ensure, as far as possible, public order. Moreover, insofar as it may call for the promulgation of laws by the Occupying Power, article 4(3) is consonant with the second paragraph of article 64 of the fourth Geneva Convention, also reflective of custom, which permits an Occupying Power to subject the population of the occupied territory 'to provisions which are essential to enable [it] ... to maintain the orderly government of the territory'.

Omitted from article 4(3) was any express obligation on a Party, in the context of belligerent occupation, to prohibit, prevent and, if necessary, put a stop to archaeological excavations not authorised by the competent national authorities, and, implicit within this, a prohibition on unauthorised digs by the Occupying Power itself. It is also difficult to see how such an obligation and prohibition could be read into the article, especially in the light of its drafting history: the insertion in the Regulations of an explicit provision to this effect was suggested by the Greek delegate to the intergovernmental conference but was rejected, although only just and partly on procedural grounds, the amendment having been proposed orally during the closing stages of the plenary.[174] Nor does the Parties' subsequent practice run unambiguously counter to this – if anything, the converse.[175] Moreover, the inclusion in the Second Protocol of articles 9(1)(b) and 9(2), dealing specifically with archaeological excavations in occupied territory, supports the view (albeit inconclusively, since they may have been inserted *ex abundante cautela*) that archaeological digs as such are not encompassed by article 4(3) of the Convention.[176] That said, it may be that the formal or effective assertion of ownership over an archaeological site not authorised by the competent national authorities, or over movables unearthed at such a site, would count as misappropriation of cultural property within the meaning of article 4(3), although this would depend on the law of the occupied territory. Misappropriation is the exercise of proprietary rights over property belonging to another. In many states, archaeological finds are the property of the finder and, as such, no act of misappropriation could be said to take place. In other states, all archaeological finds vest in the state (that is, they are public property), in this case the state whose territory is occupied. The assertion of title to archaeological finds in these circumstances would constitute misappropriation.

Article 4(3) makes no mention either of alterations to cultural property, and only in accordance with loose, polemical usage, as opposed to the ordinary meaning of the word, could such acts be termed 'vandalism' for the purposes of the provision. Subsequent practice is again generally uninstructive, perhaps even tending in the other direction,[177] and the adoption of articles 9(1)(c) and 9(2) of the Second Protocol, which expressly regulate the question, does suggest that alterations to cultural property under belligerent occupation fall outside the purview of article 4(3) of the Convention.[178]

Reprisals

By virtue of article 4(4), the High Contracting Parties 'shall refrain from any act directed by way of reprisals against cultural property'.

---

[174] *Records 1954*, paras. 1912–15. The margin was 8:9:22.
[175] See below.
[176] Recall, however, the implications of art. 43 of the Hague Rules for archaeological excavations.
[177] See below.
[178] Recall, however, the implications of art. 43 of the Hague Rules for alterations to cultural property.

Like article 4(3), article 4(4) is absolute: no waiver is available for military necessity. Although reprisals against cultural property are unknown in modern times, the provision was nonetheless something of an achievement, given the continued potential for such acts. That said, as long as reprisals against surrounding property remained lawful, cultural property remained at risk.

Belligerent occupation

Article 5 of the Convention, which applies only to belligerent occupation, deals with the crucial issue of the relationship between the Occupying Power and the competent national authorities of the occupied territory insofar as it impinges on the safeguard and preservation of cultural property situated in that territory. The article's provisions are to be read against the backdrop of the pre-existing customary law of belligerent occupation, especially the rule reflected in article 43 of the Hague Rules, which obliges the Occupying Power – unless absolutely prevented from doing so, and within the parameters set by the powers vested in and obligations imposed on it by specific rules – to leave existing administrative authority intact and free to operate. In this light, the task of preserving cultural property under belligerent occupation continues to fall to the competent national authorities.[179]

Article 5(1) states that a 'High Contracting Party in occupation of the whole or part of the territory of another High Contracting Party shall as far as possible support the competent national authorities of the occupied territory in the safeguarding and preserving of its cultural property'. The provision was probably inspired by the practice of the Office of Military Government (OMG) for Germany in the US Zone of Occupation, which promulgated Title 18 ('Monuments, Fine Arts and Archives') of the Military Government Regulations, obliging the OMG of the various Länder within the US Zone to make available to the competent German authorities, if requested by them, 'such assistance in the protection of cultural structures as appear[ed] appropriate'.[180]

---

[179] But recall that the Occupying Power's obligation of respect under art. 4(3) of the Convention requires it to prohibit, prevent and, if necessary, put a stop to any form of theft, pillage, misappropriation or vandalism of cultural property in the territory. In addition, an Occupying Power is competent to apply for the entry of cultural property in the International Register of Cultural Property under Special Protection: 1954 Hague Regulations, art. 13(2).

[180] Military Government Regulations 18–201.

The obligation in article 5(1) to support the national authorities is a positive one, going beyond the obligation merely to refrain from hampering them to include, as far as possible, assistance. In this light, it could be characterised as a reflection of the obligation imposed on an Occupying Power by the customary rule in article 43 of the Hague Rules to ensure, as far as possible, the maintenance of civil affairs. At the same time, the drafters of article 5(1) made it clear that it does not require the Occupying Power to take measures *proprio motu* to preserve cultural property in the territory (as distinct from the obligation to respect it), since such measures remain the responsibility of the competent national authorities.[181]

The words 'safeguarding' and 'preserving' in article 5(1) denote two distinct things. The former refers to the measures of safeguard mandated by article 3, namely measures designed to protect cultural property from the foreseeable effects of armed conflict. In other words, along the lines of the efforts by the German Kunstschutz in the Second World War, in co-operation with the relevant national authorities, to protect immovable and movable cultural property in the occupied Netherlands, Belgium, France and especially Italy from damage or destruction in hostilities, this first element of article 5(1) obliges the Occupying Power to work, as far as possible, with the competent authorities in their efforts to move cultural property away from the shifting frontline and/or to reinforce and insulate it *in situ*. The concept of 'preserving' refers to measures taken after the cessation of active hostilities to conserve and protect cultural property in the occupied territory – measures which, but for the state of belligerent occupation, would be considered peacetime measures. That is, this second element of article 5(1) obliges the Occupying Power to co-operate with the competent national authorities, as far as possible, in implementing the legislative and administrative regime in force in the occupied territory for the preservation of its cultural property, such as ensuring compliance with local planning regulations and enforcing criminal laws against the illegal trade in antiquities, and in taking any other practical measures as may be necessary to this end.

Should the competent national authorities request technical assistance from UNESCO under article 23(1) in organising the protection of their cultural property, or should UNESCO offer them assistance *proprio motu* under article 23(2), the obligation imposed on the Occupying

---

[181] 7 C/PRG/7, Annex I, p. 9.

Power by article 5(1) would encompass the obligation to grant the Organisation's representatives access to the property in question, to refrain from obstructing their work and even to lend them assistance, as far as possible. Indeed, when, after Israel's invasion and occupation of the south of the country, the Lebanese authorities asked the Director-General of UNESCO to send a personal representative to the archaeological site at Tyre, then in Israeli-occupied territory, the Director-General simply informed the Israeli authorities of his decision to dispatch a team, on the apparent assumption that Israel was bound to agree to this, which it did;[182] seemingly on the same assumption, he later appointed an expert to assist in placing the Convention's distinctive emblem around the site,[183] followed, at the request of the Lebanese government, by two archaeologists.[184]

Paragraph 2 of article 5 provides that '[s]hould it prove necessary to take measures to preserve cultural property situated in occupied territory and damaged by military operations, and should the competent national authorities be unable to take such measures, the Occupying Power shall, as far as possible and in close co-operation with such authorities, take the most necessary measures of preservation'. This provision, and its very careful wording, seems to have been a response to several practices manifest in the Second World War – first, the reluctance of some Occupying Powers, usually for logistical reasons, to intervene to shore up monuments damaged in the course of hostilities; secondly, the over-exuberance and insensitivity of some engineering corps when charged with clearing encumbering 'debris' and structurally unsound 'ruins'; and, thirdly, the deliberate modification 'contrary to ... national traditions' of certain cultural property in German-occupied territory on the pretext of restoration.[185] In other words, article 5(2) is designed to impose on the Occupying Power a positive obligation to take measures to prevent the deterioration of cultural property damaged in the course of hostilities, but only such measures as are strictly essential to this end, only in the event that the competent national authorities should prove unable to undertake such measures themselves, and only in collaboration with these authorities. It will tend to be only in the most urgent of circumstances that these conditions are satisfied, since it remains open to

---

[182] UNESCO Doc. 22 C/INF.8, para. 7; *1984 Reports*, paras. 14 and 17–18.
[183] 22 C/INF.8, para. 8.
[184] *Ibid.*, para. 10.
[185] 7 C/PRG/7, Annex I, p. 9. The Germans altered Wawel Castle in Cracow.

the competent national authorities, should they prove unable to take the requisite measures, to request technical assistance from UNESCO under article 23(2).

Like article 4(3), article 5 does not, on its face, include a prohibition on the conduct, sponsorship or authorisation of archaeological excavations by an Occupying Power without the consent of the competent national authorities, something which has proved a major source of controversy in the light of Israel's extensive digs in the Occupied Palestinian Territories, especially in the Old City of Jerusalem. It was dissatisfaction with the absence from the Convention of any explicit rules on archaeological excavations in occupied territory which led to the adoption of articles 9(1)(b) and 9(2) of the Second Protocol, which now make provision in this regard. It had earlier been hoped by its drafters that article 32 of UNESCO's Recommendation on International Principles Applicable to Archaeological Excavations,[186] a hortatory provision adopted by the Organisation's General Conference in 1956, would be incorporated, along with implementing regulations, in an addendum to the Convention, but this was never to be the case. Article 32 of the Recommendation provides that, in the event of armed conflict, 'any Member State occupying the territory of another State should refrain from carrying out archaeological excavations in the occupied territory'.[187] A proposal by UNESCO in 1970 to call a meeting of the High Contracting Parties to amend the Convention,[188] after the furore over Israel's practices had emphasised the lacuna in respect of archaeological excavations and alterations to cultural property in occupied territory, was also still-born.

The fact that article 5 does not expressly embody a prohibition on the conduct, sponsorship or authorisation of archaeological digs by the Occupying Power without the agreement of the competent national authorities does not rule out the possibility that such a ban is implied in the provision, and it might be argued that article 5 is premised on the

---

[186] *Records of the General Conference, Ninth Session, New Delhi 1956: Resolutions*, p. 40.
[187] Article 32 continues: 'In the event of chance finds being made, particularly during military works, the occupying Power should take all possible measures to protect these finds, which should be handed over, on the termination of hostilities, to the competent authorities of the territory previously occupied, together with all documentation relating thereto.'
[188] UNESCO Doc. DG/6/A/2620, pursuant to 83 EX/Decision 4.3.1, para. 8, in which the Executive Board requested the Director-General 'to consult the Governments Parties to The Hague Convention on the advisability of calling, as soon as possible, a meeting of the High Contracting Parties with a view to studying means whereby the scope of the said Convention can be made clear and its efficacy enhanced'.

assumption that the regulation in occupied territory of matters bearing on cultural property [except for those questions governed by article 4(3) and by relevant, specific customary rules[189]] remains the exclusive prerogative of the competent national authorities. The critical question, however, is whether a prohibition to the effect has in fact been recognised by the Parties as forming an aspect of article 5 of the Convention. In this regard, while the adoption of articles 9(1)(b) and 9(2) of the Second Protocol militates against this, it is not conclusive of the matter, as they may have been included for the avoidance of doubt.

The relevant practice of the Parties consists solely of Israel's excavations since 1967 in the occupied West Bank, including the Old City of Jerusalem, and, more representatively, of reactions to it by the other Parties (via their respective representations at UNESCO's biennial General Conference, comprising delegates from each Member State) and by the Executive Board of UNESCO. In the final analysis, this practice is too ambiguous to afford compelling enough evidence to establish that the Parties interpret article 5 – or article 4(3) or, indeed, any other provision of the Convention – to include a prohibition on the conduct, sponsorship or authorisation of archaeological excavations by an Occupying Power without the agreement of the competent national authorities. If anything, it favours the contrary.[190]

---

[189] Recall again the implications of art. 43 of the Hague Rules for archaeological excavations.

[190] The various resolutions and decisions make unspecific, indiscriminate and inconsistent reference to the Convention, to other resolutions of UNESCO's General Conference and decisions of its Executive Board, to resolutions of the UN General Assembly and Security Council, and, in later examples, to other international conventions; the acts impugned include not just archaeological digs but also, *inter alia*, acts of destruction clearly violative of the Convention; and it is not clear whether UNESCO is intervening in the matter under art. 23(2) of the Convention or pursuant to its mandate under art. I(3) of its Constitution to maintain, increase and diffuse knowledge '[b]y assuring the conservation and protection of the world's inheritance of books, works of art and monuments of history and science'. See 15 C/Resolution 3.342, 15 C/Resolution 3.343, 82 EX/Decision 4.4.2, 83 EX/Decision 4.3.1, 89 EX/Decision 4.4.1, 17 C/Resolution 3.422, 18 C/Resolution 3.427, 19 C/Resolution 4.129 and, more recently, 121 EX/Decision 5.4.1, 23 C/Resolution 11.3, 127 EX/Decision 5.4.1, 24 C/Resolution 11.6, 25 C/Resolution 3.6, 26 C/Resolution 3.12, 140 EX/Decision 5.5.1, 142 EX/Decision 5.5.1, 27 C/Resolution 3.8, 145 EX/Decision 5.5.1, 147 EX/Decision 3.6.1, 29 C/Resolution 22, 30 C/Resolution 28 and 31 C/Resolution 31. But *cf.* 125 EX/Decision 5.4.1, where para. 10 '[r]equests consequently that, in accordance with the provisions of the 1954 Hague Convention and the resolution of the General Conference adopted at its ninth session (New Delhi, 1956), no excavation should be resumed'. For his part, one of the Commissioners-General for Cultural Property appointed in respect of the Arab–Israeli conflict in 1967 took the view that the Convention does not deal with archaeological digs in occupied territory: 82 EX/29, Annex I, p. 4.

The evidence, reasoning and conclusions in respect of archaeological excavations in occupied territory apply *mutatis mutandis* to the alteration of cultural property under occupation with only slightly less force.[191]

Special protection

Chapter II of the Convention (articles 8 to 11) establishes a regime of 'special protection' applicable above and beyond the general protection provided for in chapter I. This supplementary regime, modelled on article 26 of the Air Rules and article 5(2) of the OIM draft, is designed to provide a higher standard of protection in respect of a narrower range of property, a higher standard which relates specifically to the obligation to refrain from using cultural property and its surroundings for military purposes and the obligation to refrain from directing acts of hostility against it, as laid down in respect of general protection in the two limbs of article 4(1). These twin obligations aside, all the obligations otherwise applicable to movables and immovables which satisfy the definition of cultural property under article 1 are equally applicable to property which additionally qualifies for special protection under article 8. Special protection is available only in respect of refuges intended to shelter movable cultural property, centres containing monuments and other immovable cultural property. It is not available for movable cultural property as such. Moreover, refuges, centres containing monuments and other immovable cultural property are entitled to special protection only if they satisfy strict criteria.

The difference between the standards imposed during armed conflict by the regime of special protection and the respect owed to cultural property under general protection is extraordinarily minor. Although labelled 'immunity', the additional restraints mandated in relation to specially protected property amount to no more than a tweaking of the conditions under which the waiver as to military necessity may be invoked. Any greater substantive protection that such property may stand to enjoy effectively derives from the regime's

---

[191] Dissatisfaction with this state of affairs, specifically in the light of Israel's contentious activities in Jerusalem and at the Mosque of Ibrahim at the Cave of the Patriarchs in Hebron, led to the adoption of arts. 9(1)(c) and 9(2) of the Second Protocol. Recall also the implications of art. 43 of the Hague Rules for alterations to cultural property.

criteria for eligibility, which prescribe a *cordon sanitaire* around the property.¹⁹²

As it transpires, '[t]he success of the arrangements for special protection has proved very limited'.¹⁹³ Putting it more bluntly, chapter II is a white elephant. Only one centre containing monuments, the Vatican City, and eight refuges for movable cultural property, six of them in the Netherlands, have ever been entered in the International Register of Cultural Property under Special Protection. (Three of the Dutch refuges and the single Austrian refuge have since been removed at the request of the respective governments, leaving the Register to comprise four refuges and a lone centre containing monuments.¹⁹⁴) The reasons for this underwhelming uptake are obvious: the criteria of eligibility for special protection are cripplingly difficult to satisfy, the procedure by which such protection is granted is potentially tortuous and time-consuming, and, with precious little reward for success, it must seem hardly worth the effort.¹⁹⁵

Granting of special protection

Article 8 specifies the types of cultural property eligible for special protection and the conditions under which they may be granted it. The gist of the provision, as with the provisions of the Air Rules and of the OIM draft convention which inspired it, is selectivity, with the committee of experts responsible for the UNESCO draft warning that 'States would be ill-advised to increase [the] number [of immovables under special protection] unduly, as this would inevitably make it more difficult to obtain the protection applied for'.¹⁹⁶ The committee accepted pessimistically that it was 'unfortunately impossible to provide [special] protection for monuments ... located in large towns', and foresaw that

---

[192] The *travaux* reveal, however, that protection was not in fact the motivation behind these criteria: see below. Moreover, even if one were to put a humanitarian spin on its *raison d'être*, art. 8(1)(a)'s requirement of an adequate distance from a large industrial centre or from a military objective constituting a vulnerable point would reflect a perverse logic: if cultural property is so situated as to satisfy art. 8(1)(a), it is unlikely to need legal protection in the event of armed conflict.

[193] Toman, *Protection of Cultural Property*, p. 108.

[194] In addition to the three remaining refuges in the Netherlands, there is a refuge under special protection at Oberried in Germany.

[195] The failure of the regime of special protection under chap. II of the Convention led to the regime of 'enhanced protection' under chap. 3 of the Second Protocol.

[196] 7 C/PRG/7, Annex I, p. 16.

'most immovable monuments [would] only enjoy the general protection provided for in Chapter I of the Convention'.[197] But that such an extreme degree of selectivity was reflected in the final version of article 8 was ultimately the result of US and especially UK brinkmanship at the intergovernmental conference: a majority of delegates agreed unenthusiastically to the eventual text as the price of the British and Americans' signatures. The UK's avowed aim was markedly to limit the amount of cultural property entitled to special protection. 'In the difficult conditions of warfare', the UK delegate claimed, 'it would be found necessary to raise the immunity more and more frequently, and eventually the whole "currency" of special protection would be debased.'[198] The Israeli representative responded diplomatically that he 'did not think the dangers referred to by the delegate of the United Kingdom were likely to materialize'.[199] Other delegates weighed in with more trenchant criticism. The Soviet representative stated bluntly that the UK position 'took military necessity more into account than the defence of cultural property',[200] and the UK stood accused by Poland of wanting 'the exclusion of the most precious of cultural property from special protection'.[201] The French delegate went so far as to allege that the upshot of the UK's position 'would be that, in the end, no monument would be [specially] protected'.[202]

Paragraph 1 of article 8 outlines the basic criteria for special protection. The chapeau to article 8(1) provides that there may be placed under special protection 'a limited number of refuges intended to shelter movable property in the event of armed conflict, of centres containing monuments and other immovable property of very great importance'. It is clear from this that movable cultural property – the works of art, manuscripts, books and other objects of artistic, historical or archaeological interest, and so on, mentioned in article 1(a) – cannot enjoy special protection in its own right. That said, movables can benefit from *de facto* protection, but only insofar as they are housed in a specially protected refuge or situated with a specially protected centre containing monuments.[203] Similarly, it appears that 'buildings whose

---

[197] *Ibid.*, p. 17.
[198] *Records 1954*, para. 470. See also *ibid.*, para. 523.
[199] *Ibid.*, para. 524.
[200] *Ibid.*, para. 527.
[201] *Ibid.*, para. 1929.
[202] *Ibid.*, para. 528.
[203] Recall that 'centres containing monuments' are defined in art. 1(c) as 'centres containing a large amount of cultural property as defined sub-paragraphs (a) and (b)'.

main and effective purpose is to preserve or exhibit ... movable cultural property ... such as museums, large libraries and depositories of archives', as referred to in article 1(b), are also ineligible for special protection in their own right. They will, however, benefit in effect from such protection if they incorporate within them refuges under special protection or if they are situated within a centre containing monuments under such protection.

The ironically prophetic term 'a limited number' used in the chapeau to paragraph 1 is no more than impressionistic, serving to underline the selective character of special protection without imposing an enforceable legal limit on the total property eligible. As for 'of very great importance', the immediately preceding use of the term 'other immovable cultural property' indicates that the phrase qualifies not only this last-mentioned category of property but also the two before it, both of them species of immovable cultural property. In other words, in order to enjoy special protection, refuges too must be of very great importance, as must centres containing monuments. A refuge's importance is judged by reference to the importance of the movable cultural property it is intended to shelter. The same goes *mutatis mutandis* for centres containing monuments. Curiously, in both the final version of article 8 and in UNESCO's draft article, the expression 'of very great importance' is not followed − as is the analogous phrase in article 1, applicable to general protection − by the phrase 'to the cultural heritage of every people'. Nothing, however, turns on this: there is no suggestion in the *travaux* that this aspect of the wording of the chapeau to article 8(1) was intended as anything other than shorthand for the compendious expression 'of very great importance to the cultural heritage of every people', in counterpoint to article 1. In other words, the immovables intended to be eligible for special protection are the more important examples of each Party's national cultural heritage, as determined by that Party. This was confirmed by the first meeting of the High Contracting Parties, held in 1962, where 'it was pointed out that the importance of cultural property might be assessed not only from a world but also from a national standpoint'.[204] As for the difference between 'great importance' under article 1 (general protection) and 'very great importance' under article 8(1) (special protection), the qualification 'very' is again merely

---

Sub-paragraph (a) of art. 1 encompasses movable cultural property in its own right. Sub-paragraph (b) encompasses 'buildings whose main or effective purpose is to preserve or exhibit the movable cultural property defined in sub-paragraph (a)'.

[204] CUA/120, para. 12.

impressionistic, indicating a higher degree of significance without positing an enforceable legal standard. It is unimaginable that a Party would object[205] to the entry of a given immovable in the International Register of Cultural Property under Special Protection on the sole ground that it is of great but not very great importance to the cultural heritage of the Party requesting entry.

The most severe restriction placed on the eligibility of cultural property for special protection is that such property must be, in the words of article 8(1)(a), 'situated at an adequate distance from any large industrial centre or from any important military objective constituting a vulnerable point, such as, for example, an aerodrome, broadcasting station, establishment engaged upon work of national defence, a port or railway station of relative importance or a main line of communication'. This criterion is generally acknowledged as the single most influential reason why there are only five (formerly nine) entries in the International Register of Cultural Property under Special Protection, why only one of these, the Vatican City, is not a refuge,[206] and why the Vatican City's entry was possible only on account of a special undertaking by Italy under article 8(5) – that is, not through its fulfilment of the conditions laid down in article 8(1). The requirement came in for stiff criticism at the intergovernmental conference. The Polish delegate complained that it would mean that 'only the Pyramids of Egypt would be entitled to such protection';[207] and while the UK delegate sanguinely predicted that 'Westminster Abbey would not qualify for special protection', indeed that he could not think of any monuments in the whole of the UK which would qualify for it,[208] the Soviet representative 'was of the opinion that Westminster Abbey and a great deal more cultural property in England deserved [such] protection'.[209]

Amid the gloomy predictions of the drafters, however, there was never any discussion as to precisely what distance was to be deemed 'adequate'. Similarly, the first meeting of the High Contracting Parties, which considered the question, 'was unable to arrive at a more precise definition ... partly because of the different conditions which prevailed

---

[205] See 1954 Hague Regulations, art. 14.
[206] As for the eight (now five) refuges, it is unclear whether they were granted special protection pursuant to art. 8(1) or in accordance with the exception to the requirement of adequate distance provided for in art. 8(2).
[207] *Records 1954*, para. 469.
[208] *Ibid.*, para. 470.
[209] *Ibid.*, para. 987.

in the various particular cases and made it impossible to adopt uniform and universally valid rules'.[210] Given that 'some uncertainty exist[ed] regarding the interpretation of Article 8 relating to special protection and, in particular of the concept of "adequate distance"', the meeting passed a resolution recommending that a proposed 'technical advisory committee' be seized of the problem so as 'to make a thorough study of it and submit its proposals for a solution to a subsequent Meeting of the High Contracting Parties'.[211] (The committee in question, whose establishment was recommended in a separate resolution,[212] was never created.) The meeting also expressed the hope 'that in evaluating the "adequate distance" for purposes of special protection, the High Contracting Parties [would] bear in mind first and foremost the very purpose of the Convention, which is to provide the widest possible protection for cultural property throughout the world'.[213]

The subsequent practice of the Parties, while not suggesting any more specific a distance, tends to endorse the drafters' view that very few examples of immovable cultural property are to be considered an adequate distance from any large industrial centre or from any important military objective constituting a vulnerable point. It is not that the entry of immovable cultural property in the Register has been objected to on this ground; rather, the Parties have refrained from applying for special protection in the first place. Italy contemplated requesting the entry of Venice, Vicenza, the centre of Florence, Siena, Assisi, Rome within the Aurelian walls, Caserta and Monreale in the International Register of Cultural Property under Special Protection,[214] but the plan was thwarted. Austria drew up a list of twenty-one items of immovable cultural property of very great importance, for which it proposed to request registration,[215] but this too proceeded no further. The former USSR, pointing out that the immovable cultural property in its territory worthy of special protection was concentrated in centres such as Moscow, Leningrad, Kiev, Riga and Tallinn, similarly explained its unsuitability, on the whole, for special protection by stating that 'these

---

[210] CUA/120, para. 13. 'It was noted, in particular, that the concept of "adequate distance" was liable to change according to the development of the means of destruction employed': *ibid.*, para. 12.
[211] *Ibid.*, para. 18.
[212] *Ibid.*, para. 16.
[213] *Ibid.*, para. 18.
[214] *1967 Reports*, p. 27.
[215] *1979 Reports*, p. 13.

traditional cultural centres are also major centres of political and industrial power and major links in the communications system'.[216] The United Arab Republic (Egypt) proposed to request the entry in the Register of the temples of Abu Simbel and the necropolis of Thebes, comprising the Valley of the Kings, the Valley of the Queens, the Tombs of the Nobles, the temples of Deir el Bahari, the colossi of Memnon and so on.[217] While it is unclear why this proposal was never pursued, the most likely explanation is the requirement of adequate distance: in the case of the necropolis of Thebes, the problem would likely have been the railway station at Luxor; in the case of Abu Simbel, it would seem that the Aswan High Dam was deemed an important military objective constituting a vulnerable point, that an isolated desert road to the temples represented the same, or that what was considered an 'adequate' distance from other potential targets, such as the railhead at Aswan, was simply vast. Poland 'has not availed itself of the privilege of obtaining the special protection provided for' by article 8, 'owing to the restrictions set out in [paragraph] 1 of the article and particularly to the fact that the majority of the most important museums and historic monuments are situated near bridges, stations and major lines of communication'.[218] One of the 'several reasons' why Switzerland has not yet requested the Director-General of UNESCO to inscribe any of its cultural property in the Register is that 'the strict application of Article 8, paragraph 1, of the Hague Convention makes it difficult to select this type of property in a small country where all the built-up areas are extremely close together'.[219]

Nor is the term 'large industrial centre' clear. Quite apart from the vagueness of the adjective 'large', neither the *travaux* nor the subsequent practice of the Parties points to whether 'centre' is used in the sense of 'concentration of buildings', and thereby refers only to those parts of a city or town which are themselves of an industrial character (such as factories, warehouses, gasworks and the like), or whether it indicates the city or town itself, in its entirety. This was a source of confusion at the intergovernmental conference, where the ICRC observer asked 'what was meant by a large industrial centre and whether, in cities such as Turin or Oxford, the expression referred solely to the industrial

---

[216] *1970 Reports*, pp. 22–3.
[217] *Ibid.*, p. 24.
[218] *1979 Reports*, p. 27. See also *1989 Reports*, p. 31.
[219] *1995 Reports*, p. 45.

districts, the Fiat or Morris factories, or also included the Piazza San Carlo or the wonderful old colleges'.[220]

The phrase 'important military objective constituting a vulnerable point' is similarly opaque. A US military expert explained to the main commission of the intergovernmental conference that the term 'vulnerable point' signified 'a higher strategic reference', that is 'an objective of much greater significance' than a garden-variety tactical military objective.[221] The Commission deferred to the expert's knowledge,[222] accepting his and the French delegate's assurances that 'vulnerable point' was a term of art recognised 'by all General Staffs'.[223] But while providing evidence that a special meaning was to be given to the phrase,[224] the records of the conference do little to flesh out its precise content. Furthermore, what is an 'important' military objective and whether it constitutes a 'vulnerable point' will vary according to the military circumstances prevailing at any given time: they cannot be determined *a priori*. The former USSR highlighted the contingent nature of the concept of a vulnerable point in one of its implementation reports. Vulnerability, the report stated, can be 'radically affected by the changing situation, the development of more sophisticated means of attack, and so on'.[225]

Even more to the point, the concept of a military objective itself, as today understood, is a contingent one. According to the now-customary definition, an object will be rendered a military objective only if its total or partial destruction, capture or neutralisation offers a definite military advantage in the circumstances ruling at the time.[226] Again, this cannot be determined in advance. Circumstances change: this week's vital airfield may be next week's waste of ordnance.

A further charge levelled by the ICRC observer to the conference, a criticism which applies with even greater force today, was that article 8(1)(a)'s reference to 'large industrial centres', especially if interpreted to mean industrial cities and towns taken as a whole, implies that such places can be bombed in their entirety, without any attempt to distinguish between military objectives, on the one hand, and civilians

---

[220] *Records 1954*, para. 773.
[221] *Ibid.*, para. 669.
[222] *Ibid.*, para 670.
[223] *Ibid.*, para. 667. See also 7 C/PRG/7, Annex I, p. 17.
[224] See Vienna Convention on the Law of Treaties, art. 31(4).
[225] *1970 Reports*, p. 23.
[226] Additional Protocol I, art. 52(2), as consonant with custom.

and civilian objects on the other. The ICRC observer pointed out that indiscriminate bombing of this sort was forbidden by article 27 of the Hague Rules and by the provisions of the Geneva Conventions relating to hospitals.[227] Today indiscriminate bombing is outlawed by generally applicable customary rules rooted in the principle of distinction: neither the civilian population[228] nor civilian objects[229] shall be the object of attack – that is, attacks shall be limited strictly to military objectives;[230] and, as a consequence, indiscriminate attacks are prohibited,[231] including attacks by bombardment which treat as a single military objective a number of clearly separated and distinct military objectives located in cities and towns.[232] Indeed, the ICJ has referred to the basic rules of the international law of armed conflict, among which the rules embodying the principle of distinction are to be counted, as 'intransgressible',[233] which the International Law Commission has interpreted to mean peremptory norms, that is, rules having the character of *jus cogens*.[234]

In fact, article 8(1)(a) would still not reflect the modern law of armed conflict even if 'large industrial centres' were to be interpreted more narrowly – and somewhat contrary to the ordinary meaning(s) of the words – to refer only to individual industrial installations. For an object to satisfy the customary definition of a military objective, it must, by its nature, location, purpose or use, make an effective contribution to military action,[235] the term 'military action' being interpreted restrictively. While munitions factories and production facilities for military avionics, for example, can be considered military objectives (subject, in principle, to their neutralisation offering a definite advantage in the circumstances ruling at the time), a state's general industrial capacity is not. The modern customary definition of a military objective rejects the doctrine of economic warfare, in which every element of a country's economic life is potentially marked for destruction. In this light, with the

---

[227] *Records 1954*, para. 773.
[228] Additional Protocol I, art. 51(2), as consonant with custom.
[229] *Ibid.*, art. 52(1), as consonant with custom.
[230] *Ibid.*, art. 52(2), as consonant with custom.
[231] *Ibid.*, art. 51(4), chapeau, as consonant with custom.
[232] *Ibid.*, art. 51(5)(a), as consonant with custom.
[233] *Legality of the Threat or Use of Nuclear Weapons*, Advisory Opinion, ICJ Reports 1996 (I), p. 226 at para. 79.
[234] Articles on Responsibility of States for Internationally Wrongful Acts, para. 5 of commentary to art. 40, *International Law Commission: Report on the work of its fifty-third session (23 April–1 June and 2 July–10 August 2001)*, UN Doc. A/56/10, p. 284.
[235] Additional Protocol I, art. 52(2), as consonant with custom.

exception of 'establishments engaged upon work of national defence', none of the examples cited in article 8(1)(a) of an 'important military objective constituting a vulnerable point' can be deemed a military objective *in se*. Aerodromes, broadcasting stations, ports, railway stations 'of relative importance' and 'main' lines of communication may be put to use in the service of military operations, but they may equally not be, thereby remaining civilian objects which shall not be the object of attack.

Subparagraph (b) of article 8(1) specifies that, in addition to the restrictions imposed by subparagraph (a), refuges, centres containing monuments and other immovable property of the requisite importance may not be placed under special protection if used for military purposes. The provision is a condition precedent to the grant of special protection in the first place, as distinct from a justification for the release of a Party from its obligation to ensure the immunity of cultural property already granted special protection, as provided for in article 11(1). No definition is given in article 8(1)(b) of use for military purposes. Article 8(3), however, clarifies the concept as it applies to centres containing monuments, stating that a centre containing monuments shall be deemed to be used for military purposes whenever it is used for the movement of military personnel or material, even in transit. Article 8(3) continues that the same shall apply whenever activities directly connected with military operations, the stationing of military personnel or the production of war material are carried on within the centre. Article 8(4) provides, on the other hand, that the guarding of cultural property of very great importance by 'armed custodians specially empowered to do so' or the presence in the vicinity of 'police forces normally responsible for the maintenance of public order' does not amount to use for military purposes.

Article 8(5) provides for an exception to the requirement of adequate distance. It states that if any cultural property of very great importance is situated near an important military objective as defined in article 8(1)(a), 'it may nonetheless be placed under special protection if the High Contracting Party asking for that protection undertakes, in the event of armed conflict, to make no use of the objective and particularly, in the case of a port, railway station or aerodrome, to divert all traffic therefrom'. In such cases, the provision stipulates, the diversion must be prepared in peacetime. Article 8(5) applies compendiously to 'any cultural property mentioned in paragraph 1' of article 8, namely to refuges intended to shelter movable cultural property, to centres containing monuments and to other immovable cultural property of very great importance. Declarations made under the provision constitute binding unilateral statements.[236] In contrast to article 8(1)(a), article 8(5) makes no mention of large industrial centres, the reference being only to important military objectives, and it is unclear whether cultural property situated near such centres may also benefit from an undertaking made in accordance with the provision. As it turns out, the only state to have made a peacetime undertaking in accordance with article 8(5) has been Italy, and in relation to cultural property situated in the Vatican City, a separate state. The former undertook in 1959 not to use the Via Aurelia for military purposes in the event of armed conflict, in order that the latter could be entered in the International Register of Cultural Property under Special Protection. Italy's undertaking was formally invalid: the Holy See, not Italy, was 'the High Contracting Party asking for [special] protection', in the words of article 8(5); and Italy undertook to make no use of the Via Aurelia for military purposes, whereas article 8(5) requires that the Party undertake to make no use whatsoever of the objective. That said, none of the other Parties objected at the time to the Vatican City's entry in the Register, and none has objected since. Given this acquiescence, the grant of special protection can be considered effective.[237]

One other exception to the requirement of adequate distance is found in article 8(2), which, in contrast to article 8(5), is applicable only to refuges intended to shelter movable cultural property. Article 8(2) states that a refuge for movable cultural property may also be placed under special protection, whatever its location, 'if it is so constructed that, in all probability, it will not be damaged by bombs'.[238] [The obligation not to

---

[236] See *Nuclear Tests (Australia v. France)*, ICJ Reports 1974, p. 253; *Nuclear Tests (New Zealand v. France)*, ICJ Reports 1974, p. 457; *Frontier Dispute (Burkina Faso/Mali)*, ICJ Reports 1986, p. 554.

[237] '[Subsequent] practice or conduct may affect the legal relations of the Parties even though it cannot be said to be practice in the application of the [t]reaty or to constitute an agreement between them': *Decision Regarding the Delimitation of the Border between The State of Eritrea and The Federal Democratic Republic of Ethiopia*, 41 ILM 1057 (2002), para. 3.6. In such cases, 'the effect of subsequent conduct may be so clear in relation to matters that appear to be the subject of a given treaty that the application of an otherwise pertinent treaty provision may be varied, or may even cease to control the situation, regardless of its original meaning': *ibid.*, para. 3.8. See also *Serbian Loans*, PCIJ Reports Series A Nos. 20/21 (1929) at p. 38; *Temple of Preah Vihear (Cambodia v. Thailand)*, Merits, ICJ Reports 1962, p. 6 at pp. 23, 30–1 and 32.

[238] Like the requirement of adequate distance in art. 8(1), art. 8(2) reflects a perverse logic: if a refuge can withstand bombs, it is scarcely in need of additional legal protection in the event of armed conflict.

use such refuges for military purposes, as laid down in article 8(1)(b), remains unaffected.] Article 8(2) makes it possible for works of art, manuscripts, books and the like, as referred to in article 1(a) of the Convention, to benefit *de facto* from special protection even if the refuge in which they are sheltered is situated in the heart of a city. In this way, the provision facilitates the special protection *in situ* of the collections of art galleries, museums, libraries and archives:[239] major institutions of this sort tend to possess underground storage space which could be made impervious to bombs, if it is not already; and, at least as a legal matter, not all of the movable cultural property held by the relevant institution need fit within the bombproof part of the building. Moreover, as long as the subterranean part of the building were to enjoy special protection as a refuge under article 8(2), the whole of the edifice would, in practice, enjoy such protection. The logical extension of this would be to use the provision to secure what would, in practice, be special protection for any immovable cultural property amenable to the construction within it of a refuge for movable property of very great importance. In other words, article 8(2) could potentially be used to accord special protection, in effect, to culturally important buildings, archaeological sites and the like. A suggestion to this effect was made by the committee of experts which prepared the UNESCO draft. Indeed, the OIM draft had originally stated that refuges for movables 'may take the form either of buildings erected for the purpose or of existing historic buildings and groups of buildings'.[240] The committee expressed the view that 'governments might do well to turn monuments or even groups of monuments of artistic value into refuges', adding that 'States wishing to claim immunity for such architectural monuments would then have to ensure that they fulfil the conditions entitling refuges to immunity'.[241] The Netherlands adopted this approach to article 8(2) in respect of bombproof refuges it built beneath the Royal Picture Gallery in the Mauritshuis, The Hague, and beneath St John's Cathedral in 's-Hertogenbosch with a view to their being 'deemed refuges which may be placed under special protection in accordance with the provisions of Article 8 of the Convention'.[242] It stated at the time that these two

---

[239] Such protection was foreshadowed by the drafters: 7 C/PRG/7, Annex I, p. 18; *Records 1954*, p. 318.
[240] OIM Draft, art. 4(2).
[241] 7 C/PRG/7, Annex I, p. 16. The suggestion was omitted from the UNESCO Secretariat's comments on the draft.
[242] *1989 Reports*, p. 29.

buildings are important 'both because of the priceless treasures housed in them and because they themselves are irreplaceable objects of value to [the country's] cultural heritage'.[243]

Article 8(6) states that special protection 'is granted to cultural property by its entry in the "International Register of Cultural Property under Special Protection"'.[244] This has two corollaries. First, eligible cultural property does not enjoy special protection unless and until it is entered in the Register.[245] Second, the entry of cultural property in the Register is conclusive proof of its grant of special protection.[246] Under article 12(2) of the Regulations, the duty to maintain the Register is vested in the Director-General of UNESCO, who is obliged to furnish copies of it to the Parties and to the UN Secretary-General. It is the Director-General who, in accordance with article 15(1) of the Regulations, is mandated to enter eligible cultural property in the Register. Article 8(6) of the Convention stipulates that such entry may be made only in accordance with the provisions of the Convention and its Regulations.

Chapter II of the Regulations spells out in detail the procedure for the entry of cultural property in the Register. In accordance with article 13(1) of the Regulations, it is up to the Party in whose territory the relevant refuge, centre containing monuments or other immovable cultural property is situated to submit to the Director-General of UNESCO an application for its entry in the Register. Article 13(2) specifies, however, that the Occupying Power is competent to make such an application in the event of belligerent occupation. Copies of applications, which article 13(1) stipulates must contain a description of the location of the property in question and a certification of its compliance with the provisions of article 8 of the Convention, are to be sent by the Director-General to all the Parties, pursuant to article 13(3). In contrast to general protection, the grant of special protection, effected by way of entry in the Register, is subject to a right of objection on the part of each of the other

---

[243] Ibid.
[244] The Register is prepared in accordance with art. 12 of the Regulations and with rules of 18 August 1956 prepared by the Director-General of UNESCO in the exercise of his mandate under that provision.
[245] See also 1954 Hague Convention, art. 9, pursuant to which the Parties are to ensure the immunity of cultural property under special protection 'from the time of entry in the International Register'.
[246] Note, however, that the entry in the Register does not itself become effective until thirty days after the dispatch by the Director-General of UNESCO to the UN Secretary-General and the Parties of a certified copy of the entry, in accordance with art. 15(4) of the Regulations.

Parties, a right for which highly detailed provision is made in article 14 of the Regulations. Article 14(1) grants any Party the right to object to the registration of given cultural property within four months of the date on which the Director-General sent the Party its copy of the application. The only valid reasons for objection are that the property is not cultural property as defined in article 1 of the Convention or that it does not comply with the conditions laid down in article 8 of the Convention.[247] The Director-General and the Party applying for registration are authorised under article 14(4) to make 'whatever representations they deem necessary to the High Contracting Parties which lodged the objection, with a view to causing the objection to be withdrawn'. An objecting Party is given six months in which to withdraw its objection before the Party which entered the application is authorised under article 14(6) to request arbitration in accordance with a procedure laid down in article 14(7). Alternatively, either or any of the Parties in question may opt under article 14(8) for the matter to be decided by a vote of all the Parties, to be taken by correspondence over a maximum period of six months, with a two-thirds majority of those Parties voting required in support of the objection. In the event of the withdrawal of the objection or of its failure to be confirmed following the arbitration procedure under article 14(7) or the vote of the Parties under article 14(8), the Director-General shall enter the cultural property in question in the Register.[248] Given the potentially protracted time-frame involved under article 14 of the Regulations, article 14(5) makes sensible provision in the event that a Party which has made an application for registration in peacetime becomes involved in an armed conflict before the relevant entry has been made. In these circumstances, 'the cultural property concerned shall at once be provisionally entered in the Register, by the Director-General, pending the confirmation, withdrawal or cancellation of any objection that may be, or may have been, made'. The reference to the cancellation of an objection is to its failure to be confirmed after the application of either article 14(7) or article 14(8).

The objection procedure established under article 14 of the Regulations has been invoked only once. When armed conflict spread across the Cambodian province of Siem Reap in 1972, the government of the then Khmer Republic applied for the entry in the Register of the centres containing monuments at Angkor and Roluos, of the monuments of

[247] 1954 Hague Regulations, art. 14(2).
[248] *Ibid.*, art. 15(2).

Phnom Bok and Phnom Kron, and of a refuge for movable cultural property at the headquarters of the Angkor Conservancy. The Director-General of UNESCO sent copies of the application to all the Parties, in accordance with article 13(3) of the Regulations. Four Parties (Cuba, Egypt, Romania and Yugoslavia) objected to the requested entries on the ground that 'the request for the registration of the cultural property in question had not been submitted by the authority which they considered to be the only government which had the right to represent the Khmer Republic'.[249] Entry in the Register did not proceed, despite the fact that the stated ground for the objection was not valid under article 14(2). At a meeting of experts convened in Vienna in 1983, it was complained that the Director-General did not use all the means at his disposal under article 14 to resolve the matter. The Director-General's representative responded that the deadlock procedure provided for in paragraph 6 of the provision had not been invoked, as required, by the Party seeking registration and that, in this light, no further action could be taken.[250] This does not explain why the five requested entries in the Register could not have been made provisionally, in accordance with article 14(5), although the explanation would seem to lie in the fact that this provision only applies in cases where the application for registration has been 'made ... in time of peace'.

It is hard to resist the conclusion that the laborious and potentially costly procedure by which applications for and objections to entry in the Register are made and resolved is unrealistic, indeed faintly absurd, given the minimal additional legal protection at stake. In this light, it is no surprise that only four Parties have ever applied for special protection for immovable cultural property in their territory. Nor can Cambodia be blamed for failing to pursue the registration of the treasures of Siem Reap.

In addition to the special protection available to refuges for movable cultural property under articles 8(1), 8(2) and 8(5), article 11 of the Regulations makes emergency provision for the grant of special protection to any improvised refuges that a Party may set up in the course of an armed conflict. The creation of *ad hoc* refuges for works of art, collections of books and the like was common during the Second World War, particularly during the Italian campaign. Article 11(1) of the Regulations states that if, during an armed conflict, 'any High Contracting Party is

---

[249] *1979 Reports*, para. 9.
[250] UNESCO Doc. CLT.83/CONF.641/1, para. 24.

induced by unforeseen circumstances to set up an improvised refuge and desires that it should be placed under special protection, it shall communicate this fact forthwith to the Commissioner-General accredited to that Party'.[251] In accordance with article 11(2), the Commissioner-General accredited to the Party in question may authorise the display of the Convention's distinctive emblem (repeated three times[252]) on an improvised refuge if he or she considers the measure justified by the circumstances and by the importance of the cultural property sheltered in the refuge. He or she must communicate this decision to the delegates of the relevant Protecting Powers,[253] any of whom may order the immediate withdrawal of the emblem within 30 days. If no objection is entered within 30 days, or if the delegates of the Protecting Powers agree sooner, the Commissioner-General, provided he or she is satisfied that the refuge fulfils the conditions of article 8 of the Convention, may request the Director-General of UNESCO to enter the improvised refuge in the Register.[254] The proviso is important: to benefit from special protection, an improvised refuge must effectively be situated, like any other eligible refuge, an adequate distance from any large industrial centre or from any important military objective, and must not be used for military purposes; alternatively, whatever its location, it must be so constructed that, in all probability, it will not be damaged by bombs. What is not clear is whether a unilateral undertaking pursuant to article 8(5) can also ground the grant of special protection to an improvised refuge. On the one hand, article 11(3) of the Regulations refers simply to 'the conditions laid down in Article 8 of the Convention', which would include paragraph 5 of that provision; on the other hand, the second sentence of article 8(5) requires that, in the case of ports, railway stations and aerodromes, the necessary diversion of all traffic is to be prepared in time of peace. But given that the second sentence of article 8(5) refers to a special case and that the object and purpose of its requirement is to facilitate the special protection of cultural property, it is logical to read the reference in article 11(3) of the Regulations 'to the conditions laid down in Article 8' as including article 8(5); as such, a unilateral undertaking pursuant to the latter

---

[251] As regards Commissioners-General for Cultural Property, see below.
[252] 1954 Hague Convention, art. 17(1)(c). In accordance with art. 17(1)(a), the distinctive emblem repeated three times is the mark of immovable cultural property under special protection.
[253] For the institution of Protecting Powers, see below.
[254] 1954 Hague Regulations, art. 11(3). In this event, the Director-General is directed by art. 15(3) of the Regulations to enter the property in the Register.

should be capable of forming the basis of a grant of such protection to an improvised refuge.

The interrelationship between article 11 of the Regulations and article 8(6) of the Convention calls for attention. Under article 8(6) of the Convention, special protection is granted to cultural property by its entry in the Register – that is, registration is the *sine qua non* of special protection.[255] Nothing in article 11 of the Regulations states or necessarily implies otherwise. As such, while a Commissioner-General for Cultural Property may, pursuant to article 11(2), authorise during armed conflict the display of the distinctive emblem on cultural property, that property will not enjoy special protection *de jure* unless and until the Director-General of UNESCO has, on the request of the Commissioner-General pursuant to article 11(3), entered the refuge in the Register. In this light, the display of the emblem in accordance with article 11(2) is presumably intended to afford improvised refuges *de facto* special protection insofar as a commander in the field confronted with a refuge bearing the distinctive emblem repeated three times is likely to assume, unless informed otherwise, that it benefits from special protection as a matter of law.

The Director-General of UNESCO is directed by article 16(1) of the Regulations to cancel the entry of cultural property in the Register at the request of the Party in whose territory it is situated[256] or if that Party denounces the Convention.[257] In addition, the Director-General must cancel a provisional entry made pursuant to the emergency procedure in article 14(5) in the event that the objection to the original application for registration is confirmed on the basis of article 14(7) or article 14(8).[258]

Immunity and its withdrawal

Article 9 embodies what is supposed to be the *raison d'être* of chapter II, namely the immunity of cultural property under special protection. Pursuant to this provision, the Parties undertake 'to ensure the immunity of cultural property under special protection by refraining, from the time of entry in the International Register, from any act of hostility directed

---

[255] See also 1954 Hague Convention, art. 9.
[256] 1954 Hague Regulations, art. 16(1)(a).
[257] *Ibid.*, art. 16(1)(b).
[258] *Ibid.*, art. 16(1)(c). In all cases provided for in art. 16 of the Regulations, cancellation takes effect thirty days after the dispatch by the Director-General to the UN Secretary-General and the Parties of a certified copy of the cancellation, in accordance with art. 16(2) of the Regulations.

against such property and, except for the cases provided for in paragraph 5 of Article 8, from any use of such property or its surroundings for military purposes'. The term 'act of hostility' in article 9 bears the same meaning as it does in article 4(1), extending beyond attacks to encompass demolitions. As for the second aspect of immunity, whereas article 4(1) speaks of any use of the property, of its immediate surroundings or of the appliances in use for its protection 'for purposes which are likely to expose it to destruction or damage in the event of armed conflict', article 9 prohibits any use of the property or its surroundings 'for military purposes'. In practice, there seems no real difference between the two expressions, and there is no evidence in the *travaux* that any was intended. The same goes for the omission from article 9 of article 4(1)'s reference to the appliances in use for the protection of the property. In both cases, it is reasonable to assume that the language of article 9 was intended by way of shorthand for the more detailed wording employed in article 4(1). As it is, when it comes to the use for military purposes of the appliances in use for the protection of cultural property under special protection, this would fall foul of article 9 as being use, in effect, of the cultural property itself or of its surroundings. The phrase 'from the time of entry in the International Register' makes it clear that the obligation to refrain from the use of specially protected cultural property for military purposes enures in peacetime as much as during armed conflict.[259] The exception in respect of 'the cases provided for in paragraph 5 of Article 8' is more cryptic, but its effect would seem to be to exempt a Party, in respect of cultural property granted special protection under article 8(5), from the obligation to refrain from using its surroundings for military purposes to the extent that this obligation applies during peacetime. As for hostilities, on the other hand, article 8(5) itself stipulates, and the object and purpose of article 9 make plain, that the surroundings of cultural property granted special protection by virtue of the former provision, like the surroundings of all other specially protected property, are not to be used for military purposes in the event of armed conflict.

Article 9 must be read, however, in conjunction with article 11, which deals with the withdrawal of the immunity enjoyed by cultural property under special protection. The cornerstone of article 11 is paragraph 2, the first sentence of which provides that, aside from the cases provided for in paragraph 1, 'immunity shall be withdrawn from cultural property under

---

[259] Recall, in this light, 1954 Hague Convention, art. 18(1): 'Apart from the provisions which shall take effect in time of peace, the present Convention shall apply'.

special protection only in exceptional cases of unavoidable military necessity, and only for such time as that necessity continues'. This constitutes the essence of special protection: in relation to cultural property under general protection, the obligation to refrain from any use of it, its immediate surroundings or the appliances in use for its protection for purposes which are likely to expose it to destruction or damage, and the obligation to refrain from any act of hostility directed against such property, may both be waived 'in cases where military necessity imperatively requires such a waiver', whereas, when it comes to cultural property under special protection, these same obligations may be waived only 'in exceptional cases of unavoidable military necessity'. In addition, the second sentence of article 11(2) specifies that such necessity can be established 'only by the officer commanding a force the equivalent of a division in size or larger'. The final sentence adds that, whenever circumstances permit, the opposing Party is to be notified a reasonable time in advance of the decision to withdraw immunity.

As with cultural property under general protection, the inclusion as regards cultural property under special protection of what is effectively a waiver in respect of military necessity proved controversial throughout the drafting process. But the committee of governmental experts responsible for the UNESCO draft thought that '[o]bviously, the military authorities could not accept so complete a prohibition' and that 'it must be accepted that exceptions will sometimes have to be made to this immunity',[260] a view that the majority of delegations were reluctantly prepared to accommodate to secure maximum participation in the Convention.[261]

The expression 'in exceptional cases of unavoidable military necessity', in contradistinction to 'where military necessity imperatively requires' as used in article 4(2), was intended, in the words of the committee of experts, to be understood 'as reflecting the greater degree of protection provided for in Chapter II'.[262] Beyond this, little more of use can be said,[263] and 'there is room for scepticism as to whether the semantic

---

[260] 7 C/PRG/7, Annex I, p. 10.
[261] A proposal to delete all reference to military necessity in relation to special protection was rejected in the Main Commission by 9:22:6. An analogous proposal was defeated in the Plenary Session by 7:20:14. The whole of art. 11 was eventually adopted by 28:0:14.
[262] 7 C/PRG/7, Annex I, p. 10.
[263] It should be borne in mind that what was said in the context of general protection as to the application of the concept of military necessity goes equally in the context of special protection; so too as regards incidental damage. Note also that the implication in *Kordić*,

difference resonates with practical consequences'.[264] It is not a difference which would commend itself to a court, especially one adjudicating charges of war crimes. Nor does the rider that the immunity may be withdrawn 'only for such time as [the military] necessity continues' add anything to the position which prevails under general protection, since it is a qualification already implicit in the words 'where military necessity imperatively requires'.[265] As for the obligation to notify, '[w]henever circumstances permit', the opposing Party a reasonable time in advance of the decision to withdraw immunity, in an ideal world this too would be taken as read in any genuine notion of imperative (and, *a fortiori,* unavoidable) military necessity, which presupposes that the military advantage in pursuit of which cultural property is used or made the object of an act of hostility cannot feasibly be attained any other way, since unless the opposing Party is put on notice and given the opportunity to come to an arrangement which does not demand the notifying Party's withdrawal of immunity from the cultural property in question, it cannot be said that this withdrawal is either imperatively or unavoidably necessary. (This world not being ideal, an explicit requirement of notice is a useful addition.)

Article 11(2)'s stipulation as to the level of command at which the unavoidable necessity to withdraw immunity must be established is potentially worthwhile. Presumably, the further up the chain of command the decision is taken, the fuller the intelligence-gathering and consultation possible, including the more likely the involvement of the specialist military personnel, along the lines of the MFA&A officers in the Second World War, provided for in article 7(2). In short, the higher the level of decision-making, the more informed the decision, it is to be hoped. Given that wrong or incomplete information – particularly as to whether an immovable is being used for military purposes – has regularly been the cause of the destruction and damage of significant cultural property, this practical provision is not to be dismissed lightly and is probably the major substantive difference between general and

Trial Chamber Judgment, para. 362, that use for military purposes is the sole reason for invoking military necessity in respect of cultural property under special protection is incorrect.

[264] Y. Dinstein, *The Conduct of Hostilities under the Law of International Armed Conflict* (Cambridge: Cambridge University Press, 2004), p. 159. See also S. E. Nahlik, 'La protection internationale des biens culturels en cas de conflit armé', 120 RCADI (1967-II) 61 at 132; Rogers, *Law on the Battlefield,* p. 145.

[265] It is also implicit in the words 'unavoidable military necessity' in art. 11(2).

special protection. That said, best practice dictates that a decision to waive the respect owed to generally protected cultural property should also be taken at the highest possible level.

Paragraph 1 of article 11 provides that if one of the Parties 'commits, in respect of any item of cultural property under special protection, a violation of the obligations under Article 9, the opposing Party shall, so long as this violation persists, be released from the obligation to ensure the immunity of the property concerned'.[266] In other words, in an exception to the non-synallagmatic nature of international humanitarian undertakings, article 11(1) states that the obligations assumed by way of article 9 are reciprocal, so that the principle *inadimplenti non est adimplendum* applies. This does not, however, mean that the opposing Party is thereby freed from all its obligations under the Convention in respect of that property: while it is released from the obligation laid down in article 9 to ensure its immunity, it remains bound by article 4(1) to respect the property in question – which remains cultural property within the meaning of article 1 – by refraining from any use of it and its surroundings or of the appliances in use for its protection[267] for purposes which are likely to expose it to destruction or damage and from any act of hostility directed against such property, except, as provided for by article 4(2), in cases where military necessity imperatively requires the waiver of the relevant obligation of respect. In short, the removal of immunity is not the removal of protection. The formal effect of article 11(1) is merely to allow the opposing Party to invoke the standard of military necessity available under article 4(2) ('in cases where military necessity imperatively requires'), instead of the stricter standard embodied in article 11(2) ('in exceptional cases of unavoidable military necessity'), and to free it from the procedural requirements as to

---

[266] A meeting of independent experts suggested in 1994 that 'the lifting of immunity from property under special protection only applied where it was the State where the property was located which had committed the violations of the Convention': UNESCO Doc. CLT/CH/94/608/2, pp. 6–7. There is no basis for this in the text of art. 11(1); indeed, the suggestion is contradicted by the provision's opening words, 'If one of the High Contracting Parties commits, in respect of any item of cultural property under special protection...'.

[267] In this light, a further reason for concluding that art. 4(1)'s reference to the appliances in use for the protection of cultural property should be read into art. 9 is to avoid the absurd result whereby the obligation to refrain from any use of such appliances for purposes likely to expose cultural property to damage or destruction would enure in respect of specially protected property stripped of its immunity under art. 11(1) but not in respect of property which continued to enjoy immunity under art. 9.

notification and the rank of the decision-maker stipulated in the latter. It is important to note too the requirement in article 11(1) that, before it can be released from article 9's obligation to ensure the immunity of cultural property under special protection, a Party must first, whenever possible, request the opposing Party to cease its violation of that obligation.

Article 11(3) states that the Party withdrawing immunity shall inform the Commissioner-General for Cultural Property as soon as possible in writing, stating the reasons. The word 'withdrawing' suggests that this obligation applies only to what is effectively the waiver of special protection under article 11(2), where the word 'withdraw' is used, and not also to a Party's so-called 'release', in accordance with article 11(1), from its obligation to ensure immunity in the first place. The *travaux* shed no light on this.

Identification and control

Article 10 provides that, during an armed conflict, cultural property under special protection is to be marked with the distinctive emblem. The emblem is repeated three times in the case of such property, in accordance with article 17(1)(a) of the Convention. Article 17(4), applicable to both special and general protection, further requires that the display of the emblem on immovable cultural property be accompanied by an authorisation duly dated and signed by the Party's competent authority. As article 10 itself makes clear, and in contradistinction to general protection, the use of the distinctive emblem to identify cultural property under special protection is mandatory during armed conflict. At the same time, as a function of the non-synallagmatic nature of humanitarian obligations, the failure to mark specially protected cultural property does not relieve the opposing Party of its obligation to ensure the immunity of the property, although it may have an impact on war crimes proceedings for a violation of the obligation.

In further accordance with article 10, cultural property under special protection 'shall be open to international control as provided for in the Regulations for the Execution of the Convention'. The stipulation is a curious one. No similar statement is to be found in relation to cultural property under general protection, which would appear to imply that the international control regime provided for in the Regulations applies only to cultural property under special protection. This is clearly not the case. The Regulations themselves are stated in terms applicable to special and general protection alike. Nor do the *travaux* suggest that the control regime is limited to the former. As for the subsequent practice of the Parties, the sole armed conflict in which Commissioners-General for Cultural Property have been appointed, namely the Six-Day War of 1967 and Israel's ensuing occupation of the territories overrun during the conflict, involved no specially protected cultural property. In this light, the second limb of article 10 is probably no more than a redundant and overlooked vestige of the drafting process.

Transport of cultural property

The vivid memory of truckloads of Renaissance Masters careering across Italy ahead of an Allied artillery barrage inspired the drafters of the Convention to make special provision for the transport of cultural property during armed conflict of an international character. The rules eventually adopted in chapter III ('Transport of cultural property') of the Convention and chapter III of the Regulations are equally applicable to transport by land, sea or air. The gist of these rules is the absolute immunity of duly authorised transports of cultural property.

The Convention's regime for the transport of cultural property has never formally[268] been put to use. For a start, *in situ* protection of movable cultural property has, from the point of view of conservation, always been preferable to relocation. Dismantling, packing, transport and storage all pose substantial risks, even in peacetime, to which curators are loathe to expose their exhibits if they can avoid it; and during the far more fraught conditions of war, no amount of legal restraint can insure against an adversary's mistake or malice.[269] Moreover, modern warfare tends not to involve clearly demarcated areas of opposing territorial control delineated by a firm and more-or-less predictable frontline, making the identification of in-country safe havens to which movables can be evacuated very difficult. In fact, a group of experts convened at the first

---

[268] During the international armed conflict in Cambodia in 1972, to which the Convention did not actually apply, many treasures were transported from Angkor to Phnom Penh on trucks displaying the distinctive emblem and driven by personnel wearing the armlet provided for in art. 21 of the Regulations: E. Clément and F. Quinio, 'La protection des biens culturels au Cambodge pendant la période des conflits armés, à travers l'application de la Convention de La Haye de 1954' (2004) 86 IRRC 389 at 394.

[269] The prospect, fanciful or real, of the latter was highlighted by Croatia when reporting on measures taken to safeguard cultural property during the war there in the early 1990s: *1995 Reports*, p. 22. (The conflict in Croatia in 1991, however, is best characterised as non-international, with the consequence that the Convention's regime for the transport of cultural property was not formally applicable.)

meeting of the High Contracting Parties to the Convention in 1962 considered that 'the principle of the protection of cultural property by removing it to safety should be abandoned in favour of the more realistic principle of immediate if incomplete protection on the spot'.[270] Added to this, the procedure under the Regulations for obtaining immunity for the transport of cultural property is unduly complicated and cedes an element of veto to the relevant Commissioner-General for Cultural Property with which Parties may be uncomfortable. Finally, the regime for the transport of cultural property depends on there having been appointed a Commissioner-General for Cultural Property, delegates of the Protecting Powers and, for that matter, Protecting Powers in the first place.[271] In other words, it depends on the functioning as intended of the Convention's regime of control. But the Convention's regime of control has never functioned as intended.

Article 12 of the Convention provides that means of transport exclusively engaged in the transfer of cultural property, within a territory or to another territory, may be placed under special protection at the request of the Party concerned.[272] The upshot is that the Parties must refrain from any act of hostility directed against them,[273] and that both they and the movable cultural property they are transporting are immune from seizure, placing in prize or capture.[274] The transport used must display the distinctive emblem repeated three times.[275] In accordance with article 17 of the Regulations, the Party wishing to obtain immunity for the transport of cultural property must address a request and requisite details to the Commissioner-General for Cultural Property accredited to it,[276] who, if satisfied that the transfer of the property to the proposed location is justified 'after taking such opinions as he [or she] deems fit', must consult the delegates of the Protecting Powers concerned as to the measures proposed for effecting it.[277] The Commissioner-General must then appoint one or more inspectors whose tasks it is, *inter alia*, to verify that only the cultural property listed in the request is to be transferred and to accompany the property to its destination.[278]

[270] CUA/120, p. 9.
[271] See 1954 Hague Regulations, art. 17.
[272] 1954 Hague Convention, art. 12(1).
[273] *Ibid.*, art. 12(3).
[274] *Ibid.*, art. 14(1).
[275] *Ibid.*, arts. 12(2) and 17(1)(b).
[276] 1954 Hague Regulations, art. 17(1). See also *ibid.*, art. 18(d).
[277] *Ibid.*, art. 17(2).
[278] *Ibid.*, art. 17(3).

In addition to the requirements of article 12 of the Convention and article 17 of the Regulations, article 18 of the Regulations makes supplementary provision for the transport of cultural property abroad. The subject was of concern to the drafters of the Convention in the combined light of Germany's specious claim during the Second World War that its removal of collections to the Reich was a protective measure; of the controversy over 202 artworks taken from Allied-occupied Wiesbaden at the end of the war for exhibition in the USA; of the dispute over certain Polish national treasures removed, just before the German invasion, eventually to Canada, where they remained long after the war was over; and of the analogous diplomatic tussle between the USA and Hungary over the crown of St Stephen and other coronation regalia.[279] Article 18 stipulates that as long as cultural property remains in the territory of another state, that state 'shall be its depositary and shall extend to it as great a measure of care as that which it bestows upon its own cultural property of comparable importance'.[280] It must continue to act as depositary until the end of the conflict, being obliged only then to return the property.[281] The property is to be exempt from confiscation and is not to be disposed of by either the depositary or, for the matter, the depositor, although the latter may consent to its transfer to a third country, should its safety require it.[282]

Article 13 of the Convention provides for an exception to the procedure for the transport of cultural property laid down in article 12 of the Convention and article 17 of the Regulations. In cases where the safety of cultural property requires its transfer, where the matter is of such urgency that the usual regime cannot be followed,[283] and where an application for immunity under article 12 has not already been refused, the means of transport used to transfer cultural property may display the

---

[279] As regards the last, see *Dole v. Carter*, 444 F Supp 1065 (1977), affirmed 569 F 2d 1109 (10th Cir. 1977).
[280] 1954 Hague Regulations, art. 18(a).
[281] *Ibid.*, art. 18(b).
[282] *Ibid.*, art. 18(c).
[283] Also relevant in this regard is art. 19 of the Regulations, which specifies that '[w]henever a High Contracting Party occupying territory of another High Contracting Party transfers cultural property to a refuge situated elsewhere in that territory, without being able to follow the procedure provided for in Article 17 of the Regulations, the transfer in question shall not be regarded as misappropriation within the meaning of Article 4 [paragraph 3] of the Convention, provided that the Commissioner-General for Cultural Property certifies in writing, after having consulted the usual custodians, that such transfer was rendered necessary by circumstances'.

distinctive emblem;[284] and although transport bearing the emblem pursuant to article 13 does not enjoy the immunity granted by article 12, the Parties are obliged to take, as far as possible, the necessary precautions to avoid acts of hostility against it.[285] Notification of any such transfer should, as far as possible, be given to the opposing Parties.[286] The emergency procedure provided for in article 13 is not, however, available when cultural property is transferred abroad. In such cases, means of transport may bear the distinctive emblem only when they are expressly granted immunity.[287]

Execution of the Convention

Convinced, curiously, that the destruction and plunder of cultural property in the First and Second World Wars was, to a considerable extent, a function of the absence of purpose-dedicated mechanisms to ensure compliance with the relevant international rules, the committee of experts brought together by UNESCO to prepare a draft text emphasised the need for a stringent regime for the execution of the Convention. At the same time, it eschewed as 'relatively complex and costly' the creation of a special international body to oversee compliance with the instrument.[288] Nor did UNESCO wish to take on the role, partially on account of not wanting to discourage non-Member States from becoming Parties to the Convention. In the event, the delegates to the intergovernmental conference agreed on a regime (embodied in chapter VII of the Convention) which, during armed conflict, combines the traditional reliance on so-called 'Protecting Powers' with an innovative, tripartite system of international 'control', and which allocates to UNESCO a subsidiary role exercisable also in peacetime. Breaches of the Convention are to be punished by penal or disciplinary sanctions imposed by the Parties. In addition, the Parties are to give an account of their implementation of the Convention in supposedly quadrennial reports, and can, if it be so desired, come together in meetings of the High Contracting Parties to discuss the application of the instrument.

---

[284] 1954 Hague Convention, art. 13(1).
[285] *Ibid.*, art. 13(2).
[286] *Ibid.*, art. 13(1).
[287] *Ibid.*
[288] 7 C/PRG/7, Annex I, p. 13.

Protecting Powers

Article 21 of the Convention states that the Convention and its Regulations are to be applied 'with the co-operation of the Protecting Powers responsible for safeguarding the interests of the Parties to the conflict'. The institution of the Protecting Power, a third state chosen by a belligerent Power to perform certain functions on its behalf vis-à-vis an opposing Power, is a venerable one, originating in the pragmatic need for channels of communication between hostile Powers against the backdrop of their likely severance of diplomatic relations. In accordance with article 22(1) of the Convention, the Protecting Powers are to lend their good offices in all cases where they may deem it useful in the interests of cultural property, particularly if there is disagreement between the belligerents as to the application or interpretation of the provisions of the Convention or Regulations. To this end, article 22(2) provides for a conciliation procedure whereby each of the Protecting Powers may – at the invitation of a Party or of the Director-General of UNESCO, or on its own initiative – propose to the Parties in conflict a meeting of their representatives, especially of the authorities responsible for the protection of cultural property, to be chaired by an independent person approved by the Parties; for their part, the Parties are bound to give effect to the proposals for meeting made to them. Both article 21 and article 22 are based on provisions common to the four Geneva Conventions.[289]

On the outbreak of an international armed conflict to which the Convention applies, the Protecting Power acting for a Party involved in the conflict is to appoint delegates accredited to the Party or Parties with which the latter is in conflict, as part of the regime of international control provided for by the Regulations.[290] In addition, the Protecting Power acting for a Party plays a role in the appointment of the respective Commissioners-General for Cultural Property to be accredited to the opposing Parties as another limb of the control regime.[291]

There is, however, no obligation on a state under either the Convention or customary international law to appoint a Protecting Power in the event of its involvement in an international armed conflict. Moreover, states have for decades eschewed the practice as cumbersome, an interference

---

[289] Geneva Convention I, arts. 8 and 11; Geneva Convention II, arts. 8 and 11; Geneva Convention III, arts. 8 and 11; Geneva Convention IV, arts. 9 and 12.
[290] 1954 Hague Regulations, art. 2(b).
[291] *Ibid.*, art. 4(1). A neutral state may be substituted for a Protecting Power when appointing a Commissioner-General for Cultural Property: *ibid.*, art. 9.

in high matters of state and obsolete. Indeed, the institution of the Protecting Power has effectively fallen into desuetude. Certainly in no conflict to which the Convention has applied has any of the Parties entrusted to a Protecting Power the safeguarding of its interests. As a result, the conciliation procedure provided for in article 22(2) of the Convention has never been put into effect.

Control regime

Chapter I of the Regulations provides for a regime of control to facilitate and supervise the execution of the Convention in the event of 'an armed conflict to which Article 18 of the Convention applies'.[292] This regime goes beyond that established under the Geneva Conventions in its elaborateness, and represented a notable innovation at the time. But it has never operated as designed. In no armed conflict has chapter I of the Regulations been implemented in whole. Indeed, in only a single conflict to which article 18 has applied[293] has any provision of chapter I been invoked, and even then dysfunctionally. The reasons for this are plain. First, the regime of control provided for is unwieldy and impractical. Its implementation depends on a degree of organisation, bureaucratic formality, agreement between the Parties and, quite simply, time that it is utterly unrealistic to wish for, let alone demand, under the conditions of modern armed conflict. Secondly, despite the considerable limitations it places on the freedom of action of the various functionaries,[294] it is still considerably more intrusive than most states at war could realistically be expected to stomach. Finally, with the benefit of modern telecommunications and the possibility of more flexible reliance on the arm's-length good offices of UNESCO, the UN Secretary-General,

---

[292] *Ibid.*, art. 2, chapeau. The reference to art. 18 of the Convention excludes, *inter alia*, non-international armed conflicts.

[293] Although Cambodia appointed a representative for cultural property in 1970, the armed conflict in question – of an international character involving, at a minimum, Cambodian, North Vietnamese and Viet Cong forces – was not one to which art. 18 and thus the regime of control actually applied, since only Cambodia was a Party to the Convention.

[294] Many of the powers of control are subject to the approval of the relevant Party to the conflict. In addition, art. 8 of the Regulations stipulates that the Commissioners-General for Cultural Property, delegates of the Protecting Powers, inspectors and experts 'shall take account of the security needs of the High Contracting Party to which they are accredited and shall in all circumstances act in accordance with the requirements of the military situation as communicated to them by that High Contracting Party'.

regional organisations and the ICRC, the regime of control envisaged in chapter I is all but redundant.

In accordance with article 2 of the Regulations, the Convention's regime of control has three distinct but complementary elements, namely the Parties' respective representatives for cultural property, the delegates of the respective Protecting Powers and the Commissioners-General for Cultural Property. Of this troika, the Commissioner-General appointed to each Party involved in the conflict was intended to have 'the supreme task of, and [be] responsible for, control'.[295] All three elements are designed to come into play immediately upon the outbreak of armed conflict. The result is supposed to be that each Party has its own representative for cultural property (as well as a representative for any and each territory occupied by it) and to have accredited to it delegates of the Protecting Power of each opposing Party and a Commissioner-General for Cultural Property.

Turning to the details of the scheme, article 2(a) of the Regulations stipulates that as soon as a Party is engaged in an international armed conflict governed by the Convention, it must appoint a representative for cultural property situated in its territory. In addition, if that Party is in belligerent occupation of any territory, it must appoint a special representative for cultural property situated in that territory. The functions of these representatives and special representatives for cultural property are not specified in the Regulations, although a fleeting reference in article 6(1) implies that their general mandate is to act in conjunction with the Commissioner-General for Cultural Property accredited to the Party they represent, and with the delegates of the relevant Protecting Powers, in dealing with all matters referred to the former in connection with the application of the Convention. But despite the obligation imposed by article 2(a), only once have representatives for cultural property been appointed in respect of an armed conflict to which article 18 of the Convention has applied[296] – namely, in respect of the Six-Day War between Israel and the Arab states in 1967 – and, even then, not until after the cessation of active hostilities.[297]

Pursuant to article 2(b) of the Regulations, on the outbreak of an international armed conflict to which the Convention applies, the

---

[295] 7 C/PRG/7, Annex I, p. 15.
[296] For Cambodia's appointment of a representative in 1970, see above.
[297] See *1970 Reports*, para. 15.

Protecting Power acting for a Party involved in the conflict is to appoint delegates accredited to the Party or Parties with which the latter is in conflict. Delegates are to be appointed from among the Protecting Power's diplomatic or consular staff, unless the Party to which they will be accredited agrees otherwise.[298] The functions of the delegates of a Protecting Power are to 'take note of violations of the Convention, investigate, with the approval of the Party to which they are accredited, the circumstances in which they have occurred, make representations locally to secure their cessation and, if necessary, notify the Commissioner-General [for Cultural Property] of such violations', and to keep the last informed of their activities.[299] They also play a role in relation to improvised refuges[300] and in obtaining immunity for the transport of cultural property.[301] But since no Party involved in an international armed conflict to which the Convention applied has ever appointed a Protecting Power, delegates of Protecting Powers have never been appointed either.

Finally, article 2(c) of the Regulations states that a Commissioner-General for Cultural Property is to be appointed to each Party involved in the conflict. In accordance with article 4(1), he or she shall be chosen from an international list, compiled by the Director-General of UNESCO pursuant to article 1, of persons nominated by the Parties as qualified to carry out the functions of Commissioner-General. The choice is to be made by joint agreement between the Party to which the Commissioner-General will be accredited and the Protecting Powers acting on behalf of the opposing Parties.[302] (Should any of the opposing Parties not benefit from the services of a Protecting Power, a neutral state may be substituted, as provided for in article 9.) In the event of a failure to reach agreement within three weeks, the Party in question and the Protecting Powers must request the president of the ICJ to appoint the Commissioner-General, an appointment which remains subject to the approval of that Party.[303] The respective Commissioners-General

---

[298] 1954 Hague Regulations, art. 3. In the event that a Party to the conflict does not benefit from the services of a Protecting Power, the Commissioners-General for Cultural Property accredited to the respective opposing Parties may entrust the functions of the Protecting Power's delegates to inspectors for cultural property: *ibid.*, art. 9. As regards inspectors for cultural property, see *ibid.*, art. 7.
[299] *Ibid.*, art. 5.
[300] *Ibid.*, art. 11.
[301] *Ibid.*, art. 17.
[302] *Ibid.*, art. 4(1).
[303] *Ibid.*, art. 4(2).

for Cultural Property are mandated to deal with all matters referred to them in connection with the application of the Convention, in conjunction with the representative for cultural property of the Party to which they are accredited and with the delegates of the Protecting Powers concerned.[304] Subject to the agreement of the Party to which they are accredited, they have the right to order or conduct an investigation.[305] They are also authorised to make any representations to the Parties to the conflict or to their Protecting Powers which they deem useful for the application of the Convention.[306] If necessary, they shall prepare reports on the application of the Convention for communication to the Parties concerned and to their Protecting Powers, sending copies to the Director-General of UNESCO.[307] The Commissioner-General for Cultural Property is also mandated to exercise the functions of Protecting Power should the Party to which he or she is accredited not benefit from one.[308] In addition, he or she may propose an inspector of cultural property to be charged with a special mission, along with relevant experts, and may, in the absence of a Protecting Power, entrust the functions of such Power's delegates to inspectors.[309] He or she also enjoys powers in relation to improvised refuges,[310] immunity for the transport of cultural property[311] and the transport of cultural property within occupied territory.[312]

On only a single occasion have Commissioners-General for Cultural Property been appointed,[313] and in that case two months after the cessation of active hostilities. In August 1967, in the wake of the Six-Day War, a Commissioner-General accredited to Israel and a single Commissioner-General accredited to the Arab states collectively were chosen according to the special procedure provided for in article 9

---

[304] Ibid., art. 6(1).
[305] Ibid., art. 6(3).
[306] Ibid., art. 6(4).
[307] Ibid., art. 6(5). The Director-General 'may make use only of [the] technical contents' of the reports: ibid.
[308] Ibid., art. 6(6).
[309] Ibid., arts. 7(1), 7(2) and 9 respectively. These are the powers of appointment of the Commissioner-General referred to in art. 6(2).
[310] Ibid., art. 11.
[311] Ibid., art. 17.
[312] Ibid., art. 19.
[313] The failure of the system of Commissioners-General for Cultural Property led a meeting of legal experts held in Vienna in 1983 to question whether UNESCO should play a wider role in their appointment: CLT.83/CONF.641/1, para. 34.

of the Regulations. No Parties to the conflict having designated a Protecting Power, Switzerland agreed as a neutral state to undertake, in respect of each of them, the function of the Protecting Power under article 4(1) in the appointment of a Commissioner-General.[314] While their presence would have been advantageous during the fighting, the assumption by the Commissioners-General of their duties after combat operations had ceased was far from pointless, given Israel's presence as belligerent occupant in the West Bank (including, and especially, the Old City of Jerusalem), Gaza and the Golan Heights. Moreover, the Commissioner-General accredited to the Arab side visited a range of museums and archaeological sites in Egypt with a view to assisting the Egyptian authorities to select immovable cultural property for special protection.[315] In support of these various endeavours, the Executive Board of UNESCO approved the setting up of 'a special fund, supplied by a contribution from the countries concerned and a sum allocated by the Organisation, to be used ... for the payment of the salaries and expenses of the Commissioners-General in accordance with Article 10 of the Regulations for the execution of the Convention'[316] – even though article 10 itself provides that the remuneration and expenses of Commissioners-General for Cultural property are to be met by the Party to which they are accredited. The Board also invited the Director-General to make the necessary arrangements to enable the Commissioners-General to enjoy the privileges and immunities granted to senior officials of UN specialised agencies under the Convention on the Privileges and Immunities of the Specialized Agencies.[317] On the death in 1972 of the Commissioner-General accredited to the Arab states, a replacement was successfully appointed. When both Commissioners-General stepped down separately in 1977, Switzerland again undertook to discharge the functions of the respective Protecting Powers under article 4(1).[318] A Commissioner-General to be accredited to Israel was agreed on and appointed, but the Commissioner-General chosen for the Arab states was unable to take up his

---

[314] *1970 Reports*, para. 15.
[315] *Ibid.*, p. 24. In the event, no applications for special protection were made.
[316] 77 EX/Decision 4.4.4, para. 6.
[317] *Ibid.*, para. 5(a). See Convention on the Privileges and Immunities of the Specialized Agencies, New York, 21 November 1947, 33 UNTS 261.
[318] *1979 Reports*, paras. 13–17.

appointment, and a replacement had to be found.[319] Agreement was never reached.[320]

UNESCO's role

The idea that UNESCO might act as 'the supreme controlling body' in relation to the Convention was dispensed with by the drafters out of a desire to see non-Members of the Organisation become Parties.[321] UNESCO's functions under the Convention were instead to be 'subsidiary': in addition to its role as depositary, the Organisation was envisaged as providing 'purely technical assistance, i.e. non-financial assistance' to the Parties.[322]

Pursuant to article 23(1) of the Convention, the Parties may call upon UNESCO 'for technical assistance in organizing the protection of their cultural property, or in connexion with any other problem arising out of the application of the ... Convention or the Regulations for its execution'. The reference to 'protection' includes, as defined in article 2, both safeguard and respect; and, as a corollary, article 23(1) may be invoked both in peacetime and during armed conflict. UNESCO, for its part, is mandated to accord such assistance 'within the limits fixed by its programme and by its resources', in the words of article 23(1). That is, technical assistance may 'not involve expenditure over and above that provided for in the UNESCO programme and budget approved by its Member States'.[323]

The drafters used the term 'technical' assistance to refer to non-financial assistance, and such assistance has typically taken the form of the provision of expertise. So, for example, at the request of the Egyptian (and Israeli) authorities for technical assistance in preserving the monastery of St Catherine in the wake of the Sinai War in 1956, UNESCO sent an expert 'to ascertain that this monument and the valuable collections housed in it were in a satisfactory state of

---

[319] UNESCO Doc. 120 EX/14, para. 10.
[320] Similarly, in the Iran−Iraq War of 1980−8, to which art. 18 applied and which saw considerable destruction of Iranian cultural property, a failure to agree stymied the application of chap. I of the Regulations for the duration of the conflict: see *1989 Reports*, paras. 12−14.
[321] 7 C/PRG/7, Annex I, p. 13.
[322] *Ibid.* The Organisation accepted the role conferred on it by the Convention and First Protocol in 8 C/Resolution 4.1.4.133, para. 3, reaffirming this in 24 C/Resolution 11.2, para. 1.
[323] Toman, *Protection of Cultural Property*, p. 263.

preservation after the military operations in the region'.³²⁴ In response to Cambodia's request in June 1970 for technical assistance in organising the protection of its cultural property in the face of North Vietnamese and Viet Cong attacks, the Director-General dispatched an expert to assess the situation and to make recommendations accordingly, followed by a team of technical experts with special equipment to facilitate the packing and storage of movable cultural property at the Angkor Conservancy and at the National Museum in Phnom Penh.³²⁵ When, in June 1982, the Lebanese authorities requested that the Director-General send a personal representative to the archaeological site at Tyre in southern Lebanon after fighting between Israeli and PLO forces in the area, the Director-General sent a team comprising two members of the UNESCO Secretariat and two international experts to report to him on the state of preservation of the site and to propose emergency measures to protect and preserve it, followed by an expert to advise on placing 150 signs bearing the Convention's distinctive emblem, prepared at UNESCO's expense, around it.³²⁶ At the further request of the Lebanese government, UNESCO sent two archaeologists to Tyre in February 1983.³²⁷

[324] *1967 Reports*, para. 14; *1970 Reports*, para. 14. See also *UNESCO Chronicle*, vol. III, no. 3, March 1957, p. 56.
[325] UNESCO Doc. 85 EX/9; *1979 Reports*, paras. 19–21; Clément and Quinio, 'La protection des biens culturels au Cambodge', at 391–2. Others measures initiated by the expert were the preparation of the armlets and identification cards provided for in art. 21 of the Regulations for personnel at the Angkor Conservancy and the placing of the distinctive emblem on several monuments at Angkor, on the National Museum, the National Library and the Archives in Phnom Penh and on the museum at Wat Po Veal in Battambang. Another expert mission was sent soon afterwards to formulate a long-term plan for the protection of cultural property in Cambodia.
[326] 22 C/INF.8, paras. 7–8; *1984 Reports*, paras. 15, 17 and 19. The Lebanese request was prompted by the Director-General's offer of 'such technical assistance as [Lebanon] might wish in order to organize the protection of its cultural property affected by the conflict': *1984 Reports*, para. 14. The offer was made pursuant to art. 23(2) and to para. 1 of 21 C/Resolution 4/13, adopted after Lebanon's request in 1980 for measures in respect of Tyre, in which the General Conference authorised the Director-General 'to continue his action ... by all means available to him' 'to promote the preservation of [the] site and the invaluable relics which it contains'. Lebanon also requested the Director-General to remind the Israeli authorities that 'they were forbidden by international law to do any damage or carry out any archaeological excavation whatsoever': *1984 Reports*, para 15.
[327] 22 C/INF.8, para. 10; *1984 Reports*, para 19. The Director-General later appointed an advisor on the preservation of the site, pursuant to the mandate granted him by the General Conference in para. 2 of 21 C/Resolution 4/13 'to appoint an adviser for the cultural heritage of the archaeological site of Tyre and its surrounding area, whose duty it will be to report to him on the situation and to assist all concerned to determine the emergency measures to be taken to protect and preserve the cultural heritage of all the civilizations concerned'.

The qualifier 'in connexion with any other problem arising out of the application of the present Convention or the Regulations' is open-textured enough to accommodate requests for most forms of non-financial assistance. Certainly, when on 7 June 1982 the Lebanese government appealed to the Director-General to call for a halt to all military operations between Israeli and PLO forces on the archaeological site at Tyre and the surrounding area, the Director-General requested that 'military operations cease immediately in the region of Tyre and that the necessary measures be taken to safeguard this irreplaceable cultural property'.[328] He also 'urgently requested the Member States and all the national and international organizations to use their influence to put an end to all hostilities'.[329] Some have argued that technical assistance under article 23(1) may even extend to forms of non-legal dispute settlement such as conciliation and mediation.[330] It seems, however, that technical assistance in connection with a problem arising out of the application of the Convention does not extend to the quasi-judicial function of construing the text for the Parties. When, pursuant to article 23(1), Japan sought an interpretation of the First Protocol, UNESCO declined, on the ground that interpretation of the instrument was a matter for the Parties; and to Switzerland's request for clarification of article 34 of the Convention, the UNESCO Secretariat merely referred the Swiss authorities to certain passages of the *travaux préparatoires*, without comment or elucidation.[331]

In contrast with the Convention's regime of control, which is applicable only to armed conflicts to which article 18 applies,[332] the sole limitation on the invocation of article 23(1) during armed conflict, including belligerent occupation, is the same one applicable during

---

[328] 22 C/INF.8, para. 6; *1984 Reports*, paras. 12–13. The Director-General's appeal also rested on the mandate given him by the General Conference in para. 1 of 21 C/Resolution 4/13. In response, the PLO 'assured the Director-General that it would do its utmost to safeguard Tyre and all the cultural property situated in Lebanon and to preserve them from the ... hostilities': *1984 Reports*, para. 16. Israel replied that 'the presence of "terrorist groups" of the Palestine Liberation Organization using the archaeological site as an ammunition depot and as an artillery emplacement was what, until then, had prevented the site from being adequately protected': *ibid.*, para. 18.

[329] 22 C/INF.8, para. 6; *1984 Reports*, para. 13.

[330] J. A. R. Nafziger, 'UNESCO-Centred Management of International Conflict Over Cultural Property' (1976) 27 Hastings LJ 1051 at 1061 and 1067; Toman, *Protection of Cultural Property*, p. 261; Chamberlain, *War and Cultural Heritage*, p. 79.

[331] Toman, *Protection of Cultural Property*, p. 261. See also Chamberlain, *War and Cultural Heritage*, p. 79.

[332] 1954 Hague Regulations, art. 2, chapeau.

peacetime, namely whether the state requesting technical assistance is a Party to the Convention. This is borne out by the practice of UNESCO. When the Organisation dispatched its expert to the Sinai in 1956, only Egypt, formally the requesting state, was a Party, and the request was later explicitly characterised as pursuant to article 23.[333] The same is true *mutatis mutandis* of Cambodia's request and UNESCO's response in 1970.

In accordance with the principle, reflected in article 5, that the safeguard and preservation of cultural property in occupied territory remains the responsibility of the competent national authorities, the Party whose territory is partially or totally occupied remains competent to call upon UNESCO for technical assistance in organising the protection of cultural property in the territory under occupation. This is clear from article 23(1), with its reference to 'their' cultural property. In 1956, while both Egypt and Israel requested UNESCO's assistance in respect of St Catherine's monastery in the occupied Sinai, only the former – the state whose territory was partially occupied – was a Party to the Convention, meaning that only it could possibly, as a matter of treaty law, have been competent to make the request; and the fact that the request was acceded to meant that it was, in fact, competent. In 1982, when the archaeological site at Tyre came under Israeli occupation, it was the Lebanese authorities which requested the Director-General's technical assistance; indeed, it was the Lebanese authorities that the Director-General, acting pursuant to article 23(2), prompted to make this request and to whom the report of the resulting expert mission was transmitted.[334] As for the Israeli authorities, the Director-General simply informed them of his decision to send a team of experts to Tyre.[335]

Under article 23(2), UNESCO is authorised to make, on its own initiative, proposals to the Parties on technical assistance in organising the protection of their cultural property or in connection with any other problem arising out of the application of the Convention. As with article 23(1), such assistance may relate both to peacetime measures of safeguard and to measures of respect in armed conflict. At the intergovernmental conference, the UK delegate 'objected very strongly' to the conferral of this right of initiative on the Organisation, foreseeing that '[d]ifficulties would arise if international organizations were to approach

---

[333] *1967 Reports*, para. 14; *1970 Reports*, para. 14.
[334] *1984 Reports*, paras. 14 and 19.
[335] *Ibid.*, para. 17. In reply, the Israeli authorities expressed their readiness to receive the team: *ibid.*, para. 18.

sovereign governments with suggestions as to what those governments were to do'.³³⁶ He thought that 'if a country were approached by Unesco with offers of assistance which it had not invited, it would be placed in an invidious and embarrassing position'.³³⁷ His proposal to delete the provision was soundly defeated.³³⁸ As it is, UNESCO is, on the one hand, prohibited by article I(3) of its Constitution 'from intervening in matters which are essentially within [Member States'] domestic jurisdiction'. On the other hand, the Parties acknowledge in the preamble to the Convention that the Convention's concerns are not matters within their *domaine réservé*: they declare themselves 'convinced that damage to cultural property belonging to any people whatsoever means damage to the cultural heritage of all mankind', and they consider, in this light, that 'the preservation of the cultural heritage is of great importance for all peoples of the world and that it is important that this heritage should receive international protection'. Article 23(2) reflects these statements of principle.³³⁹ Nonetheless, while the Parties are estopped from objecting to a proposal for technical assistance on the ground that it is an internal matter in which UNESCO has no right to intervene, they are under no obligation to accept any proposal made.

At the first meeting of the High Contracting Parties, held in 1962, it was recommended – in the spirit of suggestions made by some states during the drafting³⁴⁰ – that the Director-General of UNESCO set up a technical advisory committee to assist him in discharging the duties assigned to the Organisation in article 23, especially as regards '(a) the drawing up of a programme of action with a view to the application of the Convention by the different States, (b) the entry of cultural property under special protection in the International Register, (c) the dissemination of information and documents on the application of the Convention, [and] (d) the co-ordination of the activities of the national advisory committee, the establishment of which is advocated in resolution II, appended to the Final Act of the International Conference at The Hague'.³⁴¹ The committee 'would consist of some 20 members of different

---

[336] *Records 1954*, para. 736.
[337] *Ibid.*, para. 767.
[338] The margin was 20:4:6.
[339] 'In giving UNESCO this mandate, the [Parties] thereby recognized that the protection of cultural property was no longer an internal affair but a question of concern to the whole of humanity and the international community in general': Toman, *Protection of Cultural Property*, p. 259.
[340] CBC/DR/129 and 130.
[341] CUA/120, para. 16.

nationalities serving in their personal capacity and appointed by the Director-General from among the best qualified experts of the High Contracting Parties to the Convention',[342] by which the meeting meant 'experts on the different matters covered by the Convention (viz. legal, technical, military and organisational questions)'.[343] It was thought desirable for this committee to meet at least once a year.[344] The meeting acknowledged that a committee of this sort could be established only with UNESCO's co-operation, and considered that the assistance of the Organisation's Secretariat, authorised by a decision of the General Conference, 'could ensure possession by the proposed body of the necessary means, authority and prestige'.[345] The recommendation appears not to have been welcomed by the Director-General, who did nothing in furtherance of it, and it sank without a trace.[346]

The textbook example of a proposal made under article 23(2) was when, just after the Six-Day War of 1967, the Director-General of UNESCO offered and lent his services to facilitate the appointment, with the co-operation of Switzerland as neutral Power, of a Commissioner-General for Cultural Property accredited to each side, eventually hosting a meeting of representatives of the Parties to the conflict at UNESCO headquarters in Paris.[347] When replacement Commissioners-General were required ten years later, both sides were informed 'that the Secretariat remained – within the limits of its competence – at the disposal of the parties concerned in connection with further steps to be taken'.[348] In June 1982, on Israel's invasion of Lebanon, the Director-General offered 'such technical assistance as [Lebanon] might wish in order to organize the protection of its cultural property affected by the conflict', within the limits of the Organisation's programme and the resources available.[349] In 1984–5, during the Iran–Iraq War, the Director-General offered technical assistance to the belligerents in more general terms.[350] He also negotiated with them until the ceasefire in July 1988 with a view to implementing the Convention's regime of control,

---

[342] *Ibid.*
[343] *Ibid.*, para. 13.
[344] *Ibid.*, para. 16.
[345] *Ibid.*, para. 15.
[346] The idea was revived in the 1990s and eventually embodied, in modified form, in arts. 24–8 of the Second Hague Protocol.
[347] UNESCO Doc. 77 EX/32.
[348] *1979 Reports*, para. 16.
[349] *1984 Reports*, para. 14.
[350] UNESCO Doc. 121 EX/INF.3 (prov.), p. 17.

especially as regards the appointment of Commissioners-General, sending personal representatives to Iran in October 1985, to Iraq in January 1986, and again to Iran in March 1987.[351] The High Contracting Parties to the Convention subsequently 'endorse[d] the initiatives taken by the Director-General during armed conflicts in offering to send his personal representatives in order to advise on the implementation of the Convention'.[352]

As it has transpired, with the moribundity of the Convention's regime of control, the intervention of UNESCO on the outbreak of and during hostilities, and during belligerent occupation, has assumed the character of a compliance mechanism, with the apparent acquiescence of the Parties. The Organisation has consistently taken it upon itself to call on Parties involved in an armed conflict to adhere to their conventional obligations. The precise legal basis on which it has done this in any given case has never been specified: in some instances, it is possible to see UNESCO's intervention as an exercise of its right of initiative under article 23(2) 'in connexion with any ... problem arising out of the application' of the Convention; on other occasions, the interventions in question have more likely – and, where they have gone beyond the scope of the Convention altogether, must have – been based on the Organisation's general mandate under article I(2)(c) of its Constitution to assure 'the conservation and protection of the world's inheritance of books, works of art and monuments of history and science'.

The Director-General has established a routine practice of communicating with the hostile Parties on the outbreak of an armed conflict to which the Convention applies to remind them of their obligations under the Convention. When fighting broke out in the Middle East on 5 June 1967, the Director-General sent telegrams to the ministers for foreign affairs of Israel, Jordan, Lebanon, Syria and the United Arab Republic (Egypt), drawing their attention to their respective states' obligations under the Convention, especially the obligation to respect cultural property laid down in article 4(1), and the provisions of the Regulations establishing the regime of international control.[353] He followed this up with a note-verbale of 8 June 1967 to all the Parties to the conflict emphasising the duty to implement the control regime,

---

[351] *1989 Reports*, paras. 12 and 14.
[352] Resolution adopted by the second meeting of the High Contracting Parties to the Convention, UNESCO Doc. CLT-95/CONF.009/5, Annex I, para. 3.
[353] 77 EX/32, para. 1.

along with a note to Israel of the same date reminding it of its obligations under article 5.[354] When India invaded East Pakistan in 1971 and Turkey invaded Cyprus in 1974, the Acting Director-General sent telegrams to the belligerent states — all of which were Parties to the Convention — drawing their attention, in particular, to article 4's obligation of respect and to the obligation to implement the regime of control.[355] The Director-General did the same on Iraq's invasion of Iran in 1980, both states being Parties to the Convention.[356] In the case of Cyprus, '[n]ot having received any ackowledgement from the Government of Turkey the Acting Director-General sent a further telegram to that Government ... recalling the terms of the previous telegram and expressing his concern [over] the fate of important archaeological and historical monuments and sites as well as other cultural property in areas controlled by the Turkish army; he also appealed to the Government of Turkey to do its utmost to safeguard this cultural property and referred again to Article 4, paragraph 1 of the Convention'.[357] Following Iraq's invasion of Kuwait, also a High Contracting Party, in August 1990, the Director-General wrote to the former's Permanent Delegate to UNESCO to remind him of Iraq's obligations under the Convention and First Protocol.[358] Later, as the armed forces of the multinational coalition opposing Iraq amassed on its border in January 1991, the Director-General made two public appeals for observance by all the parties of the Hague Convention.[359] In addition, he drew the attention of the UN Secretary-General to resolution I of the Final Act of the Intergovernmental Conference, which expressed the hope that, in the event of military action under chapter VII of the Charter, the competent organs of the UN would ensure the application of the Convention's provisions by the armed forces involved.[360] When Coalition forces finally commenced Operation Desert Storm in February 1991 with the aim of removing Iraq from Kuwait, the

---

[354] *Ibid.*, para. 4.
[355] *1979 Reports*, paras. 22–3.
[356] *1984 Reports*, para. 22. Iraq took a month to reply, and then simply asserted its compliance. Iran took a year and a half, stating eventually that, as it had ratified the Convention, it went without saying that it would 'continue to comply with it as it ha[d] done to date': *ibid.*
[357] *1979 Reports*, para. 22.
[358] UNESCO Doc. 136 EX/31, para. 2.
[359] *1995 Reports*, para. 13. While Iraq and twenty-seven member states of the multinational coalition opposing it were Parties to the Convention, the USA and UK, the major contributors of forces to the coalition, were not.
[360] 136 EX/31, para. 2; *1995 Reports*, para. 13.

Director-General called for 'scrupulous compliance with the obligations and duties imposed by international law and in particular by the ... Convention'.[361]

The Director-General has also on occasion intervened in the course of hostilities when notified of possible breaches of the Convention. When the team of archaeologists sent by him to Tyre in February 1983 reported that earthworks being carried out by Israeli forces were encroaching on one area of the site, the Director-General wrote to draw the Israelis' attention 'to the care that should be taken to preserve the archaeological area of the hippodrome of Tyre'.[362] He wrote again when Israel's reply failed to mention the specific issue of the earthworks.[363] On 27 March 1985, after reports that Iraqi bombardment had damaged the Friday Mosque in Isfahan, the Director-General telexed the Ministry of Foreign Affairs of Iraq, drawing attention once more to the Convention and asking Iraq to refrain from action which might damage or destroy such property. Three days later, he telexed the Iranian Ministry of Foreign Affairs to the same effect, after Iraqi allegations of damage to the Imam Ali mosque in Basra caused by Iranian attacks. He also urged both Parties to implement the regime of control.[364]

In addition to the activities of the Director-General, both the General Conference and Executive Board of UNESCO have sought, within the scope of their respective competences, to secure compliance with the Convention during armed conflict, including belligerent occupation, issuing public calls in their respective resolutions and decisions for adherence to its provisions. In 1968, à propos of Israel's conduct in the Palestinian territories occupied by it the previous year, especially the Old City of Jerusalem, the General Conference recommended Member States 'to take, with the help of the two Commissioners-General, all necessary measures to conform to the articles of the Convention'.[365] The following

---

[361] UNESCO Doc. 136 EX/INF.3, para. 49.
[362] 22 C/INF.8, para. 10. See also *1984 Reports*, para. 19.
[363] 22 C/INF.8, para. 10; *1984 Reports*, para. 19. See also the Director-General's much later interventions when renewed fighting threatened Tyre: UNESCOPRESS No. 96–77, 23 April 1996; UNESCOPRESS No. 96–85, 3 May 1996.
[364] 121 EX/INF.3 (prov.), pp. 16–17.
[365] 15 C/Resolution 3.342, para. 2. In 15 C/Resolution 3.343, the General Conference – '[a]ware of the exceptional importance of the cultural property in the old city of Jerusalem, particularly the Holy Places, not only to the States directly concerned but to all humanity, on account of their artistic, historical and religious value', and '[n]oting resolution 2253 (ES-V) ['Measures taken by Israel to change the status of the City of Jerusalem'] adopted by the United Nations General Assembly on 4 July 1967,

year, the Executive Board asked the Israeli occupation authorities 'to conform strictly to the obligations set out in the Hague International Convention'.[366] Subsequently, expressing 'its deep concern at the violations by Israel of The Hague Convention', it invited Israel 'to adhere scrupulously' to the instrument.[367] Almost identically to these and later decisions of the Executive Board,[368] the General Conference urgently called upon Israel in 1972 'to adhere scrupulously to the provisions of the Convention for the Protection of Cultural Property in the Event of Armed Conflict (The Hague, 1954)'.[369] As regards the Iran–Iraq War of 1980–8, the General Conference appealed to the governments of both countries at its twenty-third and twenty-fourth sessions 'to abide strictly by international humanitarian principles and regulations, and particularly by those relating to the protection of the cultural and natural heritage'.[370] In November 1991, after Iraq's invasion and occupation of Kuwait, the Executive Board expressed

---

concerning the city of Jerusalem' – urgently called upon Israel, 'in accordance with the said United Nations resolution', 'to preserve scrupulously all the sites, buildings, and other cultural properties, especially in the old city of Jerusalem', and 'to desist from any archaeological excavations, transfer of such properties and changing of their features [or] their cultural and historical character'. It invited the Director-General 'to use all the influence and means at his disposal, in co-operation with all parties concerned, to ensure the best possible implementation of this resolution'. Pursuant to this mandate, the Director-General dispatched a special consultant to Jerusalem.

[366] 82 EX/Decision 4.4.2, para. 4.
[367] 83 EX/Decision 4.3.1, paras. 5 and 6(c). The Executive Board also invited the Director-General to 'seek the means of ensuring the rigorous and effective application' of the Convention: *ibid.*, para. 7(b). In para. 8, the Board further requested the Director-General 'to consult the Governments Parties to The Hague Convention on the advisability of calling, as soon as possible, a meeting of the High Contracting Parties with a view to studying means whereby the scope of the said Convention can be made clear and its efficacy enhanced and to report to the Board at its next session on the application of this decision'.
[368] See 88 EX/Decision 4.3.1, para. 6(c); 89 EX/Decision 4.4.1, para. 7(c).
[369] 17 C/Resolution 3.422, para. 2(d). After this, the question of the conduct of the Israeli occupation authorities in Jerusalem took on a life of its own within UNESCO's programme, becoming a matter of Israel's failure to comply with the decisions of the Executive Board and the resolutions of the General Conference. The relevant resolutions at the eighteenth to twenty-second sessions of the General Conference make no mention of the Convention. Since then, the routine resolutions and decisions on Jerusalem recall the Convention in the preamble but make no reference to it in the operative provisions. But *cf.* 121 EX/Decision 5.4.1 and 125 EX/Decision 5.4.1, referring to the Convention in the operative paragraphs.
[370] 23 C/Resolution 28, para. 2; 24 C/Resolution 29, para. 2. See also 121 EX/Decision 7.9; 129 EX/Decision 8.10.

its deep anxiety at 'the wilful damaging of ... cultural institutions and property and the destruction of the national cultural identity of the Kuwaiti people', and strongly condemned such measures.[371]

UNESCO also enjoys a right of initiative in respect of non-international armed conflict. Paragraph 3 of article 19, dealing with conflicts not of an international character, provides that UNESCO 'may offer its services to the parties to the conflict'. The provision was modelled on the ICRC's right of initiative under article 3 common to the Geneva Conventions. It is not clear whether the word 'services' in article 19(3) was intended to have a wider meaning than the term 'technical assistance' used in article 23, although on the ordinary meaning of the language it does. That said, given that article 23 has been interpreted broadly, there is probably very little, if any, difference in scope between UNESCO's rights of initiative in international and non-international armed conflict respectively. The most straightforward invocation of article 19(3) came in 1968 when, on a visit to Nigeria to discuss the application of the Convention in the civil war of 1966–70, the Director-General offered the Organisation's services to the parties to the conflict.[372] More creatively, when Israel's military reoccupation of the West Bank towns administered by the Palestinian Authority under the Oslo Accords triggered fighting with Palestinian militants in April 2002, resulting in extensive damage to the medina in Nablus and threatening other immovable cultural property, the Director-General expressed his readiness to lend his services to 'any mediation that might help to save lives and irreplaceable monuments'.[373]

Like article 23, article 19(3) has been used by the various organs of UNESCO as a basis on which to appeal for compliance with the Convention. In mid-1991, as war loomed in Yugoslavia after Slovenia and Croatia's respective declarations of independence, the Director-General contacted the relevant authorities to remind them of their

---

[371] 135 EX/Decision 8.4.
[372] *1970 Reports*, para. 16. The Nigerian government replied a year and a half later, stating 'that it was not inclined to accept an offer of services'. But it assured the Director-General 'that the Federal Military Government and its agencies had scrupulously observed the provisions of the Convention and forwarded to him a code of behaviour to be observed by the armed forces, a report drawn up by international observers in the country and the text of the law on antiquities which protects cultural property': *ibid*. In the event, the Oron Museum in Cross River State was destroyed and 600 of its 800 wood-carved ancestral figures were looted.
[373] Executive Office of the Director-General, 'The Director-General of UNESCO Launches an Appeal for the Protection of Historic, Cultural and Religious Heritage in the Palestinian Autonomous Towns', Press Release, 11 April 2002.

obligations under the Convention and First Protocol, and sent several missions to Belgrade and Zagreb to this end.[374] After the outbreak of hostilities in August in Croatia, the Director-General sent a telegram to the Yugoslav minister for foreign affairs, calling for compliance with the Convention by the Yugoslav National Army (JNA), with particular emphasis on the World Heritage sites of the Old City of Dubrovnik and Diocletian's Palace in Split.[375] He appealed twice more in 1991 to both the Yugoslav and Croatian authorities for observance of the provisions of the Convention,[376] and in October that year issued a joint appeal with the UN Secretary-General to this effect.[377] For its part, the General Conference 'urgently appeal[ed] to the conflicting parties in Yugoslavia to take all necessary measures, under the terms of the Hague Convention, to protect the cultural ... heritage'; in particular, it 'urge[d] the opposing forces to withdraw from the city of Dubrovnik which is included in the World Heritage List and whose splendour belongs to the whole of humanity'.[378] The Director-General subsequently dispatched two observers to Dubrovnik's Old City from 27 November to 22 December in the hope of deterring further attacks after incidents on 23–24 October and 9–12 November.[379] When, on 6 December 1991, members of the JNA fired hundreds of shells at the Old City (in violation of 'JNA orders and directives emphasising the requirement to avoid engaging or damaging the Old Town under any circumstances'[380]), the observer mission contacted the Director-General, who immediately requested the Yugoslav federal minister for defence to put a stop to the bombardment.[381] He protested again after subsequent shelling in May and June 1992, and, following renewed threats against the Old City in August 1995,

---

[374] *1995 Reports*, para. 16.
[375] UNESCO Doc. 137 EX/INF.5, para. 37. UNESCO characterised the conflict at that point as non-international. The respective Trial Chambers of the ICTY in *Prosecutor v. Jokić*, IT-01-42/1-S, Trial Chamber Sentencing Judgment, 18 March 2004 and in *Strugar* were not required to decide the question.
[376] UNESCO Docs. 140 EX/INF.3, para. 10 and 141 EX/22, para. 157; *Records of the General Conference, Twenty-sixth session*, Vol. 3: *Proceedings*, pp. 632–3; *1995 Reports*, paras. 16–17. Furthermore, in October 1991, the Director-General contacted the Chairman of the EC Conference on Yugoslavia, asking him to draw the attention of the relevant parties to the need to protect the cultural heritage: *1995 Reports*, para. 16.
[377] *Records of the General Conference, Twenty-sixth session*, p. 633.
[378] 26 C/Resolution 0.10.
[379] UNESCO Doc. 139 EX/INF.3, para. 74.
[380] *Jokić*, para. 39. The Trial Chamber in *Strugar* concluded at para. 280 that 'there was no possible military necessity for the attack on the Old Town on 6 December 1991'.
[381] *1995 Reports*, para. 18.

warned against further attacks, recalling once more the obligations laid down in the Convention.[382] Similarly, when the Israel Defence Forces reoccupied the Palestinian autonomous towns of the West Bank in April 2002, the Director-General wrote to both the Israeli minister for foreign affairs and the president of the Palestinian Authority, calling on them to do everything within their power to ensure compliance with the Convention.[383]

In addition, UNESCO has acted pursuant to the general mandate conferred on it by article I(2)(c) of its Constitution, that is, to ensure 'the conservation and protection of the world's inheritance of books, works of art and monuments of history and science',[384] to urge Member States not Parties to the Convention nonetheless to act in accordance with its provisions, by which it has really meant the fundamental obligations of respect in article 4. It has similarly called for observance of the Convention by Member States which are High Contracting Parties during armed conflicts to which the instrument has not actually applied. In November 1956, against the backdrop of the Sinai War between Israel and Egypt (only the latter being a Party to the Convention at the time) and of the Soviet invasion of Hungary (ditto), the General Conference – considering 'that a Convention for the Protection of Cultural Property in the Event of Armed Conflict was adopted by the international conference, convened by Unesco, which met at The Hague from 21 April to 14 May 1954, and that the aforesaid Convention came into force on 7 August 1956'; and also considering 'that, on account of recent and current events in the Middle East and in other regions of the world, monuments and other cultural property of great value, the destruction of which would

---

[382] Ibid., para. 19.
[383] Executive Office of the Director-General, 'The Director-General of UNESCO Launches an Appeal'.
[384] See 140 EX/13, para. 46: 'UNESCO's Constitution states under the heading "Purposes and functions" that the Organization will "maintain, increase and diffuse knowledge: by assuring the conservation and protection of the world's inheritance of books, works of art and monuments of history and science, and recommending to the nations concerned the necessary international conventions". Although the Organization's standard-setting action is stressed, political or operational work is by no means excluded. It is above all in the light of this provision of the Constitution that the Executive Board can, if need be, take the initiative either of "intervening" directly or of recommending to the General Conference to do so. There is nothing to prevent the Executive Board, if it so wishes, from inviting a Member State to take or avoid taking certain action. Nothing prevents it, either, from inviting the Director-General, under the Constitution, to take certain steps in peacetime or in time of war or to act or try to act in a particular situation for the protection of heritage located on the territory of a Member State.'

be a serious loss to the cultural heritage of the world, are in danger' — expressed the hope 'that all the necessary measures [would] be taken as soon as possible by the governments of the States concerned to ensure protection of and respect for the cultural property situated in the regions in question', and invited the states concerned which were not yet Parties to the Hague Convention (namely, Israel and the USSR) 'to make declarations giving undertakings to that effect, in accordance with Article 18 [paragraph 3] of the said Convention'.[385] The General Conference also drew 'special attention to the sanctity and sacredness of the Monastery of St Catherine in Sinai, which contains manuscripts and treasures of great historical and artistic interest, which has always enjoyed complete protection in time of war and peace, and which must not be touched or tampered with in any way whatsoever'.[386] Following the outbreak of hostilities in July 1969 between El Salvador and Honduras (neither of them a Party to the Convention at the time), the Director-General sent a telegram to the belligerent states drawing their attention to the provisions of the Convention and appealing to them to protect cultural property situated in the territory of each.[387] Similarly, on the launch in June 1970 of North Vietnamese and Viet Cong attacks in Cambodia, only Cambodia being a Party to the Convention, the Executive Board — '[a]ware of the exceptional importance of Angkor Wat and other ancient temples not only to Cambodia but also to all humanity, as artistic, historic and religious monuments'; '[r]ecognizing that it is the common obligation of all humanity to preserve them'; and '[e]xpressing grave concern over the spread of hostilities which threaten to destroy the ancient temples' — addressed 'an urgent international appeal to all those concerned to respect and preserve from destruction all monuments of the ancient Cambodian culture'.[388] It also invited the Director-General 'to establish contacts with all those concerned, in the spirit of The Hague Convention, with a view to preserving the monuments of Cambodia's cultural heritage from destruction, profanation and

---

[385] 9 C/Resolution 7.91, preamble and paras. 1–2.
[386] *Ibid.*, para. 3.
[387] *1970 Reports*, para. 17.
[388] 84 EX/Decision 4.3.3, paras. 2–6. Similarly, the UN Secretary-General issued a statement on 8 June 1970 urging the sparing of Angkor Wat and appealing to all concerned 'to respect, and to take every possible precaution to preserve the many religious and cultural edifices in the fighting zone and elsewhere in Indo-China': UNESCO Doc. 84 EX/37, Annex II.

pillage'.³⁸⁹ In 1997, when civil war in Afghanistan (not a Party to the Convention) threatened the Buddhas of Bamiyan, then under the control of forces hostile to the Taliban, the Director-General called on 'the people of Afghanistan' to observe the Convention, drawing attention to the obligation not to attack cultural property and to the preambular statement that 'damage to cultural property belonging to any people whatsoever means damage to the cultural heritage of all mankind'.³⁹⁰ He similarly appealed to all the parties to the Kosovo conflict in 1999 to respect cultural property, '[a]s custom dictates and as the UNESCO Convention for the Protection of Cultural Property in the Event of Armed Conflict (The Hague, 1954) stipulates'.³⁹¹ Most recently, in the leadup to the invasion of Iraq in March 2003, the Director-General alerted the various parties involved to the dangers to which the Iraqi cultural heritage would be exposed in the event of armed conflict, and drew attention to the provisions of the Convention. As a useful practical measure, he also sent detailed maps indicating the locations of archaeological sites, monuments and museums in Iraq to the UN Secretary-General and to the US State Department (the USA not being a Party to the Convention). As news arrived of the looting and burning of major museums, libraries and manuscript collections in Baghdad and Mosul, UNESCO increased its contacts with the USA and UK (the latter not a Party to the Convention either), encouraging them to take immediate steps to guard Iraq's archaeological sites and cultural institutions.³⁹²

UNESCO's general mandate under article I(3) of its Constitution also provided a useful means by which to urge respect for cultural property during the war in Bosnia-Herzegovina without having to engage with the thorny legal question of succession to the Convention by the independent states that emerged from the dissolution of the Socialist Federal Republic of Yugoslavia.³⁹³ In this way, the Executive Board, echoing an appeal

---

³⁸⁹ 84 EX/Decision 4.3.3, para. 7. In the event, the Director-General was able to provide technical assistance pursuant to art. 23(1), since the requesting state, Cambodia, was a Party to the Convention.
³⁹⁰ UNESCOPRESS No. 97–61, 18 April 1997; UNESCOPRESS No. 97–151, 16 September 1997.
³⁹¹ UNESCOPRESS No. 99–99, 5 May 1999.
³⁹² UNESCO Doc. DG/2003/064, pp. 2–3. Neither the USA nor the UK, which between them contributed the overwhelming bulk of coalition forces, was a Party to the Convention. Iraq, Australia and Poland were, as was Spain, which committed naval forces. Denmark, which also sent a naval contingent, ratified the Convention on 26 March 2003, six days after fighting commenced.
³⁹³ In April 1992, 'rump' Yugoslavia reconstituted itself to comprise only Serbia and Montenegro, and renamed itself the Federal Republic of Yugoslavia (FRY). The FRY claimed to be the continuation of the Socialist Federal Republic of Yugoslavia (SFRY),

by the Director-General[394] and recalling the Convention, was able in 1992 to reiterate 'its concern about the damage done to many secular and religious buildings of historical significance and to the 400-year-old sites which embody the historical and spiritual values of the Islamic, Catholic, Orthodox and Jewish communities living on the territory of Bosnia-Herzegovina', condemning 'all violent actions that ... destroy the historical, religious and cultural heritage as well as educational and scientific institutions in Bosnia-Herzegovina'.[395]

As for whether UNESCO's intervention has been successful in securing compliance with the Convention, it is simply impossible to tell. There are too many variables to enable one to ascribe cause and effect. It would certainly be too easy to write off the Organisation's role as so much pious verbiage. Good faith and the mobilisation of shame are not to be underestimated, and it is a fact, for example, that the shelling of Dubrovnik ceased soon after the Director-General contacted the Yugoslav minister for defence.[396] At the same time, it would be wise not to adopt too optimistic a view of the efficacy of UNESCO's efforts in bringing about adherence to the Convention. The unresolved saga of Israel's contentious activities in the Old City of Jerusalem and elsewhere in the Occupied Palestinian Territories, the destruction of cultural property in the Iran–Iraq War, the looting of Kuwait's museums during Iraq's invasion and occupation, the shelling of Dubrovnik in the first place and the devastation of the cultural heritage of Bosnia-Herzegovina are sober reminders of the limits of the Organisation's

and declared on 27 April 1992 that it considered itself bound by all treaties to which the SFRY had been a Party, which included the Convention and First Protocol. The claim to continuation was rejected by the UN, which considered the FRY a successor state to the SFRY and, as such, required to apply for admission *de novo* to the Organisation. The standoff was resolved, in the UN's favour, only in 2001. On 11 September 2001, the state which now styles itself Serbia and Montenegro transmitted to UNESCO a notification of succession to the Convention. For its part, Bosnia-Herzegovina claimed to succeed to the SFRY's obligations under the Convention and First Protocol on 6 March 1992, before its admission to the UN as an independent state. Its succession was accepted only after a subsequent notification of 12 July 1993. On 6 July 1992, after its admission to the UN, Croatia made a declaration of succession to Yugoslavia's ratification of the Convention and the First Protocol.

[394] *1995 Reports*, para. 20.
[395] 139 EX/Decision 7.5. The later 140 EX/Decision 8.4 and 141 EX/Decision 9.3, both similar to 139 EX/Decision 7.5, do not mention the Convention. The same is true of the General Conference's 27 C/Resolution 4.8. At the same time, all are cited at *1995 Reports*, para. 20 under the rubric of 'Measures taken in connection with the implementation of the Convention'.
[396] *1995 Reports*, para. 18.

diplomatic muscle – but also, to be fair, of the limits of any compliance mechanism when it comes to the laws of war.

Finally, UNESCO has become increasingly active in promoting the Convention and its Protocols, in encouraging and assisting states to become Parties to them, and in facilitating compliance with their obligations. In the past decade, in co-operation with the ICRC, the Organisation has given numerous regional seminars on the Convention and, in 2004, held a series of regional expert meetings to mark its fiftieth anniversary, having commemorated its thirtieth anniversary in 1984 with a ceremony at UNESCO headquarters. It has sponsored a commentary on the Convention,[397] prepared an information kit on the Convention and its Protocols,[398] and produced a leaflet in Albanian, Serbian and English outlining the basic rules on the protection of cultural property for distribution among the population of Kosovo.[399] Most importantly, with the assistance of the Netherlands government, it set in motion and saw to conclusion the process of the Convention's review, which led to the adoption of its Second Protocol in 1999.

Sanctions

The UNESCO Secretariat's first report to the General Conference on the drafting of the Convention was entitled 'Report on the International Protection of Cultural Property, by Penal Measures, in the Event of Armed Conflict'.[400] The Secretariat, while pointing out that reparation would be owed in principle under the law of state responsibility for the destruction of cultural property contrary to the laws of war, added that there was 'no need to stress ... that the possibility of civil reparations is of very minor interest when we are concerned with property which is essentially irreplaceable'.[401] It was in this light that the intergovernmental conference adopted article 28 of the Convention – 'one of the most difficult of all', involving as it did international criminal law, which was then in its infancy.[402]

Article 28 requires the High Contracting Parties 'to take, within the framework of their ordinary criminal jurisdiction, all necessary steps to

---

[397] See Toman, *Protection of Cultural Property*.
[398] See UNESCO, *Protect Cultural Property in Armed Conflict* (2 May 2004).
[399] See (2001) 83 IRRC 862.
[400] 5 C/PRG/6, Annex I; 6 C/PRG/22, Annex, p. 3.
[401] 5 C/PRG/6, Annex I, para. 3.
[402] 7 C/PRG/7, Annex I, p. 14; *Records 1954*, p. 314.

prosecute and impose penal or disciplinary sanctions upon those persons, of whatever nationality, who commit or order to be committed a breach of the ... Convention'. The equally authoritative[403] French version of the words 'within the framework of their ordinary criminal jurisdiction', that is 'dans le cadre de leur système de droit pénal', clarifies the meaning of this phrase to some extent. So do the *travaux*: as drafted by the 1952 committee of governmental experts, what was to become the English version of article 28 had read 'within the framework of their legal systems',[404] but the UNESCO draft had replaced 'legal systems' with 'ordinary criminal jurisdiction'.[405] The word 'ordinary' is, nonetheless, a little cryptic, and might be thought to suggest that article 28 stipulates prosecution strictly before civil (that is, non-military) courts under the general (that is, non-military) criminal law. This is not the case. The reference to the alternative of disciplinary sanctions, which are imposable only upon persons subject to military discipline, necessarily implies that trial before a military tribunal under military law is permissible; and it is a fact that many of the Parties rely for their implementation of article 28 on military criminal law, as part of their 'système de droit pénal'. As it is, the *travaux* reveal that the words 'within the framework of their ordinary criminal jurisdiction' were inserted for an altogether different purpose.[406]

In common with most provisions of international criminal law, article 28 does not stipulate, beyond the specific mention of actual commission and command responsibility, the modes of participation in the various possible breaches of the Convention that are to be rendered punishable by the Parties' respective courts (for example, attempt, conspiracy and complicity), nor the requisite mental element (*mens rea*), nor the maximum or minimum penalties imposable. The intention of the drafters was a broad text which would 'leave the Parties free to decide on the nature of the crime and the sanctions to be adopted'.[407] The drafters did not wish to oblige a Party to take measures which were not already

---

[403] 1954 Hague Convention, art. 29(1). Vienna Convention on the Law of Treaties, art. 33(3) states that the terms of a treaty are presumed to have the same meaning in each authentic text.
[404] 7 C/PRG/7, Annex II, p. 26.
[405] UNESCO Doc. CBC/3, *Records*, p. 389. The French text was amended from 'système juridique' to 'système de droit pénal'.
[406] See below.
[407] *Records 1954*, para. 1612 (Italy).

permitted under the principles of its public law, 'principles it [was] not prepared to change'.[408] The aim was an open-textured provision capable of implementation by states of every criminal justice tradition and peculiarity, a provision to whose bare bones each Party's own corpus of criminal law would add flesh.

Nonetheless, when it came to the mental element of an offence pursuant to article 28, the USA and UK – whose criminal justice traditions did not countenance criminal responsibility on the basis of strict liability – pushed during the drafting for a requirement of knowledge, believing that the 'somewhat vague' definition of cultural property in article 1 'made it possible for a Party to violate the Convention unwittingly'.[409] Their proposal to insert the word 'knowingly'[410] was not, however, reflected in the final version of the provision, and, in the end, the matter is one for the domestic criminal law of each Party, given the deliberate unspecificity of article 28. That said, as a matter of customary international law, war crimes can only be committed with intent and knowledge,[411] the latter meaning 'awareness that a circumstance exists'.[412] The question is what that circumstance might be. It is perhaps relevant only that the accused is aware that the object in question is a 'monument of architecture, art or history, whether religious or secular', an archaeological site, or any other sort of movable or immovable property referred to in article 1 of the Convention. On the other hand, it could be argued by analogy with grave breaches of the Geneva Conventions that the perpetrator must have been aware of the factual circumstances which established that the object was protected by the Convention.[413] Either way, the fact that the cultural property was marked with the distinctive emblem of the Convention will be relevant. In *Strugar*, as 'a further evidentiary issue' regarding the intent to destroy cultural property in the Old Town of Dubrovnik, the ICTY 'accept[ed] the evidence that protective UNESCO emblems were visible, from the JNA positions at Žarkovica and elsewhere, above the Old Town on 6 December 1991'.[414] Marking, however, is not the sole means by which

---

[408] 7 C/PRG/7, Annex I, p. 14.
[409] *Records 1954*, para. 1610 (UK). See also *ibid.*, para. 1613 (US).
[410] UNESCO Docs. CBC/DR/87 (UK) and CBC/DR/124 (US), *ibid.*, p. 390.
[411] ICC Statute, art. 30(1).
[412] *Ibid.*, art. 30(3).
[413] Elements of Crimes, ICC Doc. ICC-ASP/1/3 (part II-B), art. 8(2)(a)(iv) ('War crime of destruction and appropriation of property'), p. 20 at p. 21, para. 5.
[414] *Strugar*, Trial Chamber Judgment, para. 329.

an attacker may gain knowledge of the Convention's application to given property.

Article 28 also leaves open the basis or bases under international law on which High Contracting Parties are to assert jurisdiction over criminal breaches of the Convention. The provision expressly states that such offences are to be punishable whatever the nationality of the offender, but this does not advance things very far, since the real question is whether this includes offences committed by non-nationals outside the territory of the forum state. The USSR had argued in favour of explicit provision for universal jurisdiction over 'serious violations of the Convention', including, *inter alia*, all destruction of specially protected property not justified by military necessity. Basing itself on article 146 of the fourth Geneva Convention, it suggested the following text:

Each of the High Contracting Parties undertakes to seek persons accused of committing or causing the commission of serious violations of the Convention, and to bring them to trial, before its own courts, whatever nationality they may be. In accordance with the provisions of its legislation, it may, if it so desires, hand them over for trial to another Party concerned, if the latter possesses evidence constituting counts of indictment against such persons.[415]

Nor was there any objection as a matter of international law to a Party's exercise of universal jurisdiction over criminal breaches of the Convention. The USA, however, drew attention to the practical hurdle posed by the constitutional incapacity of its federal government to expand the territorial jurisdiction of the criminal courts of its various states,[416] a problem shared by some other federal countries. In the event, the Soviet delegation was prepared to withdraw its amendment and to support the Legal Committee's proposed text,[417] which suggests that it was content that the final version of article 28 did not rule out universality. On the other hand, the more non-committal wording and the insertion of the phrase 'within the framework of their ordinary criminal jurisdiction' indicate that universality is not obligatory. In the final analysis, going both on the plain meaning of the provision and on

---

[415] UNESCO Doc. CBC/DR/71, *Records 1954*, p. 390.
[416] *Records 1954*, para. 1613.
[417] *Ibid.*, para. 1614.

the *travaux préparatoires*, the obligation imposed by article 28 permits but does not compel a Party to empower its courts to exercise universal jurisdiction over criminal breaches of the Convention.[418]

It is not clear whether the obligation laid down in article 28 applies only to breaches of the Convention committed during international armed conflict, including belligerent occupation, or whether it extends to breaches committed during armed conflict not of an international character. On a narrow reading of article 19(1), article 4 is the only provision which relates to respect for cultural property, and, in this light, article 28 does not apply in the event of non-international armed conflict. On another view, article 28 is indeed a provision which relates to respect for cultural property, albeit in an adjectival sense: where article 4 of the Convention lays down the primary rules relevant to respect, article 28 provides for a special secondary rule in the event of the breach of one of these primary rules – namely, that such a breach is to give rise, ultimately under the domestic law of the respective Parties, to the individual criminal responsibility of the perpetrator. Putting it another way, the legal consequence of article 19 is that failure to observe article 4 in the course of non-international armed conflict is a breach of the Convention, and article 28 obliges the Parties to prosecute and impose penal or disciplinary sanctions on those persons who commit or who order to be committed a breach of the Convention. Subsequent practice is unhelpful, since there has never been a trial in the courts of any High Contracting Party for a criminal breach of the Convention. For its part, the UN's Group of Experts for Cambodia established pursuant to General Assembly resolution 52/135 suggested that breaches of the Convention committed during non-international armed conflict 'perhaps' gave rise to individual criminal responsibility.[419]

---

[418] See also A. R. Carnegie, 'Jurisdiction over Violations of the Laws and Customs of War' (1963) 39 BYIL 402 at 409; Y. Dinstein, 'International Criminal Law' (1985) 20 Isr. LR 206 at 216. The claim by Toman, *Protection of Cultural Property*, p. 294, that art. 28 obliges Parties to assert universal criminal jurisdiction is unsustainable and ascribes an object and purpose to the provision which goes beyond what is warranted by its wording or drafting history.

[419] See UN Doc. A/53/850-S/1999/231, Annex, para. 76. Cambodia's subsequent Law on the Establishment of Extraordinary Chambers in the Courts of Cambodia for the Prosecution of Crimes Committed During the Period of Democratic Kampuchea, as amended 27 October 2004, provides in art. 7 that the Extraordinary Chambers 'shall have the power to bring to trial all suspects most responsible for the destruction of cultural property during armed conflict pursuant to the 1954 Hague Convention for Protection of Cultural Property in the Event of Armed Conflict, and which were

Implementation reports

Article 26(2) of the Convention stipulates that, 'at least once every four years', the High Contracting Parties shall forward to the Director-General of UNESCO 'a report giving whatever information they think suitable concerning any measures being taken, prepared or contemplated by their respective administrations in fulfilment of the ... Convention and of the Regulations for its execution'. The wording of article 26(2) makes it clear that, while Parties are obliged to submit reports, those unwilling to disclose relevant facts are under no requirement to do so. Israel, for example, restricts its implementation reports to measures taken within the territory of Israel itself, excluding all mention of its activities in the Occupied Palestinian Territories, including the Old City of Jerusalem.[420] Many Parties' reports to date have been perfunctory. Many others include much extraneous fact, with no indication of how it relates to the implementation of the Convention. Moreover, few Parties submit reports at all: it has been estimated that only about 20% of the reports owed in the past have been transmitted.[421]

Implementation reports are received, collated and disseminated by UNESCO, with the earliest compilation of reports[422] distributed in 1962 at the first meeting of the High Contracting Parties and subsequent

---

committed during the period from 17 April 1975 to 6 January 1979'; and art. 2 of the Agreement between the United Nations and the Royal Government of Cambodia concerning the Prosecution under Cambodian Law of Crimes Committed During the Period of Democratic Kampuchea, 6 June 2003, 'recognizes that the Extraordinary Chambers have subject matter jurisdiction consistent with that set forth in "the Law on the Establishment of the Extraordinary Chambers in the Courts of Cambodia for the Prosecution of Crimes Committed During the Period of Democratic Kampuchea"..., as adopted and amended by the Cambodian Legislature under the Constitution of Cambodia'. But it does not appear that the Extraordinary Chambers will be called upon to answer the question at issue here, since the armed conflicts in question, which pitted Kampuchea (Cambodia) against Vietnamese and Thai forces respectively, were of an international character. Reydams, who asserts that breaches of the Convention 'necessarily imply an international element', bases his claim on the mistaken belief that the Convention 'applies only to international armed conflicts (article 18)': L. Reydams, *Universal Jurisdiction. International and Municipal Legal Perspectives* (Oxford: OUP, 2003), p. 57.

[420] *1970 Reports*, p. 15.
[421] P. J. Boylan, *Review of the Convention for the Protection of Cultural Property in the Event of Armed Conflict (The Hague Convention of 1954)*, UNESCO Doc. CLT-93/WS/12, para. 8.6.
[422] UNESCO Doc. CA/RBC.1/3, Annex II and Add. 1 to 6.

compilations published more formally in 1967, 1970, 1979, 1984, 1989 and 1995.[423] The Organisation does not, however, comment on reports,[424] and has no power of sanction over Parties evidencing unsatisfactory implementation of the Convention. It is also powerless to sanction Parties which fail to submit reports.[425]

Meetings of the High Contracting Parties

In accordance with article 27(1) of the Convention, the Director-General of UNESCO 'may, with the approval of the Executive Board, convene meetings of representatives of the High Contracting Parties', and 'must convene such a meeting if at least one-fifth of the High Contracting Parties so request'. Article 27(2) explains that the purpose of such meetings is 'to study problems concerning the application of the Convention and of the Regulations for its execution, and to formulate recommendations in respect thereof'. In addition, pursuant to article 27(3), a meeting of the High Contracting Parties may, if the majority of the Parties are represented, undertake a revision of the Convention in accordance with article 39 ('Revision of the Convention and of the Regulations for its execution').

In the first forty years of the Convention's life, only a single meeting of the High Contracting Parties was held, lasting ten days, from 16 to 25 July 1962.[426] In 1970, after the controversy over Israel's practices in the occupied West Bank, especially in the Old City of Jerusalem, had highlighted the lacuna in the Convention as regards archaeological excavations and alterations to cultural property in occupied territory, the Director-General circulated a letter canvassing the desirability of calling a second meeting of the High Contracting Parties with a view to amending the Convention.[427] While many Parties were in favour, enough were not.

---

[423] The publication of the next round of reports was still pending at the time of going to press.
[424] It did, however, prepare a perfunctory 'analysis' of the first set of reports for presentation to the first meeting of the High Contracting Parties: see CA/RBC.1/3.
[425] Dissatisfaction with the toothlessness of the system of implementation reports led to art. 27(1)(d) of the Second Protocol, pursuant to which the Committee for the Protection of Cultural Property in the Event of Armed Conflict established under the Protocol is authorised 'to consider and comment on reports of the Parties, to seek clarifications as required, and [to] prepare its own report on the implementation of [the] Protocol for the Meeting of the Parties'.
[426] See CUA/120.
[427] DG/6/A/2620, pursuant to 83 EX/Decision 4.3.1, para. 8.

There have now been five more such meetings, each lasting only a single day – two in the mid to late 1990s,[428] under the impetus of UNESCO's review of the Convention, and three since the adoption of the Second Protocol, one of them after its entry into force.[429] None has undertaken a revision of the Convention.

Special agreements

Article 24(1) of the Convention, curiously placed within chapter VII ('Execution of the Convention'), provides that the High Contracting Parties 'may conclude special agreements for all matters concerning which they deem it suitable to make separate provision'. The thinking behind the provision – which, along with article 24(2), was modelled on a provision common to the Geneva Conventions[430] – was that 'various States should, if they deem it possible in their relations with one another, accept obligations in excess of the minimum provided for in the Convention'.[431] In line with article 6 of the OIM draft, the most obvious use to which article 24(1) could be put is to arrange for the immunity of immovable cultural property, particularly centres containing monuments, which do not satisfy the criteria for special protection laid down in article 8, although the possibility is already catered for to some extent by article 8(5). The provision is, nonetheless, of general application. Article 24(2) inserts the caveat that no special agreement which would diminish the protection afforded by the Convention to cultural property and to personnel engaged in its protection may be concluded.

The First Protocol

The systematic removal by Nazi Germany of artworks and antiquities from the countries occupied by it[432] and the subsequent entry of many

---

[428] UNESCO Docs. CLT-95/CONF.009/5 and CLT-97/CONF.208/3.
[429] UNESCO Docs. CLT-99/CONF.206/4, CLT-01/CONF/204/4. The official report of the sixth meeting of the High Contracting Parties, held on 26 October 2005, was not yet available at the time of going to press.
[430] Geneva Convention I, art. 6; Geneva Convention II, art. 6; Geneva Convention III, art. 6; Geneva Convention IV, art. 7.
[431] CL/484, Annex, p. 17.
[432] The Nazis also seized the collections of German, Austrian and Sudeten Jews, but these seizures fell outside the laws of armed conflict, as they did not take place in occupied territory.

of these pieces into the market (where they were purchased by private collectors and public institutions alike) motivated the drafters of the Convention to address the question of the exportation and importation of cultural property from occupied territory. Given, however, that many of the proposed obligations implicated private-law rights of ownership with which some governments were reluctant to interfere or even barred from interfering, it was thought more appropriate to deal with them by way of a separate, optional instrument, so as not to deter participation in the Convention. So it was that the Protocol to the Convention for the Protection of Cultural Property in the Event of Armed Conflict (now called the First Protocol), which was adopted and came into force at the same time as the Convention, took on a life of its own. Despite its loose drafting, it has assumed increasing significance in the fifty years since its adoption, as the main danger to cultural property in armed conflict has changed from its destruction during bombardment to its illicit removal.

Section I (paragraphs[433] 1 to 4) of the Protocol deals with the exportation of cultural property from occupied territory, section II (paragraph 5) with the deposit of cultural property abroad for safekeeping. Section III contains final provisions. In accordance with paragraph 9, High Contracting Parties may declare that they will not be bound by the provisions of section I or, alternatively, by those of section II. No state has done so to date.

Scope of application

Paragraph 6 of the First Protocol states that the Protocol shall remain open for signature 'by all States invited to the Conference which met at The Hague from 21 April, 1954 to 14 May, 1954'. On its face, there is no requirement that signatories – and hence, by operation of paragraphs 7 and 8, High Contracting Parties – also be signatories/High Contracting Parties to the Convention. Presumably on the strength of this, some authors suggest that it is unnecessary for a state to be a Party to the Convention for it to be a Party to the Protocol.[434] This assertion is untenable. Although it is true that, in contrast with the First Protocol, the Second Protocol to the Convention explicitly provides in article 40 that

---

[433] Although the provisions of binding international agreements are usually called 'articles', the First Protocol refers to its provisions as 'paragraphs'.

[434] P. J. O'Keefe, 'The First Protocol to the Hague Convention Fifty Years On' (2004) 9 *Art Antiquity and Law* 99 at 113; Chamberlain, *War and Cultural Heritage*, pp. 140 and 150.

it shall be open for signature, ratification, acceptance or approval and accession by 'High Contracting Parties', defined in article 1(d) to mean 'a State Party to the Convention', no implication *a contrario* can be drawn in relation to the First Protocol. Indeed, there is every reason to conclude that a provision to the effect of article 40 of the Second Protocol is to be read into the First. The term 'protocol' is customarily used to refer to an optional international agreement parasitic, as it were, upon another (customarily a 'convention'), with Parties to the former required to be Parties to the latter.[435] Even more to the point, paragraph 1 of the First Protocol speaks of 'cultural property as defined in Article 1 of the Convention for the Protection of Cultural Property in the Event of Armed Conflict, signed at The Hague on 14 May, 1954', while paragraph 10(c) states that the 'situations referred to in Articles 18 and 19 of the Convention for the Protection of Cultural Property in the Event of Armed Conflict, signed at The Hague on 14 May, 1954, shall give immediate effect to ratifications and accessions deposited by the Parties to the conflict either before or after the beginning of hostilities or occupation'. These references clearly presuppose that a Party to the Protocol will also be a Party to the Convention. Indeed, the straightforward explanation for the absence from the First Protocol of any explicit requirement of participation in the Convention – opened for signature in The Hague on the very same day – was that such a requirement went without saying. It is also telling that of the Parties to the First Protocol, every single one of them is a Party to the Convention as well.

In this light, and especially given paragraph 10(c)'s express reference to articles 18 and 19 of the Convention, it is clear that the Protocol's scope of application is in principle identical to that of the Convention, although very definitely *mutatis mutandis*, since the Protocol deals only with the incidents of belligerent occupation. The reference in paragraph 10(c) of the Protocol to article 18 of the Convention *in toto* and to article 19[436] stems from no more than the unthinking transposition of article 33(3) of the Convention to the final provisions of the Protocol. In short, the First Protocol applies in respect of the belligerent occupation of the territory of one Party to the Protocol by

---

[435] Consider e.g. the Geneva Conventions and their two Additional Protocols or the European Convention on Human Rights and its thirteen Protocols.
[436] Recall that there is no such thing as belligerent occupation during non-international armed conflict.

another Party to the Protocol.[437] This being the case, assertions to the effect that it is immaterial for the purposes of section I whether the state whose territory is occupied is a Party to the Protocol[438] cannot be sustained. The same goes for Chamberlain's view that paragraph 2 and, by implication, paragraph 3 apply whether the Occupying Power is a Party to the Protocol or not.[439]

Obligations

Paragraph 1 of the First Protocol requires each Party to prevent the exportation, from territory occupied by it during armed conflict, of cultural property as defined in article 1 of the Convention. The obligation imposed on an Occupying Power goes beyond ensuring that its own occupation authorities or military forces do not export cultural property from the territory: paragraph 1 encompasses a duty to prevent private parties from doing so. Nor is the obligation limited to exportation contrary to local law; rather, paragraph 1 obliges a belligerent occupant to prevent all exportation of cultural property.

Paragraphs 2 and 3 impose obligations not on the Occupying Power itself but on the other Parties to the Protocol. The first sentence of paragraph 2 obliges each Party to take into its custody cultural property imported into its territory either directly or indirectly from any occupied territory. 'Indirectly' means via a third state or third states. The second sentence provides that such custody 'shall either be effected automatically upon the importation of the property or, failing this, at the request of the authorities of that territory'. As under paragraph 1, the obligation applies in respect of all cultural property exported from occupied territory and not just to cultural property exported in contravention of local law. Paragraph 3 imposes a duty on each Party 'to return, at the close of hostilities, to the competent authorities of the territory previously occupied, cultural property which is in its territory', if such property has been exported in contravention of the principle embodied in paragraph 1, adding, with an eye to the so-called 'trophy art' taken by the Soviet Union at the end of the Second World War, that such property 'shall never be retained as war reparations'.

---

[437] Or, in either case, a state accepting and applying the provisions of the Protocol, as per art. 18(3) of the Convention as transposed to the Protocol.
[438] Toman, *Protection of Cultural Property*, p. 344; O'Keefe, 'The First Protocol', at 100; Chamberlain, *War and Cultural Heritage*, pp. 144, 145, 146 and 149.
[439] Chamberlain, *War and Cultural Heritage*, p. 145.

The wording of paragraph 3 presupposes that the close of hostilities and the end of the occupation of the territory from which the cultural property was exported are simultaneous.[440] This poses a conundrum in situations such as Cyprus where, no legal state of war existing between the hostile Parties, it can be said that hostilities, in the sense of combat operations, have come to a close, but where occupation of part of the territory persists and has persisted for over thirty years. In such cases, unless the Party subject to the duty laid down in paragraph 3 is to retain custody over cultural property exported from the occupied territory until a final settlement is reached, which may be *ad infinitum*, it would seem in keeping with the object and purpose of the provision to return the property to the government of the unoccupied part of the territory. But paragraph 3 would not mandate this.

Paragraph 4 focuses once more on the Occupying Power – or, in this case, the former Occupying Power. It states that the Party whose obligation it was to prevent the exportation of cultural property from the territory occupied by it shall pay an indemnity to the holders in good faith of any cultural property which has to be returned in accordance paragraph 3.

Paragraph 5, the sole provision in section II, deals with cultural property deposited abroad for safekeeping for the duration of hostilities. It states that '[c]ultural property coming from the territory of a High Contracting Party and deposited by it in the territory of another High Contracting Party for the purpose of protecting such property against the dangers of an armed conflict, shall be returned by the latter, at the end of hostilities, to the competent authorities from the territory from which it came'. This obligation is independent of the Convention's regime for the transport of cultural property abroad under special protection, which contains an analogous obligation of return in article 18 of the Regulations. Like article 18 of the Regulations, paragraph 5 of the First Protocol was inspired by the dispute over certain Polish national treasures sent abroad for their protection just prior

---

[440] This reflects the situation which prevailed when war was formally and mutually declared. Hostilities were deemed not to have closed until a peace settlement was agreed between the belligerents, and, once a peace settlement was reached, control over territory occupied during the war reverted to the displaced sovereign (unless the latter ceded it). In short, the cessation of hostilities implied the cessation of belligerent occupation; conversely, continuing occupation presupposed continuing hostilities.

to the German invasion in 1939, ending up in Canada, and by the diplomatic wrangle over the return of the crown of St Stephen and other Hungarian coronation regalia sent to the USA in the closing stages of the Second World War.

When adopted in 1954, the Convention for the Protection of Cultural Property in the Event of Armed Conflict was a curious mix. The obligations it imposed vis-à-vis cultural property under general protection represented a modest advance on the Hague Rules and prevailing custom, but the regime of special protection, originally intended as the centrepiece of the instrument, became, in its final form, a waste of time. For its part, the regime of international control, also conceived of as a vital part of the Convention's rationale, was highly progressive and hopelessly overambitious in equal measure. Moreover, while the drafters cannot be blamed for this, the Convention did not address what, in terms of substantive law, was the most crucial issue for the protection of cultural property in armed conflict, namely incidental damage.

The subsequent application of the Convention has served to highlight its flaws. Only four refuges and a single centre containing monuments, representing a mere three High Contracting Parties, are entered in the International Register of Cultural Property under Special Protection, and on no occasion has the system of international control been implemented as planned. In addition, the majority of the Parties have ignored the obligation to submit implementation reports.

Nor has the Convention aged well. Indeed, in many ways, its adoption in 1954 was particularly poor timing. It came into being on the cusp of a period of great flux in the laws of armed conflict. Only two years later, in its Draft Rules for the Limitation of the Dangers incurred by the Civilian Population in Time of War, the ICRC would state the rules governing targeting not in broad terms of military necessity but by reference to the more precise concept of the military objective,[441] and would posit a rule of proportionality in relation to incidental damage.[442] Twenty years after the Intergovernmental Conference on the Protection of Cultural Property in the Event of Armed Conflict, the Diplomatic Conference on the Reaffirmation and Development of International Humanitarian Law Applicable in Armed Conflict would open in Geneva, eventually adopting

---

[441] ICRC Draft Rules, art. 7.
[442] *Ibid.*, art. 8(b).

Protocols I and II Additional to the Geneva Conventions, against whose rules on attacks the Convention's looked sorely dated.

Forty years of discontent with the Convention and a marked lack of interest in it among non-Parties and Parties alike eventually prompted UNESCO to undertake a review of the instrument in the 1990s, a process which led to the adoption in 1999 of a Second Protocol designed to revamp the agreement.

4 The 1977 Additional Protocols

After decades of calls for reform, 1974 saw the opening in Geneva of the Diplomatic Conference on the Reaffirmation and Development of International Humanitarian Law Applicable in Armed Conflicts. Three years later, the conference adopted two new instruments, framed as optional protocols supplementing the 1949 Geneva Conventions. Additional Protocol I,[1] dealing with international armed conflicts, and Additional Protocol II,[2] dealing with their non-international counterparts, codified and, in many respects, progressively developed the modern laws of armed conflict.

Both Protocols embody brief provisions relating specifically to cultural property, which prohibit attacks against it, prohibit its use in support of the military effort and, in the case of international armed conflict, prohibit making it the object of reprisals. They do so, moreover, without exception for military necessity – a notable departure, as regards attacks against and military use of such property, from the situation under the 1954 Hague Convention. That said, the Protocols' relevant provisions are stated to be without prejudice to the Convention, with the result that High Contracting Parties to both are not prevented from availing themselves of the waiver in respect of military necessity embodied in article 4(2) of the Convention.

In addition, and in practice of far greater significance to the wartime fate of cultural property, Protocol I remedies, at least in theory, the three

---

[1] Protocol Additional to the Geneva Conventions of 12 August 1949, and Relating to the Protection of Victims of International Armed Conflicts, Geneva, 8 June 1977, 1125 UNTS 3.

[2] Protocol Additional to the Geneva Conventions of 12 August 1949, and Relating to the Protection of Victims of Non-International Armed Conflicts, Geneva, 8 June 1977, 1125 UNTS 609.

cardinal reasons for its past destruction in bombardment. First, as proposed over fifty years earlier in the Air Rules, it prohibits attacks on the civilian population and civilian objects, restricting the lawful object of attack to military objectives. Next, in a repudiation of the thinking underpinning the Allies' strategic air offensive in the Second World War, it narrows the definition of a military objective, limiting permissible targets to those which make an effective contribution to military action, thereby excluding purely civilian infrastructure and industry and, as a result, dramatically reducing the number of military objectives to be found in any urban concentration. Most crucially, Protocol I outlaws excessive incidental harm to the civilian population and civilian objects – of which cultural property constitutes a species – during attacks on military objectives, positing a rule of proportionality which weighs death and injury to protected persons and damage to protected objects against the concrete and direct military advantage anticipated. These rules apply to all attacks, whether by land, sea or air. For its part, Protocol II, an attenuated, impressionistic version of Protocol I, prohibits attacks against civilians.

For the most part, Protocol I backs up the rules, both specific and general, relevant to the protection of cultural property in international armed conflict with penal sanctions.

Additional Protocol I

Scope of application

Additional Protocol I, on international armed conflicts, is stated in article 1(3) to apply in the situations referred to in article 2 common to the Geneva Conventions. Common article 2 provides that, in addition to the provisions to be implemented in peacetime, each of the four Conventions 'shall apply to all cases of declared war or of any other armed conflict which may arise between two or more of the High Contracting Parties, even if the state of war is not recognized by one of them'. It also applies 'to all cases of partial or total occupation of the territory of a High Contracting Party, even if the said occupation meets with no armed resistance'. Moreover, even if one of the parties to the conflict is not a Party to the Protocol, those states which are Parties to the latter remain bound by it in their mutual relations, and are bound by it vis-à-vis the state not Party not to it 'if the latter accepts and applies the provisions thereof'. It is no coincidence that this scope of application is identical to that of the 1954 Hague Convention, since article 18 of the latter was modelled on common article 2.

In a divergence both from the Geneva Conventions and from the 1954 Hague Convention, Protocol I also applies, via a deeming provision in article 1(4), to 'armed conflicts in which peoples are fighting against colonial domination and alien occupation and against racist régimes in the exercise of their right to self-determination, as enshrined in the Charter of the United Nations and the Declaration of Principles of International Law concerning Friendly Relations and Co-operation among States in accordance with the Charter of the United Nations'.

Civilian objects

Article 52 of Additional Protocol I posits in final, binding form the legal approach to targeting suggested over fifty years earlier in article 24(1) of the Air Rules.[3] The first sentence of article 52(1) of Protocol I states that '[c]ivilian objects shall not be the object of attack or of reprisals',[4] with the second sentence adding that civilian objects 'are all objects which are not military objectives as defined in paragraph 2'. In turn, restating in the converse the rule laid down in paragraph 1, the first sentence of paragraph 2 provides that attacks 'shall be limited strictly to military objectives'. However, it is the second sentence of paragraph 2 which is the crux. Article 52(2) specifies that, '[i]n so far as objects are concerned, military objectives are limited to those objects which by their nature, location, purpose or use make an effective contribution to military action and whose total or partial destruction, capture or neutralization, in the circumstances ruling at the time, offers a definite military advantage'. 'In case of doubt', article 52(3) elaborates, 'whether an object which is normally dedicated to civilian purposes, such as a place of worship, a house or other dwelling or a school, is being used to make an effective contribution to military action, it shall be presumed not to be so used'.

Cultural property will, in the overwhelming majority of cases, constitute a civilian object within the meaning of article 52(2) – presumptively

---

[3] See also, more generally, Additional Protocol I, art. 48: 'In order to ensure respect for and protection of the civilian population and civilian objects, the Parties to the conflict shall at all times distinguish between the civilian population and combatants and between civilian objects and military objectives and accordingly shall direct their operations only against military objectives'.

[4] As made clear in art. 49(1), the word 'attacks' refers to 'acts of violence against the adversary, whether in offence or defence'.

so, in accordance with article 52(3) – and will thereby, at a minimum, be protected by the prohibition on attack laid down in article 52(1). There are, however, rare circumstances in which targeting certain cultural property may be lawful under the provision. Historic fortresses, barracks, arsenals and the like might be said to make, by their nature, an effective contribution to military action, although when decommissioned they are better characterised as historic monuments and when still in service are better seen as contributing to military action by their use. Historic bridges, railway stations, docks and other forms of civil infrastructure could conceivably, by their purpose (defined as 'the future intended use of an object'[5]), make an effective contribution to military action, even if today one might expect more modern transport links to bear most of the military burden. The location of cultural property – that is, its position on the battlefield in relation to the positions of the opposing parties – may make an effective contribution to either's military action, for example by obstructing a line of sight or line of fire, although, in cases where a party has deliberately positioned itself so as to take advantage of this, the contribution to military action is better characterised as a function of the passive or *de facto* use of the property in question. In practice, of the four bases on which an object can be rendered a military objective under article 52(2), it is its use to make an effective contribution to military action which will be the principal one on which a Party to Protocol I may be expected to rely to justify attacking cultural property. In all cases, however, whatever the effective contribution cultural property makes to military action, attacking it will be lawful only if its total or partial destruction, capture or neutralisation, in the circumstances ruling at the time, offers a definite military advantage. In 'extremely simple terms', any attack 'must be militarily necessary in order to reach a permissible operative goal'.[6]

In its application to cultural property as a species of civilian object, article 52 of Protocol I represents little more than a useful fine-tuning of the rule of military necessity which had governed the legality of attacks against cultural property since early modern times, and which was already reflected in article 27 of the Hague Rules and embodied in articles 4(1) and 4(2) of the 1954 Hague Convention. Where article 52 does,

---

[5] *Partial Award: Western Front, Aerial Bombardment and Related Claims. Eritrea's Claims 1, 3, 5, 9–13, 14, 21, 25 & 26*, Eritrea Ethiopia Claims Commission, 19 December 2005, para. 120, endorsing *UK Manual*, para. 5.4.4, in turn endorsing Sandoz *et al.*, *Commentary*, para. 2022 ('intended future use').

[6] S. Oeter, 'Methods and Means of Combat', in Fleck, *Handbook*, p. 105 at para. 442(6).

however, constitute a marked advance on the previous regime is in its application to many other civilian objects, which, although covered by the customary rule of military necessity with its incipient principle of distinction, were vulnerable in the past to the creeping logic of total war, by which every element of the infrastructure and economy of a country was considered a permissible target. The requirement in article 52(2) that an object make an effective contribution to 'military action' – that is, to military operations, rather than to the adversary's general capacity to continue to wage war[7] – has the effect of markedly restricting the range and number of lawful military objectives. To the extent that cultural property had consistently been damaged and destroyed incidentally in the course of attacks on railways, roads, docks and factories not involved in the production of *matériel*, most signally during the Second World War, this narrowing of the legal notion of a military objective amounts to an enormous improvement in the protection of such property in the event of armed conflict.

The more circumscribed definition of a military objective in article 52(2) comes on top of the positing in article 51, for the first time in binding form, of a specific rule prohibiting attacks against civilians themselves. Article 51(2) states that '[t]he civilian population as such, as well as individual civilians, shall not be the object of attack'; and in a rejection of the doctrine espoused by Trenchard, Harris and their ilk, it continues: 'Acts or threats of violence the primary purpose of which is to spread terror among the civilian population are prohibited.'[8] Given that the 'secondary' targeting of civilians from the air so as to undermine the adversary's will to fight had been another principal cause of the devastation of cultural property in the Second World War, article 51(2)'s ban on this practice represents a landmark in the wartime legal protection not only of human life but also of humanity's cultural heritage.

The prohibitions on attacking civilian objects and the civilian population and individual civilians are backed up by the precautions in attack mandated in article 57.[9] Article 57(1) provides generally that, in the

---

[7] *Ibid.*, para. 442(5); Rogers, *Law on the Battlefield*, p. 71.
[8] See also Additional Protocol I, art. 51(6), prohibiting attacks against the civilian population or civilians by way of reprisals.
[9] In addition to art. 57's precautions in attack, art. 58 mandates precautions against the effects of attacks. Article 58(a) provides that the Parties to the conflict shall, to the maximum extent feasible, endeavour to remove civilian objects under their control from the vicinity of military objectives. Article 58(c) states that the Parties shall, again to the maximum extent feasible, 'take the other necessary precautions to protect ... civilian objects under their control against the dangers resulting from military operations'.

conduct of military operations, 'constant care shall be taken to spare the civilian population, civilians and civilian objects'. More specifically, article 57(2)(a)(i) requires that those who plan or decide upon an attack do everything feasible to verify that the objectives to be attacked are neither civilians nor civilian objects but are military objectives within the meaning of article 52(2) and that it is not prohibited by the Protocol to attack them. Article 57(2)(b) states that an attack must be cancelled or suspended if it becomes apparent that the objective is not a military one. Paragraph 3 of article 57, reflecting the classical rule of military necessity, stipulates that, when a choice is possible between several military objectives for obtaining a similar military advantage, the objective to be selected 'shall be that the attack on which may be expected to cause the least danger to civilian lives and to civilian objects'. Lastly, paragraph 5 of article 57 provides, for the avoidance of doubt, that no provision of article 57 is to be construed as authorising any attacks against the civilian population, civilians or civilian objects.

Cultural property

Over and above its protection as a civilian object under article 52, cultural property benefits under article 53 of Additional Protocol I from a special regime of protection. Article 53, applicable to 'a limited class of objects which, because of their recognized importance, constitute a part of the cultural heritage of mankind',[10] reads:

Without prejudice to the provisions of the Hague Convention for the Protection of Cultural Property in the Event of Armed Conflict of 14 May 1954, and of other relevant international instruments, it is prohibited:

(a) to commit any acts of hostility directed against the historic monuments, works of art or places of worship which constitute the cultural or spiritual heritage of peoples;
(b) to use such objects in support of the military effort;
(c) to make such objects the object of reprisals.

The ICRC had originally seen no need to include an article to this effect in its draft texts of the Additional Protocols, given that cultural property

[10] CDDH/SR.41, Annex, *Official Records of the Diplomatic Conference on the Reaffirmation and Development of International Humanitarian Law Applicable in Armed Conflicts, Geneva (1974–1977)*, 17 vols. (Bern: Federal Political Department, 1978), vol. VI, p. 195 (Netherlands); CDDH/SR.42, Annex, *ibid.*, p. 224 (Canada). See also, almost identically, CDDH/SR.42, para. 16, *ibid.*, p. 207 (Netherlands); CDDH/SR.42, Annex, *ibid.*, pp. 225 (FRG), 239 (UK) and 240 (USA).

was already afforded legal protection in both international and non-international armed conflict by the 1954 Hague Convention. Similarly, it was agreed from the outset at the Geneva diplomatic conference 'that there was no need to revise the existing rules on the subject'.[11] Nonetheless, many delegations felt 'that the protection and respect for cultural objects should be confirmed'[12] by inserting a short mention of the subject in each Protocol. The fact that the Convention enjoyed far from universal participation was relevant to the final decision in this regard. In short, the motivation behind article 53 of Protocol I was to affirm in a single provision the essential obligations of respect in international armed conflict embodied more exhaustively in the 1954 Hague Convention.[13] The derivative or secondary nature of article 53 is emphasised in the chapeau's 'without prejudice' clause, inserted to make it clear that article 53 is not intended to modify the existing legal obligations of those Parties to Protocol I which are also Parties to the Convention.[14] The point was underlined by the adoption of resolution 20(IV) of the Diplomatic Conference of Geneva:

Welcoming the adoption of Article 53 relating to the protection of cultural objects and places of worship as defined in the said Article, contained in the Protocol Additional to the Geneva Conventions of 12 August 1949, and relating to the Protection of Victims of International Armed Conflicts (Protocol I),

Acknowledging that the Convention for the Protection of Cultural Property in the Event of Armed Conflict and its Additional Protocol, signed at The Hague on 14 May 1954, constitutes an instrument of paramount importance for the international protection of the cultural heritage of all mankind against the effects of armed conflict and that the application of this Convention will in no way be prejudiced by the adoption of the Article referred to in the preceding paragraph,

Urges States which have not yet done so to become Parties to the aforementioned Convention.[15]

The desire was to avoid the 'parallel application of two divergent systems for the protection of cultural property, which could only be a source of

---

[11] Sandoz et al., *Commentary*, para. 2046.
[12] *Ibid.*
[13] *Ibid.*, paras. 2039–40. See also *ibid.*, paras. 4826–7 (as regards the identical description of the property protected in art. 16 of Additional Protocol II).
[14] *Ibid.*, para. 2046. See also *ibid.*, para. 4832 (Additional Protocol II).
[15] *Records 1974–77*, vol. I, part I, p. 213.

confusion',[16] with several delegates placing the emphasis on the Convention.[17]

Since the object and purpose of article 53 of Protocol I was to restate the fundamental obligations of respect laid down in the 1954 Hague Convention, it stands to reason that the property protected by the provision, viz. 'historic monuments, works of art or places of worship which constitute the cultural or spiritual heritage of peoples', should equate, as far as the ordinary meaning of the text permits, with cultural property within the meaning of its predecessor. The wording of article 53 was intended as an abbreviation or simplification of the formula used in article 1 of the Convention, the relevant working group speaking of 'the cultural heritage of peoples, in the words of the Hague Convention of 1954'.[18] Indeed, in the equally authentic French and Spanish texts of both instruments, the language is (except for the insertion of the words 'or spiritual') identical: the French and Spanish texts of article 1 of the Convention make no use of the word 'every' found in the English version, referring simply to 'le patrimoine culturel des peuples' and 'el patrimonio cultural de los pueblos' respectively, while the French and Spanish texts of article 53 speak of 'le patrimoine culturel ou spirituel des peuples' and 'el patrimonio cultural o espiritual de los pueblos'. For its part, the ICRC commentary, referring to the superficial divergence between the relative clause 'which constitute the cultural and spiritual heritage of peoples' in article 53 and the clause 'which are of great importance to the cultural heritage of every people' in the Convention, states that '[i]t does not seem that these expressions have a different meaning',[19] and makes it clear that 'there was no question of creating a new category of cultural objects'.[20] The ICRC's view was endorsed by the Appeals Chamber of the

---

[16] CDDH/SR.53, para. 4, ibid., vol. VII, p. 142 (FRG).
[17] As regards Additional Protocol I, see CDDH/SR.42, para. 12, ibid., vol. VI, p. 207 (Belgium); CDDH/SR.42, Annex, ibid., pp. 224 (Canada) and 234 (Poland); CDDH/III/SR.15, para. 22, ibid., vol. XIV, p. 121 (USSR); CDDH/III/SR.16, para. 15, ibid., p. 129 (Poland); CDDH/III/SR.24, paras. 28–30, ibid., pp. 221–2 (Netherlands). As regards Additional Protocol II, see CDDH/SR.52, paras. 2 and 7, ibid., vol. VII, pp. 125 and 126 (Belgium).
[18] CDDH/III/224, ibid., vol. XV, p. 333. See also the report of Committee III: CDDH/215/Rev.1, para. 69, ibid., p. 278.
[19] Sandoz et al., Commentary, para. 4844 (Additional Protocol II). See also ibid., para. 2064; J. Toman, 'La protection des biens culturels en cas de conflit armé non international', in W. Haller et al. (eds.), Im Dienst an der Gemeinschaft. Festschrift für Dietrich Schindler zum 65. Geburtstag (Basel/Frankfurt am Main: Helbing & Lichtenhahn, 1989), p. 311 at pp. 333–4.
[20] Sandoz et al., Commentary, para. 2064 n. 23.

ICTY in *Kordić*, where, drawing attention to the variation in wording between article 53 of Protocol I and article 1 of the 1954 Hague Convention, it cited the ICRC commentary to hold that, 'despite this difference in terminology, the basic idea is the same'.[21]

In this light, the terms 'historic monuments' and 'works of art' in article 53 should be seen as shorthand for the full panoply of immovable and movable cultural property referred to article 1 of the Convention.[22] In addition, the former's reference to the cultural or spiritual heritage 'of peoples' is correctly to be construed as meaning the cultural or spiritual heritage of each respective people – that is, of each Party, as determined by it according to its own criteria. In other words, as under the Convention, so too under article 53 is it the case that the precise property protected is left to the determination of the Party in whose territory it is situated. The initial draft of the provision had in fact spoken of 'the cultural heritage of a country',[23] and the earliest draft of the analogous provision (article 16) in Protocol II had used the expression 'the national heritage of a country'.[24] Moreover, in its discussion of the differences of opinion which arose, in relation to an intermediate draft,[25] over the application to places of worship of the clause 'which constitute the cultural heritage of peoples', a Report of Committee III of the Diplomatic Conference – in a statement applicable *mutatis mutandis* to historic monuments and works of art – suggested that '[h]ere cultural heterogeneity may be the key, for among some peoples any place of worship may be part of the cultural heritage, while among others only some places

---

[21] *Prosecutor* v. *Kordić and Čerkez*, IT-95-14/2-A, Appeals Chamber Judgment, 17 December 2004, para. 91, followed in *Prosecutor* v. *Strugar*, IT-01-42-T, Trial Chamber Judgment, 31 January 2005, para. 307. The latter, however, left open '[w]hether there may be precise differences': *ibid*. The former reference is to Sandoz *et al.*, *Commentary*, para. 2064.

[22] See also Sandoz *et al.*, *Commentary*, para. 2068 and para. 4838 (Additional Protocol II); Partsch, 'Protection of Cultural Property', para. 901(3).

[23] CDDH/III/17 and Rev.1, *Records 1974–77*, vol. III, p. 213.

[24] CDDH/III/GT/95, *ibid.*, vol. IV, p. 65. See also the Greek delegate's reference to 'the national heritage of a country' and to 'the cultural heritage of a people': CDDH/III/SR.49, paras. 13 and 14 respectively, *ibid.*, vol. XV, p. 110. She spoke of both Additional Protocol I, art. 53 and Additional Protocol II, art. 16 as protecting cultural property of value 'to the history of the country concerned and to the culture of its people': *ibid.*, para. 14. The Netherlands delegate referred to art. 53 of Additional Protocol I as protecting 'cultural riches and historic monuments constituting the cultural heritage of an entire nation and even of mankind as a whole': CDDH/III/SR.24, para. 29, *ibid.*, vol. XIV, p. 222.

[25] CDDH/215/Rev.1, Annex, *ibid.*, vol. XV, p. 307, which reads 'historic monuments, places of worship, or works of art which constitute the cultural heritage of peoples'.

of worship may be so described'.²⁶ Similarly, the ICRC commentary's gloss on the notion of the spiritual heritage of peoples — applicable *mutatis mutandis* to the idea of the cultural heritage of peoples — is instructive: acknowledging that 'the expression remains rather subjective', it suggests that, in case of doubt, 'reference should be made in the first place to the value or veneration ascribed to the object by the people whose heritage it is'.[27]

The conclusion that article 53 serves to protect the national cultural and spiritual heritage of each Party as determined by that Party is not undermined by the ICRC commentary's additional assertion that 'the Conference intended to protect in particular the most important objects, a category akin to property granted special protection as provided in Article 8 of the Hague Convention'.[28] The apparent attribution to the Protocol's drafters of explicit reference to article 8 of the Convention is editorial licence.[29] The *travaux* reveal no such reference or, indeed, specificity. In fact, Committee III spoke only of 'objects of considerable historical, cultural, and artistic importance'.[30] Furthermore, the suggestion that article 53 applies to a category of cultural property akin to that covered by article 8 of the Convention fails to account for the fact that the latter encompasses only immovable cultural property, with movables enjoying only *de facto* protection insofar as they are placed in specially protected refuges or situated in specially protected centres containing monuments. Article 53, on the contrary, expressly applies to 'works of art' in their own right. It is also hard to imagine that the Geneva diplomatic conference would have troubled itself to debate and adopt article 53 for the benefit of what was then eight examples of immovable cultural property, as inscribed in the International Register of Cultural Property under Special Protection.

---

[26] CDDH/236/Rev.1, para. 62, *ibid.*, p. 395 (Additional Protocols I and II). See also CDDH/III/353, *ibid.*, p. 437.
[27] Sandoz *et al.*, *Commentary*, para. 2065.
[28] *Ibid.*, para. 4844 (Additional Protocol II). Recall that at the time of the Geneva diplomatic conference and the preparation of the ICRC commentary, the regime of 'enhanced protection' in chap. 3 of the Second Hague Protocol did not exist.
[29] So too the hyperbole indulged in by the ICRC commentary *ibid.*, para. 2064 and para. 4840 (Additional Protocol II), based solely on an intervention by the Greek delegate at the diplomatic conference (CDDH/III/SR.59, para. 69, *Records 1974–77*, vol. XV, p. 220, subsequently cited in *Kordić*, Appeals Chamber Judgment, para. 91.
[30] CDDH/215/Rev.1, para. 69, *Records 1974–77*, vol. XV, p. 278. See also CDDH/III/224, *ibid.*, p. 333.

Nonetheless, the ICRC has persisted, in its recent study on customary international humanitarian law, in drawing a distinction between cultural property 'which forms part of the cultural or spiritual heritage of "peoples" (i.e. mankind)', as protected by article 53, and the 'broader' scope of the 1954 Hague Convention, 'which covers property which forms part of the cultural heritage of "every people" ',[31] concluding that '[t]he property covered by the Additional Protocols must be of such importance that it will be recognised by everyone'.[32] This is to commit the elementary mistake of considering only the English-language texts. As seen above, leaving aside article 53's reference to the spiritual heritage, the equally authentic French and Spanish texts of the respective wordings are identical: both translate as 'the cultural heritage ... of peoples'. Additionally, even restricting one's attention to the English text, the ICRC's construction of the word 'mankind' overlooks the key statement in the preamble to the 1954 Hague Convention that 'damage to cultural property belonging to any people whatsoever means damage to the cultural heritage of all mankind, since each people makes its contribution to the culture of the world'. The ICRC study claims support for its view in the interpretative declarations entered by several states at the time of article 53's adoption.[33] But, as reproduced in the study itself, the distinction drawn by these states is between the scope of application of article 53 of Protocol I and the scope of application of article 27 of the Hague Rules, not of article 1 of the 1954 Hague Convention.[34]

The obvious textual divergence between article 1 of the 1954 Hague Convention and article 53 of Protocol I is the insertion in the latter of places of worship and of the concept of the spiritual heritage of peoples. The ICRC commentary elaborates that in general 'the adjective "cultural" applies to historic monuments and works of art, while the adjective "spiritual" applies to places of worship', yet emphasises that a religious building may qualify for protection on account of its cultural value, just as under the Convention.[35] Putting it more simply,

---

[31] J.-M. Henckaerts and L. Doswald-Beck, *Customary International Humanitarian Law*, 3 vols. (Cambridge: Cambridge University Press, 2005), vol. I, pp. 130 and 132.

[32] *Ibid.*, p. 130.

[33] *Ibid.*, especially n. 19.

[34] See the statements of Canada, FRG, UK and USA, *ibid.*, vol. II, part 1, chap. 12, paras. 180, 193, 220 and 227 respectively. The statement by the Netherlands cited by the ICRC, as reproduced and in the original, makes no reference either to art. 1 of the 1954 Hague Convention or to art. 27 of the Hague Rules, and the Australian statement cited deals with a different question altogether.

[35] Sandoz *et al.*, *Commentary*, para. 2065. See also *ibid.*, para. 4843 (Additional Protocol II).

and although there was some dissent on this point at the diplomatic conference, the majority of delegates, who adopted article 53 by consensus, took the unequivocal view that not all places of worship are protected by article 53 but rather only those which constitute the cultural or spiritual heritage of peoples.[36]

In practice, the addition of places of worship which constitute part of the cultural or spiritual heritage of peoples should not make a difference to the relative scope of application of article 53 vis à vis article 1 of the 1954 Hague Convention. Those places of worship important enough to constitute part of the spiritual heritage of a people will, in practice, also be historic monuments forming part of the cultural heritage of that people for the purposes of both article 53 and article 1 of the Convention.[37] In this light, the insertion of the two terms would seem to have no more than rhetorical significance. Indeed, rhetorical significance was precisely the motivation behind the amendment, as proposed by Saudi Arabia, the Holy See, Italy and a coalition of Islamic states.[38] The delegate to the Holy See, acting as unofficial spokesman for the group, elaborated:

In the opinion of the delegation of the Holy See, the addition of the words 'spiritual' and 'places of worship' to the original text ... shows a better understanding of what is most mysterious and most precious in man's heritage ... If all one sees in the stained glass at Chartres, in the frescoes at Assisi, in the pure lines of the mosques at Fez, are artistic creations, no matter how admirable – one is missing the essential. Truly to comprehend these objects of sacred art, to grasp their uniqueness, one has to discover and comprehend their *spirit*, the spiritual motives which inspired the artist's hand.[39]

In short, 'places of worship symbolized and gave expression to basic human values which were not only historic or artistic'.[40]

In the final analysis, then, there is sufficient evidence to conclude that, despite its different wording, article 53 rightly applies to cultural property within the meaning of the 1954 Hague Convention – that is,

---

[36] *Ibid.*, para. 2067. Places of worship not constituting the cultural or spiritual heritage of peoples are nonetheless protected as civilian objects by art. 52 of Additional Protocol I, as made clear by the reference to them in art. 52(3).

[37] When, at one point in the drafting, the reference to places of worship was deleted, the Irish delegate expressed the view 'that the words "historic monuments or works of art" applied to the major places of worship of every nation and religion': CDDH/III/SR.59, para. 61, *Records 1974–77*, vol. XV, p. 219.

[38] CDDH/412/Rev. 1 to 3, *ibid.*, vol. III, p. 215.

[39] CDDH/SR.42, Annex, *ibid.*, vol. VI, p. 227, original emphasis.

[40] CDDH/SR.41, para. 167, *ibid.*, p. 171.

to immovables and movables comprising each Party's cultural (and spiritual) heritage as determined by it. Going on the practice of Parties to the Convention, this generally means that, as applied to immovables, article 53 will serve to protect the full panoply of buildings, sites and monuments listed or scheduled in accordance with the relevant domestic conservation legislation of the Party in whose territory they are situated, or to a sizeable proportion thereof. Its application to movables is less clear, as is the case under the Convention.

That said, there remained among the delegations at Geneva 'a measure of disagreement' on the effect of the modifying clause 'which constitute the cultural [or spiritual] heritage of peoples', as acknowledged by Committee III of the Diplomatic Conference;[41] and, as with article 1 of the 1954 Hague Convention, uncertainty appears to persist today as to the proper interpretation and application of article 53. Nor, unlike under the Convention, is there probative evidence of the subsequent practice of the Parties in interpreting and applying the relevant part of the provision.[42] A few leading jurists, for their part, continue to take their lead from the ICRC commentary's misleading assertion to construe article 53 highly restrictively,[43] as has the Eritrea Ethiopia Claims Commission.[44] The result is a highly unsatisfactory state of affairs which can only undermine the wartime protection of the cultural and spiritual heritage of peoples.

As again seen under the 1954 Hague Convention, it should be emphasised that, while in principle article 53 leaves it to the Party in whose territory the relevant historic monument, work of art or place of worship is situated to determine whether or not this object constitutes part of its cultural or spiritual heritage and is therefore protected by

---

[41] CDDH/III/353, *ibid.*, vol. XV, p. 437. See also CDDH/236/Rev. 1, *ibid.*, p. 395.

[42] Parties to Additional Protocol I are not required to submit periodic implementation reports, as Parties to the 1954 Hague Convention are. Nor, in contrast to the latter, does the former embody a regime of distinctive marking by which one might tentatively gauge the range of property in its territory to which a Party considers art. 53 applicable.

[43] See W. A. Solf, 'Cultural property, protection in armed conflict', in R. Bernhardt (ed.), *Encyclopedia of Public International Law*, 5 vols. (Amsterdam: North-Holland, 1992), vol. I, p. 892 at pp. 895–6; J. de Preux, 'La Convention de La Haye et le récent développement du droit des conflits armés', in Istituto Internazionale di Diritto Umanitario (ed.), *The International Protection of Cultural Property. Acts of the Symposium organized on the occasion of the 30th Anniversary of the Hague Convention on the Protection of Cultural Property in the Event of Armed Conflicts* (Rome: Fondazione Europea Dragan, 1986), p. 107 at pp. 112–13; Rogers, *Law on the Battlefield*, p. 153; Wolfrum, 'Protection of Cultural Property', at 316–17.

[44] *Partial Award: Central Front. Eritrea's Claims 2, 4, 6, 7, 8 and 22*, 43 ILM 1249 (2004), para. 113.

the provision, in practice the determination tends ultimately to fall by default to the opposing Party, unless the former has notified the latter in advance of the objects it considers protected. In other words, the non-territorial Party will in practice often be called upon to assess the cultural or spiritual importance of the object in question to the opposing Party. The safest course in this event is to err on the side of caution and to presume that every historic monument and work of art and most places of worship constitute part of the cultural or spiritual heritage of the adversary, and are thereby protected by article 53.

Like article 4 of the Convention, article 53 of Protocol I applies as much to cultural property situated within a Party's own territory as to cultural property in the territory of an opposing Party,[45] and as much to belligerent occupation as to hostilities.[46] As for the nature of the obligations it imposes, the term 'acts of hostility' in article 53(a) bears the same meaning as under article 4(1) of the Convention. In other words, article 53(a) forbids not just attacks against the objects in question but also their demolition.[47] As for article 53(b), the concept of 'the military effort' is arguably wider than the notion of 'military action' referred to in article 52(2). According to the ICRC commentary, the military effort is 'a very broad concept, encompassing all military activities connected with the conduct of a war'.[48] For example, the use of the cellars of a historic castle a long way behind the front line to store rations might be considered supportive of the military effort but might not be thought to make an effective contribution to military action. The same might go for the billeting of non-frontline troops there. Such use might be held to violate article 53(b) but would arguably not justify an attack against the castle under article 52(2).

The thrust of article 53 is to affirm the Convention's essential obligations. But whereas the obligations of respect in article 4(1) of the Convention are subject to article 4(2), article 53 contains no exception in respect of military necessity. That is, military necessity, as such, provides no justification for directing acts of hostility against historic monuments, works of art or places of worship which constitute the cultural or spiritual heritage of peoples, for using them in support of the military effort or for making them the object of reprisals. Nor are paragraphs (a)

---

[45] Sandoz *et al.*, *Commentary*, para. 2073.
[46] Additional Protocol I, art. 1(3) and, in turn, Geneva Conventions I to IV, common art. 2.
[47] Sandoz *et al.*, *Commentary*, para. 2070, including n. 27; Bothe *et al.*, *New Rules*, para. 2.5.2.
[48] Sandoz *et al.*, *Commentary*, para. 2078.

and (b) of article 53 reciprocal,[49] either as a matter of construction or of broader principle.

That said, if and for as long as an object covered by article 53 is used in support of the military effort contrary to paragraph (b), the legality of any attack against that object – and only that object – falls to be determined by reference to article 52(2),[50] and will be lawful provided such use makes an effective contribution to military action and the object's total or partial destruction, capture or neutralisation, in the circumstances ruling at the time, offers a definite military advantage. In other words, despite the unavailability under article 53 of an exception as to military necessity and despite the non-synallagmatic character of the obligations imposed by the provision, objects falling within its scope do not, in the final analysis, enjoy unconditional immunity from attack; rather, if used to make an effective contribution to military action, they may be targeted by operation of article 52(2), as long as the second limb of the provision is satisfied. In terms of attack, then, whereas other civilian objects may be targeted pursuant to article 52(2) on account of their nature, location, purpose or use, the practical effect of the additional protection afforded by article 53 is that historic monuments, works of art and places of worship which constitute the cultural or spiritual heritage of peoples may be attacked only on account of their use. Note that this is not the same as saying that article 53(a) and article 53(b) are reciprocal obligations – in other words, that the use of cultural property by one Party in support of the military effort, contrary to article 53(b), releases the other Party from its obligation under article 53(a) not to direct acts of hostility against cultural property. The result of such a relationship would be that the latter Party would be freed from the obligation not to attack cultural property as it applies to all cultural property under article 53 – the lawfulness of an attack against any of this property then falling to be determined under article 52(2) – and not just as it applies to the specific item of cultural property used by the opposing Party in support of the military effort. This is not the case.

Article 53 interacts with article 52(2) only in the context of attacks, in accordance with the wording of the latter provision, which is restricted to attacks. All other acts of hostility, including demolitions, remain absolutely prohibited by article 53.

---

[49] *Ibid.*, para. 2079.
[50] Sandoz *et al.*, *Commentary*, para. 2079; Toman, *Protection of Cultural Property*, p. 390; Solf, 'Cultural property', at 895.

The *travaux préparatoires* give no hint whether the exclusion of military necessity was deliberate or not. Rogers, for one, expresses surprise at this progressive reform.[51] On the other hand, insofar as it applies to bombardment, article 53 is in keeping with the better reading of article 27 of the Hague Rules. Either way, the practical impact of the change should not be overestimated in the case of attacks, where article 53 effectively eliminates nature, location and purpose as grounds for targeting cultural property, since, even where these three grounds are formally available under article 52(2), use remains by far the principal way in which such property could, in practice, make an effective contribution to military action. In the context of demolitions, however, the omission of a waiver as to military necessity is a considerable advance. The same goes in respect of the use of cultural property in support of the military effort, as absolutely prohibited by article 53(b).

The protection granted by article 53 is buttressed by the precautions in attack required by article 57, for the purposes of which historic monuments, works of art and places of worship which constitute the cultural or spiritual heritage of peoples are characterised as civilian objects.

It is crucial, nonetheless, to recall that article 53 of Protocol I is stated to be without prejudice to the provisions of the 1954 Hague Convention. As a consequence, where the parties to an international armed conflict are Parties both to Protocol I and to the Convention, conduct covered by both article 53 and the Convention is governed by the provisions of the Convention.[52] The result is that Parties to both instruments are entitled to invoke the waiver as to military necessity embodied in article 4(2) of the Convention to justify directing an act of hostility (be it an attack or demolitions) against cultural property or to justify using such property for purposes likely to expose it to destruction or damage.[53] Ironically, then, participation in the Convention, the specialist instrument, by Parties to Protocol I can serve to weaken, in this limited respect at least, the protection of cultural property in armed conflict.

---

[51] Rogers, *Law on the Battlefield*, p. 154.
[52] See Vienna Convention on the Law of Treaties, art. 30(2).
[53] *Strugar*, Trial Chamber Judgment, para. 309. See also Sandoz *et al.*, *Commentary*, para. 2072 n. 28; Toman, *Protection of Cultural Property*, p. 389; E. David, *Principes de droit des conflits armés*, 3rd edn (Brussels: Bruylant, 2002), para. 2.59; R. Kolb, *Ius in bello. Le droit international des conflits armés* (Basle/Brussels: Helbing & Lichtenhahn/Bruylant, 2003), para. 298. But in accordance with 1954 Hague Convention, art. 4(4), it remains absolutely prohibited to direct any act of hostility against such property by way of reprisal.

The reference in article 53's 'without prejudice' clause to 'other relevant international instruments' would appear to be to the Roerich Pact, in force when the provision was adopted, and still in force, among a small number of American states. But the ordinary meaning of the phrase would also encompass any similar specialist international agreement for the protection of cultural property in the event of armed conflict as may be concluded in the future. In this light, where parties to an international armed conflict are Parties to both Protocol I and to the Second Protocol to the 1954 Hague Convention, conduct covered by both instruments is governed by the provisions of the Second Protocol.

Incidental damage

In a watershed in the history of the laws of war, Protocol I repudiates the doctrine of double effect by embodying in binding form a rule as to incidental damage resulting from attacks against lawful military objectives. Article 51(4) states that '[i]ndiscriminate attacks are prohibited', and article 51(5)(b) defines as indiscriminate, *inter alia*, 'an attack which may be expected to cause incidental loss of civilian life, injury to civilians, damage to civilian objects, or a combination thereof, which would be excessive in relation to the concrete and direct military advantage anticipated'. The prohibition on such attacks is backed up by article 57(2)(a)(iii), which specifies that those who plan or decide upon an attack shall 'refrain from deciding to launch any attack which may be expected to cause incidental loss of civilian life, injury to civilians, damage to civilian objects, or a combination thereof, which would be excessive in relation to the concrete and direct military advantage anticipated'; and by article 57(2)(b), which provides that an attack shall be cancelled or suspended if it becomes apparent that it may be expected to cause such loss, injury or damage.[54] For the purposes of all three provisions, historic monuments, works of art and places of worship covered by article 53 are characterised as civilian objects. The test is one of proportionality,[55] even if the word is not used; and although

---

[54] See also Additional Protocol I, art. 57(2)(a)(ii), obliging those who plan or decide upon an attack to 'take all feasible precautions in the choice of means and methods of attack with a view to avoiding, and in any event to minimizing, incidental loss of civilian life, injury to civilians and damage to civilian objects'.

[55] In this light, Sandoz *et al.*, *Commentary*, para. 1980, and the reference *ibid.*, para. 2218 to 'extensive' destruction of civilian objects, are manifestly wrong.

the assessment called for is not an exact science, it must be made in good faith.

As applied to cultural property, proportionality implicates qualitative as much as quantitative factors. In other words, the extent of incidental loss occasioned by damage to or destruction of historic monuments, works of art or places of worship is a question not just of square metres but also of the cultural value represented thereby. In this light, it is significant that property protected by article 53 is, by definition, of sufficient cultural importance as to constitute the cultural or spiritual heritage of a people. Moreover, resolution 20(IV) of the Diplomatic Conference of Geneva implies that, as under the 1954 Hague Convention, the ultimate concern of article 53 is the wartime protection of 'the cultural heritage of all mankind'. Since elements of this heritage are often irreplaceable, only the anticipation of very considerable concrete and direct military advantage, in many cases overwhelming, will, in practice, suffice to justify an attack likely to cause incidental damage to cultural property. A textbook example of the application of the rule of proportionality came during the Gulf War in 1991, when Iraq positioned two fighter aircraft next to the ancient ziggurat of Ur. Coalition commanders decided not to attack the aircraft 'on the basis of respect for cultural property and the belief that positioning of the aircraft adjacent to Ur (without servicing equipment or a runway nearby) effectively had placed each out of action, thereby limiting the value of their destruction by Coalition air forces when weighed against the risk of damage to the temple'.[56]

Given the fate of cultural property during attacks against military targets since the advent of the practice of bombardment, and especially since the rise of aerial bombardment, the adoption in Protocol I of a strict rule of proportionality in respect of incidental damage is one of the most crucial advances in the history of the legal protection of cultural property in armed conflict.

Other indiscriminate attacks

Article 50(4)'s prohibition on indiscriminate attacks is not limited to excessive incidental harm. In addition to the definition in article 51(5)(b), article 51(5)(a) defines as indiscriminate 'an attack by bombardment by any methods or means which treats as a single military objective a number of clearly separated and distinct military objectives located

---

[56] Department of Defense, *Report to Congress on the Conduct of the Persian Gulf War, Appendix O: The Role of the Law of War*, 31 ILM 612 (1992) at 626.

in a city, town, village or other area containing a similar concentration of civilians or civilian objects'. In short, article 51(5)(4), referable back to article 50(4), forbids area bombing, responsible for the devastation in the Second World War of the cultural heritage of Germany and Japan. Other attacks deemed indiscriminate include, in the words of article 51(4)(b), 'those which employ a method or means of combat which cannot be directed at a specific military objective'. This serves to outlaw the use of, *inter alia*, unguided or insufficiently guided ballistic missiles, which caused considerable damage to Iranian cultural property in the Iran–Iraq War.

Localities and zones under special protection

Part IV, section I, chapter V of Additional Protocol I makes provision for localities and zones under special protection – provision not specifically aimed at the protection of cultural property but which nonetheless has considerable potential in this regard. The relevant articles, namely articles 59 and 60, have their origins in the concept of 'open' towns and cities, as promoted in the 1930s, used to minor effect in the Spanish Civil War and Sino-Japanese War, and bandied about with little common understanding or success in the Second World War.

Article 59 deals with the essentially unilateral[57] device of non-defended localities. Unlike the regime of special protection for cultural property under chapter II of the 1954 Hague Convention, such localities are designed to come into being only once armed conflict has broken out: they are not established in advance in peacetime. Paragraph 1 of article 59 embodies the gist of the concept, namely absolute immunity from attack, stating that it is prohibited for the Parties to the conflict to attack, by any means whatsoever, non-defended localities. Paragraph 2 defines the concept and specifies the conditions for it.[58] It provides that the appropriate authorities of a Party to the conflict 'may declare as a non-defended locality any inhabited place near or in a zone where armed forces are in contact which is open for occupation by an adverse Party'. The cumulative conditions for such a locality are fourfold. First, in

---

[57] In an exception to this unilateral character, art. 59(5) provides for the establishment, by way of agreement between or among the Parties to the conflict, of non-defended localities even if they do not fulfil the conditions specified in paragraph 2.
[58] Article 59(7) states that a locality loses its status as non-defended when it ceases to fulfil the conditions in para. 2 or, if established pursuant to para. 5, the conditions in the agreement referred to therein.

accordance with article 59(2)(a), all combatants, as well as mobile weapons and mobile military equipment, must have been evacuated. Subparagraph (b) stipulates that no hostile use is to be made of fixed military installations or establishments. Subparagraph (c) requires that no acts of hostility are to be committed by the authorities or by the population. Finally, pursuant to article 59(2)(d), no activities in support of military operations may be undertaken. Article 59(3) adds that the presence in the locality of persons specially protected under the Geneva Conventions and Protocol I, and of police forces retained for the sole purpose of maintaining law and order, is not contrary to the conditions laid down in article 59(2).[59] The ICRC commentary adds that, '[a]lthough Article 59 does not mention this explicitly, it is clear that personnel assigned to the protection of cultural objects defined by the Hague Convention of 1954 are also covered by this paragraph'.[60]

As a means by which to immunise cultural property unilaterally from the effects of armed conflict, non-defended localities offer several advantages over the regime of special protection provided for in chapter II of the 1954 Hague Convention. In terms of the substantive obligations imposed on the Parties to the conflict, article 59 of Protocol I recognises no exception to the immunity it accords: the prohibition on attacking non-defended localities is absolute. As regards the conditions for the enjoyment of this immunity, article 59 – in contrast to article 8, paragraphs 1(a) and 5 respectively of the Convention – does not require that such localities be situated an adequate distance from transport and communications infrastructure or, in the alternative, that the relevant Party undertake to make no use of these during armed conflict: railways, main lines of communication, broadcasting stations and the like may be situated even within such localities, and may continue to be used as long as no activities in support of military operations are undertaken. Nor is the establishment of such a locality dependent on the tortuous registration process outlined in articles 13 to 15 of the Regulations for the Execution of the Convention, with its possibility that another Party may object to the grant of immunity. Finally, the protection afforded by non-defended localities would not be limited *de jure* to the immovable cultural

---

[59] Persons specially protected under the Geneva Conventions and Additional Protocol I include medical units (Additional Protocol I, art. 12) and civilian medical and religious personnel (*ibid.*, art. 15).
[60] Sandoz et al., *Commentary*, para. 2277. Consider also, in this light, 1954 Hague Convention, art. 8(4).

property protected by article 8 but would permissibly embrace all cultural property within the meaning of article 1 of the Convention.

The advantages of non-defended localities over the 'enhanced protection' provided for in chapter 3 of the Second Protocol to the Convention are fewer: use in support of military operations in either context leads to the loss of immunity; neither regime is conditional upon an adequate distance between the property in question and transport and communications infrastructure; and both regimes can cover movables. But to share in the immunity of a non-defended locality, cultural property need not be 'of the greatest importance for humanity', nor 'protected by adequate domestic legal and administrative measures recognising its exceptional cultural and historic value and ensuring the highest level of protection'.[61] Nor need the procedure laid down in article 11 of the Second Protocol be followed.

For its part, article 60 of Additional Protocol I relates to the mutual device of demilitarised zones, the essence of which, *viz.* absolute immunity from attack, is the same as that of non-defended localities. In accordance with paragraph 1 of article 60, it is prohibited for the Parties to the conflict 'to extend their military operations to zones on which they have conferred by agreement the status of demilitarized zone, if such extension is contrary to the terms of the agreement'.[62] In contrast with declarations or agreements establishing non-defended localities, agreements setting up demilitarised zones may be concluded in peacetime, and there is no requirement that such zones be inhabited. While the terms of any agreement establishing a demilitarised zone are at the discretion of the relevant Parties, article 60(3) states that the subject of such an agreement 'shall normally be any zone which fulfils [four] conditions',[63] the first three of which, as spelled out in subparagraphs (a), (b) and (c), are identical to those laid down in article 59(2)(a) to (c). Article 60(3)(d) additionally requires

---

[61] Second Hague Protocol, arts. 10(a) and 10(b) respectively.

[62] As specified in art. 60(2), such agreements must be express, although they may be concluded verbally and may consist of reciprocal and concordant declarations. They may also be concluded through the good offices of a Protecting Power or of any impartial humanitarian organisation, among the latter of which can be numbered – in addition to the ICRC – the International Committee of the Blue Shield (ICBS), with its mandate in respect of certain cultural property.

[63] Article 60(7) provides that if one of the Parties to the conflict commits a material breach of the provisions of para. 3, the other Party is released from its obligations under the agreement.

that 'any activity linked to the military effort' must have ceased, the interpretation of this condition being left to the agreement of the Parties to the conflict. Insofar as it might be used to immunise cultural property, article 60 provides those Parties to Additional Protocol I which are not also Parties to the 1954 Hague Convention an opportunity to make the sort of special agreements provided for in article 24 of the latter.

Misuse of recognised emblems

Article 38(1) of Additional Protocol I forbids the improper use and deliberate misuse of certain emblems, signs and signals. Of relevance in the present context is the second sentence of the provision, by which it is prohibited to misuse deliberately in an armed conflict 'the protective emblem of cultural property', a reference to the distinctive emblem of the 1954 Hague Convention, as regulated by chapter V of the Convention and by chapter IV of the Regulations for its Execution.[64] The reference in article 38(1) of Protocol I to the protective emblem, in the singular, suggests that the Convention's emblem was the only one the drafters had in mind.[65] At the same time, the use of the generic term 'protective emblem', in contradistinction to the term 'distinctive emblem' employed throughout the Convention, might be taken to imply that the improper use during armed conflict of other emblems for the protection of cultural property, such as the 'visible signs' prescribed during naval bombardment by article 5 of Hague Convention IX and the 'distinctive flag' provided for in article 3 of the Roerich Pact, is similarly prohibited by article 38(1). The question is academic, however, given that article 38(1) also forbids the deliberate misuse in armed conflict of 'other internationally recognized protective emblems, signs or signals', a category which clearly encompasses these other markers.[66] The prohibition may even extend to the World Heritage emblem, adopted in 1978 as the official symbol of the World Heritage Convention and used to identify properties on the World Heritage List,[67] although this is not, strictly speaking, a 'protective' emblem.

---

[64] The improper use of the distinctive emblem is similarly prohibited during armed conflict by art. 17(3) of the Convention.
[65] See also Sandoz et al., *Commentary*, paras. 1529 and 1550, although n. 33 of the latter refers also to the Roerich Pact.
[66] *Ibid.*, paras. 1529, n. 4 and 1557, referring to Hague Convention IX, art. 5.
[67] See Operational Guidelines for the Implementation of the World Heritage Convention, UNESCO Doc. WHC.05/2, paras. 258–79.

Certain improper use of the distinctive emblem of the 1954 Hague Convention would also amount to perfidy, within the meaning of article 37 of Protocol I. Article 37(1) states that it is prohibited to kill, injure or capture an adversary 'by resort to perfidy', the term being defined to comprise '[a]cts inviting the confidence of an adversary to lead him to believe that he is entitled to, or is obliged to accord, protection under the rules of international law applicable in armed conflict, with intent to betray that confidence'.[68] While it is unlikely that the use on cultural property of the distinctive emblem of the 1954 Hague Convention could ever be perfidious within the meaning of article 37, as distinct from merely improper within the meaning of article 38, it is not hard to imagine the perfidious use of an armlet bearing the distinctive emblem by soldiers feigning to be personnel engaged in the protection of cultural property or even persons responsible for the duties of control.[69]

Criminal sanctions

Part V, section II of Additional Protocol I provides for criminal sanctions for the suppression of certain breaches of its obligations, operable via the penal provisions of the Geneva Conventions,[70] to which Parties to the Protocol must also be Parties. Article 85(1) states that the provisions of the Geneva Conventions relating to the repression of breaches and grave breaches, supplemented by part V, section II of the Protocol, are to apply to the repression of breaches and grave breaches of the Protocol. This means that Parties are required to enact any legislation necessary to provide effective penal sanctions for persons committing, or ordering to be committed, any of the grave breaches of the Protocol.[71] They are also obliged to search for persons alleged to have committed, or to have ordered to be committed, grave breaches of the Protocol and to bring them, regardless of their nationality, before their courts. This last imposes a duty on Parties to empower their criminal courts to exercise

---

[68] Note that subparas. (a) to (d) of Additional Protocol I, art. 37(1) are illustrative, not exhaustive.
[69] See 1954 Hague Convention, arts. 17(2)(c) and 17(2)(b) respectively and 1954 Hague Regulations, art. 21(1).
[70] Geneva Convention I, arts. 49 and 50; Geneva Convention II, arts. 50 and 51; Geneva Convention III, arts. 129 and 130; Geneva Convention IV, arts. 146 and 147.
[71] The obligation to search for suspects is limited to situations where a Party realises that such a person is on its territory: Pictet, *Commentary (IV)*, p. 593.

universal jurisdiction over grave breaches,[72] along with a duty to prosecute such breaches. As an alternative to prosecution, a Party 'may also, if it prefers, and in accordance with the provisions of its own legislation, hand such persons over for trial to another High Contracting Party concerned, provided such High Contracting Party has made out a *prima facie* case'. Additionally, each Party is to take measures necessary for the suppression of all acts contrary to the Protocol other than grave breaches. Municipal criminalisation of what might be called 'non-grave' breaches is a permissible and appropriate means of giving effect to this obligation, as is the assertion by a Party of universal criminal jurisdiction over such breaches.[73] Lastly, Protocol I supplements the obligations laid down by the provisions of the Geneva Conventions relating to the suppression of grave and other breaches with some obligations of its own. Article 86 deals with culpable omissions, recognising in paragraph 2 the doctrines of command and superior responsibility. Article 87 obliges Parties and the Parties to the conflict to impose on commanders duties of prevention, suppression and punishment in respect of breaches of the Conventions and of Protocol I. Article 88 imposes on Parties and the Parties to the conflict obligations of mutual assistance in criminal matters related to grave breaches, but seemingly not other breaches, of the Conventions and Protocol.

Precisely which breaches are to be considered grave breaches of Protocol I is spelled out in paragraphs 2 to 4 of article 85, with article 85(4) identifying a range of acts not necessarily causing death or serious injury which constitute grave breaches 'when committed wilfully and in violation of the Conventions or the Protocol'. Of particular relevance is article 85(4)(d), a curiously drafted provision which defines as a grave breach of the Protocol 'making the clearly-recognized historic monuments, works of art or places of worship which constitute the cultural or spiritual heritage of peoples and to which special protection has been

---

[72] *Arrest Warrant of 11 April 2000 (Democratic Republic of the Congo v. Belgium)*, ICJ Reports 2002, p. 3, sep. op. Bula-Bula at para. 65; *ibid.*, diss. op. Van den Wyngaert at para. 59; *ibid.*, sep. op. Rezek at para. 7, more ambiguously. This is the long-established position of the ICRC: see Pictet, *Commentary (IV)*, pp. 587 and 592; ICRC, *Advisory Service 1999 Annual Report. National Implementation of International Humanitarian Law* (Geneva: ICRC, 2000), p. 4; F. Kalshoven and L. Zegveld, *Constraints on the Waging of War. An Introduction to International Humanitarian Law*, 3rd edn (Geneva: ICRC, 2001), p. 80. But *cf.*, perhaps *contra*, *Arrest Warrant of 11 April 2000*, sep. op. Guillaume at para. 17; *ibid.*, dec. Ranjeva at para.7; *ibid.*, sep. op. Higgins, Kooijmans and Buergenthal at paras. 28–32.

[73] See also T. Meron, 'International Criminalization of Internal Atrocities' (1995) 89 AJIL 554 at 568–71.

given by special arrangement, for example, within the framework of a competent international organization, the object of attack, causing as a result extensive destruction thereof, where there is no evidence of the violation by the adverse Party of Article 53, sub-paragraph (b), and when such historic monuments, works of art and places of worship are not located in the immediate proximity of military objectives'. The requirement in the chapeau to article 85(4) that the acts enumerated must be committed in violation of the Conventions or the Protocol means, in effect, that, for the purposes of article 85(4)(d), the attack in question must constitute a breach of article 53 of the Protocol.

It is not clear what is meant in article 85(4)(d) by 'special protection ... by special arrangement, for example, within the framework of a competent international organization'. It is likely, in the light of the privileged status accorded it by article 53 of Protocol I and by resolution 20(IV) of the Diplomatic Conference of Geneva, that the 1954 Hague Convention constitutes a 'special arrangement' within the meaning of the provision. But it is less certain whether the drafters envisaged that all cultural property protected by the Convention, as *lex specialis* to the *lex generalis* of Protocol I, was to be considered under 'special protection' or only those immovables enjoying special protection within the meaning of chapter II of the Convention by virtue of their entry in the International Register of Cultural Property under Special Protection.[74] Given, however, that 'works of art', as mentioned in article 85(4)(d) of Protocol I, cannot enjoy special protection under chapter II of the Convention in their own right, it must be the case that all cultural property covered by the Convention falls within the provision.[75] In addition, it has been suggested, with good reason, that those historic monuments inscribed on the World Heritage List in accordance with the provisions of the World Heritage Convention would equally satisfy the description in article 85(4)(d).[76] So too would those under the protection of the Roerich Pact and those the subject of any *ad hoc* arrangement. Specifics aside, the bottom line is that the special protection of the object in question

---

[74] Recall that, at the time of the Geneva diplomatic conference, the regime of 'enhanced protection' in chap. 3 of the Second Hague Protocol did not exist.

[75] For this reason, the assertion in Henckaerts and Doswald-Beck, *Customary International Humanitarian Law*, vol. I, p. 580 that '[i]n practice' art. 85(4)(d) 'refers to the special protection regime created by the Hague Convention for the Protection of Cultural Property' is unsustainable.

[76] E. J. Roucounas, 'Les infractions graves au droit humanitaire (Article 85 du Protocole additionnel I aux Conventions de Genève)' (1978) 31 RHDI 57 at 113–14.

by some sort of special arrangement is an essential material element of a war crime under article 85(4)(d): the protection of article 53 of the Protocol is not enough. But what is not indicated is whether the special arrangement in question must be in force as between both the attacking Party and the Party whose cultural property is the object of attack, or whether it suffices that the latter alone is a Party to such an arrangement.[77] On the whole, article 85(4)(d)'s condition precedent of special protection pursuant to a special agreement is an odd one, perhaps being intended as a means of urging states which have not yet done so to become Parties to the 1954 Hague Convention, in the words of resolution 20(IV).

The phrase 'clearly-recognized', which introduces a requirement of knowledge into the *mens rea* of the offence, is ambiguous. It may refer simply to the identification of the object of attack as a historic monument, work of art or place of worship. Alternatively, it may refer to the additional recognition of the historic monument, work of art or place of worship in question as one which constitutes the cultural or spiritual heritage of a people and to which special protection has been given by special arrangement.[78] The *travaux préparatoires* are silent on the question.[79] Either way, the fact that the object attacked was marked at the time with the distinctive emblem of the 1954 Hague Convention would serve as evidence from which to infer that the accused both recognised it as cultural property[80] and recognised that special protection had been given it by special agreement. The same can be said, with less force, of the object's entry in the International Register of Cultural Property under Special Protection or on the List of Cultural Property under Enhanced Protection, as long as this is adequately publicised. The inscription of the attacked object on the World Heritage List, again if

---

[77] Needless to say, both must be Parties to Additional Protocol I, in the light of which it cannot be said that the second alternative violates the *pacta tertiis* principle, as reflected in Vienna Convention on the Law of Treaties, art. 34.

[78] J. de Breucker, 'La répression des infractions graves aux dispositions du premier Protocole additionel aux quatre Conventions de Genève du 12 août 1949' (1977) 16 RDPMDG 497 at 505.

[79] For its part, the ICRC commentary misses the point: see Sandoz et al., *Commentary*, para. 3517 n. 36.

[80] See *Strugar*, Trial Chamber Judgment, para. 329, reference omitted: 'As a further evidentiary issue regarding [the intent to destroy cultural property], the Chamber accepts the evidence that protective UNESCO emblems were visible, from the JNA positions at Žarkovica and elsewhere, above the Old Town on 6 December 1991.'

sufficiently publicised and/or if signalled at the site by the display of the World Heritage emblem, would serve the same purpose.[81]

The stipulation that the attack cause extensive destruction of the historic monument, work of art or place of worship, a *de minimis* provision taken from article 50 of the first Geneva Convention, article 51 of the second and article 147 of the fourth, is what distinguishes a grave breach of the Protocol from other breaches which also relate solely to property. The word 'extensive' has no precise legal content and remains a matter of appreciation in each case.

The stipulation that the historic monument, work of art or place of worship the object of attack not be located in the immediate proximity of military objectives does not imply that objects so located may lawfully be attacked. Rather, it is an evidentiary precaution, linked to the requirement that the attack be committed wilfully, and seeks to obviate the imposition of criminal responsibility on the basis of negligence. It is designed to ensure that an accused is convicted under article 85(4)(d) only for deliberately making cultural property protected by article 53 the object of attack, and not for either a misdirected attack against a legitimate military objective or a well-directed attack against a military objective which causes extensive damage to cultural property nearby. An analogous issue was raised under the customary international law of war crimes in *Strugar*, dealing with the attack on the Old Town of Dubrovnik on 6 December 1991. There a Trial Chamber of the ICTY, considering 'that the special protection awarded to cultural property itself may not be lost simply because of military activities or military installations in the immediate vicinity of the cultural property', added that in such a case, however, 'the practical result may be that it cannot be established that the acts which caused destruction of or damage to cultural property were "directed against" that cultural property, rather than the military installation or use in its immediate vicinity'.[82]

Article 85(3)(b) establishes the grave breach of launching an indiscriminate attack affecting the civilian population or civilian objects in the knowledge that the attack will cause excessive loss of life, injury to civilians or damage to civilian objects, 'as defined in Article 57, paragraph 2(a)(iii)'. The reference to article 57(2)(a)(iii), although

---

[81] See *ibid.*, references omitted: '[T]he direct perpetrators' intent to deliberately destroy cultural property is inferred by the Chamber from the evidence of the deliberate attack on the Old Town, the unique cultural and historical character of which was a matter of renown, as was the Old Town's status as a UNESCO World Heritage site.'

[82] *Ibid.*, para. 310.

confusingly placed, is to the term 'indiscriminate attack', and means an attack 'which may be expected to cause incidental loss of civilian life, injury to civilians, damage to civilian objects, or a combination thereof, which would be excessive in relation to the concrete and direct military advantage anticipated'. Cultural property is a species of civilian object for the purposes of article 85(3)(b).

Finally, article 85(3)(f) states that 'the perfidious use, in violation of Article 37, of the distinctive emblem of the red cross, red crescent or red sun and lion or of other protective signs recognized by the Conventions or [the] Protocol' constitutes a grave breach of the Protocol. The ICRC commentary suggests that a perfidious use of the distinctive emblem of the 1954 Hague Convention causing death or serious injury would constitute a grave breach of the Protocol under article 85(3)(f),[83] and it would certainly appear that the phrase 'other protective signs recognized by the Conventions or [the] Protocol' used in the provision was intended as an omnibus expression encompassing both the 'other emblems, signs or signals provided for by the Conventions or by [the] Protocol' referred to in article 38(1)[84] and the 'other internationally recognized protective emblems, signs or signals, including the flag of truce, and the protective emblem of cultural property' mentioned in the same article.

Additional Protocol II

Scope of application

According to article 1(1) of Additional Protocol II, which governs non-international armed conflicts, the Protocol 'develops and supplements Article 3 common to the Geneva Conventions ... without modifying its existing conditions of application'. But whereas common article 3 applies in the event of 'armed conflict not of an international character occurring in the territory of one of the High Contracting Parties', Protocol II is stated to apply to armed conflicts 'which take place in the territory of a High Contracting Party between its armed forces and

---

[83] Sandoz et al., *Commentary*, para. 3498. See also Toman, *Protection of Cultural Property*, p. 187.
[84] See e.g. the signs, 'as may be agreed upon with the other Party', to be displayed, in accordance with art. 59(6), by the Party in control of a non-defended locality established by mutual agreement pursuant to art. 59(5) and, in accordance with art. 60(5), by the Party in control of a demilitarised zone: Sandoz et al., *Commentary*, para. 3495.

dissident armed forces or other organized armed groups which, under responsible command, exercise such control over a part of its territory as to enable them to carry out sustained and concerted military operations and to implement [the] Protocol'. In other words, the scope of application of Protocol II is narrower than that of common article 3: it applies only to conflicts between the armed forces of the government of a High Contracting Party and dissident armed forces or other organised armed groups, whereas common article 3 is capable of applying to internal armed conflicts between or among non-governmental forces or other groups; and it applies only in the event that the non-government party satisfies specified conditions relating to its command, its control over territory, the nature of its military operations and its capacity to implement the Protocol. Since common article 3 was the model for article 19 of the 1954 Hague Convention, the scope of application of Protocol II is therefore also narrower than the scope of the Convention, insofar as the latter applies to non-international armed conflicts.

Article 1(2) of Protocol II adds, for the avoidance of doubt, that the Protocol is inapplicable 'to situations of internal disturbances and tensions, such as riots, isolated and sporadic acts of violence and other acts of a similar nature, as not being armed conflicts'. The participial clause 'as not being armed conflicts' indicates that such acts are to be considered beneath the threshold of organised armed violence required, by virtue of the term 'armed conflict', both by the Protocol itself, on the one hand, and by common article 3 and article 19 of the 1954 Hague Convention, on the other.

Cultural property

During the drafting of Protocol II, the Greek delegate to the Geneva diplomatic conference 'pointed out that many of the world's treasures were in danger of being destroyed in the course of internal armed conflicts, among others the temples of Angkor Wat, which the United Nations Educational, Scientific and Cultural Organization had asked all combatants to protect'.[85] In response, article 16 of Protocol II, a condensed version of article 53 of Protocol I,[86] provides that, '[w]ithout prejudice to the provisions of the Hague Convention for

---

[85] CDDH/SR.51, para. 59, *Records 1974–77*, vol. VII, p. 115.
[86] That Additional Protocol II, art. 16 was intended as a simplified version of Additional Protocol I, art. 53 was made clear by the Rapporteur of the Working Group on the draft provision: CDDH/III/SR.49, para. 3, *ibid.*, vol. XV, p. 107.

the Protection of Cultural Property in the Event of Armed Conflict of 14 May 1954, it is prohibited to commit any acts of hostility directed against historic monuments, works of art or places of worship which constitute the cultural or spiritual heritage of peoples, and to use them in support of the military effort'. Like article 53 of Protocol I, article 16 embodies no exception in respect of military necessity. In contrast to article 53, article 16 makes no mention of reprisals against cultural property.

The interpretation and application of article 16 of Protocol II accord *mutatis mutandis* with the interpretation and application of article 53 of Protocol I. It should be noted, however, that Protocol II contains no provision equivalent to article 52(2)'s definition of a military objective. Indeed, nowhere does Protocol II embody a prohibition on attacking civilian objects as such or the concomitant obligation to limit attacks strictly to military objectives. So whereas the use of cultural property contrary to article 53(b) of Protocol I results in the legality of an attack against that particular object falling to be assessed by reference to article 52(2), the use of an item of cultural property contrary to article 16(b) of Protocol II results in the lawfulness of any attack against it falling to be determined by reference to the customary international law of targeting in non-international armed conflict. In this regard, it is now sufficiently clear that, whatever the position in respect of civilian objects generally, customary international law prohibits attacks on cultural property in the course of non-international armed conflict unless such property, by its nature, location, purpose or use, makes an effective contribution to military action and its total or partial destruction, capture or neutralisation, in the circumstances ruling at the time, offers a definite military advantage. In the final analysis, then, while differing as to formal source, the rules applied in international and non-international armed conflict in relation to attacks against cultural property are in substance the same.

As noted in the Report of Committee III of the Diplomatic Conference, the reference in article 16's 'without prejudice'[87] clause to the 1954 Hague Convention 'is intended to point in particular to Article 19 of that Convention, which deals with non-international armed conflicts'.[88]

---

[87] Whereas the French text of Additional Protocol I, art. 53 uses the expression 'Sans préjudice de', the French version of Additional Protocol II, art. 16 uses the phrase 'Sous réserve de'. The divergence, not found in the equally authentic English, Spanish and Russian versions, is simply a case of lax *nettoyage*.

[88] CDDH/236/Rev.1, para. 61, *Records 1974–77*, vol. XV, p. 395.

In turn, the effect of article 19 is to make the obligations of respect for cultural property laid down in article 4 of the Convention, as well as the exception for military necessity embodied in paragraph 2 of that article, applicable in the event of non-international armed conflict. The upshot is that, where the relevant states are Parties to both Protocol II and the Convention, conduct covered by both the Convention and article 16 is governed by the provisions of the Convention.[89] Consequently, either Party is entitled to invoke the waiver as to military necessity embodied in article 4(2) of the Convention to justify directing an act of hostility, whether an attack or demolitions, against cultural property or to justify using such property for purposes likely to expose it to destruction or damage.[90] As with Protocol I, then, participation in the Convention by Parties to Protocol II can have the perverse effect, at least in this limited respect, of weakening the protection of cultural property in armed conflict.

In contrast to article 53 of Protocol I, article 16's 'without prejudice' clause makes no mention of 'other relevant international instruments'. This would seem to reflect the fact that, insofar as it applies during wartime, the Roerich Pact applies only to wars between states, and not to civil wars. It does raise the question, however, of the relationship between article 16 and the subsequently adopted provisions of the Second Protocol to the 1954 Hague Convention. Given the relationship between article 53 of Protocol I and the Second Protocol to the Convention, and in the light of the drafters' intention that article 16 should not affect the application of the specialist regime represented at the time of drafting by the Convention, it is reasonable to treat the Second Protocol as *de facto* an integral part of the Convention for the specific purposes of article 16, with the result that article 16 is without prejudice to the provisions of the Second Protocol. As such, where a state involved in a non-international armed conflict within its territory is a Party to both Protocol II and the Second Protocol, conduct by that state which is covered by both instruments is governed by the provisions of the Second Protocol.

---

[89] See Vienna Convention on the Law of Treaties, art. 30(2).
[90] *Strugar*, Trial Chamber Judgment, para. 309. See also Sandoz et al., *Commentary*, para. 2072 n. 28 (as regards Additional Protocol I, art. 53); Toman, *Protection of Cultural Property*, p. 389; David, *Principes*, para. 2.59; Kolb, *Ius in bello*, para. 298.

Civilian population

Protocol II embodies no prohibition, equivalent to article 52(1) of Protocol I, on attacks or reprisals against civilian objects as such, nor any concomitant obligation, equivalent to article 52(2), to limit attacks strictly to military objectives; *a fortiori*, it contains no definition of a military objective, as found in the latter provision. Equally, Protocol II incorporates no prohibition on excessive incidental damage to civilian objects, nor on excessive incidental loss of civilian life or injury to civilians, or any combination thereof, as posited in article 51(5)(b) of Protocol I. Subsequent developments under customary international law fill the lacunae. But the Protocol itself is silent on these matters.

On the other hand, article 13 of Protocol II, corresponding to the first three paragraphs of article 51 of Protocol I, provides in paragraph 1 that the civilian population and individual civilians are to enjoy general protection against the dangers arising from military operations. In an application of this rule, article 13(2) stipulates that the civilian population and individual civilians must not be the object of attack, adding that acts or threats of violence 'the primary purpose of which is to spread terror among the civilian population' are prohibited. As in international armed conflict, so too is it the case in non-international armed conflict that the prohibition on making the civilian population the object of attack stands to benefit the cultural property in its midst.

Criminal sanctions

In contrast to Protocol I, Protocol II contains no grave breaches regime. Indeed, it makes no provision for the repression of breaches of its obligations. That said, article 1(1) of Protocol II declares the Protocol to develop and supplement article 3 common to the Geneva Conventions. In turn, the Parties to the Conventions are under an obligation to take measures necessary for the suppression of all acts contrary to the provisions of the Conventions other than grave breaches.[91] As with common article 3 itself, the municipal criminalisation of, and provision for universal jurisdiction over, breaches of Protocol II is a permissible and appropriate means of giving effect to this obligation.[92]

---

[91] Geneva Convention I, art. 49; Geneva Convention II, art. 50; Geneva Convention III, art. 129; Geneva Convention IV, art. 146.
[92] See also Meron, 'International Criminalization', at 568–71.

The role of the ICRC

The ICRC has proved active in promoting the protection of cultural property in armed conflict. Its delegates played useful expert roles during the drafting of the 1954 Hague Convention and First Protocol and, later, of the Second Protocol. Over the past decade, in co-operation with UNESCO, its Advisory Service has organised regional seminars and expert meetings on the protection of cultural property in the event of armed conflict, as well as events to commemorate the fiftieth anniversary of the 1954 Hague Convention. It has also disseminated a number of relevant publications.[93] Nor has the ICRC shied away from action on the ground: in late 1956, during Israel's occupation of the Sinai peninsula, it exercised the right of initiative granted it under the fourth Geneva Convention to send a delegate to check on the state of the monastery of St Catherine and its residents.[94] The International Red Cross and Red Crescent Movement, of which the ICRC is a part, has also taken an interest in cultural property, with the 2001 session of the Council of Delegates adopting Resolution 11, entitled 'Protection of Cultural Property in the Event of Armed Conflict'.[95]

The comprehensive updating of the rules on targeting by way of Additional Protocol I, in general and as specifically regards cultural property, left the relevant articles of the 1954 Hague Convention looking antiquated. In addition, the criminal sanctions laid down by the Protocol for grave breaches of these rules was a considerable advance on the Convention's single, sketchy penal provision. Even the far less developed Protocol II had its comparative advantages. In short, the specialist instrument for the protection of cultural property in armed conflict had been outstripped in several crucial respects by the wider law.

---

[93] See M. T. Dutli (ed.), *Protection of Cultural Property in the Event of Armed Conflict. Report on the Meeting of Experts (Geneva, 5–6 October 2000)* (Geneva: ICRC, 2002); *Practical Advice for the Protection of Cultural Property in the Event of Armed Conflict* (Geneva: ICRC, 2002); *1954 Convention on the Protection of Cultural Property in the Event of Armed Conflict and its Protocols,* Factsheet (September 2002); *1954 Convention for the Protection of Cultural Property in the Event of Armed Conflict and its Protocols. Advice and model instruments of ratification/accession* (31 May 2003); and the June 2004 issue (No. 854) of the *International Review of the Red Cross.* In addition, national laws for the protection of cultural property in armed conflict are featured in the ICRC's National Implementation Database (< http://www.icrc.org/ihl-nat>).

[94] *UNESCO Chronicle*, vol. III, no. 3, March 1957, p. 56; (1957) 39 RICR 26.

[95] (2002) 84 IRRC 284.

To make matters worse, given that the relevant provisions of the Additional Protocols are without prejudice to the application of the Convention, participation in the Convention by Parties to the Protocols actually served to undermine, to an extent, the protection afforded cultural property by the latter. It was no wonder, then, that interest in the Convention faded after 1977. But events in the Persian Gulf and south-central Europe would change that.

5 The 1999 Second Hague Protocol

By the 1980s, the 1954 Hague Convention was suffering from 'benign neglect'.[1] Underwhelming participation in it[2] and the High Contracting Parties' lacklustre response to calls for their implementation reports reflected a loss of interest in the instrument. Nor was this hard to explain: among other things, its regimes of special protection and international control were failures, its provisions on attack had been eclipsed by those of the 1977 Additional Protocols, as had the sanctions prescribed for its breach, and the lack of a prohibition on unauthorised archaeological excavations by an Occupying Power had been exposed as a serious omission.

With the outbreak in 1980 of the Iran–Iraq War, which wrought considerable destruction on the cultural heritage of Iran, the Convention and its inadequacies were thrust into the spotlight. In 1983, the Director-General of UNESCO convened a meeting of legal experts to discuss it.[3] In 1987, Iran asked the Director-General to include on the agenda of the twenty-fourth session of the General Conference an item entitled 'The role played by UNESCO in ensuring the application and implementation of the provisions of the 1954 Hague Convention for the Protection of Cultural Property, the protection of educational establishments and historic monuments and the conservation of the human and natural environment, in the event of armed conflict'.[4] The General Conference, considering it constitutionally incumbent on the Organisation to promote the protection and conservation of the cultural

---

[1] UNESCO Doc. 142 EX/15, Annex, para. 6.6.
[2] On 1 January 1980, there were 68 High Contracting Parties to the Convention.
[3] UNESCO Doc. CLT.83/CONF.641/1.
[4] UNESCO Doc. 24 C/105.

heritage, and recognising that 'damage to cultural property belonging to any people whatsoever means damage to the cultural heritage of all mankind', reaffirmed 'the role of UNESCO with respect to the application of the Convention, as set out in the relevant articles of the Convention and of the Regulations for its execution', and invited the Director-General 'to further study the mechanisms for the implementation of the aforementioned articles of the Hague Convention, and of the Regulations for its execution, so as to contribute to the attainment of the objectives of this Convention'.[5] As the attacks on its cultural heritage continued, Iran further requested that the implementation of this mandate be placed on the agenda of the Executive Board, considering it 'appropriate once more to ask what UNESCO, as depositary of the Hague Convention and an agency directly concerned with the protection of cultural property and historic monuments, ha[d] undertaken in pursuance of the [General Conference's] resolution'.[6] In response, the Executive Committee requested the Secretariat 'to speed up the implementation of [the resolution] concerning further study of the Hague Convention for the protection of cultural property'.[7] But with the end of the Iran–Iraq conflict in 1988, the question was deferred 'to a future session'.[8]

It was not long before the Convention and its discontents were back centre stage. Iraq's invasion and occupation of Kuwait in August 1990 was accompanied by the plunder of Kuwaiti cultural institutions, and, throughout 1991, war in Yugoslavia threatened the historic cities and towns of the Dalmatian coast, with the first shells hitting the Old Town of Dubrovnik in October. The following month, the twenty-sixth session of the UNESCO General Conference noted that 'the international system of safeguards of the world cultural heritage [did] not appear to be satisfactory, as indicated by the ever-increasing dangers due [*inter alia*] to armed conflicts'.[9] It called on all states 'to increase their efforts to achieve better implementation of the existing instruments and to reinforce UNESCO's action', and invited the Director-General to report on the matter to the Executive Board 'and to formulate suggestions on ways and means of reinforcing UNESCO's action, including the possibility and desirability of a revision of the existing provisions regulating the

---

[5] 24 C/Resolution 11.2.
[6] UNESCO Doc. 129/EX 27.
[7] 129 EX/Decision 8.10, para. 8.
[8] 131 EX/Decision 9.1, para. 3.
[9] 26 C/Resolution 3.9, preamble, third recital.

protection and conservation of the world cultural heritage'.[10] The subsequent bombardment of Dubrovnik and the destruction of the Oriental Institute and National and University Library in Sarajevo lent impetus to the call.

In late 1992, the Director-General reported to the Executive Board the prevailing view that the Convention 'no longer me[t] current requirements'[11] – a conclusion recalled by the Executive Board in its consequent decision[12] – and announced the commissioning of a study with a view to the Convention's revision or supplementing with a further protocol.[13] The study, prepared by an independent expert, Professor Patrick Boylan, and submitted in early 1993, concluded, however, that the Convention and its Protocol remained 'valid and realistic' and 'relevant to present circumstances', and that 'the problem [was] essentially one of failure in the application of the Convention and Protocol rather than of inherent defects in the international instruments themselves'.[14] For example, while conceding that the regime of special protection had 'clearly not been effective', the Boylan report ascribed this to 'the almost total failure of High Contracting Parties to submit proposals' for entry in the Register, acknowledging only in a footnote the obstacles posed by the conditions laid down in article 8 of the Convention.[15] The report took the view that '[t]echnical improvements to the detailed provisions of the Convention' would perhaps be desirable 'in the long term' but that 'the over-riding priority' was to secure their 'greater recognition, acceptance and application'.[16] In this light, it did not formally propose amending the Convention.[17] Nonetheless, the Boylan report did identify 'significant issues' which deserved 'to be incorporated into the provisions' of the Convention 'as soon as circumstances permit[ted], probably by means of an Additional Protocol, rather than by a revision of the Convention itself', although the latter would perhaps 'be desirable in the future'.[18]

---

[10] *Ibid.*, paras. 1 and 2 respectively.
[11] UNESCO Doc. 140 EX/13, para. 11. The Director-General's conclusions and proposals were echoed in a note submitted by the Netherlands, UNESCO Doc. 140 EX/26.
[12] 141 EX/Decision 5.5.1, para. 6.
[13] 140 EX/13, para. 15.
[14] P. J. Boylan, *Review of the Convention for the Protection of Cultural Property in the Event of Armed Conflict (The Hague Convention of 1954)*, UNESCO Doc. CLT-93/WS/12, para. A.2.
[15] *Ibid.*, para. A.7, including n. 4.
[16] *Ibid.*, para. A.4.
[17] *Ibid.*
[18] *Ibid.*, para. G.1.

An expert meeting held in The Hague in July 1993 – the year that the Old Bridge at Mostar in Herzegovina and the Ferhat Pasha and Arnaudija mosques in Bosnia were destroyed – nuanced the Boylan report's findings, declaring that 'the object and purpose of the Convention' were still valid and realistic,[19] a conclusion subsequently endorsed by UNESCO's Executive Board and General Conference,[20] but laying emphasis on 'apparent weaknesses' in its provisions.[21] The issues identified and suggestions made by the Boylan report and by the Hague meeting of experts were discussed at a further meeting of experts held in early 1994 at Lauswolt, the Netherlands, where detailed proposals for amendments (the so-called 'Lauswolt document') were put forward,[22] and a third expert meeting took place in Paris in late 1994 to discuss these.[23] In November 1995, during the twenty-eighth session of the UNESCO General Conference, a one-day meeting of the High Contracting Parties to the Convention, only the second in its history, was convened to discuss the instrument's review and the proposals put forward.[24] A majority supported the adoption of an additional protocol to supplement the provisions of the Convention, which the meeting reaffirmed as 'an essential instrument of international humanitarian law'.[25] The meeting invited all Parties to submit to the UNESCO Secretariat written comments on the proposals for the improvement of the Convention; emphasised the importance of a further expert meeting; and invited the Director-General to convene another meeting of the High Contracting Parties during the twenty-ninth session of the General Conference 'to discuss and possibly decide on matters related to the strengthening

---

[19] 142 EX/15, Annex, para. 5.
[20] 142 EX/Decision 5.5.2, para. 5(a) and 27 C/Resolution 3.5, preamble, recital (a) respectively. See also the preamble to the resolution later adopted by the second meeting of the High Contracting Parties to the Convention, UNESCO Doc. CLT-95/CONF.009/5, Annex I.
[21] 142 EX/15, Annex, para. 5.
[22] The same year also saw the publication of a UNESCO-sponsored commentary on the Convention: see J. Toman, *La protection des biens culturels en cas de conflit armé. Commentaire de la Convention et du Protocole de La Haye du 14 mai 1954 pour la protection des biens culturels en cas de conflit armé ainsi que d'autres instruments de droit international relatifs à cette protection* (Paris: UNESCO, 1994), published in English two years later.
[23] See UNESCO Doc. CLT/CH/94/608/2.
[24] See CLT-95/CONF.009/5. Sixty-nine of the then eighty-seven High Contracting Parties sent representatives.
[25] Resolution adopted by the Second Meeting of the High Contracting Parties, *ibid.*, Annex I, preamble, second recital.

and the implementation of the Convention'.[26] Pursuant to this mandate, a meeting of governmental experts was held in Paris in March 1997,[27] which refined the proposals without deciding on what form any new instrument would take. A subsequent meeting of the High Contracting Parties,[28] convened during the twenty-ninth session of the General Conference in November 1997, was 'in favour of adopting a new instrument which would bridge the existing gaps in the Hague Convention'.[29] Written comments were invited once again, and one last meeting of governmental experts was urged before the convening of a diplomatic conference.[30] The majority of delegations to the meeting, which took place in Vienna in May 1998[31] and was attended by representatives from fifty-seven of the then ninety Parties, were of the view that the most suitable form of instrument was an optional protocol to the Convention.[32]

On 15 March 1999, the Diplomatic Conference on the Second Protocol to the Hague Convention for the Protection of Cultural Property in the Event of Armed Conflict opened in The Hague, attended by delegates from seventy-four High Contracting Parties to the Convention out of ninety-five, along with observers from nineteen non-Party states and Palestine, as well as from the ICRC and the International Committee of the Blue Shield (ICBS), a non-governmental organisation comprising the International Council on Archives (ICA), the International Council of Museums (ICOM), the International Council on Museums and Sites (ICOMOS) and the International Federation of Library Associations and Institutions (IFLA).[33] On 26 March 1999, ninety-nine years and eight months after the conclusion of the First Hague Peace Conference in 1899, the Second Protocol to the Hague Convention for the Protection

---

[26] *Ibid.*, paras. 2, 7 and 9 respectively.
[27] See UNESCO Doc. CLT-96/CONF.603/5.
[28] See UNESCO Doc. CLT-97/CONF.208/3. Sixty-five of the then ninety High Contracting Parties were represented.
[29] *Ibid.*, para. 5(i).
[30] Resolution adopted by the Third Meeting of the High Contracting Parties, *ibid.*, Annex I.
[31] See UNESCO Doc. 155 EX/51, Annex.
[32] *Ibid.*, para. 10.
[33] See *Diplomatic Conference on the Second Protocol to the Hague Convention for the Protection of Cultural Property in the Event of Armed Conflict (The Hague, 15–26 March 1999), Summary Report*, UNESCO, Paris, June 1999 and UNESCO's daily *précis* of the proceedings, <www.unesco.org/culture/legalprotection/war/html_eng/precis.htm>. The full proceedings of the diplomatic conference were not yet published at the time of going to press.

of Cultural Property in the Event of Armed Conflict was adopted.[34] Unlike the Convention, it was not accompanied by regulations for its execution. The Second Protocol entered into force on 9 March 2004 and, as of 1 January 2006, had thirty-seven States Parties.[35]

As made clear in the preamble, the Second Protocol is designed to supplement, not supplant, the provisions of the Convention, ostensibly 'through measures to reinforce their implementation'. While the latter is a somewhat misleading characterisation of its practical effect, the Protocol nonetheless leaves intact the basic architecture of the Convention and operates, on a technical level, by reference back to it, elaborating on, refining and in places adding to its various obligations as between States Parties to the later instrument (which, as a precondition to participation, must also be High Contracting Parties to the earlier one[36]). The Protocol maintains the distinction between general and special protection of cultural property, albeit radically overhauling the content of the latter – one of the main rationales for the new instrument – and renaming it 'enhanced' protection. In substantive terms, in addition to the reform of special protection to render it more accessible, objective and worthwhile, the Second Protocol revamps general protection to reflect developments in international humanitarian and cultural heritage law since 1954. In a major advance on article 28 of the Convention, it embodies a comprehensive and weighty regime of penal sanctions for breach. A further *raison d'être* of the Protocol was its establishment of a formalised institutional framework to facilitate and supervise the protection of cultural property in the event of armed conflict, comprising a biennial meeting of the Parties, an intergovernmental committee and a centralised fund. The instrument also incorporates obligations relating to the dissemination of information and to international assistance. In terms of its scope of application, the Second Protocol is noteworthy in applying *in toto* to both international and non-international armed conflicts, without distinction.

---

[34] The Hague, 26 March 1999, UN Reg. No. 3511.
[35] For an updated list of States Parties, see <http://portal.unesco.org/la/convention.asp?KO=15207&language=E>. Note that, where the Convention uses the term 'High Contracting Parties', the Second Protocol uses 'States Parties'. The meaning is identical, as made clear in Second Hague Protocol, arts. 1(a) and 1(d).
[36] Second Hague Protocol, arts 40–2, referring to 'High Contracting Parties', defined in art. 1(d) to mean Parties to the Convention.

Relationship to the Convention

The precise relationship between the Second Protocol and the Convention remained a thorny issue at the Hague diplomatic conference. While a consensus had been arrived at early in the drafting process on the desirability of a new instrument bearing on the Convention in some way, argument persisted over the details. Three options presented themselves: a new convention replacing the 1954 Hague Convention; an instrument formally amending the Convention, in accordance with the procedure for its revision laid down in article 39; and an optional protocol supplementing the Convention. At the final intergovernmental meeting of experts in May 1998, most delegates agreed that the Convention should be retained, and that states wishing to accede to it as it stood should not be precluded from doing so,[37] with the result that an optional protocol emerged as the favoured means for addressing 'the need to improve the protection of cultural property in the event of armed conflict'.[38] Such an approach, provided for in article 41 of the Vienna Convention on the Law of Treaties, would permit willing states to agree on a reformed regime among themselves without the need for its acceptance by every High Contracting Party to the Convention, as required in the case of amendments by article 39(5) of the latter.[39] Some delegates, however, insisted that article 39 of the Convention was the only proper means by which to supplement it, and would have the advantage of maintaining a uniform regime. The debate carried over to the diplomatic conference, where the possibility of replacing the Convention was also reopened. In the event, most delegates plumped for an optional protocol supplementary to the Convention and were satisfied that such an instrument could be validly adopted by the diplomatic conference. Three states,

---

[37] 1954 Hague Convention, art. 39(7) states that after the entry into force of amendments to the Convention only the text as amended shall remain open for ratification or accession.

[38] Second Hague Protocol, preamble, first recital.

[39] 1954 Hague Convention, art. 39(1) provides for the Convention's revision with or without a Conference of the High Contracting Parties. In the event of a Conference, art. 39(5) states that amendments to the Convention 'shall enter into force only after they have been unanimously adopted by the High Contracting Parties represented at the Conference and accepted by each of the High Contracting Parties'. Acceptance of amendments by the Parties is effected by the deposit of a formal instrument with the Director-General of UNESCO, in accordance with art. 39(6).

however, insisted on article 39(5) until the bitter end, with Israel making a declaration to this effect.[40]

The relationship between the Second Protocol and the Convention is stipulated in article 2, which states that the Protocol 'supplements the Convention in relations between the Parties'. ['Party' is defined in article 1(a) to mean a State Party to the Second Protocol, and articles 40 to 42, cross-referenced with article 1(d), reflect that States Parties to the Second Protocol must also be High Contracting Parties to the Convention.] At the diplomatic conference, the chairperson of the working group on chapters 1 and 5 'noted the clarification provided by the working group that the word "supplements" in Article 2 signifies that the Protocol does not affect the rights and obligations of States Parties to the Convention'.[41] In short, Parties to both the Convention and the Protocol are bound by both, to the extent that their provisions are compatible, in their mutual relations,[42] and Parties to the Convention alone remain bound in their mutual relations only by the Convention, its provisions unaffected.[43] As for a Party to both Convention and Protocol and a Party to the Convention alone, they are bound in their mutual relations by the Convention alone.[44]

In a partial exception, however, to the general rule laid down in article 2, article 4(b) of the Protocol makes special provision for the relationship between chapter 3 of the Protocol, embodying the new, improved version of special protection for cultural property known as enhanced protection, and chapter II of the Convention, the original regime of special protection. Article 4(b) states that the application of the provisions of chapter 3 of the Protocol is without prejudice to the application of the provisions of chapter II of the Convention, 'save that, as between Parties to [the] Protocol . . ., where cultural property has been granted both special protection and enhanced protection, only the provisions of enhanced protection shall apply'.[45] In other words, whereas

---

[40] See *Summary Report*, Annex 3: 'It should be noted that some delegations were of the opinion that the provisions of Article 39(5) of the 1954 Hague Convention should have been applied in relation to the adoption of this Protocol.'

[41] Final Act of the Diplomatic Conference on the Second Protocol to the Hague Convention for the Protection of Cultural Property in the Event of Armed Conflict, *Summary Report*, Annex 1, para. 11.

[42] See Vienna Convention on the Law of Treaties, art. 30(4)(a).

[43] See *ibid.*, art. 34.

[44] See *ibid.*, art. 30(4)(b).

[45] Second Hague Protocol, art. 4(b) further provides that the rule as between Parties to the Protocol also applies as between a Party to the Protocol and a state which accepts and applies the Protocol in accordance with art. 3(2).

the rest of the Protocol supplements the Convention in relations between the Parties, the regime of enhanced protection under the Protocol replaces the regime of special protection under the Convention as between Parties to both Protocol and Convention, but only in cases where the cultural property in question has been granted both special and enhanced protection. Where both states are Parties to the Protocol but the cultural property in question has been granted only special protection in accordance with the provisions of article 8 of the Convention, the obligations laid down in chapter II (specifically, articles 9 to 11) of the Convention continue to govern their conduct in respect of that property.

Article 4 also specifies, for the avoidance of doubt, the relationship between enhanced protection and the general provisions regarding protection laid down in chapter 1 of the Convention and chapter 2 of the Protocol. Article 4(a) states that the application of chapter 3 of the Protocol is without prejudice to the application of the provisions of chapter I of the Convention and of chapter 2 of the Protocol. In other words, except for where chapter 3 constitutes *lex specialis*, the general provisions regarding protection embodied in both the Convention and the Protocol apply as much to cultural property under enhanced protection as they do to all other cultural property encompassed by these instruments. In practical terms, this means that cultural property under enhanced protection is protected not just by article 12 of the Protocol, as refined by article 13, but also by articles 3, 4(3), 4(4), 4(5) and 5 of the Convention and by articles 5, 7, 8 and 9 of the Protocol. It also means that it is protected by article 4(1) of the Convention to the extent that the expression 'act of hostility' used in this provision is more compendious than the term 'attack' used in articles 12 and 13 of the Protocol. Furthermore, when articles 4(a) and 4(b) are read together, it is apparent that, where the parties to the conflict are Parties to both the Convention and the Protocol, cultural property which remains under the regime of special protection embodied in chapter II of the Convention nonetheless benefits – to the extent that the provisions of chapter II do not constitute *lex specialis* – not just from article 9 of the Convention, as modified by article 11, and from the general provisions regarding protection laid down in chapter I of that instrument but also from the general provisions regarding protection laid down in chapter 2 of the Protocol, namely articles 5, 7, 8 and 9.

There is no doubt that the Second Protocol is a valid means of modifying the Convention as between Parties to both. Such a modification is not prohibited by the Convention, it does not affect the enjoyment by the other High Contracting Parties to the Convention of their rights under the Convention or the performance of their obligations, and it does not relate to a provision derogation from which is incompatible with the effective execution of the object and purpose of the Convention as a whole;[46] indeed, the Protocol furthers the effective execution of that object and purpose. It was also the only realistic way of proceeding. Replacing the Convention was never a serious option, for political as much as practical reasons, and amending it was unfeasible in the light of the requirement of unanimity in article 37(5). The differentiated obligations which result may be messy, but no more so than in a host of other treaty regimes, among them the Geneva Conventions and their Additional Protocols.

Scope of application

Article 3(1) provides that, in addition to the provisions which are to apply in time of peace, the Second Protocol is to apply in the situations referred to in article 18, paragraphs 1 and 2 of the Convention, namely in the event of declared war or any other armed conflict arising between two or more States Parties, even if the state of war is not recognised by one of them, and in all cases of partial or total occupation of the territory of a State Party, even if the occupation meets with no armed resistance. Article 3(1) further states that the Protocol shall apply in the situations referred to in article 22(1) of the Protocol. In turn, article 22(1) provides that the Protocol – and not just those provisions of it 'which relate to respect for cultural property', as is the case under article 19(1) of the Convention – shall apply in the event of armed conflict not of an international character occurring within the territory of one of the States Parties. It is logical to assume that this refers to non-international armed conflicts within the meaning of article 3 common to the four Geneva Conventions, rather than to those covered by Additional Protocol II: first, article 22(1) of the Second Protocol contains no words of limitation analogous to those in article 1(1) of Protocol II; secondly, the Second Protocol is intended 'to supplement [the Convention's] provisions through measures to reinforce their implementation',[47] and, insofar as it applies

---

[46] See Vienna Convention on the Law of Treaties, art. 41(1).
[47] Second Hague Protocol, preamble, second recital.

to non-international armed conflicts, the Convention applies to those covered by common article 3, on which article 19(1) of the Convention was modelled. Article 22(2) of the Second Protocol, mirroring article 1(2) of Protocol II on which it is based, clarifies that the Protocol 'shall not apply to situations of internal disturbances and tensions, such as riots, isolated and sporadic acts of violence and other acts of a similar nature'.

In short, the Second Protocol applies equally to both international and non-international armed conflicts. That this should eventually be the case was not, however, a foregone conclusion. The issue was a fraught one from the earliest expert meetings. On the one hand, it was pointed out that 'the overwhelming majority of cultural property destroyed since the adoption of the Hague Convention' had been in conflicts of a non-international kind.[48] Several states, on the other hand, resisted encroachment on what they viewed as their *domaine réservé*, fearing that the regulation of internal armed conflicts would be used as a pretext for interference in the internal affairs of states. Indeed, at the Paris meeting of governmental experts in 1997, some delegates sought an end to discussion of the issue, believing the question to be sufficiently regulated by Additional Protocol II.[49] While the issue remained controversial at the diplomatic conference, agreement was ultimately reached on article 22, which many states welcomed 'in view of the loss of cultural heritage in recent non-international armed conflict'.[50]

To assuage the discomfort felt in some quarters with the Second Protocol's application in its entirety to internal armed conflicts, the drafters inserted several clarificatory paragraphs into article 22. In a provision lifted directly from article 3(1) of Additional Protocol II, article 22(3) states that nothing in the Second Protocol 'shall be invoked for the purpose of affecting the sovereignty of a State or the responsibility of the government, by all legitimate means, to maintain or re-establish law and order in the State or to defend the national unity and territorial integrity of the State'. Article 22(5) mirrors article 3(2) of Protocol II in saying that nothing in the Second Protocol 'shall be invoked as

---

[48] CLT-96/CONF.603/5, para. 20.
[49] CLT-97/CONF.208/3, para. 5(vi).
[50] *Summary Report*, para. 33. As noted by the ICRC observer, the equal application of the Second Protocol to international and non-international armed conflicts also obviates the complex questions of factual appreciation and, at times, excessive legal formalism involved in distinguishing between the two: *ibid.*, para. 34.

a justification for intervening, directly or indirectly, for any reason whatever, in the armed conflict or in the internal or external affairs of the Party in the territory of which that conflict occurs'. Neither provision, however, prevents States Parties to the Second Protocol from criticising another Party's breach of the Protocol in the course of a non-international armed conflict occurring within its territory: in the *Nicaragua* case, the ICJ characterised an unlawful intervention as 'one bearing on matters in which each State is permitted, by the principle of State sovereignty, to decide freely',[51] and by consenting via article 22(1) to making their treatment of cultural property during an internal armed conflict on their territory the subject of international obligations, States Parties to the Second Protocol concede that this is no longer such a matter. For its part, article 22(4) was drafted in response to concerns, especially on the part of China and India, over the application of chapter 4, the regime of penal sanctions for serious violations of the Second Protocol, to non-international armed conflicts. It provides that nothing in the Protocol 'shall prejudice the primary jurisdiction of a Party in whose territory an armed conflict not of an international character occurs over the violations set forth in Article 15'. Finally, mirroring article 19(4) of the Convention, article 22(6) makes it clear that the application of the Second Protocol to non-international armed conflicts does not affect the legal status of the parties to the conflict.

The first limb of article 3(2) of the Second Protocol, analogous to the first limb of article 18(3) of the Convention, establishes that a *si omnes* clause is not to be read into article 3(1) of the Protocol insofar as it relies on article 18, paragraphs 1 and 2 of the Convention. It provides that when one of the parties to the armed conflict in question is not bound by the Protocol, the Parties to the Protocol involved in the conflict remain bound by the Protocol in their mutual relations. The second limb of article 3(2), reproducing *mutatis mutandis* the second limb of article 18(3) of the Convention, adds that the Parties to the Protocol shall also be bound by it in relation to any state involved in the conflict which is not Party to it 'if the latter accepts the provisions of [the] Protocol and so long as it applies them'.

---

[51] *Military and Paramilitary Activities In and Against Nicaragua (Nicaragua v. United States of America)*, Merits, ICJ Reports 1986, p. 14 at para. 205.

General provisions regarding protection

Chapter 2 of the Second Protocol ('General provisions regarding protection') supplements chapter I of the Convention, the general provisions regarding protection embodied in the earlier instrument. Article 5 ('Safeguarding of cultural property') and article 6 ('Respect for cultural property') are glosses on provisions of the Convention, the first elaborating on article 3, the second refining the concept of imperative military necessity embodied in article 4(2) as applied to article 4(1). Article 7 ('Precautions in attack'), article 8 ('Precautions against the effects of hostilities') and article 9 ('Protection of cultural property in occupied territory') are, on the other hand, stand-alone provisions, adding to the sum of obligations imposed on Parties to the Convention as regards cultural property within the meaning of article 1 of that instrument.

Definition of 'cultural property'

The definition of cultural property under article 1 of the Convention was the subject of adverse comment early in the review process. The Boylan report referred to it as 'very imprecise' and noted its divergence from the definitions used in later UNESCO instruments (without acknowledging that none of these definitions is the same as another, each convention having its specific object and purpose).[52] At the 1993 meeting of experts, however, '[t]he definition given in Article 1 of the Convention still seemed largely acceptable to the participants, for it was considered broad enough to cover all of the cultural heritage in need of protection'.[53] This view prevailed throughout the review process, and the question of the definition of cultural property for the purposes of the Convention and Second Protocol was never reopened. In the event, article 1(b) of the latter states that 'cultural property' for the purposes of the Second Protocol means cultural property as defined in article 1 of the Convention.

Moreover, the 1993 meeting of experts elaborated on how the open-textured definition laid down in article 1 was properly to be applied by the Parties. In the course of discussing possible co-ordination between the World Heritage Convention and the 1954 Hague Convention, 'the experts noted that the protections of The Hague Convention apply to many more cultural sites than those inscribed on the World Heritage List',

---

[52] Boylan, *Review of the Convention*, para. G.2. See also 140 EX/26, p. 1 (Netherlands).
[53] 142 EX/15, Annex, para. 6.2.

and 'further noted that efforts to enhance the protection during armed conflict of cultural sites inscribed on the World Heritage List, which are already subject to The Hague Convention, should in no way lessen the protection of other immovable cultural property not of outstanding universal significance but of national or local significance and not, therefore, liable to inscription on the World Heritage List'.[54] These statements were endorsed by UNESCO's Executive Board and General Conference – the latter comprising all Member States of the Organisation, many of them Parties to the Convention – which both, in identical terms, requested the Director-General 'to draw the attention of States that are party to the [World Heritage Convention], but are not party to the 1954 Hague Convention, to the fact that the latter Convention offers protection to cultural property that is of national and local importance as well as to sites of outstanding universal importance'.[55]

Safeguarding

There was general agreement during the process of review that article 3 of the Convention, on peacetime measures of safeguard, was unhelpfully impressionistic. A more programmatic provision was needed, 'listing steps to be taken in peacetime to ensure overall risk-prevention'.[56] The ICOMOS observer at the 1994 expert meeting suggested that a provision of this sort 'would enable cultural professionals ... to begin dialogue on protection with local authorities'.[57] In particular, the preparation of inventories of protected property had long been recommended, both as a means of alerting potential adversaries to its location and because 'the organization of proper documentation on protected property, combined with easy access thereto, would facilitate the taking of preparatory steps to protect cultural property'.[58] In this regard, 'military experts on the whole agreed that fear on the part of States about publishing detailed data on their cultural property ... was no longer justified',

---

[54] 142 EX/15, para. 8.
[55] 27 C/Resolution 3.5, para. 3. See also 142 EX/Decision 5.5.2, para. 7(c). In a declaration annexed to its instrument of ratification, Iran speaks consistently of 'the cultural heritage of nations', which it bears in mind 'is deemed as part of [the] cultural heritage of humanity': http://portal.unesco.org/en/ev.php-URL_ID=15207&URL_DO =DO_TOPIC& URL_SECTION=201.html#RESERVES.
[56] CLT/CH/94/608/2, p. 6.
[57] Ibid.
[58] Ibid., p. 2.

since '[b]oth military and civilian technological advances were such that any such information that was not supplied by the States Parties could readily be obtained through other means'.[59]

As a result, article 5 of the Second Protocol seeks to put flesh on the bare bones of article 3 of the Convention, providing that '[p]reparatory measures taken in time of peace for the safeguarding of cultural property against the foreseeable effects of an armed conflict pursuant to Article 3 of the Convention shall include, as appropriate, the preparation of inventories, the planning of emergency measures for protection against fire or structural collapse, the preparation for the removal of cultural property or the provision for adequate *in situ* protection of such property, and the designation of competent authorities responsible for the safeguarding of cultural property'. The provision is designed to function as a concise set of operational guidelines to the implementation of the obligation already imposed by article 3 of the Convention. At the same time, the measures listed are 'merely indicative and not exhaustive'.[60]

In the light of the expenditure and expertise needed to implement article 5, the Fund for the Protection of Cultural Property in the Event of Armed Conflict established pursuant to article 29 of the Second Protocol is to provide financial or other assistance in support of preparatory or other measures to be taken in peacetime in accordance with, *inter alia*, article 5.[61] A Party may also call on UNESCO for technical assistance in organising preparatory action to safeguard cultural property, in accordance with article 33(1), and article 33(2) encourages Parties to provide technical assistance either bilaterally or multilaterally. In addition, the diplomatic conference adopted a related resolution geared towards the needs of developing States Parties. 'Stressing that safeguarding measures such as the compilation of national inventories of cultural property, taken in peacetime, are essential in preventing foreseeable effects of armed conflicts', and '[r]ecognising that a number of developing countries may have difficulty in fully implementing the provision of the Hague Convention, its First Protocol and [its Second] Protocol', the diplomatic conference urged all States Parties to the Protocol 'to give careful consideration to requests from developing countries

---

[59] *Ibid.*
[60] *Ibid.*, p. 6.
[61] Second Hague Protocol, art. 29(1)(a).

either at [the] bilateral level or within the framework of intergovernmental organisations'.[62]

Respect

The question of the waiver in respect of military necessity contained in article 4(2) of the Convention was a contentious topic throughout the review process, after the Boylan report had floated its deletion.[63] Those in favour of the abolition of the waiver invoked its potential for abuse, and pointed to the fact that neither article 53 of Additional Protocol I nor article 16 of Additional Protocol II recognised military necessity as such as justifying an act of hostility against cultural property. Proponents of the waiver's retention argued that any new instrument had to be acceptable to states and their military authorities, and drew attention to the longstanding allowance for military necessity in the customary and conventional laws of war, as now embodied in the guise of the definition of a military objective in article 52(2) of Protocol I. To an extent, the protagonists of the debate were arguing at cross-purposes. Those against article 4(2) seemed to imply that the abolition of military necessity as such in articles 53 and 16 of the respective Additional Protocols meant that cultural property would 'remain untouched in any circumstances',[64] overlooking the fact that its use for military purposes results in its amenability to attack if its total or partial destruction, capture or neutralisation, in the circumstances ruling at the time, offers a definite military advantage, in the words of article 52(2) of Protocol I. Equally, those in favour of keeping the waiver ignored the fact that article 53 of Protocol I and article 16 of Protocol II had indeed excluded military necessity as such in relation to cultural property, and that both Protocols had since proved acceptable to the very large numbers of states which had become Parties to them. By the third meeting of the High Contacting Parties to the Convention, a majority was in favour of retaining the waiver in principle but also of defining more strictly and precisely the circumstances in which it could be invoked. It was suggested that the relevant provisions of the Additional Protocols could serve as a useful basis for drafting such refinements.

---

[62] Diplomatic Conference on the Second Protocol to the Hague Convention for the Protection of Cultural Property in the Event of Armed Conflict, Resolution, *Summary Report*, Annex 2.
[63] Boylan, *Review of the Convention*, para. G.4.
[64] 155 EX/51, Annex, para. 14.

As finally adopted, article 6 of the Second Protocol, on respect for cultural property, is not a freestanding rule but an explicitly supplementary provision, referable back to article 4 of the Convention. 'With the goal of ensuring respect for cultural property in accordance with Article 4 of the Convention', in the words of the chapeau, it seeks to structure article 4(2)'s broad-brush reservation as to military necessity by 'outlining the conditions under which the concept [can] be invoked',[65] positing relatively precise and restrictive criteria. It does this separately as regards acts of hostility directed against cultural property, on the one hand, and the use of cultural property for purposes likely to expose it to destruction or damage, on the other. As regards the former, the term 'act of hostility'[66] encompasses both attacks and demolitions. Insofar as it applies to attacks, it does so whether they be by land, sea or air.

Article 6(a) deals with the waiver of the obligation to refrain from acts of hostility directed against cultural property, that is, the second limb of article 4(1) of the Convention as modified by article 4(2). It states that a waiver on the basis of imperative military necessity pursuant to article 4(2) of the Convention may be invoked to direct an act of hostility against cultural property only when, and for as long as, two cumulative conditions are met: first, as provided for in subparagraph (i), when and for as long as the cultural property in question 'has, by its function, been made into a military objective'; and, secondly, as provided for in subparagraph (ii), when and for as long as there is 'no feasible alternative available to obtain a similar military advantage to that offered by directing an act of hostility against that objective'. In turn, the term 'military objective' is defined in article 1(f) in accordance with the now-customary definition found in article 52(2) of Additional Protocol I, namely as 'an object which by its nature, location, purpose, or use makes an effective contribution to military action and whose total or partial destruction, capture or neutralisation, in the circumstances ruling at the time, offers a definite military advantage'.

A terminological disjuncture is immediately apparent. Article 6(a)(i) refers to cultural property being made into a military objective by its 'function', whereas article 1(f) speaks of its 'nature, location, purpose,

---

[65] *Summary Report*, para. 11.
[66] See also 1954 Hague Convention, art. 4(1); Additional Protocol I, art. 53; Additional Protocol II, art. 16.

or use'. The daily *précis* and summary report of the proceedings of the diplomatic conference reveal the explanation. Opinion was sharply divided at the conference between those states which supported reference to cultural property which 'has, by its use, become a military objective',[67] 'feeling that "nature", "purpose" and/or "location" were not on their own sufficient to define a military objective',[68] and those which sought a full restatement of the definition of a military objective found in article 1(f). That is, some delegates favoured the higher standard of protection afforded cultural property by article 53 of Additional Protocol I and article 16 of Additional Protocol II, whereas others wished simply to endorse the emergent customary standard of protection conferred on cultural property as a species of civilian object by the rule encapsulated in article 52(2) of Protocol I. Faced with this impasse, the chairman of the conference invited the informal working group on chapter 2 of the draft Second Protocol to reconvene 'in order to try to find a balance between the need to protect cultural property, and the actions that have to be taken in certain military situations'.[69] The upshot was the compromise word 'function', a term open-textured enough to accommodate both positions. In other words, article 6(a)(i) appears deliberately designed to permit a degree of discretion in its interpretation and application. Those states favouring the lower standard are free to hold that cultural property can become a military objective under article 6(a)(i) by virtue of its nature, location or purpose, in addition to its use. At the same time, states supporting the higher standard are not precluded from maintaining that only its use can make cultural property a military objective. Room is also left for the possibility that the higher standard may emerge in the future as customary international law, in which case article 6(a)(i) will have to be read consistently with it. It is true that when one delegate to the diplomatic conference proposed substituting the word 'function' for the word 'use' in article 13(1)(b) – which specifies the circumstances in which the immunity of cultural property under enhanced protection is to be lost – so as to bring chapter 3 (enhanced protection) into conformity with chapter 2 (general protection), the majority of delegates objected, stressing 'that the different wording marked the distinction between the different levels

---

[67] Draft art. 4 (eventually art. 6) prepared by the working group on chapter 2, <www.unesco.org/culture/legalprotection/war/html_eng/hc1995.htm>, p. 2.
[68] <www.unesco.org/culture/legalprotection/war/html_eng/precis24.htm>, p. 2.
[69] *Ibid.*, p. 3.

of protection in each Chapter'.[70] But this reflects the view of the majority only, a view not rendered mandatory by the text of article 6(a)(i), which was adopted by consensus and was intended to straddle the opposing positions. It should be emphasised, however, that the effective difference between the two levels of protection is unlikely to be great, given that, in practice, by far the most common ground on which cultural property will be made a military objective is its use. Indeed, today it is extremely hard to envisage a Party citing the nature, location or purpose of given cultural property to justify an attack against it.[71]

The formulation of article 6(a) represents an improvement over the modern statement of the customary law drawn from article 52(2) of Additional Protocol I insofar as subparagraph (ii) imposes the express condition 'that there is no feasible alternative available to obtain a similar military advantage to that offered by directing an act of hostility against that objective'. The requirement is really no more than an explicit elaboration of the limits imposed by the concept of imperative military necessity, as embodied in article 4(2) of the Convention and in the classical customary law codified in article 23(g) of the Hague Rules and reflected in article 57(3) of Protocol I.[72] Yet while the more rigorous view has always been that imperative military necessity implies the indispensability of the act of hostility foreshadowed, another approach has been to invoke the concept in support of actions with equally viable alternatives, a construction to which the formulation used in article 52(2) of Protocol I lends itself, with its reference to military 'advantage', rather than 'necessity'. Article 6(a)(ii) scotches this permissive school of thought in respect of cultural property covered by the Second Protocol.

---

[70] *Summary Report*, para. 22. See also <www.unesco.org/culture/legalprotection/war/html_eng/precis25.htm>, pp. 2–3. In accordance with Second Hague Protocol, art. 13(1)(b), the immunity granted cultural property under enhanced protection may be lost only 'if, and for as long as, the property has, by its use, become a military objective'.

[71] That said, Canada annexed to its instrument of accession to the Second Protocol a 'statement of understanding', para. 6 of which declares it to be 'the understanding of the Government of Canada that under Article 6(a)(i), cultural property can be made into a military objective because of its nature, location, purpose or use': http://portal.unesco.org/en/ev.php-URL_ID=15207&URL_DO=DO_TOPIC&URL_SECTION=201.html #RESERVES.

[72] Additional Protocol I, art. 57(3) provides that when a choice is possible between several military objectives for obtaining a similar military advantage, 'the objective to be selected shall be that the attack on which may be expected to cause the least danger to civilian lives and to civilian objects'.

The fact that, in accordance with article 6(a)(i), military necessity may be invoked to justify an act of hostility against cultural property only when that property has been made into a military objective necessarily implies that military necessity may never be invoked to justify demolishing such property, since it is only attacks which depend on whether an object is a military objective.[73] One effect of article 6 of the Second Protocol on article 4(2) of the Convention is therefore that the obligation to respect cultural property laid down in article 4(1) of the latter is, in the case of cultural property covered by both instruments, absolute when it comes to demolitions. In short, for Parties to the Second Protocol, military necessity can never justify the demolition of cultural property.

No provision was included in the Second Protocol explaining its relationship to the 1977 Additional Protocols. It will be recalled, however, that article 53 of Protocol I is expressed to be without prejudice to the provisions not only of the Convention but also of 'other relevant international instruments'. Going on its ordinary meaning, the phrase encompasses not only past specialist international agreements for the protection of cultural property in armed conflict, such as the Roerich Pact, but also any that may be concluded in the future. In this light, it would seem that where the parties to an international armed conflict are Parties to both Additional Protocol I and the Second Protocol, conduct covered by both instruments is governed by the provisions of the Second Protocol. So while Parties to Protocol I alone are obliged not to attack cultural property unless, on account of its use, and its use only, it becomes a military objective, Parties to both Protocol I and the Second Protocol – and permitted therefore to invoke article 6(a) of the latter in place of article 53 of the former – may target cultural property if it is made a military objective through its nature, location, purpose or use. In short, as with the Convention, so too with the Second Protocol: participation by a Party to Protocol I in the specialist instrument, that is, the Second Protocol, has the potential to weaken, in this specific respect, the protection from attack afforded cultural property in international armed conflict.

In contrast, however, to article 53 of Protocol I, article 16 of Protocol II's 'without prejudice' clause makes no mention of 'other relevant international instruments', probably in reflection of the fact that, insofar as it applies wartime, the Roerich Pact applies only to wars between states and

---

[73] See, in this light, Second Hague Protocol, art. 6(d), referring explicitly to 'an *attack* based on a decision taken in accordance with sub-paragraph (a)' (emphasis added).

not to civil wars. This omission poses the question of the relationship between article 16 of Protocol II and article 6(a) of the Second Protocol. Considering the relationship between article 53 of Protocol I and article 6(a), and given the drafters' intention that article 16 of Protocol II should not affect the application of the specialist regime represented at the time of drafting by the Convention, it is reasonable to treat the Second Protocol as *de facto* an integral part of the Convention for the limited purposes of article 16, with the result that article 16 is without prejudice to article 6(a) of the Second Protocol. In this light, where a state involved in a non-international armed conflict within its territory is a Party to both Protocol II and the Second Protocol, conduct covered by both instruments is governed by the provisions of the Second Protocol.

Article 6(d) of the Second Protocol, based on article 57(2)(c) of Additional Protocol I, adds a procedural obligation, providing that, in the event of an attack based on a decision taken in accordance with article 6(a), 'an effective advance warning shall be given whenever circumstances enable'. The word 'effective' implies both that the warning is successfully transmitted and received and that it is given long enough in advance to enable the opposing party either to cease its use of the cultural property or, in the far less likely event that the property has been made a military objective on another account, to enable the opposing party to come to some other arrangement to obviate an attack on the property.

In relation to the first limb of article 4(1) of the Convention as modified by article 4(2), article 6(b) of the Second Protocol states that a waiver on the basis of imperative military necessity pursuant to article 4(2) of the Convention may be invoked to use cultural property for purposes which are likely to expose it to destruction or damage only when, and for as long as, 'no choice is possible between such use of the cultural property and another feasible method for obtaining a similar military advantage'. The provision is no more than a codified statement of the proper application of article 4(2) as it applies to the use of cultural property, but this is precisely its value, explicitly ruling out, as it does, a permissive construction of the notion of imperative military necessity.

Whereas the Convention does not specify the level in the chain of command at which a decision to invoke article 4(2) must be taken,[74]

---

[74] In contrast, see 1954 Hague Convention, art. 11(2), applicable to cultural property under special protection.

article 6(c) of the Second Protocol stipulates that the decision to invoke military necessity 'shall only be taken by an officer commanding a force the equivalent of a battalion in size or larger, or a force smaller in size where circumstances do not permit otherwise'.

Precautions in attack

There was consensus from early on in the review process that the Convention would benefit from an obligation to take precautions in attack along the lines of article 57 of Additional Protocol I. The result was article 7 of the Second Protocol, which is stated in the chapeau to be without prejudice 'to other precautions required by international humanitarian law in the conduct of military operations'. The provision is a freestanding one, not an elaboration or refinement of any article in the Convention, although it is premised on the protection afforded by article 4. Article 7 imposes four distinct but related obligations. Reference in its various provisions to 'cultural property protected by Article 4 of the Convention' is intended to encompass not just cultural property under general protection alone but also property additionally under special protection (Convention, chapter II) and enhanced protection (Second Protocol, chapter 3).

Article 7(a), modelled on article 57(2)(a)(i) of Additional Protocol I, requires each Party to the conflict to do everything feasible to verify that the objectives to be attacked are not cultural property protected under article 4 of the Convention. At the expert drafting meeting held in 1994, 'it was thought that military personnel should, at the very least, consult [any] available lists of protected cultural property'[75] before launching an attack. Paragraph (b) of article 7, drawn from article 57(2)(a)(ii) of Protocol I, obliges Parties to the conflict to take all feasible precautions in the choice of means and methods of attack 'with a view to avoiding, and in any event to minimizing, incidental damage to cultural property protected under Article 4 of the Convention'.

Article 7(c) is one of the most significant provisions of the whole Second Protocol. It compels Parties to the conflict to 'refrain from deciding to launch any attack which may be expected to cause incidental damage to cultural property protected under Article 4 of the Convention which would be excessive in relation to the concrete and direct military advantage anticipated'. As under article 57(2)(a)(iii) of Additional Protocol I on which it is based, the test under article 7(c) is one of

---

[75] CLT/CH/94/608/2, p. 3.

proportionality, even if the term is not employed. Again, too, the calculus calls for consideration of qualitative as well as quantitative factors. The quantum of incidental damage caused to cultural property comprises not only the raw amount destroyed or otherwise harmed but also its cultural significance. In this connection, it must be taken into account that cultural property, within the meaning of the Convention and Second Protocol, is, by definition, 'of great importance to the cultural heritage of [a] people',[76] and that the Parties declare in the preamble to the Convention that 'damage to cultural property belonging to any people whatsoever means damage to the cultural heritage of all mankind'. Since elements of this heritage are often irreplaceable, only the anticipation of very considerable concrete and direct military advantage will, in practice, be enough to justify an attack likely to cause incidental damage to cultural property. This goes even more so for cultural property under special protection (defined to be of 'very great importance'[77]) and cultural property under enhanced protection ('cultural heritage of the greatest importance for humanity'[78]). In that article 7(c) simply restates article 57(2)(a)(iii) of Protocol I as it applies to cultural property, and with it the now-customary rule to be superimposed on the Convention even by High Contracting Parties not also Parties to the Second Protocol, the provision breaks no new ground in relation to armed conflicts of an international character – even if it is an extremely useful endorsement of what is the single most important rule today in the protection of cultural property during attack. It is, however, a landmark as regards non-international armed conflict, being the first time that such a rule has been posited in treaty form. While it is arguably the case under modern customary international law, to be overlaid on the Convention by Parties to it, that a rule of proportionality governs incidental damage to cultural property in internal armed conflicts, this is not a view shared by all, and its explicit recognition puts the question beyond doubt as regards cultural property within the meaning of the Convention and Protocol.

The last paragraph of article 7, namely paragraph (d), based on Additional Protocol I, article 57(2)(b), obliges Parties to the conflict to cancel or suspend an attack in two circumstances – first, in accordance with subparagraph (i), if it becomes apparent that the objective of the attack is cultural property protected under article 4 of the Convention;

---

[76] 1954 Hague Convention, art. 1(a), incorporated as the definition of cultural property for the purposes of the Second Protocol by Second Hague Protocol, art. 1(b).
[77] 1954 Hague Convention, art. 8(1), chapeau.
[78] Second Hague Protocol, art. 10(a).

and, alternatively, in accordance with subparagraph (ii), if it becomes apparent that the attack may be expected to cause incidental damage to cultural property protected under article 4 of the Convention which would be excessive in relation to the concrete and direct military advantage anticipated.

Precautions against the effects of hostilities

As well as mandating precautions in attack, the Second Protocol imposes obligations to take precautions against the effects of hostilities. Article 8, modelled on article 58(a) and (b) of Additional Protocol I, stipulates in subparagraph (a) that the Parties to the conflict shall, to the maximum extent feasible, remove movable cultural property from the vicinity of military objectives or provide for adequate *in situ* protection; and, in subparagraph (b), that they shall avoid locating military objectives near cultural property. Just as in article 58 of Protocol I, article 8's use of the term 'Parties to the conflict' indicates that the obligations it imposes arise only after the outbreak of hostilities. Indeed, subparagraph (a) of article 8 was intended specifically to complement two of the peacetime measures of safeguard specified in article 5, namely the preparation for the removal of movable cultural property and the provision for its adequate *in situ* protection, since there was little point making Parties prepare to safeguard movables in the event of armed conflict without making them follow through when war broke out. The potentially costly measures required for the implementation of article 8(a) may attract disbursements from the Fund for the Protection of Cultural Property in the Event of Armed Conflict established under article 29 of the Second Protocol. Article 29(1)(b) authorises the Fund 'to provide financial or other assistance in relation to emergency, provisional or other measures to be taken in order to protect cultural property during periods of armed conflict or of immediate recovery after the end of hostilities in accordance with, *inter alia*, Article 8 sub-paragraph (a)'. As for article 8(b), this is a crucial provision, given the history of the destruction of cultural property through incidental damage.

Protection in occupied territory

Every obligation of respect mandated by the Convention and Second Protocol is applicable as much to belligerent occupation as to active hostilities. Nonetheless, just as article 5 of the former makes special, additional provision in respect of occupation alone, so too article 9 of the latter lays down a set of obligations specific to this aspect of international armed conflict. These obligations are supplementary and without prejudice to the provisions of articles 4 and 5 of the Convention, as made clear in the chapeau to article 9.

The transnational market in archaeological and other historico-artistic objects misappropriated in and exported from territories under occupation emerged after 1954 as a very grave threat to the material cultural heritage of many countries. The matter was already addressed to an extent by the First Protocol and by article 11 of the Convention on the Means of Prohibiting the Illicit Import, Export and Transfer of Ownership of Cultural Property,[79] but not all Parties to the 1954 Hague Convention were Parties to these other instruments. In light of the pillage at Angkor during the Vietnamese occupation of Cambodia,[80] the plunder of Kuwaiti cultural institutions by Iraqi forces and, less explicitly but no less seriously, of the continuing theft of cultural property from Turkish-occupied northern Cyprus, a desire was expressed during the review process to insert a single, brief provision on the illicit export of cultural property from occupied territory. In response, article 9(1)(a) of the Second Protocol requires an Occupying Power, in respect of the occupied territory, to prohibit and prevent any illicit export, other removal or transfer of ownership of cultural property. The provision's generic reference to 'cultural property' comprehends not only movables (even if, in practice, the activities of export and removal can only relate to these) but also immovables. As such, an Occupying Power is obliged to prohibit and prevent the illicit transfer of ownership not only of antiquities, works of art and the like but also of buildings, archaeological sites and monuments in the narrow sense. Like article 4(3) of the Convention, article 9 obliges Parties to prohibit and prevent the impugned acts not only when committed by their own forces and occupation authorities but also – and this is the thrust of both provisions – when committed by private persons. Again like article 4(3) of the Convention, article 9 of the Protocol does not, on its face, prohibit a State Party from engaging in such activities itself: the obligation, strictly speaking, is to prohibit and prevent. But, just as with article 4(3), a prohibition to this effect must

---

[79] Paris, 14 November 1970, 823 UNTS 231.
[80] Ironically, it was only after the departure of Vietnamese troops from the site in 1982 that Angkor was systematically looted and vandalised: Clément and Quinio, 'La protection des biens culturels au Cambodge', at 395–6.

be read into article 9, reasoning *a fortiori*. Any other result would be absurd and would contradict the provision's object and purpose.

The term 'illicit' is defined in article 1(g) to mean 'under compulsion or otherwise in violation of the applicable rules of the domestic law of the occupied territory or of international law'. The applicable rules of international law for the purposes of article 1(g) comprise, first, the relevant rules of the law of international armed conflict applicable during belligerent occupation, namely the customary prohibitions on the misappropriation and seizure of private property and of publicly owned cultural property reflected in articles 46 and 56 respectively of the Hague Rules, as well as the customary ban on pillage recognised in article 47 of the Hague Rules and in article 33 of the fourth Geneva Convention; the prohibition on any form of theft, pillage or misappropriation of cultural property implicit in article 4(3) of the 1954 Hague Convention, to which Parties to the Second Protocol are per force also Parties; and, where the relevant Parties are also Parties to the First Protocol to the Convention, article 1 of that Protocol, which obliges each Party to prevent the export of cultural property from territory occupied by it. In addition, where the Occupying Power is also a Party to the Convention on the Means of Prohibiting the Illicit Import, Export and Transfer of Ownership of Cultural Property,[81] article 11 of that instrument, which provides that the 'export and transfer of ownership of cultural property under compulsion arising directly or indirectly from the occupation of a country by a foreign power shall be regarded as illicit', is a relevant rule of international law within the meaning of article 1(g).

At the 1996 meeting of governmental experts, the participants also 'expressed their concern over archaeological excavations undertaken by an occupying power which may lead to the destruction of valuable information concerning the culture of the local population'.[82] The immediate reference was to Israeli-sponsored digs in the occupied West Bank and East Jerusalem, which had been the subject of international concern since 1967.[83] Archaeological excavations in occupied territory had formed the subject in 1956 of article 32 of the Recommendation on

---

[81] No provision of the 1970 UNESCO Convention requires that the occupied state must also be a Party to it. Moreover, its obligations are of a paradigmatic character.
[82] CLT-96/CONF.603/5, para. 15.
[83] In addition to the references above in chapter 3, see GA res. 3240A (XXIX), 29 November 1974, para. 3(g); GA res. 3525A (XXX), 15 December 1975, para. 5(g); GA res. 31/106C, 16 December 1976, para. 5(h); *et seq.*

International Principles Applicable to Archaeological Excavations, but there was no express provision on point in the legally binding Convention. A related concern was the alteration or change of use of cultural property in occupied territory, as at the Mosque of Ibrahim at the Cave of the Patriarchs in Hebron, part of which was converted into a synagogue after Israel occupied the West Bank, a measure noted with concern and declared null and void by the UN General Assembly in 1975.[84]

At the Hague diplomatic conference, the delegates reached consensus on three interrelated provisions. Paragraph (1)(b) of article 9 requires an Occupying Power to prohibit and prevent any archaeological excavation in the occupied territory, 'save where this is strictly required to safeguard, record or preserve cultural property'. On its face, the obligation extends even to digs authorised by the competent national authorities, including digs in progress, which at first blush seems odd. It is unclear if this is what was intended. On the one hand, with the exception of those matters falling expressly or necessarily within the rights ceded to and duties imposed on the Occupying Power by specific rules,[85] the regulation of cultural property in occupied territory remains the province of these competent national authorities, and there seems no reason why they should not be free to authorise whatever archaeological excavations they see fit. On the other hand, it is possible that the provision is a precautionary one, premised on the calculation that the only way to prevent illicit excavations in occupied territory is to ban all excavations for the duration of the occupation. Either way, it may be that the exception in respect of excavations strictly required to safeguard, record or preserve cultural property would permit the continuation of digs in progress insofar as this is necessary to enable the recording of finds already unearthed and to prepare the site for suspension of the work. For its part, paragraph 1(c) obliges the Occupying Power to prohibit and prevent, in relation to the territory, 'any alteration to, or change of use of, cultural property which is intended to conceal or destroy cultural, historical or scientific evidence'. Lastly, article 9(2) provides that '[a]ny archaeological excavation of, alteration to, or change of use of, cultural

---

[84] GA res. 3525D (XXX), 15 December 1975, preamble, third recital and para. 1. See also GA res. 31/106C, para. 5(i).

[85] For example, the obligation to prohibit and prevent the illicit export, other removal or transfer of ownership of cultural property from or within the territory, as laid down in art. 9(1)(a) of the Protocol.

property in occupied territory shall, unless circumstances do not permit, be carried out in close cooperation with the competent national authorities of the occupied territory'. One delegate 'expressed his strong opposition' to the qualification of article 9(2), since 'in some occupied territories, activities of national institutions are curtailed or even subjected to closure'.[86] But he was prepared, in a spirit of consensus, to tolerate the provision as drafted.

Enhanced protection

The dominant view from the start of the review process was that the regime of special protection established under chapter II of the Convention had been a failure, and, while doubts were expressed as to the utility of maintaining two different levels of protection, it was generally agreed that the relevant provisions called for improvement. In particular, the conditions of eligibility for special protection were roundly criticised for their parsimony and inflexibility – the Vatican City being the only cultural site on the World Heritage List[87] to be entered in the International Register of Cultural Property under Special Protection – and the procedure for entry in the Register, which had led to the failure to inscribe Angkor in 1972, was condemned as being too open to politicisation. In the event, the reform of special protection through the new regime of enhanced protection created in chapter 3 ('Enhanced protection') emerged as one of the core rationales of the Second Protocol, a centrality underscored in the first recital of the preamble, whereby the Parties declare themselves conscious of the need 'to establish an enhanced system of protection for specifically designated cultural property'.

Enhanced protection, unlike special protection and inclusion on the World Heritage List, is available for immovable and movable cultural property alike. Its conditions of eligibility are intended to be more realisable than those for special protection, with the absence of any requirement that the property in question be situated an adequate distance from military objectives. The procedure by which enhanced protection is granted is designed to be more objective and transparent, with the final decision being taken by the Committee for the Protection of

---

[86] *Summary Report*, para. 13.
[87] See Convention concerning the Protection of the World Cultural and Natural Heritage, Paris, 16 November 1972, 1037 UNTS 151 (the World Heritage Convention), art. 11(2).

Cultural Property in the Event of Armed Conflict established under article 24, as well as more multilateral, in keeping with the protected property's characterisation as being of the greatest importance 'for humanity'. The immunity afforded is more substantial than is the case under special protection: cultural property under enhanced protection and its immediate surroundings may never be used in support of military action, it may never be subject to demolitions and it may only be attacked if its use renders it a military objective. In addition, chapter 4, the Second Protocol's regime of penal sanctions, embodies two war crimes specifically relating to cultural property under enhanced protection. It is worth noting, however, as remarked upon at the fourth meeting of the High Contracting Parties to the Convention, that the Protocol makes no provision for the distinctive marking of cultural property under enhanced protection.[88]

The relationship between chapter 3 of the Second Protocol (enhanced protection) and chapter II of the Convention (special protection) is outlined in article 4(b) of the former: as between States Parties to the Protocol,[89] where cultural property has been granted both special protection and enhanced protection, the rules on enhanced protection alone apply. For its part, article 4(a) states that chapter 3 of the Protocol is without prejudice to chapter I of the Convention and chapter 2 of the Protocol. As a result, cultural property under enhanced protection continues to enjoy the benefit of the general provisions regarding protection laid down in the Convention and the Protocol, except to the extent that the provisions of chapter 3 constitute *lex specialis*. The upshot is that cultural property under enhanced protection is protected not just by article 12 of the Protocol, as refined by article 13, but also by articles 3, 4(3), 4(4), 4(5) and 5 of the Convention and by articles 5, 7, 8 and 9 of the Protocol. It also means that it is protected by article 4(1) of the Convention to the extent that the expression 'act of hostility' used in that provision is more compendious than the term 'attack' used in articles 12 and 13 of the Protocol.

Conditions of eligibility

The conditions of eligibility for enhanced protection are laid down in article 10 of the Second Protocol, which provides that cultural property

---

[88] UNESCO Doc. CLT-99/CONF.206/4, para. 10(v).
[89] And as between a Party and a state which accepts and applies the Second Protocol in accordance with art. 3(2).

may be placed under enhanced protection if it meets three cumulative criteria. Paragraph (a) requires that it be 'cultural heritage of the greatest importance for humanity'; paragraph (b) that it is protected by 'adequate domestic legal and administrative measures recognising its exceptional cultural and historic value and ensuring the highest level of protection'; and paragraph (c) that it is not used for military purposes or to shield military sites and that a declaration has been made by the Party which has control over it, confirming that it will not be used this way. Article 10 represents a liberalisation of the availability of supplementary protection when compared with the conditions of eligibility for special protection specified in article 8 of the Convention. First, it is not limited to immovable cultural property, so that works of art, antiquities and other movable cultural property of the greatest importance for humanity housed in museums and galleries which do not themselves satisfy the criteria for enhanced protection will nonetheless be eligible for the protection of chapter 3 of the Second Protocol. Secondly, article 10 contains no requirement that cultural property under enhanced protection be situated an adequate distance from the nearest military objective. All the same, the criteria laid down by article 10 are demanding.

Article 10(a)'s requirement that the cultural property in question constitute 'cultural heritage of the greatest importance to humanity' is stricter than the requirement in article 8 of the Convention, which speaks of 'very great importance'. This tough threshold criterion was the *quid pro quo* for the freeing up of what might be called the objective criteria for enhanced protection. It does not, however, represent a quantifiable legal standard, and its satisfaction will be a matter of factual appreciation in each case, to be undertaken by the Committee for the Protection of Cultural Property in the Event of Armed Conflict, one of whose tasks is to decide upon any request for inclusion in the International List of Cultural Property under Enhanced Protection.[90] The term 'heritage', as distinct from 'property', and the word 'humanity', as compared to the draft text 'all peoples', were settled on for rhetorical reasons, the former to connote intergenerational ethical responsibilities of a fiduciary character, the latter to emphasise 'the common interest in safeguarding important cultural heritage'.[91] The drafters eschewed the expression 'outstanding universal value', used in article 1 of the World Heritage Convention, so as to underline that the items on the International List of Cultural Property

---

[90] Second Hague Protocol, art. 11(5).
[91] *Summary Report*, para. 15.

under Enhanced Protection will not necessarily be coextensive with the cultural sites inscribed on the World Heritage List pursuant to article 11 of the World Heritage Convention. At the same time, there is no textual indication of whether the standard of cultural importance demanded by article 10(a) of the Second Protocol is to be construed as being higher or lower than the standard demanded by article 1 of the World Heritage Convention.[92] Presumably the open-textured formulation of the provision, reached by consensus, was a means of accommodating both inclusivist and exclusivist schools of thought, deferring the debate to the case-by-case deliberations of the Committee, where inclusion on the List is determined by a majority of four-fifths of its members present and voting.[93]

The requirement in article 10(b), akin to one of the criteria for inscription on the World Heritage List laid down in the Operational Guidelines for the Implementation of the World Heritage Convention,[94] responds to the view expressed by a majority of delegates to the 1998 meeting of governmental experts 'that any special protection regime on an intergovernmental level has to be complemented by appropriate national legislation'.[95] Its appropriateness to a conventional regime on the protection of cultural property in the event of armed conflict is open to question. Such a condition is one thing, and eminently sensible, if the domestic legal and administrative measures it contemplates are measures of safeguard as per article 3 of the Convention and article 5 of the Second Protocol, designed as they are to ensure the property's

[92] The UK currently proposes to request enhanced protection for its twenty-two cultural sites on the World Heritage List. 'In the case of movable cultural property the situation is less clear as there is no equivalent for museums and galleries to designation as a World Heritage Site.' 'In the absence of any internationally agreed criteria for designating the collections of museums', or of galleries or archives, the UK proposes to request enhanced protection for the contents of twenty-six museums and galleries, as well as of the National Record Offices and the country's five legal deposit libraries: Department of Culture, Media and Sport Cultural Property Unit, *Consultation Paper*, pp. 30–3, quotes at p. 31.
[93] Second Hague Protocol, art. 11(5).
[94] UNESCO Doc. WHC.05/2. Paragraph 97 of the Operational Guidelines reads: 'All properties inscribed on the World Heritage List must have adequate long-term legislative, regulatory, institutional and/or traditional protection and management to ensure their safeguarding. This protection should include adequately delineated boundaries. Similarly States Parties should demonstrate adequate protection at the national, regional, municipal, and/or traditional level for the nominated property. They should append appropriate texts to the nomination with a clear explanation of the way this protection operates to protect the property.'
[95] 155 EX/51, Annex, para. 12.

protection should armed conflict break out. But if what is meant in article 10(b) are more general measures geared towards the preservation of the relevant property in time of peace, this amounts to an expansion of the object and purpose of the Convention and Second Protocol beyond the strictly humanitarian. For their part, some delegates to the diplomatic conference felt that the provision 'did not take into consideration ... the difficulty that poorer countries could have in implementing [it], especially without international technical assistance'.[96] This concern was eventually reflected in several provisions – first, article 29(1)(a) of the Second Protocol, in accordance with which the Fund for the Protection of Cultural Property in the Event of Armed Conflict is authorised to provide financial or other assistance in support of preparatory or other measures to be taken in peacetime in accordance with, *inter alia*, article 10(b);[97] next, article 32(1), under which a Party may request from the Committee international assistance 'with respect to the preparation, development or implementation of the laws, administrative provisions and measures referred to in Article 10'; and article 33, pursuant to paragraph 1 of which Parties may call upon UNESCO for technical assistance in connection with any problem arising out of the application of the Convention, and in paragraph 2 of which Parties are encouraged to provide technical assistance bilaterally or multilaterally. In addition, linked to article 33(2) is the resolution adopted by the diplomatic conference, which reiterates 'the importance of adoption and implementation of adequate legal standards to protect cultural property within the framework of national cultural heritage protection policy'; recognises 'that a number of developing countries may have difficulty in fully implementing the provisions of the Hague Convention, its First Protocol and [its Second] Protocol'; and urges 'all States Parties to the [Second] Protocol to give careful consideration to requests from developing countries either at [the] bilateral level or within the framework of intergovernmental organisations'. The reference in article 10(b) to 'cultural and historic' value, where 'cultural' alone would have sufficed – the greater including

---

[96] *Summary Report*, para. 15.
[97] Note that art. 29(1)(a) does not assist in construing the 'domestic legal and administrative measures' required by art. 10(b). The former's full reference is to 'preparatory or other measures to be taken in peacetime in accordance with, *inter alia*, Article 5, Article 10 sub-paragraph (b) and Article 30'. Measures to be taken under art. 5 are obviously preparatory, and those under art. 30 ('Dissemination') most likely 'other', with the result that the measures to be taken under art. 10(b), as contemplated by art. 29(1)(a), are not obviously one or the other.

the lesser – is poor drafting: it wrongly implies that the adjectives are mutually exclusive, is inconsistent with article 10(a), which uses 'cultural' only, and sits uncomfortably with article 1 of the Convention, which employs 'cultural' as a catch-all term for 'historical', 'artistic', 'archaeological', 'scientific' and even bibliographical and archival.

The stipulation in article 10(1)(c) that cultural property for which enhanced protection is sought not be used for military purposes or to shield military sites is analogous to article 8(1)(b) of the Convention. The requirement that the Party in control of the cultural property in question make a declaration that it will not be used in a manner contrary to article 10(1)(c) is akin to that laid down in article 8(5) of the Convention, the difference being that the latter speaks only of the property's use in the event of armed conflict, whereas the requirement in article 10(1)(c) of the Second Protocol relates to peacetime use as well. The declaration provided for would constitute a binding unilateral statement.[98]

Granting of enhanced protection

The granting of enhanced protection is regulated by article 11 of the Second Protocol, which is closely linked to articles 25 to 27, whereby the twelve-person intergovernmental Committee for the Protection of Cultural Property in the Event of Armed Conflict is established. One of the Committee's functions is 'to grant, suspend or cancel enhanced protection for cultural property and to establish, maintain and promote the List of Cultural Property under Enhanced Protection'.[99] Another is to 'promote the identification of cultural property under enhanced protection'.[100]

In accordance with article 11(1), inspired by article 11(1) of the World Heritage Convention and its practice of 'tentative lists',[101] each Party to the Second Protocol should submit to the Committee a list of cultural property for which it intends to request the granting of enhanced protection. As indicated by the word 'should', article 11(1) is hortatory, not mandatory: there is no obligation to submit a list. Nor is there a requirement that property on any list submitted be situated in the

---

[98] See *Nuclear Tests (Australia v. France)*, ICJ Reports 1974, p. 253; *Nuclear Tests (New Zealand v. France)*, ICJ Reports 1974, p. 457; *Frontier Dispute (Burkina Faso/Mali)*, ICJ Reports 1986, p. 554.
[99] Second Hague Protocol, art. 27(1)(b).
[100] *Ibid.*, art. 27(1)(c).
[101] See UNESCO Doc. WHC-05/29.COM/8A.

sovereign territory of the Party submitting the list: the reference in paragraph 2 of article 11 to 'control' over the cultural property implies that an Occupying Power is entitled to request that property situated in territory it occupies be granted enhanced protection, and, *a fortiori*, is entitled to include such property on its list; and paragraph 4 of article 11 implies that cultural property in disputed territory may be listed by a Party.[102]

Article 11(2) provides that the Party which has jurisdiction or control over the cultural property may request that it be included in 'the List to be established in accordance with Article 27 sub-paragraph 1(b)'. A request must include 'all necessary information related to the criteria mentioned in Article 10'. The List referred to, as made clear in article 1(h), is the International List of Cultural Property under Enhanced Protection,[103] which is to chapter 3 of the Second Protocol what the International Register of Cultural Property under Special Protection is to chapter II of the Convention. The implication to be drawn from the purely hortatory nature of paragraph 1 of article 11, an implication not rebutted by the text of paragraph 2, is that a Party may request the inclusion of cultural property regardless of whether it has submitted a list under article 11(1); and, as noted above, article 11(2)'s reference to 'control' implies that an Occupying Power is authorised to request the inclusion of cultural property located in the territory it occupies.

In a significant internationalisation of the procedure for entry on the List, article 11(2) further provides that the Committee may invite a Party to request that cultural property be included in the List. Furthermore, article 11(3) authorises other States Parties, the ICBS 'and other non-governmental organisations with relevant expertise' to recommend cultural property to the Committee. 'In such cases', article 11(3) continues, 'the Committee may decide to invite a Party to request inclusion of that cultural property in the List'. But in neither of the cases foreshadowed in paragraphs 2 and 3 respectively of article 11 is the Party with jurisdiction or control over the property under any obligation to accept the Committee's invitation.

---

[102] Article 11(4) reads: 'Neither the request for inclusion of cultural property situated in a territory, sovereignty or jurisdiction over which is claimed by more than one State, nor its inclusion, shall in any way prejudice the rights of the parties to the dispute.'

[103] In a drafting incongruity, art. 1(h) refers to 'the *International* List of Cultural Property under Enhanced Protection established in accordance with Article 27, sub-paragraph 1(b)' (emphasis added), whereas art. 27(1)(b) refers simply to 'the List of Cultural Property under Enhanced Protection'.

The Committee is to inform all the Parties of the receipt of a request for inclusion in the List, in accordance with article 11(5), and any Party may submit representations regarding the request within sixty days. In response to the debacle in 1972 when the entry of Angkor in the International Register of Cultural Property under Special Protection was stymied by objections relating to the non-recognition of the government of the Khmer Republic, article 11(5) stipulates that representations by States Parties 'shall be made only on the basis of the criteria mentioned in Article 10' and 'shall be specific and related to the facts'. The Committee is to consider the representations, 'providing the Party requesting inclusion with a reasonable opportunity to respond before taking the decision'.

Under article 27(1)(b), the power to grant enhanced protection is vested in the Committee. In accordance with article 26(2), decisions of the Committee, including decisions whether to grant enhanced protection, require a two-thirds majority of its members voting. But article 11(5) specifies that in cases where the Committee has received representations from other States Parties, decisions on inclusion in the List must be taken, notwithstanding article 26, by a majority of four-fifths of its members present and voting. Article 11(6), which is of hortatory value only, states that, when deciding upon a request, the Committee 'should ask the advice of governmental and non-governmental organisations, as well as of individual experts'. Mirroring article 11(5)'s stipulation regarding representations by States Parties, article 11(7) makes it clear that decisions to grant or deny enhanced protection may be made only on the basis of the criteria in article 10. In an oddly drafted provision, article 11(10) specifies that enhanced protection 'shall be granted to cultural property by the Committee from the moment of its entry in the List', which would seem to mean simply that enhanced protection is effective from, and only from, the time of such entry. The Director-General of UNESCO, in accordance with article 11(11), is mandated to notify all the Parties, as well as the UN Secretary-General, of any decision to include cultural property on the List.

Article 11(8) provides for an extraordinary procedure whereby, '[i]n exceptional cases, when the Committee has concluded that the Party requesting inclusion of cultural property in the List cannot fulfil the criteria of Article 10 sub-paragraph (b), the Committee may decide to grant enhanced protection, provided that the requesting Party submits a request for international assistance under Article 32'. In other words, a Party's lack of the technical or financial wherewithal to put in place adequate domestic legal and administrative measures recognising the exceptional cultural value of the cultural property in question and ensuring the highest level of protection for it is not necessarily a bar to the inclusion of that property on the List, provided that the Party in question asks for assistance from the Committee pursuant to article 32(1). Article 11(9) posits another exception to the usual procedure in the event of armed conflict. On the outbreak of hostilities, a Party involved in the conflict may, on an emergency basis, communicate to the Committee a request for enhanced protection for cultural property under its jurisdiction or control. The Committee is bound to transmit any such request to all the Parties to the conflict (as distinct from all the Parties to the Second Protocol) and is to consider representations from the Parties concerned on an expedited basis. It is required to take its decision as soon as possible, and must do so – representations or no representations – by a majority of four-fifths of its members present and voting. An affirmative vote results in the grant by the Committee of provisional enhanced protection, 'pending the outcome of the regular procedure for the granting of enhanced protection', provided that paragraphs (a) and (c) of article 10 are satisfied.

Immunity and its loss

From early in the review process, the maintenance of the waiver in respect of military necessity, controversial in the context of general protection, was doubly so in the context of special protection. Some Parties to the Convention expressed the view that 'a small number of cultural properties, due to their exceptional value, should remain untouched in any circumstances'.[104] As with general protection, however, the majority favoured keeping the waiver in some form in the context of what was to become the regime of enhanced protection laid down in chapter 3 of the Second Protocol, although there was a consensus that its availability ought to be markedly curtailed. The result was articles 12 and 13, the former stating the basic rule as to the immunity of cultural property under enhanced protection, the latter the circumstances in which this immunity is lost.

Article 12 provides that the Parties to the conflict 'shall ensure the immunity of cultural property under enhanced protection by refraining from making such property the object of attack or from any use of the property or its immediate surroundings in support of military action'.

---

[104] 155 EX/51, Annex, para. 14.

For no obvious reason, the phrase 'by refraining from making such property the object of attack' is used in preference to the more compendious 'by refraining ... from any act of hostility directed against such property', the latter being employed in article 9 of the Convention (special protection), as well, *mutatis mutandis*, as in article 4(1) of the Convention and article 6 of the Second Protocol (general protection) and in article 53 of Additional Protocol I and article 16 of Additional Protocol II. As a result of its more restrictive formulation, article 12 does not encompass demolitions. But it must be kept in mind that, in cases where chapter 3 of the Second Protocol does not constitute *lex specialis* to chapter I of the Convention and chapter 2 of the Second Protocol, cultural property under enhanced protection benefits from the general provisions regarding protection embodied in the latter two chapters. In this light, the prohibition on demolitions inherent in the obligation in article 4(1) of the Convention to refrain from directing acts of hostility against cultural property applies to cultural property under enhanced protection.

Article 12 of the Second Protocol uses the expression 'in support of military action', as found in article 52(2) of Additional Protocol I, rather than 'in support of the military effort', as contained in article 53(b) of Protocol I and article 16 of Protocol II. The concept of 'military action', referring to military operations,[105] is arguably more restrictive than the notion of 'the military effort', which is 'a very broad concept, encompassing all military activities connected with the conduct of a war',[106] with the result that the protection granted by article 12 against military use, generically speaking, is possibly narrower than that provided by articles 53 and 16 of the respective Additional Protocols.

Article 13(1) specifies the only two circumstances in which cultural property under enhanced protection can 'lose such protection', in the words of the chapeau. The wording is unfortunate, since what the cultural property is better characterised as losing in the second of the two circumstances is its immunity, rather than its enhanced protection as such. It is, however, a distinction without a difference, given the exact formulation of article 13(1)(b).

The first situation in which enhanced protection can be lost, as spelled out in article 13(1)(a), is if such protection is suspended or cancelled in accordance with article 14. In turn, article 14(1) states that, where cultural property no longer meets any one of the three criteria specified

---

[105] Oeter, 'Methods and means of combat', para. 442(5).
[106] Sandoz *et al.*, *Commentary*, para. 2078.

in article 10, 'the Committee may suspend its enhanced protection status or cancel that status by removing that cultural property from the List'. Pursuant to article 14(2), the Committee may further suspend cultural property's enhanced protection in the event of a serious violation of article 12 arising from its use in support of military action, and may exceptionally cancel enhanced protection by removing cultural property from the List in cases where such violations are continuous. The Committee is obliged by article 11(4) to afford an opportunity to the Parties to make their views known before it takes any decision to suspend or cancel enhanced protection.[107]

The other circumstance in which cultural property can lose its enhanced protection, as provided for in article 13(1)(b), is 'if, and for as long as, the property has, by its use, become a military objective'. Two crucial implications can be drawn from this provision. First, provided it is not suspended or cancelled, enhanced protection can be lost only in relation to attacks, since it is only attacks which depend on whether an object is a military objective. In other words, in contrast to the immunity granted specially protected cultural property under the Convention, but no different from that afforded cultural property more generally by article 53 of Additional Protocol I and article 16 of Additional Protocol II, the immunity of cultural property under enhanced protection is absolute when it comes to demolitions, on the one hand, and to the use of such property in support of military action, on the other. Military necessity can never justify either act. Secondly, whereas cultural property under general protection can become a military objective through any one of its nature, location, purpose or use, cultural property under enhanced protection, like the cultural property protected by articles 53 and 16 of the respective Additional Protocols, can become a military objective only through its use.[108] It was this that a majority of delegates to the diplomatic conference saw as the main difference in the level of protection provided by each regime.[109]

---

[107] In addition, art. 11(3) obliges the Director-General of UNESCO to notify all the Parties to the Second Protocol, as well as the UN Secretary-General, of any decision to suspend or cancel enhanced protection.

[108] In another drafting inconsistency, Second Hague Protocol, art. 6(a)(i) refers to situations where cultural property under general protection has 'been made into' a military objective, whereas art. 13(1)(b) refers to when cultural property under enhanced protection has 'become' a military objective. The distinction is meaningless.

[109] *Summary Report*, para. 22; <www.unesco.org/culture/legalprotection/war/html_eng/precis25.htm>, pp. 2–3.

The invocation of article 13(1)(b) is subject to additional, cumulative conditions as specified in article 13(2), although it is unclear to what extent, if any, they constitute a real advance over the relevant provisions of the Additional Protocols. In accordance with subparagraph (a), cultural property which has, by its use, become a military objective may only be the object of attack if the attack is the only feasible means of terminating such use. Subparagraph (b) compels the taking of all feasible precautions in the choice of means and methods of attack, 'with a view to terminating such use and avoiding, or in any event minimising, damage to the cultural property'. Subparagraph (c) specifies three requirements, all of which must be met 'unless circumstances do not permit, due to requirements of immediate self-defence'. First, pursuant to article 13(2)(c)(i), the attack must be ordered 'at the highest operational level of command', meaning the highest level of military command.[110] Next, 'effective advance warning', that is, advance warning successfully transmitted and received, must be issued to the opposing forces requiring the termination of the cultural property's use in support of military action, as stipulated in article 13(2)(c)(ii). Finally, article 13(2)(c)(iii) requires that reasonable time be given to the opposing forces to 'redress the situation'.

Penal sanctions

The process of the Convention's review revealed dissatisfaction with the penal sanctions prescribed by article 28, a provision seen as too weak. The simplistic view expressed by some – ignoring customary international law, article 85(4)(d) of Additional Protocol I and elementary criminology – was that a stiffer criminal-law deterrent might have prevented the ravaging of cultural property during the wars in Croatia and Bosnia-Herzegovina. The adoption in 1993 of article 3(d) of the Statute of the International Criminal Tribunal for the former Yugoslavia,[111] vesting the Tribunal with jurisdiction over the customary war crime of 'seizure of, destruction or wilful damage done to institutions dedicated to ... the arts and sciences, historic monuments and works of art and science', represented a vindication of the Convention's object and purpose, and, at the same time, threw into even sharper relief the

---

[110] As earlier drafted, the provision had spoken of 'the highest political level', but this was objected to on account of its perceived impracticality: *Summary Report*, para. 19.
[111] UN Doc. S/25704, Annex, as amended.

inadequacy of its penal regime. The contrast was made starker still by the adoption in 1998 of articles 8(2)(b)(ix) and 8(2)(e)(iv) of the Rome Statute of the International Criminal Court,[112] recognising the Court's jurisdiction over the war crime, committed in international and non-international armed conflict respectively, of intentionally directing attacks against buildings dedicated to, *inter alia*, art or science or against historic monuments, provided they are not military objectives. Ultimately, the regime of penal sanctions established in chapter 4 became one of the major *raisons d'être* of the Second Protocol, one of the measures to reinforce the implementation of the Convention cited as necessary in the preamble's second recital; and while some delegates to the diplomatic conference thought that its provisions 'should exactly reflect those in Additional Protocol I',[113] and others those in the Rome Statute, those eventually adopted differ from both.

Chapter 4, like the Second Protocol as a whole, applies to armed conflicts of an international and non-international character alike. The extension of the Protocol's penal regime to internal conflicts was initially opposed by some delegates, who resisted the incursion into what they saw as their *domaine réservé*. The *quid pro quo* for their eventual acceptance of chapter 4 as adopted was article 22(4), which states that nothing in the Protocol is to prejudice 'the primary jurisdiction of a Party in whose territory an armed conflict not of an international character occurs over the violations set forth in Article 15'. Article 22(4) must be read in the light of article 16(1), which obliges States Parties to establish their criminal jurisdiction over serious violations of the Protocol not only on the basis of territoriality[114] but also on two extraterritorial bases, namely nationality[115] and universality,[116] and in the light of article 16(2)(a), which states that the Protocol does not preclude 'the exercise of jurisdiction under national and international law that may be applicable, or affect the exercise of jurisdiction under customary international law'. The effect of article 22(4) is to assert a hierarchy among these potentially concurrent prescriptive jurisdictions in cases of serious violations committed during a non-international armed conflict on the territory of a State Party. It implies that a Party seeking to exercise an

---

[112] Rome, 17 July 1998, 2187 UNTS 3.
[113] *Summary Report*, para. 7. See also *ibid.*, para. 28.
[114] Second Hague Protocol, art. 16(1)(a), applicable to all serious violations.
[115] *Ibid.*, art. 16(1)(b), applicable to all serious violations.
[116] *Ibid.*, art. 16(1)(c), applicable only to those serious violations set forth in art. 15(1), subparagraphs (a) to (c).

extraterritorial head of prescriptive jurisdiction over such a violation must, if requested, defer to the jurisdiction of the Party in whose territory the armed conflict, and hence the alleged serious violation, took place. This was something of a concession, given the classical position that no hierarchy pertains among concurrent criminal jurisdictions.[117]

Chapter 4 imposes on Parties two distinct sets of obligations. The first mandates legislative measures of a specifically penal nature, the second legislative and other measures which may include those of a penal nature. The first set of obligations are those attaching to the five 'serious violations' of the Protocol defined in article 15(1) – the label being settled on as a means of both likening them to and distinguishing them from the grave breaches of the Geneva Conventions and of Additional Protocol I. These obligations are to be found in articles 15(2) to 19. The second set of obligations are those attaching to the two 'other violations' referred to in article 21. These obligations are to be found in article 21 itself.

Article 38, included *ex abundante cautela* in chapter 8 ('Execution of this Protocol'), emphasises that nothing in the Protocol relating to individual criminal responsibility affects the responsibility of states under international law for breaches of the Protocol, referring specifically to the secondary obligation to provide reparation.

Serious violations

Definition

Article 15(1) enumerates five offences within the meaning of the Second Protocol, known collectively as serious violations of the Protocol. The chapeau to article 15(1) provides that a person commits an offence within the meaning of the Protocol if he or she intentionally and in violation of the Convention or the Protocol commits any of the acts outlined. In other words, the requirements of intent and of a relevant breach of the Convention or Protocol apply to each of the five serious violations defined in the provision.

The first two acts relate solely to cultural property under enhanced protection. Subparagraph (a) cites making cultural property under enhanced protection the object of attack as an offence within the meaning of the Protocol. The chapeau's requirement that the acts in

---

[117] Indeed, any hierarchy asserted has usually been in favour of the suspect's state of nationality: see e.g. *The S. S. 'Lotus'*, PCIJ Reports Series A No. 10 (1927), diss. op. Altamira at p. 95.

question be committed in violation of the Convention or the Protocol indicates that not every attack against cultural property under enhanced protection constitutes an offence for the purposes of article 15(1)(a), but only those incapable of justification by reference to article 13 ('Loss of enhanced protection') of the Protocol. Like article 12 of the Protocol, *viz.* the substantive provision establishing the immunity of cultural property under enhanced protection, article 15(1)(a) refers specifically – and inexplicably – to making such property the object of attack, as distinct from directing any act of hostility against it, with the result that the provision does not, on its face, recognise as a serious violation of the Protocol the demolition of cultural property under enhanced protection. Such a construction is completely at odds with the provision's object and purpose. Since the word 'attack' is nowhere defined in the Protocol, and since the meaning ascribed to it in Additional Protocol I – where the term, as herein used, was coined – is a special meaning,[118] not the ordinary meaning of the word, there is maybe room to argue that, as specifically employed in article 15(1)(a), 'attack' can encompass demolitions. But the argument is tenuous and smacks of special pleading. Moreover, if the accused is tried under a municipal provision in precisely the same terms as article 15(1)(a), this sort of expansive interpretation to his or her detriment is likely to offend against the requirement of certainty inherent in the principle *nullum crimen sine lege*, recognised as a general principle of law within the meaning of article 38(1)(c) of the Statute of the International Court of Justice and accorded the status of an international human right in, *inter alia*, article 15(1) of the International Covenant on Civil and Political Rights.[119] In the end, the best way to fill the lacuna is for Parties to legislate in more precise terms when establishing as an offence under their domestic law the offence embodied in article 15(1)(a). As for article 15(1)(b), this deems using cultural property under enhanced protection, or its immediate surroundings, in support of military action to be an offence within the meaning of the Protocol. The substantive provision of the Protocol to which article 15(1)(b) relates is again article 12, to which, as specifically regards the use of cultural

---

[118] See Additional Protocol I, art. 49(1): '"Attacks" means acts of violence against the adversary, whether in offence or defence.'

[119] New York, 16 December 1966, 999 UNTS 171. The first sentence of art. 15(1) of the ICCPR reads: 'No one shall be held guilty of any criminal offence on account of any act or omission which did not constitute a criminal offence, under national or international law, at the time when it was committed.'

property, article 13 provides no exception. It is crucial to note that neither provision stipulates destruction or damage of the relevant cultural property as a material element of the offence: criminal responsibility is imposed under articles 15(1)(a) and 15(1)(b) regardless of the result of the acts impugned.

Subparagraph (c) of article 15(1) recognises as an offence within the meaning of the Protocol extensive destruction or appropriation of cultural property protected under the Convention and the Protocol. The phrase 'under the Convention and [the] Protocol', as used also in the following provision, indicates that the cultural property in question is that protected by the general provisions regarding protection embodied in chapter I of the Convention and chapter 2 of the Protocol. In this connection, it must again be recalled that, insofar as chapter 3 of the Protocol does not constitute *lex specialis* to them, cultural property under enhanced protection benefits as much from these general provisions of the Convention and Protocol as does cultural property covered only by these provisions. As a consequence, article 15(1)(c) relates to the destruction and appropriation of cultural property solely under general protection as well as to cultural property additionally under enhanced protection. It also extends to cultural property which remains under the regime of special protection provided for in chapter II of the Convention, given that, where the parties to the conflict are Parties to both instruments, specially protected cultural property enjoys the benefits – to the extent that the provisions of chapter II do not constitute *lex specialis* – not only of the general provisions regarding protection laid down in chapter I of the Convention but also of those laid down in chapter 2 of the Protocol. In the light of the specific provision in articles 15(1)(a) and 15(1)(d) for making cultural property under enhanced and general protection respectively the object of attack, the reference to 'destruction' in article 15(1)(c) must refer to destruction caused by other means. The first such means is by demolitions contrary to article 4(1) of the Convention, even if, in the case of cultural property under enhanced protection, it is perverse that such acts must cause extensive destruction, in accordance with subparagraph (c) of article 15(1), while the unlawful acts vis-à-vis such property recognised as offences in subparagraphs (a) and (b) do not. The other destruction encompassed by article 15(1)(c), in relation to cultural property under general and enhanced protection alike, is by way of incidental damage, in circumstances where the attacking party has failed to take the precautions in attack specified in either article 7(c) or article 7(d)(ii) of the Protocol, both of which demand the application of a rule of proportionality. It must, however, be kept in mind that occasioning incidental damage will constitute a crime under the provision only when committed intentionally, in accordance with the chapeau to article 15(1): negligently inflicting incidental damage to cultural property covered by article 15(1)(c) is not a serious violation of the Protocol. The requirement that, in order for it to amount to a war crime, incidental damage to cultural property must be 'extensive' is drawn from article 85(4)(d) of Additional Protocol I, where it derives in turn from article 50 of the first Geneva Convention, article 51 of the second and article 147 of the fourth. As for appropriation, which, if extensive and of cultural property protected under the Convention and the Protocol, is also an offence for the purposes of article 15(1)(c), the relevant substantive prohibitions are that implied in article 4(3) of the Convention, namely the prohibition on any form of theft, pillage or misappropriation of, and acts of vandalism against, cultural property, and, insofar as any of the relevant acts amount to 'appropriation', the prohibition implied in article 9(1)(a) of the Second Protocol on any illicit export, other removal or transfer of ownership of cultural property. Although article 4(3) of the Convention is reflected more explicitly in subparagraph (e) of article 15(1), this latter provision relates only to 'cultural property protected under the Convention', whereas article 15(1)(c) relates to cultural property protected under the Convention and the Protocol.

Article 15(1)(d) embodies the offence of making cultural property protected under the Convention and the Protocol the object of attack. Since cultural property under enhanced protection is specifically covered by subparagraph (a) of article 15(1), subparagraph (d) relates to cultural property under general protection only. The substantive prohibition in question is article 4(1) of the Convention, as modified by article 4(2), as refined in turn by article 6(a) of the Second Protocol. As with article 15(1)(a), article 15(1)(d)'s use of the term 'making cultural property ... the object of attack', as opposed to the more inclusive 'directing an act of hostility against' such property, has the perverse effect of excluding demolitions from the ambit of the offence. Again, there is some room for reading demolitions into the provision; but, again, the argument is a weak one. In the final analysis, it is up to the Parties to remedy this oversight when enacting article 15(1)(d) into domestic law.

Lastly, paragraph (e) of article 15(1) recognises the offence of theft, pillage or misappropriation of, or acts of vandalism directed against cultural property protected under the Convention. The substantive provision to which article 15(1)(e) relates is article 4(3) of the Convention. The cultural property in question is cultural property under general protection alone. The term 'protected under the Convention' is somewhat misleading, in that, as regards Parties to the Second Protocol, cultural property under general protection enjoys the benefit of the general provisions regarding protection laid down in both the Convention and the Protocol. It would seem that the expression is intended to convey that the substantive rule implicated by article 15(1)(e) is found only in the Convention.

It is unclear whether the requirement of intent in the chapeau to article 15(1) implies knowledge that the property in question has been placed under enhanced protection, is protected by the Convention and Protocol or is protected by the Convention, as the case may be, or simply that the property is a 'monument of architecture, art or history, whether religious or secular', an archaeological site, or any other sort of movable or immovable property referred to in article 1 of the Convention.

Obligations on States Parties

The first limb of the first sentence of article 15(2) lays down the most fundamental obligation imposed on States Parties in respect of serious violations of the Second Protocol. It provides that each Party 'shall adopt such measures as may be necessary to establish as criminal offences under its domestic law the offences set forth' in article 15(1). The obligation applies to all the offences defined in subparagraphs (a) to (e) of that provision. The precise measures necessitated by the first limb of the first sentence of article 15(2) depend on the domestic law of the Party in question.

The second limb of the first sentence of article 15(2) further obliges Parties to adopt such measures as may be necessary to make the offences in question punishable by 'appropriate penalties'. The provision itself contains no indication of what penalties are to be considered appropriate. In this light, the first limb of the second sentence of article 15(2) is relevant. This provides that, when implementing their obligations under the first sentence, the Parties 'shall comply with general principles of law and international law'. International legal principles regarding the imposition of penalties for war crimes and, *a fortiori*, for war crimes specifically in respect of cultural property are at present embryonic. What seems clear, however, is that imprisonment is the only appropriate penalty.[120] Fines and forfeiture alone are inappropriate for war crimes, although they may be imposed in addition to a custodial sentence. As regards the maximum sentence which may be appropriate, it is instructive that Trial Chamber I of the ICTY, in its Sentencing Judgment in *Jokić*, which related to the bombardment in 1991 of the Old Town of Dubrovnik, referred to the war crime of destroying or wilfully damaging, *inter alia*, historic monuments and works of art – as per article 3(d) of the ICTY Statute – as 'a violation of values especially protected by the international community'.[121] It took the view that, 'since it is a serious violation of international humanitarian law to attack civilian buildings, it is a crime of even greater seriousness to direct an attack on an especially protected site, such as the Old Town, constituted of civilian buildings',[122] and that any sentence had to acknowledge that the attack on the Old Town was an attack 'against the cultural heritage of humankind'.[123] Similarly, '[a]s regards the seriousness of the offence of damage to cultural property', the Trial Chamber in *Strugar*, also relating to Dubrovnik, observed 'that such property is, by definition, of "great importance to the cultural heritage of every people"', citing article 1(a) of the 1954 Hague Convention.[124] The Tribunal in *Jokić* further noted that restoration of buildings of this kind, 'when possible, can never return [them] to their state prior to the attack because a certain amount of original, historically authentic, material will have been destroyed, thus affecting the inherent value of the buildings'.[125]

The relevance of the second sentence of article 15(2) is not limited to the penalties to attach under domestic law to the offences enumerated in article 15(1), but encompasses all aspects of the domestic criminalisation of serious violations of the Protocol. The second sentence of article 15(2)

---

[120] See e.g. ICC Statute, art. 77; ICTY Statute, art. 24; Statute of the International Criminal Tribunal for Rwanda, UN Doc. S/RES/955 (1994), Annex, as amended, art. 23; Statute of the Special Court for Sierra Leone, as amended, art. 19. Each of these provisions pertains to trial by the international tribunal in question. All the same, they are indicative of the principles one could expect to be embodied in domestic war crimes legislation.
[121] *Prosecutor v. Jokić*, IT-01-42/1-S, Trial Chamber Sentencing Judgment, 18 March 2004, para. 46.
[122] *Ibid.*, para. 53.
[123] *Ibid.*, para. 51.
[124] *Prosecutor v. Strugar*, IT-01-42-T, Trial Chamber Judgment, 31 January 2005, para. 232, reference omitted.
[125] *Jokić*, para. 52.

states in full that, when adopting the measures required by the first sentence of the provision, Parties are to comply with 'general principles of law and international law, including the rules extending individual criminal responsibility to persons other than those who directly commit the act'. The provision relates in particular to the material scope of the offences defined in article 15(1) – that is, to the various forms of conduct for which an individual may be held responsible for a serious violation.[126] The various modes of participation in an offence recognised by international law are derived from general principles of criminal responsibility common to national legal traditions, and include both participation in the offence and secondary forms of criminal responsibility. The most basic mode of participation is actual commission of the offence:[127] in the words of article 15(2), criminal responsibility attaches, first of all, to 'those who directly commit the act'. Commission can include omission, in cases where an individual is under a legal duty to act.[128] International law most likely also recognises criminal responsibility for the inchoate offence of attempt.[129] Next, given that the second sentence of article 15(2) makes special reference to 'the rules extending criminal responsibility to persons other than those who directly commit the act', an important mode of participation in an offence recognised by international law is ordering, soliciting or inducing the commission of an offence which occurs or is attempted.[130] Responsibility as principal in the second degree for ordering the commission of an offence is to be distinguished from command and superior responsibility, forms of secondary

---

[126] Recall that the mental element required for serious violations (*viz.* intent) is specified in the chapeau to art. 15(1).

[127] See ICC Statute, art. 25(3)(a), adding the rider 'whether as an individual, jointly with another or through another person, regardless of whether that other person is criminally responsible'. See also ICTY Statute, art. 7(1); ICTR Statute, art. 6(1).

[128] *Prosecutor* v. *Tadić*, IT-94-1-A, Appeals Chamber Judgment, 15 July 1999, para. 188. See also, in this light, Additional Protocol I, art. 86(1).

[129] See ICC Statute, art. 25(3)(f), adding the rider 'by taking action that commences its execution by means of a substantial step, but the crime does not occur because of circumstances independent of the person's intentions'. The article goes on to say: 'However, a person who abandons the effort to commit the crime or otherwise prevents the completion of the crime shall not be liable for punishment under this Statute for the attempt to commit that crime if that person completely and voluntarily gave up the criminal purpose.' But the inchoate offence of attempt is not embodied in the statute of either the ICTY or ICTR.

[130] See ICC Statute, art. 25(3)(b). See also, as regards ordering, ICTY Statute, art. 7(1); ICTR Statute, art. 6(1). Recall that the sanctions envisaged in 1954 Hague Convention, art. 28 are to be imposed not only on those who commit a breach of the Convention but also on those who order the commission of a breach.

criminal responsibility involving failure to act. International law also embodies criminal responsibility where, for the purpose of facilitating the commission of an offence, a person aids, abets or otherwise assists in its commission or attempted commission, including providing the means for its commission.[131] Criminal responsibility is further imposed in cases where a person contributes in any other way to the commission or attempted commission of an offence by a group of persons acting with a common purpose.[132] A contribution of this sort must be made either with the aim of furthering the criminal activity or criminal purpose of the group, where such activity or purpose involves the commission of an offence, or be made in the knowledge of the group's intention to commit the offence.[133] Finally, international law recognises secondary criminal responsibility in the form of command and superior responsibility.[134]

Article 16(1) obliges each Party to the Protocol to take the necessary legislative measures to establish its jurisdiction over the offences set forth in article 15 on three specific bases, two of which are applicable to all serious violations, the third only to those serious violations laid down in article 15(1) subparagraphs (a) to (c). As regards all offences within the meaning of the Protocol, article 16(1) obliges a Party to establish jurisdiction when the offence is committed in the territory of that state, as provided for in subparagraph (a), and when the alleged offender is a national of that state, in accordance with subparagraph (b). In other words, a Party must vest its domestic criminal courts with jurisdiction over all the offences set forth in article 15(1) on the basis of territoriality and, in relation to extraterritorial conduct, on the basis of nationality (or 'active personality'). As regards only those offences defined in subparagraphs (a) to (c) of article 15(1), each Party is further obliged to

---

[131] See ICC Statute, art. 25(3)(c). See also ICTY Statute, art. 7(1); ICTR Statute, art. 6(1).
[132] See ICC Statute, art. 25(3)(d). This mode of commission is not embodied in the statute of either the ICTY or ICTR, but criminal responsibility for a 'common purpose', 'common design' or 'joint criminal enterprise' has been recognised in the jurisprudence of both tribunals: see *Tadić*, Appeals Chamber Judgment, paras. 185–229; *Prosecutor v. Ntakirutimana*, ICTR-96-10-A and ICTR-96-17-A, Appeals Chamber, Judgment, 13 December 2004, especially paras. 461–8.
[133] See ICC Statute, art. 25(3)(d)(i) and (ii).
[134] See *ibid.*, art. 28. See also Additional Protocol I, art. 86, especially para. (2). ICTY Statute, art. 7(3) and ICTR Statute, art. 6(3) refer only to a 'superior', but it was held by the ICTY Appeals Chamber in *Prosecutor v. Delalić, Mucić, Delić and Landžo (Čelebići* case), IT-96-21-A, Appeals Chamber Judgment, 20 February 2001, para. 195, that 'the principle of superior responsibility reflected in Article 7(3) of the Statute encompasses political leaders and other civilian superiors in positions of authority'.

establish jurisdiction 'when the alleged offender is present in its territory'. That is, a Party must establish jurisdiction over the offences set forth in article 15(1)(a) to (c) on the basis of universality. Note, however, that this obligation is limited to situations where the alleged offender is subsequently present in the territory of the prosecuting state: there is no obligation on Parties to make legislative provision, even where domestically permissible, for trial *in absentia* pursuant to universal prescriptive jurisdiction.

Paragraph 1 of article 16 is stated to be without prejudice to paragraph 2, which contains two provisions of a clarificatory nature. Subparagraph (a) provides that the Protocol 'does not preclude the incurring of individual criminal responsibility or the exercise of jurisdiction under national and international law that may be applicable, or affect the exercise of jurisdiction under customary international law'. A provision to the effect that nothing in a convention mandating the establishment of specific heads of jurisdiction excludes the exercise of jurisdiction in accordance with national law is a common feature of international criminal conventions, even if its meaning is opaque. It is unclear whether such a clause effectively constitutes an agreement among the Parties that the exercise of any head of prescriptive jurisdiction, including universal jurisdiction,[135] over the offences provided for in the instrument is to be treated as permissible – but not mandatory, in contrast to the heads of jurisdiction cited in article 16(1) – as among the Parties, or whether its effect is simply to leave unaffected the exercise under national law of such jurisdiction as may be permissible under customary international law or another convention. The insertion in article 16(2)(a) of additional reference to the incurring of individual criminal responsibility, of the words 'and international law', and of the second clause relating to customary international law does nothing to clarify the situation. In the final analysis, however, it is likely that the second alternative is the correct one, and that article 16(2)(a) is intended to clarify that article 16(1) is without prejudice to existing national legislation criminalising and establishing jurisdiction over those grave breaches of the Geneva Conventions and of Additional Protocol I, and

---

[135] In *Arrest Warrant*, diss. op. Van den Wyngaert at para. 61, Judge *ad hoc* Van den Wyngaert expressed the view that such provisions did not exclude the exercise of universal jurisdiction over the offences in question, but this conclusion is predicated on her affirmation, at least in principle, of the '*Lotus* presumption' (see *The S. S. 'Lotus'*, at p. 19). Judges Higgins, Kooijmans and Buergenthal were noticeably more cautious: *Arrest Warrant*, sep. op. Higgins, Kooijmans and Buergenthal at para. 51.

those war crimes under customary international law, the subject matter of which potentially overlaps with serious violations of the Protocol. As for subparagraph (b) of article 16(2), it provides that, '[e]xcept in so far as a State which is not Party to this Protocol may accept and apply its provisions in accordance with Article 3 paragraph 2, members of the armed forces and nationals of a State which is not Party to this Protocol, except for those nationals serving in the armed forces of a State which is Party to this Protocol, do not incur individual criminal responsibility by virtue of this Protocol, nor does this Protocol impose an obligation to establish jurisdiction over such persons or to extradite them'. The provision, inserted at the instigation of the USA, is intended to acknowledge the effect of the *pacta tertiis* rule of the law of treaties.[136] Article 16(2)(b) does not, however, render impermissible the exercise by a Party of prescriptive criminal jurisdiction over a third-party national on the basis of any head of jurisdiction permitted by customary international law.[137] One of these, namely service in the armed forces of the prescribing Party, is expressly mentioned.

Article 16(2) is itself stated to be without prejudice to article 28 of the Convention. It will be recalled that the obligation imposed by article 28 permits but does not compel a Party to empower its courts to exercise universal jurisdiction over criminal breaches of the Convention. Nothing in article 16 of the Protocol thus precludes this.

It should lastly be noted that, at the diplomatic conference, the chairperson of the working group on chapter 4 made an interpretative statement with regard to article 16. By way of further reassurance of those states concerned by chapter 4's application to non-international armed conflict,[138] he made it clear that nothing in the Protocol, including article 16, 'in any way limits the State's ability to legislate, criminalize or otherwise deal with any substantive offences including conduct addressed in [the] Protocol'. He also stated, for the avoidance of doubt, that nothing in article 16(2)(b) 'should be interpreted as in any way affecting the application of Article 16(1)(a)'.[139]

---

[136] See Vienna Convention on the Law of Treaties, art. 34: 'A treaty does not create either obligations or rights for a third State without its consent.'

[137] As for extradition, as long as the suspect is present in the territory of the requested state, that state enjoys enforcement jurisdiction over him or her. Whether it also needs to point to some permissible head of prescriptive jurisdiction over the offence depends on whether any relevant treaty and/or the state's domestic extradition law imposes a requirement of double criminality.

[138] See also, in this light, Second Hague Protocol, art. 22(4).

[139] Final Act of the Diplomatic Conference, para. 11.

As regards those serious violations of the Second Protocol embodied in article 15(1) subparagraphs (a) to (c), article 17(1) imposes on a Party in whose territory the alleged offender is found the obligation, if it does not extradite that person, to 'submit, without exception whatsoever and without undue delay, the case to its competent authorities, for the purpose of prosecution, through proceedings in accordance with its domestic law or with, if applicable, the relevant rules of international law'. This obligation, again common to many international criminal conventions, is usually referred to as the obligation to try or extradite (*aut dedere aut judicare*) or to prosecute or extradite (*aut dedere aut prosequi*) an alleged offender. But it is more precisely an obligation on the Parties, in the event that they do not extradite the suspect, to submit the case to their prosecuting authorities with a view to prosecution: these authorities are not obliged, in the absence of a satisfactory case, to proceed to trial. Although it is by no means clear, the cryptic reference in article 17(1) to the relevant rules of international law, a reference not found in other international criminal conventions, would appear to make somewhat pedantic allowance for the possible prosecution of serious violations of the Protocol before a mixed criminal tribunal established on the territory of a Party and regulated by international law.

Article 17(2) embodies fundamental procedural safeguards for alleged offenders. 'Without prejudice to, if applicable, the relevant rules of international law', it stipulates that 'any person regarding whom proceedings are being carried out in connection with the Convention or [the] Protocol shall be guaranteed fair treatment and a fair trial in accordance with domestic law and international law at all stages of the proceedings, and in no cases shall be provided guarantees less favorable to such person than those provided by international law'. These guarantees are not limited to proceedings in respect of the serious violations provided for in article 15(1) subparagraphs (a) to (c), but extend to all serious violations of the Protocol, as well as to proceedings pursuant to legislative measures of a penal nature taken by Parties in accordance with article 21. Nor are the guarantees in question restricted to prosecution, but equally apply to extradition proceedings.

Article 18, applicable only to those serious violations of the Protocol set forth in article 15(1), subparagraphs (a) to (c), contains a range of technical provisions relevant to extradition. Article 19(1), inspired by article 88 of Additional Protocol I and the more recent international criminal conventions, obliges Parties to afford one another 'the greatest measure of assistance in connection with investigations or criminal or extradition proceedings brought in respect of the offences set forth in Article 15, including assistance in obtaining evidence at their disposal necessary for the proceedings'. The obligation of mutual legal assistance applies to all serious violations of the Protocol. For its part, article 20 clarifies the permissible grounds on which a Party may refuse a request for extradition in respect of the offences set forth in article 15(1)(a) to (c) or for mutual legal assistance in respect of any of the offences in article 15(1). In line with the recent trend in international criminal conventions, paragraph 1 of article 20 abrogates the 'political offence exception', as occasionally invoked to resist requests for extradition or mutual legal assistance, in relation to the offences in question. It states that the relevant offences 'shall not be regarded as political offences nor as offences connected with political offences nor as offences inspired by political motives', so that a request for extradition or for mutual legal assistance based on such offences 'may not be refused on the sole ground that it concerns a political offence or an offence connected with a political offence or an offence inspired by political motives'. Paragraph 2, again in keeping with recent treaty developments in international criminal law, qualifies paragraph 1 by providing that nothing in the Protocol shall be interpreted as imposing an obligation to extradite or to afford mutual legal assistance if the requested Party has substantial grounds for believing that the request for extradition or for mutual legal assistance 'has been made for the purpose of prosecuting or punishing a person on account of that person's race, religion, nationality, ethnic origin or political opinion or that compliance with the request would cause prejudice to that person's position for any of these reasons'.

Other violations

Article 21 of the Second Protocol – relating to 'other violations', as distinct from the serious violations of the Protocol enumerated in article 15(1) – imposes on Parties an obligation to adopt 'such legislative, administrative or disciplinary measures as may be necessary to suppress' two specified acts, when committed intentionally. Subparagraph (a) of article 21 cites any use of cultural property in violation of the Convention or the Protocol, and subparagraph (b) any illicit export, other removal or transfer of ownership of cultural property in violation of the Convention or the Protocol. Article 21 would justify, although not require, legislative measures by a Party to establish as criminal offences under its domestic law the violations referred to in subparagraphs (a) and (b). It would also justify, but not compel, the establishment by a Party of universal jurisdiction over the offences in question. The obligation laid down in article 21 of the Protocol is declared to be without prejudice to article 28 of the Convention.

Institutional issues

There was consensus from the very start of the review process that the regime of international control established under the Convention was an abject failure. No one disputed that it was too complicated and cumbersome, and the adoption of a 'flexible and simplified regime' was deemed crucial to the Convention's implementation.[140] The only question was the form that this should take. One view was that the UNESCO Secretariat should be reinforced, another that more use should be made of meetings of the High Contracting Parties. Most Parties to the Convention, however, favoured a purpose-built supervisory body, in the form of either an intergovernmental committee like the World Heritage Committee[141] or a smaller, lighter bureau. At the diplomatic conference, proponents of an intergovernmental committee argued that a body charged with 'taking decisions on the protection of cultural property of importance to all humankind' needed 'political weight and [a] representative character'.[142] Those preferring a bureau queried whether this 'political character' made an intergovernmental committee the best forum for taking such decisions, and commended instead an 'impartial, expert body', which would also be cheaper and easier to administer.[143]

In the event, chapter 6 of the Second Protocol ('Institutional Issues') creates an intergovernmental committee, but a trim one assisted by the UNESCO Secretariat, with an emphasis on the relevant expertise of its members. The Committee for the Protection of Cultural Property in the Event of Armed Conflict is supported by a specially created Fund for the Protection of Cultural Property in the Event of Armed Conflict. The Protocol further provides for a biennial Meeting of the Parties. The importance of this institutional regime is emphasised in the preamble's

---

[140] 142 EX/15, Annex, para. 6.6. See also CLT-95/CONF.009/5, p. 3.
[141] See the Intergovernmental Committee for the Protection of the World Cultural and Natural Heritage (the World Heritage Committee) established under chap. III of the World Heritage Convention.
[142] *Summary Report*, para. 23.
[143] *Ibid.*

third recital, which speaks of the desire 'to provide the High Contracting Parties to the Convention with a means of being more closely involved in the protection of cultural property in the event of armed conflict by establishing appropriate procedures therefor'.

But chapter 6 does not, as between Parties to the Second Protocol, replace the regime of international control established under the Convention and its Regulations. As provided for in article 2 of the Protocol, the latter merely supplements the Convention and its Regulations in this regard. Parties to the Protocol remain bound by their obligations under article 20 of the Convention and chapter I of the Regulations to put the regime of control into effect, despite general dissatisfaction with it. In this regard, it is worth noting that the Protocol, like the Convention, 'shall be applied with the co-operation of the Protecting Powers responsible for safeguarding the interests of the Parties to the conflict', as provided for in article 34.

The Committee

In accordance with article 24(1) of the Second Protocol, the Committee for the Protection of Cultural Property in the Event of Armed Conflict is established. The Committee is intergovernmental in character — that is, it comprises representatives of the States Parties, rather than independent persons. In contrast to the twenty-one member World Heritage Committee, it is composed of only twelve Parties. Parties members of the Committee are to be elected by the biennial Meeting of the Parties, which, as stipulated in article 24(3), must seek to ensure an equitable distribution of the different regions and cultures of the world. A Party is elected to the Committee for a four-year term of office, with the possibility of a single successive re-election.[144] In a more detailed provision than its analogue under the World Heritage Convention, article 24(4) specifies that 'Parties members of the Committee shall choose as their representatives persons qualified in the fields of cultural heritage, defence or international law, and they shall endeavour, in consultation with one another, to ensure that the Committee as a whole contains adequate expertise in all these fields'.[145] The Committee

---

[144] Second Hague Protocol, art. 25(1).
[145] World Heritage Convention, art. 9(3) requires more basically that States members of the World Heritage Committee are to choose as their representatives 'persons qualified in the field of the cultural or natural heritage'.

is to meet once a year in ordinary session and in extraordinary session whenever it deems necessary,[146] and shall adopt its own Rules of Procedure.[147] Decisions of the Committee, including decisions to grant, suspend or cancel enhanced protection, are to be taken by a majority of two-thirds of its members voting,[148] except in two cases: when representations submitted by the Parties in accordance with article 11(5) are before the Committee, a decision for inclusion in the List must be taken by a majority of four-fifths of its members present and voting, and the same goes for a decision to grant provisional enhanced protection pursuant to article 11(9). A Party member of the Committee is not permitted to participate in the voting on any decision relating to cultural property affected by an armed conflict to which it is party.[149]

The Committee's functions – which article 27(2) provides shall be performed in co-operation with the Director-General of UNESCO – are enumerated in article 27(1). First, in an idea borrowed from the established practice of the World Heritage Committee,[150] the Committee is to develop Guidelines for the implementation of the Protocol.[151] Next, and central to the implementation of chapter 3, it is to grant, suspend or cancel enhanced protection for cultural property and to establish, maintain and promote the List of Cultural Property under Enhanced Protection.[152] It is also to 'promote the identification' of cultural property eligible for enhanced protection.[153] Thirdly, in response to the perceived need for closer, more consistent attention to the question, the Committee enjoys a mandate 'to monitor and supervise' the implementation of the Protocol.[154] The Committee's monitoring and supervising functions do not, however, substitute for the regime of international control established pursuant to article 20 of the Convention and chapter I of its Regulations. Nor is it clear whether its

---

[146] Second Hague Protocol, art. 24(2).
[147] Ibid., art. 26(1).
[148] Ibid., art. 26(2).
[149] Ibid., art. 26(3).
[150] Recall the Operational Guidelines for the Implementation of the World Heritage Convention. The Convention does not itself make express provision for the Operational Guidelines.
[151] Second Hague Protocol, art. 27(1)(a).
[152] Ibid., art. 27(1)(b).
[153] Ibid., art. 27(1)(c).
[154] Ibid.

mandate extends to diplomatic calls for compliance with the Convention. As it is, since article 27(2) stipulates that the functions of the Committee are to be performed in co-operation with the Director-General of UNESCO, and since the Organisation enjoys both an express right of initiative under article 33(3) of the Protocol and an implied right under article I(3) of its Constitution, the Committee can rely on the Director-General to call on the relevant Party or Parties. Fourthly, with the intention of making the submission of implementation reports a more serious and useful exercise, the Committee is empowered 'to consider and comment on' the reports demanded of the Parties by article 37(2), as well as to 'seek clarifications as required' and to 'prepare its own report on the implementation of [the] Protocol for the Meeting of the Parties'.[155] Fifthly, it is to receive and consider requests for international assistance under article 32,[156] paragraph 3 of which requires the Committee to adopt rules for the submission of such requests and to define the forms such assistance may take. Next, it is to determine the use of the Fund for the Protection of Cultural Property in the Event of Armed Conflict established under article 29.[157] Finally, the Committee is to perform any other function which may be assigned to it by the Meeting of the Parties.[158]

In a provision blending elements of articles 8(3) and 13(7) of the World Heritage Convention, and significantly widening the pool of expertise open to the Committee, article 27(3) instructs the latter to co-operate with organisations – 'international and national', 'governmental and non-governmental' – which have objectives similar to those of the Convention and its First and Second Protocols. 'To assist in the implementation of its functions', the Committee is authorised to invite to its meetings, in an advisory capacity, 'eminent professional organisations such as those which have formal relations with UNESCO, including the International Committee of the Blue Shield (ICBS) and its constituent bodies', *viz.* ICA, ICOM, ICOMOS and IFLA. It may also invite, in the same capacity, representatives of the International Centre for the Study of the Preservation and Restoration of Cultural Property (the Rome Centre or ICCROM) and of the ICRC.

---

[155] *Ibid.*, art. 27(1)(d).
[156] *Ibid.*, art. 27(1)(e).
[157] *Ibid.*, art. 27(1)(f).
[158] *Ibid.*, art. 27(1)(g).

Whereas the World Heritage Committee has its own secretariat,[159] article 28 specifies that the Committee for the Protection of Cultural Property in the Event of Armed Conflict shall be assisted by the UNESCO Secretariat, which is charged with preparing the Committee's documentation and the agenda for its meetings, and which is responsible for implementing its decisions.

The Fund

Inspired by the Fund for the Protection of the World Cultural and Natural Heritage (the World Heritage Fund) established under chapter IV of the World Heritage Convention, article 29 of the Second Protocol establishes the Fund for the Protection of Cultural Property in the Event of Armed Conflict. The purpose of the Fund – which article 29(2) designates as a trust fund, in conformity with the provisions of the financial regulations of UNESCO – is twofold. Pursuant to article 29(1)(a), it is to provide financial or other assistance in support of preparatory or other measures to be taken in peacetime in accordance with, *inter alia*, articles 5, 10(b) and 30 of the Protocol; and, pursuant to article 29(1)(b), it is to provide financial or other assistance in relation to emergency, provisional or other measures to be taken in order to protect cultural property during periods of armed conflict or of immediate recovery after the end of hostilities in accordance with, *inter alia*, article 8(a).[160] Article 29(3) stipulates that disbursements from the Fund are to be used only for such purposes as the Committee shall decide in accordance with guidelines for the use of the Fund to be provided by the Meeting of the Parties under article 23(3)(c). There is nothing in article 29 to suggest that such disbursements are conditional on a request from a Party under article 32. The Fund's capital is to be drawn from a range of sources specified in

---

[159] World Heritage Convention, art. 14(1). Since 1992, the role of Secretariat to the World Heritage Committee has been performed by the World Heritage Centre: Operational Guidelines, para. 27. Similarly, while World Heritage Convention, art. 14(2) provides that the Director-General of UNESCO 'shall prepare the Committee's documentation and the agenda of its meetings and shall have the responsibility for the implementation of its decisions', these tasks too are now carried out by the World Heritage Centre: *ibid.*, para. 28.

[160] A form of 'other assistance' which could, for example, be supported by a disbursement from the Fund under art. 29(1)(b) would be the technical assistance in damage and needs assessment envisaged in the Joint Declaration for the Safeguarding, Rehabilitation and Protection of Cultural and Natural Heritage adopted by UNESCO and Italy: see UNESCOPRESS, Press Release 2004–97, 28 October 2004.

article 29(4), including voluntary contributions from the Parties,[161] as well as contributions, gifts or bequests from other States,[162] from UNESCO or other organisations within the UN,[163] from other intergovernmental or non-governmental organisations,[164] and from public or private bodies or individuals.[165] Article 29(3) makes it clear that the Committee may accept contributions to be used only for a certain programme or project, provided it has decided on the implementation of that programme or project. Unlike under the World Heritage Convention,[166] Parties to the Second Protocol are not compelled to contribute to the Fund.

The Meeting of the Parties

Article 23 provides for a biennial Meeting of the Parties to carry out certain functions related to the implementation of the Protocol. For States Parties to the Protocol, the Meeting is additional to the Meeting of the High Contracting Parties to the Convention which the Director-General of UNESCO may convene under article 27 of the latter.[167] In accordance with article 23(1) of the Protocol, the Meeting of the Parties to the Protocol shall be convened to coincide with the General Conference of UNESCO, which takes place once every two years, and in co-ordination with the Meeting of the High Contracting Parties to the Convention, if the Director-General has called one. In addition, article 23(4) provides that the Director-General must convene an Extraordinary Meeting of the Parties if requested to do so by at least one-fifth of the Parties to the Protocol. The Meeting of the Parties has several functions conferred on it by article 23(3). It is to elect the twelve Members of the Committee;[168] to endorse the Guidelines for the implementation

---

[161] Second Hague Protocol, art. 29(4)(a).
[162] Ibid., art. 29(4)(b)(i).
[163] Ibid., art. 29(4)(b)(ii).
[164] Ibid., art. 29(4)(b)(iii).
[165] Ibid., art. 29(4)(b)(iv). The Fund's other sources comprise any interest accruing on the Fund, funds raised by collections and receipts from events organised for the benefit of the Fund, and all other resources authorised by the guidelines for the use of the Fund to be provided by the Meeting of the Parties: ibid., art. 29(4)(c), (d) and (e) respectively.
[166] World Heritage Convention, arts. 15(3)(a) and 16.
[167] The first Meeting of the Parties took place on 26 October 2005, the same day as the sixth meeting of the High Contracting Parties to the Convention and five days after the close of the thirty-third session of the General Conference of UNESCO. The official report of the Meeting was not yet available at the time of going to press.
[168] Second Hague Protocol, art. 23(3)(a).

of the Protocol which the Committee is charged under article 27(1)(a) with developing;[169] to provide the Committee with the guidelines for the use of the Fund referred to in article 29(3), and to supervise this use;[170] to consider the report on the implementation of the Protocol which the Committee is charged with submitting under article 27(1)(d);[171] and to discuss any problem related to the application of the Protocol, and to make recommendations, as appropriate.[172] The Meeting shall adopt its own Rules of Procedure.[173]

Dissemination, co-operation and assistance

Convinced that public and professional awareness of the Second Protocol is essential to its success, the drafters adopted article 30, a provision incorporating elements of articles 7 and 25 of the 1954 Hague Convention, the analogous provisions of the Geneva Conventions and Additional Protocols,[174] and article 27 of the World Heritage Convention. Article 30(1) addresses the single most important precondition to the achievement of the objective and purpose of the Protocol, although perhaps the least amenable to government action. It obliges Parties to 'endeavour, by appropriate means, and in particular by educational and information programmes, to strengthen appreciation and respect for cultural property by their entire population'. Linked to this, article 30(2) requires that Parties disseminate the Protocol as widely as possible, both in peacetime and during armed conflict. On the professional level, article 30(3) insists that any military or civilian authorities who, in time of armed conflict, assume responsibilities with respect to the application of the Protocol be fully acquainted with its text. In furtherance of this, the Parties must incorporate guidelines and instructions on the protection of cultural property into their military regulations,[175] and develop and implement, in co-operation with UNESCO and relevant

---

[169] *Ibid.*, art. 23(3)(b).
[170] *Ibid.*, art. 23(3)(c).
[171] *Ibid.*, art. 23(3)(d).
[172] *Ibid.*, art. 23(3)(e).
[173] *Ibid.*, art. 23(2).
[174] See Geneva Convention I, arts. 47 and 48; Geneva Convention II, arts. 48 and 49; Geneva Convention III, arts. 127 and 128; Geneva Convention IV, arts. 144 and 145; Additional Protocol I, arts. 83 and 84; Additional Protocol II, art. 19.
[175] Second Hague Protocol, art. 30(3)(a).

governmental and non-governmental organisations, peacetime training and educational programmes,[176] communicating with one another, via the Director-General of UNESCO, information on the laws and administrative provisions adopted and others measures taken to these ends.[177] They must also communicate to one another as soon as possible, again through the Director-General, any laws and administrative provisions which they may adopt to ensure the application of the Protocol.[178]

Article 31 states that, '[i]n situations of serious violations of [the] Protocol', the Parties undertake to act, jointly through the Committee for the Protection of Cultural Property in the Event of Armed Conflict, or individually, in co-operation with UNESCO and the UN, and in conformity with the UN Charter. The provision is modelled on article 89 of Protocol I, which also refers to 'serious violations', as distinct from grave breaches, the implication being that Parties to Protocol I are bound to act in relation to all serious infringements of the Geneva Conventions or the Protocol, and not merely in relation to those which implicate the individual criminal responsibility of the perpetrator under the grave breaches provisions of the relevant instrument. Given, however, the special meaning of the term 'serious violations' in the Second Protocol, its scope in article 31 would appear restricted to those violations amounting under article 15(1) to an offence within the meaning of the Protocol. The obligation on Parties to 'act' is deliberately unprescriptive, although the object and purpose of the Protocol leaves no doubt that such action must be directed towards bringing such violations to an end.[179] The requirement of conformity with the UN Charter amounts to a requirement that action pursuant to article 31 not contravene the prohibition on the unlawful use of force in article 2(4) of the Charter.

Under paragraph 1 of article 32, a Party is entitled to request from the Committee international assistance for cultural property under enhanced protection, as well as international assistance in respect of 'the preparation, development and implementation of the laws, administrative provisions and measures referred to in Article 10'. The right to

---

[176] Ibid., art. 30(3)(b).
[177] Ibid., art. 30(3)(c).
[178] Ibid., art. 30(3)(d).
[179] Consider, in this connection, the subsequently elaborated art. 41(1) of the International Law Commission's Articles on Responsibility of States for Internationally Wrongful Acts, annexed to GA res 56/82, 12 December 2001. This is applicable, however, only to serious (that is, gross or systematic) breaches by a state of an obligation arising under a peremptory norm of general international law, in accordance with art. 40 of the ILC's Articles.

request such assistance does not, however, presuppose the right to receive it.[180] On its face, the unspecific reference in the first limb of article 32(1) to 'international assistance for cultural property under enhanced protection' would encompass assistance in the preservation of such property during peacetime, although such a grant of international assistance would represent an expansion of the Protocol's remit beyond the strictly humanitarian. The reference in the second limb of article 32(1) is to the 'adequate domestic legal and administrative measures' recognising the 'exceptional cultural and historic value' of cultural property and ensuring the 'highest level of protection' for it specified in article 10(b) as a condition to the grant of enhanced protection by the Committee; and it will be recalled in this connection that, when the Committee concludes that the Party requesting enhanced protection cannot satisfy article 10(b), article 11(8) permits the former, in exceptional cases, to grant enhanced protection on the proviso that the requesting Party submit a request for international assistance under article 32. But nothing in article 32(1) indicates that a Party must wait until the Committee concludes that it cannot satisfy article 10(b) before it is entitled to request such assistance.

Pursuant to paragraph 2 of article 32, a party to the conflict which is not a Party to the Protocol but which accepts and applies its provisions in accordance with article 3(2) may request 'appropriate international assistance' from the Committee. This entitlement does not, however, extend to the non-government party or parties to an armed conflict not of an international character: article 3(2) of the Protocol refers expressly to 'a State party to the conflict', the non-government party or parties to a non-international armed conflict being putatively bound by the Protocol by operation of article 22(1).

Article 32(3) requires the Committee to adopt rules for the submission of requests for international assistance and to define the forms such assistance may take. If a request for international assistance is for one of the purposes specified in subparagraphs (a) and (b) of article 29(1), there is no reason why any assistance granted may not be supported by a disbursement from the Fund for the Protection of Cultural Property in the Event of Armed Conflict.[181] For their part, Parties are encouraged by article 32(4) to give technical assistance of all kinds, through the

---

[180] The point is underlined in Second Hague Protocol, art. 27(1)(e), under which the Committee is mandated to receive and 'consider' such requests for international assistance.

[181] Recall, however, that there is nothing in art. 29 to suggest that disbursements from the Fund are conditional on a request under art. 32.

Committee, to those 'Parties or parties to the conflict' which request it, the latter term referring again, in the light of article 32(2), to those parties to the conflict which, although not Parties to the Protocol, accept and apply its provisions in accordance with article 3(2).

Modelled on article 23 of the Convention, article 33 of the Protocol entitles a Party to call upon UNESCO for technical assistance in organising the protection of its cultural property – by which is meant activities 'such as preparatory action to safeguard cultural property, preventive and organizational measures for emergency situations and compilation of national inventories of cultural property' – or in connection with any other problem arising out of the application of the Protocol. As under the Convention, the Organisation shall accord such assistance within the limits fixed by its programme and by its resources. The Parties are encouraged by article 33(2) to provide technical assistance, either bilaterally or multilaterally. As under article 23(2) of the Convention, UNESCO is authorised under article 33(3) of the Protocol to make, on its own initiative, 'proposals on these matters' to the Parties.

Pursuant to article 22(7) of the Protocol, analogous to article 19(3) of the Convention, UNESCO is also authorised to 'offer its services' to the parties to a non-international armed conflict to which the former applies. It almost goes without saying that the reference here is to the non-governmental party or parties as much as to the government.

Execution of the Protocol

Although there was agreement from early in the process of review that the Convention's confidence in the institution of Protecting Powers had been misplaced, the drafters of the Second Protocol were reluctant to do away with the system altogether, and the ICRC appealed for its retention.[182] In the end, the conference adopted article 34, reproducing almost verbatim article 21 of the Convention and providing that the Protocol is to be applied with the co-operation of the Protecting Powers responsible for safeguarding the interests of 'the Parties to the conflict'. The use of the upper case indicates that the reference is to States Parties involved in the conflict, reflecting the view of many delegates that the system of Protecting Powers is inapplicable to non-international armed conflicts.[183] Similarly, article 35 reproduces *mutatis mutandis*

---

[182] *Summary Report*, para. 42.
[183] *Ibid.*

article 22 of the Convention. As in article 34, on which it is premised, the use in article 35 of the capitalised term 'Parties' makes it clear that the provision, relying as it does on Protecting Powers, does not apply to non-international armed conflicts. In the light of lingering doubts as to the likely efficacy of the foregoing provisions, article 36 provides for conciliation in the absence of Protecting Powers. Paragraph 1 of article 36 states that, in a conflict where no Protecting Powers are appointed, the Director-General of UNESCO may lend his or her good offices or act by any other form of conciliation or mediation, with a view to settling 'the disagreement', the term referring back to the 'disagreement between the Parties to the conflict as to the application or interpretation of the provisions of [the] Protocol' in article 35(1). Paragraph 2 of article 36 provides that, at the invitation of one Party or of the Director-General, the Chairman of the Committee for the Protection of Cultural Property in the Event of Armed Conflict may propose to the Parties to the conflict a meeting of their representatives, and in particular of the authorities responsible for the protection of cultural property, if considered appropriate, on the territory of a State not party to the conflict. Whether the Party entitled to invite the Chairman of the Committee to act must be a Party to the conflict is unclear.

Article 37(2) maintains in relation to the Second Protocol the system of implementation reports provided for in article 26(2) of the Convention, but with modifications to make it more rigorous. Instead of 'giving whatever information they think suitable concerning any measures being taken, prepared or contemplated by their respective administrations' in fulfilment of the Convention,[184] Parties to the Second Protocol are obliged to submit, every four years, a report 'on the implementation of [the] Protocol'; and rather than submitting these reports to the Director-General of UNESCO, the Parties are required to submit them to the Committee, which is mandated to consider and comment on them, to seek clarifications as required, and to prepare its own report on the implementation of the Protocol for the Meeting of the Parties.[185]

It obviously remains to be seen what difference, if any, the Second Protocol will make to the protection of cultural property in armed conflict. It is doubtless an improvement on the Convention, even if several of its

---

[184] 1954 Hague Convention, art. 26(2).
[185] Second Hague Protocol, art. 27(1)(d).

substantive advances merely codify the overlay of contemporary customary international law which must now be applied on top of the earlier instrument. But whether it is more is hard to tell.

The reform of the Convention by way of a supplementary protocol makes for a maze of legal relationships as among Parties to any or all or none of the Convention, the Second Protocol, Additional Protocol I and Additional Protocol II which, as well as potentially discouraging participation in the most recent instrument, threatens to undermine the clarity, and hence the implementation by members of the armed forces, of the applicable rules. That said, a sensible military handbook on the laws of armed conflict, a sensible programme of instruction and a sensible drill will stick at all times to the stricter or strictest standard of the possible permutations.

In substantive terms, the Second Protocol represents a retreat from the Additional Protocols, under which all cultural property – and not just the relatively small range of cultural property eligible for the Second Protocol's enhanced protection – is immune during armed conflict unless, by its use and use alone, it has been rendered a military objective.[186] The point is worthy of remark, although it is also worth emphasising that the practical difference is probably not too great, and that customary international law may, in future, intervene to make use the sole justification for attacking any cultural property covered by the Second Protocol. There remains, nonetheless, the risk that the Protocol's maintenance of two different levels of protection for cultural property, with the emphasis seemingly on enhanced protection, may serve in practice to devalue the general provisions regarding protection. If nothing else, the different levels of protection on paper make things more complicated than they need be, and experience shows that complexity is to be avoided in the laws of armed conflict. As for the regime of enhanced protection, while it is certainly superior to the Convention's regime of special protection, it still seems a lot of bother for little real reward.

The obligation regarding the illicit import, export and transfer of ownership of cultural property from occupied territory is very welcome, addressing what is today a grave threat to the cultural heritage of many states, although it does not address the equally grave threat posed by the

---

[186] To make matters worse, recall that Parties to the Additional Protocols which are also Parties to the Second Protocol may avail themselves of the more permissive standard of protection granted cultural property by the latter.

traffic in cultural property illicitly removed during non-international armed conflict. The prohibitions on unauthorised archaeological excavations and alterations to cultural property in occupied territory are long overdue, but will presumably never apply to the concrete situation the drafters had in mind. For their part, the Protocol's penal provisions have real bite. At the same time, the deterrent value of criminal sanctions can be overstated.

The establishment of the Committee for the Protection of Cultural Property in the Event of Armed Conflict stands to facilitate the implementation of the Protocol during peacetime and, just as importantly, connotes the degree of seriousness with which this — and, more broadly, the object and purpose of the Protocol and Convention — is to be taken. It will probably not, however, do much to improve the implementation of, and compliance with, the provisions of the former and, *a fortiori*, of the latter in the course of armed conflict, which was seemingly its most basic rationale: the Committee does not replace the dysfunctional system of international control established under the Convention and its Regulations, and its mandate to 'monitor and supervise the implementation of [the] Protocol' is unlikely, in the end, to prove more potent a check on wartime breach than UNESCO's existing and continuing rights of initiative (through the exercise of which any diplomatic intervention may anyway have to come). As it is, the idea that the destruction of cultural property in the armed conflicts of the 1980s and 1990s reflected a failure of implementation seems a misdiagnosis. It must seriously be questioned whether the breaches of the Convention during the Iran–Iraq War, the invasion of Kuwait and the wars in the former Yugoslavia would have been prevented by stronger international institutional oversight. Even the most intrusive mechanisms for compliance with the laws of war (among which the Committee cannot be counted) are powerless against malice and contumacious outlawry. Time will tell, too, whether the financial and bureaucratic implications of another intergovernmental committee — albeit a light, comparatively cheap one — deter states from becoming Parties to the Protocol. The related Fund for the Protection of Cultural Property in the Event of Armed Conflict is another good idea, and the voluntary nature of contributions may stave off criticisms, although it may also stave off contributions.

In the final analysis, the value of the Second Protocol is as much rhetorical as legal. In the wake of the destruction and plunder of cultural property in the wars of the 1980s and 1990s, the High Contracting Parties to the Convention, along with UNESCO itself and interested non-governmental organisations, reaffirmed the values reflected in that instrument, reasserting 'that the preservation of the cultural heritage is of great importance for all peoples of the world and that it is important that this heritage should receive international protection'.[187] Whether the concrete form this reassertion takes contributes to that protection is a question for the future.

[187] 1954 Hague Convention, preamble, third recital.

6   Other relevant bodies of law

In addition to the law outlined in the preceding chapters, there is a miscellany of other international rules relevant to the protection of cultural property in armed conflict. Some are treaty-based, some customary. Some are rules of international humanitarian law,[1] some not. Many illustrate the wider normative influence of the vision of a universal cultural heritage and, in some cases, of the 1954 Hague Convention specifically.

Treaties

1980 and 1996 Protocols on Prohibitions or Restrictions on the Use of Mines, Booby-Traps and Other Devices

In 1980, the Convention on Prohibitions or Restrictions on the Use of Certain Conventional Weapons Which May be Deemed to be Excessively Injurious or to Have Indiscriminate Effects was adopted, along with three Protocols to it,[2] among them the Protocol on Prohibitions or Restrictions on the Use of Mines, Booby-Traps and Other Devices. The Convention and its Protocols apply to those situations outlined in article 2 common to the four Geneva Conventions, namely international armed conflicts, and to those conflicts deemed international by article 1(4) of Additional Protocol I.

Article 6(1)(b)(ix) of 1980 Protocol II, which is without prejudice to those rules of the law of armed conflict relating to treachery and perfidy,

---

[1] Note that the law of war crimes is a subset both of international humanitarian law and of international criminal law. It is dealt with below under the second rubric.

[2] Geneva, 10 October 1980, 1342 UNTS 137.

prohibits in all circumstances the use of booby-traps[3] which are in any way attached to or associated with historic monuments, works of art or places of worship which constitute the cultural or spiritual heritage of peoples. The property protected is identical to the property covered by articles 53 and 16 of Additional Protocols I and II respectively, which in turn is essentially the same as cultural property within the meaning of article 1 of the 1954 Hague Convention. Article 6(1)(b)(i) prohibits the use of booby-traps which are in any way attached to or associated with, *inter alia*, internationally recognised protective emblems, signs or signals, such as the distinctive emblem of the 1954 Hague Convention. More generally, article 3(3) prohibits the indiscriminate use of mines, booby-traps or other devices.[4] The expression 'indiscriminate use' is defined in the provision to mean any placement of such weapons which is not on, or directed against, a military objective;[5] which employs a method or means of delivery which cannot be directed at a specific military objective;[6] or which may be expected to cause incidental loss of civilian life, injury to civilians, damage to civilian objects, or a combination thereof, which would be excessive in relation to the concrete and direct military advantage anticipated.[7] The term 'military objective' is defined in article 2(4) according to the formula used in article 52(2) of Additional Protocol I to mean, as far as objects are concerned, any object which by its nature, location, purpose or use makes an effective contribution to military action and whose total or partial destruction, capture or neutralisation, in the circumstances ruling at the time, offers a definite military advantage. 'Civilian objects' are defined in article 2(5) to mean all objects which are not military objectives as defined in article 2(4). In this light, cultural property qualifies as a civilian object for the purposes of the prohibition laid down in article 3(3) of 1980 Protocol II,

---

[3] 'Booby-trap' is defined in art. 2(2) to mean 'any device or material which is designed, constructed or adapted to kill or injure and which functions unexpectedly when a person disturbs or approaches an apparently harmless object or performs an apparently safe act'.

[4] 'Mine' is defined in art. 2(1) to mean 'any munition placed under, on or near the ground or other surface area and designed to be detonated or exploded by the presence, proximity or contact of a person or vehicle'. 'Other devices' is defined in art. 2(3) to mean 'manually-emplaced munitions and devices designed to kill, injure or damage and which are actuated by remote control or automatically after a lapse of time'.

[5] 1980 Protocol II, art. 3(3)(a).

[6] *Ibid.*, art. 3(3)(b).

[7] *Ibid.*, art. 3(3)(c).

unless it has been rendered a military objective by virtue of its nature, location, purpose or use.

Dissatisfaction with some aspects of 1980 Protocol II led in 1996 to the adoption of the Amended Protocol on Prohibitions or Restrictions on the Use of Mines, Booby-Traps and Other Devices.[8] In addition to the situations to which 1980 Protocol II applies, 1996 Amended Protocol II applies to non-international armed conflicts as referred to in article 3 common to the Geneva Conventions[9] (as distinct from the non-international armed conflicts referred to in article 1(1) of Additional Protocol II). Article 7(1)(i) of 1996 Amended Protocol II mirrors the prohibition laid down in article 6(1)(b)(ix) of 1980 Protocol II on the use in all circumstances of booby-traps[10] which are in any way attached to or associated with historic monuments, works of art or places of worship which constitute the cultural or spiritual heritage of peoples, but extends this prohibition to the use of certain other devices.[11] Article 7(1)(a) does the same vis-à-vis the prohibition in article 6(1)(b)(i) of 1980 Amended Protocol II relating to internationally recognised protective emblems, signs or signals. Article 3(8) parallels the prohibition on the indiscriminate use of mines, booby-traps and other devices[12] found in article 3(3) of 1980 Protocol II, the term 'indiscriminate' being defined the same way.[13] Article 3(9) adds that several clearly separated and distinct military objectives located in a city, town, village or other area containing a similar concentration of civilians or civilian objects are not to be treated as a single military objective. The terms 'military objective' and 'civilian object' are defined as in 1980 Protocol II,[14] so that cultural property is

---

[8] Geneva, 3 May 1996, UK Misc. No. 2 (1997), Cm 3507.
[9] 1996 Amended Protocol II, art. 1(2). Article 1(2) makes it clear that the Protocol does not apply to situations of internal disturbances and tensions, such as riots, isolated and sporadic acts of violence and other acts of a similar nature, 'as not being armed conflicts'.
[10] 'Booby-trap' is defined in art. 2(4) in a manner identical to 1980 Protocol II, art. 2(2).
[11] 'Other devices' is defined in art. 2(5) to mean 'manually-emplaced munitions and devices including improvised explosive devices designed to kill, injure or damage and which are actuated manually, by remote control or automatically after a lapse of time'.
[12] The difference is that 'other devices' is defined more expansively in 1996 Amended Protocol II, art. 2(5) than in 1980 Protocol II, art. 2(3).
[13] 1996 Amended Protocol II, art. 3(8)(a), (b) and (c). Article 3(8)(a) adds that in case of doubt as to whether an object which is normally dedicated to civilian purposes, such as a place of worship, a house or other dwelling or a school, is being used to make an effective contribution to military action, it shall be presumed not to be so used.
[14] Ibid., arts. 2(6) and 2(7).

again to be characterised as a civilian object unless it has become a military objective on account of its nature, location, purpose or use.

International human rights law

Article 15(1)(a) of the International Covenant on Economic, Social and Cultural Rights[15] guarantees the right to take part in cultural life.[16] As interpreted by the Committee on Economic, Social and Cultural Rights, the provision encompasses an obligation of '[p]reservation and presentation of mankind's cultural heritage'[17] – in other words, a duty to preserve cultural property.[18] The duty includes an obligation to protect such property from vandalism and theft,[19] as well as a prohibition on its wilful destruction.[20] For example, the Special Representative of the Secretary-General on the situation of human rights in Cambodia characterised the vandalism and looting of Angkor Wat as an issue going to article 15 of the ICESCR.[21] Far less specifically, the destruction and looting of the cultural heritage of Afghanistan have been considered by both the UN General Assembly[22] and the UN Commission on Human Rights[23] as human rights issues.

---

[15] New York, 16 December 1966, 993 UNTS 3.

[16] Article 15(1)(a) embodies in binding treaty form 'the right freely to participate in the cultural life of the community' recognised in art. 27 of the Universal Declaration of Human Rights, GA res. 217A (III), 10 December 1948.

[17] Revised Guidelines regarding the Form and Contents of Reports to be submitted by States Parties under Articles 16 and 17 of the International Covenant on Economic, Social and Cultural Rights, UN Doc. E/1991/23, p. 88 at p. 108, para. 1(f). See also General Discussion on the Right to Take Part in Cultural Life as recognised in Article 15 of the International Covenant on Economic, Social and Cultural Rights, UN Doc. E/1993/22, chap. VII, para. 213.

[18] See the Committee's comments at UN Docs. E/1991/23, para. 79; E/1992/23, paras. 310 and 312; E/1993/22, para. 186.

[19] UN Doc. E/1993/22, para. 186.

[20] UN Doc. E/1995/22, para. 136.

[21] UN Doc. E/CN.4/1994/73, paras. 118–22. The UN Commission on Human Rights took note of the Special Representative's report, recommendations and conclusions 'with interest', 'in particular the identification of priority areas requiring urgent attention': Commission on Human Rights res. 1994/61, 4 March 1994, para. 8, chapeau. The first of these priority areas was '[t]he devotion of proper resources ... for [inter alia] the defence of cultural treasures, especially Angkor Wat': ibid., para. 8(a).

[22] GA res. 52/145, 12 December 1997, para. 17; GA res. 53/165, 9 December 1998, para. 16; GA res. 54/185, 17 December 1999, para. 16; GA res. 55/119, 4 December 2000, para. 19.

[23] Commission on Human Rights res. 1998/70, 21 April 1998, para. 2, chapeau and subpara. (g); Commission on Human Rights res. 1999/9, 23 April 1999, para. 12, chapeau and subpara. (e); Commission on Human Rights res. 2000/18, 18 April 2000, para. 14.

The nature of a State Party's obligations under the ICESCR is one of progressive realisation to the maximum of that Party's available resources, in accordance with article 2(1). This may have a bearing on the measures required of a Party to acquit its positive duty to protect cultural property from vandalism and theft. It does not, however, affect the negative obligation to refrain from wilfully destroying such property. In addition, States Parties may subject rights guaranteed by the Covenant to such limitations as are determined by law, insofar as this is compatible with the nature of these rights and for the purpose of promoting the general welfare in a democratic society, in accordance with article 4.

In terms of the ICESCR's scope of application *ratione loci*, the International Court of Justice in *Legal Consequences of the Construction of a Wall in the Occupied Palestinian Territory* considered it 'not to be excluded' that the Covenant 'applies both to territories over which a State party has sovereignty and to those over which that State exercises territorial jurisdiction'; and, recalling the view of the Committee on Economic, Social and Cultural Rights that Israel's obligations under the Covenant extended to all territories and populations under its effective control, it held that the ICESCR applied in the Occupied Palestinian Territory, including East Jerusalem.[24] At the same time, the Court characterised the rights guaranteed by the ICESCR as 'essentially territorial',[25] suggesting that their extraterritorial application was possible only in circumstances where the Party in question exercised a sufficient degree of control over the relevant territory.

The issue of the relationship between international human rights law and the laws of armed conflict was also discussed by the ICJ in the *Wall* opinion. The Court first recalled what it had said in *Legality of the Threat or Use of Nuclear Weapons* when it rejected the contention that the loss of life in hostilities was governed by the laws of armed conflict to the exclusion of the International Covenant on Civil and Political Rights:[26]

[T]he protection of the International Covenant on Civil and Political Rights does not cease in times of war, except by operation of Article 4 of the Covenant whereby certain provisions may be derogated from in a time of national emergency. Respect for the right to life is not, however, such a provision. In principle, the

---

[24] *Legal Consequences of the Construction of a Wall in the Occupied Palestinian Territory*, ICJ General List No. 131, Advisory Opinion, 9 July 2004, para. 112, quoting UN Doc. E/C.12/1/Add.90, paras. 15 and 31.
[25] *Ibid.*
[26] New York, 16 December 1966, 999 UNTS 171.

right not arbitrarily to be deprived of one's life applies also in hostilities. The test of what is an arbitrary deprivation of life, however, then falls to be determined by the applicable *lex specialis*, namely, the law applicable in armed conflict which is designated to regulate the conduct of hostilities.[27]

The Court then continued in its own words:

More generally, the Court considers that the protection offered by human rights conventions does not cease in case of armed conflict, save through the effect of provisions for derogation of the kind to be found in Article 4 of the International Covenant on Civil and Political Rights. As regards the relationship between international humanitarian law and human rights law, there are thus three possible situations: some rights may be exclusively matters of international humanitarian law; others may be exclusively matters of human rights law; yet others may be matters of both these branches of international law.[28]

As a consequence, in order to answer the question put to it, the Court had 'to take into consideration both these branches of international law, namely human rights law and, as *lex specialis*, international humanitarian law'.[29]

What exactly the ICJ meant by referring to international humanitarian law as *lex specialis* to international human rights law is not altogether clear. It may have meant that, while human rights law does not cease to apply by mere virtue of the existence of a state of armed conflict, the conduct of hostilities is regulated by the laws of armed conflict and, for these specific purposes, the laws of armed conflict apply instead of human rights law. In other words, derogation aside, there is nothing to stop human rights law applying in armed conflict, but the conduct of hostilities, as a specific aspect of armed conflict, is governed exclusively by humanitarian law. Presumably this would also be the case *mutatis mutandis* for belligerent occupation: in short, where there is an applicable rule of the laws of armed conflict, it effectively ousts the applicable human rights law to the extent of any overlap. Alternatively, the Court's

---

[27] *Construction of a Wall in the Occupied Palestinian Territory*, para. 105, quoting *Legality of the Threat or Use of Nuclear Weapons*, Advisory Opinion, ICJ Reports 1996 (I), p. 226 at para. 25.
[28] *Ibid.*, para. 106, affirmed in *Armed Activities on the Territory of the Congo (Democratic Republic of the Congo v. Uganda)*, ICJ General List No. 116, Judgment, 19 December 2005, para. 216.
[29] *Construction of a Wall in the Occupied Palestinian Territory*, para. 106, affirmed in *Armed Activities on the Territory of the Congo (DRC v. Uganda)*, para. 216.

final sentence ('The test of what is an arbitrary deprivation of life ... then falls to be determined by ... the law applicable in armed conflict') gives rise to a second possibility, namely that human rights law does continue to apply even to the conduct of hostilities but that a tribunal charged with determining whether, in this context, a Party has adequately secured the relevant right must assess that Party's conduct by reference to the standard embodied in the laws of armed conflict. A violation of the relevant rule of humanitarian law will, in this context, be conclusive of the violation of the applicable human rights guarantee. In other words, both international humanitarian law and international human rights law can apply to the conduct of hostilities: if a tribunal is charged with determining whether a violation of humanitarian law has occurred, it simply looks to the applicable rule of humanitarian law; if a tribunal is charged with determining whether a violation of human rights law has occurred, it looks to the relevant rule of humanitarian law as the standard for assessing whether the applicable rule of human rights law has been breached. For what it is worth, this second construction of the Court's dictum in *Nuclear Weapons* is the one placed on it by the Inter-American Commission on Human Rights.[30] Moreover, that the second construction was the one intended by the ICJ is made clearer by the last sentence of the quoted paragraph, which was omitted by the Court in the *Wall* opinion and which reads 'Thus whether a particular loss of life, through the use of a certain weapon in warfare, is to be considered an arbitrary deprivation of life contrary to Article 6 of the Covenant, can only be decided by reference to the law applicable in armed conflict and not deduced from the terms of the Covenant itself.'[31] If the second construction is indeed what the Court meant in *Nuclear Weapons*, and hence in the *Wall* opinion, what goes for the conduct of hostilities would again presumably go *mutatis mutandis* for belligerent occupation: in short, the applicable rules of international humanitarian law can be used to determine whether any applicable rules of international human rights law have been breached.

If the second construction were to represent the law, a State Party to the ICESCR would be obliged by article 15(1)(a) of the Covenant not wilfully to destroy cultural property in the course of at least

---

[30] *Coard v. United States of America*, 123 ILR 156 (1999), para. 42; *Decision on Request for Precautionary Measures (Detainees at Guantánamo Bay, Cuba)*, 41 ILM 532 (2002) at 532–3.

[31] *Legality of the Threat or Use of Nuclear Weapons*, para. 25.

non-international armed conflict on its own territory and when in belligerent occupation of the territory of another state, insofar as it had not in either case limited the right in article 15(1)(a) in accordance with article 4 of the Covenant. Whether or not the Party had acquitted its obligation in any given situation would then fall to be determined by the applicable rule of international humanitarian law: if destruction were to take place by way of an attack, the standard applied would be the customary prohibition on attacking cultural property unless it has become a military objective; if it were to take place by way of demolition for military purposes, the test would be that of military necessity; and if it were to take place to no military end during belligerent occupation, the applicable standard would be the absolute customary prohibition reflected in article 56 of the Hague Rules, with the result that article 15(1)(a) of the ICESCR would *ipso facto* be violated. Article 15(1)(a) would also be breached, in the course of at least non-international armed conflict on its own territory and during the belligerent occupation of another state's, where the armed forces of a State Party seized or pillaged cultural property in violation of the customary international humanitarian prohibitions on such acts, and where that Party failed to acquit its customary international humanitarian obligation to prohibit, prevent and, if necessary, put a stop to any form of theft, pillage, misappropriation and vandalism of cultural property.

As well as itself respecting article 15(1)(a) of the ICESCR when it is a Party to it, a state in the position of an Occupying Power is further obliged to ensure, as far as possible, that the competent national authorities respect article 15(1)(a) too in the event that the displaced Power is a Party to the Covenant. In *Armed Activities on the Territory of the Congo*, the ICJ stated that an Occupying Power's customary obligation, reflected in article 43 of the Hague Rules, to ensure, as far as possible, 'l'ordre et la vie publics' encompasses 'the duty to secure respect for the applicable rules of international human rights law'.[32] So, for example, if the displaced Power were a Party to the ICESCR and the competent local authorities were to authorise the razing of an integral and irreplaceable part of the cultural heritage in violation of article 15(1)(a), the Occupying Power would be compelled to intervene by virtue of its duty to ensure the enforcement of the existing legal order in the territory.

Although the protection of cultural property as an aspect of international human rights law is most developed under the rubric of

---

[32] *Armed Activities on the Territory of the Congo (DRC v. Uganda)*, para. 178.

article 15(1)(a) of the ICESCR, other provisions are also potentially engaged by the destruction of such property in the course of at least non-international armed conflict and belligerent occupation. Obvious candidates include article 27 of the International Covenant on Civil and Political Rights[33] and articles 2 and 5 of the Convention on the Elimination of All Forms of Racial Discrimination.[34]

World Heritage Convention

In language reminiscent of the 1954 Hague Convention, the preamble to the Convention concerning the Protection of the World Cultural and Natural Heritage[35] (the World Heritage Convention) testifies to the States Parties' conviction 'that deterioration or disappearance of any item of the cultural or natural heritage constitutes a harmful impoverishment of the heritage of all the nations of the world'. It speaks of the 'importance, for all the peoples of the world, of safeguarding this unique and irreplaceable property, to whatever people it may belong', and declares 'that parts of the cultural or natural heritage ... need to be preserved as part of the world heritage of mankind as a whole'. Motivated by this awareness of a universal interest in 'the conservation and protection of the world's heritage',[36] each Party recognises in article 4 its 'duty of ensuring the identification, protection, conservation, presentation and transmission to future generations' of the cultural and natural heritage situated in its territory, and undertakes to 'do all it can to this end, to the utmost of its

---

[33] ICCPR, art. 27 provides: 'In those States in which ethnic, religious or linguistic minorities exist, persons belonging to such minorities shall not be denied the right, in community with the other members of their group, to enjoy their own culture, to profess and practise their own religion, or to use their own language.' Under the rubric of art. 27, the Human Rights Committee has asked one State Party to 'provide information about the arrangements for preservation of religious, cultural and ancestral sites of indigenous peoples': UN Doc. CCPR/C/69/L/AUS, para. 8.

[34] New York, 7 March 1966, 660 UNTS 195. Articles 2 and 5 embody a range of measures, general and specific, which States Parties are obliged to take to eliminate racial discrimination in all its forms. The Committee on the Elimination of Racial Discrimination has expressed concern over insufficient measures taken by one State Party to prevent the destruction of the cultural heritage of indigenous peoples: UN Doc. CERD/C/304/Add.17, para. 12. In its Statement on the human rights of the Kurdish people, UN Doc. A/54/18, 10 March 1999, para. 22, the Committee declared itself 'profoundly alarmed about widespread and systematic violations of human rights inflicted on people because of their ethnic or national origin', which 'cause immense suffering, including ... the destruction of cultural heritage'.

[35] Paris, 16 November 1972, 1037 UNTS 151.

[36] World Heritage Convention, preamble, fourth recital.

own resources and, where appropriate, with any international assistance and co-operation ... it may be able to obtain'. In fulfilment of this duty, each Party subscribes in article 5 to a set of specific obligations in respect of cultural and natural heritage situated in its territory, 'in so far as possible, and as appropriate for each country'. Parties recognise in article 6(1) that 'such heritage constitutes a world heritage for whose protection it is the duty of the international community as a whole to co-operate', and undertake in article 6(3) 'not to take any deliberate measures which might damage directly or indirectly the cultural and natural heritage ... situated on the territory of other States Parties to [the] Convention'.

The term 'cultural heritage' is defined in article 1 to mean monuments, groups of buildings and sites – in other words, immovable cultural property – 'of outstanding universal value' from a cultural point of view. (The term 'natural heritage' is defined in article 2.) The Intergovernmental Committee for the Protection of the World Cultural and Natural Heritage (the World Heritage Committee), established under article 8, is authorised by article 11(2) to select, on the basis of 'tentative lists' submitted by the Parties pursuant to article 11(1) and in accordance with criteria established by the Committee,[37] certain property forming part of the cultural and natural heritage for inclusion on the World Heritage List. A Fund for the Protection of the World Cultural and Natural Heritage (the World Heritage Fund) is established under article 15. Properties inscribed on the World Heritage List are eligible for international assistance in accordance with the provisions of chapter V. The Committee is further mandated by article 11(4) to maintain the List of World Heritage in Danger, an inventory of those properties on the World Heritage List threatened by 'serious and specific dangers' – among them 'the outbreak or the threat of an armed conflict' – for the conservation of which 'major operations' are necessary and for which assistance has been requested under the Convention.

The obligations imposed by articles 4 and 6(3) respectively of the World Heritage Convention arise regardless of whether the cultural heritage in question is inscribed on the World Heritage List. Both provisions speak of 'the cultural and natural heritage referred to in Articles 1 and 2' (that is, all heritage protected by the Convention), rather than 'the cultural and natural heritage referred to in paragraphs 2 and 4 of Article 11'

---

[37] See also *ibid.*, art. 11(5). These criteria are outlined in Operational Guidelines for the Implementation of the World Heritage Convention, UNESCO Doc. WHC.05/2, paras. 45–168.

(that is, heritage included in the World Heritage List and List of World Heritage in Danger respectively), as used in articles 6(2) and 12. Moreover, article 12 makes it clear that the fact that property forming part of the cultural or natural heritage has not been included in the World Heritage List 'shall in no way be construed to mean that it does not have an outstanding universal value for purposes other than those resulting from inclusion' in the List. In practical terms, articles 4 and 6(3) apply to all cultural and natural heritage inscribed on the World Heritage List, or included in a tentative list submitted in accordance with article 11(1) by the Party in whose territory it is situated, or otherwise identified and delineated by that Party in accordance with article 3.[38]

No provision states that the Convention is inapplicable in situations of armed conflict. By analogy with the relationship between the laws of armed conflict and international human rights law, the sounder conclusion is that the World Heritage Convention continues to apply in armed conflict[39] but that, in such circumstances, the applicable rules of international humanitarian law constitute *lex specialis* to the *lex generalis* represented by article 4's obligation to protect, preserve and transmit to future generations items of the cultural heritage situated in a Party's own territory and by article 6's obligation not to take any deliberate measures which might damage, directly or indirectly, items of the cultural heritage situated in the territory of other Parties. At the same time, the jurisprudence on the relationship between international humanitarian and human rights law is ambiguous as to the precise relationship between the special and general rules. In the present context, it may be

---

[38] See e.g. *Queensland v. Commonwealth of Australia*, 90 ILR 115 (1988) at 129–31, per Mason CJ, Brennan, Deane, Toohey, Gaudron and McHugh JJ, and especially at 134, per Dawson J. See also *Richardson v. Forestry Commission*, 90 ILR 58 (1988), where a conclusion to the same effect is implicit in the various judgments.

[39] See also Toman, *Protection of Cultural Property*, p. 369. This is also the suggestion in *Prosecutor v. Strugar*, IT-01-42-T, Trial Chamber Judgment, 31 January 2005, para. 279, where the ICTY, referring to Dubrovnik and the attack against it on 6 December 1991, stated: 'The Old Town is also legally distinct from the rest of the wider city because the Old Town, in its entirety including the medieval walls, enjoys a World Heritage listing and the protections and immunities that are consequent on that listing.' But cf. *Bureau of the World Heritage Committee, Twenty-fifth session, 25–30 June 2001. Report of the Rapporteur*, UNESCO Doc. WHC-2001/CONF.205/10, 17 August 2001, para. I.9, where it was suggested by the director of UNESCO's Division of Cultural Heritage, Sector for Culture, that the Convention 'does not apply to civil conflicts'. Others are non-committal: see J. Simmonds, 'UNESCO World Heritage Convention' (1997) 2 *Art Antiquity and Law* 251 at 274; Chamberlain, *War and Cultural Heritage*, p. 18.

that, while the World Heritage Convention does not cease to apply by mere virtue of the existence of a state of armed conflict, the treatment of cultural property[40] during hostilities and belligerent occupation is regulated by the laws of armed conflict, and, for these specific purposes, the laws of armed conflict apply in preference to articles 4 and 6(3) of the Convention, ousting them to the extent of any overlap. The other possibility is that articles 4 and 6(3) of the World Heritage Convention continue to apply even to the treatment of cultural heritage[41] during hostilities and belligerent occupation, but that whether a Party to the Convention has complied with these provisions in relevant circumstances is to be assessed by reference to the standards embodied in the applicable laws of armed conflict. On such a reading, a violation of the relevant rule of the laws of armed conflict is conclusive of the violation of the applicable provision of the World Heritage Convention.

The second construction accords more closely with the jurisprudence, insofar as it is applicable by analogy to the relationship between the laws of armed conflict and the World Heritage Convention. If this reading were indeed to represent the law, it would mean that an act of hostility directed in the course of armed conflict by a Party to the Convention against an item of cultural heritage would, if it failed to satisfy the applicable rule of international humanitarian law, amount to a breach of either article 4[42] (in the case of cultural heritage situated in that Party's territory[43]) or of article 6(3) (in the case of cultural heritage situated in another Party's territory[44]) of the Convention. The same would go for acts of vandalism against cultural heritage during hostilities or, in the case of article 6(3), belligerent occupation, and for making it the object of reprisals. But the Convention, like the relevant rules of international humanitarian law, imposes no positive obligation on States Parties to preserve cultural heritage in territories occupied by them: while article 4,

---

[40] As defined in the applicable rule of the laws of armed conflict, be it art. 1 of the 1954 Hague Convention, arts. 53 and 16 of Additional Protocols I and II respectively, or customary international law.
[41] As defined in World Heritage Convention, art. 1.
[42] Although the precise obligation imposed on a State Party by art. 4 is 'to do all it can ... to the utmost of its own resources' to, *inter alia*, protect cultural heritage situated in its territory, the qualification is irrelevant when the conduct required is simply to refrain from actively destroying or damaging that heritage.
[43] That is, as regards conduct during an international or non-international armed conflict on that Party's territory.
[44] That is, as regards conduct during an international armed conflict, whether in the form of hostilities or belligerent occupation, on that other Party's territory.

applicable to a Party's own territory, encompasses a positive duty to conserve, article 6(3), applicable to cultural heritage in the territory of another Party, embodies the more limited duty not to take deliberate measures which might damage it.

As for the *sui generis* situation of the Old City of Jerusalem, as a matter of international law this is neither the sovereign territory of another State Party nor the sovereign territory of Israel, the Occupying Power, with the result that, as a formal matter, neither article 6(3) nor article 4 applies. In this light, despite the controversy over Jordan's irregular but successful nomination for the inscription of the Old City of Jerusalem and its walls on the World Heritage List,[45] no legal consequences for Israel could flow from this.[46] At the same time, the presence on the World Heritage List of cultural heritage situated in territory occupied by it has obvious diplomatic repercussions for an Occupying Power. This goes doubly for inscription on the List of World Heritage in Danger, which Jordan successfully proposed for the Old City of Jerusalem and its walls in 1982.[47] Similarly, in the context of active hostilities, the World Heritage Committee placed the Old Town of Dubrovnik on the List of World Heritage in Danger in December 1991, within a fortnight of its most serious bombardment and as units of the Yugoslav National Army continued to lay siege to the city.[48]

Convention on the Means of Prohibiting and Preventing the Illicit Import, Export and Transfer of Ownership of Cultural Property

In article 2(2) of the UNESCO-sponsored Convention on the Means of Prohibiting and Preventing the Illicit Import, Export and Transfer of Ownership of Cultural Property,[49] adopted in 1970, States Parties undertake to oppose the illicit import, export and transfer of ownership of

---

[45] *World Heritage Committee, First Extraordinary Session, Paris, 10 and 11 September 1981. Report of the Rapporteur*, UNESCO Doc. CC-81/CONF.008/2 Rev., 30 September 1981. Note that, in accordance with World Heritage Convention, art. 11(3), the 'inclusion of a property situated in a territory, sovereignty or jurisdiction over which is claimed by more than one State shall in no way prejudice the rights of the parties to the dispute'.

[46] As it was, Israel did not become a Party to the World Heritage Convention until 1999.

[47] *World Heritage Committee, Sixth Session, Paris, 13–17 December 1982. Report of the Rapporteur*, UNESCO Doc. CLT-82/CH/CONF.015/8, 17 January 1983, paras. 28–35. The site remains on the List of World Heritage in Danger.

[48] *World Heritage Committee, Fifteenth Session (Carthage, 9–13 December 1991)*, UNESCO Doc. SC-91/CONF.002/15, 12 December 1991, para. 29.

[49] Paris, 14 November 1970, 823 UNTS 231.

movable cultural property – recognised in article 2(1) as 'one of the main causes of the impoverishment of the cultural heritage of the countries of origin' – with the means at their disposal. For the purposes of the Convention, the term 'cultural property' is defined in article 1 to mean 'property which, on religious or secular grounds, is specifically designated by each State as being of importance for archaeology, prehistory, history, literature, art or science' and which belongs to one of the categories of movables listed in subparagraphs (a) to (k) of the provision. Article 3 states that the import, export or transfer of ownership of cultural property 'effected contrary to the provisions adopted under [the] Convention by the States Parties thereto' shall be illicit. More specifically, article 11 provides that the export and transfer of ownership of cultural property 'under compulsion arising directly or indirectly from the occupation of a country by a foreign power' shall be regarded as illicit, although there remains no conclusive indication of how this is to be interpreted.

In pursuance of the general obligation laid down in article 2(2), States Parties to the 1970 UNESCO Convention undertake in article 6, subparagraph (a), to introduce an export certification scheme and, in subparagraph (b), to prohibit the export from their territory of uncertified cultural property. Under article 7(a), the Parties are required to take the necessary measures, 'consistent with national legislation', to prevent museums and similar institutions within their territories from acquiring cultural property originating in another State Party which has been illicitly exported after the entry into force of the Convention in the relevant states. Under article 7(b), they must prohibit the import of cultural property stolen from a museum or religious or secular public monument or similar institution in another Party after the Convention's entry into force in the relevant states, 'provided that such property is documented as appertaining to the inventory of that institution'. Article 8 obliges the Parties to impose penalties or administrative sanctions on any person responsible for infringing the prohibitions in articles 6(b) and 7(b). In article 10(a), the Parties undertake to require antique dealers, subject to penal or administrative sanctions, to maintain a register recording the origin, the names and addresses of suppliers, a description and the price of each item of cultural property sold, and to inform the purchaser of the export prohibition to which the property may be subject.

The 1970 UNESCO Convention plays a central role in legal attempts to combat the import, export and transfer of ownership of cultural property misappropriated during armed conflict, including belligerent occupation.⁵⁰ Its significance in this context was highlighted in 2003, when the Director-General of UNESCO drew the attention of the prospective parties to the armed conflict in Iraq to it and invited INTERPOL, the World Customs Organisation and the International Confederation of Art Dealers to ensure its application.⁵¹

Customary international law

At its twenty-seventh session, the General Conference of UNESCO declared that 'the fundamental principles of protecting and preserving cultural property in the event of armed conflict' — by which it appeared to mean the obligations of respect embodied in article 4 of the 1954 Hague Convention, the only ones applicable under the Convention to both international and non-international armed conflict⁵² — 'could be considered part of international customary law'.⁵³ While the statement is a useful indicator, its generality does not advance things very far. In determining the extent to which customary international law regulates the protection of cultural property in armed conflict, it is necessary to examine each potential rule on its own merits, and to examine its application during international and non-international armed conflict respectively. The exercise is per force a rough and ready one. Cogent evidence of relevant state practice and *opinio juris* is not easy to come by. Most, and in the case of Additional Protocol I the overwhelming majority of states are Parties to the various treaties that embody the rules in question, thereby reducing the number of

---

⁵⁰ For consideration of the 1970 UNESCO Convention in this context, see *Autocephalous Greek-Orthodox Church of Cyprus and the Republic of Cyprus* v. *Goldberg and Feldman Fine Arts, Inc.*, 108 ILR 488 (7th Cir. 1990) at 507–9, concerning four Byzantine mosaics illicitly removed from the Kanakaria church in the Turkish-occupied north of Cyprus. But the assertion of Cudahy, Circuit Judge, at 508, that the 1954 Hague Convention 'applies to international trafficking during peacetime in cultural property unlawfully seized during an armed conflict' is plainly mistaken.

⁵¹ UNESCO Doc. DG/2003/064, pp. 2–3.

⁵² See *Delimitation of the Maritime Boundary in the Gulf of Maine Area (Canada/United States of America)*, ICJ Reports 1984, p. 246 at para. 79: '[I]n this context, "principles" clearly means principles of law, that is, it also includes rules of international law in whose case the use of the term "principles" may be justified because of their more general and more fundamental character.'

⁵³ 27 C/Resolution 3.5, preamble, recital (b). See also 142 EX/Decision 5.5.2, para. 5(b).

non-Parties whose practice it is which is most compelling.[54] Hard practice, in the form of conduct in respect of cultural property in the course of armed conflict, is thankfully sparse. Other material sources are not always readily available. In addition, the judgments of the ICTY, while a useful subsidiary source of customary rules going to individual criminal responsibility and state responsibility alike, must sometimes be taken with a grain of salt. Some reliance can be placed on the repeated embodiment of a rule in different treaties, although, as a matter of strict logic, this need not be persuasive of custom. In the end, the discernment of rules of customary international law is not rigorously scientific, and relies to a considerable degree on attempting to gauge an often unspoken consensus. Many conclusions can be no more than tentative.

International humanitarian law

Obligation of peacetime safeguard

It is unlikely that customary international law imposes on states a positive obligation to take peacetime measures of safeguard in respect of cultural property, as envisaged in article 3 of the 1954 Hague Convention and article 5 of its Second Protocol. Article 3 was not codificatory of any pre-existing customary rule. No such duty was recognised in the Hague Rules and, while states took preparatory measures prior to the outbreak of the Second World War, there is no indication, and no likelihood, that they did this out of a sense of international legal obligation. Quite simply, they viewed it as a good thing to safeguard their national collections and architectural heritage from the destructive effects of the imminent conflict. Nor does the rule embodied in article 3 of the Convention constitute a satisfactory basis for the development of a parallel customary rule of identical or very similar content. The words 'by taking such measures as they consider appropriate' would seem to deny the provision the fundamentally norm-creating character necessary for the formation

---

[54] Even very widespread participation in a treaty is not of itself an indication of the customary character of a rule embodied therein, since becoming Party to and, *a fortiori*, applying a treaty obligation is not necessarily predicated on a belief in its consonance with custom – indeed, often quite the opposite. In this regard, much of the state practice presented in the ICRC study on customary international humanitarian law, in the form of the military manuals of States Parties to the various conventions, is beside the point: see J.-M. Henckaerts and L. Doswald-Beck, *Customary International Humanitarian Law*, 3 vols. (Cambridge: CUP, 2005). The study nonetheless has its uses.

of a rule of custom.⁵⁵ The subsequent practice of states does little to change the situation. Again, states tend to, although do not always, make arrangements to insulate and isolate cultural property from the effects of hostilities, but again there is insufficient evidence to indicate that this is viewed as a customary obligation. The majority of the states in question, being Parties to the Convention, take the relevant measures in fulfilment of their treaty obligation under article 3. The rest as likely as not just consider such measures good policy. In this light, there is not enough evidence to suggest that states are custom-bound to prepare in time of peace for the safeguarding of cultural heritage situated within their territory against the foreseeable effects of an armed conflict.⁵⁶

Prohibition on making cultural property the object of attack

In the context of international armed conflict, the rule that civilian objects are not to be made the object of attack – a basic function of the 'cardinal' principle⁵⁷ of distinction, one of the 'intransgressible principles of international customary law',⁵⁸ and reflected in articles 48 and 52(1) of Additional Protocol I – is solidly established as customary international law.⁵⁹ Custom dictates, in the words of article 52(2) of Protocol I, that attacks shall be limited strictly to military objectives.⁶⁰

---

⁵⁵ *North Sea Continental Shelf (Federal Republic of Germany/Denmark; Federal Republic of Germany/ Netherlands)*, ICJ Reports 1969, p. 3 at para. 74.
⁵⁶ See also Henckaerts and Doswald-Beck, *Customary International Humanitarian Law*, vol. I, chap. 12 ('Cultural Property'), which does not include such a rule.
⁵⁷ *Legality of the Threat or Use of Nuclear Weapons*, para. 78.
⁵⁸ *Ibid.*, para. 79.
⁵⁹ See e.g.*Prosecutor* v. *Strugar, Jokić and others*, IT-01-42-AR72, Appeals Chamber Decision on Interlocutory Appeal, 22 November 2002, paras. 9–10 and 13; *Partial Award: Western Front, Aerial Bombardment and Related Claims. Eritrea's Claims 1, 3, 5, 9–13, 14, 21, 25 and 26*, Eritrea Ethiopia Claims Commission, 19 December 2005, para. 95.
⁶⁰ See also Henckaerts and Doswald-Beck, *Customary International Humanitarian Law*, vol. I, pp. 25–9 (Rule 7), as well as *ibid.*, pp. 34–6 (Rule 10). As a corollary, customary international law prohibits attacks during international armed conflict which are not directed at a specific military objective and attacks which employ a method or means of combat which cannot be directed at a specific military objective. These rules, embodied in art. 51(4)(a) and (b) of Additional Protocol I, were restated in 1980 Protocol II, art. 3(3)(a) and (b), and in 1996 Amended Protocol II, art. 3(8)(a) and (b). Custom also prohibits attacks by bombardment or any method or means which treats as a single military objective a number of clearly separated and distinct military objectives located in a city, town, village or other area containing a similar concentration of civilians or civilian objects, as laid down in Additional Protocol I, art. 51(5)(a). See Henckaerts and Doswald-Beck, *Customary International Humanitarian Law*, vol. I, pp. 37–45 (Rules 11–13). See also *Prosecutor* v. *Blaškić*, IT-95-14-A, Appeals Chamber Judgment, 29 July 2004, para. 157. In *Armed Activities on the Territory of the Congo (DRC v. Uganda)*, para. 208, the ICJ stated 'that indiscriminate shelling is ... a grave violation of humanitarian law'.

As for what constitutes a military objective, customary international law accords with the definition laid down in article 52(2) of that Protocol: insofar as objects are concerned, military objectives are limited to those objects which by their nature, location, purpose or use make an effective contribution to military action and whose total or partial destruction, capture or neutralisation, in the circumstances ruling at the time, offers a definite military advantage.[61] Applying this definition, cultural property – in the generic sense of the 'buildings dedicated to religion, art, science or charitable purposes [and] historic monuments' referred to in article 27 of the Hague Rules; in the technical sense of 'movable or immovable property of great importance to the cultural heritage of every people', within the meaning of article 1 of the 1954 Hague Convention; and in the generic sense once more of the 'historic monuments, works of art or places of worship which constitute the cultural or spiritual heritage of peoples' cited in article 53(a) of Protocol I – can be expected to constitute *prima facie* a civilian object.[62] Although the precise definition embodied in article 52(2) of Protocol I is no longer accepted in its entirety by the USA,[63] the most influential state not Party to Protocol I, the contested elements have no direct bearing on cultural property. Moreover, the USA has incorporated article 52(2) verbatim into two of its military manuals.[64] Its revised position has not altered the established customary definition, which has been entrenched by its recodification in successive treaties[65] and by judicial

---

[61] See e.g. *Western Front, Aerial Bombardment and Related Claims*, para. 113. See also Henckaerts and Doswald-Beck, *Customary International Humanitarian Law*, vol. I, pp. 29–32 (Rule 8).

[62] See also Henckaerts and Doswald-Beck, *Customary International Humanitarian Law*, vol. I, pp. 32–4 (Rule 9), especially p. 34, listing 'historic monuments, places of worship and cultural property' as *prima facie* civilian objects, 'provided, in the final analysis, they have not become military objectives'.

[63] See Department of the Navy, *The Commander's Handbook on the Law of Naval Operations*, Naval Warfare Publication 1–14M, October 1995, para. 8.1.1; Department of Defense, Military Commission Instruction No. 2, 30 April 2003, para. 5(D).

[64] See Department of the Army, *The Law of Land Warfare*, Field Manual No. 27–10, as amended 15 July 1976, para. 40(c); Department of the Air Force, *International Law: The Conduct of Armed Conflict and Air Operations*, Air Force Publication 110–31, November 1976, para. 5–3(b)(1). See also Department of the Air Force, *USAF Intelligence Targeting Guide*, Air Force Pamphlet 14–210 Intelligence, 1 February 1998, Attachment 4 ('Targeting and International Law'), para. A4.2.2.

[65] See 1980 Protocol II, art. 2(4); Protocol on Prohibitions or Restrictions on the Use of Incendiary Weapons (1980 Protocol III), Geneva, 10 October 1980, 1342 UNTS 137, art. 1(3); 1996 Amended Protocol II, art. 2(6); Second Hague Protocol, art. 1(f).

support.⁶⁶ In the final analysis, there is no doubt whatsoever that cultural property, in the broadest sense of the term, is protected during international armed conflict by the customary prohibition on attacks against civilian objects.

Whether, in the course of international armed conflict, customary international law accords greater protection from attack to cultural property *quâ* cultural property is more difficult. In terms of state practice, very wide participation in Additional Protocol I is not of itself an indication of the customary character of article 53(a), which effectively makes an exception to the protection against acts of hostility afforded to historic monuments, works of art or places of worship which constitute the cultural or spiritual heritage of peoples only where they are used for military purposes. Moreover, article 53(a) arguably lacks the fundamentally norm-creating character needed to form the basis of a rule of custom, since it is stated to be without prejudice to the provisions of the 1954 Hague Convention, article 4(2) of which embodies a general waiver in respect of military necessity. On the other hand, use for military purposes is the sole ground on which a Party to the Roerich Pact may deny cultural property 'the privileges recognized' in that instrument.⁶⁷ As for the practice of states not Parties to Protocol I, there is not much of this to be found, and, as it is, the more Parties there are to the Protocol, the less capable the non-Parties are of making custom on their own, given the requirement of widespread and representative practice. Nonetheless, it is not without evidentiary weight that the US Department of Defense – the USA being the most influential state not Party to Protocol I – stated in 1992 that 'cultural . . . objects are protected from direct, intentional attack unless they are used for military purposes'.⁶⁸ This view is reflected in US military handbooks.⁶⁹ But the US position may have since changed: the Department of Defense's

---

[66] *Prosecutor* v. *Brdjanin*, IT-99-36-T, Trial Chamber Judgment, 1 September 2004, para. 596 n. 1509.
[67] Roerich Pact, art. 5.
[68] Department of Defense, *Report to Congress on the Conduct of the Persian Gulf War, Appendix O: The Role of the Law of War*, 31 ILM 612 (1992) at 622. See also Department of Defense, *Report to Congress on International Policies and Procedures regarding the Protection of Natural and Cultural Resources during Times of War*, reproduced in Boylan, *Review*, appendix VIII, pp. 202 and 204.
[69] Department of the Army, *Law of Land Warfare*, para. 45(a); Department of the Navy, *Commander's Handbook*, paras. 8.5.1.6, 8.6.2 and 8.6.2.2. See also Department of the Air Force, *Targeting Guide*, Attachment 4, para. A4.5.2.

Military Commission Instruction No. 2 of 30 April 2003 defines the term 'protected property' to mean 'property specifically protected by the law of armed conflict such as buildings dedicated to religion, education, art, science or charitable purposes [or] historic monuments... provided they are not being used for military purposes or are not otherwise military objectives'.[70] As for judicial decisions, a Trial Chamber of the ICTY in *Strugar*, dealing with the attack on the Old Town of Dubrovnik in the context of the war crime of destruction or wilful damage done to 'institutions dedicated to religion, charity and education, the arts and sciences, historic monuments and works of art and science' within the meaning of article 3(d) of the Tribunal's Statute, suggested that the only exception to the customary protection of such property from acts of hostility is when it is being used for military purposes.[71] But the Trial Chamber's reasoning is unconvincing. For a start, it elides article 27 of the Hague Rules,[72] and its proviso as to military use, with articles 4(1) and 4(2) of the 1954 Hague Convention, the latter referring more broadly to cases where imperative military necessity requires a waiver.[73] Perhaps more to the point, it pays no attention to subsequent practice in the interpretation of article 27, which seems to favour a construction whereby the provision prohibits only such bombardment of protected property as is not imperatively demanded by the necessities of war. Furthermore, while the Trial Chamber relies on what it calls 'the established jurisprudence of the Tribunal', all this consists of is a strikingly bald and brief assertion by the Trial Chamber in *Blaškić*,[74] as followed without serious analysis by the Trial Chambers in *Kordić*,[75] *Naletilić*[76] and *Brdjanin*[77] respectively.[78] For its

---

[70] Military Commission Instruction No. 2, para. 5(F).
[71] *Strugar*, Trial Chamber Judgment, para. 312.
[72] In *Construction of a Wall in the Occupied Palestinian Territory*, para. 89, as affirmed in *Armed Activities on the Territory of the Congo (DRC v. Uganda)*, para. 217, the ICJ noted that 'the provisions of the Hague Regulations have become part of customary law'. In the latter case, the Court held that damage caused by Ugandan shelling to the cathedral in Kisangani (*ibid.*, para. 208) was 'in clear violation' of Hague Rules, art. 27, an obligation binding on Uganda as a matter of customary international law (*ibid.*, para. 219). But the Court was not called on to consider the provision in any detail.
[73] *Strugar*, Trial Chamber Judgment, para 309. See also *ibid.*, para. 229.
[74] *Prosecutor v. Blaškić*, IT-95-14-T, Trial Chamber Judgment, 3 March 2000, para. 185.
[75] *Prosecutor v. Kordić and Čerkez*, IT-95-14/2-T, Trial Chamber Judgment, 26 February 2001, paras. 361–2.
[76] *Prosecutor v. Naletilić and Martinović*, IT-98-34-T, Trial Chamber Judgment, 31 March 2003, paras. 603 and 605.
[77] *Brdjanin*, para. 598.
[78] As for earlier judicial pronouncements, the Nuremberg tribunal was not called on to deal with Hague Rules, art. 27.

part, article 8(2)(b)(ix) of the Rome Statute of the International Criminal Court gives the Court jurisdiction over the war crime of '[i]ntentionally directing attacks against buildings dedicated to religion, education, art, science or charitable purposes [and] historic monuments ... provided they are not military objectives'. Given the customary definition of a military objective, it is reasonable to construe this as lending support to the view that its use for military purposes is not the sole ground on which cultural property may lawfully be attacked, but that its nature, location and purpose may also, in appropriate circumstances, be invoked. At the same time, the ICC Statute does not itself define the term 'military objectives', leaving room to argue the contrary. Both the crime embodied in article 8(2)(b)(ix) of the ICC Statute[79] and the absence of a definition of 'military objectives' are features of the Statute of the Iraqi Special Tribunal, drafted by US and UK lawyers and promulgated by the Coalition Provisional Authority.

The most probative evidence militating against a higher customary standard of protection in respect of attacks against cultural property *quâ* cultural property than that accorded it as a civilian object can be drawn from the drafting of the Second Protocol. Although delegates to the 1999 Hague diplomatic conference eventually settled on the compromise word 'function' in article 6(a)(i), which was adopted by consensus, it will be recalled that the majority was against citing use alone as grounds on which cultural property, as defined in article 1 of the 1954 Hague Convention, can be made into a military objective.[80] It is unthinkable that these states wished to derogate from custom. As for the Second Protocol's regime of enhanced protection, which excludes nature, location and purpose as justifications for attack, this is clearly not customary. Indeed, it is difficult to see how it could become so, given the inextricable link between the obligations it imposes and the International List of Cultural Property under Enhanced Protection, as determined by the Committee for the Protection of Cultural Property in

---

[79] See Statute of the Iraqi Special Tribunal, 43 ILM 231 (2004), art. 13(b)(10). Although the Iraqi Special Tribunal was replaced on 18 October 2005 by the Iraqi Higher Criminal Court, the latter is in substance a continuation of the former: see Law of the Iraqi Higher Criminal Court, Law No. (10) 2005, *Official Gazette of the Republic of Iraq*, No. 4006, 18 October 2005.

[80] And thus grounds on which a Party may invoke the waiver as to military necessity embodied in 1954 Hague Convention, art. 4(2) to justify launching an attack against it.

the Event of Armed Conflict — both institutions inescapably creatures of treaty.

In this light, it is hard to conclude otherwise than that, while a higher standard of protection is probably *de lege ferenda*, at present the protection granted cultural property against attack by customary international law is the same as that granted other civilian objects: it is not to be attacked unless by its nature, location, purpose or use it makes an effective contribution to military action and its total or partial destruction, capture or neutralisation, in the circumstances ruling at the time, offers a definite military advantage.[81] It should again be stressed, however, that the difference between the two standards is, practically speaking, slight: its use is by far and away the main way in which cultural property could be expected to make an effective contribution to military action, and it is highly unlikely that a state would cite any other ground for attacking it. It should also be added, although article 52(2) of Protocol I does not make this clear, that an otherwise lawful military objective may be attacked only when and for as long as there is no feasible alternative available for obtaining a similar military advantage to that offered by attacking that objective. This is a straightforward function of the general customary rule on the destruction of enemy property, as embodied in article 23(g) of the Hague Rules, that such destruction is lawful only if imperatively demanded by the necessities of war. It finds further expression in article 57(3) of Protocol I, which provides that when a choice is possible between several military objectives for obtaining a similar military advantage, the objective to be selected shall be that the attack on which may be expected to cause the least danger to civilian lives and to civilian objects. The general rule is reflected in the context of cultural property in article 4(2) of the 1954 Hague Convention, which provides that the obligation to refrain from directing acts of hostility against such property may be waived only in cases where military necessity imperatively requires such a waiver — one of the 'fundamental principles' of the protection of cultural property in armed conflict recognised as customary by the twenty-seventh General Conference of UNESCO. The requirement that there be no feasible alternative available

---

[81] While the ICRC study on customary international law is problematic in this respect, misconstruing as it does the property protected by art. 53 of Additional Protocol I, its conclusions do not diverge from the conclusion reached here: see Henckaerts and Doswald-Beck, *Customary International Humanitarian Law*, vol. I, pp. 127–30 (Rule 38).

for obtaining a similar military advantage was codified in article 6(a)(ii) of the Second Protocol, a provision which proved uncontroversial at the Hague diplomatic conference.

Turning to armed conflicts not of an international character,[82] it will be recalled that the effect of article 19 of the 1954 Hague Convention is to make the obligations of respect embodied in article 4, the 'fundamental principles' characterised by the General Conference of UNESCO as customary, applicable to non-international armed conflicts. As for civilian objects in general, it will also be recalled that, while Additional Protocol II prohibits attacks on the civilian population and individual civilians,[83] it makes no mention of civilian objects. In 1995, however, the ICTY Appeals Chamber concluded in the *Tadić* decision on jurisdiction that the rules of customary international law which have developed to regulate non-international armed conflict cover not only the protection of civilians from hostilities but also the protection of civilian objects; and in its interlocutory decision in 2005 in *Hadžihasanović and Kubura*, the Appeals Chamber was satisfied that a specific prohibition on attacks against civilian objects in non-international armed conflict 'has attained the status of customary international law'.[84] In *Tadić*, the Appeals Chamber considered in particular that the customary international law of non-international armed conflict protected cultural property,[85] citing as one of the 'treaty rules [which] have gradually become part of

---

[82] The distinction drawn in conventional law between non-international armed conflicts within the meaning of common art. 3 of the Geneva Conventions (and art. 19 of the 1954 Hague Convention, and thus the Second Hague Protocol) and non-international armed conflicts within the meaning of Additional Protocol II appears to have been effaced at customary international law, which would seem to reflect the former's inclusive standard. No such distinction features in the jurisprudence of the ICTY and ICTR. ICC Statute, art. 8(2)(f) – reproducing verbatim the non-international limb of the definition of an armed conflict given by the Appeals Chamber of the ICTY in *Prosecutor* v. *Tadić*, IT-94-1, Appeals Chamber Decision on Defence Motion for Interlocutory Appeal on Jurisdiction, 2 October 1995, para. 70 – speaks of 'armed conflicts that take place in the territory of a State when there is protracted armed conflict between governmental authorities and organized armed groups or between such groups'. Nor is the divergence between common art. 3 and Additional Protocol II reflected in the ICRC's *Customary International Humanitarian Law*. The customary concept of non-international armed conflict does, however, exclude situations of internal disturbances and tensions, such as riots, isolated and sporadic acts of violence or other acts of a similar nature.

[83] Additional Protocol II, art. 13(2).

[84] *Prosecutor* v. *Hadžihasanović and Kubura*, IT-01-47-AR73.3, Appeals Chamber Decision on Joint Defence Interlocutory Appeal of Trial Chamber Decision on Rule 98 *bis* Motions for Acquittal, 11 March 2005, para. 30.

[85] *Tadić*, Appeals Chamber Decision on Jurisdiction, para. 127.

customary law' article 19 of the 1954 Hague Convention,[86] by which it clearly meant the obligations of respect laid down in article 4 of the Convention, as made applicable to non-international armed conflict by article 19. This was followed in *Strugar* in the context of the attack on the Old Town of Dubrovnik.[87] For its part, however, the ICC Statute makes no mention, in the context of non-international armed conflicts, of attacks against civilian objects generally, although one might perhaps seek to distinguish between a customary rule binding on states and the further question of individual criminal responsibility. The ICC Statute does, on the other hand, vest the ICC in article 8(2)(e)(iv) with jurisdiction over the war crime of intentionally directing attacks against, *inter alia*, buildings dedicated to religion, education, art, science or charitable purposes and historic monuments during non-international armed conflict, 'provided they are not military objectives'. Similarly, the Statute of the Iraqi Special Tribunal, while silent on civilian objects generally in non-international armed conflict, vests the Tribunal with jurisdiction over the war crime referred to in article 8(2)(e)(iv) of the ICC Statute, provided again that protected buildings and historic monuments are not military objectives.[88] Finally, although it is not necessarily indicative of a belief as to custom, it is not without relevance that the delegates to the 1999 Hague diplomatic conference chose to supplement article 4(2) of the 1954 Hague Convention, applicable via article 19 to non-international armed conflict, with article 6(a) of the Second Protocol, applicable also to non-international armed conflict via articles 3(1) and 22(1), and that the majority were of the view, despite the compromise word 'function', that cultural property can become a military objective by any one of its nature, location, purpose or use.

It will be recalled, however, that article 16(a) of Protocol II, applicable to non-international armed conflict, posits a higher standard of protection for cultural property, in effect permitting its attack only when it is used for military purposes. At the same time, it will also be recalled that article 16 is stated to be without prejudice to the provisions of the 1954 Hague Convention, article 4(2) of which makes allowance for military necessity more generally. In *Tadić*, the Appeals Chamber of the ICTY was of the view

---

[86] *Ibid.*, para. 98. See also *Hadžihasanović and Kubura*, Appeals Chamber Decision on Joint Defence Interlocutory Appeal of Trial Chamber Decision on Rule 98 *bis* Motions for Acquittal, paras. 44 and 46–7.
[87] *Strugar*, Trial Chamber Judgment, para. 229.
[88] Iraqi Special Tribunal Statute, art. 13(d)(4).

that the 'core' of Protocol II could be included among the 'treaty rules [which] have gradually become part of customary law'.[89] Although the Tribunal gave no conclusive indication as to which provisions it considered this core to comprise, it did not cite article 16 anywhere in its judgment, despite the fact that it made particular reference to the protection of cultural property in armed conflicts not of an international character. Indeed, in this regard, it referred solely to article 19 of the 1954 Hague Convention. As for the ICC Statute and the Statute of the Iraqi Special Tribunal, the relevant war crimes, mentioned above, contain the condition 'provided they are not military objectives', and the customary definition of a military objective encompasses not just use but also nature, location and purpose; that said, no definition of the term is included in either statute. As regards the Second Protocol, its regime of enhanced protection recognises use as the sole justification for attacking cultural property within its scope. But this regime is not and, given the indispensable role it accords treaty-based bodies, cannot become customary.

In the light of all of the above, it is sufficiently clear that customary international law prohibits attacks in the course of non-international armed conflict against cultural property, as defined in article 1 of the 1954 Hague Convention, unless by its nature, location, purpose or use it makes an effective contribution to military action and provided its total or partial destruction, capture or neutralisation, in the circumstances ruling at the time, offers a definite military advantage.[90] It should again be added – in the light of the general rule on the destruction of enemy property reflected in article 23(g) of the Hague Rules (itself consistently recognised to apply, as a matter of custom, to non-international armed conflicts), as well as of article 4(2) of the 1954 Hague Convention and article 6(a)(ii) of the Second Protocol, both applicable to non-international armed conflict – that cultural property which has been made into a military objective may be attacked only when and for as long as there is no feasible alternative available for obtaining a similar military advantage to that offered by directing an act of hostility against that objective.

---

[89] *Tadić*, Appeals Chamber Decision on Jurisdiction, para. 98.
[90] Henckaerts and Doswald-Beck, *Customary International Humanitarian Law*, vol. I, pp. 127–30 (Rule 38) is compatible with this conclusion.

Incidental damage

While certain questions regarding the precise formulation and application of the rule remain unsettled, there is now no doubt that, in the context of international armed conflict, customary international law regulates incidental damage to civilian objects, including cultural property in the broadest sense of the term, in accordance with a rule of proportionality corresponding in all essential respects to article 51(5)(b) of Additional Protocol I.[91] The USA has acknowledged the customary status of essentially the same rule. Its Department of Defense has recognised as customary a rule precluding 'collateral damage of civilian objects ... that is clearly disproportionate to the military advantage gained in the attack of military objectives', and has spoken of 'the principle of proportionality [which] prohibits military action in which the negative effects (such as collateral civilian casualties) clearly outweigh the military gain'.[92] A rule to this effect is included in several US military handbooks.[93] As specifically regards cultural property, the Department of Defense has stated that, under customary international law, '[c]ultural property ... is protected from collateral damage that is clearly disproportionate to the military advantage to be gained in the attack of military objectives'.[94] In the 1991 Gulf War, some targets were 'specifically avoided' by Coalition forces 'because the value of destruction of each target was outweighed by the potential risk ..., as in the case of certain archaeological or religious sites, to civilian objects'.[95] For example, when Iraq parked two fighter aircraft next to the ancient ziggurat at Ur, Coalition commanders opted not to attack them 'on the basis of respect for cultural property and the belief that positioning of the aircraft adjacent to Ur (without servicing equipment or a runway nearby) effectively had placed each out of action, thereby limiting the value of their destruction by Coalition air forces when weighed against the risk

---

[91] See also *ibid.*, pp. 46–50 (Rule 14); F. Pocar, 'Protocol I Additional to the 1949 Geneva Conventions and Customary International Law' (2001) 31 Isr. YHR 145 at 153–4; J. Gardam, *Necessity, Proportionality and the Use of Force by States* (Cambridge: Cambridge University Press, 2004), p. 136.

[92] Department of Defense, *Conduct of the Persian Gulf War, Appendix O*, at 622.

[93] Department of the Army, *Law of Land Warfare*, para. 41; Department of the Air Force, *Conduct of Armed Conflict*, paras. 1–3a(2) and 5–3c(1)(b); Department of the Navy, *Commander's Handbook*, paras. 8.1.2.1 and 8.5.1.1. See also Department of the Air Force, *Targeting Guide*, Attachment 4, paras. A4.3 and A4.3.1.2.

[94] Department of Defense, *Protection of Natural and Cultural Resources*, at p. 202.

[95] Department of Defense, *Conduct of the Persian Gulf War, Appendix O*, at 622.

of damage to the temple'.[96] It is worth noting further that the rule on proportionality of incidental damage as formulated in article 51(5)(b) of Protocol I is restated verbatim in article 3(3)(c) of 1980 Protocol II and in article 3(8)(c) of 1996 Amended Protocol II; that the Appeals Chamber of the ICTY implied in *Blaškić* that the rule in article 51(5)(b) of Protocol I was customary,[97] a position taken by an earlier Trial Chamber in *Galić*;[98] that article 8(2)(b)(iv) of the ICC Statute and article 13(b)(4) of the Statute of the Iraqi Special Tribunal vest their respective judicial bodies with jurisdiction over the war crime of intentionally launching an attack in the knowledge that such attack will cause incidental damage to civilian objects 'which would be clearly excessive in relation to the concrete and direct overall military advantage anticipated'; and that the drafters of the Second Protocol adopted article 7(c) – which obliges Parties to refrain from deciding to launch any attack which may be expected to cause incidental damage to cultural property, as defined in article 1 of the 1954 Hague Convention, which would be excessive in relation to the concrete and direct military advantage anticipated – and article 7(d)(ii), obliging them to cancel or suspend an attack if it becomes apparent that it may be expected to cause such damage. The customary status of the rule posited in article 51(5)(b) of Protocol I was most recently acknowledged by the Eritrea Ethiopia Claims Commission in one of its partial awards of 19 December 2005.[99]

Whether an analogous rule of proportionality as regards incidental damage to civilian objects is applicable as a customary matter to non-international armed conflicts is harder to say.[100] No such rule was included in Additional Protocol II, although 1996 Amended Protocol II, applicable to international and non-international armed conflicts alike, contains in article 3(8)(c) a rule stated in identical terms to that laid down in article 51(5)(b) of Additional Protocol I. For its part, the ICTY Appeals Chamber in *Tadić* held that the customary international law of

---

[96] Ibid., at 626. 'Other cultural property similarly remained on the Coalition no-attack list, despite Iraqi placement of valuable military equipment in or near those sites.': ibid.
[97] *Blaškić*, Appeals Chamber Judgment, para. 157.
[98] *Prosecutor v. Galić*, IT-98-29-T, Trial Chamber Judgment, 5 December 2003, paras. 57–8.
[99] *Western Front, Aerial Bombardment and Related Claims*, para. 95. See also ibid., para. 97.
[100] Firmly in the 'pro' camp, see Henckaerts and Doswald-Beck, *Customary International Humanitarian Law*, vol. I, pp. 46–50 (Rule 14). Gardam is far more cautious, concluding merely that it is 'becoming increasingly realistic to argue that proportionality will soon have a role to play in some internal conflicts': Gardam, *Necessity, Proportionality*, p. 127.

non-international armed conflicts 'covers such areas as protection of civilians from hostilities, in particular from indiscriminate attacks, [and] protection of civilian objects, in particular cultural property',[101] although it did not specify whether this included the particular prohibition on attacks causing excessive incidental damage to civilians and civilian objects. In *Blaškić*, the Appeals Chamber, like the earlier Trial Chamber in *Galić*,[102] proceeded as though the rule in article 51(5)(b) of Protocol I applied equally to armed conflicts not of an international character.[103] On the other hand, neither the ICC Statute nor the Statute of the Iraqi Special Tribunal grants jurisdiction over a war crime of intentionally launching an attack during non-international armed conflict in the knowledge that the attack will cause excessive incidental damage to civilians or civilian objects, although one should again be cautious when using individual criminal responsibility as the index of a rule pertaining to states. As specifically regards cultural property, it will be recalled that articles 7(c) and 7(d)(ii) of the Second Protocol, regarding attacks that may be expected to cause incidental damage which would be excessive in relation to the concrete and direct military advantage anticipated, apply to non-international armed conflicts by virtue of articles 3(1) and 22(1). That said, this does not necessarily indicate a belief in the customary character of these rules. In the final analysis, however, it is not too rash to suggest that customary international law prohibits attacks in the course of non-international armed conflict which may be expected to cause incidental damage to cultural property, at least as defined in article 1 of the 1954 Hague Convention, which would be excessive in relation to the concrete and direct military advantage anticipated.

Precautions in attack

As a corollary of the prohibitions on attacks against cultural property, provided it has not been made a military objective, and on attacks likely to cause disproportionate incidental damage to cultural property, customary international law also imposes on states positive obligations to do everything feasible to verify that the objectives to be attacked are not cultural property, in the broadest sense; to take all feasible

---

[101] *Tadić*, Appeals Chamber Decision on Jurisdiction, para. 127.
[102] *Galić*, paras. 57–8.
[103] *Blaškić*, Appeals Chamber Judgment, para. 157.

precautions in the choice of means and method of attack with a view to avoiding, and in any event minimising, incidental damage to cultural property; to refrain from deciding to launch any attack which may be expected to cause incidental damage to cultural property which would be excessive in relation to the concrete and direct military advantage anticipated; and to cancel or suspend an attack if it becomes apparent that the objective is cultural property which has not been made a military objective or that the attack may be expected to cause incidental damage to cultural property which would be excessive in relation to the concrete and direct military advantage anticipated.[104] These rules, posited in relation to civilian objects generally in article 57(2) of Additional Protocol I, are restated in the specific context of cultural property in article 7 of the Second Protocol. Article 57 of Protocol I was considered customary by a Trial Chamber of the ICTY in *Kupreškić*[105] and by the Eritrea Ethiopia Claims Commission in a partial award of 19 December 1995.[106] The rules embodied in article 57 are treated as customary by the USA, not a Party to Protocol I.[107] In the lead-up to the 1991 Gulf War, US military planners prepared an official 'Joint No-Fire Target List' on which they placed, *inter alia*, significant cultural sites,[108] a procedure repeated before the 2003 invasion of Iraq.

As for non-international armed conflict, given that customary international law forbids attacks against cultural property unless it is made a military objective, as well as attacks which may be expected to cause disproportionate incidental damage to such property, reason suggests that states are also obliged to take the range of precautions in attack specified in respect of international armed conflict by the rules in article 57(2) of Protocol I. That said, reason and positive law do not always march side by side. Protocol II contains no analogous rules. On the other hand, a Trial Chamber of the ICTY in *Kupreškić* proceeded as if the

---

[104] See also Henckaerts and Doswald-Beck, *Customary International Humanitarian Law*, vol. I, pp. 51–62 (Rules 15–19). As regards the rules embodied in Additional Protocol I, arts. 57(2)(a)(iii) and 57(2)(b), see Gardam, *Necessity, Proportionality*, p. 136.

[105] *Prosecutor* v. *Kupreškić and others*, IT-95-16-T, Trial Chamber Judgment, 14 January 2000, para. 524. See also *Galić*, paras. 57–8.

[106] *Western Front, Aerial Bombardment and Related Claims*, para. 95.

[107] Department of Defense, *Conduct of the Persian Gulf War, Appendix O*, at 625; Department of the Army, *Law of Land Warfare*, para. 41; Department of the Air Force, *Targeting Guide*, Attachment 4, paras. A4.3–A4.3.1.3 and A4.5.2.

[108] M. W. Lewis, 'The Law of Aerial Bombardment in the 1991 Gulf War' (2003) 97 AJIL 481 at 487.

obligations embodied in article 57(2) of Protocol I applied to international and non-international armed conflict alike.[109] As for the Second Protocol, the application of the obligations laid down in article 7 to non-international armed conflict by virtue of articles 3(1) and 22(1) was uncontroversial, and, while this does not of itself indicate their customary status, it is possible that the negotiating process has crystallised a customary rule to this effect. In the final analysis, however, while it is not an enormous leap to suggest that custom requires states to take the precautionary measures outlined in article 7 of the Second Protocol in the context of non-international armed conflict, the evidence to establish this is not yet conclusive.[110]

Acts of hostility other than attacks

Article 4(1) of the 1954 Hague Convention and article 53(a) of Additional Protocol I apply to more than just attacks against cultural property. The broader term used in both provisions, 'acts of hostility', encompasses demolitions. The classic customary rule on such acts, as reflected in article 23(g) of the Hague Rules, was that they were permissible if imperatively demanded by the necessities of war. This applied as much to belligerent occupation as to international hostilities. In the former context, the rule in article 23(g) was endorsed in article 53 of the fourth Geneva Convention, which provides that any destruction by the Occupying Power of real or personal property belonging individually or collectively to private persons, to the State, to other public authorities or to social or co-operative organisations is prohibited, except where such destruction is rendered absolutely necessary by military operations. In the context of both occupation and hostilities, the rule was restated in article 4(2), modifying article 4(1), of the 1954 Hague Convention, which permits Parties to waive the prohibition on acts of hostility against cultural property in cases where military necessity imperatively requires such a waiver. On the other hand, article 53(a) of Protocol I and article 6(a) of the Second Protocol, both applicable to international hostilities and belligerent occupation alike, make no allowance for military necessity in relation to acts of hostility other than attacks. For its part, the case-law of the ICTY on the war crime of destruction or wilful damage done to

---

[109] *Kupreškić*, Trial Chamber Judgment, para. 524.
[110] But see *contra* Henckaerts and Doswald-Beck, *Customary International Humanitarian Law*, vol. I, pp. 51–62 (Rules 15–19).

institutions dedicated to religion, charity and education, the arts and sciences, historic monuments and works of art and science under article 3(d) of its Statute does not distinguish between destruction caused by attacks and destruction caused by other acts of hostility, and is therefore not directly on point. Nonetheless, the Tribunal's view that such destruction is permissible only when the property in question is being used at that moment for military purposes[111] would seem to prohibit demolitions, which, when motivated by considerations of the property's military use, are intended to prevent such use or its recurrence.[112] As discussed above, however, this jurisprudence is not at all convincing. Nor has the Tribunal made any sustained attempt to explain the relationship between the crime recognised in article 3(d) of the Statute and that in article 3(b) ('wanton destruction of cities, towns or villages, or devastation not justified by military necessity'). As for the ICC Statute, as mirrored in the Statute of the Iraqi Special Tribunal,[113] it distinguishes between attacks against and other destruction of buildings dedicated to religion, education, art, science or charitable purposes and historic monuments: as regards the latter, which encompasses demolitions, the property in question is treated the same as all other enemy property, with article 8(2)(b)(xiii) vesting the ICC with jurisdiction over the war crime of destroying it unless such destruction be imperatively demanded by the necessities of war. Finally, it will be recalled that the twenty-seventh General Conference of UNESCO recognised the 'fundamental principles' of the Convention, which must be taken to include the waiver laid down in article 4(2), modifying article 4(1), as customary.

In this light, the customary rule applicable during international armed conflict, including belligerent occupation, to acts of hostility other than attacks against cultural property, in the broadest sense, is that such acts are prohibited unless imperatively demanded by the necessities of war, or, to paraphrase article 4(2) of the 1954 Hague Convention, unless military necessity imperatively requires it.[114] In addition, in the specific context of belligerent occupation, destruction of or damage to cultural property not linked to military operations constitutes a breach of the

---

[111] *Blaškić*, Trial Chamber Judgment, para. 185; *Kordić*, Trial Chamber Judgment, paras. 361–2; *Naletilić*, paras. 603 and 605; *Brdjanin*, para. 598.

[112] Property being used at that moment for military purposes will be attacked, not demolished.

[113] Iraqi Special Tribunal Statute, arts. 13(b)(10) and 13(b)(14).

[114] See, in this light, *Hess v. Commander of the IDF in the West Bank*, 58(3) PD 443 (2004).

special rule on destroying or damaging cultural property during belligerent occupation reflected in article 56 of the Hague Rules. Article 56 was explicitly recognised as consonant with custom at Nuremberg.[115] It was reaffirmed as such in 2004 by the Eritrea Ethiopia Claims Commission, which held that the toppling of the Stela of Matara – an obelisk 'perhaps about 2,500 years old' and 'of great historical and cultural significance to both Eritrea and Ethiopia'[116] – by way of a military explosive fastened at its base by one or several soldiers of the Ethiopian army, which was at that point in belligerent occupation of the part of Eritrea's territory on which the stela stood, constituted a violation of customary international law.[117]

As regards non-international armed conflict, article 4(2) of the 1954 Hague Convention, modifying article 4(1), applies to international and non-international armed conflicts alike to prohibit acts of hostility against cultural property unless military necessity imperatively requires them. Although article 16(a) of Additional Protocol II and article 6(a) of the Second Protocol, both applicable to armed conflicts not of an international character, make no allowance for military necessity, and while the ICTY has made an exception only for military use,[118] the ICC Statute and the Statute of the Iraqi Special Tribunal permit the destruction of cultural property (as a species of 'property of an adversary') during non-international armed conflict if imperatively demanded by the necessities of the conflict.[119] Moreover, the General Conference of UNESCO has recognised the 'fundamental principles' of the Convention as consonant with custom, and the Appeals Chamber of the ICTY in *Tadić*, as followed in *Strugar*,[120] cited as one of the 'treaty rules [which] have gradually become part of customary law' article 19 of the 1954 Hague Convention,[121] by which it meant the obligations of respect

---

[115] See Judgment of the International Military Tribunal for the Trial of German Major War Criminals, Nuremberg, 30 September and 1 October 1946, Misc. No. 12 (1946), Cmd 6964, pp. 64–5.
[116] *Partial Award: Central Front. Eritrea's Claims 2, 4, 6, 7, 8 and 22*, 43 ILM 1249 (2004), para. 107.
[117] Ibid., para 113. Neither Eritrea nor Ethiopia was a Party at the time to the 1954 Hague Convention. Recall also the view of the ICJ that the Hague Rules reflect customary international law: *Construction of a Wall in the Occupied Palestinian Territory*, para. 89; *Armed Activities on the Territory of the Congo (DRC v. Uganda)*, para. 217.
[118] *Blaškić*, Trial Chamber Judgment, para. 185; *Kordić*, Trial Chamber Judgment, paras. 361–2; *Naletilić*, paras. 603 and 605; *Brđanin*, para. 598.
[119] ICC Statute, art. 8(2)(e)(xii); Iraqi Special Tribunal Statute, art. 13(d)(12).
[120] *Strugar*, Trial Chamber Judgment, para. 229.
[121] *Tadić*, Appeals Chamber Decision on Jurisdiction, para. 98.

laid down in article 4 of the Convention, as made applicable to non-international armed conflict by article 19. As such, it is clear that, in non-international armed conflict, customary international law prohibits acts of hostility other than attacks against cultural property – at least as the term is defined in article 1 of the 1954 Hague Convention, and probably in the broadest sense – unless military necessity imperatively requires it.

Acts of vandalism against cultural property are specifically, albeit implicitly, prohibited by article 4(3) of the 1954 Hague Convention, which applies to international armed conflict, including belligerent occupation, and non-international armed conflict alike. Article 4(3) is undoubtedly one of the 'fundamental principles' of the Convention recognised as customary by the twenty-seventh General Conference of UNESCO.[122] As it is, the prohibition on vandalism is simply an application of the broader customary prohibition on damage to or destruction of cultural property when not imperatively required by military necessity.

Prohibition on certain use

Article 4(1) of the 1954 Hague Convention, applicable to international armed conflict, including belligerent occupation, and non-international armed conflict alike, was the first provision of the laws of war to prohibit the use of cultural property for purposes likely to expose it to damage or destruction in the event of armed conflict. Classical custom, as manifest in the consistent practice of states, had permitted such use. Article 4(1), however, is subject to article 4(2), which allows for waiver of this prohibition when military necessity imperatively requires it. In contrast, article 53(b) of Additional Protocol I and article 16(b) of Protocol II make no exception for military necessity: the use of cultural property 'in support of the military effort' is absolutely prohibited. But the General Conference of UNESCO has recognised the 'fundamental principles' of the 1954 Hague Convention as customary, and, as specifically regards non-international armed conflict, the Appeals Chamber of the ICTY stated in *Tadić* that article 19 of the 1954 Hague Convention, by which article 4's obligations of respect apply to conflicts not of an international character, has come to reflect custom. Moreover, the Convention's exception in respect of military necessity was maintained, albeit tightened, in

---

[122] See also Henckaerts and Doswald-Beck, *Customary International Humanitarian Law*, vol. I, pp. 132–3 (Rule 40(A)).

the context of the use of cultural property in article 6(b) of the Second Protocol, applicable once more to both international and non-international armed conflict.[123] As such, it can be accepted that customary international law prohibits the use of cultural property, as defined in article 1 of the 1954 Hague Convention, for any purpose likely to expose it to damage or destruction in the event of international or non-international armed conflict, unless such use is imperatively required by military necessity.[124] It should be added that how the proviso as to military necessity is to be applied is codified in article 6(b) of the Second Protocol – namely, when and for as long as no choice is possible between such use of the cultural property and another feasible method for obtaining a similar military advantage.

Prohibition on reprisals

Article 4(4) of the 1954 Hague Convention, applicable via article 19 to both international and non-international armed conflicts, prohibits reprisals against cultural property, a prohibition reproduced in the context of international armed conflict in article 53(c) of Protocol I[125] and probably counted among the 'fundamental principles' of the Convention considered customary by the General Conference of UNESCO. While the matter is not beyond doubt, it is probably safe to say that customary international law prohibits reprisals against cultural property during international armed conflict.[126] The situation in non-international armed conflict is more doubtful, given that article 16 of Protocol II contains no provision analogous to article 53(c) of Protocol I. *Pace* the UNESCO General Conference, there is probably insufficient evidence to conclude that reprisals against cultural property are forbidden as a customary matter during non-international armed conflict.[127]

---

[123] For its part, the USA, the most powerful state Party neither to the 1954 Hague Convention and its Protocols nor to Additional Protocols I and II, recognises that the improper use of privileged buildings for military purposes constitutes a war crime: Department of the Army, *Law of Land Warfare*, para. 504(h). See also Military Commission Instruction No. 2, para. 6(A)(10) (use of protected property to shield military objectives from attack a war crime).

[124] See also Henckaerts and Doswald-Beck, *Customary International Humanitarian Law*, vol. I, pp. 131–2 (Rule 39).

[125] When ratifying Additional Protocol I, the UK entered a reservation in which it regarded itself as entitled to take reprisals against property protected by art. 53, subject to strict conditions, in the event of the provision's breach by an adverse Party by way of serious and deliberate attacks against such property: see *ibid.*, vol. II, part 2, p. 3453, para. 955.

[126] See also *ibid.*, vol. I, pp. 523–5 (Rule 147).

[127] See also *ibid.*, p. 523.

Prohibition on plunder

Customary international law has long regulated certain takings of cultural property in international armed conflict, including belligerent occupation. The longstanding customary rule reflected in article 23(g) of the Hague Rules is that the seizure of any enemy property is prohibited unless imperatively demanded by the necessities of war. Since there can be no legitimate military reason for seizing cultural property, the rule amounts, in practice, to an absolute prohibition in this regard. Similarly, article 4(3) of the 1954 Hague Convention, applicable to both international armed conflict, including belligerent occupation, and non-international armed conflict, and without doubt one of the 'fundamental principles' of the Convention recognised as consonant with customary international law by the twenty-seventh General Conference of UNESCO, can be taken to prohibit under its first limb the theft, pillage and misappropriation of cultural property as defined in the Convention, with its second limb explicitly obliging states to refrain from requisitioning movable cultural property situated in the territory of another state. Article 4(3) is not subject to article 4(2)'s waiver in respect of military necessity. In the specific context of cultural property under belligerent occupation, the customary rule reflected in article 56 of the Hague Rules expressly forbids in absolute terms all seizure of institutions dedicated to religion, charity and education, the arts and sciences, and of historic monuments and works of art and science, stipulating that it should be made the subject of legal proceedings. Article 56 also provides that such institutions shall be treated as private property, meaning that they must be respected and must not be confiscated, as laid down in article 46.[128] These provisions were recognised as customary at Nuremberg,[129] article 6(b) of the London Charter having granted the IMT jurisdiction over the war crime of plunder of public or private property[130] – one of the offences of which Rosenberg was convicted. Article 3(e) of the Statute of the ICTY vests the Tribunal with jurisdiction over the same war crime, and the Tribunal has held that the offence, which it has recognised as

---

[128] Article 46 of the Hague Rules was explicitly treated as customary by the ICJ in *Armed Activities on the Territory of the Congo (DRC v. Uganda)*, para. 219.

[129] Nuremberg Judgment, pp. 64–5.

[130] See also Control Council Law No. 10, Punishment of Persons Guilty of War Crimes, Crimes Against Peace and Against Humanity, 20 December 1945, 3 *Official Gazette Control Council for Germany* 50 (1946), art. II(1)(b).

customary,[131] should be understood to embrace 'all forms of unlawful appropriation of property in armed conflict ..., including those acts traditionally described as "pillage" '.[132] The specific customary prohibition on pillage in international armed conflict is reflected in article 28 (hostilities) and article 47 (belligerent occupation) of the Hague Rules[133] and in article 33 (both hostilities and belligerent occupation) of the fourth Geneva Convention. In addition to the offence of plunder of public or private property in article 3(e), article 3(d) of the Statute of the ICTY grants the Tribunal jurisdiction over the war crime of seizure of institutions dedicated to religion, charity and education, the arts and sciences, historic monuments and works of art and science. For its part, in the context of international armed conflict, the ICC Statute recognises the war crimes of seizing the enemy's property unless such seizure be imperatively demanded by the necessities of war and of pillaging a town or place, even when taken by assault.[134] The same goes for the Statute of the Iraqi Special Tribunal.[135] It is absolutely clear, therefore, that customary international law forbids the seizure of cultural property, in the broadest sense, in international armed conflict, including belligerent occupation, unless such seizure be imperatively demanded by the necessities of war. It also prohibits the pillage of such property.

It is also probably the case that the same customary prohibitions apply during non-international armed conflict. While Additional Protocol II contains only the prohibition on pillage,[136] the ICTY has held that the war crime of plunder is applicable to international and non-international armed conflict alike.[137] Similarly, both the ICC Statute and the Statute of the Iraqi Special Tribunal vest their respective judicial bodies with jurisdiction over the war crimes, committed in non-international armed conflict, of seizing the property of an adversary unless such seizure be

---

[131] *Hadžihasanović and Kubura*, Appeals Chamber Decision on Joint Defence Interlocutory Appeal of Trial Chamber Decision on Rule 98 *bis* Motions for Acquittal, para. 37.
[132] *Ibid*.
[133] Articles 28 and 47 of the Hague Rules were explicitly treated as customary by the ICJ in *Armed Activities on the Territory of the Congo (DRC v. Uganda)*, para. 219.
[134] ICC Statute, arts. 8(2)(b)(xiii) and 8(2)(b)(xvi) respectively.
[135] Iraqi Special Tribunal Statute, arts. 13(b)(14) and 13(b)(17) respectively.
[136] Additional Protocol II, art. 4(g).
[137] *Hadžihasanović and Kubura*, Appeals Chamber Decision on Joint Defence Interlocutory Appeal of Trial Chamber Decision on Rule 98 *bis* Motions for Acquittal, para. 37.

imperatively demanded by the necessities of the conflict[138] and of pillaging a town or place, even when taken by assault.[139]

Obligation to prohibit, prevent and put a stop to theft, pillage, misappropriation and vandalism

It will be recalled that article 4(3) of the 1954 Hague Convention, applicable to both international armed conflict, including belligerent occupation, and non-international armed conflict, obliges the Parties to prohibit, prevent and, if necessary, put a stop to any form of theft, pillage or misappropriation of, or acts of vandalism against, cultural property. Article 4(3) is without doubt one of the 'fundamental principles' of the Convention recognised as consonant with customary international law by the twenty-seventh General Conference of UNESCO and, in the specific context of belligerent occupation, accords with Allied practice during the Second World War. Moreover, in the context of occupation, the rule is little more than a gloss on the obligation imposed on an Occupying Power by the general customary rule reflected in article 43 of the Hague Rules to take all measures in its power to restore, and ensure, as far as possible, public order.[140] In this light, while it does not necessarily reflect *opinio juris* going to a rule of custom, nor is it irrelevant that the twelfth recital of the preamble to UN Security Council resolution 1483 (2003) of 22 May 2003 – adopted in the wake of the failure of US and other military forces involved in the invasion of Iraq to prevent the looting by the local populace of many of the country's cultural institutions, including the National Museum in Baghdad, and of archaeological sites such as Isin, Tell Bismaya, Umma and Umm al Aqarib – stressed 'the need ... for the continued protection of archaeological, historical, cultural, and religious sites, museums, libraries, and monuments', a statement reproduced almost verbatim in the ninth recital of the preamble to Security Council resolution 1546 (2004) of 8 June 2004.[141] As for non-international armed conflict specifically, the Appeals Chamber of the ICTY in *Tadić* held that article 19 of the 1954 Hague Convention, by which article 4(3) is made

---

[138] ICC Statute, art. 8(2)(e)(xii); Iraqi Special Tribunal Statute, art. 13(d)(12).
[139] ICC Statute, art. 8(2)(e)(v); Iraqi Special Tribunal Statute, art. 13(d)(5).
[140] Article 43 of the Hague Rules was explicitly treated as customary by the ICJ in *Armed Activities on the Territory of the Congo (DRC v. Uganda)*, para. 219.
[141] See also the Bruges Declaration on the Use of Force adopted by the Institut de droit international in 2003, which states that 'the occupying power assumes the responsibility and the obligation to maintain order and ... to protect [the territory]'s historical heritage [and] cultural property ...': (2003) 70-II AIDI 285 at 287.

applicable to non-international armed conflict, was consonant with customary international law;[142] and, although this again was not necessarily a statement of *opinio juris*, the General Assembly – '[r]eiterat[ing] that the cultural and historic relics and monuments of Afghanistan belong to the common heritage of mankind' – repeatedly called upon all parties to the civil war in that country, in particular the Taliban government, 'to protect the cultural and historic relics and monuments of Afghanistan from acts of vandalism, damage and theft'.[143] In the light of all of this, it is reasonably well settled that customary international law obliges states during international armed conflict, including belligerent occupation, to prohibit, prevent and, if necessary, put a stop to any form of theft, pillage and misappropriation of, and acts of vandalism against, cultural property, as defined in article 1 of the 1954 Hague Convention, and it is more likely than not that the same customary obligation applies to non-international armed conflict.[144]

Obligations with respect to belligerent occupation

While many customary rules applicable to international armed conflict apply as much during belligerent occupation as during hostilities, customary international law also embodies rules applicable only to the former. As a customary matter, as affirmed by the ICJ,[145] the definition of belligerent occupation is that laid down in article 42 of the Hague Rules: territory is considered occupied 'when it is actually placed under the authority of the hostile army', and the occupation 'extends only to the territory where such authority has been established and can be exercised'. Although the ICTY Trial Chamber in *Naletilić*, relying on the ICRC commentary to the fourth Geneva Convention, highlighted the more flexible notion of belligerent occupation applicable under the latter instrument to the treatment of persons who fall into the enemy's hands, it equally stated that the definition embodied in article 42 of the Hague Rules was the one applicable as a customary matter to the destruction

---

[142] *Tadić*, Appeals Chamber Decision on Jurisdiction, para. 98.
[143] GA res. 53/203A, 18 December 1998, para. 21; GA res. 54/189A, 17 December 1999, para. 30; GA res. 55/174A, 19 December 2000, para. 30. These resolutions are to be distinguished from those, seen above, adopted to similar effect under the rubric of the question of human rights in Afghanistan.
[144] See also Henckaerts and Doswald-Beck, *Customary International Humanitarian Law*, vol. I, pp. 132–5 (Rule 40(A)); Wolfrum, 'Protection of Cultural Property', at 323.
[145] *Construction of a Wall in the Occupied Palestinian Territory*, para. 78; *Armed Activities on the Territory of the Congo (DRC v. Uganda)*, para. 172.

(and, by implication, to the treatment generally) of property in occupied territory.[146]

The cardinal customary rule of belligerent occupation reflected in article 43 of the Hague Rules obliges an Occupying Power to take all measures in its power to restore, and ensure, as far as possible, public order and civil affairs, while respecting, unless absolutely prevented, the laws in force in the country.[147] The second limb of the provision obliges a belligerent occupant, unless absolutely prevented from doing so, to leave in place and abide by any existing laws providing for the protection and preservation of immovable and movable cultural property in the territory, which entails an obligation to allow the competent national authorities to fulfil any duties or exercise any rights they may have under such laws. The Occupying Power must leave intact and comply with any existing local laws relating *inter alia* to the authorisation of archaeological excavations, the alteration of cultural property and the trade in art and antiquities. The first limb of the customary rule reflected in article 43 of the Hague Rules requires an Occupying Power to put a stop to and prevent, as far as possible, the breakdown of law and order, and insofar as the latter involves looting and vandalism of cultural property, the obligation chimes with the customary rule obliging a belligerent occupant to prohibit, prevent and, if necessary, put a stop to any form of theft, pillage, misappropriation and vandalism of cultural property. More generally, a belligerent occupant must ensure, as far as possible, the adequate enforcement of existing laws aimed at preventing any form of misappropriation of and wilful damage to cultural property in the territory, and of laws for the preservation more broadly of cultural property, including town planning laws requiring permits for construction on sensitive sites, laws regulating the upkeep and alteration of historic buildings, laws relating to the authorisation of archaeological excavations and laws governing the trade in art and antiquities, including export controls. This may require the Occupying Power to help the competent national authorities to perform their functions, an obligation codified in article 5(1) of the 1954 Hague Convention, which

---

[146] *Naletilić*, paras. 219–22.
[147] The general duty to leave the local law and administrative structures untouched is subject always to the authority expressly vested in the Occupying Power, and the obligations expressly imposed on it, by any specific rules, among them the customary rule obliging it to prohibit, prevent and, if necessary, put a stop to any form of theft, pillage, misappropriation and vandalism of cultural property in the territory.

requires a Party in occupation of the whole or part of the territory of another Party to support, as far as possible, these authorities in safeguarding and preserving the territory's cultural property. Evidence for the customary nature of this rule is provided by Part 2 ('Protection and Preservation of Cultural Structures') of Title 18 ('Monuments, Fine Arts and Archives') promulgated at the end of the Second World War by the Office of Military Government for Germany in the US Zone of Occupation, which authorised the OMG of the various Länder within the US Zone to make available, if requested by the competent German authorities, 'such assistance in the protection of cultural structures as appear[ed] appropriate'.[148] Israel's conduct after its occupation of the Sinai in 1956, when it co-operated with the Egyptian authorities to request UNESCO's assistance in safeguarding and preserving the ancient monastery of St Catherine on Mount Sinai,[149] could also be cited. There may be circumstances too where the Occupying Power is obliged by the default of the local authorities to enforce the relevant legal regime itself. For example, in *Shikhrur v. Military Commander of the Judea and Samaria Region*, the Supreme Court of Israel, sitting as the High Court of Justice, upheld the decision of the military commander in the occupied West Bank to use the occupant's military courts, instead of relying on the local courts, to prosecute residents charged under the Jordanian Antiquities Law (No. 51) 1966 with damaging antiquities, on the ground that a number of antiquities had been damaged in the territory and the local courts were not treating this with sufficient gravity.[150] In *Candu v. Minister of Defence*, the Supreme Court of Israel, sitting again as the High Court of Justice, upheld the decision of the Israeli occupation authorities, which have assumed powers over antiquities in the West Bank in place of the Jordanian authorities,[151] to refuse the petitioner permission to build

---

[148] Military Government Regulations 18–201.
[149] *1967 Reports*, para. 14; *1970 Reports*, para. 14. Israel was not, at that point, a Party to the 1954 Hague Convention.
[150] 44(2) PD 233 (1990) at 234–5. Although the first paragraph of the customary rule reflected in art. 64 of Geneva Convention IV provides that the tribunals of the occupied territory shall continue to function in respect of all offences covered by the penal laws of that territory, the court noted that this is expressly subject to 'the necessity for ensuring the effective administration of justice'.
[151] By way of Military Order 119, 6 July 1967, the commanding officer of the IDF in the West Bank cancelled all appointments made and jurisdiction granted by the Jordanian government or any of its institutions under the Jordanian Antiquities Law (No. 51) 1966, transferring them to the Israeli official-in-charge, who was empowered to appoint persons in their place. The Israeli authorities in the West Bank continue to apply the Jordanian Antiquities Law.

on his land unless a well which was part of the ancient pools of King Solomon was preserved in accordance with the same Jordanian Antiquities Law. The court held that customary international law imposed on an Occupying Power an obligation 'to protect and preserve cultural treasures in occupied territory, including archaeological treasures',[152] a statement endorsed in *Hess* v. *Commander of the IDF in the West Bank*;[153] and while the court's words are too broad if read in isolation, they are accurate in the context of an Occupying Power's duty, in the absence (for whatever reason) of competent national authorities, to ensure the enforcement of the existing legal regime for the protection and preservation of antiquities in the territory. Finally, the first limb of the customary rule reflected in article 43 of the Hague Rules permits, if necessary, the promulgation by the Occupying Power of laws for the maintenance of public order and civil affairs, including laws for the protection and preservation of cultural property. Furthermore, where required, the promulgation of laws specifically to prohibit the theft, pillage, misappropriation and vandalism of cultural property is obligatory, by virtue of the Occupying Power's customary duty to prohibit, prevent and, if necessary, put a stop to all forms of these acts.

The customary rule embodied in article 43 of the Hague Rules obliges an Occupying Power to comply with and ensure the enforcement of any existing export controls in relation to cultural property.[154] Where such controls do not exist, the same customary rule would permit their promulgation. It is also more likely than not that a rule of customary international humanitarian law[155] obliges an Occupying Power to prohibit and prevent any illicit export, other removal or transfer of ownership of cultural property from territory occupied by it.[156] Article 1 of the First Protocol to the 1954 Hague Convention obliges the Parties to prevent the exportation of cultural property, as defined in article 1 of the Convention, from territory occupied by them. Similarly, article 2(2) of the Convention on the Means of Prohibiting and Preventing the Illicit Import,

---

[152] 43(1) PD 738 (1989) at 742.
[153] *Hess*, Judgment, para. 17.
[154] The enforcement of the export licence requirement of the Jordanian Antiquities Law (No. 51) 1966 by the Israeli occupation authorities in the West Bank formed the background to *Ruidi and Maches* v. *Military Court of Hebron*, 24(2) PD 419 (1970).
[155] For such a rule as a function of international human rights law, see above.
[156] See also, more confidently, Henckaerts and Doswald-Beck, *Customary International Humanitarian Law*, vol. I, pp. 135–6 (Rule 41).

Export and Transfer of Ownership of Cultural Property requires Parties to oppose with the means at their disposal the illicit export or transfer of ownership of movable cultural property, as defined in article 1 of that Convention; and article 11 of the Convention provides that the export or transfer of ownership of cultural property under compulsion arising directly or indirectly from the occupation of a country by a foreign power is to be regarded as illicit. Finally, article 9(1)(a) of the Second Protocol requires Parties acting as Occupying Powers to prohibit and prevent any illicit export, other removal or transfer of ownership of cultural property from the occupied territory. The practice of states not Parties to these treaty provisions is not, however, readily available, making it difficult to conclude with any certainty that customary international law embodies a rule to this effect.

International criminal law

War crimes

There is no doubt that customary international law recognises individual criminal responsibility for unlawfully directing attacks against cultural property in the generic sense of the term, whether in international or non-international armed conflict. This responsibility is over and above that recognised for unlawfully directing attacks against civilian objects.[157] In *Strugar*, a Trial Chamber of the ICTY found the accused guilty of the war crime of 'destruction or wilful damage done to institutions dedicated to religion, charity and education, the arts and sciences, historic monuments and works of art and science', within the meaning of article 3(d) of the Tribunal's Statute, for his role in the bombardment of the Old Town of Dubrovnik on 6 December 1991. It stated that such conduct was a war crime regardless of whether the conflict was international or non-international,[158] a position endorsed by the Appeals Chamber in *Hadžihasanović and Kubura*.[159] The accused

---

[157] The Appeals Chamber of the ICTY has held that individual criminal responsibility attaches under customary international law to attacks against civilian objects in both international and non-international armed conflict: *Hadžihasanović and Kubura*, Appeals Chamber Decision on Joint Defence Interlocutory Appeal of Trial Chamber Decision on Rule 98 *bis* Motions for Acquittal, para. 30. See also *Strugar, Jokić and others*, Appeals Chamber Decision on Interlocutory Appeal, para. 10.

[158] *Strugar*, Trial Chamber Judgment, para. 230.

[159] *Hadžihasanović and Kubura*, Appeals Chamber Decision on Joint Defence Interlocutory Appeal of Trial Chamber Decision on Rule 98 *bis* Motions for Acquittal, paras. 44 and 46–8.

in Jokić[160] pleaded guilty to the same offence in respect of the same attack. For its part, articles 8(2)(b)(ix) and 8(2)(e)(iv) of the ICC Statute give the Court jurisdiction over the war crime, in international and non-international armed conflicts respectively, of '[i]ntentionally directing attacks against buildings dedicated to religion, art, science or charitable purposes [and] historic monuments ... provided they are not military objectives'. Both provisions of the ICC Statute are reproduced in the Statute of the Iraqi Special Tribunal.[161] The US's Military Commission Instruction No. 2 recognises the war crime of 'attacking protected property',[162] by which it means 'property specifically protected by the law of armed conflict such as buildings dedicated to religion, education, art, science or charitable purposes [or] historic monuments'.[163]

The requisite material elements (*actus reus*) of the offence are to be derived from the substantive customary rule governing attacks against cultural property. It will be recalled in this regard that, although a Trial Chamber of the ICTY in *Strugar* – endorsing the 'established jurisprudence' of the Tribunal in *Blaškić*,[164] *Kordić*,[165] *Naletilić*[166] and *Brdjanin*[167] – stated that the only exception to the prohibition on acts of hostility against cultural property is when it is used for military purposes,[168] this does not accurately state the true customary rule, which presently accepts that attacks against cultural property are not unlawful if by its nature, location, purpose or use such property makes an effective contribution to military action and its total or partial destruction, capture or neutralisation, in the circumstances ruling at the time, offers a definite military advantage. On the other hand, the Trial Chambers in both *Strugar* and *Naletilić* rightly rejected the stipulation posited in *Blaškić*[169] that the cultural property attacked must not have been in the immediate vicinity of military objectives.[170] As for whether destruction

---

[160] *Prosecutor v. Jokić*, IT-01-42/1-S, Trial Chamber Sentencing Judgment, 18 March 2004.
[161] Iraqi Special Tribunal Statute, arts. 13(b)(10) (international armed conflict) and 13 (d)(4) (non-international armed conflict).
[162] Military Commission Instruction No. 2, para. 6(A)(4).
[163] *Ibid.*, para. 5(F).
[164] *Blaškić*, Trial Chamber Judgment, para. 185.
[165] *Kordić*, Trial Chamber Judgment, paras. 361–2.
[166] *Naletilić*, paras. 603 and 605.
[167] *Brdjanin*, para. 598.
[168] *Strugar*, Trial Chamber Judgment, para. 312.
[169] *Blaškić*, Trial Chamber Judgment, para. 185.
[170] *Strugar*, Trial Chamber Judgment, para. 310; *Naletilić*, para. 604.

or damage is a necessary element of the offence, the position under the Statute of the ICTY differs from that under the ICC Statute. Article 3(d) of the former speaks of 'destruction or ... damage' to cultural property, whereas articles 8(2)(b)(ix) and 8(2)(e)(iv) of the latter refer to 'directing attacks against' such property.[171] Reason suggests that the ICC position is the better, since the underlying substantive rule of customary international law prohibits directing attacks against cultural property. Articles 13(b)(10) and 13(d)(4) of the Statute of the Iraqi Special Tribunal reproduce verbatim articles 8(2)(b)(ix) and 8(2)(e)(iv) of the ICC Statute; and, when enumerating the elements of the war crime of 'attacking protected property', US Military Commission Instruction No. 2 includes no requirement of destruction or damage.[172]

In terms of the *mens rea* of the offence, the attack in question must be committed with intent and knowledge,[173] the latter meaning 'awareness that a circumstance exists'.[174] That is, the accused must intentionally direct an attack against the relevant object in the knowledge that it is cultural property, generically speaking. Although the Trial Chamber in *Blaškić* posited the requirement that the object 'may be clearly identified' as cultural property,[175] this was probably no more than a clumsy way of demanding knowledge on the part of the accused that the object was, in fact, cultural property. The Tribunal's choice of words has not been reproduced in later cases, and the ICC's Elements of Crimes embody no explicit requirement that the institutions and historic monuments referred to in articles 8(2)(b)(ix) and 8(2)(e)(iv) of the ICC Statute may be clearly identified as such.[176] The accused's intent and

---

[171] Nor do the respective Elements of Crimes require destruction or damage: Elements of Crimes, ICC Doc. ICC-ASP/1/3 (part II-B), art. 8(2)(b)(ix), p. 135 and art. 8(2)(e)(v), p. 149. This accords with the ICRC's commentary to the reference in art. 53 of Additional Protocol I to acts of hostility 'directed against' cultural property: Sandoz *et al.*, *Commentary*, para. 2070.

[172] Military Commission Instruction No. 2, para. 6(A)(4).

[173] ICC Statute, arts. 8(2)(b)(ix) and 8(2)(e)(iv), and, more generally, art. 30(1); Military Commission Instruction No. 2, paras. 4(A), 6(A)(4)(a)(3) and 6(A)(4)(a)(4). See also *Blaškić*, Trial Chamber Judgment, para. 185; *Kordić*, Trial Chamber Judgment, para. 361; *Naletilić*, para. 605; *Brdjanin*, para. 599; *Strugar*, Trial Chamber Judgment, para. 312, although the ICTY jurisprudence is complicated by the requirement of damage in ICTY Statute, art. 3(d). The ICTY has never expressly required knowledge that the object is cultural property, but this is a necessary corollary of its requirement of intent; moreover, it seems to be what the Trial Chamber was asking for in *Blaškić*, Trial Chamber Judgment, para. 185.

[174] ICC Statute, art. 30(3).

[175] *Blaškić*, Trial Chamber Judgment, para. 185.

[176] Elements of Crimes, pp. 135 and 149 respectively.

knowledge can be inferred from relevant facts and circumstances.[177] In *Strugar*, the fact that copies of the distinctive emblem of the 1954 Hague Convention 'were visible, from the JNA positions at Žarkovica and elsewhere, above the Old Town [of Dubrovnik] on 6 December 1991' was evidence going to the intent of the accused to destroy cultural property, 'as was the Old Town's status as a UNESCO World Heritage site'.[178]

As for unlawful indiscriminate attacks causing incidental damage to cultural property, the implication from the ICTY Trial Chamber judgment in *Galić*[179] and from the Appeals Chamber judgment in *Blaškić*[180] is that the customary international law applicable in both international and non-international armed conflict recognises individual criminal responsibility for intentional attacks causing incidental damage to civilians and/or civilian objects which is excessive in relation to the concrete and direct military advantage anticipated. It will also be recalled that article 8(2)(b)(iv) of the ICC Statute and article 13(b)(4) of the Statute of the Iraqi Special Tribunal vest their respective judicial bodies with jurisdiction over the war crime of intentionally launching an attack during an international armed conflict in the knowledge that the attack will cause incidental damage to civilian objects 'which would be clearly excessive in relation to the concrete and direct overall military advantage anticipated'. Neither statute, however, accords jurisdiction over the equivalent war crime in non-international armed conflict.

Unlawful acts of hostility against cultural property other than attacks also give rise to individual criminal responsibility under customary international law, regardless of whether the acts take place in international or non-international armed conflict. In the international context, it will be recalled that several of the major German war criminals tried at Nuremberg were convicted for their roles in the razing of cultural property in occupied territory. For the purposes of the ICTY, attacks and other acts of hostility against cultural property are both dealt with under article 3(d) of the Tribunal's Statute, which vests it with jurisdiction over the war crime of 'destruction or wilful damage done to institutions dedicated to religion, charity and education, the arts and sciences, historic monuments and works of art and science'; and, taking just two

---

[177] Elements of Crimes, general introduction, para. 3, *ibid.*, p. 5. See also *Prosecutor v. Tadić*, IT-94-1-T, Trial Chamber Judgment, 7 May 1997, para. 676.
[178] *Strugar*, Trial Chamber Judgment, para. 329.
[179] *Galić*, paras. 57–8.
[180] *Blaškić*, Appeals Chamber Judgment, para. 157.

relevant cases, the accused in *Blaškić* was convicted under article 3(d) for mining mosques, while the accused in *Brdjanin* was found guilty under the same provision for destroying mosques and churches with mines and other explosives, for tearing them down with heavy machinery and for setting fire to them. For its part, the ICC Statute treats acts of hostility against cultural property not amounting to attacks under the general rubric of the customary war crime of destroying the enemy's property unless such destruction be imperatively demanded by the necessities of war.[181] The same goes for the Statute of the Iraqi Special Tribunal.[182]

Again, the requisite material elements of the offence derive from the substantive customary rules on destruction of or damage to cultural property by acts of hostility other than attacks. In this regard, it will be recalled that, *pace* the ICTY, the better view is that such destruction and damage is not unlawful if imperatively demanded by the necessities of war. As for *mens rea*, intent and knowledge are again required.[183]

When it comes to sentencing in respect of the war crimes in question, it is instructive that a Trial Chamber of the ICTY in the Sentencing Judgment in *Jokić*, relating to the attack on the Old Town of Dubrovnik, referred to the war crime in article 3(d) of the ICTY Statute of destroying or wilfully damaging, *inter alia*, historic monuments and works of art as 'a violation of values especially protected by the international community'.[184] It observed that, 'since it is a serious violation of international humanitarian law to attack civilian buildings, it is a crime of even greater seriousness to direct an attack on an especially protected site, such as the Old Town, constituted of civilian buildings',[185] and that any sentence had to acknowledge that the attack on the Old Town was an attack 'against the cultural heritage of humankind'.[186] Similarly, '[a]s regards the seriousness of the offence of damage to cultural property', the Trial Chamber in *Strugar*, also relating to Dubrovnik, noted 'that such

---

[181] ICC Statute, art. 8(2)(b)(xiii) (international armed conflict) and art. 8(2)(e)(xii) (non-international armed conflict).
[182] Iraqi Special Tribunal Statute, art. 13(b)(14) (international) and art. 13(d)(12) (non-international).
[183] ICC Statute, art. 30(1). See also *Blaškić*, Trial Chamber Judgment, para. 185; *Kordić*, Trial Chamber Judgment, para. 361; *Naletilić*, para. 605; *Brdjanin*, para. 599; *Strugar*, Trial Chamber Judgment, para. 312.
[184] *Jokić*, para. 46.
[185] *Ibid.*, para. 53.
[186] *Ibid.*, para. 51.

property is, by definition, of "great importance to the cultural heritage of [a] people"', citing article 1(a) of the 1954 Hague Convention.[187] The presence of Dubrovnik on the World Heritage List appeared to add to the gravity of the offence in both cases,[188] with the Trial Chamber in *Jokić* drawing attention to the statement in the preamble to the World Heritage Convention that 'deterioration or disappearance of any item of the cultural or natural heritage constitutes a harmful impoverishment of the heritage of all the nations of the world'.[189] The extent of the damage also weighed against both accused.[190] The Trial Chamber in *Jokić* added that '[r]estoration of buildings of this kind, when possible, can never return the buildings to their state prior to the attack because a certain amount of original, historically authentic, material will have been destroyed, thus affecting the inherent value of the buildings'.[191] In the Sentencing Judgment in *Plavšić*, the following considerations, among many others relating to other offences, were taken into account:

Some 29 of the 37 municipalities listed in the Indictment possessed cultural monuments and sacred sites that were destroyed. This includes the destruction of over 100 mosques, 2 mektebs and 7 Catholic churches. Some of these monuments were located in the Foča, Višegrad and Zvornik municipalities, and dated from the Middle Ages. They were, quite obviously, culturally, historically and regionally significant sites. As one example, the Prosecution referred to the wanton destruction of the Alidža mosque in Foča, which had been in existence since the year 1550. According to the witness, this mosque was a 'pearl amongst the cultural heritage in this part of Europe'.[192]

For these and numerous other reasons, the Tribunal concluded that the accused was guilty of 'a crime of the utmost gravity'.[193]

Customary international law further recognises individual criminal responsibility for the unlawful plunder of public or private property, including cultural property, whether in international or non-international armed conflict. Article 6(b) of the London Charter vested the IMT at Nuremberg with jurisdiction over the war crime of 'plunder of

---

[187] *Strugar*, Trial Chamber Judgment, para. 232, reference omitted.
[188] *Jokić*, paras. 49 and 66–7; *Strugar*, Trial Chamber Judgment, para. 461.
[189] *Jokić*, para. 49, emphasis omitted.
[190] *Ibid.*, para. 53; *Strugar*, Trial Chamber Judgment, para. 461.
[191] *Jokić*, para. 52.
[192] *Prosecutor v. Plavšić*, IT-00-39&40/1-S, Trial Chamber Sentencing Judgment, 27 February 2003, para. 44, references omitted.
[193] *Ibid.*, para. 52.

public or private property',[194] and, in the context of belligerent occupation, the Tribunal held the accused Rosenberg 'responsible for a system of organised plunder of both public and private property throughout the invaded countries of Europe'.[195] Article 3(e) of the Statute of the ICTY vests the Tribunal with jurisdiction over the same war crime, and the Tribunal has held that the offence, which it has recognised as customary,[196] 'should be understood to embrace all forms of unlawful appropriation of property in armed conflict for which individual criminal responsibility attaches under international criminal law, including those acts traditionally described as "pillage"'.[197] In addition to the offence in article 3(e), article 3(d) of the Statute of the ICTY grants the Tribunal jurisdiction over the specific war crime of 'seizure of institutions dedicated to religion, charity and education, the arts and sciences, historic monuments and works of art and science'. The relevant case-law of the ICTY has proceeded on the basis that the war crimes referred to in articles 3(d) and 3(e) of the Statute apply to international and non-international armed conflict alike. For its part, the ICC Statute recognises, in both international and non-international armed conflict, the war crimes of seizing the enemy's property unless such seizure be imperatively demanded by the necessities of war[198] and of pillaging a town or place, even when taken by assault.[199] The same is the case under the Statute of the Iraqi Special Tribunal.[200]

The material elements of the respective offences are to be drawn from the substantive customary rules which underlie them. In the case of seizure, while military necessity is formally accommodated in the substantive customary rule embodied in article 23(g) of the Hague Rules, in practice there can never be a legitimate military rationale for the seizure of cultural property, a point reflected, in the context of belligerent occupation, in the customary rule laid down in article 56 of

---

[194] See also Control Council Law No. 10, art. II(1)(b).
[195] Nuremberg Judgment, p. 95.
[196] Hadžihasanović and Kubura, Appeals Chamber Decision on Joint Defence Interlocutory Appeal of Trial Chamber Decision on Rule 98 bis Motions for Acquittal, para. 37.
[197] Ibid.
[198] ICC Statute, art. 8(2)(b)(xiii) (international armed conflict) and art. 8(2)(e)(xii) (non-international armed conflict).
[199] Ibid., art. 8(2)(b)(xvi) (international) and art. 8(2)(e)(v) (non-international).
[200] In respect of seizing the enemy's property, see Iraqi Special Tribunal Statute, art. 13(b)(14) (international) and 13(d)(12) (non-international). In respect of pillage, see ibid., art. 13(b)(17) (international) and art. 13(d)(5) (non-international).

the Hague Rules, where the specific prohibition on the seizure of such property is stated in absolute terms. The requisite *mens rea* is intent and knowledge.[201]

Crimes against humanity

The IMT at Nuremberg held that the unlawful destruction and plunder of cultural property in the occupied territories of the East amounted not only to war crimes on a vast scale but also to crimes against humanity.[202] In *Blaškić*, a Trial Chamber of the ICTY held that the specific crime against humanity of 'persecutions on political, racial and religious grounds' recognised in article 5(h) of the Tribunal's Statute[203] 'encompasses not only bodily and mental harm and infringements upon individual freedom but also acts ... such as those targeting property, so long as the victimised persons were specially selected on grounds linked to their belonging to a particular community'.[204] The Tribunal accepted the prosecution's contention that persecution could take the form of the confiscation or destruction of symbolic buildings belonging to the Muslim population of Bosnia-Herzegovina.[205] The Trial Chamber in *Kordić* similarly held that destruction of or wilful damage to religious buildings, if discriminatory, may amount to persecution as a crime against humanity;[206] and in *Brdjanin*, having found that the destruction of and wilful damage to Bosnian Muslim and Bosnian Croat religious and cultural buildings in which the accused was involved was in fact

---

[201] ICC Statute, art. 30(1).
[202] Nuremberg Judgment, p. 65.
[203] See also ICTR Statute, art. 3(h). Although these provisions all refer conjunctively to persecution on 'political, racial and religious grounds', the ICTY has held that this should be read disjunctively, in accordance with customary international law, so that persecution on any one of these grounds suffices: *Tadić*, Trial Chamber Judgment, para. 713, affirmed in *Prosecutor v. Kunarac, Kovač and Vuković*, IT-96-23 & IT-96-23/1-A, Appeals Chamber Judgment, 12 June 2002, paras. 93 and 97. See also Nuremberg Charter, art. 6(c); Control Council Law No. 10, art. II(1)(c); ICC Statute, art. 7(1)(h); Iraqi Special Tribunal Statute, art. 12(a)(8). Article 5 of the Law on Establishment of Extraordinary Chambers in the Courts of Cambodia for the Prosecution of Crimes Committed During the Period of Democratic Kampuchea, as amended 27 October 2004, refers in the chapeau to 'national, political, ethnical, racial or religious grounds' but to 'political, racial, and religious grounds' in the specific provision on persecutions.
[204] *Blaškić*, Trial Chamber Judgment, para. 233. See also, previously, *Tadić*, Trial Chamber Judgment, paras. 703–4.
[205] *Blaškić*, Trial Chamber Judgment, para. 227.
[206] *Kordić*, Trial Chamber Judgment, para. 207.

discriminatory (Bosnian Serb buildings having been spared), the Trial Chamber held that this qualified as the crime against humanity of persecution.[207] In all three cases, the accused was convicted of both war crimes and crimes against humanity for the same conduct. In addition, in *Plavšić*, the accused pleaded guilty to acts of persecution constituting crimes against humanity for her role in the 'destruction of cultural and sacred objects' belonging to the Muslim and Croat populations of Bosnia-Herzegovina.[208] In a like manner, several Trial Chambers of the ICTY have held that the plunder of public or private property, if discriminatory, can amount to the crime against humanity of persecution for the purposes of article 5(h) of the Tribunal's Statute.[209] The case-law of the ICTY in both these respects is in no way contradicted by article 7(1)(h) of the ICC Statute, as reproduced in article 12(a)(8) of the Statute of the Iraqi Special Tribunal, which recognises as a crime against humanity '[p]ersecution against any identifiable group or collectivity on political, racial, national, ethnic, cultural, religious, gender ... or other grounds that are universally recognized as impermissible under international law, in connection with any [other crime against humanity] or any crime within the jurisdiction of the Court'.[210] Since unlawful destruction and plunder of cultural property constitute war crimes under article 8 of the ICC Statute, they may also constitute crimes against humanity under article 7(1)(h).

As for the other material elements of the offence, the cardinal feature of a crime against humanity is that it is directed against a civilian population (meaning any civilian population, not just the civilian population of occupied territory).[211] In addition, for the destruction and plunder of cultural property in armed conflict to constitute crimes against humanity and not just war crimes, they must be committed 'as part of a widespread or systematic attack' on that civilian

---

[207] *Brdjanin*, paras. 1022–3.
[208] *Plavšić*, para. 15.
[209] *Tadić*, Trial Chamber Judgment, para. 704; *Kordić*, Trial Chamber Judgment, para. 205; *Naletilić*, para. 698. See also *Plavšić*, para. 15.
[210] 'Persecution' is defined in ICC Statute, art. 7(2)(g) to mean 'the intentional and severe deprivation of fundamental rights contrary to international law by reason of the identity of the group or collectivity'. See also, identically, Iraqi Special Tribunal Statute, art. 12(b)(6).
[211] See Nuremberg Charter, art. 6(c); Control Council Law No. 10, art. II(1)(c); ICTY Statute, art. 5; ICTR Statute, art. 3; ICC Statute, art. 7(1); Iraqi Special Tribunal Statute, art. 12(a); Law on Cambodian Extraordinary Chambers, art. 5.

population.²¹² In *Kunarac*, the Appeals Chamber of the ICTY made it clear that 'only the attack, not the individual acts of the accused, must be widespread or systematic': 'all other conditions being met, a single or relatively limited number of acts on his or her part would qualify as a crime against humanity, unless those acts may be said to be isolated or random'.²¹³ The Appeals Chamber in *Kunarac* also rejected the condition posited by earlier Trial Chambers that crimes against humanity must be committed in pursuance of some sort of policy.²¹⁴ It is unclear, however, whether this accords with custom.²¹⁵ Finally, given that crimes against humanity need not be committed in armed conflict,²¹⁶ it is *a fortiori* immaterial whether, if they are committed in armed conflict, the conflict is international or non-international.

The requisite *mens rea* for a crime against humanity is intent to commit the underlying offence, combined with knowledge of the widespread and systematic attack on the civilian population.²¹⁷ The latter means that the perpetrator 'knew that the conduct was part of or intended the conduct to be part of a widespread or systematic attack against a civilian population'.²¹⁸ For the specific crime against humanity of persecution,

---

²¹² *Report of the Secretary-General pursuant to paragraph 2 of Security Council resolution 808 (1993)*, UN Doc. S/25704, 3 May 1993, para. 48; ICTR Statute, art. 3; Draft Code of Crimes against the Peace and Security of Mankind, *Report of the International Law Commission on the work of its forty-eighth session, 6 May–26 July 1996*, UN Doc. A/51/10, para. 50, art. 18 ('committed in a systematic manner or on a large scale'); ICC Statute, art. 7(1); Iraqi Special Tribunal Statute, art. 12(a); Law on Cambodian Extraordinary Chambers, art. 5.

²¹³ *Kunarac*, Appeals Chamber Judgment, para. 96.

²¹⁴ Ibid., para. 98.

²¹⁵ See *contra* the definition of the expression 'attack directed against any civilian population' in ICC Statute, art. 7(2)(a) ('pursuant to or in furtherance of a State or organizational policy to commit such attack'). See also, identically, Iraqi Special Tribunal Statute, art. 12(b)(1).

²¹⁶ *Tadić*, Trial Chamber Judgment, para. 713; ICTR Statute, art. 3; Draft Code of Crimes, art. 18 and especially para. (6) of commentary thereon; ICC Statute, art. 7; Iraqi Special Tribunal Statute, art. 12; Law on Cambodian Extraordinary Chambers, art. 5. While ICTY Statute, art. 5 makes the existence of an armed conflict (international or non-international) a condition of a crime against humanity for the purposes of the Tribunal's jurisdiction, it was recognised by the drafters that customary international law was not so restrictive: *Report of the Secretary-General pursuant to paragraph 2 of Security Council resolution 808 (1993)*, para. 47.

²¹⁷ *Kunarac*, Appeals Chamber Judgment, para. 102; ICC Statute, arts. 7(1) and 30(1); Iraqi Special Tribunal Statute, art. 12(a).

²¹⁸ Elements of Crimes, art. 7, pp. 116–24. But this 'should not be interpreted as requiring proof that the perpetrator had knowledge of all the characteristics of the attack or the precise details of the plan or policy of the State or organization.

the accused must also have acted with the intent to discriminate on one of the specified grounds.[219]

Genocide

In General Assembly resolution 96 (I) of 11 December 1946, the Member States of the United Nations affirmed that genocide was a crime under general international law.[220] This affirmation was confirmed in article I of the Convention on the Prevention and Punishment of the Crime of Genocide,[221] adopted in 1948, which specifies that genocide is a crime under international law 'whether committed in time of peace or in time of war'.[222] Article II of the Genocide Convention defines the international crime of genocide as

any of the following acts committed with intent to destroy, in whole or in part, a national, ethnical, racial or religious group, as such:

(a) Killing members of the group;
(b) Causing serious bodily or mental harm to members of the group;
(c) Deliberately inflicting on the group conditions of life calculated to bring about its physical destruction in whole or in part;
(d) Imposing measures intended to prevent births within the group;
(e) Forcibly transferring children of the group to another group.

Draft versions of the Convention had encompassed the concept of 'cultural genocide', which included, in the earliest draft, '[s]ystematic destruction of historical or religious monuments or their diversion to alien uses' and 'destruction or dispers[al] of documents and objects of historical, artistic, or religious value and of objects used in religious

---

In the case of an emerging widespread or systematic attack against a civilian population, the intent clause of the last element indicates that this mental element is satisfied if the perpetrator intended to further such an attack.': *ibid.*, art. 7, introduction, p. 116, para. 2. See, similarly, *Kunarac*, Appeals Chamber Judgment, para. 102.

[219] *Prosecutor v. Tadić*, IT-94-1-A, Appeals Chamber Judgment, 15 July 1999, para. 305; *Brdjanin*, para. 1024.

[220] The word 'affirmed' is rhetorical, since the genocidal acts of Nazi Germany were prosecuted after the Second World War as a species of crime against humanity, not as the crime of genocide as such. Moreover, only those genocidal acts committed after the outbreak of the war were prosecuted.

[221] Paris, 9 December 1948, 78 UNTS 277.

[222] *A fortiori*, it is immaterial whether its wartime commission is in international or non-international armed conflict.

worship';[223] and, in a later version, '[d]estroying ... libraries, museums, schools, historical monuments, places of worship and other cultural institutions and objects of the group' with the intent to destroy the culture of that group.[224] But the concept was rejected by the Sixth Committee of the General Assembly,[225] which prepared the final text of the Convention as adopted by the Assembly in plenary.

In *Reservations to the Convention on Genocide*, the ICJ stated that the principles of the Genocide Convention 'are principles which are recognized by civilized nations as binding on States, even without any conventional obligation',[226] a statement which applied as much to the definition of the crime as to the obligations arising for states. The definition laid down in article II of the Genocide Convention was subsequently reproduced verbatim in article 4(2) of the Statute of the ICTY, the UN Secretary-General having taken the view that the Convention's definition of genocide accorded with customary international law,[227] and in article 2(2) of the Statute of the International Criminal Tribunal for Rwanda. It was again restated unamended in article 17 of the International Law Commission's Draft Code of Crimes against the Peace and Security of Mankind, as finally adopted by the Commission in 1996. Paragraph 12 of the ILC's commentary to article 17 of the Draft Code explicitly dismisses the concept of 'cultural genocide':

As clearly shown by the preparatory work for the Convention, the destruction in question is the material destruction of a group either by physical or by biological

---

[223] Article II(2)(e) of the Draft Convention for the Prevention and Punishment of Genocide (UN Doc. E/447), annexed to ECOSOC res. 77 (V), 6 August 1947.

[224] Article III(2) of the Draft Convention on the Prevention and Punishment of the Crime of Genocide (UN Doc. E/794), *United Nations Economic and Social Council, Third Year, Seventh Session, Supplement No. 6*, Annex.

[225] Many delegates to the Sixth Committee opposed, in the words of the South African representative, 'any attempt to destroy the cultural heritage of a group or to prevent a group from making its specific contribution to the cultural heritage of mankind': *United Nations. Official Records of the Third Session of the General Assembly, Part I. Sixth Committee, Summary Records of Meetings 21 September–10 December 1948*, p. 202. But they equally thought that a convention on genocide was not the place to express this opposition. In the event, the motion to remove reference to cultural genocide was carried 25:16:4, with 13 delegations absent during the vote.

[226] *Reservations to the Convention on Genocide*, Advisory Opinion, ICJ Reports 1951, p. 15 at p. 23. See also *Armed Activities on the Territory of the Congo (New Application: 2002) (Democratic Republic of the Congo v. Rwanda)*, ICJ General List No. 126, Jurisdiction and Admissibility, 3 February 2006, para. 64.

[227] *Report of the Secretary-General pursuant to paragraph 2 of Security Council resolution 808 (1993)*, para. 45, citing *Reservations to the Convention on Genocide*.

means, not the destruction of the national, linguistic, religious, cultural or other identity of a particular group. The national or religious element and the racial or ethnic element are not taken into consideration in the definition of the word 'destruction', which must be taken only in its material sense, its physical or biological sense. It is true that the 1947 draft Convention prepared by the Secretary-General and the 1948 draft prepared by the *Ad Hoc* Committee on Genocide contained provisions on 'cultural genocide' covering any deliberate act committed with the intent to destroy the language, religion or culture of a group, such as prohibiting the use of the language of the group in daily intercourse or in schools or the printing and circulation of publications in the language of the group or destroying or preventing the use of libraries, museums, schools, historical monuments, places of worship or other cultural institutions and objects of the group. However, the text of the Convention, as prepared by the Sixth Committee and adopted by the General Assembly, did not include the concept of 'cultural genocide' contained in the two drafts and simply listed acts which come within the category of 'physical' or 'biological' genocide. The first three subparagraphs of the present article list acts of 'physical genocide', while the last two list acts of 'biological genocide'.[228]

Three years later, article 6 of the ICC Statute again reproduced word for word the definition of genocide used in article II of the Genocide Convention. Never at any point during the proceedings of the Ad Hoc Committee on the Establishment of an International Criminal Court, the Preparatory Committee on the Establishment of an International Criminal Court or the United Nations Diplomatic Conference of Plenipotentiaries on the Establishment of an International Criminal Court was it proposed to widen the definition of genocide to embrace the concept of 'cultural genocide'.

The idea of cultural genocide was rejected once more by a Trial Chamber of the ICTY in *Krstić*. Recalling the drafting of the Genocide Convention and the view of the ILC, the Tribunal concluded that 'customary international law limits the definition of genocide to those acts seeking the physical or biological destruction of all or part of the group', with the consequence that 'an enterprise attacking only the cultural or sociological characteristics of a human group in order to annihilate these elements which give to that group its own identity

---

[228] *Report of the International Law Commission on the work of its forty-eighth session*, pp. 90–1, reference omitted.

distinct from the rest of the community would not fall under the definition of genocide'.[229] But the Tribunal added a rider:

> The Trial Chamber however points out that where there is physical or biological destruction there are often simultaneous attacks on the cultural and religious property and symbols of the targeted group as well, attacks which may legitimately be considered as evidence of an intent to physically destroy the group. In this case, the Trial Chamber will thus take into account as evidence of intent to destroy the group the deliberate destruction of mosques and houses belonging to members of the group.[230]

The Appeals Chamber subsequently affirmed that the conventional definition of genocide represents customary international law[231] and that the Trial Chamber had 'correctly identified the governing legal principle'.[232] In his partial dissenting opinion, Judge Shahabuddeen, accepting that the notion of 'cultural genocide' fell outside the *actus reus* of genocide as defined by customary international law, nonetheless emphasised what the Trial Chamber had suggested in its rider, namely that '[t]he destruction of culture may serve evidentially to confirm an intent, to be gathered from other circumstances, to destroy the group as such'.[233] In *Krstić* itself, 'the razing of the principal mosque confirm[ed] an intent to destroy the Srebrenica part of the Bosnian Muslim group'.[234]

The customary definition of genocide in article II of the Genocide Convention has most recently been embodied in article 11 of the Statute of the Iraqi Special Tribunal and in article 4 of the Law on the Establishment of Extraordinary Chambers in the Courts of Cambodia for the Prosecution of Crimes Committed During the Period of Democratic Kampuchea.

UNESCO Declaration concerning the Intentional Destruction of Cultural Heritage

At its thirty-first session in 2001, in the immediate wake of the wilful destruction of the Buddhas of Bamiyan by the Taliban government of

---

[229] *Prosecutor v. Krstić*, IT-98-33-T, Trial Chamber Judgment, 2 August 2001, para. 580.
[230] *Ibid*.
[231] *Prosecutor v. Krstić*, IT-98-33-A, Appeals Chamber Judgment, 19 April 2004, para. 25.
[232] *Ibid*., para. 26.
[233] *Ibid*., partial diss. op. Shahabuddeen, para. 53.
[234] *Ibid*.

Afghanistan, the General Conference of UNESCO adopted a resolution entitled 'Acts constituting a crime against the common heritage of humanity'.[235] Calling on all Member States of the Organisation and all other states of the world — 'in order to maximize the protection of the cultural heritage of humanity, and in particular, against destructive acts'[236] — to become Parties to the 1954 Hague Convention and its two Protocols, as well as to the Convention on the Means of Prohibiting and Preventing the Illicit Import, Export and Transfer of Ownership of Cultural Property, the World Heritage Convention and the UNIDROIT Convention on Stolen or Illicitly Exported Cultural Objects, the General Conference noted and reiterated 'the fundamental principles included in these instruments to prevent the destruction of the cultural heritage including looting and illicit excavations',[237] and invited the Director-General of UNESCO to formulate, on the basis of these principles, 'a Draft Declaration concerning the Intentional Destruction of Cultural Heritage'.[238]

The upshot was the UNESCO Declaration concerning the Intentional Destruction of Cultural Heritage,[239] adopted by the General Conference in 2003 at its thirty-second session.

Recalling the principles of all UNESCO's conventions, recommendations, declarations and charters for the protection of cultural heritage,
Mindful that cultural heritage is an important component of the cultural identity of communities, groups and individuals, and of social cohesion, so that its intentional destruction may have adverse consequences on human dignity and human rights,
Reiterating one of the fundamental principles of the Preamble of the 1954 Hague Convention for the Protection of Cultural Property in the Event of Armed Conflict providing that 'damage to cultural property belonging to any people whatsoever means damage to the cultural heritage of all mankind, since each people makes its contribution to the culture of the world',
Recalling the principles concerning the protection of cultural heritage in the event of armed conflict established in the 1899 and 1907 Hague Conventions and, in particular, in Articles 27 and 56 of the Regulations of the 1907 Fourth Hague Convention, as well as other subsequent agreements,

---

[235] 31 C/Resolution 26.
[236] *Ibid.*, para. 1.
[237] *Ibid.*, paras. 2 and 3.
[238] *Ibid.*, para. 4. See also, previously, 161 EX/Decision 3.1.1(III).
[239] 32 C/Resolution 33, Annex.

Mindful of the development of rules of customary international law as also affirmed by the relevant case-law, related to the protection of cultural heritage in peacetime as well as in the event of armed conflict,

Also recalling Articles 8(2)(b)(ix) and 8(2)(e)(iv) of the Rome Statute of the International Criminal Court, and, as appropriate, Article 3(d) of the Statute of the International Criminal Tribunal for the former Yugoslavia, related to the intentional destruction of cultural heritage, ...[240]

the General Conference resolved that states 'should take all appropriate measures to prevent, avoid, stop and suppress acts of intentional destruction of cultural heritage, wherever such heritage is located'.[241] The Declaration provides that, where they have not already done so, states should become Parties to the 1954 Hague Convention and its two Protocols, as well as to the two Additional Protocols to the Geneva Conventions,[242] and that, '[w]hen involved in an armed conflict, be it of an international or non-international character, including the case of occupation, States should take all appropriate measures to conduct their activities in such a manner as to protect cultural heritage, in conformity with customary international law and the principles and objectives of international agreements and UNESCO recommendations concerning the protection of such heritage during hostilities'.[243] It further declares that a state 'that intentionally destroys or intentionally fails to take appropriate measures to prohibit, prevent, stop, and punish intentional destruction of cultural heritage of great importance for humanity, whether or not it is inscribed on a list maintained by UNESCO or another international organization, bears the responsibility for such destruction, to the extent provided for by international law';[244] that states 'should take all appropriate measures, in accordance with international law, to establish jurisdiction over, and provide effective criminal sanctions against, those persons who commit, or order to be committed, acts of intentional destruction of cultural heritage of great importance for humanity, whether or not it is inscribed on a list maintained by UNESCO or another international organization';[245] and that, '[f]or the purposes of more comprehensive protection, each State is encouraged to

---

[240] *Ibid.*, preamble.
[241] *Ibid.*, para. III(1).
[242] *Ibid.*, para. III(4)(a).
[243] *Ibid.*, para. V.
[244] *Ibid.*, para. VI.
[245] *Ibid.*, para. VII.

take all appropriate measures, in accordance with international law, to cooperate with other States concerned with a view to establishing jurisdiction over, and providing effective criminal sanctions against, those persons who have committed or have ordered to be committed acts referred to above ... and who are found present on its territory, regardless of their nationality and the place where such act occurred'.[246]

The Declaration does not itself impose obligations on Member States of UNESCO. Its hortatory and thus not fundamentally norm-creating language is incapable of doing so, and the *travaux préparatoires* show that this was not the intention.[247] Rather, the *travaux* and the consistent references in the text to existing conventional and customary international law make it clear that the instrument is a restatement of the *droit acquis*, as well as a statement of political consensus and intent.[248]

The above rules and recommendations testify to the normative resonance of the conviction that cultural property should be spared in war and to the wider practical influence of the bodies of law outlined in the preceding chapters. They also show how an exclusive focus on the Hague Rules, the 1954 Hague Convention and Protocols, and the 1977 Additional Protocols does not give a full picture of the international legal protection of cultural property in armed conflict.

---

[246] *Ibid.*, para. VIII(2), referring to the acts mentioned in para. VII.
[247] The Director-General of UNESCO stated in UNESCO Doc. 31 C/46, para. 6(c) that the then-proposed Declaration 'would not be intended to create obligations for States, but would restate the fundamental principles of the existing legal instruments'.
[248] The UN General Assembly welcomed the adoption of the Declaration in GA res. 58/17, 3 December 2003, para. 3.

Epilogue

With the adoption and coming into force of the Second Hague Protocol and the Rome Statute of the International Criminal Court, the international law on the protection of cultural property in armed conflict has assumed a shape that will probably remain unchanged for quite some time. Given this, it would be pointless for this book to prescribe reform. It would also be unwise: a period of consolidation is needed now.

Nor do the preceding chapters adopt a theoretical or critical approach. It is doubtful such a stance could do justice to the complexities, contradictions and quiddities of this (or any other) messy human endeavour. Moreover, this is a work of law, and law is, at some irreducible level, a practical undertaking.

Rather, this book sets itself a more limited task, but hopefully a useful one. In seeking to acquit it, it reveals the perhaps surprising degree of attention paid by states over the past two hundred years, mostly in good faith, to sparing cultural property from destruction and misappropriation in war, and it suggests that, while experience dictates caution, today's legal and technological conditions give grounds for sober optimism that such efforts stand a decent chance of success. The vision of cultural property as a shared heritage – shared by a people, shared by present humanity and shared with generations to come – has driven the evolution of international rules and institutions adherent to its logic, continues to inform how the rules are interpreted and applied, and serves as both an internal draw towards compliance and a conceptual framework for international mobilisation in defence of cultural treasures.

The preceding chapters also reveal, through a detailed analysis of the law and practice of the first half of the twentieth century, how this body of law has little hope of proving effective unless states manifest as much legal and practical concern for the wartime fate of human beings – for whose benefit cultural property is protected in armed conflict – as they show for that cultural property itself. Excepting campaigns of contumacious outlawry, which law can hope to punish but not prevent, the destruction of cultural property in armed conflict over the past hundred years has largely reflected the weakness of the rules on the wartime protection of the civilian population and civilian objects. Conversely, greater interest in sparing people from attack has improved cultural heritage's chances. In turn, leaving monuments untouched almost always saves the people living near them. *Ars longa, vita longa.*

But there is no cause for complacency. While the law and technology of targeting have gone some way to addressing one problem, the gravest threat today to cultural property in armed conflict is its theft by private, civilian actors not bound in this regard by the laws of war. The breakdown of order that accompanies armed conflict and the corrupting lure of the worldwide illicit trade in art and antiquities continue to drive the looting of archaeological sites and museums in war-zones and occupied territory, depriving the world of their scientific value and causing grievous material damage. International rules are in place to combat the phenomenon, but watertight compliance regimes are what is needed now.

Ultimately, cultural property and human beings will always suffer in war. A surefire protection is not to wage it.

Bibliography

Abi-Saab, G., 'The Specificities of Humanitarian Law', in Swinarksi, C. (ed.), *Studies and Essays on International Humanitarian Law and Red Cross Principles in Honour of Jean Pictet* (Geneva/The Hague: ICRC/Martinus Nijhoff, 1984), p. 265
  'Non-International Armed Conflicts', in *International Dimensions of Humanitarian Law* (Geneva/Paris/Dordrecht: Henry Dunant Institute/UNESCO/Martinus Nijhoff, 1988), p. 217
  '"Humanité" et "communauté internationale" dans la dialectique du droit internationale', in *Humanité et droit international. Mélanges René-Jean Dupuy* (Paris: Pedone, 1991), p. 1
Abi-Saab, R., *Droit humanitaire et conflits internes. Origines et évolution de la réglementation internationale* (Geneva/Paris: Henry Dunant Institute/Pedone, 1986)
Abtahi, H., 'The Protection of Cultural Property in Times of Armed Conflict: The Practice of the International Criminal Tribunal for the Former Yugoslavia' (2001) 14 *Harvard Human Rights Journal* 1
Agius, E. and Busuttil, S. (eds.), *Future Generations in International Law* (London: FIELD/Earthscan, 1998)
'Agora: What Obligation Does Our Generation Owe to the Next? An Approach to Global Environmental Responsibility' (1990) 84 *American Journal of International Law* 190
'A Hard Look at Soft Law' (1988) 82 *Proceedings of the American Society of International Law* 371
Ago, R., 'La codification du droit international et les problèmes de sa réalisation', in *Recueil d'études de droit international en hommage à Paul Guggenheim* (Geneva: Faculté de droit de l'Université de Genève/IUHEI, 1968), p. 93
Aldrich, G. H., 'Progressive Development of the Laws of War: A Reply to Criticisms of the 1977 Geneva Protocol I' (1986) 26 *Virginia Journal of International Law* 693
  'The Laws of War on Land' (2000) 94 *American Journal of International Law* 42
'Area Bombing', in Dear, I. C. B. and Foot, M. R. D. (eds.), *The Oxford Companion to the Second World War* (Oxford: Oxford University Press, 1995), p. 53

Alexandrov, E., *International Legal Protection of Cultural Property* (Sofia: Sofia Press, 1979)
Aubry, C. and Rau, C., *Cours de droit civil français d'après la méthode de Zachariae*, 6th edn, 12 vols. (Paris: Marchal et Billard, 1935−58), vol. IX
Audoin-Rouzeau, S., 'Paris bombardé 1914−1918', in Chassaigne, P. and Largeaud, J.-M. (eds.), *Villes en guerre (1914−1945)* (Paris: Armand Colin, 2004), p. 31
Ayala, B., *De Jure et Officiis Bellicis et Disciplina Militari Libri III*, text of 1582, translated by J.P. Bate (Washington, DC: Carnegie Institution, 1912)
Babelon, J.-P. and Chastel, A., 'La notion de patrimoine' (1980) 49 *Revue de l'art* 5
'Baedeker Raids', in Dear, I.C.B. and Foot, M.R.D. (eds.), *The Oxford Companion to the Second World War* (Oxford: Oxford University Press, 1995), p. 101
Baker, P.J., 'The Codification of International Law' (1924) 5 *British Yearbook of International Law* 38
Baker, S. (ed.), *Halleck's International Law*, 3rd edn (London: Kegan Paul, Trench, Trübner, 1893)
Balladore Pallieri, G., *Diritto bellico*, 2nd edn (Padua: Cedam, 1954)
Bardonnet, D., 'Quelques observations sur le principe de proportionnalité en droit international', in *International Law in an Evolving World. Liber Amicorum in Tribute to Professor Eduardo Jiménez de Aréchaga*, 3 vols. (Montevideo: FCU, 1994), vol. II, p. 995
Bassiouni, M.C., 'Reflections on Criminal Jurisdiction in International Protection of Cultural Property' (1983) 10 *Syracuse Journal of International Law and Commerce* 281
Baxter, R.R., 'The Effects of Ill-Conceived Codification and Development of International Law', in *Recueil d'études de droit international en hommage à Paul Guggenheim* (Geneva: Faculté de droit de l'Université de Genève/IUHEI, 1968), p. 146
  'International Law in "Her Infinite Variety"' (1980) 29 *International and Comparative Law Quarterly* 549
Bayle, P., *Dictionnaire Historique et Critique Par Monsieur Bayle*, 4 vols. (Rotterdam: Reinier Leers, 1697)
Bedjaoui, M. (ed.), *International Law: Achievements and Prospects* (Paris/Dordrecht: UNESCO/Martinus Nijhoff, 1991)
Beer Poortugael, J.C.C. Jonkheer den, *Le droit des gens en marche vers la paix et la guerre de Tripoli* (The Hague: Martinus Nijhoff, 1912)
Belli, P., *De Re Militari et Bello Tractatus*, text of 1563, translated by H.C. Nutting (Oxford: Clarendon, 1936)
Benvenisti, E., *The International Law of Occupation*, with new preface by the author (Princeton, NJ: Princeton University Press, 2004)
Berman, S., 'Antiquities in Israel in a Maze of Controversy' (1987) 19 *Case Western Reserve Journal of International Law* 343
Best, G., *Humanity in Warfare. The Modern History of the International Law of Armed Conflicts* (London: Weidenfeld and Nicolson, 1980)
  'World War Two and the Law of War' (1981) 7 *Review of International Studies* 67
  'The Restraint of War in Historical and Philosophical Perspective', in Delissen, A.J.M. and Tanja, G.J. (eds.), *Humanitarian Law of Armed Conflict,*

Challenges Ahead. Essays in Honour of Frits Kalshoven (Dordrecht: Martinus Nijhoff, 1991), p. 3

War and Law Since 1945 (Oxford: Clarendon Press, 1994)

Biddle, T.D., 'British and American Approaches to Strategic Bombing: Their Origins and Implementation in the World War II Combined Bomber Offensive' (1995) 18 *Journal of Strategic Studies* 91

Birkenhead, The Earl of (F.E. Smith), *International Law*, 6th edn, edited by R.W. Moelwyn-Hughes (London: Dent, 1927)

Birov, V., 'Prize or Plunder: The Pillage of Works of Art and the International Law of War' (1997–8) 30 *New York University Journal of International Law and Policy* 201

Blet, P. et al. (eds.), *Actes et Documents du Saint Siège relatifs à la Seconde Guerre Mondiale*, 11 vols. (Vatican City: Libreria Editrice Vaticana, 1965–81)

Blix, H., 'Area Bombardment: Rules and Reasons' (1978) 49 *British Yearbook of International Law* 31

Blumenson, M., *United States Army in World War II, The Mediterranean Theater of Operations: Salerno to Cassino* (Washington, DC: Office of the Chief of Military History, United States Army, 1969)

Bluntschli, J.-C., *Le droit international codifié*, translated by M.C. Lardy (Paris: Guillaumin, 1870)

'Droit de la guerre et coutume de guerre, à propos des attaques du colonel von Rüstow contre le droit des gens' (1876) 8 *Revue de Droit International* 663

Le droit international codifié, 3rd edn, translated by M.C. Lardy (Paris: Guillaumin, 1881)

'Lettre de M. Bluntschli à M. le comte de Moltke' (1881) 13 *Revue de Droit International* 82

Boog, H., 'The Luftwaffe and Indiscriminate Bombing up to 1942', in Boog, H. (ed.), *The Conduct of the Air War in the Second World War. An International Comparison* (New York/Oxford: Berg, 1992), p. 373

'Concluding Remarks', in Boog, H. (ed.), *The Conduct of the Air War in the Second World War. An International Comparison* (New York/Oxford: Berg, 1992), p. 706

Bothe, M., 'Legal Restraints on Targeting: Protection of Civilian Population and the Changing Faces of Modern Conflicts' (2001) 31 *Israel Yearbook on Human Rights* 35

Bothe, M., Kurzidem, T. and Macalister-Smith, P. (eds.), *National Implementation of International Humanitarian Law. Proceedings of an International Colloquium held at Bad Homburg, June 17–19, 1988* (Dordrecht: Martinus Nijhoff, 1990)

Bothe, M., Partsch, K.J. and Solf, W.A., *New Rules for Victims of Armed Conflicts* (The Hague: Martinus Nijhoff, 1982)

Bots, H. and Waquet, F., *La République des Lettres* (Paris: Belin, 1997)

Boulting, N., 'The Law's Delays: Conservationist Legislation in the British Isles', in Fawcett, J. (ed.), *The Future of the Past. Attitudes to Conservation 1174–1974* (London: Thames and Hudson, 1976), p. 9

Bourquin, M., 'L'humanisation du droit des gens' in *La technique et les principes du droit public. Études en l'honneur de Georges Scelle*, 2 vols. (Paris: LGDP, 1950), vol. I, p. 21

Bouwsma, W. J., *The Waning of the Renaissance, 1550–1640* (London: Yale University Press, 2000)

Bretton, P., 'Actualité du droit international humanitaire applicable dans les conflits armés', in *Mélanges offerts à Hubert Thierry. L'évolution du droit international* (Paris: Pedone, 1998), p. 57

Breucker, J. de, 'La réserve des nécessités militaires dans la Convention de la Haye du 14 mai 1954 sur la protection des biens culturels' (1975) 14 *Revue de Droit Pénal Militaire et Droit de la Guerre* 225

'Pour les vingt ans de la Convention de la Haye du 14 Mai 1954 pour la protection des biens culturels' (1975) 11 *Revue Belge de Droit International* 525

'La répression des infractions graves aux dispositions du premier Protocole additionel aux quatre Conventions de Genève du 12 août 1949' (1977) 16 *Revue de Droit Pénal Militaire et Droit de la Guerre* 497

Brocher, H., 'Les principes naturels du droit de la guerre (Chapitre III)' (1873) 5 *Revue de Droit International* 321

Brown Scott, J., 'The Work of the Second Hague Peace Conference' (1908) 2 *American Journal of International Law* 1

'Bombardment by Naval Forces' (1908) 2 *American Journal of International Law* 285

'The Codification of International Law' (1924) 18 *American Journal of International Law* 260

'La genèse du traité du Droit de la Guerre et de la Paix' (1925) 6 *Revue de Droit International (3ème série)* 481

Brown Weiss, E., *In Fairness to Future Generations: International Law, Common Patrimony, and Intergenerational Equity* (Dobbs Ferry: Transnational, 1989)

Bruha, T., 'Bombardment', in Bernhardt, R. (ed.), *Encyclopedia of Public International Law*, 5 vols. (Amsterdam: North-Holland, 1992), vol. I, p. 419

Büchel, R., 'Mesures préventatives prises en Suisse dans le cadre de la protection des biens culturels' (2004) 86 *International Review of the Red Cross* 325

Bugnion, F., 'La genèse de la protection juridique des biens culturels en cas de conflit armé' (2004) 86 *International Review of the Red Cross* 313

Burckhardt, J., *The Civilization of the Renaissance in Italy*, text of 1860, translated by S. G. C. Middlemore (London: Penguin, 1990)

Burlamaqui, J. J., *Principes du Droit Politique*, 2 vols. (Amsterdam: Chatelain, 1751)

Butler, J. R. M., *Grand Strategy. Volume II. September 1939–June 1941* (London: HMSO, 1957)

Calvo, C., *Le droit international théorique et pratique*, 5th edn, 5 vols. (Paris: Rousseau, 1896)

Canestaro, N. A., 'Legal and Policy Constraints on the Conduct of Aerial Precision Warfare' (2004) 37 *Vanderbilt Journal of Transnational Law* 431

Canino, G., 'Il ruolo svolto dall'UNESCO nella tutela del patrimonio mondiale culturale e naturale', in Ciciriello, M. C. (ed.), *La protezione del patrimonio mondiale culturale e naturale a venticinque anni dalla Convenzione dell'UNESCO* (Naples: Editoriale Scientifica, 1997), p. 1

Cannizzaro, E., *Il principio della proporzionalità nell'ordinamento internazionale* (Milan: Giuffrè, 2000)
Carnahan, B. M., 'The Law of Air Bombardment in its Historical Context' (1975) 17 *Air Force Law Review* 39
  'Lincoln, Lieber and the Laws of War: The Origins and Limits of the Principle of Military Necessity' (1998) 92 *American Journal of International Law* 213
Carnegie, A. R., 'Jurisdiction over Violations of the Laws and Customs of War' (1963) 39 *British Yearbook of International Law* 402
Castrén, E., *The Present Law of War and Neutrality* (Helsinki: Suomalaisen Tiedeakatemian Toimituksia, 1954)
Chamberlain, K., 'The Protection of Cultural Property in Armed Conflict' (2003) 8 *Art Antiquity and Law* 209
  War and Cultural Heritage. An Analysis of the 1954 Convention for the Protection of Cultural Property in the Event of Armed Conflict and its Two Protocols (Leicester: Institute of Art and Law, 2004)
Chklaver, G., 'Projet d'une Convention pour la Protection des Institutions et Monuments consacrés aux Arts et aux Sciences' (1930) 6 *Revue de Droit International* (Paris) 589
Choay, F., *The Invention of the Historic Monument* (Cambridge: Cambridge University Press, 2001)
Chrétien, M., 'La "guerre totale" du Japon en Chine' (1939) 46 *Revue Générale de Droit International Public* 229
Clausewitz, C. von, *On War*, text of 1832 (London: Penguin, 1982)
Clemen, P., *Kunstschutz im Kriege: Berichte über den Zustand der Kunstdenkmäler auf den verschiedenen Kriegsschauplätzen und über die deutschen und österreichischen Massnahmen zu ihrer Erhaltung, Rettung, Erforschung* (Leipzig: Seeman, 1919)
Clémens, R., *Le Projet de Monaco, le droit et la guerre. Villes sanitaires et villes de sécurité. Assistance sanitaire internationale* (Paris: Sirey, 1937)
Clément, E., 'Le concept de *responsabilité collective* de la communauté internationale pour la protection des biens culturels dans les conventions et racommendations de l'UNESCO' (1993) 26 *Revue Belge de Droit International* 534
  'Some Recent Practical Experience in the Implementation of the 1954 Hague Convention' (1994) 3 *International Journal of Cultural Property* 11
Clément, E. and Quinio, F., 'La protection des biens culturels au Cambodge pendant la période des conflits armés, à travers l'application de la Convention de La Haye de 1954' (2004) 86 *International Review of the Red Cross* 389
Cobban, A., 'The Fall of France', in Toynbee, A. and Toynbee, V. M. (eds.), *The Initial Triumph of the Axis* (London: Oxford University Press/Royal Institute of International Affairs, 1958), p. 190
Colby, E., 'Aërial Law and War Targets' (1925) 19 *American Journal of International Law* 702
Colin, J.-P. and Lang, J., 'La culture entre les peuples et les états: vers un nouveau droit international', in *Le droit des peuples à disposer d'eux-mêmes. Méthodes*

d'analyse du droit international. Mélanges offerts à Charles Chaumont (Paris: Pedone, 1984), p. 179

Colley, L., 'Looking for Ourselves. Uses and Abuses of the Heritage Idea', Times Literary Supplement, 2 May 1997, p. 8

Collier, B., The Defence of the United Kingdom (London: HMSO, 1957)

Collins, L. and Lapierre, D., Is Paris Burning? (London: GraftonBooks, 1991)

Colwell-Chanthaphonh, C. and Piper, J., 'War and Cultural Property: The 1954 Hague Convention and the Status of US Ratification' (2001) 10 International Journal of Cultural Property 217

'Combined Bomber Offensive (CBO)', in Dear, I.C.B. and Foot, M.R.D. (eds.), The Oxford Companion to the Second World War (Oxford: Oxford University Press, 1995), p. 253

'Commission of Jurists to Consider and Report upon the Revision of the Rules of Warfare. General Report' (1938) 32 American Journal of International Law Supplement 1

Conforti, B., 'Humanité et renouveau de la production normative', in Humanité et droit international. Mélanges René-Jean Dupuy (Paris: Pedone, 1991), p. 113

Cornu, M., Le droit culturel des biens. L'intérêt culturel juridiquement protégé (Brussels: Bruylant, 1996)

Cox, S. (ed.), The Strategic Air War Against Germany 1939–1945. Report of the British Bombing Survey Unit (London: Frank Cass, 1998)

Craven, W.F. and Cate, J.L. (eds.), The Army Air Forces In World War II, 7 vols. (Chicago: University of Chicago Press, 1948–58)

'Customary Law and Additional Protocol I to the Geneva Conventions for Protection of War Victims: Future Directions in Light of the US Decision Not to Ratify' (1987) 81 Proceedings of the American Society of International Law 26

D'Amato, A., 'Good faith', in Bernhardt, R. (ed.), Encyclopedia of Public International Law, 5 vols. (Amsterdam: North-Holland, 1992), vol. II, p. 599

'Megatrends in the Use of Force' (1998) 71 Naval War College International Law Studies 1

Danse, M., 'Communication relative à la formation culturelle dans l'armée aérienne au regard des dispositions de l'article 7, §1er de la Convention du 14 mai 1954' (1963) 2 Recueils de la Société de Droit Pénal Militaire et de Droit de la Guerre 147

Dansette, A., Histoire de la libération de Paris, text of 1946 (Paris: Perrin, 1994)

David, E., Principes de droit des conflits armés, 3rd edn (Brussels: Bruylant, 2002)

Davis, G.B., 'Doctor Francis Lieber's Instructions for the Government of Armies in the Field' (1907) 1 American Journal of International Law 13

Debeyre, G., 'Localités et zones sanitaires en temps de guerre' (1939) 46 Revue Générale de Droit International Public 600

Department of the Air Force, International Law: The Conduct of Armed Conflict and Air Operations, Air Force Publication 110–31, November 1976

USAF Intelligence Targeting Guide, Air Force Pamphlet 14–210 Intelligence, 1 February 1998

Department of the Army, International Law. Volume II, PAM 27-161-2, October 1962

The Law of Land Warfare, Field Manual No. 27–10, as amended 15 July 1976

Department of the Navy, *The Commander's Handbook on the Law of Naval Operations*, Naval Warfare Publication 1–14M, October 1995

Desch, T., 'The Second Protocol to the 1954 Hague Convention for the Protection of Cultural Property in the Event of Armed Conflict' (1999) 2 *Yearbook of International Humanitarian Law* 63

Desvallées, A., 'Emergence et cheminements du mot patrimoine', *Musées & Collections publiques de France*, No. 208, September 1995, p. 6

Dibon, P., 'L'Université de Leyde et la République des Lettres au 17e Siècle' (1975) 5 *Quaerendo* 4

Diderot D. and d'Alembert, J.L. (eds.), *Encyclopédie, ou Dictionnaire Raisonné des Sciences, des Arts et des Métiers, par une Société des Gens de Lettres*, 17 vols. (Paris: Briasson, David, Le Breton, Durand, 1751–7)

Dinstein, Y., 'International Criminal Law' (1985) 20 *Israel Law Review* 206

'Military Necessity', in Bernhardt, R. (ed.), *Encyclopedia of Public International Law*, 5 vols. (Amsterdam: North-Holland, 1992), vol. III, p. 395

'The Laws of Air, Missile and Nuclear Warfare' (1998) 27 *Israel Yearbook on Human Rights* 1

'Legitimate Military Objectives under the Current *Jus in Bello*' (2001) 31 *Israel Yearbook on Human Rights* 1

The Conduct of Hostilities under the Law of International Armed Conflict (Cambridge: Cambridge University Press, 2004)

Donnison, F.S.V., *Civil Affairs and Military Government North-West Europe 1944–46* (London: HMSO, 1961)

Dörmann, K., 'The Protection of Cultural Property as Laid Down in the Roerich-Pact of 15 April 1935' (1993) 6 *Humanitäres Völkerrecht Informationsschriften* 230

Doswald-Beck, L., 'Implementation of International Humanitarian Law in Future Wars' (1998) 71 *Naval War College International Law Studies* 39

Draper, G.I.A.D., 'The Geneva Conventions of 1949', 114 *Recueil des Cours de l'Académie de Droit International* (1965-I) 59

'Grotius' Place in the Development of Legal Ideas about War', in Bull, H., Kingsbury, B. and Roberts, A. (eds.), *Hugo Grotius and International Relations* (Oxford: Clarendon Press, 1992), p. 177

'Indiscriminate Attack', in Bernhardt, R. (ed.), *Encyclopedia of Public International Law*, 5 vols. (Amsterdam: North-Holland, 1992), vol. II, p. 953

Driver, M.C., 'The Protection of Cultural Property During Wartime' (2000) 9 *Review of European Community and International Environmental Law* 1

Drost, P.N., *The Crime of State. Penal Protection for Fundamental Freedoms of Persons and Peoples*, 2 vols. (Leyden: Sythoff, 1959)

Duff, K., 'Liberated Italy: from September 1943 to February 1947', in Toynbee, A. and Toynbee, V.M. (eds.), *The Realignment of Europe* (London: Oxford University Press/Royal Institute of International Affairs, 1955), p. 409

Dupuy, P.-M., 'Humanité, communauté, et efficacité du droit', in *Humanité et droit international. Mélanges René-Jean Dupuy* (Paris: Pedone, 1991), p. 133

Dupuy, R.-J., 'Communauté internationale et disparités de développement. Cours général de droit international public', 165 *Recueil des Cours de l'Académie de Droit International* (1979-IV) 9

'Conclusions du colloque', in Dupuy, R.-J. (ed.), *L'avenir du droit international dans un monde multiculturel. Colloque, La Haye, 17–19 novembre 1983* (The Hague: Martinus Nijhoff, 1984), p. 447

'La Révolution française et le droit international actuel', 214 *Recueil des Cours de l'Académie de Droit International* (1989-II) 9

'Les ambiguïtés de l'universalisme', in *Le droit international au service de la paix, de la justice et du développment. Mélanges Michel Virally* (Paris: Pedone, 1991), p. 273

Dupuy, R. J. and Leonetti, A., 'La notion de conflit armé à caractère non international', in Cassese, A. (ed.), *The New Humanitarian Law of Armed Conflict* (Naples: Editoriale Scientifica, 1979), p. 258

Dutli, M. T. (ed.), *Protection of Cultural Property in the Event of Armed Conflict. Report on the Meeting of Experts (Geneva, 5–6 October 2000)* (Geneva: ICRC, 2002)

'National Implementation of International Humanitarian Law, the Work of the ICRC Advisory Service and the Protection of Cultural Property, Including Strategies for the Ratification of the Relevant Humanitarian Law Treaties', in Dutli, M. T. (ed.), *Protection of Cultural Property in the Event of Armed Conflict. Report on the Meeting of Experts (Geneva, 5–6 October 2000)* (Geneva: ICRC, 2002), p. 69

Edmonds, J. E. and Oppenheim, L., *Land Warfare. An Exposition of the Laws and Usages of War on Land, for the Guidance of Officers of His Majesty's Army* (London: HMSO, 1911)

Eide, A., 'The New Humanitarian Law in Non-International Armed Conflict', in Cassese, A. (ed.), *The New Humanitarian Law of Armed Conflict* (Naples: Editoriale Scientifica, 1979), p. 277

Eirenberg, K. W., 'The United States Reconsiders the 1954 Hague Convention' (1994) 3 *International Journal of Cultural Property* 27

Eisenstein, E. L., *The Printing Press as an Agent of Change. Communications and Cultural Transformations in Early-Modern Europe*, 2 vols. (Cambridge: Cambridge University Press, 1979)

Ellis, J., *Cassino: The Hollow Victory. The Battle for Rome January–June 1944* (London: André Deutsch, 1984)

Ellis, L. F., *Victory in the West*, 2 vols. (London: HMSO, 1962–8)

Elsner, J. and Cardinal, R. (eds.), *The Cultures of Collecting* (London: Reaktion, 1994)

Eustathiades, C. T., 'La réserve des nécessités militaires et la Convention de La Haye pour la protection des biens culturels en cas de conflit armé', in *Hommage d'une génération de juristes au Président Basdevant* (Paris: Pedone, 1960), p. 183

Facon, P., 'Les bombardements alliés sur la France. Stratégies politiques et mémoire 1940–1945', in Chassaigne, P. and Largeaud, J.-M. (eds.), *Villes en guerre (1914–1945)* (Paris: Armand Colin, 2004), p. 73

Falk, S. L., 'Strategic Air Offensives. 3. Against Japan', in Dear, I. C. B. and Foot, M. R. D. (eds.), *The Oxford Companion to the Second World War* (Oxford: Oxford University Press, 1995), p. 1076

Fauchille, P., 'Les attentats allemands contre les biens et les personnes en Belgique et en France' (1915) 22 *Revue Générale de Droit International Public* 249

Traité de Droit International Public (Paris: Rousseau, 1921)

Fawcett, J. (ed.), *The Future of the Past. Attitudes to Conservation 1174–1974* (London: Thames and Hudson, 1976)

Fechner, F. G., 'The Fundamental Aims of Cultural Property Law' (1998) 7 *International Journal of Cultural Property* 376

Fenrick, W. J., 'The Rule of Proportionality and Protocol I in Conventional Warfare' (1982) 98 *Military Law Review* 91

Fiore, P., *Trattato di diritto internazionale pubblico*, 2nd edn, 3 vols. (Turin: Unione Tipografico-Editrice, 1884)

'La véritable mission de la science du droit international pour donner à la société internationale son organisation juridique' (1910) 12 *Revue de Droit International (2ème série)* 169

Fischer, H., 'The Protection of Cultural Property in Armed Conflicts: After the Hague Meeting of Experts' (1993) 6 *Humanitäres Völkerrecht Informationsschriften* 188

Fleck, D. (ed.), *The Handbook of Humanitarian Law in Armed Conflicts* (Oxford: Oxford University Press, 1995)

'Strategic Bombing and the Definition of Military Objectives' (1998) 27 *Israel Yearbook on Human Rights* 41

Foot, M. R. D., 'Paris rising', in Dear, I. C. B. and Foot, M. R. D. (eds.), *The Oxford Companion to the Second World War* (Oxford: Oxford University Press, 1995), p. 865

Forget, M., 'Co-operation between Air Force and Army in the French and German Air Forces during the Second World War', in Boog, H. (ed.), *The Conduct of the Air War in the Second World War. An International Comparison* (New York/Oxford: Berg, 1992), p. 415

Francioni, F., 'World Cultural Heritage List and National Sovereignty' (1993) 6 *Humanitäres Völkerrecht Informationsschriften* 195

'Patrimonio comune della cultura. Sovranità et conflitti armati', in *Studi in ricordo di Antonio Filippo Panzera*, 3 vols. (Bari: Cacucci, 1995), vol. I, p. 381

Francioni, F. and Lenzerini, F., 'The Destruction of the Buddhas of Bamyan and International Law' (2003) 14 *European Journal of International Law* 619

Frankland, A. N., 'Strategic Air Offensives. 1. Against Germany', in Dear, I. C. B. and Foot, M. R. D. (eds.), *The Oxford Companion to the Second World War* (Oxford: Oxford University Press, 1995), p. 1066

Friedmann, W., 'International Law and the Present War' (1941) 26 *Transactions of the Grotius Society* 211

Frigo, M., *La protezione dei beni culturali nel diritto internazionale* (Milan: Giuffrè, 1986)

'Reflexions sur quelques aspects juridiques de la protection internationale des biens culturels', in Istituto Internazionale di Diritto Umanitario (ed.), *The International Protection of Cultural Property. Acts of the Symposium organized on the occasion of the 30th Anniversary of the Hague Convention on the Protection of Cultural Property in the Event of Armed Conflicts* (Rome: Fondazione Europea Dragan, 1986), p. 215

'Cultural property v. cultural heritage: A "battle of concepts" in international law?' (2004) 86 *International Review of the Red Cross* 367

Frowein, J., 'The Relationship between Human Rights Regimes and Regimes of Belligerent Occupation' (1998) 28 *Israel Yearbook on Human Rights* 1

Fussell, P., *The Great War and Modern Memory* (Oxford: Oxford University Press, 1975)

Galenskaya, L., 'International Co-operation in Cultural Affairs', 198 *Recueil des Cours de l'Académie de Droit International* (1986-III) 265

Gamboni, D., *The Destruction of Art. Iconoclasm and Vandalism since the French Revolution* (London: Reaktion, 1997)

Gardam, J. G., *Non-Combatant Immunity as a Norm of International Humanitarian Law* (Dordrecht: Martinus Nijhoff, 1993)

  'Proportionality and Force in International Law' (1993) 87 *American Journal of International Law* 391

Gardam, J., 'Necessity and Proportionality in *Jus ad Bellum* and *Jus in Bello*', in Boisson de Chazournes, L. and Sands, P. (eds.), *International Law, the International Court of Justice and Nuclear Weapons* (Cambridge: Cambridge University Press, 1999), p. 275

  Necessity, Proportionality and the Use of Force by States (Cambridge: Cambridge University Press, 2004)

Garner, J. W., 'Some Questions of International Law in the European War' (1915) 9 *American Journal of International Law* 72

  International Law and the World War (London: Longmans, Green, 1920)

  'La réglementation internationale de la guerre aérienne' (1923) 30 *Revue Générale de Droit International Public* 372

  'Proposed Rules for the Regulation of Aerial Warfare' (1924) 18 *American Journal of International Law* 56

  'Some Observations on the Codification of International Law' (1925) 19 *American Journal of International Law* 327

  'International Regulation of Air Warfare' (1932) 3 *Air Law Review* 103

  'Les lois de la guerre. Leur valeur, leur avenir' (1936) 17 *Revue de Droit International (3ème série)* 96

Garrett, S. A., *Ethics and Airpower in World War II. The British Bombing of German Cities* (New York: St Martin's Press, 1993)

Gasser, H.-P., 'Protection of the Civilian Population', in Fleck, D. (ed.), *The Handbook of Humanitarian Law in Armed Conflicts* (Oxford: Oxford University Press, 1995), p. 209

Gentili, A., *De Jure Belli Libri Tres*, first published 1598, text of 1612, translated by J. C. Rolfe (Oxford: Clarendon Press, 1933)

Georgopoulos, T., 'Avez-vous bien dit "crime contre la culture"? La protection internationale des monuments historiques' (2001) 54 *Revue Hellénique de Droit International* 459

Giannini, M. S., 'I beni culturali' (1976) 26 *Rivista trimestriale di diritto pubblico* 3

Gimbrère, S. and Pronk, T., 'The Protection of Cultural Property: From UNESCO to the European Community with Special Reference to the Case of the Netherlands' (1992) 28 *Netherlands Yearbook of International Law* 223

Glaser, S., 'La protection internationale des valeurs humaines' (1957) 61 *Revue Générale de Droit International Public* 211

Goldberg, A., 'Commentary', in Boog, H. (ed.), *The Conduct of the Air War in the Second World War. An International Comparison* (New York/Oxford: Berg, 1992), p. 270

Goldgar, A., *Impolite Learning. Conduct and Community in the Republic of Letters 1680–1750* (New Haven: Yale University Press, 1995)

Goldmann, K., 'The Treasure of the Berlin State Museums and Its Allied Capture: Remarks and Questions' (1998) 7 *International Journal of Cultural Property* 308

Goodman, D., *The Republic of Letters. A Cultural History of the French Enlightenment* (Ithaca: Cornell University Press, 1994)

Gordon, J. B., 'The UNESCO Convention on the Illicit Movement of Art Treasures' (1971) 12 *Harvard International Law Journal* 537

Goy, R. H. M., 'The International Protection of the Cultural and Natural Heritage' (1973) 4 *Netherlands Yearbook of International Law* 117

Goy, R., 'La question de Jérusalem à l'UNESCO' (1976) 22 *Annuaire Français de Droit International* 420

'La destruction intentionnelle du patrimoine culturel en droit international' (2005) 109 *Revue Générale de Droit International Public* 273

Goyder, J., 'Scheduling Monuments: The Rose Theatre Case' (1992) 1 *International Journal of Cultural Property* 353

Graham, G. M., 'Protection and Reversion of Cultural Property: Issues of Definition and Justification' (1987) 21 *International Lawyer* 755

Graven, J., *Le difficile progrès du règne de la justice et de la paix internationales par le droit des origines à la Société des Nations* (Paris: Pedone, 1970)

Graves, R., *Goodbye to All That*, text of 1929 (London: Penguin, 1960)

Green, L., 'What is – Why Is There – the Law of War?' (1998) 71 *Naval War College International Law Studies* 141

Green, L. C., *The Contemporary Law of Armed Conflict*, 2nd edn (Manchester: Manchester University Press, 2000)

Greenspan, M., *The Modern Law of Land Warfare* (Berkeley: University of California Press, 1959)

Greenwood, C., 'The Relationship between *Ius ad Bellum* and *Ius in Bello*' (1983) 9 *Review of International Studies* 221

'The Concept of War in Modern International Law' (1987) 36 *International and Comparative Law Quarterly* 283

'Customary Law Status of the 1977 Geneva Protocols', in Delissen, A. J. M. and Tanja, G. J. (eds.), *Humanitarian Law of Armed Conflict, Challenges Ahead. Essays in Honour of Frits Kalshoven* (Dordrecht: Martinus Nijhoff, 1991), p. 93

'The Administration of Occupied Territory in International Law', in Playfair, E. (ed.), *International Law and the Administration of Occupied Territories. Two Decades of Israeli Occupation of the West Bank and Gaza Strip* (Oxford: Clarendon Press, 1992), p. 242

'Customary International Law and the First Geneva Protocol of 1977 in the Gulf Conflict', in Rowe, P. (ed.), *The Gulf War 1990–91 in International and English Law* (London: Routledge/Sweet & Maxwell, 1993), p. 63

'Historical Development and Legal Basis', in Fleck, D. (ed.), *The Handbook of Humanitarian Law in Armed Conflicts* (Oxford: Oxford University Press, 1995), p. 1

'Scope of Application of Humanitarian Law', in Fleck, D. (ed.), *The Handbook of Humanitarian Law in Armed Conflicts* (Oxford: Oxford University Press, 1995), p. 39

'International Humanitarian Law and the Tadic Case' (1996) 7 *European Journal of International Law* 265

'Jus ad bellum and jus in bello in the Nuclear Weapons Advisory Opinion', in Boisson de Chazournes, L. and Sands, P. (eds.), *International Law, the International Court of Justice and Nuclear Weapons* (Cambridge: Cambridge University Press, 1999), p. 247

Grégoire, l'abbé, *Œuvres de l'abbé Grégoire. Tome II. Grégoire député à la Convention nationale* (Nendeln/Paris: KTO Press/EDHIS), (1977)

Grotius, H., *De Jure Belli ac Pacis Libri Tres*, first published 1625, text of 1646, translated by F.W. Kelsey (Oxford: Clarendon Press, 1925)

Guelle, J., *Précis des lois de la guerre sur terre. Commentaire pratique à l'usage des officiers de l'armée active, de la réserve et de la territoriale*, 2 vols. (Paris: Pedone-Lauriel, 1884)

Guggenheim, P., 'La souveraineté dans l'histoire du droit des gens. De Vitoria à Vattel', in Ibler, V. (ed.), *Mélanges offerts à Juraj Andrassy* (The Hague: Martinus Nijhoff, 1968), p. 111

Henckaerts, J.-M., 'New Rules for the Protection of Cultural Property in Armed Conflict' (1999) 81 *International Review of the Red Cross* 593

Henckaerts, J.-M. and Doswald-Beck, L., *Customary International Humanitarian Law*, 3 vols. (Cambridge: Cambridge University Press, 2005)

Haggenmacher, P., *Grotius et la doctrine de la guerre juste* (Paris: PUF, 1983)

'Grotius and Gentili: A Reassessment of Thomas E. Holland's Inaugural Lecture', in Bull, H., Kingsbury, B. and Roberts, A. (eds.), *Hugo Grotius and International Relations* (Oxford: Clarendon Press, 1992), p. 133

Hale, J., *The Civilization of Europe in the Renaissance* (London: Fontana, 1993)

Hampson, F.J., 'Proportionality and Necessity in the Gulf Conflict' (1992) 86 *Proceedings of the American Society of International Law* 45

'Means and Methods of Warfare in the Conflict in the Gulf', in Rowe, P. (ed.), *The Gulf War 1990–91 in International and English Law* (London: Routledge/Sweet & Maxwell, 1993), p. 89

Hanke, H.M., 'The 1923 Hague Rules of Air Warfare. A Contribution to the Development of International Law Protecting Civilians from Air Attack' (1993) 75 *International Review of the Red Cross* 12

Hanson, J., 'Warsaw Risings', in Dear, I.C.B. and Foot, M.R.D. (eds.), *The Oxford Companion to the Second World War* (Oxford: Oxford University Press, 1995), p. 1260

Hapgood, D. and Richardson, D., *Monte Cassino* (London: Angus & Robertson, 1984)

Hardesty, V., 'The Soviet Air Force: Doctrine, Organisation and Technology', in Boog, H. (ed.), *The Conduct of the Air War in the Second World War. An International Comparison* (New York/Oxford: Berg, 1992), p. 207

Harris, A., *Bomber Offensive* (London: Collins, 1947)

Hartigan, R.S., *Lieber's Code and the Law of War* (Chicago: Precedent, 1983)

Haunton, M., 'Peacekeeping, Occupation and Cultural Property' (1993) 6 *Humanitäres Völkerrecht Informationsschriften* 199

Hecks, K., *Bombing 1939–45. The Air Offensive Against Land Targets in World War II* (London: Robert Hale, 1990)

Herczegh, G., *Development of International Humanitarian Law* (Budapest: Akadémiai Kiadó, 1984)

Heydte, F.A. Freiherr von der, 'Military Objectives', in Bernhardt, R. (ed.), *Encyclopedia of Public International Law*, 5 vols. (Amsterdam: North-Holland, 1992), vol. III, p. 397

Hladík, J., 'Meeting of the High Contracting Parties to the Hague Convention for the Protection of Cultural Property in the Event of Armed Conflict of 1954' (1996) 5 *International Journal of Cultural Property* 339

Hladík, J., 'The Third Meeting of the High Contracting Parties to the Hague Convention for the Protection of Cultural Property in the Event of Armed Conflict of 1954 (Paris, November 13, 1997)' (1998) 7 *International Journal of Cultural Property* 268

'The Review Process of the 1954 Hague Convention for the Protection of Cultural Property in the Event of Armed Conflict and Its Impact on International Humanitarian Law' (1998) 1 *Yearbook of International Humanitarian Law* 313

'The 1954 Hague Convention for the Protection of Cultural Property in the Event of Armed Conflict and the Notion of Military Necessity' (1999) 81 *International Review of the Red Cross* 621

'Reporting System Under the 1954 Convention for the Protection of Cultural Property in the Event of Armed Conflict' (2000) 82 *International Review of the Red Cross* 1001

'The Control System under the Hague Convention for the Protection of Cultural Property in the Event of Armed Conflict 1954 and its Second Protocol' (2001) 4 *Yearbook of International Humanitarian Law* 419

'Protection of Cultural Property during Hostilities: Meeting of Experts in Latin America' (2002) 84 *International Review of the Red Cross* 697

'UNESCO's Activities for the Implementation and Promotion of the 1954 Hague Convention for the Protection of Cultural Property in the Event of Armed Conflict and its Two Protocols', in Dutli, M.T. (ed.), *Protection of Cultural Property in the Event of Armed Conflict. Report on the Meeting of Experts (Geneva, 5–6 October 2000)* (Geneva: ICRC, 2002), p. 57

'Marking of Cultural Property with the Distinctive Emblem of the 1954 Hague Convention for the Protection of Cultural Property in the Event of Armed Conflict' (2004) 86 *International Review of the Red Cross* 379

'The UNESCO Declaration Concerning the Intentional Destruction of Cultural Heritage' (2004) 9 *Art Antiquity and Law* 215

'Fiftieth Anniversary of the Hague Convention: Commemorative Symposium, Paris, 14th May 2004' (2004) 9 *Art Antiquity and Law* 413

Holland, T.E., *Studies in International Law* (Oxford: Clarendon Press, 1898)

The Laws of War on Land (Written and Unwritten) (Oxford: Clarendon Press, 1908)

Lectures on International Law, edited by T.A. Walker and W.L. Walker (London: Sweet & Maxwell, 1933)

Hollander, B., *The International Law of Art for Lawyers Collectors and Artists* (London: Bowes & Bowes, 1959)

Horne, J. and Kramer, A., *German Atrocities 1914. A History of Denial* (New Haven/ London: Yale University Press, 2001)

Hornung, J., 'Note sur la répression des délits contre le droit des gens et plus spécialement sur celle des délits contre les lois de la guerre' (1880) 12 *Revue de Droit International* 104

Howard, M., 'The Battle in the Air Ministry', *Times Literary Supplement*, 21 August 1998, p. 10

Iluyomade, B. O., 'The Scope and Content of a Complaint of Abuse of Right in International Law' (1975) 16 *Harvard International Law Journal* 47

'Implementing Limitations on the Use of Force: The Doctrine of Proportionality and Necessity' (1992) 86 *Proceedings of the American Society of International Law* 39

Institut de droit international, IVme Commission, 'Déclaration de Bruxelles concernant les lois et coutumes de la guerre' (1875) 7 *Revue de Droit International* 284

  IVme Commission, 'Lois et coutumes de la guerre. Examen de la déclaration de Bruxelles. Rapport de M. Rolin-Jaequemyns' (1875) 7 *Revue de Droit International* 447

'Les lois de la guerre – Appel aux belligérants et à la presse' (1877) 9 *Revue de Droit International* 133

'Les lois de la guerre sur terre. Manuel publié par l'Institut de droit international' (1881–2) 5 *Annuaire de l'Institut de Droit International* 157

Israel National Section of the International Commission of Jurists, *The Rule of Law in the Areas Administered by Israel* (1981)

Jackson, W., *The Mediterranean and Middle East. Volume VI. Part II* (London: HMSO, 1987)

  The Mediterranean and Middle East. Volume VI. Part III (London: HMSO, 1988)

Jardine, L., *Worldly Goods. A New History of the Renaissance* (London: Papermac, 1997)

Jayme, E., 'Antonio Canova, la repubblica delle arti ed il diritto internazionale' (1992) 75 *Rivista di diritto internazionale* 889

Jenks, C. W., 'The General Welfare as a Legal Interest', in *Jus et Societas. Essays in Tribute to Wolfgang Friedmann* (The Hague: Martinus Nijhoff, 1979), p. 151

Jennings, R. Y., 'Open Towns' (1945) 22 *British Yearbook of International Law* 258

Jovanović, S., *Restriction des compétences discrétionnaires des états en droit international* (Paris: Pedone, 1988)

Kalshoven, F., *Assisting the Victims of Armed Conflict and Other Disasters* (Dordrecht: Martinus Nijhoff, 1989)

Kalshoven, F. and Sandoz, Y. (eds.), *Implementation of International Humanitarian Law* (Dordrecht: Martinus Nijhoff, 1989)

Kalshoven, F. and Zegveld, L., *Constraints on the Waging of War. An Introduction to International Humanitarian Law*, 3rd edn (Geneva: ICRC, 2001)

Kastenberg, J. E., 'The Legal Regime for Protecting Cultural Property During Armed Conflict' (1997) 42 *Air Force Law Review* 277

Keen, M. H., *The Laws of War in the Late Middle Ages* (London: Routledge & Kegan Paul, 1965)

Kiss, A., 'Abuse of Rights', in Bernhardt, R. (ed.), *Encyclopedia of Public International Law*, 5 vols. (Amsterdam: North-Holland, 1992), vol. I, p. 4

Kiss, A.-C. (ed.), *Répertoire de la Pratique Française en matière de Droit International Public*, 7 vols. (Paris: Editions du CNRS, 1962–72)

Klüber, J.-L., *Droit des gens moderne de l'Europe*, 2 vols. (Paris: J.-P. Aillaud, 1831)

Kolb, R., *Ius in bello. Le droit international des conflits armés* (Basel/Brussels: Helbing & Lichtenhahn/Bruylant, 2003)

Kooijmans, P. H., 'In the Shadowland between Civil War and Civil Strife: Some Reflections on the Standard-Setting Process', in Delissen, A. J. M. and Tanja, G. J. (eds.), *Humanitarian Law of Armed Conflict, Challenges Ahead. Essays in Honour of Frits Kalshoven* (Dordrecht: Martinus Nijhoff, 1991), p. 225

Kowalski, W. W., *Art Treasures and War*, edited by T. Schadla-Hall (Leicester: Institute of Art and Law, 1998)

Krebs, G., 'The Japanese Air Forces', in Boog, H. (ed.), *The Conduct of the Air War in the Second World War. An International Comparison* (New York/Oxford: Berg, 1992), p. 228

Kunz, J. L., 'Plus de lois de la guerre?' (1934) 41 *Revue Générale de Droit International Public* 22

 'The Chaotic Status of the Laws of War' (1951) 45 *American Journal of International Law* 37

Kwakwa, E. K., *The International Law of Armed Conflict: Personal and Material Fields of Application* (Dordrecht: Kluwer, 1992)

La Guerre de 1914. Recueil de documents intéressant le droit international, 2 vols. (Paris: Pedone, undated)

Lauterpacht, H., 'Règles générales du droit de la paix', 62 *Recueil des Cours de l'Académie de Droit International* (1937-IV) 95

 'The Problem of the Revision of the Law of War' (1952) 29 *British Yearbook of International Law* 360

 'Codification and Development of International Law' (1955) 49 *American Journal of International Law* 16

Lawrence, B., 'Extrait d'une lettre adressée par M. Beach Lawrence au Secrétaire-Général de l'Institut' (1875) 7 *Revue de Droit International* 526

Lawrence, T. J., *The Principles of International Law*, 7th edn, Winfield, P. H. (ed.) (London: Macmillan, 1930)

Lefranc, O., 'Les problèmes juridiques posés devant la XIIe session de la Conférence Générale de l'UNESCO (Novembre–Décembre 1962)' (1962) 8 *Annuaire Français de Droit International* 638

Le Goff, M., 'Les bombardements aériens dans la guerre civile espagnole' (1938) 45 *Revue Générale de Droit International Public* 581

Lemaire, R. M., 'La doctrine contemporaine de sauvegarde du patrimoine monumental' (1982) 49 *Rivista di Studi Politici Internazionali* 587

Levie, H. S., *Protection of War Victims: Protocol I to the 1949 Geneva Conventions*, 4 vols. (Dobbs Ferry: Oceana, 1979–81)

Levine, A. J., *The Strategic Bombing of Germany, 1940–1945* (Westport: Praeger, 1992)

Levy, M. and Salvadori, M., *Why Buildings Fall Down. How Structures Fail* (New York: Norton, 1992)

Lewis, M. W., 'The Law of Aerial Bombardment in the 1991 Gulf War' (2003) 97 *American Journal of International Law* 481
Liddell Hart, B. H., *History of the Second World War* (London: Cassell, 1970)
Lindop, G., 'With a Cold Tongue or a Piece of Beef', *Times Literary Supplement*, 31 July 1998, p. 9
Lindqvist, S., *A History of Bombing* (London: Granta, 2001)
Lippmann, M., 'Art and Ideology in the Third Reich: The Protection of Cultural Property and the Humanitarian Law of War' (1998–9) 17 *Dickinson Journal of International Law* 1
Lough, J., *The Encyclopédie* (London: Longman, 1971)
Lowenthal, D., *The Past is a Foreign Country* (Cambridge: Cambridge University Press, 1985)
  'Heritages for Europe' (1995) 4 *International Journal of Cultural Property* 377
Lowenthal, D., *The Heritage Crusade and the Spoils of History* (New York: Free Press, 1996)
Lucas, C., 'La civilisation de la guerre' (1877) 9 *Revue de Droit International* 114
McCamley, N. J., *Saving Britain's Art Treasures* (Barnsley: Leo Cooper, 2003)
McCoubrey, H., *International Humanitarian Law. Modern Developments in the Limitation of Warfare*, 2nd edn (Aldershot: Ashgate/Dartmouth, 1998)
MacIsaac, D. (ed.), *The United States Strategic Bombing Survey*, 10 vols. (New York: Garland, 1976)
McNair, A., *The Law of Treaties* (Oxford: Clarendon Press, 1961)
Maier, K. A., 'Total War and Operational Air Warfare' in Maier, K. A. *et al.* (eds.), *Germany and the Second World War*, 6 vols., translated by P. S. Falla, D. S. McMurry and E. Osers (Oxford: Clarendon Press, 1991), vol. II, p. 33
  'The Operational Air War until the Battle of Britain', in Maier, K. A. *et al.* (eds.), *Germany and the Second World War*, 6 vols., translated by P. S. Falla, D. S. McMurry and E. Osers (Oxford: Clarendon Press, 1991), vol. II, p. 327
  'The Battle of Britain', in Maier, K. A. *et al.* (eds.), *Germany and the Second World War*, 6 vols., translated by P. S. Falla, D. S. McMurry and E. Osers (Oxford: Clarendon Press, 1991), vol. II, p. 374
Mailler, A., *De la distinction des combattants et non combattants comme base du droit de guerre* (Paris: Pedone, 1916)
Maine, H. S., *International Law*, 2nd edn (London: John Murray, 1894)
Mainetti, V., 'De nouvelles perspectives pour la protection des biens culturels en cas de conflit armé: l'entrée en vigueur du Deuxième Protocole relatif à la Convention de La Haye de 1954' (2004) 86 *International Review of the Red Cross* 337
Makagiansar, M., 'The Thirtieth Anniversary of the Convention for the Protection of Cultural Property in the Event of Armed Conflict (The Hague, 1954): Results and Prospects', in Istituto Internazionale di Diritto Umanitario (ed.), *The International Protection of Cultural Property. Acts of the Symposium organized on the occasion of the 30th Anniversary of the Hague Convention on the Protection of Cultural Property in the Event of Armed Conflicts* (Rome: Fondazione Europea Dragan, 1986), p. 27
Malintoppi, A., 'La protezione "speciale" della Città del Vaticano in caso di conflitto armato' (1960) 43 *Rivista di diritto internazionale* 607

Manisty, H. F., 'Aerial Warfare and the Laws of War' (1922) 7 *Transactions of the Grotius Society* 33

Manual of Air Force Law, 2nd edn (London: HMSO, 1933, reprinted without change 1939)

Marcolin, A., *Firenze 1943–'45* (Florence: Edizioni Medicea, 1994)

Marks, S. P., 'Education, Science, Culture and Information', in Schachter, O. and Joyner, C. C. (eds.), *United Nations Legal Order*, 2 vols. (Cambridge: Cambridge University Press/American Society of International Law, 1995), vol. II, p. 577

Marot, P., 'L'abbé Grégoire et le vandalisme révolutionnaire' (1980) 49 *Revue de l'art* 36

Martens, F., 'Lettre de M. de Martens à S. A. I. le Duc Nicolas de Leuchtenberg' (1881) 13 *Revue de Droit International* 309

Martens, F. de, *Traité de Droit International*, translated by A. Léo, 2 vols. (Paris: A. Marescq Ainé, 1887)

Martens, G. F. de, *Précis du Droit des Gens Moderne de l'Europe*, new edn, 2 vols. (Paris: Aillaud, Heideloff, 1831)

Mastalir, R. W., 'A proposal for protecting the "cultural" and "property" aspects of cultural property under international law' (1992–3) 16 *Fordham International Law Journal* 1033

Matteucci, M., 'Su la Convenzione per la protezione dei beni culturali in caso di conflitto armato' (1958) 41 *Rivista di diritto internazionale* 670

Mazza, R., 'La Convenzione de l'Aja del 1954 e la Convenzione di Parigi del 1972: sistema di protezioni paralleli', in Ciciriello, M. C. (ed.), *La protezione del patrimonio mondiale culturale e naturale a venticinque anni dalla Convenzione dell'UNESCO* (Naples: Editoriale Scientifica, 1997), p. 255

'La protezione internazionale dei beni culturali mobili in caso di conflitto armato: possibili sviluppi', in Paone, P. (ed.), *La protezione internazionale e la circolazione comunitaria dei beni culturali mobili* (Naples: Editoriale Scientifica, 1998), p. 119

Meranghini, U., 'Difesa dei beni culturali in caso di guerra' (1961) 2 *Recueils de la Société Internationale de Droit Pénal Militaire et Droit de la Guerre* 144

Mérignhac. A., *Traité de droit public international*, 3 vols. (Paris: LGDJ, 1905–12)

'De la responsabilité pénale des actes criminels commis au cours de la guerre de 1914–1918' (1920) 1 *Revue de Droit International (3ème série)* 34

Mérignhac, A. and Lémonon, E., *Le Droit des Gens et la Guerre de 1914–1918* (Paris: Recueil Sirey, 1921)

Meron, T., 'The Geneva Conventions as Customary Law' (1987) 81 *American Journal of International Law* 348

Human Rights and Humanitarian Norms as Customary Law (Oxford: Clarendon Press, 1989)

'International Criminalization of Internal Atrocities' (1995) 89 *American Journal of International Law* 566

War Crimes Law Comes of Age. Essays (Oxford: Clarendon Press, 1998)

'The Humanization of Humanitarian Law' (2000) 94 *American Journal of International Law* 239

Merryman, J. H., 'Two Ways of Thinking About Cultural Property' (1986) 80 *American Journal of International Law* 831
  'The Public Interest in Cultural Property' (1989) 77 *California Law Review* 339
  'The Nation and the Object' (1994) 3 *International Journal of Cultural Property* 61
  'Note on *The Marquis de Somerueles*' (1996) 5 *International Journal of Cultural Property* 321
Messenger, C., *'Bomber' Harris and the Strategic Bombing Offensive, 1939–45* (London: Arms & Armour Press, 1984)
  'Berlin Air Offensive', in Dear, I.C.B. and Foot, M.R.D. (eds.), *The Oxford Companion to the Second World War* (Oxford: Oxford University Press, 1995), p. 124
  'Dresden, Raid On', in Dear, I.C.B. and Foot, M.R.D. (eds.), *The Oxford Companion to the Second World War* (Oxford: Oxford University Press, 1995), p. 311
Meyer, D.A., 'The 1954 Hague Cultural Property Convention and its Emergence into Customary International Law' (1993) 11 *Boston University International Law Journal* 349
Meyer, M.A. (ed.), *Armed Conflict and the New Law: Aspects of the 1977 Geneva Protocols and the 1981 Weapons Convention* (London: BIICL, 1989)
Meyrowitz, H., 'Le bombardement stratégique d'après le Protocole additionnel I aux Conventions de Genève' (1981) 41 *Zeitschrift für ausländisches öffentliches Recht und Völkerrecht* 1
Michel, H., *The Second World War*, translated by D. Parmée (London: André Deutsch, 1975)
  Paris Résistant (Paris: Albin Michel, 1982)
Middlebrook, M. and Everitt, C., *The Bomber Command War Diaries. An Operational Reference Book 1939–1945*, revised edn (Leicester: Midland, 1996)
Miller, P.N., *Peiresc's Europe. Learning and Virtue in the Seventeenth Century* (London: Yale University Press, 2000)
Millin de Grandmaison, A.-L., *Antiquités nationales, ou Recueil de monumens pour servir à l'histoire générale et particulière de l'empire françois, tels que tombeaux, inscriptions, statues, vitraux, fresques, etc.; tirés des abbayes, monastères, châteaux, et autres lieux devenus domaines nationaux*, 5 vols. (Paris: Drouhin, 1790–9)
Moir, L., 'The Historical Development of the Application of Humanitarian Law in Non-International Armed Conflicts to 1949' (1998) 47 *International and Comparative Law Quarterly* 337
  The Law of Internal Armed Conflict (Cambridge: Cambridge University Press, 2002)
Molony, C.J.C., *The Mediterranean and Middle East. Volume V* (London: HMSO, 1973)
  The Mediterranean and Middle East. Volume VI. Part I (London: HMSO, 1984)
Moltke Count von, 'Lettre de M. le comte de Moltke à M. Bluntschli' (1881) 13 *Revue de Droit International* 80
Monden, A. and Wils, G., 'Art Objects as Common Heritage of Mankind' (1986) 19 *Revue Belge de Droit International* 327
'Monte Cassino, Battles for', in Dear, I.C.B. and Foot, M.R.D. (eds.), *The Oxford Companion to the Second World War* (Oxford: Oxford University Press, 1995), p. 756

Montmorency, E.G. de, 'The Washington Conference and Air-Law in Disarmament' (1922) 7 *Transactions of the Grotius Society* 109

Moore, J.B. (ed.), *A Digest of International Law*, 8 vols. (Washington, DC: Government Printing Office, 1906)

International Law and Some Current Illusions, and Other Essays (New York: Macmillan, 1924)

Mose, G.M., 'The Destruction of Churches and Mosques in Bosnia-Herzegovina: Seeking a Rights-Based Approach to the Protection of Religious Cultural Property' (1996–7) 3 *Buffalo Journal of International Law* 108

Mulder, B., 'Les lacunes de droit international public' (1926) 7 *Revue de Droit International (3ème série)* 555

Müller, M.M., 'Cultural Heritage Protection: Legitimacy, Property, and Functionalism' (1998) 7 *International Journal of Cultural Property* 395

Muranghini, U., 'Difesa dei Beni Culturali in caso di Guerra' (1961) 2 *Recueils de la Société de Droit Pénal Militaire et Droit de la Guerre* 144

Murphy, J.F., 'Some Legal (and a Few Ethical) Dimensions of the Collateral Damage Resulting from NATO's Kosovo Campaign' (2001) 31 *Israel Yearbook on Human Rights* 51

Murray, W., 'The Influence of Pre-War Anglo-American Doctrine on the Air Campaigns of the Second World War', in Boog, H. (ed.), *The Conduct of the Air War in the Second World War. An International Comparison* (New York/Oxford: Berg, 1992), p. 235

Nafziger, J.A.R., 'UNESCO-Centred Management of International Conflict Over Cultural Property' (1976) 27 *Hastings Law Journal* 1051

'International Penal Aspects of Protecting Cultural Property' (1985) 19 *International Lawyer* 835

Nahlik, S.E., 'Des crimes contre les biens culturels' (1959) 29 *Yearbook of the Association des Anciens Auditeurs* 20

'La protection internationale des biens culturels en cas de conflit armé', 120 *Recueil des Cours de l'Académie de Droit International* (1967-II) 61

'L'intérêt de l'humanité à proteger son patrimoine culturel' (1967–8) 37–8 *Yearbook of the Association des Anciens Auditeurs* 156

'International Law and the Protection of Cultural Property in Armed Conflict' (1976) 27 *Hastings Law Journal* 1069

'On Some Deficiencies of the Hague Convention of 1954 on the Protection of Cultural Property in the Event of Armed Conflict' (1976) 5 *Yearbook of the Association des Anciens Auditeurs* 100

'The Case of the Displaced Art Treasures' (1980) 23 *German Yearbook of International Law* 255

'Convention for the Protection of Cultural Property in the Event of Armed Conflict, The Hague 1954: General and Special Protection', in Istituto Internazionale di Diritto Umanitario (ed.), *The International Protection of Cultural Property. Acts of the Symposium organized on the occasion of the 30th Anniversary of the Hague Convention on the Protection of Cultural Property in the Event of Armed Conflicts* (Rome: Fondazione Europea Dragan, 1986), p. 87

'Protection of Cultural Property', in *International Dimensions of Humanitarian Law* (Geneva/Paris/Dordrecht: Henry Dunant Institute/UNESCO/Martinus Nijhoff, 1988), p. 203

Naval War College, *International Law Topics and Discussions 1914* (Washington, DC: US Government Printing Office, 1915)

International Law Documents. Regulation of Maritime Warfare 1925 (Washington, DC: US Government Printing Office, 1926)

Nicholas, L. H., *The Rape of Europa. The Fate of Europe's Treasures in the Third Reich and the Second World War* (London: Papermac, 1995)

Niecówna, H., 'Sovereign Rights to Cultural Property' (1971) 4 *Polish Yearbook of International Law* 239

Nieć, H., 'The "Human Dimension" of the Protection of Cultural Property in the Event of Armed Conflict' (1993) 6 *Humanitäres Völkerrecht Informationsschriften* 204

Noblecourt, A., *Protection of Cultural Property in the Event of Armed Conflict* (Paris: UNESCO, 1956)

Norman, G., *The Hermitage. The Biography of a Great Museum* (London: Pimlico, 1997)

Nys, E., *Études de droit international et de droit politique (1ère série)* (Brussels: Castaigne, 1896)

'François Lieber. Les Instructions pour les armées des États-Unis. Les conférences européennes' (1902) 4 *Revue de Droit International (2ème série)* 683

'La guerre et la déclaration de guerre. Quelques notes' (1905) 7 *Revue de Droit International (2ème série)* 517

Le droit international. Les principes, les théories, les faits, 3 vols. (Brussels: Castaigne, 1904–6)

'Le droit des gens et les écrits de Jean-Jacques Rousseau' (1907) 9 *Revue de Droit International (2ème série)* 77

'Le droit de la nature et le droit des gens au XVIIe siècle' (1914) 16 *Revue de Droit International (2ème série)* 245

O'Brien, W. V., *The Conduct of Just and Limited War* (New York: Praeger, 1981)

O'Connell, M. E., 'Occupation Failures and the Legality of Armed Conflict: The Case of Iraqi Cultural Property' (2004) 9 *Art Antiquity and Law* 323

O'Connor, J. F., *Good Faith in International Law* (Aldershot: Dartmouth, 1991)

Oeter, S., 'Indiscriminate Attack. Addendum', in Bernhardt, R. (ed.), *Encyclopedia of Public International Law*, 5 vols. (Amsterdam: North-Holland, 1992), vol. II, p. 956

'Methods and Means of Combat', in Fleck, D. (ed.), *The Handbook of Humanitarian Law in Armed Conflicts* (Oxford: Oxford University Press, 1995), p. 105

Official Records of the Diplomatic Conference on the Reaffirmation and Development of International Humanitarian Law Applicable in Armed Conflicts. Geneva (1974–1977), 17 vols. (Bern: Federal Political Department, 1978)

O'Keefe, P. J., *Commentary on the UNESCO 1970 Convention on Illicit Traffic* (Leicester: Institute of Art and Law, 2000)

'The First Protocol to the Hague Convention Fifty Years On' (2004) 9 *Art Antiquity and Law* 99

O'Keefe, P.J. and Prott, L.V., 'Cultural Property', in Bernhardt, R. (ed.), *Encyclopedia of Public International Law*, 5 vols. (Amsterdam: North-Holland, 1992), vol. I, p. 890

Oppenheim, L., *International Law. A Treatise*, 2 vols. (London: Longmans, Green, 1905–6)

International Law. A Treatise, 2nd edn, 2 vols. (London: Longmans, Green, 1912)

International Law. A Treatise, 3rd edn, edited by R.F. Roxburgh, 2 vols. (London: Longmans, Green, 1920–1)

International Law. A Treatise, 5th edn, edited by H. Lauterpacht, 2 vols. (London: Longmans, Green, 1935–7)

International Law. A Treatise. Volume II: Disputes, War and Neutrality, 6th edn, edited by H. Lauterpacht (London: Longmans, Green, 1940)

International Law. A Treatise. Volume II: Disputes, War and Neutrality, 6th revised edn, edited by H. Lauterpacht (London: Longmans, Green, 1944)

International Law. A Treatise, 7th edn, edited by H. Lauterpacht, 2 vols. (London: Longmans, Green, 1948–52)

Oppermann, T., 'Cultural and Intellectual Co-operation', in Bernhardt, R. (ed.), *Encyclopedia of Public International Law*, 5 vols. (Amsterdam: North-Holland, 1992), vol. I, p. 886

Osgood, R.E. and Tucker, R.W., *Force, Order, and Justice* (Baltimore: Johns Hopkins Press, 1967)

Overy, R.J., 'Air Power in the Second World War: Historical Themes and Theories', in Boog, H. (ed.), *The Conduct of the Air War in the Second World War. An International Comparison* (New York/Oxford: Berg, 1992), p. 7

Overy, R., 'Strategic Air Offensives. 2. Against Europe Outside Germany', in Dear, I.C.B. and Foot, M.R.D. (eds.), *The Oxford Companion to the Second World War* (Oxford: Oxford University Press, 1995), p. 1073

Padelford, N.J., *International Law and Diplomacy in the Spanish Civil Strife* (New York: Macmillan, 1939)

Panzera, A.F., *La tutela dei beni culturali in tempo di guerra* (Turin: Giappichelli, 1993)

Pardo, A. and Christol, C.Q., 'The Common Interest: Tension Between the Whole and the Parts', in Macdonald, R.St J. and Johnston, D.M. (eds.), *The Structure and Process of International Law: Essays in Legal Philosophy Doctrine and Theory* (The Hague: Martinus Nijhoff, 1983), p. 643

Parent, M., 'La problématique du patrimoine architectural légal: Les "monuments historiques"' (1980) 49 *Revue de l'art* 84

Parieu E. de, 'Lettre de M.E. de Parieu en réponse au questionnaire' (1875) 7 *Revue de Droit International* 519

Parks, W.H., 'Air War and the Law of War' (1990) 32 *Air Force Law Review* 1

'Air War and the Laws of War', in Boog, H. (ed.), *The Conduct of the Air War in the Second World War. An International Comparison* (New York/Oxford: Berg, 1992), p. 310

'"Precision" and "Area" Bombing: Who Did Which, and When?' (1995) 18 *Journal of Strategic Studies* 145

'The Protection of Civilians from Air Warfare' (1998) 27 *Israel Yearbook on Human Rights* 65
Partsch, K.J., 'La mise en œuvre des droits de l'homme par l'UNESCO. Remarques sur un système particulier' (1990) 36 *Annuaire Français de Droit International* 482
'Protection of Cultural Property', in Fleck, D. (ed.), *The Handbook of Humanitarian Law in Armed Conflicts* (Oxford: Oxford University Press, 1995), p. 377
Paul, V., 'The Abuse of Rights and Bona Fides in International Law' (1977) 28 *Österreichisches Zeitschrift für öffentliches Recht und Völkerrecht* 107
'Pays-Bas. La protection des monuments et objets historiques et artistiques contre les destructions de la guerre. Proposition de la Société néerlandaise d'archéologie' (1919) 26 *Revue Générale de Droit International Public* 329
Penna, L.R., 'Customary International Law and Protocol I: An Analysis of Some Provisions', in Swinarski, C. (ed.), *Studies and Essays on International Humanitarian Law and Red Cross Principles in Honour of Jean Pictet* (Geneva/ The Hague: ICRC/Martinus Nijhoff, 1984), p. 201
Phillipson, C., *International Law and the Great War* (London: T. Fisher Unwin/Sweet & Maxwell, 1915)
Phuong, C., 'The Protection of Iraqi Cultural Property' (2004) 53 *International and Comparative Law Quarterly* 985
Pictet, J. (ed.), *Geneva Convention relative to the Protection of Civilian Persons in Time of War. Commentary* (Geneva: ICRC, 1958)
Pictet, J., *Development and Principles of International Humanitarian Law* (Dordrecht/ Geneva: Martinus Nijhoff/Henry Dunant Institute, 1985)
Pillet, A., *Les lois actuelles de la Guerre* (Paris: Rousseau, 1898)
'La guerre actuelle et le droit des gens' (1916) 23 *Revue Générale de Droit International Public* 1
Pocar, F., 'Protocol I Additional to the Geneva Conventions and Customary International Law' (2001) 31 *Israel Yearbook on Human Rights* 145
Politis, N., 'Le problème des limitations de la souveraineté et la théorie de l'abus des droits dans les rapports internationaux', 6 *Recueil des Cours de l'Académie de Droit International* (1925-I) 1
Post, H.H.G., 'Some Curiosities in the Sources of the Law of Armed Conflict Conceived in a General International Legal Perspective', in Barnhoorn, L.A. and Wellens, K.C. (eds.), *Diversity in Secondary Rules and the Unity of International Law* (The Hague: Martinus Nijhoff, 1995), p. 83
'Practical Advice for the Protection of Cultural Property in the Event of Armed Conflict', in Dutli, M.T. (ed.), *Protection of Cultural Property in the Event of Armed Conflict. Report on the Meeting of Experts (Geneva, 5–6 October 2000)* (Geneva: ICRC, 2002), p. 143
Preston, P., *A Concise History of the Spanish Civil War*, revised edn (London: Fontana, 1996)
Preux, J. de, 'La Convention de La Haye et le récent développement du droit des conflits armés', in Istituto Internazionale di Diritto Umanitario (ed.), *The International Protection of Cultural Property. Acts of the Symposium organized on the occasion of the 30th Anniversary of the Hague Convention on the Protection of*

Cultural Property in the Event of Armed Conflicts (Rome: Fondazione Europea Dragan, 1986), p. 107
'Protecting the Public Interest in Art' (1981) 91 *Yale Law Journal* 121
Prott, L.V., 'Commentary: the 1954 Hague Convention for the Protection of Cultural Property in the Event of Armed Conflict', in Ronzitti, N. (ed.), *The Law of Naval Warfare* (Dordrecht: Martinus Nijhoff, 1988), p. 582
'Cultural Rights as Peoples' Rights in International Law', in Crawford, J. (ed.), *The Rights of Peoples* (Oxford: Clarendon Press, 1988), p. 93
'The Protocol to the Convention for the Protection of Cultural Property in the Event of Armed Conflict (The Hague Convention) 1954' (1993) 6 *Humanitäres Völkerrecht Informationsschriften* 191
'The Development of Legal Concepts Connected with the Protection of the Cultural Heritage', in Blanpain, R. (ed.), *Law in Motion. International Encyclopaedia of Laws World Law Conference, Brussels, 9–12 September 1996* (The Hague: Kluwer, 1996)
Prott, L.V. and O'Keefe, P.J., *Law and the Cultural Heritage. Volume I: Discovery and Excavation* (Abingdon: Professional Books, 1984)
Law and the Cultural Heritage. Volume III: Movement (Butterworths: London, 1989)
'"Cultural Heritage" or "Cultural Property"?' (1992) 1 *International Journal of Cultural Property* 307
Provost, R., 'Reciprocity in Human Rights and Humanitarian Law' (1994) 65 *British Yearbook of International Law* 383
International Human Rights and Humanitarian Law (Cambridge: Cambridge University Press, 2002)
Przyborowska-Klimcak, A., 'Les notions des "biens culturels" et du "patrimoine culturel mondial" dans le droit international' (1989–90) 18 *Polish Yearbook of International Law* 47
Pufendorf, S., *Elementorum Jurisprudentiae Universalis Libri Duo*, first published 1660, text of 1672, translated by W.A. Oldfather (Oxford: Clarendon Press, 1931)
De Jure Naturae et Gentium Libri Octo, first published 1672, text of 1688, translated by C.H. and W.A. Oldfather (Oxford: Clarendon Press, 1934)
Quatremère de Quincy, A.C., *Lettres à Miranda sur le déplacement des monuments de l'art de l'Italie (1796)*, 2nd edn, introduction and notes by E. Pommier (Paris: Macula, 1996)
Quindry, F.E., 'Aerial Bombardment of Civilian and Military Objectives' (1931) 2 *Journal of Air Law* 474
Rachel, S., *De Jure Naturae et Gentium Dissertationes*, text of 1676, translated by J.P. Bate (Washington, DC: Carnegie Institution, 1916)
Randelzhofer, A., 'Civilian Objects', in Bernhardt, R.(ed.), *Encyclopedia of Public International Law*, 5 vols. (Amsterdam: North-Holland, 1992), vol. I, p. 603
Records of the Conference convened by the United Nations Educational, Scientific and Cultural Organization held at The Hague from 21 April to 14 May 1954 (The Hague: Staatsdrukkerij- en uitgeverijbedrijf, 1961)
Redslob, R., *Histoire des grands principes du droit des gens depuis l'antiquité jusqu'à la veille de la Grande Guerre* (Paris: Rousseau, 1923)
Reichelt, G., 'La protection des biens culturels' (1985) 1 *Uniform Law Review* 42

Reid, B. H., 'Italian Campaign', in Dear, I. C. B. and Foot, M. R. D. (eds.), *The Oxford Companion to the Second World War* (Oxford: Oxford University Press, 1995), p. 572

Renoliet, J.-J., *L'UNESCO oubliée. La Société des Nations et la coopération intellectuelle (1919–1946)* (Paris: Publications de la Sorbonne, 1999)

Report of the American Commission for the Protection and Salvage of Artistic and Historic Monuments in War Areas (Washington, DC: Government Printing Office, 1946)

Reydams, L., *Universal Jurisdiction. International and Municipal Legal Perspectives* (Oxford: Oxford University Press, 2003)

Riegl, A., *Le Culte Moderne des Monuments: Son Essence et Sa Genèse*, text of 1903, translated by D. Wieczorek (Paris: Seuil, 1984)

Ritter, W., 'The Soviet Spoils Commissions: On the Removal of Works of Art from German Museums and Collections' (1998) 7 *International Journal of Cultural Property* 446

Rivier, A., *Principes du droit des gens*, 2 vols. (Paris: Rousseau, 1896)

Robbins, K. et al., 'Religion', in Dear, I. C. B. and Foot, M. R. D. (eds.), *The Oxford Companion to the Second World War* (Oxford: Oxford University Press, 1995), p. 937

Roberts, A., 'What is Military Occupation?' (1984) 55 *British Yearbook of International Law* 249

'The Laws of War: Problems of Implementation in Contemporary Conflicts', in *Law in Humanitarian Crises*, 2 vols. (Luxembourg: Office for Official Publications of the European Communities, 1995), vol. I, p. 13

'Implementation of the Laws of War in Late-Twentieth-Century Conflicts' (1998) 71 *Naval War College International Law Studies* 359

'The Laws of War After Kosovo' (2001) 31 *Israel Yearbook on Human Rights* 79

Roberts, A. and Guelff, R. (eds.), *Documents on the Laws of War*, 3rd edn (Oxford: Oxford University Press, 2000)

Robisch, T. G., 'General William T. Sherman: Would the Georgia Campaigns of the First Commander of the Modern Era Comply with Current Law of War Standards?' (1995) 9 *Emory International Law Review* 459

Rodgers, W. L., 'The Laws of War Concerning Aviation and Radio' (1923) 17 *American Journal of International Law* 629

Rodick, B. C., *The Doctrine of Necessity in International Law* (New York: Columbia University Press, 1928)

Rogers, A. P. V., *Law on the Battlefield*, 2nd edn (Manchester: Manchester University Press, 2004)

'What is a Legitimate Military Target?', in Burchill, R., White, N. D. and Morris, J. (eds.), *International Conflict and Security Law. Essays in Memory of Hilaire McCoubrey* (Cambridge: Cambridge University Press, 2005), p. 160

Rolin, A., 'Les fossoyeurs du droit de la guerre' (1919) 26 *Revue Générale de Droit International Public* 29

Le Droit Moderne de la Guerre. Les principes. Les conventions. Les usages et les abus (Brussels: Dewit, 1920)

Rolin-Jaequemyns, G., 'Chronique du droit international' (1869) 1 *Revue de Droit International* 138

'La guerre actuelle' (1870) 2 *Revue de Droit International* 643
'Essai complémentaire sur la guerre franco-allemande dans ses rapports avec le droit international' (1871) 3 *Revue de Droit International* 288
'Conférence de Bruxelles' (1875) 7 *Revue de Droit International* 87
Rolland, L., 'Les pratiques de la guerre aérienne dans le conflit de 1914 et le droit des gens' (1916) 23 *Revue Générale de Droit International Public* 497
Ronzitti, N., *Diritto internazionale dei conflitti armati* (Turin: Giappichelli, 1998)
Roscini, M., 'Targeting and Contemporary Aerial Bombardment' (2005) 54 *International and Comparative Law Quarterly* 411
Roszkowski, G., 'De la codification du droit international' (1889) 21 *Revue de Droit International* 521
Rothnie, N., *The Baedeker Blitz. Hitler's Attack on Britain's Historic Cities* (Shepperton: Ian Allen, 1992)
Roucounas, E.J., 'Les infractions graves au droit humanitaire (Article 85 du Protocole additionnel I aux Conventions de Genève)' (1978) 31 *Revue Hellénique de Droit International* 57
Rousseau, C., *Le droit des conflits armés* (Paris: Pedone, 1983)
Rousseau, J.-J., *The Social Contract*, text of 1762, translated by M. Cranston (London: Penguin, 1968)
Saba, H., 'Unesco and Human Rights', in Vasak, K. and Alston, P. (eds.), *The International Dimensions of Human Rights*. (Westport/Paris: Greenwood Press/ UNESCO, 1982), Vol. II p. 401
Sabelli, D., 'La Convenzione sul patrimonio mondiale: limiti giuridico-politici', in Ciciriello, M. C. (ed.), *La protezione del patrimonio mondiale culturale e naturale a venticinque anni dalla Convenzione dell'UNESCO* (Naples: Editoriale Scientifica, 1997), p. 143
Salmon, J.J.A., 'Le concept de raisonnable en droit international public', in *Le droit international: unité et diversité. Mélanges offerts à Paul Reuter* (Paris: Pedone, 1981), p. 447
Samuel, R., *Theatres of Memory. Volume I: Past and Present in Contemporary Culture* (London: Verso, 1984)
Sandiford, R., *Diritto aeronautico di guerra* (Rome: Foro Italiano, 1937)
Sandoz, Y., 'Competing Priorities: Placing Cultural Property on the Humanitarian Law Agenda', in Dutli, M.T. (ed.), *Protection of Cultural Property in the Event of Armed Conflict. Report on the Meeting of Experts (Geneva, 5–6 October 2000)* (Geneva: ICRC, 2002), p. 21
Sandoz, Y., Swinarski, C. and Zimmermann, B., *Commentary on the Additional Protocols of 8 June 1977 to the Geneva Conventions of 12 August 1949* (Geneva: ICRC/ Martinus Nijhoff, 1987)
Sassòli, M., 'Legislation and Maintenance of Public Order and Civil Life by Occupying Powers' (2005) 16 *European Journal of International Law* 661
Sassoon, S., *Memoirs of an Infantry Officer*, text of 1930 (London: Faber and Faber, 1997)
Sax, J.L., 'Heritage Preservation as a Public Duty: The Abbé Grégoire and the Origins of an Idea' (1990) 88 *Michigan Law Review* 1142

'Is Anyone Minding Stonehenge? The Origins of Cultural Property Protection in England' (1990) 78 *California Law Review* 1543
Playing Darts with a Rembrandt: Public and Private Rights in Cultural Treasures (Ann Arbor: University of Michigan Press, 1999)
Schaffer, R., *Wings of Judgment. American Bombing in World War II* (New York: Oxford University Press, 1985)
Schabas, W. A., *Genocide in International Law* (Cambridge: Cambridge University Press, 2000)
Schama, S., *Landscape and Memory* (London: HarperCollins, 1995)
Schindler, D., 'The Different Types of Armed Conflicts According to the Geneva Conventions and Protocols', 163 *Recueil des Cours de l'Académie de Droit International* (1979-II) 117
Schindler, D. and Toman, J. (eds.), *The Laws of Armed Conflicts. A Collection of Conventions, Resolutions and Other Documents*, 4th revised and completed edn (Leiden/Boston: Martinus Nijhoff, 2004)
Schmitt, M. N., 'Future War and the Principle of Discrimination' (1998) 28 *Israel Yearbook on Human Rights* 51
'Targeting and Humanitarian Law: Current Issues' (2004) 34 *Israel Yearbook on Human Rights* 59
Schorlemer, S. von, 'Legal Changes in the Regime of the Protection of Cultural Property in Armed Conflict' (2004) 9 *Art Antiquity and Law* 43
Schwarzenberger, G., *International Law and Totalitarian Lawlessness* (London: Jonathan Cape, 1943)
A Manual of International Law (London: Stevens & Sons, 1947)
International Law as Applied by International Courts and Tribunals. Volume II. The Law of Armed Conflict (London: Stevens & Sons, 1968)
Scott-Clark, C. and Levy, A., *The Amber Room* (London: Atlantic Books, 2004)
Seidl-Hohenveldern, I., 'Artefacts as National Cultural Heritage and as Common Heritage to Mankind', in Bello, E. G. and Ajibola, B. A. (eds.), *Essays in Honour of Judge Taslim Olawale Elias*, 2 vols. (Dordrecht: Martinus Nijhoff, 1992), vol. I, p. 163
Seidl-Hohenveldern, I., 'La protection internationale du patrimoine culturel national' (1993) 97 *Revue Générale de Droit International Public* 395
Seršić, M., 'Protection of Cultural Property in Time of Armed Conflict' (1996) 27 *Netherlands Yearbook of International Law* 3
Sibert, M., 'Les bombardements aériens et la protection des populations civiles' (1930) 37 *Revue Générale de Droit International Public* 621
Simmonds, J., 'UNESCO World Heritage Convention' (1997) 2 *Art Antiquity and Law* 251
Sloutzki, N., 'Les Combattants et les non-Combattants dans les Guerres Modernes' (1928) 9 *Revue de Droit International (3ème série)* 346
Smith, H. A., 'The Government of Occupied Territory' (1944) 21 *British Yearbook of International Law* 151
Smith, M., 'The Air Threat and British Foreign and Domestic Policy: The Background to the Strategic Air Offensive', in Boog, H. (ed.), *The Conduct of the*

Air War in the Second World War. An International Comparison (New York/Oxford: Berg, 1992), p. 609

Solf, W. A., 'Cultural Property, Protection in Armed Conflict', in Bernhardt, R. (ed.), *Encyclopedia of Public International Law*, 5 vols. (Amsterdam: North-Holland, 1992), vol. I, p. 892

Spaight, J. M., *Aircraft In War* (London: Macmillan, 1914)
  'Air Bombardment' (1923–4) 4 *British Yearbook of International Law* 21
  Air Power and War Rights (London: Longmans, Green, 1924)
  Air Power and War Rights, 2nd edn (London: Longmans, Green, 1933)
  'Legitimate Objectives in Air Warfare' (1944) 21 *British Yearbook of International Law* 158
  Air Power and War Rights, 3rd edn (London: Longmans, Green, 1947)

Stephens, D. and Lewis, M., 'The Law of Armed Conflict – A Contemporary Critique' (2005) 6 *Melbourne Journal of International Law* 55

Stone, J., *Legal Controls of International Conflict. A Treatise on the Dynamics of Disputes- and War-Law* (New York: Rinehart, 1954)

Suárez, F., 'On Charity', text of 1621, in *Selections from Three Works of Francisco Suárez, S. J.*, translated by G. L. Williams, *et al.* (Oxford: Clarendon Press, 1944), p. 797

Sykes, K., 'The Trade in Iraqi Antiquities' (2003) 8 *Art Antiquity and Law* 299

Sykes, M. H., *Manual on Systems of Inventorying Immovable Cultural Property* (Paris: UNESCO, 1984)

Symonides, J., 'The United Nations Educational, Scientific and Cultural Organization (UNESCO) and the Promotion and Protection of Human Rights', in Danieli, Y., Stamatopolou, E. and Dias, C. J. (eds.), *The Universal Declaration of Human Rights: Fifty Years and Beyond* (Amityville: Baywood, 1999), p. 45

Tadashi, T., '*Temperamenta* (Moderation)', in Yasuaki, O. (ed.), *A Normative Approach to War. Peace, War, and Justice in Hugo Grotius* (Oxford: Clarendon Press, 1993), p. 276

Tanja, G. J., 'Recent Developments Concerning the Law for the Protection of Cultural Property in the Event of Armed Conflict' (1994) 7 *Leiden Journal of International Law* 115

Tavernor, R., *On Alberti and the Art of Building* (New Haven: Yale University Press, 1999)

Taylor, A. J. P., *From the Boer War to the Cold War. Essays on Twentieth-Century Europe* (London: Hamish Hamilton, 1995)

Taylor, G. D. S., 'The Content of the Rule Against Abuse of Rights in International Law' (1972–3) 46 *British Yearbook of International Law* 323

Terraine, J., 'Theory and Practice of the Air War: The Royal Air Force', in Boog, H. (ed.), *The Conduct of the Air War in the Second World War. An International Comparison* (New York/Oxford: Berg, 1992), p. 467

Textor, J. W., *Synopsis Juris Gentium*, text of 1680, translated by J. P. Bate (Washington, DC: Carnegie Institution, 1916)

The German War Book being 'The Usages of War on Land' Issued by the Great General Staff of the German Army, translated by J. H. Morgan (London: John Murray, 1915)

'The International Protection of Cultural Property' (1977) 71 *Proceedings of the American Society of International Law* 196

The Law of War on Land being Part III of the Manual of Military Law (London: HMSO, 1958)

The Proceedings of the Hague Peace Conferences. Translation of the Official Texts, 4 vols. (New York: Oxford University Press, 1920–1)

The Protection of Movable Cultural Property. Compendium of Legislative Texts, 2 vols. (Paris: UNESCO, 1984)

'The Use of Balloons in the War between Italy and Turkey' (1912) 6 *American Journal of International Law* 485

Thurlow, M. D., 'Protecting Cultural Property in Iraq: How American Military Policy Comports with International Law' (2005) 8 *Yale Human Rights and Development Law Journal* 153

Toman, J., 'La protection des biens culturels dans les conflits armés internationaux; cadre juridique et institutionnel', in Swinarski, C. (ed.), *Studies and Essays on International Humanitarian Law and Red Cross Principles in Honour of Jean Pictet* (Geneva/The Hague: ICRC/Martinus Nijhoff, 1984), p. 559

'La protection des biens culturels en cas de conflit armé non international', in Haller, W. et al. (eds.), *Im Dienst an der Gemeinschaft. Festschrift für Dietrich Schindler zum 65. Geburtstag* (Basel: Helbing & Lichtenhahn, 1989), p. 311

The Protection of Cultural Property in the Event of Armed Conflict. Commentary on the Convention for the Protection of Cultural Property in the Event of Armed Conflict and its Protocol, signed on 14 May 1954 in The Hague, and on other Instruments of International Law Concerning Such Protection (Paris/Aldershot: UNESCO/Dartmouth, 1996)

Tombs, R., 'The Wars against Paris', in Förster, S. and Nagler, J. (eds.), *On the Road to Total War. The American Civil War and the German Wars of Unification, 1861–1871* (Washington, DC/Cambridge: German Historical Institute/ Cambridge University Press, 1997), p. 541

Toynbee, A. J. (ed.), *Documents on International Affairs 1939–1946. Volume I. March–September 1939* (London: Oxford University Press/Royal Institute of International Affairs, 1951)

Twiss, T., *The Law of Nations Considered as Independent Political Communities. On the Rights and Duties of Nations in Time of War*, 2nd edn revised (Oxford/London: Clarendon Press/Longmans, 1875)

UK Ministry of Defence, *The Manual of the Law of Armed Conflict* (Oxford: Oxford University Press, 2004)

United Nations War Crimes Commission, *History of the United Nations War Crimes Commission and the Development of the Laws of War* (London: HMSO, 1948)

USAF Judge Advocate General School, *The Military Commander and the Law*, 3rd edn (Maxwell: AFJAGS Press, 1996)

Vattel, E. de, *Le Droit des Gens, ou Principes de la Loi Naturelle, appliqués à la Conduite et aux Affaires des Nations et des Souverains*, text of 1758 (Washington, DC: Carnegie Institution, 1916)

Vauthier, M., 'La doctrine du contrat social' (1914) 16 *Revue de Droit International (2ème série)* 325

Vedovato, G., 'La protezione del patrimonio storico artistico e culturale nella guerra moderna' (1961) 2 *Recueils de la Société Internationale de Droit Pénal Militaire et Droit de la Guerre* 117

Vergier-Boimond, J., *Villes sanitaires et cités d'asile* (Paris: Éditions Internationales, 1939)

Verri, P., 'Le destin des biens culturels dans les conflits armés. De l'Antiquité à la deuxième guerre (Avant-propos & Première partie)' (1985) 67 *International Review of the Red Cross* 67

'Le destin des biens culturels dans les conflits armés. De l'Antiquité à la deuxième guerre (Deuxième partie & Considérations finales)' (1985) 67 *International Review of the Red Cross* 127

Verzijl, J. H. W., *International Law in Historical Perspective, Volume IX: The Laws of War* (Alphen aan den Rijn: Sijthoff and Noordhoff, 1978)

Visscher, C. de, 'Les lois de la guerre et la théorie de la nécessité' (1917) 24 *Revue Générale de Droit International Public* 74

Visscher, C. de, 'La codification du droit international', 6 *Recueil des Cours de l'Académie de Droit International* (1925-I) 325

'La protection internationale des objets d'art et des monuments historiques. Première partie. La conservation du patrimoine artistique et historique en temps de paix' (1935) 16 *Revue de Droit International (3ème série)* 32

'La protection internationale des objets d'art et des monuments historiques. Deuxième Partie. Les monuments historiques et les œuvres d'art en temps de guerre et dans les traités de la paix' (1935) 16 *Revue de Droit International (3ème série)* 246

'La Conférence internationale des fouilles (Le Caire, 9–15 mars 1937) et l'œuvre de l'Office internationale des musées' (1937) 18 *Revue de Droit International (3ème série)* 700

Vitoria, F. de, 'De Indis Relectio Posterior, sive De Jure Belli Hispanorum in Barbaros', first published 1557, text of 1696, in *De Indis et De Jure Belli Relectiones*, translated by J.P. Bate (Washington, DC: Carnegie Institution, 1917), p. 163

Vyverberg, H., *Human Nature, Cultural Diversity, and the French Enlightenment* (New York: Oxford University Press, 1989)

Walker, C.J., 'The Meaning of Genocide', *Times Literary Supplement*, 7 August 1998, p. 17

Walker, T.A. and Walker, W.L. (eds.), *Lectures on International Law by Thomas Erskine Holland* (London: Sweet and Maxwell, 1933)

Walzer, M., *Just and Unjust Wars. A Moral Argument with Historical Illustrations* (New York: Basic Books, 1977)

'War Damage: The Cultural Heritage of Bosnia-Herzegovina, London Seminar' (1994) 3 *International Journal of Cultural Property* 355

Waxman, M.C., 'Siegecraft and Surrender: The Law and Strategy of Cities as Targets' (1999) 39 *Virginia Journal of International Law* 353

Webster, C. and Frankland, N., *The Strategic Air Offensive against Germany 1939–1945*, 4 vols. (London: HMSO, 1961)

Weinberg, G.L., *A World At Arms: A Global History of World War II* (Cambridge: Cambridge University Press, 1994)

Westlake, J., *International Law*, 2nd edn, 2 vols. (Cambridge: Cambridge University Press, 1910–13)
Wheaton, H., *Histoire des progrès du droit des gens en Europe depuis la Paix de Westphalie jusqu'au Congrès de Vienne* (Leipzig: Brockhaus, 1841)
Elements of International Law, 8th edn, edited by R.H. Dana (London: Sampson Low, 1866)
White, G., 'The Principle of Good Faith', in Lowe, V. and Warbrick, C. (eds.), *The United Nations and the Principles of International Law. Essays in Memory of Michael Akehurst* (London: Routledge, 1994), p. 230
Whiteman, M.M. (ed.), *Digest of International Law*, 15 vols. (Washington, DC: US Government Printing Office, 1963–73)
Wilhelm, R.-J., 'La "Croix-Rouge des Monuments"' (1954) 36 *Revue Internationale de la Croix-Rouge* 793
Williams, S., 'The Polish Art Treasures in Canada 1940–1960' (1977) 15 *Canadian Yearbook of International Law* 146
Williams, S.A., *The International and National Protection of Movable Cultural Property: A Comparative Study* (Dobbs Ferry: Oceana, 1978)
Winter, J., *Sites of Memory, Sites of Mourning. The Great War in European Cultural History* (Cambridge: Cambridge University Press, 1995)
Wolff, C., *Jus Gentium Methodo Scientifica Pertractatum*, first published 1740–9, text of 1764, translated by J.H. Drake (Oxford: Clarendon Press, 1934)
Wolfrum, R., 'Protection of Cultural Property in Armed Conflict' (2003) 32 *Israel Yearbook on Human Rights* 305
Wolfrum, R. and Philipp, C. (eds.), *United Nations: Law, Policies and Practice*, revised English edn (Munich/Dordrecht: Beck/Martinus Nijhoff, 1995)
Woolley, L., *A Record of the Work Done by the Military Authorities for the Protection of the Treasures of Art and History in War Areas* (London: HMSO, 1947)
Worsley, G., 'Stately Homes Relived', *Times Literary Supplement*, 21 November 1997, p. 4
Wright, P., *On Living in an Old Country* (London: Verso, 1985)
Wright, Q., *A Study of War*, 2nd edn (Chicago: University of Chicago Press, 1965)
Wyss, M.P., 'The Protection of the Cultural Heritage and its Legal Dimensions: The Heidelberg Symposium 22–23 June 1990' (1992) 1 *International Journal of Cultural Property* 232
Zargar, A. and Samadi, Y., 'Experience of the Islamic Republic of Iran in the Preservation of Cultural Property Against War Damages (The Hague Convention, 1954)' (1993) 6 *Humanitäres Völkerrecht Informationsschriften* 213
Zoller, E., *La bonne foi en droit international public* (Paris: Pedone, 1977)
Zouche, R., *Iuris et Iudicii Fecialis, sive, Iuris Inter Gentes, et Quaestionum de Eodem Explicatio*, text of 1650, translated by J.L. Brierly (Washington, DC: Carnegie Institution, 1911)

Index

Abu Simbel 146
Additional Protocol I (Protocol Additional to the Geneva Conventions of 12 August 1949, and Relating to the Protection of Victims of International Armed Conflicts) 4, 100, 202, 203–29
  civilian objects 203, 204–7, 318, 330
  civilian population 203, 204, 206
  criminal sanctions 224–9
  demilitarised zones 222–3
  grave breaches 224–9, 284
  incidental damage 132, 218–19, 257–8, 327
  indiscriminate attacks 148, 218–20, 328
  military objectives 128, 203, 204–7, 318
  misuse of recognised emblems 223–4
  non-defended localities 220–2
  proportionality 132, 218–19, 257–8, 327–9
  scope of application 203–4
  special regime for cultural property 100, 207–18
Additional Protocol II (Protocol Additional to the Geneva Conventions of 12 August 1949, and Relating to the Protection of Victims of Non-International Armed Conflicts) 4, 202, 203, 229–33, 246
  civilian objects 231, 324
  civilian population 233, 324
  criminal sanctions 233
  scope of application 229–30, 245, 246, 324
  special regime for cultural property 230–2
Afghanistan 99, 185, 305, 339, 357
  destruction of Buddhas of Bamiyan 98, 356–7
agreements, ad hoc/special 42, 58, 80, 98, 195, 223, 226
Ahnenerbe 79, 81

Alembert, Jean d' 9
Alidža mosque 348
Alt Aussee 87
Altstadt 67
Amber Room 81
America
  Central 17
  North 19
  South 17
American Civil War 19, 20
Ancona 37, 79
Angkor/Angkor Wat 153–4, 162, 173, 185, 260, 263, 270, 305
Anglo-American War 16
antiquities 2, 9–10, 14, 17, 31, 79, 80, 83, 84, 92, 114, 182, 195, 260, 265, 341–2
  market/trade in 2, 32, 33, 136, 195–6, 260, 340, 361
Arabia 40
Arab states 168, 170, 171
archaeological sites 2, 10, 28, 99, 101, 107, 132, 151, 171, 186, 260, 338, 361
archives 21, 29, 39, 80, 82, 86, 92, 101, 103, 107, 113, 143, 151, 266
armed conflict
  definition 96
  international 96, 97, 98, 124, 128, 162, 166–9, 174, 182, 192, 202, 203, 208, 217, 218, 236, 241, 245, 255, 258–61, 275, 302, 316, 318, 320, 326, 328, 330, 332–9, 343–4, 346, 348, 349, 352, 358
  non-international 59–61, 96–8, 124, 128, 192, 208, 229–32, 241, 245, 246, 247, 256, 258, 275, 296–300, 304, 309–10, 316, 324–6, 328–31, 333, 343–4, 346, 348, 349, 352, 358
  laws of 30, 99, 128, 132, 148, 182, 200, 202, 233, 236, 261, 299, 302, 306–9, 312, 313, 321
Arnaudija mosque 239

393

art 2, 15, 17, 20, 24–5, 27–9, 37, 40, 42, 46, 60, 68, 71, 76–8, 81–2, 84, 87–8, 99, 101, 103, 190, 198, 213, 280, 315, 319, 321–2, 325, 332, 343–4, 361
  galleries: *see* galleries
  protection corps 41, 77–80, 119
  works of 6, 8–9, 12, 13, 14, 20, 21, 22, 31, 39, 41, 42, 53, 55, 56, 58–60, 61, 62, 66, 70, 76, 78, 82, 83, 92, 99, 101, 139, 142, 151, 154, 174, 184, 207, 209, 210, 211, 212, 214–19, 225, 226, 227, 228, 231, 260, 265, 274, 275, 281, 303, 304, 319–21, 331, 336–7, 343, 346–7, 349; *see also* artworks
arts 9, 11, 14–16, 21–2, 29, 31, 40, 51, 274, 321, 331, 336–7, 346
  fine 9, 15, 78
artworks 9, 13, 15, 16, 79–84, 88, 92, 114, 164, 195, 349
  market/trade in 2, 32, 33, 195–6, 340, 361
Assisi 71, 80, 213
Athens Conference (First International Conference of Architects and Technicians of Historic Monuments) 95
attacks
  definition 4, 130, 204
  indiscriminate 218–20, 228–9, 346
Aubry, Charles 95
Australia 186, 212
Austria 16, 19, 36–8, 87, 105, 107, 141, 145
Ayala, Baltasar 6

Babylon 125
Baedeker raids 63
Baghdad 186, 338
Basra 180
Bath 63
Bayle, Pierre 9
Belgium 39, 40, 41, 44, 61, 67, 83, 87, 136, 209
Belgrade 38, 62, 182
belligerent occupation 21–2, 30–3, 80–6, 97–8, 120–1, 126, 130, 133–4, 135–40, 197–8, 259–63, 307–9, 313, 316, 332, 336–7, 338–43
belligerent reprisals 37, 42, 63, 134–5, 204, 207, 231, 335
Berlin 40, 68, 87
Bethlehem 130
Bismarck, Otto von 20, 66
bombardment/bombing 2, 11–12, 19–20, 23–30, 35–9, 43, 49, 66, 80, 90, 114, 117, 126–7, 131, 147, 148, 196, 203, 217, 219, 238, 318, 321
  area 49, 65, 67–9, 72, 220
  aerial 26–7, 35–9, 44–51, 54, 61–73, 76, 89–91, 117, 219

  inaccuracy of 11, 24, 34, 37, 42, 49, 67, 72, 73
  land 25, 26, 27, 74
  morale/terror 20, 46, 50, 62, 64–5, 67–8
  naval 22, 24–5, 45, 223
  rationale of 11, 19–20, 23, 36, 67
  strategic 36–7, 49, 61–73, 90
  tactical 62, 76, 77, 90
Bomber Command 62, 67
books 14, 92, 101, 139, 142, 151, 154, 178, 184
Bormann, Martin 81
Bosnia-Herzegovina, war in 186–7, 238–9, 274, 350–1, 356
Botta, Paul-Emile 17
Boxer Rebellion 22
Boylan, Patrick 238
  report 238, 239, 248, 251
Britain 16, 36, 40, 50, 62, 63, 64, 65, 67, 69, 70, 80, 84, 86, 88, 142; *see also* UK
British Court of Vice-Admiralty 16
British Military Court, Hamburg 90
British Museum 86
Bruges 42, 103, 338
Buddhas of Bamiyan 98–9, 185, 356
Bulgaria 36, 105, 107, 112
Burckhardt, Jakob 9, 17
Burlamaqui, Jean-Jacques 10, 12, 13
Butt report 67
Byelorussia/Byelorussian SSR 81, 82, 104, 105, 107

Cairo 69
Cambodia
  war in 153–4, 162, 172–3, 185
  Law on the Establishment of Extraordinary Chambers in the Courts of Cambodia for the Prosecution of Crimes Committed During the Period of Democratic Kampuchea 192–3, 350–2, 356
Canada 87, 164, 200, 207, 209, 212, 254
Canova, Antonio 16
Canterbury 63
Caserta 145
Castel Gandolfo 72
Castlereagh, Robert Stewart, Lord 16
Catania 76
Catherine Palace 81
Cave of the Patriarchs 131, 140, 262
Chamberlain, Kevin 198
Champollion, Jean-François 17
charitable purposes/charity 20, 22, 24–6, 29, 31, 32, 44, 46, 56, 88, 101, 127, 319, 321, 322, 325, 331, 332, 336, 337, 343, 344, 346, 349

INDEX

China 247
Chinese imperial summer palace 21
Chklaver, Georges 51–2
Choltitz, General Dietrich von 76
churches 26, 28, 37–40, 82–4, 87, 112, 347, 348
Church of the Eremitani 73
Church of the Nativity 130
Church, Roman Catholic 71
cities, open 58, 69, 72, 80, 120
civil affairs 33, 84, 136, 340, 342
civilian districts/quarters 11, 19, 20, 25, 34, 36, 62
civilian objects/property 3, 6, 11–12, 18, 34–8, 46, 50, 148, 149, 203, 204–7, 213, 216–18, 220, 228–9, 233, 253, 281, 303, 304, 318, 319, 320, 322, 323–5, 327, 328, 329, 343, 346, 347, 361
civilian populace/population 3, 12, 27, 35, 45, 46, 50–1, 58, 62, 67, 75, 80, 88, 90, 131, 149, 200, 203, 204, 206, 207, 228, 233, 324, 351–3
civilian service 112, 115
civilians 3, 6, 7, 11, 12, 35, 46, 51, 64, 66–9, 73, 84, 89, 90, 147, 203, 206–7, 218, 220, 228, 229, 233, 303, 304, 318, 324, 327, 328, 329, 346, 361
Clemen, Paul 41
Coalition Provisional Authority 322
Codex Aesinas of Tacitus's Germania 79
collections 14, 16, 21, 60, 68, 80, 81, 83, 86–9, 101, 107, 113, 114, 151, 154, 164, 172, 186, 195, 266, 317
Cologne 68
Combined Bomber Offensive (CBO) 67
Commission of Jurists 44–9
Commission on Responsibilities, Sub-Commission III 26, 32, 43–4, 127
  draft list of war crimes 26, 43–4
Control Council Law No.10 336, 349–51
Convention on the Elimination of All Forms of Racial Discrimination 310
  Committee on the Elimination of Racial Discrimination 310
Convention on the Means of Prohibiting the Illicit Import, Export and Transfer of Ownership of Cultural Property 3, 260, 261, 314–16, 342–3, 357
Convention on the Prevention and Punishment of the Crime of Genocide (Genocide Convention) 95, 353–6
Cracow 87, 137
criminal/penal sanctions 31, 43–4, 88–91, 188–92, 203, 224–9, 233, 241, 274–88, 300, 343–56
  aut dedere aut judicare/prosequi 286

command/superior responsibility 282, 283
crimes against humanity 88, 350–3
extradition 44, 285–7
genocide 353–6
jurisdiction 188–9, 191–2, 224–5, 233, 247, 274, 275, 283–5, 288, 322, 324, 325, 328, 329, 332, 336–7, 344, 346, 348–9, 351, 352, 358–9
mens rea 189, 227, 345, 347, 350, 352
mutual legal assistance 287, 350, 352
nullum crimen sine lege 277
participation, modes of 189, 282–3
penalties 280–1, 315
sentencing 281, 347, 348
universality 191–2, 224–5, 233, 275, 284
war crimes 31, 43–4, 88–91, 228, 280–1, 284, 326, 336, 337, 343–50, 351
Croatia 105, 182, 187
  war in 112, 114, 162, 182
Cuba 154
cultural heritage 2–4, 35, 61, 65, 69, 91, 94–5, 97, 100, 101–6, 108–11, 113, 118, 123, 133, 143, 144, 152, 176, 181, 183–7, 206–17, 219–20, 225, 227, 231, 236–8, 241, 246, 248, 258, 260, 264–5, 267, 281, 289, 299, 301–5, 309–15, 317–20, 347–8, 354, 357–8, 361; *see also* heritage
cultural property
  acts of hostility 126–31, 156–61, 207, 215–17, 231–2, 244, 251–7, 264, 272, 277, 279, 313, 331–4, 346–7
  alteration 32, 134, 140, 262, 300, 340
  appropriation/misappropriation 2, 8, 13, 15–16, 21–2, 31, 33, 44, 80–3, 88–9, 100, 132–4, 260–1, 278, 279, 305, 309, 316, 336–9, 340, 342, 348–50, 351, 361
  definition 3–4, 101–11, 190, 248–9
  deposit abroad 164, 196, 199–200
  export/exportation 33, 196, 198, 199, 260–1, 287, 314–16, 340, 342–3
  identification 29–30, 46, 52, 105, 114–15, 116–18, 155, 156, 161, 268, 290
  immovable 1, 4, 27, 28, 31–2, 42, 56, 78, 83, 84, 87, 94, 98, 111–14, 117, 118, 124, 132, 136, 140–5, 149–52, 154, 155, 161, 171, 182, 190, 195, 210, 214, 221, 222, 226, 249, 260, 263, 265, 280, 319, 340
  immunity 42, 47, 57, 58, 149, 152, 156–65, 195, 216, 220–2, 264, 271–4, 299
  import/importation 94, 196, 198, 299, 314–16
  making the object of attack 128–30, 204–5, 216, 231–2, 244, 271–4, 277, 309, 318–26, 343–6

cultural property (cont.)
  movable 1, 4, 8, 27, 31, 32, 35, 39, 42, 47, 52, 56–8, 61, 77–9, 84–5, 87, 94, 98, 100–5, 107, 111–14, 117, 133–4, 136, 140–3, 149–51, 154, 162, 163, 173, 190, 210–11, 214, 222, 259–60, 263, 265–6, 280, 311, 315, 319, 336, 340, 343
  preservation 8, 16–17, 32–3, 135–8, 175, 266–7, 296, 305, 312–14, 340–2
  reprisals 37, 42, 134–5, 207, 231, 335
  requisition 120, 132, 133, 336
  seizure 22, 23, 31, 336–7, 349
  term as used throughout book 3–4
  transfer of ownership 261, 279, 287, 299, 314–15, 342–3, 357
  transport/transportation 112, 162–5, 169, 170, 199
  use 25, 38, 42, 47–8, 56, 57, 78–9, 100, 120–6, 157–61, 215–17, 231–2, 252, 256, 264, 268, 277, 287, 334–5
  vandalism 33, 77, 124, 132–4, 135, 309, 313, 334, 338–40, 342
customary international law 63, 127, 132, 133, 190, 228, 231, 233, 258, 284–5, 316–17, 324, 326, 328, 333, 336, 348
Cyprus, invasion and occupation of 178–9, 199, 260
Cyrenaica 84
Czechoslovakia 67

da Vinci, Leonardo 87
Declaration concerning the Intentional Destruction of Cultural Heritage 356–9
demilitarisation 42, 43, 48, 58
demilitarised zones 42, 43, 222–3
demolitions 76, 126, 130–31, 157, 215, 216, 232, 255, 272, 273, 332
Denmark 106, 186
Diderot, Denis 9
digs, archaeological 32, 134, 138, 139, 261–2; *see also* excavations, archaeological
Diocletian's Palace 183
Diplomatic Conference on the Reaffirmation and Development of International Humanitarian Law Applicable in Armed Conflicts 200, 202
  Committee III 210, 214, 231
  resolution 20(IV) 219
Diplomatic Conference on the Second Protocol to the Hague Convention for the Protection of Cultural Property in the Event of Armed Conflict 240
distinction, principle of 12, 13, 45, 148, 204, 206

double effect, doctrine of 6, 12, 47, 218
Dresden 68
Dubrovnik 183, 187, 190, 228, 237, 238, 281, 312, 314, 321, 325, 343, 346, 347

East Pakistan, invasion of 178
Ecuador 122
education 22, 26, 29, 31, 32, 44, 52, 56, 88, 101, 127, 187, 236, 294–5, 321, 322, 325–6, 331, 336, 337, 343, 344, 346, 349
Egypt 10, 17, 144, 146, 154, 171, 172, 174, 175, 178, 184, 341
Einsatzstab Rosenberg 81–3, 89
Eisenhower, General Dwight 74, 75, 122
Elgin, Thomas Bruce, Lord 17
Elizabeth I, Queen 28
El Salvador, war with Honduras 185
Enlightenment 9, 10
Erdut 114
Eritrea 333
Eritrea Ethiopia Claims Commission 131, 214, 328, 330, 333
Ethiopia 333
Europe 8, 9, 15–16, 17, 19, 27, 49, 62, 65, 75, 77–9, 82–3, 89, 133, 235, 348–9
excavations, archaeological 10, 17, 32–3, 78, 133–4, 138–40, 194, 261–3, 300, 340
Exeter 63
export controls 33, 340, 342

factories 36, 45, 48, 51, 68, 89, 146–8, 206
Ferhat Pasha mosque 239
First World War 3, 35–44, 51, 79, 89, 91, 119
Florence 42, 48, 72–3, 76, 78, 79, 145
Foča 348
fortresses 7, 23, 38, 115, 128, 205
France 13, 15–16, 17, 20, 28, 36, 39–41, 44, 49, 61, 64–5, 67, 74, 76, 77–9, 83, 87–8, 106, 124, 136, 142, 147
  Comité des travaux historiques 16
  Commission on Historic Monuments 16
  Commission on Monuments 13–14
  Historic Monuments Inspectorate 16
  Institut de 20
  loi du 31 décembre 1913 sur les monuments historiques 28
  National Constituent Assembly 14
  National Convention 14
  Revolution: *see* French Revolution
Francioni, Francesco 99
Franco-Prussian War 19–20
Freiburg 68
French Permanent Military Tribunal, Metz 89
French Revolution 13–15
Friday Mosque 180

galleries 26, 39, 79, 80, 86, 87, 107, 112, 117, 151, 265–6
Garner, James Wilford 37–40
General Order No. 68 74–5, 78, 79, 96–7
Geneva Conventions 4, 96–8, 119, 148, 166–7, 182, 190, 195, 197, 202–4, 221, 224–5, 229, 233, 245, 276, 284, 294–5, 302, 304, 324
Geneva Conventions, Protocols Additional to: see Additional Protocol I, Additional Protocol II
Genoa 69, 76
Gentili, Alberico 6, 8
Germany 2, 9, 35–41, 43–4, 49, 61–71, 78, 79, 81–4, 87, 90–1, 105, 107, 124–5, 129, 133, 135, 136, 137, 141, 164, 195, 220, 341, 353
  Federal Republic (FRG) 97, 318
  West 106, 107, 114
Goering, Hermann 81, 83
good faith 39, 106, 109, 187, 199, 219, 360
Göttingen 68
  University of 20
Grandmaison, Aubin-Louis Millin de 28
Great Powers 24
Greco-German Mixed Arbitral Tribunal 27
Greece 27, 117, 122, 133, 210–11, 230
Grégoire, abbé 15, 16
Grotius, Hugo 6, 7, 9
Guelle, Jules 21
Guernica 50
Gulf War 124, 179, 219, 327, 330

Hadassah Hospital 29
Hague Convention 1954 (Convention for the Protection of Cultural Property in the Event of Armed Conflict) 92–198, 200–1, 202, 204, 205, 208, 219, 236–301, 357–9
  belligerent occupation 97, 98, 118–21, 124, 126, 133–40, 152, 168, 178, 180, 192, 197, 259, 336, 338, 340–1
  centres containing monuments 102, 103, 140–3, 149, 153, 195, 211
  Commissioners-General for Cultural Property 139, 161, 163, 166–71, 177
  control, regime of 94, 163, 167–71, 174, 178, 179, 180, 200, 236, 289, 300
  definition of 'cultural property' 4, 101–11, 117, 198, 209–10, 212–14, 248–9, 319
  delegates of Protecting Powers 169
  distinctive marking 116–18, 161, 214, 227, 264, 346
  emblem 119, 161, 223, 224, 227, 229, 303, 346
  execution 94, 165–95

general protection (general provisions regarding protection) 94, 100–40, 142, 143, 152, 158, 161, 200, 241, 244, 248–63, 264, 271–3, 278–80
immunity of cultural property under special protection 140, 152, 156–61, 195, 264
implementation reports 104, 105, 193–4, 200, 214, 298
International Register of Cultural Property under Special Protection 135, 141, 144, 145, 146, 150, 152–7, 176, 200, 211, 226, 227, 263, 269
meetings of the High Contracting Parties 138, 165, 176, 194–5, 288, 293
military measures 118–20
personnel 94, 115, 116, 119, 195, 221
preamble 94–5, 104, 176, 212
Protecting Powers 155, 165–71, 289
refuges for cultural property 103, 140–4, 149–52, 154–6
Regulations for the Execution of the Convention 93, 115, 117, 119–20, 163–72, 237, 289–90
representatives for cultural property 168–9
respect for cultural property 94, 98, 116, 120–40, 186, 192, 208, 209, 215, 217, 251–7, 316, 324–5, 333
safeguarding 94, 111–16, 121, 135–6, 175, 249–51, 317–18
sanctions 188–92, 236, 241, 274
technical assistance 112, 136, 172, 174–7, 182, 297
UNESCO, role of 172–88, 297
scope of application 96–100, 196–7, 204, 230, 245–6, 324–5, 333–6, 338
special protection 94, 100, 108, 126, 140–62, 220–2, 241, 243–4, 263–5, 271, 272, 278
Hague Convention 1954, First Protocol to 94, 132, 174, 179, 182, 195–201, 234, 260–1
  prevention of exportation 132, 198, 199, 342
  return 198–9
  scope of application 196–8
  taking custody 198
Hague Convention 1954, Second Protocol to 139, 234, 236–301, 360
  belligerent occupation 259–63, 343
  Committee for the Protection of Cultural Property in the Event of Armed Conflict 241, 263–6, 265, 268–71, 288–98, 300
  co-operation 294, 295
  definition of 'cultural property' 248–9

Hague Convention 1954, Second Protocol to (*cont.*)
  dissemination 294–5
  enhanced protection 108, 241, 243, 244, 258, 263–74, 276–9, 290, 296, 299, 322, 326
  execution 297–8
  Fund for the Protection of Cultural Property in the Event of Armed Conflict 250, 259, 267, 288, 291, 292–3, 296, 300
  general protection (general provisions regarding protection) 244, 248–63, 264, 272–3, 278–80
  genesis of 236–41
  immunity of cultural property under enhanced protection 253, 271–4, 277
  international assistance 241, 267, 270, 291, 295, 296
  International List of Cultural Property under Enhanced Protection 265–6, 269–71, 273, 290
  Meeting of the Parties 241, 288, 289, 291–4, 298
  penal sanctions 241, 247, 264, 274–88, 300
  precautions against the effects of hostilities 248, 259
  precautions in attack 248, 257–9, 278, 328–31
  Protecting Powers 289, 297, 298
  relationship to 1954 Hague Convention 242–5, 264
  respect for cultural property 248, 251–7, 322, 325, 333–5
  safeguarding 248–51, 317
  scope of application 245–7, 325, 329, 330
  serious violations 247, 275–87, 295
  UNESCO, role of 297
Hague Convention IX (Convention concerning Bombardment by Naval Forces in Time of War) 22, 24, 45–7, 56, 117
Hague Draft Air Rules (Air Rules) 44–51, 56–8, 64–5, 131, 204
Hague Peace Conferences 23, 27
Hague Rules 1907 (Regulations concerning the Laws and Customs of War on Land) 5, 22–39, 43–7, 55–6, 63, 74, 83, 84, 88–9, 91, 95, 97, 101–2, 126–7, 130, 133–6, 317, 321, 323, 326, 331–2, 336–40, 342
  belligerent occupation 30–3, 83–4, 88–9, 133–6, 336–40
  bombardment 23–30, 34, 35, 36–8, 43–7, 63, 126–7, 321
  destruction of enemy property 23–6, 31, 39, 43–4, 74, 127, 130–1, 323, 326, 331

Hamburg 68, 90
Harris, Sir Arthur 62, 66, 67
Hebron 103, 131, 140, 262
Heidelberg 68
Héring, General Pierre 76
heritage 1, 5, 13, 14, 20, 21, 40, 51–2, 54, 68, 69, 71, 91, 94–5, 100, 104, 113, 131, 184, 310–11, 338, 348, 357–8, 360
  cultural: *see* cultural heritage
  spiritual 1, 100, 207, 209–17, 219, 225, 227, 231, 303–4, 319, 320, 339, 348
Hermitage Museum 41, 86
Himmler, Heinrich 79
Hohenwalde 87
holy places 40, 180
Holy See 70, 150, 213
Holy Shrines 80
Honduras, war with El Salvador: *see* El Salvador, war with Honduras
hospitals 4, 29, 80, 148
humanity 11, 18, 20, 40, 51, 55, 58, 62, 73, 91, 104, 183, 185, 206, 222, 258, 264–6, 357–8, 360
  considerations/principles of 8, 12, 19, 70
  crimes against: *see* crimes against humanity
humankind 21, 281, 288, 347
Hungary 104, 105, 164
  invasion of 184

Imam Ali mosque 180
incidental damage/harm/injury/loss 6–7, 12, 34, 37, 46–7, 49, 61, 65, 131–2, 200, 203, 206, 218–19, 229, 233, 257–9, 279, 326–30, 346
industrial centre 57, 64, 141, 144–50, 155
India 105, 247
infrastructure 36, 45, 50–1, 90, 129, 203, 205, 206, 221–2
Institut de droit international 19, 338
Inter-American Commission on Human Rights 308
Intergovernmental Conference on the Protection of Cultural Property in the Event of Armed Conflict 93, 99, 115, 200
  resolution I of Final Act 99, 179
  resolution II of Final Act 115–16, 176
International Commission on Intellectual Co-operation (Commission Internationale de Coopération Intellectuelle/CICI) 53
International Committee of the Blue Shield (ICBS) 222, 240, 291
International Committee of the Red Cross (ICRC) 58, 60, 80, 96, 146–8, 182, 200, 209–15, 221, 229, 234, 297, 323, 324, 339

INDEX 399

International Confederation of Art Dealers 316
International Council on Archives (ICA) 240
International Council of Museums (ICOM) 240
International Council on Museums and Sites (ICOMOS) 240
International Court of Justice (ICJ) 104, 127, 148, 169, 247, 306–9, 321, 333, 336–9, 354
International Covenant on Civil and Political Rights (ICCPR) 277, 306, 310
  Human Rights Committee 310
International Covenant on Economic, Social and Cultural Rights (ICESCR) 305–10
  Committee on Economic, Social and Cultural Rights 305–6
  right to take part in cultural life 305–10
International Criminal Court (ICC) 128, 275, 322, 358
  Ad Hoc Committee on the Establishment of an International Criminal Court 355
  Elements of Crimes 190, 345–6, 352
  Preparatory Committee on the Establishment of an International Criminal Court 355
  Statute 128, 190, 281–2, 322, 324–6, 328–9, 332–3, 337–8, 344–7, 349–52, 355, 360
  United Nations Conference of Plenipotentiaries on the Establishment of an International Criminal Court 355
international criminal law 188–9, 280–3, 287, 343–56
International Criminal Tribunal for Rwanda (ICTR) 283, 324
  Statute 281–3, 350–2, 354
International Criminal Tribunal for the former Yugoslavia (ICTY) 127–8, 183, 190, 210, 228, 274, 281, 283, 312, 317, 321, 324–5, 328, 330–4, 337–8, 343–8, 350–2, 355–6
  Statute 281–3, 332, 336–7, 345–7, 349–52, 354
International Federation of Library Associations and Institutions (IFLA) 240
international humanitarian law 99, 200, 202, 236, 239, 257, 281, 307–9, 312–13, 317, 342, 347
international human rights law 305–10, 312, 342
  relationship to international humanitarian law/laws of armed conflict 306–8, 312, 313

International Institute for Intellectual Co-operation (Institut Internationale de Coopération Intellectuelle/IICI) 54
International Law Commission (ILC) 148, 295, 354, 355
  Draft Code of Crimes against the Peace and Security of Mankind, and commentary 95, 352, 354–5
International Military Tribunal (IMT), Nuremberg 35, 42, 63, 89, 332, 336, 346, 348, 350–1
  Charter (London Charter) 336, 348
International Museums Office (Office International des Musées/OIM) 51, 55
  recommendations to national authorities 52–3, 57
  Declaration on the Protection of Cultural Property in the Course of Armed Conflict 61
International Red Cross and Red Crescent Movement 234
INTERPOL 316
inter-war years 44–61
inventories 111, 114, 249–50
Iran 104, 236, 237, 249
Iran-Iraq War 118, 171, 177, 181, 187, 220, 236–7, 300
Iraq 107, 118, 124, 125, 179, 219, 316, 327
  invasion of 3, 186, 316, 330, 338
Iraqi Special Tribunal, Statute of 128, 322, 325–6, 328–9, 332–3, 337–8, 344–7, 349–51, 356
Ireland, Royal Academy of 20
Isfahan 180
Isin 338
Israel 96, 105, 130–1, 138–40, 142, 162, 168, 170–5, 178, 180–2, 183–5, 193–4, 234, 243, 261, 262, 306, 314, 341–2
  Defence Forces 103, 130, 183
  Supreme Court (High Court of Justice) 103, 130, 341–2
Italy 15, 36–7, 41, 47, 69–80, 84, 87, 145, 162

Jagellonian tapestries 87
Japan 2, 17, 35, 61–2, 69, 91, 174, 220
Jeddah 40
Jerusalem 29, 138, 140, 180, 181, 187, 194, 261, 314
Jordan 104–5, 178, 314, 341
  Antiquities Law (No. 51) 1966 341–2
jus ad bellum 5
jus in bello 5
just war 5, 18

Kaiser (Wilhelm II) 40, 41
Kanakaria church 316
Kawasaki 69

400 INDEX

Kersaint, Armand-Guy-Simon de Coetnempren, comte de 13
Kesselring, Field Marshal Albert 76, 79
Kharkov 81
Khmer Republic 153, 154, 270
Kiev 81, 145
King Solomon, pools of 342
Kisangani, cathedral in 321
Kobe 69
Königsberg 81
Korean War 99
Kosovo conflict 186
Kunstschutz 41, 79, 83, 119
Kuwait, invasion and occupation of 2, 179, 181, 187, 237, 260, 300
Kyoto 3, 69

Lakanal, Joseph 14, 16
Lang of Lambeth, Cosmo, Lord 71
Lauswolt document 239
Lauterpacht, Sir Hersch 89, 109
law and order 32-3, 221, 246, 340
Layard, Sir Austen Henry 17
League of Nations Assembly 50, 60, 65
    Seventh Committee 55, 56
    Sixth Committee 53, 60, 354, 355
    Third Committee 50-1, 65
Lebanon 96, 173-4, 175, 177, 178
    invasion and occupation of 96, 130, 137, 175, 177, 180
Lenzerini, Federico 99
Le Roy, Julien-David 10
libraries 14, 21, 29, 39, 79, 81, 87, 89, 92, 100, 102, 103, 107, 108, 113, 143, 151, 186, 266, 338, 354, 355
Lieber, Francis 18, 21
Lieber Code 18, 21, 22, 27, 90
Liechtenstein 105, 114
'Lieux de Genève' movement 58, 80
lines of communication 36, 45, 57, 89, 144, 146, 149, 221
London 36, 38, 41, 86
Louvain (Leuven) 39, 40
Low Countries 64, 78
Lübeck 63, 68
Luftwaffe 49, 62
Luxembourg 105

Madagascar 105
Madrid 60
Maisonrouge, François Puthod de 14
mankind 16, 17, 40, 51, 54, 68, 89, 94, 95, 97, 104, 106, 113, 144, 176, 207, 208, 212, 219, 237, 258, 305, 310, 339, 357
Manod Quarry 86
Mantegna, Andrea 73
maps 73, 111, 114, 186

material protection 42, 45, 47, 55-7, 80, 86, 94, 95
Mauritshuis 151
mektebs 348
Merkers 87
Mesopotamia 17, 40
Messina 76
Michelangelo (Buonarotti) 76
Milan 69, 76, 87
military action 90, 99, 128, 129, 148, 179, 203-6, 215, 216, 217, 231, 264, 271-2, 277, 303, 319, 323, 326, 344
military effort 202, 207, 215, 216, 223, 231, 272, 334
military measures 118-20
military necessity 22-6, 31-2, 39, 42-3, 45, 47, 52, 56, 65, 73-7, 88, 90, 109, 121-3, 125-31, 133, 140, 158, 159, 160, 202, 205-7, 215, 217, 251-7, 271, 322, 323, 331-7, 347, 349
military operations 11, 12, 31, 130-1, 137, 149, 174, 206-7, 221-2, 230, 257, 272, 331-2
military objectives 24, 45, 49-51, 61, 63-5, 67, 70, 72-4, 117, 128, 130, 141, 144-50, 200, 203-7, 216, 219-20, 228, 231, 233, 252-6, 259, 263-4, 318-19, 321-3, 325-7, 344
military purposes 20, 25, 38, 42, 47-8, 78-80, 127, 140, 149-51, 157, 265, 268, 273, 320-2, 325, 332, 344
Monaco project (International Association for the Protection of Humanity) 58, 80
Monreale 145
Monte Cassino 77, 124, 129
Montenegro 36, 186, 187
monuments 4, 6, 8-11, 13-18, 20-2, 24-8, 30, 32, 35, 37-48, 51-62, 65-6, 68-9, 71, 73-4, 76-80, 83-6, 88-9, 91-3, 99, 101-3, 106-7, 111-13, 115, 122, 124, 129, 137, 140-4, 146, 149-53, 172, 178, 182, 184-6, 190, 195, 200, 205, 207, 209-19, 226-8, 231, 236, 260, 275, 280, 281, 303-4, 311, 315, 319-22, 325, 332, 336-9, 343-9, 353-5, 361
Monuments, Fine Arts and Archives (MFA&A) 78, 85-6, 119, 135, 341
Moore, John Bassett 45
Morris, William 17
Mosque of Ibrahim 140, 262
mosques 213, 347, 348
Mostar 239
Mosul 186
Munich 68
museums 2, 26, 29, 38-40, 52, 60, 78-82, 86-7, 89, 92, 100, 102-3, 107, 112-13,

116, 132, 143, 146, 151, 171, 186–7, 265, 315, 338, 354–5, 361
Mycenae 17

Nablus 182
Napoleon (Bonaparte) 15
Napoleonic Wars 1, 5, 13, 15, 21
Nagoya 69
Nara 69
national advisory committee 115, 176
National Gallery 86
National Trust 17
nations, law of 5, 6, 8, 10
NATO-Partnership for Peace Conference on Cultural Heritage Protection in Wartime and in State of Emergency 114, 118
nature, law of 5, 7, 11
necessity, doctrine of 5–6, 10–12
  military: see military necessity
Netherlands 41, 54, 61, 67, 83, 93, 105, 107, 113, 122, 123, 136, 141, 151, 188, 207, 209–10, 212, 238, 248
Netherlands Archaeological Society (NOB), report of 41–3, 45, 47–8, 52–3, 55–6, 58, 80, 95, 113
New World 27
Niger 105
Nigeria, civil war in 182
nineteenth century 5, 16–22, 24
non-defended localities 220, 221, 222
Norwich 63
Nuremberg 68
  International Military Tribunal (IMT): see International Military Tribunal (IMT), Nuremberg

Oberried 141
occupation: see belligerent occupation
Occupied Palestinian Territories 138, 180, 187, 193, 306
occupied territory 2, 21, 42, 78, 81, 88, 91, 94, 119, 121, 133–40, 168, 170, 174, 194, 196, 198–9, 248, 259–63, 299, 313, 340, 342, 346, 351, 361
  definition 30, 97, 339
Occupying Power 21, 31, 32, 33, 42, 130, 133, 135, 136, 137, 138–9, 152, 198, 199, 236, 260–2, 269, 309, 331, 338, 340–3
Office of Military Government (OMG) 84–5, 135, 341
Old Bridge 239
Operation Desert Storm 179
Oppenheim, Lassa 26
Oron Museum 182
Orvieto 72
Osaka 69

Oxford 42, 68, 146
Oxford Manual 19, 20–21, 22, 27

Padua 71, 72, 73
paintings 9–10, 14, 79, 81, 83, 86, 89, 112
Palermo 76
Palestine 240
Palestine Liberation Organization (PLO) 96, 130, 173, 174
Palestinian Authority 182, 184
Palestinian autonomous towns, reoccupation of 182, 183
Pan-American Union 52
Paris 14, 20, 26, 32, 36, 37, 42, 43, 63, 76, 177, 239, 240, 246
Pavlovsk 81
Peiresc, Nicolas-Claude Fabri de 9
Peking, imperial astronomical observatory in 22
penal sanctions: see criminal/penal sanctions
peoples 5, 40, 54, 62, 94, 95, 100, 103, 106, 110, 113, 118, 176, 204, 207, 209–17, 225–6, 231, 265, 301, 303, 304, 310, 319–20
perfidy 46, 224, 236
Pergamon frieze 87
persecution 88, 350–2
Perugia 71
Peterhof 81
Phillipson, Coleman 40
Phnom Bok 154
Phnom Kron 154
Phnom Penh 162, 173
pillage 8, 13, 22, 30, 33, 44, 77, 89, 100, 120, 132–3, 185, 260–1, 279, 309, 336–40, 342, 349
Pisa 71, 72
Pius II, Pope 9
Pius XII, Pope 71
plunder 1, 2, 5, 15–16, 21, 35, 62, 81–3, 87–9, 91, 132, 142, 146, 165, 237, 260, 300, 336–7, 348–51
Ponte Santa Trinità 76
Ponte Vecchio 76
Portal, Sir Charles 64
Portalis, Jean-Etienne-Marie 13
Poznan 87
Prado 60
precautions against effects of hostilities 206
precautions in attack 206–7, 217, 257–9, 329–31
Preliminary Draft International Convention for the Protection of Historic Buildings and Works of Art in Times of War (OIM draft) 53–61, 80, 93–5, 101, 140–1, 151, 195

Preliminary Peace Conference of Paris 26, 32, 43–4, 127; *see also* Commission on Responsibilities
preservationism 17, 95
prize 13, 163
proportionality 7, 12, 34, 46–7, 49, 50–1, 61, 65–6, 131–2, 218–19, 228–9, 233, 257–9, 278, 326–31, 346
Protecting Powers 155, 163, 165–71, 289, 297, 298
   delegates 155, 168–9
   desuetude of institution 166–7
Protocols on Prohibitions or Restrictions on the Use of Mines, Booby-Traps and Other Devices 302–5, 318, 327–8
Provost, René 126
Prussia 16, 20, 31
public order 32–3, 84, 133, 149, 338, 340, 342
Pyramids 144

Quatremère de Quincy, Antoine 15–16, 28

Radetzky, Field Marshal Joseph 19
Ramsay, Andrew Michael 9
Rau, Charles 95
Ravenna 71, 72
Recommendation on International Principles Applicable to Archaeological Excavations 138, 261
Red Army 81, 82
refuges 57–8, 79, 83, 87, 102–3, 112, 120, 140–4, 149–52, 154–6, 164, 169–70, 200, 211
Reichenau, Field Marshal Walter 82
religion 22, 24, 25, 28, 29, 31, 56, 70–1, 101, 287, 310, 319, 321, 322, 325, 331–2, 336–7, 343–4, 346, 349, 355
Renaissance 5, 8–9, 80, 94, 162
reprisals: *see* belligerent reprisals
republic
   of letters (respublica literaria/République des Lettres) 8–9
   of the arts 15–16
Revett, Nicholas 10
Rheims cathedral 37, 39, 40
Ribbentrop, Joachim von 81
Riegl, Alois 18, 28
Riga 87, 145
Roberts, Justice Owen 77
Roberts Commission (American Commission for the Protection and Salvage of Artistic and Historic Monuments in War Areas) 77, 116
Roerich, Nikolai 40, 51–2
Roerich Pact 51–2, 95, 102, 114, 117, 218, 223, 226, 232, 255, 320

Rogers, A P V 217
Roluos 153
Romania 154
Rome 3, 42, 69–73, 76, 78, 80, 145
Rome Centre (International Centre for the Study of the Preservation and Restoration of Cultural Property/ICCROM) 291
Roosevelt, President Franklin 64, 70–1, 77, 116
Rosenberg, Albert 81–3, 88–9, 336, 349
Rothenburg 42
Rotterdam 62, 64
Rousseau, Jean-Jacques 12–13
Royal Air Force (RAF) 49, 62, 64–5
Ruskin, John 17
Russia 16, 41, 82
Russo-Japanese War 51

St Catherine, monastery of 172, 175, 185, 234, 341
St Denis, abbey of 20
St Gervais, church of 37
St John's Cathedral 151
St Paul's Cathedral 41
St Petersburg (Leningrad) 41, 86, 145
St Stephen, crown of 164, 200
San Gimignano 72
San Lorenzo Fuori le Mure, papal basilica of 71, 72
Santa Maria delle Grazie, convent of 87
Santa Maria della Scala 29
San Marino 105
Sarajevo 238
Saud, King Abdul Aziz ibn 80
Saudi Arabia 80, 213
Schliemann, Heinrich 17, 87
Second Opium War 21
Second World War 2–3, 35, 61–91, 133, 137, 154, 165, 206, 220, 317; *see also* World War Two
   belligerent occupation 62, 80–6, 135–7, 338, 341, 349, 350
   home front 86–7
   land and associated air operations 74–7
   post-war trials 88–91
   special protective measures 62, 77–80
   strategic air operations 62–73, 89–91
Serbia 36, 187
Shahabuddeen, Judge Mohammed 356
Sheridan, General Philip 20
's-Hertogenbosch 151
Siberia 87
Sicily 10, 70, 74, 76, 78
Siena 72, 145
signs 29–30, 48, 117, 173, 223, 229, 303–4
signals 223, 229, 303–4

Sinai 175, 185, 234, 341
Sinai War 172, 184
Sino-Japanese War 50, 53, 58, 220
Six-Day War 161, 168, 170, 177
Slovenia 105, 107, 182
Society for the Protection of Ancient Buildings 17
Soviet Union 62, 81–2, 86, 87, 106, 121, 142, 144, 184, 191, 198; *see also* USSR
Spaight, J M 48
Spain 53, 59–60, 108–9, 122, 186
Spanish-American War 22
Spanish Civil War 44, 50, 53, 58, 60, 220
Split 183
Spoleto 72
Srebrenica 356
Stela of Matara 333
Strasbourg 20
Stuart, James 10
Suárez, Francisco 6, 7
Sverdlovsk 86
Switzerland 17, 60, 79, 105, 107, 113, 114, 146, 170–1, 174, 177
Syria 178

Taliban 99, 186, 339, 356
Tallinn 87, 145
Tate Gallery 86
Taylor, Telford 63
technical assistance 60, 112, 136, 138, 172–8, 182, 250, 267, 297
Tell Bismaya 338
Textor, Joannes 6, 7
Thebes, necropolis of 146
Tokyo 69
Toledo 103
Torcello 72
tourism 18
town planning 33, 340
towns
  defended 11, 19, 23, 24, 34, 36–8, 42, 45, 48
  demilitarised 42
  fortified 7, 11, 19
  open 19, 58, 220
  undefended 19, 23, 37, 45
  unfortified 11
  university 68
Trenchard, Sir Hugh 49, 50, 206
Trieste 37
Tripolitana 84
trophy units 82, 87
Trojan gold 87
Troy 17
Tsarskoye Selo (Pushkin) 81
Tübingen 68
Turin 69, 76, 146
Turkey 17, 36, 122, 178–9

Tyre 130, 137, 173–5, 180

Ukraine/Ukrainian SSR 81–2, 104, 105, 125
Umma 338
Umm al Aqarib 338
UNIDROIT Convention on Stolen or Illicitly Exported Cultural Objects 3, 357
United Kingdom (UK) 17, 28, 49, 50, 62, 64–6, 69, 71, 73, 78, 83, 86, 88, 107, 108, 110, 118, 122, 125, 129, 133, 142, 144, 175, 179, 186, 190, 207, 212, 266, 322, 335
  Act for the better Protection of Works of Art 17
  Ancient Monuments Protection Act 17, 28
  Ancient Monuments Consolidation and Amendment Act 28
  National Trust Act 17
  Royal Commission on Historical Monuments 17
United Nations (UN)
  Commission on Human Rights 305
  Conference of Plenipotentiaries on the Establishment of an International Criminal Court 355
  General Assembly 3, 132, 139, 180, 192, 262, 305, 339, 353–4, 359
  Group of Experts for Cambodia 192
  military forces 99
  Organization 92
  peacekeeping operations 100
  Secretary-General 99, 152, 156, 167, 179, 183, 185, 186, 270, 273, 354–5
  Security Council 139, 338
  Special Representative of the Secretary-General on the situation of human rights in Cambodia 305
United Nations Educational, Scientific and Cultural Organization (UNESCO) 92, 93, 95, 101–3, 105, 112, 114, 122, 136, 138, 141, 143, 151, 158, 165, 167, 172–9, 182, 184, 186–8, 189, 193, 195, 201, 230, 234, 236–7, 248
  Constitution 92, 176, 178, 184, 186
  Director-General 92–3, 98–9, 108, 114, 137, 138, 146, 152–6, 166, 169–71, 173–87, 193, 194, 236–9, 270, 290–1, 292, 293, 295, 298, 316, 357
  director, Sector for Culture, Division of Cultural Heritage 98, 312
  Executive Board 138, 139, 171, 180–1, 184–6, 194, 237–9, 249
  Intergovernmental Committee for Promoting the Return of Cultural Property to its Countries of Origin or Restitution in case of Illicit Appropriation 3

United Nations Educational, Scientific and Cultural Organization (UNESCO) (*cont.*)
  General Conference 92, 99, 108, 138, 139, 180–1, 184, 188, 236–7, 239–40, 249, 293, 316, 323, 324, 332–6, 338, 357, 358
  Member States 92, 100, 172, 174, 180, 184, 249, 357, 359
  Secretariat 151, 173, 174, 188, 239, 288, 292
United Nations War Crimes Commission 89
United States of America (US/USA) 27, 64, 70–3, 77–8, 83–5, 87–90, 122, 135, 142, 147, 164, 186, 190, 200, 319–22, 327, 330, 338, 341, 344–5
universal jurisdiction: *see* criminal/penal sanctions
Ur 78, 219, 327
Urbino 72
US Army Air Forces (USAAF) 69
US Military Tribunal, Nuremberg 89, 90
USSR 62, 81–3, 88, 104–5, 122, 145, 147, 185, 191, 209; *see also* Soviet Union

vandalism 15, 33, 40, 77, 100, 120, 124, 132–4, 135, 279, 305–6, 309, 313, 334, 338–9, 340, 342
van Dyck, Sir Anthony 86
Vatican/Vatican City 72, 79, 141, 144, 150, 263
Vattel, Emer de 10–13, 18
Venice 19, 37, 38, 42, 48, 71–3, 103, 145
Vicenza 145
Vicq d'Azyr, Félix 14, 16
Victoria & Albert Museum 86
Villa Reale 80
Višegrad 348
Visscher, Charles de 53
Vitoria, Fransciso de 6–8

war
  laws of 2, 12, 18–19, 21, 35, 39, 43, 55, 77, 128, 187, 188, 218, 251, 300, 334, 361
  total 35, 63, 206
  used in lay sense throughout book 4
war crimes: *see* criminal/penal sanctions
Warsaw 61–3, 82
Washington Conference on the Limitation of Armament 44
Waterloo 3

Wat Po Veal 173
Wawel Castle 87, 137
Wellington, Arthur Wellesley, Duke of 16
Weygand, General Maxime 76
West Bank 103, 131, 139, 171, 182, 183, 194, 261–2, 341–2
Westminster Abbey 144
Westwood Quarry 86
Wiesbaden 164
Whitby Abbey 37
Winckelmann, Johan Joachim 10
Winter Palace 87
Wolff, Christian 10, 13
Woolley, Sir Leonard 78, 79
World Customs Organization 316
World Heritage Convention (Convention for the Protection of the World Cultural and Natural Heritage) 108, 223, 226, 248–9, 265, 266, 268, 288, 289, 291–3, 294, 310–14, 348, 357
  List of World Heritage in Danger 311, 312, 314
  Operational Guidelines for the Implementation of the World Heritage Convention 223, 266, 290, 311
  tentative lists 108, 268, 311, 312
World Heritage Committee 108, 288–90, 292, 311, 314
World Heritage emblem 223, 228
World Heritage Fund 292, 311
World Heritage List 108, 183, 223, 226, 227, 248–9, 263, 265–6, 311–12, 314, 348
World Heritage site 183, 228, 266, 346
worship, places of 4, 10, 99, 207–10, 212–17, 219, 225–8, 231, 303–4, 319–20, 354, 355
Würzburg 68

Yokohama 69
York 63
Ypres, Cloth Hall at 39
Yugoslavia 2, 68, 154, 182–3, 186, 237, 300
Yugoslav National Army (JNA) 115, 183, 190, 227, 314, 346

Žarkovica 190, 227, 346
Zvornik 348

CAMBRIDGE STUDIES IN INTERNATIONAL AND COMPARATIVE LAW

Books in the series

The Protection of Cultural Property in Armed Conflict
Roger O'Keefe

Multinationals and Corporate Social Responsibility
Limitations and Opportunities in International Law
Jennifer A. Zerk

Judiciaries within Europe
A Comparative Review
John Bell

Law in Times of Crisis
Emergency Powers in Theory and Practice
Oren Gross and Fionnuala Ni Aoláin

Vessel-Source Marine Pollution
The Law and Politics of International Regulation
Alan Tan

Enforcing Obligations Erga Omnes *in International Law*
Christian J. Tams

Non-Governmental Organisations in International Law
Anna-Karin Lindblom

Democracy, Minorities and International Law
Steven Wheatley

Prosecuting International Crimes
Selectivity and the International Law Regime
Robert Cryer

Compensation for Personal Injury in English, German and Italian Law
A Comparative Outline
Basil Markesinis, Michael Coester, Guido Alpa, Augustus Ullstein

Dispute Settlement in the UN Convention on the Law of the Sea
Natalie Klein

The International Protection of Internally Displaced Persons
Catherine Phuong

Imperialism, Sovereignty and the Making of International Law
Antony Anghie

Necessity, Proportionality and the Use of Force by States
Judith Gardam

International Legal Argument in the Permanent Court of International Justice
The Rise of the International Judiciary
Ole Spiermann

Great Powers and Outlaw States
Unequal Sovereigns in the International Legal Order
Gerry Simpson

Local Remedies in International Law
C. F. Amerasinghe

Reading Humanitarian Intervention
Human Rights and the Use of Force in International Law
Anne Orford

Conflict of Norms in Public International Law
How WTO Law Relates to Other Rules of Law
Joost Pauwelyn

Transboundary Damage in International Law
Hanqin Xue

European Criminal Procedures
Edited by Mireille Delmas-Marty and John Spencer

The Accountability of Armed Opposition Groups in International Law
Liesbeth Zegveld

Sharing Transboundary Resources
International Law and Optimal Resource Use
Eyal Benvenisti

International Human Rights and Humanitarian Law
René Provost

Remedies Against International Organisations
Karel Wellens

Diversity and Self-Determination in International Law
Karen Knop

The Law of Internal Armed Conflict
Lindsay Moir

International Commercial Arbitration and African States
Practice, Participation and Institutional Development
Amazu A. Asouzu

The Enforceability of Promises in European Contract Law
James Gordley

International Law in Antiquity
David J. Bederman

Money Laundering
A New International Law Enforcement Model
Guy Stessens

Good Faith in European Contract Law
Reinhard Zimmermann and Simon Whittaker
On Civil Procedure
J. A. Jolowicz

Trusts
A Comparative Study
Maurizio Lupoi

The Right to Property in Commonwealth Constitutions
Tom Allen

International Organizations Before National Courts
August Reinisch

The Changing International Law of High Seas Fisheries
Francisco Orrego Vicuña

Trade and the Environment
A Comparative Study of EC and US Law
Damien Geradin

Unjust Enrichment
A Study of Private Law and Public Values
Hanoch Dagan

Religious Liberty and International Law in Europe
Malcolm D. Evans

Ethics and Authority in International Law
Alfred P. Rubin

Sovereignty Over Natural Resources
Balancing Rights and Duties
Nico Schrijver

The Polar Regions and the Development of International Law
Donald R. Rothwell

Fragmentation and the International Relations of Micro-States
Self-determination and Statehood
Jorri Duursma

Principles of the Institutional Law of International Organizations
C. F. Amerasinghe

For EU product safety concerns, contact us at Calle de José Abascal, 56–1°,
28003 Madrid, Spain or eugpsr@cambridge.org.